U.S. History

Part 1: Chapters 1–18

SENIOR CONTRIBUTING AUTHORS
P. Scott Corbett, Ventura College
Jay Precht, Pennsylvania State University, Fayette
Volker Janssen, California State University–Fullerton
John M. Lund, Keene State College
Todd Pfannestiel, Clarion University
Paul Vickery, Oral Roberts University
Sylvie Waskiewicz, Lead Editor

Pak ISBN: 978-150669-815-1
Volume 1 ISBN: 979-8-3851-4686-4

OpenStax
Rice University
6100 Main Street MS-375
Houston, Texas 77005

To learn more about OpenStax, visit https://openstax.org.
Individual print copies and bulk orders can be purchased through our website.

©2021 Rice University. Textbook content produced by OpenStax is licensed under a Creative Commons Attribution 4.0 International License (CC BY 4.0). Under this license, any user of this textbook or the textbook contents herein must provide proper attribution as follows:

- If you redistribute this textbook in a digital format (including but not limited to PDF and HTML), then you must retain on every page the following attribution:
    "Access for free at openstax.org."
- If you redistribute this textbook in a print format, then you must include on every physical page the following attribution:
    "Access for free at openstax.org."
- If you redistribute part of this textbook, then you must retain in every digital format page view (including but not limited to PDF and HTML) and on every physical printed page the following attribution:
    "Access for free at openstax.org."
- If you use this textbook as a bibliographic reference, please include
    https://openstax.org/details/books/us-history in your citation.

For questions regarding this licensing, please contact support@openstax.org.

Trademarks
The OpenStax name, OpenStax logo, OpenStax book covers, OpenStax CNX name, OpenStax CNX logo, OpenStax Tutor name, Openstax Tutor logo, Connexions name, Connexions logo, Rice University name, and Rice University logo are not subject to the license and may not be reproduced without the prior and express written consent of Rice University. Kendall Hunt and the Kendall Hunt Logo are trademarks of Kendall Hunt. The Kendall Hunt mark is registered in the United States, Canada, and the European Union. These trademarks may not be used without the prior and express written consent of Kendall Hunt.

HARDCOVER BOOK ISBN-13	978-1-938168-36-9
PAPERBACK BOOK ISBN-13	978-1-951693-04-6
B&W PAPERBACK BOOK ISBN-13	978-150669-815-1
VOLUME 1 ISBN	979-8-3851-4686-4
DIGITAL VERSION ISBN-13	978-1-947172-08-1
ENHANCED TEXTBOOK ISBN-13	978-1-938168-98-7
ORIGINAL PUBLICATION YEAR	2014

5 6 7 8 9 10 JAY 21 18 17

OpenStax

OpenStax provides free, peer-reviewed, openly licensed textbooks for introductory college and Advanced Placement® courses and low-cost, personalized courseware that helps students learn. A nonprofit ed tech initiative based at Rice University, we're committed to helping students access the tools they need to complete their courses and meet their educational goals.

Rice University

OpenStax, OpenStax CNX, and OpenStax Tutor are initiatives of Rice University. As a leading research university with a distinctive commitment to undergraduate education, Rice University aspires to path-breaking research, unsurpassed teaching, and contributions to the betterment of our world. It seeks to fulfill this mission by cultivating a diverse community of learning and discovery that produces leaders across the spectrum of human endeavor.

Philanthropic Support

OpenStax is grateful for the generous philanthropic partners who advance our mission to improve educational access and learning for everyone. To see the impact of our supporter community and our most updated list of partners, please visit openstax.org/impact.

- Arnold Ventures
- Chan Zuckerberg Initiative
- Chegg, Inc.
- Arthur and Carlyse Ciocca Charitable Foundation
- Digital Promise
- Ann and John Doerr
- Bill & Melinda Gates Foundation
- Girard Foundation
- Google Inc.
- The William and Flora Hewlett Foundation
- The Hewlett-Packard Company
- Intel Inc.
- Rusty and John Jaggers
- The Calvin K. Kazanjian Economics Foundation
- Charles Koch Foundation
- Leon Lowenstein Foundation, Inc.
- The Maxfield Foundation
- Burt and Deedee McMurtry
- Michelson 20MM Foundation
- National Science Foundation
- The Open Society Foundations
- Jumee Yhu and David E. Park III
- Brian D. Patterson USA-International Foundation
- The Bill and Stephanie Sick Fund
- Steven L. Smith & Diana T. Go
- Stand Together
- Robin and Sandy Stuart Foundation
- The Stuart Family Foundation
- Tammy and Guillermo Treviño
- Valhalla Charitable Foundation
- White Star Education Foundation

CONTENTS

Preface   1

CHAPTER 1
The Americas, Europe, and Africa Before 1492   7
Introduction   7
1.1 The Americas   8
1.2 Europe on the Brink of Change   17
1.3 West Africa and the Role of Slavery   23
Key Terms   28
Summary   28
Review Questions   29
Critical Thinking Questions   30

CHAPTER 2
Early Globalization: The Atlantic World, 1492–1650   31
Introduction   31
2.1 Portuguese Exploration and Spanish Conquest   32
2.2 Religious Upheavals in the Developing Atlantic World   39
2.3 Challenges to Spain's Supremacy   42
2.4 New Worlds in the Americas: Labor, Commerce, and the Columbian Exchange   47
Key Terms   53
Summary   53
Review Questions   54
Critical Thinking Questions   56

CHAPTER 3
Creating New Social Orders: Colonial Societies, 1500–1700   57
Introduction   57
3.1 Spanish Exploration and Colonial Society   58
3.2 Colonial Rivalries: Dutch and French Colonial Ambitions   60
3.3 English Settlements in America   64
3.4 The Impact of Colonization   76
Key Terms   82
Summary   82
Review Questions   83
Critical Thinking Questions   84

CHAPTER 4
Rule Britannia! The English Empire, 1660–1763   85
Introduction   85
4.1 Charles II and the Restoration Colonies   86
4.2 The Glorious Revolution and the English Empire   92
4.3 An Empire of Slavery and the Consumer Revolution   95
4.4 Great Awakening and Enlightenment   99
4.5 Wars for Empire   103
Key Terms   107

Summary   107
Review Questions   108
Critical Thinking Questions   110

CHAPTER 5
Imperial Reforms and Colonial Protests, 1763-1774   111
Introduction   111
5.1 Confronting the National Debt: The Aftermath of the French and Indian War   112
5.2 The Stamp Act and the Sons and Daughters of Liberty   116
5.3 The Townshend Acts and Colonial Protest   122
5.4 The Destruction of the Tea and the Coercive Acts   128
5.5 Disaffection: The First Continental Congress and American Identity   131
Key Terms   134
Summary   134
Review Questions   135
Critical Thinking Questions   136

CHAPTER 6
America's War for Independence, 1775-1783   139
Introduction   139
6.1 Britain's Law-and-Order Strategy and Its Consequences   140
6.2 The Early Years of the Revolution   146
6.3 War in the South   152
6.4 Identity during the American Revolution   155
Key Terms   161
Summary   161
Review Questions   162
Critical Thinking Questions   163

CHAPTER 7
Creating Republican Governments, 1776–1790   165
Introduction   165
7.1 Common Sense: From Monarchy to an American Republic   166
7.2 How Much Revolutionary Change?   169
7.3 Debating Democracy   176
7.4 The Constitutional Convention and Federal Constitution   182
Key Terms   188
Summary   188
Review Questions   189
Critical Thinking Questions   190

CHAPTER 8
Growing Pains: The New Republic, 1790–1820   191
Introduction   191
8.1 Competing Visions: Federalists and Democratic-Republicans   192
8.2 The New American Republic   198
8.3 Partisan Politics   203
8.4 The United States Goes Back to War   209
Key Terms   214
Summary   214
Review Questions   215

Access for free at openstax.org.

Critical Thinking Questions   216

CHAPTER 9
Industrial Transformation in the North, 1800–1850   217
Introduction   217
9.1 Early Industrialization in the Northeast   218
9.2 A Vibrant Capitalist Republic   226
9.3 On the Move: The Transportation Revolution   232
9.4 A New Social Order: Class Divisions   235
Key Terms   240
Summary   240
Review Questions   241
Critical Thinking Questions   242

CHAPTER 10
Jacksonian Democracy, 1820–1840   243
Introduction   243
10.1 A New Political Style: From John Quincy Adams to Andrew Jackson   244
10.2 The Rise of American Democracy   250
10.3 The Nullification Crisis and the Bank War   252
10.4 Indian Removal   256
10.5 The Tyranny and Triumph of the Majority   261
Key Terms   265
Summary   265
Review Questions   266
Critical Thinking Questions   268

CHAPTER 11
A Nation on the Move: Westward Expansion, 1800–1860   269
Introduction   269
11.1 Lewis and Clark   270
11.2 The Missouri Crisis   276
11.3 Independence for Texas   278
11.4 The Mexican-American War, 1846–1848   282
11.5 Free or Slave Soil? The Dilemma of the West   289
Key Terms   293
Summary   293
Review Questions   294
Critical Thinking Questions   296

CHAPTER 12
Cotton is King: The Antebellum South, 1800–1860   297
Introduction   297
12.1 The Economics of Cotton   298
12.2 African Americans in the Antebellum United States   303
12.3 Wealth and Culture in the South   310
12.4 The Filibuster and the Quest for New Slave States   319
Key Terms   322
Summary   322
Review Questions   323
Critical Thinking Questions   324

CHAPTER 13
Antebellum Idealism and Reform Impulses, 1820–1860   325
Introduction   325
13.1 An Awakening of Religion and Individualism   326
13.2 Antebellum Communal Experiments   332
13.3 Reforms to Human Health   337
13.4 Addressing Slavery   340
13.5 Women's Rights   345
Key Terms   348
Summary   348
Review Questions   349
Critical Thinking Questions   350

CHAPTER 14
Troubled Times: the Tumultuous 1850s   353
Introduction   353
14.1 The Compromise of 1850   354
14.2 The Kansas-Nebraska Act and the Republican Party   362
14.3 The Dred Scott Decision and Sectional Strife   368
14.4 John Brown and the Election of 1860   371
Key Terms   375
Summary   375
Review Questions   376
Critical Thinking Questions   377

CHAPTER 15
The Civil War, 1860–1865   379
Introduction   379
15.1 The Origins and Outbreak of the Civil War   380
15.2 Early Mobilization and War   385
15.3 1863: The Changing Nature of the War   389
15.4 The Union Triumphant   398
Key Terms   404
Summary   404
Review Questions   405
Critical Thinking Questions   406

CHAPTER 16
The Era of Reconstruction, 1865–1877   407
Introduction   407
16.1 Restoring the Union   408
16.2 Congress and the Remaking of the South, 1865–1866   412
16.3 Radical Reconstruction, 1867–1872   416
16.4 The Collapse of Reconstruction   423
Key Terms   431
Summary   431
Review Questions   432
Critical Thinking Questions   433

CHAPTER 17
Go West Young Man! Westward Expansion, 1840-1900   435

Introduction   435
17.1 The Westward Spirit   436
17.2 Homesteading: Dreams and Realities   441
17.3 Making a Living in Gold and Cattle   444
17.4 The Assault on American Indian Life and Culture   449
17.5 The Impact of Expansion on Chinese Immigrants and Hispanic Citizens   454
Key Terms   458
Summary   458
Review Questions   460
Critical Thinking Questions   461

CHAPTER 18
Industrialization and the Rise of Big Business, 1870-1900   463
Introduction   463
18.1 Inventors of the Age   464
18.2 From Invention to Industrial Growth   469
18.3 Building Industrial America on the Backs of Labor   475
18.4 A New American Consumer Culture   483
Key Terms   486
Summary   486
Review Questions   487
Critical Thinking Questions   489

CHAPTER 19
The Growing Pains of Urbanization, 1870-1900   491
Introduction   491
19.1 Urbanization and Its Challenges   492
19.2 The African American "Great Migration" and New European Immigration   500
19.3 Relief from the Chaos of Urban Life   504
19.4 Change Reflected in Thought and Writing   511
Key Terms   516
Summary   516
Review Questions   517
Critical Thinking Questions   518

CHAPTER 20
Politics in the Gilded Age, 1870-1900   521
Introduction   521
20.1 Political Corruption in Postbellum America   522
20.2 The Key Political Issues: Patronage, Tariffs, and Gold   528
20.3 Farmers Revolt in the Populist Era   535
20.4 Social and Labor Unrest in the 1890s   539
Key Terms   545
Summary   545
Review Questions   546
Critical Thinking Questions   547

CHAPTER 21
Leading the Way: The Progressive Movement, 1890-1920   549
Introduction   549
21.1 The Origins of the Progressive Spirit in America   550

21.2 Progressivism at the Grassroots Level   552
21.3 New Voices for Women and African Americans   559
21.4 Progressivism in the White House   565
Key Terms   574
Summary   574
Review Questions   576
Critical Thinking Questions   577

CHAPTER 22
Age of Empire: American Foreign Policy, 1890-1914   **579**
Introduction   579
22.1 Turner, Mahan, and the Roots of Empire   580
22.2 The Spanish-American War and Overseas Empire   586
22.3 Economic Imperialism in East Asia   592
22.4 Roosevelt's "Big Stick" Foreign Policy   594
22.5 Taft's "Dollar Diplomacy"   599
Key Terms   601
Summary   601
Review Questions   602
Critical Thinking Questions   603

CHAPTER 23
Americans and the Great War, 1914-1919   **605**
Introduction   605
23.1 American Isolationism and the European Origins of War   606
23.2 The United States Prepares for War   612
23.3 A New Home Front   617
23.4 From War to Peace   622
23.5 Demobilization and Its Difficult Aftermath   627
Key Terms   632
Summary   632
Review Questions   633
Critical Thinking Questions   635

CHAPTER 24
The Jazz Age: Redefining the Nation, 1919-1929   **637**
Introduction   637
24.1 Prosperity and the Production of Popular Entertainment   638
24.2 Transformation and Backlash   643
24.3 A New Generation   650
24.4 Republican Ascendancy: Politics in the 1920s   656
Key Terms   660
Summary   660
Review Questions   661
Critical Thinking Questions   662

CHAPTER 25
Brother, Can You Spare a Dime? The Great Depression, 1929-1932   **665**
Introduction   665
25.1 The Stock Market Crash of 1929   666

25.2 President Hoover's Response   676
25.3 The Depths of the Great Depression   681
25.4 Assessing the Hoover Years on the Eve of the New Deal   687
Key Terms   691
Summary   691
Review Questions   693
Critical Thinking Questions   694

CHAPTER 26
Franklin Roosevelt and the New Deal, 1932-1941   695
Introduction   695
26.1 The Rise of Franklin Roosevelt   696
26.2 The First New Deal   700
26.3 The Second New Deal   709
Key Terms   720
Summary   720
Review Questions   721
Critical Thinking Questions   722

CHAPTER 27
Fighting the Good Fight in World War II, 1941-1945   723
Introduction   723
27.1 The Origins of War: Europe, Asia, and the United States   724
27.2 The Home Front   730
27.3 Victory in the European Theater   741
27.4 The Pacific Theater and the Atomic Bomb   745
Key Terms   750
Summary   750
Review Questions   751
Critical Thinking Questions   752

CHAPTER 28
Post-War Prosperity and Cold War Fears, 1945-1960   753
Introduction   753
28.1 The Challenges of Peacetime   754
28.2 The Cold War   757
28.3 The American Dream   764
28.4 Popular Culture and Mass Media   770
28.5 The African American Struggle for Civil Rights   773
Key Terms   779
Summary   779
Review Questions   780
Critical Thinking Questions   782

CHAPTER 29
Contesting Futures: America in the 1960s   783
Introduction   783
29.1 The Kennedy Promise   784
29.2 Lyndon Johnson and the Great Society   791
29.3 The Civil Rights Movement Marches On   797
29.4 Challenging the Status Quo   805

Key Terms   810
Summary   810
Review Questions   811
Critical Thinking Questions   812

CHAPTER 30
Political Storms at Home and Abroad, 1968-1980   815
Introduction   815
30.1 Identity Politics in a Fractured Society   815
30.2 Coming Apart, Coming Together   822
30.3 Vietnam: The Downward Spiral   829
30.4 Watergate: Nixon's Domestic Nightmare   834
30.5 Jimmy Carter in the Aftermath of the Storm   838
Key Terms   842
Summary   842
Review Questions   843
Critical Thinking Questions   845

CHAPTER 31
From Cold War to Culture Wars, 1980-2000   847
Introduction   847
31.1 The Reagan Revolution   848
31.2 Political and Cultural Fusions   852
31.3 A New World Order   857
31.4 Bill Clinton and the New Economy   864
Key Terms   874
Summary   874
Review Questions   875
Critical Thinking Questions   876

CHAPTER 32
The Challenges of the Twenty-First Century   877
Introduction   877
32.1 The War on Terror   878
32.2 The Domestic Mission   884
32.3 New Century, Old Disputes   890
32.4 Hope and Change   894
Key Terms   902
Summary   902
Review Questions   903
Critical Thinking Questions   904

Appendix A The Declaration of Independence   905
Appendix B The Constitution of the United States   909
Appendix C Presidents of the United States of America   925
Appendix D U.S. Political Map   929
Appendix E U.S. Topographical Map   931
Appendix F United States Population Chart   933
Appendix G Further Reading   935
Answer Key   947
Index   957

Preface

Welcome to *U.S. History*, an OpenStax resource. This textbook was written to increase student access to high-quality learning materials, maintaining highest standards of academic rigor at little to no cost.

About OpenStax

OpenStax is a nonprofit based at Rice University, and it's our mission to improve student access to education. Our first openly licensed college textbook was published in 2012, and our library has since scaled to over 25 books for college and AP® courses used by hundreds of thousands of students. OpenStax Tutor, our low-cost personalized learning tool, is being used in college courses throughout the country. Through our partnerships with philanthropic foundations and our alliance with other educational resource organizations, OpenStax is breaking down the most common barriers to learning and empowering students and instructors to succeed.

About OpenStax resources

Customization

U.S. History is licensed under a Creative Commons Attribution 4.0 International (CC BY) license, which means that you can distribute, remix, and build upon the content, as long as you provide attribution to OpenStax and its content contributors.

Because our books are openly licensed, you are free to use the entire book or pick and choose the sections that are most relevant to the needs of your course. Feel free to remix the content by assigning your students certain chapters and sections in your syllabus, in the order that you prefer. You can even provide a direct link in your syllabus to the sections in the web view of your book.

Instructors also have the option of creating a customized version of their OpenStax book. The custom version can be made available to students in low-cost print or digital form through their campus bookstore. Visit your book page on OpenStax.org for more information.

Art Attribution in *U.S. History*

To maximize readability and content flow, art does not include attribution in the text. The art is openly licensed and can be reused. If you are also reusing portions of the OpenStax textbook, you must give attribution to OpenStax.

Errata

All OpenStax textbooks undergo a rigorous review process. However, like any professional-grade textbook, errors sometimes occur. Since our books are web based, we can make updates periodically when deemed pedagogically necessary. If you have a correction to suggest, submit it through the link on your book page on OpenStax.org. Subject matter experts review all errata suggestions. OpenStax is committed to remaining transparent about all updates, so you will also find a list of past errata changes on your book page on OpenStax.org.

Format

You can access this textbook for free in web view or PDF through OpenStax.org, and in low-cost print editions.

About *U.S. History*

U.S. History is designed to meet the scope and sequence requirements of most introductory courses. The text brings forth the people, events, and ideas that have shaped the United States from both the top down (politics, economics, diplomacy) and bottom up (eyewitness accounts, lived experience). *U.S. History* covers key forces that form the American experience, with particular attention to issues of race, class, and gender. It is designed to provide a balanced approach, both confronting difficult and oppressive aspects of our history and celebrating those who overcame them.

Coverage and scope

To develop *U.S. History*, we solicited ideas from historians at all levels of higher education, from community colleges to PhD-granting universities. They told us about their courses, students, challenges, resources, and how a textbook can best meet the needs of them and their students.The result is a book that covers the breadth of the chronological history of the United States and also provides the necessary depth to ensure the course is manageable for instructors and students alike.

The pedagogical choices, chapter arrangements, and learning objective fulfillment were developed and vetted with feedback from educators dedicated to the project. They thoroughly read the material and offered critical and detailed commentary. Reviewer feedback centered on achieving equilibrium between the various political, social, and cultural dynamics that permeate history.

While the book is organized primarily chronologically, as needed, material treating different topics or regions over the same time period is spread over multiple chapters. For example, chapters 9, 11, and 12 look at economic, political, social, and cultural developments during the first half of the eighteenth century in the North, West, and South respectively, while chapters 18 to 20 closely examine industrialization, urbanization, and politics in the period after Reconstruction.

In improvements to the originally published version of the text, new contributors have clarified historical events and government policies, and have detailed the related impacts on people. The chapters exploring America's relationship with and mistreatment of Native American people have been revised to improve the accuracy of the descriptions, remove historical myths, and employ more authentic language. In other parts of the text, additions highlight the contributions of Black women to the Suffrage and the Civil Rights movements. Other additions deepen the descriptions of anti-LGBTQ discrimination and the struggle for LGBTQ rights. Finally, the sections discussing the 1980s have been expanded with additional aspects of the war on drugs, mass incarceration, and more detailed explorations of cultural and political developments.

Throughout the textbook, specific language and terminology have been changed in order to provide a more inclusive, humanizing, and accurate portrayal of identity and experience.

Pedagogical foundation

U.S. History features material that takes topics one step further to engage students in historical inquiry.Our features include:

- **Americana**. This feature explores the significance of artifacts from American pop culture and considers what values, views, and philosophies are reflected in these objects.
- **Defining "American"**. This feature analyzes primary sources, including documents, speeches, and other writings, to consider important issues of the day while keeping a focus on the theme of what it means to be American.
- **My Story**. This feature presents first-person accounts (diaries, interviews, letters) of significant or exceptional events from the American experience.
- **Click and Explore**. This feature is a very brief introduction to a website with an interactive experience, video, or primary sources that help improve student understanding of the material.

Questions for each level of learning

U.S. History offers two types of end-of-module questions for students:

- **Review Questions** are simple recall questions from each module in the chapter and are in either multiple-choice or open-response format. The answers can be looked up in the text.
- **Critical Thinking Questions** are higher-level, conceptual questions that ask students to demonstrate their understanding by applying what they have learned in each module to the whole of the chapter. They ask for outside-the-box thinking and reasoning about the concepts pushing students to places they wouldn't have thought of going themselves.

Additional resources

Student and instructor resources

We've compiled additional resources for both students and instructors, including Getting Started Guides, an instructor solution guide, and PowerPoint slides. Instructor resources require a verified instructor account, which you can apply for when you log in or create your account on OpenStax.org. Take advantage of these resources to supplement your OpenStax book.

Community Hubs

OpenStax partners with the Institute for the Study of Knowledge Management in Education (ISKME) to offer Community Hubs on OER Commons – a platform for instructors to share community-created resources that support OpenStax books, free of charge. Through our Community Hubs, instructors can upload their own materials or download resources to use in their own courses, including additional ancillaries, teaching material, multimedia, and relevant course content. We encourage instructors to join the hubs for the subjects most relevant to your teaching and research as an opportunity both to enrich your courses and to engage with other faculty.

To reach the Community Hubs, visit www.oercommons.org/hubs/OpenStax.

Partner resources

OpenStax Partners are our allies in the mission to make high-quality learning materials affordable and accessible to students and instructors everywhere. Their tools integrate seamlessly with our OpenStax titles at a low cost. To access the partner resources for your text, visit your book page on OpenStax.org.

About the authors

Senior contributing authors

P. Scott Corbett, Ventura College
Dr. Corbett's major fields of study are recent American history and American diplomatic history. He teaches a variety of courses at Ventura College, and he serves as an instructor at California State University's Channel Islands campus. A passionate educator, Scott has also taught history to university students in Singapore and China.

Jay Precht, Pennsylvania State University, Fayette
Jay Precht is an associate professor of history at Penn State Fayette, where he teaches courses in history and American studies. He earned his doctorate in American history from Arizona State University and worked with the Coushatta Tribe of Louisiana Heritage Department as a post-doctoral researcher before accepting his current position. His early research focused on the Coushatta community during the twentieth century and led to publications in *Native South*, *Ethnohistory*, and the *American Indian Quarterly*. Precht is currently researching Native American communities that were legally terminated without authorization from the U.S. Congress.

Volker Janssen, California State University–Fullerton
Born and raised in Germany, Dr. Janssen received his BA from the University of Hamburg and his MA and PhD from the University of California, San Diego. He is a former Fulbright scholar and an active member of Germany's advanced studies foundation "Studienstiftung des Deutschen Volkes." Volker currently serves as Associate Professor at California State University's Fullerton campus, where he specializes in the social, economic, and institutional history of California, and more recently, the history of technology.

John M. Lund, Keene State College
Dr. Lund's primary research focuses on early American history, with a special interest in oaths, Colonial New England, and Atlantic legal cultures. John has over 20 years of teaching experience. In addition to working with students at Keene State College, he lectures at Franklin Pierce University, and serves the online learning

community at Southern New Hampshire University.

Todd Pfannestiel, Clarion University
Dr. Pfannestiel is a Professor in the history department of Clarion University in Pennsylvania, where he also holds the position of Dean of the College of Arts and Sciences. Todd has a strong history of service to his institution, its students, and the community that surrounds it.

Paul Vickery, Oral Roberts University
Educating others is one of Dr. Vickery's delights, whether in the classroom, through authoring books and articles, or via informal teaching during his travels. He is currently Professor of History at Oral Roberts University, where his emphasis is on the history of ideas, ethics, and the role of the church and theology in national development. Paul reads Portuguese, Italian, French, and Hebrew, and has taught on five continents.

Sylvie Waskiewicz, Lead Editor
Dr. Waskiewicz received her BSBA from Georgetown University and her MA and PhD from the Institute of French Studies at New York University. With over 10 years of teaching experience in English and French history and language, Sylvie left academia to join the ranks of higher education publishing. She has spent the last eight years editing college textbooks and academic journals.

Reviewers

Amy Bix, Iowa State University
Edward Bond, Alabama A&M University
Tammy Byron, Dalton State College
Benjamin Carp, Brooklyn College, CUNY
Sharon Deubreau, Rhodes State College
Gene Fein, Fordham University
Joel Franks, San Jose State University
Raymond Frey, Centenary College
Richard Gianni, Indiana University Northwest
Larry Gragg, Missouri University of Science and Technology
Laura Graves, South Plains College
Elisa Guernsey, Monroe Community College
Thomas Chase Hagood, University of Georgia
Charlotte Haller, Worcester State University
David Head, Spring Hill College
Tamora Hoskisson, Salt Lake Community College
Jean Keller, Palomar College
Kathleen Kennedy, Missouri State University
Mark Klobas, Scottsdale Community College
Ann Kordas, Johnson & Wales University
Stephanie Laffer, Miami International University of Art and Design
Jennifer Lang, Delgado Community College
Jennifer Lawrence, Tarrant County College
Wendy Maier-Sarti, Oakton Community College
Jim McIntyre, Moraine Valley Community College
Marianne McKnight, Salt Lake Community College
Brandon Morgan, Central New Mexico Community College
Caryn Neumann, Miami University of Ohio
Michelle Novak, Houston Community College
Lisa Ossian, Des Moines Area Community College
Paul Ringel, High Point University

Jason Ripper, Everett Community College
Silvana Siddali, Saint Louis University
Brooks Simpson, Arizona State University
Steven Smith, California State University, Fullerton
David Trowbridge, Marshall University
Eugene Van Sickle, University of North Georgia
Hubert van Tuyll, Augusta State University

The Americas, Europe, and Africa Before 1492

1

FIGURE 1.1 This 1507 map by cartographers Martin Waldseemüller and Matthais Ringmann is credited as the first to incorporate the word "America." Little was known about the continent at the time, as the land masses on the far left of the map reveal. But the New World offered opportunity that the Old World would exploit.

CHAPTER OUTLINE
1.1 The Americas
1.2 Europe on the Brink of Change
1.3 West Africa and the Role of Slavery

INTRODUCTION Globalization, the ever-increasing interconnectedness of the world, is not a new phenomenon, but it accelerated when western Europeans discovered the riches of the East. During the Crusades (1095–1291), Europeans developed an appetite for spices, silk, porcelain, sugar, and other luxury items from the East, for which they traded fur, timber, and Slavic people they captured and sold (hence the word *slave*). But when the Silk Road, the long overland trading route from China to the Mediterranean, became costlier and more dangerous to travel, Europeans searched for a more efficient and inexpensive trade route over water, initiating the development of what we now call the Atlantic World.

In pursuit of commerce in Asia, fifteenth-century traders unexpectedly encountered a "New World" populated by millions and home to sophisticated and numerous peoples. Mistakenly believing they had reached the East Indies, these early explorers called its inhabitants "Indians." West Africa, a diverse and culturally rich area, soon entered the stage as other nations exploited its slave trade and brought its peoples to the New World in chains. Although Europeans would come to dominate the New World, they could not have done so without Africans and Native peoples (Figure 1.1).

1.1 The Americas

LEARNING OBJECTIVES

By the end of this section, you will be able to:
- Locate on a map the major American civilizations before the arrival of the Spanish
- Discuss the cultural achievements of these civilizations
- Discuss the differences and similarities between lifestyles, religious practices, and customs among Native peoples

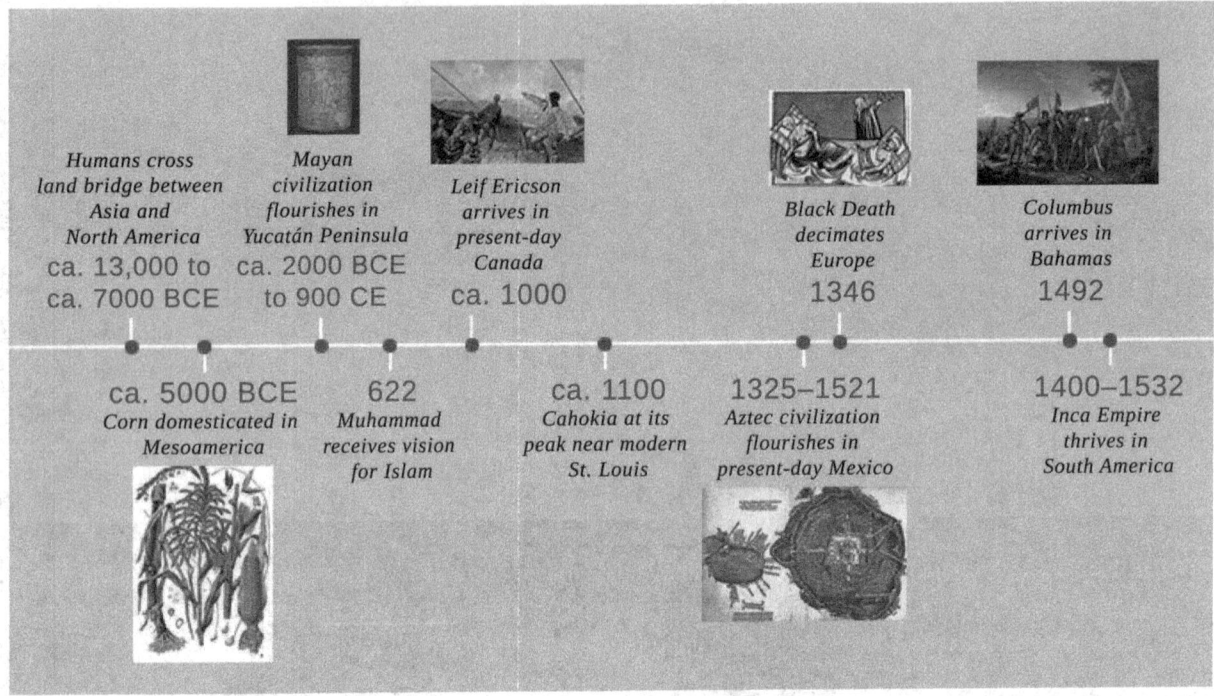

FIGURE 1.2 (credit: modification of work by Architect of the Capitol)

Most Native American origin stories assert that Native nations have always called the Americas home; however, some scholars believe that between nine and fifteen thousand years ago, a land bridge existed between Asia and North America that we now call **Beringia**. The first inhabitants of what would be named the Americas migrated across this bridge in search of food. When the glaciers melted, water engulfed Beringia, and the Bering Strait was formed. Later settlers came by boat across the narrow strait. (The fact that Asians and Native Americans share genetic markers on a Y chromosome lends credibility to this migration theory.) Continually moving southward, the settlers eventually populated both North and South America, creating unique cultures that ranged from the highly complex and urban Aztec civilization in what is now Mexico City to the woodland tribes of eastern North America. Recent research along the west coast of South America suggests that migrant populations may have traveled down this coast by water as well as by land.

Researchers believe that about ten thousand years ago, humans also began the domestication of plants and animals, adding agriculture as a means of sustenance to hunting and gathering techniques. With this agricultural revolution, and the more abundant and reliable food supplies it brought, populations grew and people were able to develop a more settled way of life, building permanent settlements. Nowhere in the Americas was this more obvious than in Mesoamerica (Figure 1.3).

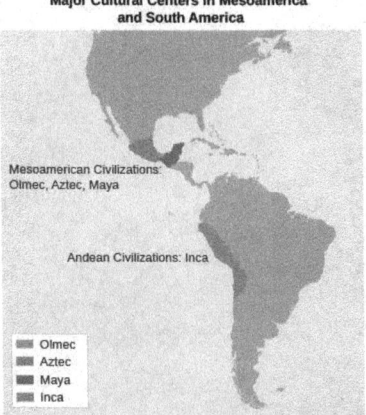

FIGURE 1.3 This map shows the extent of the major civilizations of the Western Hemisphere. In South America, early civilizations developed along the coast because the high Andes and the inhospitable Amazon Basin made the interior of the continent less favorable for settlement.

THE FIRST AMERICANS: THE OLMEC

Mesoamerica is the geographic area stretching from north of Panama up to the desert of central Mexico. Although marked by great topographic, linguistic, and cultural diversity, this region cradled a number of civilizations with similar characteristics. Mesoamericans were polytheistic; their gods possessed both male and female traits and demanded blood sacrifices of enemies taken in battle or ritual bloodletting. Corn, or maize, domesticated by 5000 BCE, formed the basis of their diet. They developed a mathematical system, built huge edifices, and devised a calendar that accurately predicted eclipses and solstices and that priest-astronomers used to direct the planting and harvesting of crops. Most important for our knowledge of these peoples, they created the only known written language in the Western Hemisphere; researchers have made much progress in interpreting the inscriptions on their temples and pyramids. Though the area had no overarching political structure, trade over long distances helped diffuse culture. Weapons made of obsidian, jewelry crafted from jade, feathers woven into clothing and ornaments, and cacao beans that were whipped into a chocolate drink formed the basis of commerce. The mother of Mesoamerican cultures was the Olmec civilization.

Flourishing along the hot Gulf Coast of Mexico from about 1200 to about 400 BCE, the Olmec produced a number of major works of art, architecture, pottery, and sculpture. Most recognizable are their giant head sculptures (Figure 1.4) and the pyramid in La Venta. The Olmec built aqueducts to transport water into their cities and irrigate their fields. They grew maize, squash, beans, and tomatoes. They also bred small domesticated dogs which, along with fish, provided their protein. Although no one knows what happened to the Olmec after about 400 BCE, in part because the jungle reclaimed many of their cities, their culture was the base upon which the Maya and the Aztec built. It was the Olmec who worshipped a rain god, a maize god, and the feathered serpent so important in the future pantheons of the Aztecs (who called him Quetzalcoatl) and the Maya (to whom he was Kukulkan). The Olmec also developed a system of trade throughout Mesoamerica, giving rise to an elite class.

FIGURE 1.4 The Olmec carved heads from giant boulders that ranged from four to eleven feet in height and could weigh up to fifty tons. All these figures have flat noses, slightly crossed eyes, and large lips. These physical features can be seen today in some of the peoples indigenous to the area.

THE MAYA

After the decline of the Olmec, a city rose in the fertile central highlands of Mesoamerica. One of the largest population centers in pre-Columbian America and home to more than 100,000 people at its height in about 500 CE, Teotihuacan was located about thirty miles northeast of modern Mexico City. The ethnicity of this settlement's inhabitants is debated; some scholars believe it was a multiethnic city. Large-scale agriculture and the resultant abundance of food allowed time for people to develop special trades and skills other than farming. Builders constructed over twenty-two hundred apartment compounds for multiple families, as well as more than a hundred temples. Among these were the Pyramid of the Sun (which is two hundred feet high) and the Pyramid of the Moon (one hundred and fifty feet high). Near the Temple of the Feathered Serpent, graves have been uncovered that suggest humans were sacrificed for religious purposes. The city was also the center for trade, which extended to settlements on Mesoamerica's Gulf Coast.

The Maya were one Mesoamerican culture that had strong ties to Teotihuacan. The Maya's architectural and mathematical contributions were significant. Flourishing from roughly 2000 BCE to 900 CE in what is now Mexico, Belize, Honduras, and Guatemala, the Maya perfected the calendar and written language the Olmec had begun. They devised a written mathematical system to record crop yields and the size of the population, and to assist in trade. Surrounded by farms relying on primitive agriculture, they built the city-states of Copan, Tikal, and Chichen Itza along their major trade routes, as well as temples, statues of gods, pyramids, and astronomical observatories (Figure 1.5). However, because of poor soil and a drought that lasted nearly two centuries, their civilization declined by about 900 CE and they abandoned their large population centers.

FIGURE 1.5 El Castillo, located at Chichen Itza in the eastern Yucatán peninsula, served as a temple for the god Kukulkan. Each side contains ninety-one steps to the top. When counting the top platform, the total number of stairs is three hundred and sixty-five, the number of days in a year. (credit: Ken Thomas)

The Spanish found little organized resistance among the weakened Maya upon their arrival in the 1520s. However, they did find Mayan history, in the form of glyphs, or pictures representing words, recorded in folding books called codices (the singular is *codex*). In 1562, Bishop Diego de Landa, who feared the converted Native people had reverted to their traditional religious practices, collected and burned every codex he could find. Today only a few survive.

CLICK AND EXPLORE

Visit the University of Arizona Library Special Collections (http://openstax.org/l/mayancodex) to view facsimiles and descriptions of two of the four surviving Mayan codices.

THE AZTEC

When the Spaniard Hernán Cortés arrived on the coast of Mexico in the sixteenth century, at the site of present-day Veracruz, he soon heard of a great city ruled by an emperor named Moctezuma. This city was tremendously wealthy—filled with gold—and took in tribute from surrounding tribes. The riches and complexity Cortés found when he arrived at that city, known as Tenochtitlán, were far beyond anything he or his men had ever seen.

According to legend, a warlike people called the Aztec (also known as the Mexica) had left a city called Aztlán and traveled south to the site of present-day Mexico City. In 1325, they began construction of Tenochtitlán on an island in Lake Texcoco. By 1519, when Cortés arrived, this settlement contained upwards of 200,000 inhabitants and was certainly the largest city in the Western Hemisphere at that time and probably larger than any European city (Figure 1.6). One of Cortés's soldiers, Bernal Díaz del Castillo, recorded his impressions upon first seeing it: "When we saw so many cities and villages built in the water and other great towns on dry land we were amazed and said it was like the enchantments . . . on account of the great towers and cues and buildings rising from the water, and all built of masonry. And some of our soldiers even asked whether the things that we saw were not a dream? . . . I do not know how to describe it, seeing things as we did that had never been heard of or seen before, not even dreamed about."

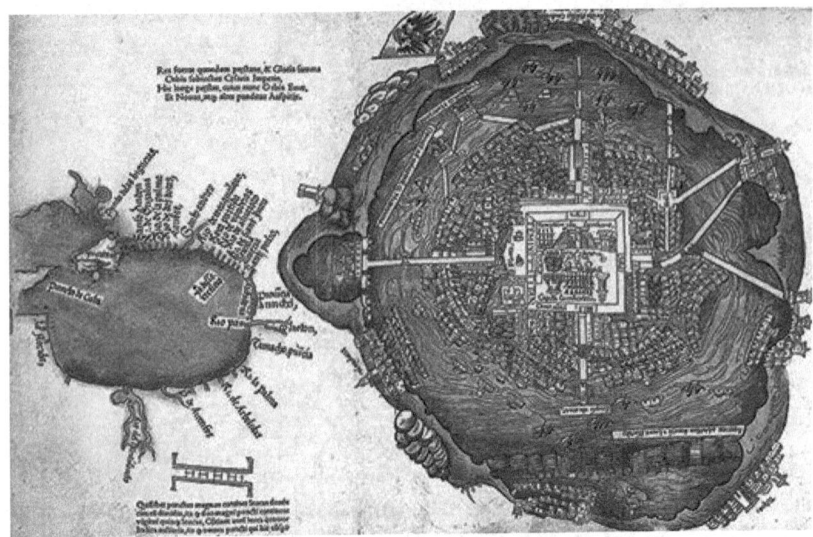

FIGURE 1.6 This rendering of the Aztec island city of Tenochtitlán depicts the causeways that connected the central city to the surrounding land. Envoys from surrounding tribes brought tribute to the Emperor.

Unlike the dirty, fetid cities of Europe at the time, Tenochtitlán was well planned, clean, and orderly. The city had neighborhoods for specific occupations, a trash collection system, markets, two aqueducts bringing in fresh water, and public buildings and temples. Unlike the Spanish, Aztecs bathed daily, and wealthy homes might even contain a steam bath. A labor force of enslaved people from subjugated neighboring tribes had built the fabulous city and the three causeways that connected it to the mainland. To farm, the Aztec constructed barges made of reeds and filled them with fertile soil. Lake water constantly irrigated these **chinampas**, or "floating gardens," which are still in use and can be seen today in Xochimilco, a district of Mexico City.

Each god in the Aztec pantheon represented and ruled an aspect of the natural world, such as the heavens, farming, rain, fertility, sacrifice, and combat. A ruling class of warrior nobles and priests performed ritual human sacrifice daily to sustain the sun on its long journey across the sky, to appease or feed the gods, and to stimulate agricultural production. The sacrificial ceremony included cutting open the chest of a criminal or captured warrior with an obsidian knife and removing the still-beating heart (Figure 1.7).

FIGURE 1.7 In this illustration, an Aztec priest cuts out the beating heart of a sacrificial victim before throwing the body down from the temple. Aztec belief centered on supplying the gods with human blood—the ultimate sacrifice—to keep them strong and well.

CLICK AND EXPLORE

Explore Aztec-History.com (http://openstax.org/l/azteccreation) to learn more about the Aztec creation story.

> **MY STORY**
>
> ### The Aztec Predict the Coming of the Spanish
> The following is an excerpt from the sixteenth-century Florentine Codex of the writings of Fray Bernardino de Sahagun, a priest and early chronicler of Aztec history. When an old man from Xochimilco first saw the Spanish in Veracruz, he recounted an earlier dream to Moctezuma, the ruler of the Aztecs.
>
> "Said Quzatli to the sovereign, "Oh mighty lord, if because I tell you the truth I am to die, nevertheless I am here in your presence and you may do what you wish to me!" He narrated that mounted men would come to this land in a great wooden house [ships] this structure was to lodge many men, serving them as a home; within they would eat and sleep. On the surface of this house they would cook their food, walk and play as if they were on firm land. They were to be White, bearded men, dressed in different colors and on their heads they would wear round coverings."
>
> Ten years before the arrival of the Spanish, Moctezuma received several omens which at the time he could not interpret. A fiery object appeared in the night sky, a spontaneous fire broke out in a religious temple and could not be extinguished with water, a water spout appeared in Lake Texcoco, and a woman could be heard wailing, "O my children we are about to go forever." Moctezuma also had dreams and premonitions of impending disaster. These foretellings were recorded after the Aztecs' destruction. They do, however, give us insight into the importance placed upon signs and omens in the pre-Columbian world.

THE INCA

In South America, the most highly developed and complex society was that of the Inca, whose name means "lord" or "ruler" in the Andean language called Quechua. At its height in the fifteenth and sixteenth centuries, the Inca Empire, located on the Pacific coast and straddling the Andes Mountains, extended some twenty-five hundred miles. It stretched from modern-day Colombia in the north to Chile in the south and included cities built at an altitude of 14,000 feet above sea level. Its road system, kept free of debris and repaired by workers stationed at varying intervals, rivaled that of the Romans and efficiently connected the sprawling empire. The Inca, like all other pre-Columbian societies, did not use axle-mounted wheels for transportation. They built stepped roads to ascend and descend the steep slopes of the Andes; these would have been impractical for wheeled vehicles but worked well for pedestrians. These roads enabled the rapid movement of the highly trained Incan army. Also like the Romans, the Inca were effective administrators. Runners called **chasquis** traversed the roads in a continuous relay system, ensuring quick communication over long distances. The Inca had no system of writing, however. They communicated and kept records using a system of colored strings and knots called the **quipu** (Figure 1.8).

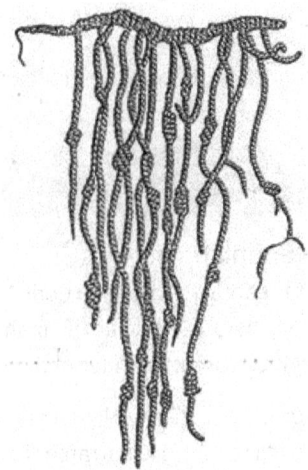

FIGURE 1.8 The Inca had no written language. Instead, they communicated and kept records by means of a system of knots and colored strings called the *quipu*. Each of these knots and strings possessed a distinct meaning intelligible to those educated in their significance.

The Inca people worshipped their lord who, as a member of an elite ruling class, had absolute authority over every aspect of life. Much like feudal lords in Europe at the time, the ruling class lived off the labor of the peasants, collecting vast wealth that accompanied them as they went, mummified, into the next life. The Inca farmed corn, beans, squash, quinoa (a grain cultivated for its seeds), and the indigenous potato on terraced land they hacked from the steep mountains. Peasants received only one-third of their crops for themselves. The Inca ruler required a third, and a third was set aside in a kind of welfare system for those unable to work. Huge storehouses were filled with food for times of need. Each peasant also worked for the Inca ruler a number of days per month on public works projects, a requirement known as the **mita**. For example, peasants constructed rope bridges made of grass to span the mountains above fast-flowing icy rivers. In return, the lord provided laws, protection, and relief in times of famine.

The Inca worshipped the sun god Inti and called gold the "sweat" of the sun. Unlike the Maya and the Aztecs, they rarely practiced human sacrifice and usually offered the gods food, clothing, and coca leaves. In times of dire emergency, however, such as in the aftermath of earthquakes, volcanoes, or crop failure, they resorted to sacrificing prisoners. The ultimate sacrifice was children, who were specially selected and well fed. The Inca believed these children would immediately go to a much better afterlife.

In 1911, the American historian Hiram Bingham uncovered the lost Incan city of Machu Picchu (Figure 1.9). Located about fifty miles northwest of Cusco, Peru, at an altitude of about 8,000 feet, the city had been built in 1450 and inexplicably abandoned roughly a hundred years later. Scholars believe the city was used for religious ceremonial purposes and housed the priesthood. The architectural beauty of this city is unrivaled. Using only the strength of human labor and no machines, the Inca constructed walls and buildings of polished stones, some weighing over fifty tons, that were fitted together perfectly without the use of mortar. In 1983, UNESCO designated the ruined city a World Heritage Site.

FIGURE 1.9 Located in today's Peru at an altitude of nearly 8,000 feet, Machu Picchu was a ceremonial Incan city built about 1450 CE.

CLICK AND EXPLORE

Browse the British Museum's World Cultures collection (http://openstax.org/l/inca) to see more examples and descriptions of Incan (as well as Aztec, Mayan, and North American Native) art.

NATIVE AMERICANS

With few exceptions, the North American Native cultures were much more widely dispersed than the Mayan, Aztec, and Incan societies, and did not have their population size or organized social structures. Although the cultivation of corn had made its way north, many Native people still practiced hunting and gathering. Horses, first introduced by the Spanish, allowed the Plains Natives to more easily follow and hunt the huge herds of bison. A few societies had evolved into relatively complex forms, but they were already in decline at the time of Christopher Columbus's arrival.

In the southwestern part of today's United States dwelled several groups we collectively call the Pueblo. The Spanish first gave them this name, which means "town" or "village," because they lived in towns or villages of permanent stone-and-mud buildings with thatched roofs. Like present-day apartment houses, these buildings had multiple stories, each with multiple rooms. The three main groups of the Pueblo people were the Mogollon, Hohokam, and Anasazi.

The Mogollon thrived in the Mimbres Valley (New Mexico) from about 150 BCE to 1450 CE. They developed a distinctive artistic style for painting bowls with finely drawn geometric figures and wildlife, especially birds, in black on a white background. Beginning about 600 CE, the Hohokam built an extensive irrigation system of canals to irrigate the desert and grow fields of corn, beans, and squash. By 1300, their crop yields were supporting the most highly populated settlements in the southwest. The Hohokam decorated pottery with a red-on-buff design and made jewelry of turquoise. In the high desert of New Mexico, the Anasazi, whose name means "ancient enemy" or "ancient ones," carved homes from steep cliffs accessed by ladders or ropes that could be pulled in at night or in case of enemy attack (Figure 1.10).

FIGURE 1.10 To access their homes, the cliff-dwelling Anasazi used ropes or ladders that could be pulled in at night for safety. These pueblos may be viewed today in Canyon de Chelly National Monument (above) in Arizona and Mesa Verde National Park in Colorado.

Roads extending some 180 miles connected the Pueblos' smaller urban centers to each other and to Chaco Canyon, which by 1050 CE had become the administrative, religious, and cultural center of their civilization. A century later, however, probably because of drought, the Pueblo peoples abandoned their cities. Their present-day descendants include the Hopi and Zuni tribes.

The Indigenous groups who lived in the present-day Ohio River Valley and achieved their cultural apex from the first century CE to 400 CE are collectively known as the Hopewell culture. Their settlements, unlike those of the southwest, were small hamlets. They lived in wattle-and-daub houses (made from woven lattice branches "daubed" with wet mud, clay, or sand and straw) and practiced agriculture, which they supplemented by hunting and fishing. Utilizing waterways, they developed trade routes stretching from Canada to Louisiana, where they exchanged goods with other tribes and negotiated in many different languages. From the coast they received shells; from Canada, copper; and from the Rocky Mountains, obsidian. With these materials they created necklaces, woven mats, and exquisite carvings. What remains of their culture today are huge burial mounds and earthworks. Many of the mounds that were opened by archaeologists contained artworks and other goods that indicate their society was socially stratified.

Perhaps the largest indigenous cultural and population center in North America was located along the Mississippi River near present-day St. Louis. At its height in about 1100 CE, this five-square-mile city, now called Cahokia, was home to more than ten thousand residents; tens of thousands more lived on farms surrounding the urban center. The city also contained one hundred and twenty earthen mounds or pyramids, each dominating a particular neighborhood and on each of which lived a leader who exercised authority over the surrounding area. The largest mound covered fifteen acres. Cahokia was the hub of political and trading activities along the Mississippi River. After 1300 CE, however, this civilization declined—possibly because the area became unable to support the large population.

NATIVE PEOPLES OF THE EASTERN WOODLAND

Encouraged by the wealth found by the Spanish in the settled civilizations to the south, fifteenth- and sixteenth-century English, Dutch, and French explorers expected to discover the same in North America. What they found instead were small, disparate communities, many already ravaged by European diseases brought by the Spanish and transmitted among the Native peoples. Rather than gold and silver, there was an abundance of land, and the timber and fur that land could produce.

The Native peoples living east of the Mississippi did not construct the large and complex societies of those to the west. Because they lived in small autonomous clans or tribal units, each group adapted to the specific environment in which it lived (Figure 1.11). These groups were by no means unified, and warfare among tribes was common as they sought to increase their hunting and fishing areas. Still, these tribes shared some common traits. A leader or group of tribal elders made decisions, and although the leader was a man, usually the women selected and counseled him. Gender roles were not as fixed as they were in the patriarchal societies of Europe, Mesoamerica, and South America.

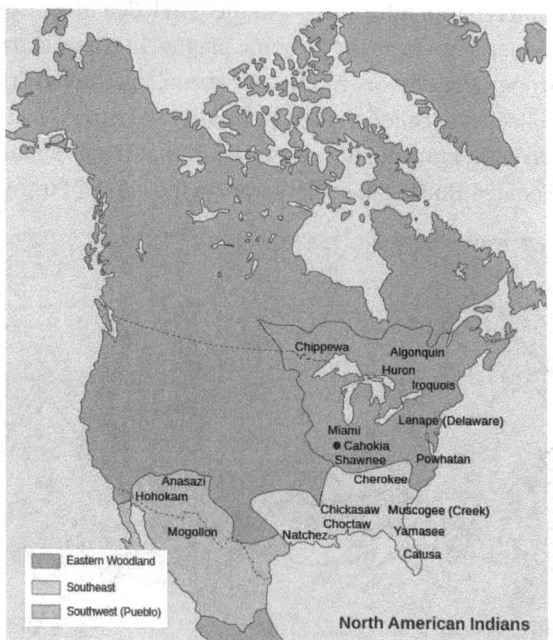

FIGURE 1.11 This map indicates the locations of the three Pueblo cultures the major Eastern Woodland Native tribes, and the tribes of the Southeast, as well as the location of the ancient city of Cahokia.

Women typically cultivated corn, beans, and squash and harvested nuts and berries, while men hunted, fished, and provided protection. But both took responsibility for raising children, and most major Native societies in the east were matriarchal. In tribes such as the Iroquois, Lenape, Muscogee, and Cherokee, women had both power and influence. They counseled and passed on the traditions of the tribe. These complementary gender roles changed dramatically with the coming of the Europeans, who introduced, sometimes forcibly, their own customs and traditions to the natives.

Clashing beliefs about land ownership and use of the environment would be the greatest area of conflict with Europeans. Although tribes often claimed the right to certain hunting grounds—usually identified by some geographical landmark—Native peoples did not practice, or in general even have the concept of, private ownership of land. The European Christian worldview, on the other hand, viewed land as the source of wealth. According to the Christian Bible, God created humanity in his own image with the command to use and subdue the rest of creation, which included not only land, but also all animal life. Land, and the game that populated it, they believed, were there for the taking.

1.2 Europe on the Brink of Change

LEARNING OBJECTIVES

By the end of this section, you will be able to:
- Describe the European societies that engaged in conversion, conquest, and commerce
- Discuss the motives for and mechanisms of early European exploration

The fall of the Roman Empire (476 CE) and the beginning of the European Renaissance in the late fourteenth century roughly bookend the period we call the Middle Ages. Without a dominant centralized power or overarching cultural hub, Europe experienced political and military discord during this time. Its inhabitants retreated into walled cities, fearing marauding pillagers including Vikings, Mongols, Arabs, and Magyars. In return for protection, they submitted to powerful lords and their armies of knights. In their brief, hard lives, few people traveled more than ten miles from the place they were born.

The Christian Church remained intact, however, and emerged from the period as a unified and powerful institution. Priests, tucked away in monasteries, kept knowledge alive by collecting and copying religious and secular manuscripts, often adding beautiful drawings or artwork. Social and economic devastation arrived in 1340s, however, when Genoese merchants returning from the Black Sea unwittingly brought with them a rat-borne and highly contagious disease, known as the bubonic plague. In a few short years, it had killed many millions, about one-third of Europe's population. A different strain, spread by airborne germs, also killed many. Together these two are collectively called the **Black Death** (Figure 1.12). Entire villages disappeared. A high birth rate, however, coupled with bountiful harvests, meant that the population grew during the next century. By 1450, a newly rejuvenated European society was on the brink of tremendous change.

FIGURE 1.12 This image depicts the bodily swellings, or buboes, characteristic of the Black Death.

CLICK AND EXPLORE

Visit EyeWitness to History (http://openstax.org/l/plague) to learn more about the Black Death.

LIFE IN FEUDAL EUROPE

During the Middle Ages, most Europeans lived in small villages that consisted of a manorial house or castle for the lord, a church, and simple homes for the peasants or **serfs**, who made up about 60 percent of western Europe's population. Hundreds of these castles and walled cities remain all over Europe (Figure 1.13).

FIGURE 1.13 One of the most beautifully preserved medieval walled cities is Carcassonne, France. Notice the use of a double wall.

Europe's **feudal society** was a mutually supportive system. The lords owned the land; knights gave military service to a lord and carried out his justice; serfs worked the land in return for the protection offered by the lord's castle or the walls of his city, into which they fled in times of danger from invaders. Much land was communally farmed at first, but as lords became more powerful they extended their ownership and rented land to their subjects. Thus, although they were technically free, serfs were effectively bound to the land they worked, which supported them and their families as well as the lord and all who depended on him. The Catholic Church, the only church in Europe at the time, also owned vast tracts of land and became very wealthy by collecting not only tithes (taxes consisting of 10 percent of annual earnings) but also rents on its lands.

A serf's life was difficult. Women often died in childbirth, and perhaps one-third of children died before the age of five. Without sanitation or medicine, many people perished from diseases we consider inconsequential today; few lived to be older than forty-five. Entire families, usually including grandparents, lived in one- or two-room hovels that were cold, dark, and dirty. A fire was kept lit and was always a danger to the thatched roofs, while its constant smoke affected the inhabitants' health and eyesight. Most individuals owned no more than two sets of clothing, consisting of a woolen jacket or tunic and linen undergarments, and bathed only when the waters melted in spring.

In an agrarian society, the seasons dictate the rhythm of life. Everyone in Europe's feudal society had a job to do and worked hard. The father was the unquestioned head of the family. Idleness meant hunger. When the land began to thaw in early spring, peasants started tilling the soil with primitive wooden plows and crude rakes and hoes. Then they planted crops of wheat, rye, barley, and oats, reaping small yields that barely sustained the population. Bad weather, crop disease, or insect infestation could cause an entire village to starve or force the survivors to move to another location.

Early summer saw the first harvesting of hay, which was stored until needed to feed the animals in winter. Men and boys sheared the sheep, now heavy with wool from the cold weather, while women and children washed the wool and spun it into yarn. The coming of fall meant crops needed to be harvested and prepared for winter. Livestock was butchered and the meat smoked or salted to preserve it. With the harvest in and the provisions stored, fall was also the time for celebrating and giving thanks to God. Winter brought the people indoors to weave yarn into fabric, sew clothing, thresh grain, and keep the fires going. Everyone celebrated the birth of Christ in conjunction with the winter solstice.

THE CHURCH AND SOCIETY

After the fall of Rome, the Christian Church—united in dogma but unofficially divided into western and eastern branches—was the only organized institution in medieval Europe. In 1054, the eastern branch of Christianity, led by the Patriarch of Constantinople (a title that because roughly equivalent to the western Church's pope), established its center in Constantinople and adopted the Greek language for its services. The western branch, under the pope, remained in Rome, becoming known as the Roman Catholic Church and continuing to use Latin. Following this split, known as the Great Schism, each branch of Christianity maintained a strict organizational hierarchy. The pope in Rome, for example, oversaw a huge bureaucracy led by cardinals, known as "princes of the church," who were followed by archbishops, bishops, and then priests. During this period, the Roman Church became the most powerful international organization in western Europe.

Just as agrarian life depended on the seasons, village and family life revolved around the Church. The sacraments, or special ceremonies of the Church, marked every stage of life, from birth to maturation, marriage, and burial, and brought people into the church on a regular basis. As Christianity spread throughout Europe, it replaced pagan and animistic views, explaining supernatural events and forces of nature in its own terms. A benevolent God in heaven, creator of the universe and beyond the realm of nature and the known, controlled all events, warring against the force of darkness, known as the Devil or Satan, here on earth. Although ultimately defeated, Satan still had the power to trick humans and cause them to commit evil or sin.

All events had a spiritual connotation. Sickness, for example, might be a sign that a person had sinned, while crop failure could result from the villagers' not saying their prayers. Penitents confessed their sins to the priest, who absolved them and assigned them penance to atone for their acts and save themselves from eternal damnation. Thus the parish priest held enormous power over the lives of his parishioners.

Ultimately, the pope decided all matters of theology, interpreting the will of God to the people, but he also had authority over temporal matters. Because the Church had the ability to excommunicate people, or send a soul to hell forever, even monarchs feared to challenge its power. It was also the seat of all knowledge. Latin, the language of the Church, served as a unifying factor for a continent of isolated regions, each with its own dialect; in the early Middle Ages, nations as we know them today did not yet exist. The mostly illiterate serfs were thus dependent on those literate priests to read and interpret the Bible, the word of God, for them.

CHRISTIANITY ENCOUNTERS ISLAM

The year 622 brought a new challenge to Christendom. Near Mecca, Saudi Arabia, a prophet named Muhammad received a revelation that became a cornerstone of the Islamic faith. The **Koran** contained his message, affirming monotheism but identifying Christ not as God but as a prophet like Moses, Abraham, David, and Muhammad. Following Muhammad's death in 632, Islam spread by both conversion and military conquest across the Middle East and Asia Minor to India and northern Africa, crossing the Straits of Gibraltar into Spain in the year 711 (Figure 1.14).

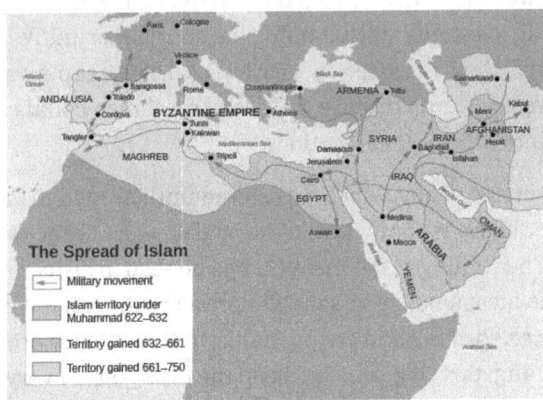

FIGURE 1.14 In the seventh and eighth centuries, Islam spread quickly across North Africa and into the Middle East. The religion arrived in Europe via Spain in 711 and remained there until 1492, when Catholic monarchs reconquered the last of Muslim-held territory after a long war.

The Islamic conquest of Europe continued until 732. Then, at the Battle of Tours (in modern France), Charles Martel, nicknamed the Hammer, led a Christian force in defeating the army of Abdul Rahman al-Ghafiqi. Muslims, however, retained control of much of Spain, where Córdoba, known for leather and wool production, became a major center of learning and trade. By the eleventh century, a major Christian holy war called the Reconquista, or reconquest, had begun to slowly push Muslims from Spain. With the start of the **Crusades**, the wars between Christians and Muslims for domination of the Holy Land (the Biblical region of Palestine), Christians in Spain and around Europe began to see the **Reconquista** as part of a larger religious struggle with Islam.

CLICK AND EXPLORE

Visit EyeWitness to History (http://openstax.org/l/crusades) to read a personal account of the Crusades.

JERUSALEM AND THE CRUSADES

The city of Jerusalem is a holy site for Jews, Christians, and Muslims. It was here King Solomon built the Temple in the tenth century BCE. It was here the Romans crucified Jesus in 33 CE, and from here, Christians maintain, he ascended into heaven, promising to return. From here, Muslims believe, Muhammad traveled to heaven in 621 to receive instructions about prayer. Thus claims on the area go deep, and emotions about it run high, among followers of all three faiths. Evidence exists that the three religions lived in harmony for centuries.

In 1095, however, European Christians decided not only to retake the holy city from the Muslim rulers but also to conquer what they called the Holy Lands, an area that extended from modern-day Turkey in the north along the Mediterranean coast to the Sinai Peninsula and that was also held by Muslims. The Crusades had begun.

Religious zeal motivated the knights who participated in the four Crusades. Adventure, the chance to win land and a title, and the Church's promise of wholesale forgiveness of sins also motivated many. The Crusaders, mostly French knights, retook Jerusalem in June 1099 amid horrific slaughter. A French writer who accompanied them recorded this eyewitness account: "On the top of Solomon's Temple, to which they had climbed in fleeing, many were shot to death with arrows and cast down headlong from the roof. Within this Temple, about ten thousand were beheaded. If you had been there, your feet would have been stained up to the ankles with the blood of the slain. What more shall I tell? Not one of them was allowed to live. They did not spare the women and children." A Muslim eyewitness also described how the conquerors stripped the temple of its wealth and looted private homes.

In 1187, under the legendary leader Saladin, Muslim forces took back the city. Reaction from Europe was swift as King Richard I of England, the Lionheart, joined others to mount yet another action. The battle for the Holy Lands did not conclude until the Crusaders lost their Mediterranean stronghold at Acre (in present-day Israel) in 1291 and the last of the Christians left the area a few years later.

The Crusades had lasting effects, both positive and negative. On the negative side, the wide-scale persecution of Jews began. Christians classed them with the infidel Muslims and labeled them "the killers of Christ." In the coming centuries, kings either expelled Jews from their kingdoms or forced them to pay heavy tributes for the privilege of remaining. Muslim-Christian hatred also festered, and intolerance grew.

On the positive side, maritime trade between East and West expanded. As Crusaders experienced the feel of silk, the taste of spices, and the utility of porcelain, desire for these products created new markets for merchants. In particular, the Adriatic port city of Venice prospered enormously from trade with Islamic merchants. Merchants' ships brought Europeans valuable goods, traveling between the port cities of western Europe and the East from the tenth century on, along routes collectively labeled the Silk Road. From the days of the early adventurer Marco Polo, Venetian sailors had traveled to ports on the Black Sea and established their own colonies along the Mediterranean Coast. However, transporting goods along the old Silk Road was costly, slow, and unprofitable. Muslim middlemen collected taxes as the goods changed hands. Robbers waited to ambush the treasure-laden caravans. A direct water route to the East, cutting out the land portion of the trip, had to be found. As well as seeking a water passage to the wealthy cities in the East, sailors wanted to find a route to the exotic and wealthy Spice Islands in modern-day Indonesia, whose location was kept secret by Muslim rulers. Longtime rivals of Venice, the merchants of Genoa and Florence also looked west.

THE IBERIAN PENINSULA

Although Norse explorers such as Leif Ericson, the son of Eric the Red who first settled Greenland, had reached Canada roughly five hundred years prior to Christopher Columbus's voyage, it was explorers sailing for Portugal and Spain who traversed the Atlantic throughout the fifteenth century and ushered in an unprecedented age of exploration and permanent contact with North America.

Located on the extreme western edge of Europe, Portugal, with its port city of Lisbon, soon became the center for merchants desiring to undercut the Venetians' hold on trade. With a population of about one million and supported by its ruler Prince Henry, whom historians call "the Navigator," this independent kingdom fostered exploration of and trade with western Africa. Skilled shipbuilders and navigators who took advantage of maps from all over Europe, Portuguese sailors used triangular sails and built lighter vessels called caravels that could sail down the African coast.

Just to the east of Portugal, King Ferdinand of Aragon married Queen Isabella of Castile in 1469, uniting two of the most powerful independent kingdoms on the Iberian peninsula and laying the foundation for the modern nation of Spain. Isabella, motivated by strong religious zeal, was instrumental in beginning the **Inquisition** in

1480, a brutal campaign to root out Jews and Muslims who had seemingly converted to Christianity but secretly continued to practice their faith, as well as other heretics. This powerful couple ruled for the next twenty-five years, centralizing authority and funding exploration and trade with the East. One of their daughters, Catherine of Aragon, became the first wife of King Henry VIII of England.

AMERICANA

Motives for European Exploration

Historians generally recognize three motives for European exploration—God, glory, and gold. Particularly in the strongly Catholic nations of Spain and Portugal, religious zeal motivated the rulers to make converts and retake land from the Muslims. Prince Henry the Navigator of Portugal described his "great desire to make increase in the faith of our Lord Jesus Christ and to bring him all the souls that should be saved."

Sailors' tales about fabulous monsters and fantasy literature about exotic worlds filled with gold, silver, and jewels captured the minds of men who desired to explore these lands and return with untold wealth and the glory of adventure and discovery. They sparked the imagination of merchants like Marco Polo, who made the long and dangerous trip to the realm of the great Mongol ruler Kublai Khan in 1271. The story of his trip, printed in a book entitled *Travels*, inspired Columbus, who had a copy in his possession during his voyage more than two hundred years later. Passages such as the following, which describes China's imperial palace, are typical of the *Travels*:

"You must know that it is the greatest Palace that ever was. . . . The roof is very lofty, and the walls of the Palace are all covered with gold and silver. They are also adorned with representations of dragons [sculptured and gilt], beasts and birds, knights and idols, and sundry other subjects. And on the ceiling too you see nothing but gold and silver and painting. [On each of the four sides there is a great marble staircase leading to the top of the marble wall, and forming the approach to the Palace.]" "The hall of the Palace is so large that it could easily dine 6,000 people; and it is quite a marvel to see how many rooms there are besides. The building is altogether so vast, so rich, and so beautiful, that no man on earth could design anything superior to it. The outside of the roof also is all colored with vermilion and yellow and green and blue and other hues, which are fixed with a varnish so fine and exquisite that they shine like crystal, and lend a resplendent lustre to the Palace as seen for a great way round. This roof is made too with such strength and solidity that it is fit to last forever."

Why might a travel account like this one have influenced an explorer like Columbus? What does this tell us about European explorers' motivations and goals?

The year 1492 witnessed some of the most significant events of Ferdinand and Isabella's reign. The couple oversaw the final expulsion of North African Muslims (Moors) from the Kingdom of Granada, bringing the nearly eight-hundred-year Reconquista to an end. In this same year, they also ordered all unconverted Jews to leave Spain.

Also in 1492, after six years of lobbying, a Genoese sailor named Christopher Columbus persuaded the monarchs to fund his expedition to the Far East. Columbus had already pitched his plan to the rulers of Genoa and Venice without success, so the Spanish monarchy was his last hope. Christian zeal was the prime motivating factor for Isabella, as she imagined her faith spreading to the East. Ferdinand, the more practical of the two, hoped to acquire wealth from trade.

Most educated individuals at the time knew the earth was round, so Columbus's plan to reach the East by sailing west was plausible. Though the calculations of Earth's circumference made by the Greek geographer Eratosthenes in the second century BCE were known (and, as we now know, nearly accurate), most scholars did not believe they were dependable. Thus Columbus would have no way of knowing when he had traveled far enough around the Earth to reach his goal—and in fact, Columbus greatly underestimated the Earth's circumference.

In August 1492, Columbus set sail with his three small caravels (Figure 1.15). After a voyage of about three thousand miles lasting six weeks, he landed on an island in the Bahamas named Guanahani by the native Lucayans. He promptly christened it San Salvador, the name it bears today.

FIGURE 1.15 Columbus sailed in three caravels such as these. The *Santa Maria*, his largest, was only 58 feet long.

1.3 West Africa and the Role of Slavery

LEARNING OBJECTIVES

At the end of this section, you will be able to:
- Locate the major West African empires on a map
- Discuss the roles of Islam and Europe in the slave trade

It is difficult to generalize about West Africa, which was linked to the rise and diffusion of Islam. This geographical unit, central to the rise of the Atlantic World, stretches from modern-day Mauritania to the Democratic Republic of the Congo and encompasses lush rainforests along the equator, savannas on either side of the forest, and much drier land to the north. Until about 600 CE, most Africans were hunter-gatherers. Where water was too scarce for farming, herders maintained sheep, goats, cattle, or camels. In the more heavily wooded area near the equator, farmers raised yams, palm products, or plantains. The savanna areas yielded rice, millet, and sorghum. Sub-Saharan Africans had little experience in maritime matters. Most of the population lived away from the coast, which is connected to the interior by five main rivers—the Senegal, Gambia, Niger, Volta, and Congo.

Although there were large trading centers along these rivers, most West Africans lived in small villages and identified with their extended family or their clan. Wives, children, and dependents (including enslaved people) were a sign of wealth among men, and **polygyny**, the practice of having more than one wife at a time, was widespread. In time of need, relatives, however far away, were counted upon to assist in supplying food or security. Because of the clannish nature of African society, "we" was associated with the village and family members, while "they" included everyone else. Hundreds of separate dialects emerged; in modern Nigeria, nearly five hundred are still spoken.

CLICK AND EXPLORE

Read The Role of Islam in African Slavery (http://openstax.org/l/islamslavery) to learn more about the African slave trade.

THE MAJOR AFRICAN EMPIRES

Following the death of the prophet Muhammad in 632 CE, Islam continued to spread quickly across North Africa, bringing not only a unifying faith but a political and legal structure as well. As lands fell under the control of Muslim armies, they instituted Islamic rule and legal structures as local chieftains converted, usually under penalty of death. Only those who had converted to Islam could rule or be engaged in trade. The first major empire to emerge in West Africa was the Ghana Empire (Figure 1.16). By 750, the Soninke farmers of the sub-Sahara had become wealthy by taxing the trade that passed through their area. For instance, the Niger River basin supplied gold to the Berber and Arab traders from west of the Nile Valley, who brought cloth, weapons, and manufactured goods into the interior. Huge Saharan salt mines supplied the life-sustaining mineral to the Mediterranean coast of Africa and inland areas. By 900, the monotheistic Muslims controlled most of this trade and had converted many of the African ruling elite. The majority of the population, however, maintained their tribal animistic practices, which gave living attributes to nonliving objects such as mountains, rivers, and wind. Because Ghana's king controlled the gold supply, he was able to maintain price controls and afford a strong military. Soon, however, a new kingdom emerged.

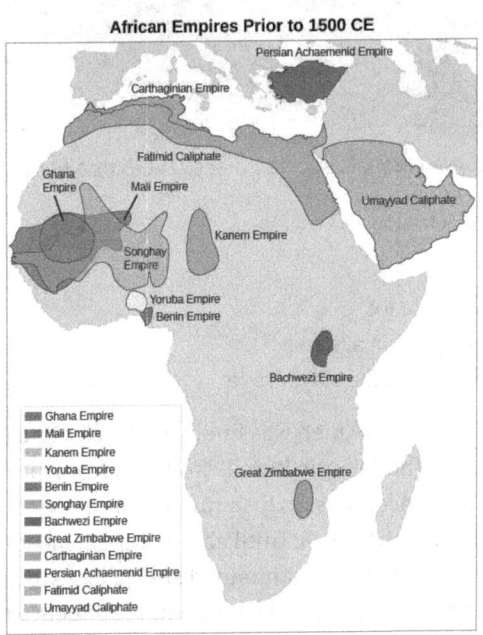

FIGURE 1.16 This map shows the general locations of major West African empires before 1492. Along the Mediterranean coast, Muslim states prevailed.

By 1200 CE, under the leadership of Sundiata Keita, Mali had replaced Ghana as the leading state in West Africa. After Sundiata's rule, the court converted to Islam, and Muslim scribes played a large part in administration and government. Miners then discovered huge new deposits of gold east of the Niger River. By the fourteenth century, the empire was so wealthy that while on a *hajj*, or pilgrimage to the holy city of Mecca, Mali's ruler Mansu Musa gave away enough gold to create serious price inflation in the cities along his route. Timbuktu, the capital city, became a leading Islamic center for education, commerce and the slave trade. Meanwhile, in the east, the city of Gao became increasingly strong under the leadership of Sonni Ali and soon eclipsed Mali's power. Timbuktu sought Ali's assistance in repelling the Tuaregs from the north. By 1500, however, the Tuareg empire of Songhay had eclipsed Mali, where weak and ineffective leadership prevailed.

THE ROLE OF SLAVERY

The institution of slavery is not a recent phenomenon. Most civilizations have practiced some form of human bondage and servitude, and African empires were no different (Figure 1.17). Famine or fear of stronger enemies might force one tribe to ask another for help and give themselves in a type of bondage in exchange. Similar to the European serf system, those seeking protection, or relief from starvation, would become the servants of those who provided relief. Debt might also be worked off through a form of servitude. Typically, these servants became a part of the extended tribal family. There is some evidence of **chattel slavery**, in which people are treated as personal property to be bought and sold, in the Nile Valley. It appears there was a slave-trade route through the Sahara that brought sub-Saharan Africans to Rome, which had enslaved people from all over the world.

FIGURE 1.17 Traders with a group of enslaved people connected at the neck. Muslim traders brought enslaved people to the North African coast, where they might be sent to Europe or other parts of Africa.

Arab slave trading, which exchanged enslaved people for goods from the Mediterranean, existed long before Islam's spread across North Africa. Muslims later expanded this trade and enslaved not only Africans but also Europeans, especially from Spain, Sicily, and Italy. Male captives were forced to build coastal fortifications and serve as enslaved galley people. Women were added to the harem.

The major European slave trade began with Portugal's exploration of the west coast of Africa in search of a trade route to the East. By 1444, enslaved people were being brought from Africa to work on the sugar plantations of the Madeira Islands, off the coast of modern Morocco. The slave trade then expanded greatly as European colonies in the New World demanded an ever-increasing number of workers for the extensive plantations growing tobacco, sugar, and eventually rice and cotton (Figure 1.18).

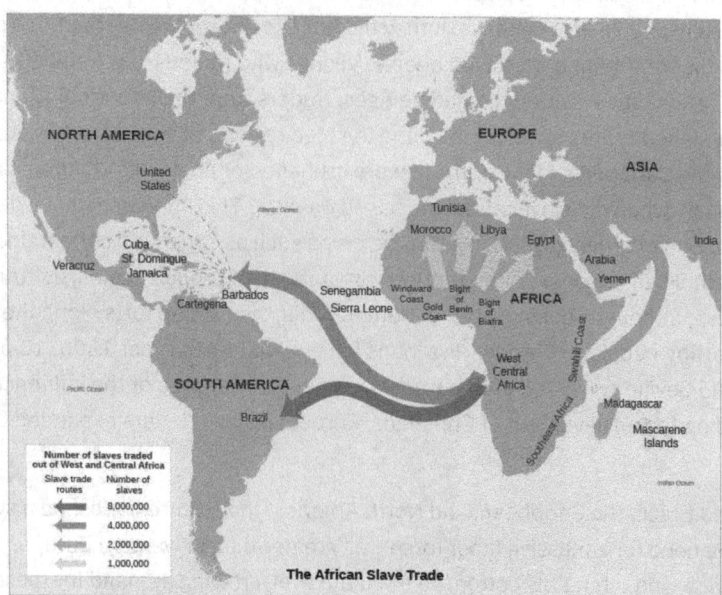

FIGURE 1.18 This map shows the routes that were used in the course of the slave trade and the number of enslaved people who traveled each route. As the figures indicate, most enslaved African were bound for Brazil and the Caribbean. While West Africans made up the vast majority of the enslaved, the east coast of Africa, too, supplied

enslaved people for the trade.

In the New World, the institution of slavery assumed a new aspect when the mercantilist system demanded a permanent, identifiable, and plentiful labor supply. Enslaved Africans were both easily identified (by their skin color) and plentiful, because of the thriving slave trade. This led to a race-based slavery system in the New World unlike any bondage system that had come before. Initially, the Spanish tried to force Native people to farm their crops. Most Spanish and Portuguese settlers coming to the New World were gentlemen and did not perform physical labor. They came to "serve God, but also to get rich," as noted by Bernal Díaz del Castillo. However, enslaved natives tended to sicken or die from disease or from the overwork and cruel treatment they were subjected to, and so the indigenous peoples proved not to be a dependable source of labor. Although he later repented of his ideas, the great defender of the Native peoples, Bartolomé de Las Casas, seeing the near extinction of the native population, suggested the Spanish send Black (and White) laborers to the Indies. These workers proved hardier, and within fifty years, a change took place: The profitability of the African slave trade, coupled with the seemingly limitless number of potential enslaved people and the Catholic Church's denunciation of the enslavement of Christians, led race to become a dominant factor in the institution of slavery.

In the English colonies along the Atlantic coast, indentured servants initially filled the need for labor in the North, where family farms were the norm. In the South, however, labor-intensive crops such as tobacco, rice, and indigo prevailed, and eventually the supply of indentured servants was insufficient to meet the demand. These workers served only for periods of three to seven years before being freed; a more permanent labor supply was needed. Thus, whereas in Africa permanent, inherited slavery was unknown, and children of those bound in slavery to the tribe usually were free and intermarried with their captors, this changed in the Americas; slavery became permanent, and children born to enslaved people became enslaved. This development, along with slavery's identification with race, forever changed the institution and shaped its unique character in the New World.

AMERICANA

The Beginnings of Racial Slavery

Slavery has a long history. The ancient Greek philosopher Aristotle posited that some peoples were *homunculi*, or humanlike but not really people—for instance, if they did not speak Greek. Both the Bible and the Koran have passages that address the treatment of enslaved people. Vikings who raided from Ireland to Russia brought back enslaved people of all nationalities. During the Middle Ages, traders from the interior of Africa brought enslaved people along well-established routes to sell them along the Mediterranean coast. Initially, slavers also brought enslaved Europeans to the Caribbean. Many of these were orphaned or homeless children captured in the cities of Ireland. The question is, when did slavery become based on race? This appears to have developed in the New World, with the introduction of gruelingly labor-intensive crops such as sugar and coffee. Unable to fill their growing need from the ranks of prisoners or indentured servants, the European colonists turned to African laborers. The Portuguese, although seeking a trade route to India, also set up forts along the West African coast for the purpose of exporting people to Europe. Historians believe that by the year 1500, 10 percent of the population of Lisbon and Seville consisted of Black enslaved people. Because of the influence of the Catholic Church, which frowned on the enslavement of Christians, European slave traders expanded their reach down the coast of Africa.

When Europeans settled Brazil, the Caribbean, and North America, they thus established a system of racially based slavery. Here, the need for a massive labor force was greater than in western Europe. The land was ripe for growing sugar, coffee, rice, and ultimately cotton. To fulfill the ever-growing demand for these crops, large plantations were created. The success of these plantations depended upon the availability of a permanent, plentiful, identifiable, and skilled labor supply. As Africans were already familiar with animal husbandry as well as farming, had an identifying skin color, and could be readily supplied by the existing African slave trade, they proved the answer to this need. This process set the stage for the expansion of New World slavery into North America.

Key Terms

Beringia   an ancient land bridge linking Asia and North America

Black Death   two strains of the bubonic plague that simultaneously swept western Europe in the fourteenth century, causing the death of nearly half the population

chasquis   Incan relay runners used to send messages over great distances

chattel slavery   a system of servitude in which people are treated as personal property to be bought and sold

chinampas   floating Aztec gardens consisting of a large barge woven from reeds, filled with dirt and floating on the water, allowing for irrigation

Crusades   a series of military expeditions made by Christian Europeans to recover the Holy Land from the Muslims in the eleventh, twelfth, and thirteenth centuries

feudal society   a social arrangement in which serfs and knights provided labor and military service to noble lords, receiving protection and land use in return

Inquisition   a campaign by the Catholic Church to root out heresy, especially among converted Jews and Muslims

Koran   the sacred book of Islam, written by the prophet Muhammad in the seventh century

matriarchy   a society in which women have political power

mita   the Incan labor tax, with each family donating time and work to communal projects

polygyny   the practice of taking more than one wife

quipu   an ancient Incan device for recording information, consisting of variously colored threads knotted in different ways

Reconquista   Spain's nearly eight-hundred-year holy war against Islam, which ended in 1492

serf   a peasant tied to the land and its lord

Summary

1.1 The Americas

Great civilizations had risen and fallen in the Americas before the arrival of the Europeans. In North America, the complex Pueblo societies including the Mogollon, Hohokam, and Anasazi as well as the city at Cahokia had peaked and were largely memories. The Eastern Woodland peoples were thriving, but they were soon overwhelmed as the number of English, French, and Dutch settlers increased.

Mesoamerica and South America had also witnessed the rise and fall of cultures. The once-mighty Mayan population centers were largely empty. In 1492, however, the Aztecs in Mexico City were at their peak. Subjugating surrounding tribes and requiring tribute of both humans for sacrifice and goods for consumption, the island city of Tenochtitlán was the hub of an ever-widening commercial center and the equal of any large European city until Cortés destroyed it. Further south in Peru, the Inca linked one of the largest empires in history through the use of roads and disciplined armies. Without the use of the wheel, they cut and fashioned stone to build Machu Picchu high in the Andes before abandoning the city for unknown reasons. Thus, depending on what part of the New World they explored, the Europeans encountered peoples that diverged widely in their cultures, traditions, and numbers.

1.2 Europe on the Brink of Change

One effect of the Crusades was that a larger portion of western Europe became familiar with the goods of the East. A lively trade subsequently developed along a variety of routes known collectively as the Silk Road to supply the demand for these products. Brigands and greedy middlemen made the trip along this route expensive and dangerous. By 1492, Europe—recovered from the Black Death and in search of new products and new wealth—was anxious to improve trade and communications with the rest of the world. Venice and Genoa led the way in trading with the East. The lure of profit pushed explorers to seek new trade routes to the Spice Islands and eliminate Muslim middlemen.

Portugal, under the leadership of Prince Henry the Navigator, attempted to send ships around the continent of Africa. Ferdinand of Aragon and Isabella of Castile hired Columbus to find a route to the East by going west. As strong supporters of the Catholic Church, they sought to bring Christianity to the East and any newly found lands, as well as hoping to find sources of wealth.

1.3 West Africa and the Role of Slavery

Before 1492, Africa, like the Americas, had experienced the rise and fall of many cultures, but the continent did not develop a centralized authority structure. African peoples practiced various forms of slavery, all of which differed significantly from the racial slavery that ultimately developed in the New World. After the arrival of Islam and before the Portuguese came to the coast of West Africa in 1444, Arabs and Berbers controlled the slave trade out of Africa, which expanded as European powers began to colonize the New World. Driven by a demand for labor, slavery in the Americas developed a new form: It was based on race, and the status of slave was both permanent and inherited.

Review Questions

1. Which of the following Native peoples built homes in cliff dwellings that still exist?
   A. Anasazi
   B. Cherokee
   C. Aztec
   D. Inca

2. Which culture developed the first writing system in the Western Hemisphere?
   A. Inca
   B. Maya
   C. Olmec
   D. Pueblo

3. Which culture developed a road system rivaling that of the Romans?
   A. Cherokee
   B. Inca
   C. Olmec
   D. Anasazi

4. What were the major differences between the societies of the Aztec, Inca, and Maya and the Native peoples of North America?

5. The series of attempts by Christian armies to retake the Holy Lands from Muslims was known as _____.
   A. the Crusades
   B. the Reconquista
   C. the Black Death
   D. the Silk Road

6. _____ became wealthy trading with the East.
   A. Carcassonne
   B. Jerusalem
   C. Rome
   D. Venice

7. In 1492, the Spanish forced these two religious groups to either convert or leave.
   A. Jews and Muslims
   B. Christians and Jews
   C. Protestants and Muslims
   D. Catholics and Jews

8. How did European feudal society operate? How was this a mutually supportive system?

9. Why did Columbus believe he could get to the Far East by sailing west? What were the problems with this plan?

10. The city of _____ became a leading center for Muslim scholarship and trade.
    A. Cairo
    B. Timbuktu
    C. Morocco
    D. Mali

11. Which of the following does *not* describe a form of slavery traditionally practiced in Africa?
    A. a system in which those in need of supplies or protection give themselves in servitude
    B. a system in which debtors repay those whom they owe by giving themselves in servitude
    C. a system in which people are treated as chattel—that is, as personal property to be bought and sold
    D. a system in which people are enslaved permanently on account of their race

Critical Thinking Questions

12. The Inca were able to control an empire that stretched from modern Colombia to southern Chile. Which of their various means for achieving such control do you think were most effective, and why?

13. How did the Olmec, Aztec, Inca, Maya, and North American Natives differ in their ways of life and cultural achievements? How did their particular circumstances—geography, history, or the accomplishments of the societies that had preceded them, for example—serve to shape their particular traditions and cultures?

14. What were the lasting effects of the Crusades? In what ways did they provide opportunities—both negative and positive—for cross-cultural encounters and exchanges?

15. Was race identified with slavery before the era of European exploration? Why or why not? How did slavery's association with race change the institution's character?

16. What are the differences between the types of slavery traditionally practiced in Africa and the slavery that developed in the New World? How did other types of servitude, such as European serfdom, compare to slavery?

Early Globalization: The Atlantic World, 1492–1650

2

FIGURE 2.1 After Christopher Columbus "discovered" the New World, he sent letters home to Spain describing the wonders he beheld. These letters were quickly circulated throughout Europe and translated into Italian, German, and Latin. This woodcut is from the first Italian verse translation of the letter Columbus sent to the Spanish court after his first voyage, *Lettera delle isole novamente trovata* by Giuliano Dati.

CHAPTER OUTLINE

2.1 Portuguese Exploration and Spanish Conquest
2.2 Religious Upheavals in the Developing Atlantic World
2.3 Challenges to Spain's Supremacy
2.4 New Worlds in the Americas: Labor, Commerce, and the Columbian Exchange

INTRODUCTION The story of the Atlantic World is the story of global migration, a migration driven in large part by the actions and aspirations of the ruling heads of Europe. Columbus is hardly visible in this illustration of his ships making landfall on the Caribbean island of Hispaniola (Figure 2.1). Instead, Ferdinand II of Spain (in the foreground) sits on his throne and points toward Columbus's landing. As the ships arrive, the Arawak people tower over the Spanish, suggesting the native population density of the islands.

This historic moment in 1492 sparked new rivalries among European powers as they scrambled to create New World colonies, fueled by the quest for wealth and power as well as by religious passions. Almost continuous war resulted. Spain achieved early preeminence, creating a far-flung empire and growing rich with treasures from the Americas. Native Americans who confronted the newcomers from Europe suffered unprecedented losses of life, however, as previously unknown diseases sliced through their populations. They also were victims of the arrogance of the Europeans, who viewed themselves as uncontested masters of the New World, sent by God to bring Christianity to the "Indians."

2.1 Portuguese Exploration and Spanish Conquest

LEARNING OBJECTIVES

By the end of this section, you will be able to:
- Describe Portuguese exploration of the Atlantic and Spanish exploration of the Americas, and the importance of these voyages to the developing Atlantic World
- Explain the importance of Spanish exploration of the Americas in the expansion of Spain's empire and the development of Spanish Renaissance culture

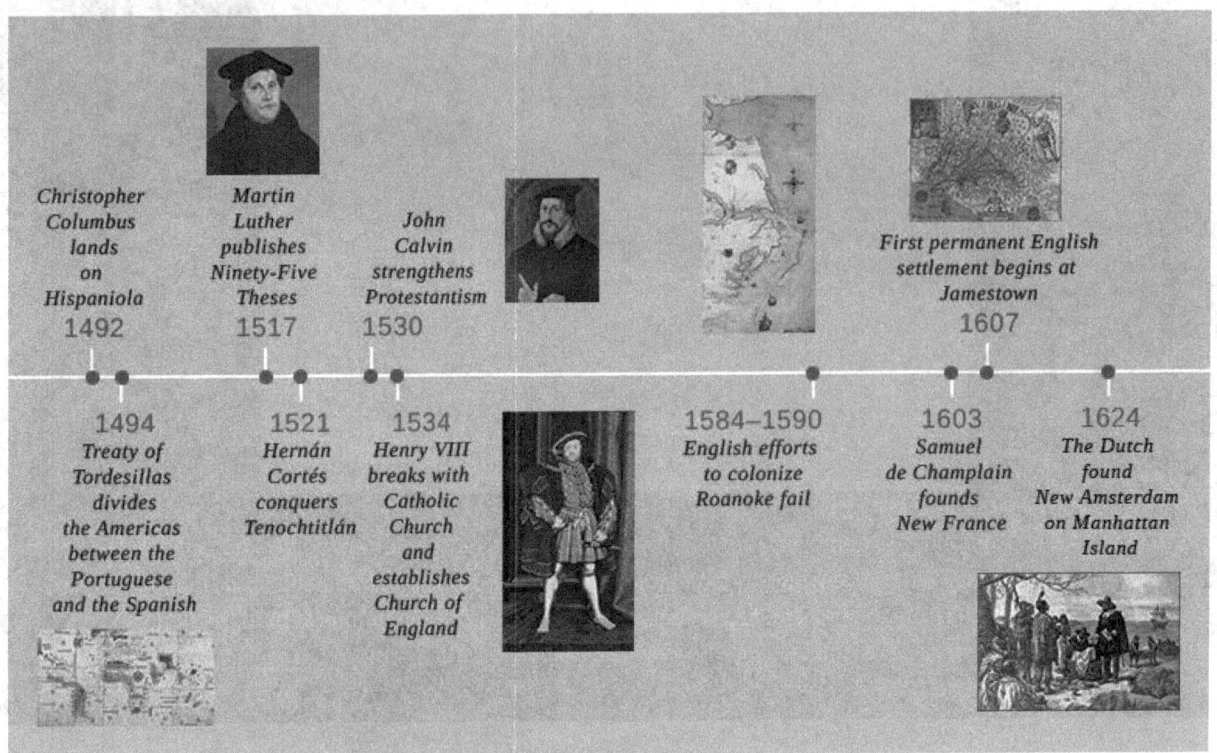

FIGURE 2.2

Portuguese colonization of Atlantic islands in the 1400s inaugurated an era of aggressive European expansion across the Atlantic. In the 1500s, Spain surpassed Portugal as the dominant European power. This age of exploration and the subsequent creation of an Atlantic World marked the earliest phase of globalization, in which previously isolated groups—Africans, Native Americans, and Europeans—first came into contact with each other, sometimes with disastrous results.

PORTUGUESE EXPLORATION

Portugal's Prince Henry the Navigator spearheaded his country's exploration of Africa and the Atlantic in the 1400s. With his support, Portuguese mariners successfully navigated an eastward route to Africa, establishing a foothold there that became a foundation of their nation's trade empire in the fifteenth and sixteenth centuries.

Portuguese mariners built an Atlantic empire by colonizing the Canary, Cape Verde, and Azores Islands, as well as the island of Madeira. Merchants then used these Atlantic outposts as debarkation points for subsequent journeys. From these strategic points, Portugal spread its empire down the western coast of Africa to the Congo, along the western coast of India, and eventually to Brazil on the eastern coast of South America. It also established trading posts in China and Japan. While the Portuguese didn't rule over an immense landmass, their strategic holdings of islands and coastal ports gave them almost unrivaled control of nautical trade routes and a global empire of trading posts during the 1400s.

The travels of Portuguese traders to western Africa introduced them to the African slave trade, already brisk among African states. Seeing the value of this source of labor in growing the profitable crop of sugar on their Atlantic islands, the Portuguese soon began exporting enslaved Africans along with African ivory and gold. Sugar fueled the Atlantic slave trade, and the Portuguese islands quickly became home to sugar plantations. The Portuguese also traded these enslaved people, introducing much-needed human capital to other European nations. In the following years, as European exploration spread, slavery spread as well. In time, much of the Atlantic World would become a gargantuan sugar-plantation complex in which Africans labored to produce the highly profitable commodity for European consumers.

AMERICANA

Elmina Castle

In 1482, Portuguese traders built Elmina Castle (also called São Jorge da Mina, or Saint George's of the Mine) in present-day Ghana, on the west coast of Africa (Figure 2.3). A fortified trading post, it had mounted cannons facing out to sea, not inland toward continental Africa; the Portuguese had greater fear of a naval attack from other Europeans than of a land attack from Africans. Portuguese traders soon began to settle around the fort and established the town of Elmina.

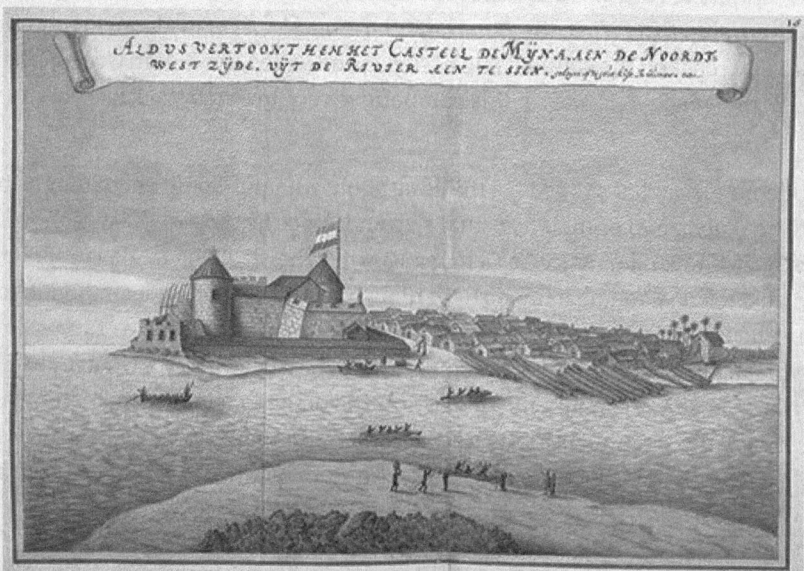

FIGURE 2.3 Elmina Castle on the west coast of Ghana was used as a holding pen for captured people before they were brought across the Atlantic and sold. Originally built by the Portuguese in the fifteenth century, it appears in this image as it was in the 1660s, after being seized by Dutch slave traders in 1637.

Although the Portuguese originally used the fort primarily for trading gold, by the sixteenth century they had shifted their focus. The dungeon of the fort now served as a holding pen for enslaved Africans from the interior of the continent, while on the upper floors Portuguese traders ate, slept, and prayed in a chapel. Enslaved people lived in the dungeon for weeks or months until ships arrived to transport them to Europe or the Americas. For them, the dungeon of Elmina was their last sight of their home country.

SPANISH EXPLORATION AND CONQUEST

The Spanish established the first European settlements in the Americas, beginning in the Caribbean and, by

1600, extending throughout Central and South America. Thousands of Spaniards flocked to the Americas seeking wealth and status. The most famous of these Spanish adventurers are Christopher Columbus (who, though Italian himself, explored on behalf of the Spanish monarchs), Hernán Cortés, and Francisco Pizarro.

The history of Spanish exploration begins with the history of Spain itself. During the fifteenth century, Spain hoped to gain advantage over its rival, Portugal. The marriage of Ferdinand of Aragon and Isabella of Castile in 1469 unified Catholic Spain and began the process of building a nation that could compete for worldwide power. Since the 700s, much of Spain had been under Islamic rule, and King Ferdinand II and Queen Isabella I, arch-defenders of the Catholic Church against Islam, were determined to defeat the Muslims in Granada, the last Islamic stronghold in Spain. In 1492, they completed the Reconquista: the centuries-long Christian conquest of the Iberian Peninsula. The Reconquista marked another step forward in the process of making Spain an imperial power, and Ferdinand and Isabella were now ready to look further afield.

Their goals were to expand Catholicism and to gain a commercial advantage over Portugal. To those ends, Ferdinand and Isabella sponsored extensive Atlantic exploration. Spain's most famous explorer, Christopher Columbus, was actually from Genoa, Italy. He believed that, using calculations based on other mariners' journeys, he could chart a westward route to India, which could be used to expand European trade and spread Christianity. Starting in 1485, he approached Genoese, Venetian, Portuguese, English, and Spanish monarchs, asking for ships and funding to explore this westward route. All those he petitioned—including Ferdinand and Isabella at first—rebuffed him; their nautical experts all concurred that Columbus's estimates of the width of the Atlantic Ocean were far too low. However, after three years of entreaties, and, more important, the completion of the Reconquista, Ferdinand and Isabella agreed to finance Columbus's expedition in 1492, supplying him with three ships: the *Nina*, the *Pinta*, and the *Santa Maria*. The Spanish monarchs knew that Portuguese mariners had reached the southern tip of Africa and sailed the Indian Ocean. They understood that the Portuguese would soon reach Asia and, in this competitive race to reach the Far East, the Spanish rulers decided to act.

Columbus held erroneous views that shaped his thinking about what he would encounter as he sailed west. He believed the earth to be much smaller than its actual size and, since he did not know of the existence of the Americas, he fully expected to land in Asia. On October 12, 1492, however, he made landfall on an island in the Bahamas. He then sailed to an island he named **Hispaniola** (present-day Dominican Republic and Haiti) (Figure 2.4). Believing he had landed in the East Indies, Columbus called the native Taínos he found there "Indios," giving rise to the term "Indian" for any native people of the New World. Upon Columbus's return to Spain, the Spanish crown bestowed on him the title of Admiral of the Ocean Sea and named him governor and viceroy of the lands he had discovered. As a devoted Catholic, Columbus had agreed with Ferdinand and Isabella prior to sailing west that part of the expected wealth from his voyage would be used to continue the fight against Islam.

FIGURE 2.4 This sixteenth-century map shows the island of Hispaniola (present-day Haiti and Dominican Republic). Note the various fanciful elements, such as the large-scale ships and sea creatures, and consider what the creator

of this map hoped to convey. In addition to navigation, what purpose would such a map have served?

Columbus's 1493 letter—or **probanza de mérito** (proof of merit)—describing his "discovery" of a New World did much to inspire excitement in Europe. *Probanzas de méritos* were reports and letters written by Spaniards in the New World to the Spanish crown, designed to win royal patronage. Today they highlight the difficult task of historical work; while the letters are primary sources, historians need to understand the context and the culture in which the conquistadors, as the Spanish adventurers came to be called, wrote them and distinguish their bias and subjective nature. While they are filled with distortions and fabrications, *probanzas de méritos* are still useful in illustrating the expectation of wealth among the explorers as well as their view that native peoples would not pose a serious obstacle to colonization.

In 1493, Columbus sent two copies of a *probanza de mérito* to the Spanish king and queen and their minister of finance, Luis de Santángel. Santángel had supported Columbus's voyage, helping him to obtain funding from Ferdinand and Isabella. Copies of the letter were soon circulating all over Europe, spreading news of the wondrous new land that Columbus had "discovered." Columbus would make three more voyages over the next decade, establishing Spain's first settlement in the New World on the island of Hispaniola. Many other Europeans followed in Columbus's footsteps, drawn by dreams of winning wealth by sailing west. Another Italian, Amerigo Vespucci, sailing for the Portuguese crown, explored the South American coastline between 1499 and 1502. Unlike Columbus, he realized that the Americas were not part of Asia but lands unknown to Europeans. Vespucci's widely published accounts of his voyages fueled speculation and intense interest in the New World among Europeans. Among those who read Vespucci's reports was the German mapmaker Martin Waldseemuller. Using the explorer's first name as a label for the new landmass, Waldseemuller attached "America" to his map of the New World in 1507, and the name stuck.

DEFINING AMERICAN

Columbus's *Probanza de mérito* of 1493

The exploits of the most famous Spanish explorers have provided Western civilization with a narrative of European supremacy and Native American savagery. However, these stories are based on the self-aggrandizing efforts of conquistadors to secure royal favor through the writing of *probanzas de méritos* (proofs of merit). Below are excerpts from Columbus's 1493 letter to Luis de Santángel, which illustrates how fantastic reports from European explorers gave rise to many myths surrounding the Spanish conquest and the New World.

"This island, like all the others, is most extensive. It has many ports along the sea-coast excelling any in Christendom—and many fine, large, flowing rivers. The land there is elevated, with many mountains and peaks incomparably higher than in the centre isle. They are most beautiful, of a thousand varied forms, accessible, and full of trees of endless varieties, so high that they seem to touch the sky, and I have been told that they never lose their foliage.... There is honey, and there are many kinds of birds, and a great variety of fruits. Inland there are numerous mines of metals and innumerable people. Hispaniola is a marvel. Its hills and mountains, fine plains and open country, are rich and fertile for planting and for pasturage, and for building towns and villages. The seaports there are incredibly fine, as also the magnificent rivers, most of which bear gold. The trees, fruits and grasses differ widely from those in Juana. There are many spices and vast mines of gold and other metals in this island. They have no iron, nor steel, nor weapons, nor are they fit for them, because although they are well-made men of commanding stature, they appear extraordinarily timid. The only arms they have are sticks of cane, cut when in seed, with a sharpened stick at the end, and they are afraid to use these. Often I have sent two or three men ashore to some town to converse with them, and the natives came out in great numbers, and as soon as they saw our men arrive, fled without a moment's delay although I protected them from all injury."

What does this letter show us about Spanish objectives in the New World? How do you think it might have influenced Europeans reading about the New World for the first time?

The 1492 Columbus landfall accelerated the rivalry between Spain and Portugal, and the two powers vied for domination through the acquisition of new lands. In the 1480s, Pope Sixtus IV had granted Portugal the right to all land south of the Cape Verde islands, leading the Portuguese king to claim that the lands discovered by Columbus belonged to Portugal, not Spain. Seeking to ensure that Columbus's finds would remain Spanish, Spain's monarchs turned to the Spanish-born Pope Alexander VI, who issued two papal decrees in 1493 that gave legitimacy to Spain's Atlantic claims at the expense of Portugal. Hoping to salvage Portugal's Atlantic holdings, King João II began negotiations with Spain. The resulting Treaty of Tordesillas in 1494 drew a north-to-south line through South America (Figure 2.5); Spain gained territory west of the line, while Portugal retained the lands east of the line, including the east coast of Brazil.

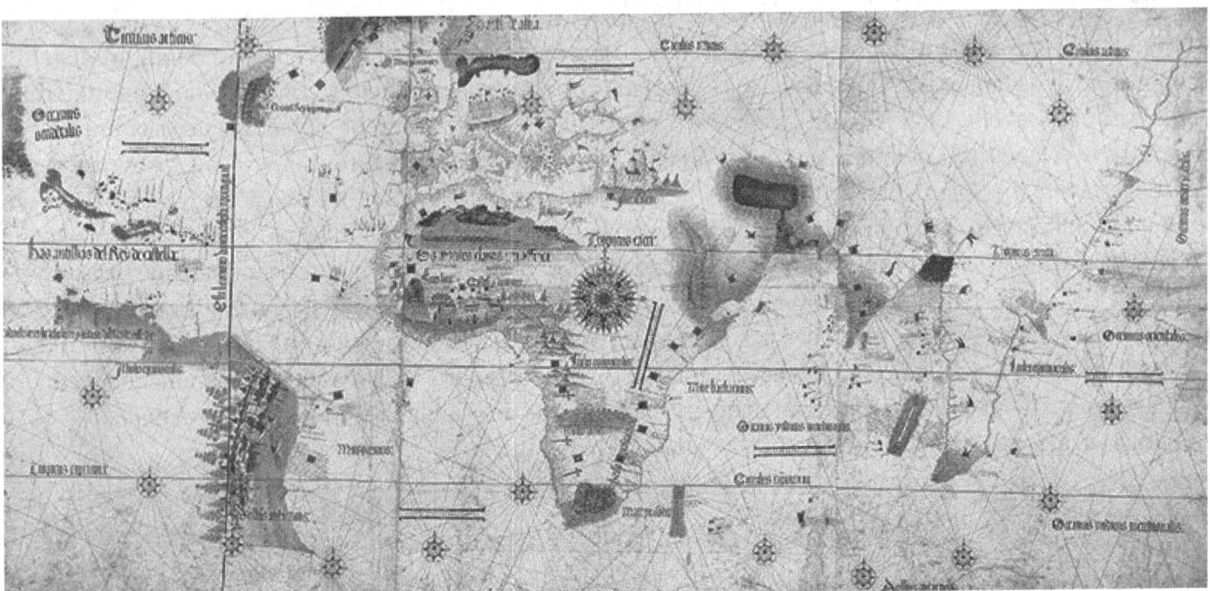

FIGURE 2.5 This 1502 map, known as the Cantino World Map, depicts the cartographer's interpretation of the world in light of recent discoveries. The map shows areas of Portuguese and Spanish exploration, the two nations' claims under the Treaty of Tordesillas, and a variety of flora, fauna, figures, and structures. What does it reveal about the state of geographical knowledge, as well as European perceptions of the New World, at the beginning of the sixteenth century?

Columbus's discovery opened a floodgate of Spanish exploration. Inspired by tales of rivers of gold and timid, malleable natives, later Spanish explorers were relentless in their quest for land and gold. Hernán Cortés hoped to gain hereditary privilege for his family, tribute payments and labor from natives, and an annual pension for his service to the crown. Cortés arrived on Hispaniola in 1504 and took part in the conquest of that island. In anticipation of winning his own honor and riches, Cortés later explored the Yucatán Peninsula. In 1519, he entered Tenochtitlán, the capital of the Aztec (Mexica) Empire. He and his men were astonished by the incredibly sophisticated causeways, gardens, and temples in the city, but they were horrified by the practice of human sacrifice that was part of the Aztec religion. Above all else, the Aztec wealth in gold fascinated the Spanish adventurers.

Hoping to gain power over the city, Cortés took Moctezuma, the Aztec ruler, hostage. The Spanish then murdered hundreds of high-ranking Mexica during a festival to celebrate Huitzilopochtli, the god of war. This angered the people of Tenochtitlán, who rose up against the interlopers in their city. Cortés and his people fled for their lives, running down one of Tenochtitlán's causeways to safety on the shore. Smarting from their defeat at the hands of the Aztec, Cortés slowly created alliances with native peoples who resented Aztec rule. It took nearly a year for the Spanish and the tens of thousands of native allies who joined them to defeat the Mexica in Tenochtitlán, which they did by laying siege to the city. Only by playing upon the disunity among the diverse groups in the Aztec Empire were the Spanish able to capture the grand city of Tenochtitlán. In August 1521, having successfully fomented civil war as well as fended off rival Spanish explorers, Cortés claimed

Tenochtitlán for Spain and renamed it Mexico City.

The traditional European narrative of exploration presents the victory of the Spanish over the Aztec as an example of the superiority of the Europeans over the "savage Indians." However, the reality is far more complex. When Cortés explored central Mexico, he encountered a region simmering with conflict. Far from being unified and content under Aztec rule, many peoples in Mexico resented it and were ready to rebel. One group in particular, the Tlaxcalan, threw their lot in with the Spanish, providing as many as 200,000 fighters in the siege of Tenochtitlán. The Spanish also brought smallpox into the valley of Mexico. The disease took a heavy toll on the people in Tenochtitlán, playing a much greater role in the city's demise than did Spanish force of arms.

Cortés was also aided by a Nahua woman called Malintzin (also known as La Malinche or Doña Marina, her Spanish name), whom the natives of Tabasco gave him as tribute. Malintzin translated for Cortés in his dealings with Moctezuma and, whether willingly or under pressure, entered into a physical relationship with him. Their son, Martín, may have been the first mestizo (person of mixed indigenous American and European descent). Malintzin remains a controversial figure in the history of the Atlantic World; some people view her as a traitor because she helped Cortés conquer the Aztecs, while others see her as a victim of European expansion. In either case, she demonstrates one way in which native peoples responded to the arrival of the Spanish. Without her, Cortés would not have been able to communicate, and without the language bridge, he surely would have been less successful in destabilizing the Aztec Empire. By this and other means, native people helped shape the conquest of the Americas.

Spain's acquisitiveness seemingly knew no bounds as groups of its explorers searched for the next trove of instant riches. One such explorer, Francisco Pizarro, made his way to the Spanish Caribbean in 1509, drawn by the promise of wealth and titles. He participated in successful expeditions in Panama before following rumors of Inca wealth to the south. Although his first efforts against the Inca Empire in the 1520s failed, Pizarro captured the Inca emperor Atahualpa in 1532 and executed him one year later. In 1533, Pizarro founded Lima, Peru. Like Cortés, Pizarro had to combat not only the natives of the new worlds he was conquering, but also competitors from his own country; a Spanish rival assassinated him in 1541.

Spain's drive to enlarge its empire led other hopeful conquistadors to push further into the Americas, hoping to replicate the success of Cortés and Pizarro. Hernando de Soto had participated in Pizarro's conquest of the Inca, and from 1539 to 1542 he led expeditions to what is today the southeastern United States, looking for gold. He and his followers explored what is now Florida, Georgia, the Carolinas, Tennessee, Alabama, Mississippi, Arkansas, Oklahoma, Louisiana, and Texas. Everywhere they traveled, they brought European diseases, which claimed thousands of native lives as well as the lives of the explorers. In 1542, de Soto himself died during the expedition. The surviving Spaniards, numbering a little over three hundred, returned to Mexico City without finding the much-anticipated mountains of gold and silver.

Francisco Vásquez de Coronado was born into a noble family and went to Mexico, then called New Spain, in 1535. He presided as governor over the province of Nueva Galicia, where he heard rumors of wealth to the north: a golden city called Quivira. Between 1540 and 1542, Coronado led a large expedition of Spaniards and native allies to the lands north of Mexico City, and for the next several years, they explored the area that is now the southwestern United States (Figure 2.6). During the winter of 1540–41, the explorers waged war against the Tiwa in present-day New Mexico. Rather than leading to the discovery of gold and silver, however, the expedition simply left Coronado bankrupt.

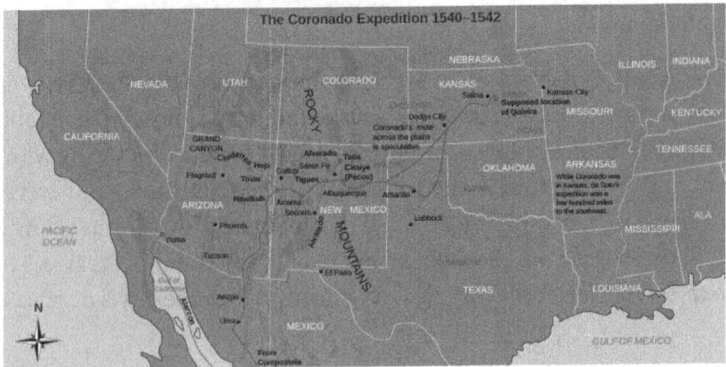

FIGURE 2.6 This map traces Coronado's path through the American Southwest and the Great Plains. The regions through which he traveled were not empty areas waiting to be "discovered": rather, they were populated and controlled by the groups of native peoples indicated. (credit: modification of work by National Park Service)

THE SPANISH GOLDEN AGE

The exploits of European explorers had a profound impact both in the Americas and back in Europe. An exchange of ideas, fueled and financed in part by New World commodities, began to connect European nations and, in turn, to touch the parts of the world that Europeans conquered. In Spain, gold and silver from the Americas helped to fuel a golden age, the Siglo de Oro, when Spanish art and literature flourished. Riches poured in from the colonies, and new ideas poured in from other countries and new lands. The Hapsburg dynasty, which ruled a collection of territories including Austria, the Netherlands, Naples, Sicily, and Spain, encouraged and financed the work of painters, sculptors, musicians, architects, and writers, resulting in a blooming of Spanish Renaissance culture. One of this period's most famous works is the novel *The Ingenious Gentleman Don Quixote of La Mancha*, by Miguel de Cervantes. This two-volume book (1605 and 1618) told a colorful tale of an *hidalgo* (gentleman) who reads so many tales of chivalry and knighthood that he becomes unable to tell reality from fiction. With his faithful sidekick Sancho Panza, Don Quixote leaves reality behind and sets out to revive chivalry by doing battle with what he perceives as the enemies of Spain.

CLICK AND EXPLORE

Explore the collection at The Cervantes Project (http://openstax.org/l/cervantes) for images, complete texts, and other resources relating to Cervantes's works.

Spain attracted innovative foreign painters such as El Greco, a Greek who had studied with Italian Renaissance masters like Titian and Michelangelo before moving to Toledo. Native Spaniards created equally enduring works. *Las Meninas (The Maids of Honor)*, painted by Diego Velázquez in 1656, is one of the best-known paintings in history. Velázquez painted himself into this imposingly large royal portrait (he's shown holding his brush and easel on the left) and boldly placed the viewer where the king and queen would stand in the scene (Figure 2.7).

FIGURE 2.7 *Las Meninas (The Maids of Honor)*, painted by Diego Velázquez in 1656, is unique for its time because it places the viewer in the place of King Philip IV and his wife, Queen Mariana.

2.2 Religious Upheavals in the Developing Atlantic World

LEARNING OBJECTIVES

By the end of this section, you will be able to:
- Explain the changes brought by the Protestant Reformation and how it influenced the development of the Atlantic World
- Describe Spain's response to the Protestant Reformation

Until the 1500s, the Catholic Church provided a unifying religious structure for Christian Europe. The Vatican in Rome exercised great power over the lives of Europeans; it controlled not only learning and scholarship but also finances, because it levied taxes on the faithful. Spain, with its New World wealth, was the bastion of the Catholic faith. Beginning with the reform efforts of Martin Luther in 1517 and John Calvin in the 1530s, however, Catholic dominance came under attack as the **Protestant Reformation**, a split or schism among European Christians, began.

During the sixteenth century, Protestantism spread through northern Europe, and Catholic countries responded by attempting to extinguish what was seen as the Protestant menace. Religious turmoil between Catholics and Protestants influenced the history of the Atlantic World as well, since different nation-states competed not only for control of new territories but also for the preeminence of their religious beliefs there. Just as the history of Spain's rise to power is linked to the Reconquista, so too is the history of early globalization connected to the history of competing Christian groups in the Atlantic World.

MARTIN LUTHER

Martin Luther (Figure 2.8) was a German Catholic monk who took issue with the Catholic Church's practice of selling **indulgences**, documents that absolved sinners of their errant behavior. He also objected to the Catholic Church's taxation of ordinary Germans and the delivery of Mass in Latin, arguing that it failed to instruct German Catholics, who did not understand the language.

FIGURE 2.8 Martin Luther, a German Catholic monk and leader of the Protestant Reformation, was a close friend of the German painter Lucas Cranach the Elder. Cranach painted this and several other portraits of Luther.

Many Europeans had called for reforms of the Catholic Church before Martin Luther did, but his protest had the unintended consequence of splitting European Christianity. Luther compiled a list of what he viewed as needed Church reforms, a document that came to be known as *The Ninety-Five Theses*, and nailed it to the door of a church in Wittenberg, Germany, in 1517. He called for the publication of the Bible in everyday language, took issue with the Church's policy of imposing tithes (a required payment to the Church that appeared to enrich the clergy), and denounced the buying and selling of indulgences. Although he had hoped to reform the Catholic Church while remaining a part of it, Luther's action instead triggered a movement called the Protestant Reformation that divided the Church in two. The Catholic Church condemned him as a heretic, but a doctrine based on his reforms, called Lutheranism, spread through northern Germany and Scandinavia.

CLICK AND EXPLORE

Visit Fordham University's Internet Medieval Sourcebook (http://openstax.org/l/fordham) for access to many primary sources relating to the Protestant Reformation.

JOHN CALVIN

Like Luther, the French lawyer John Calvin advocated making the Bible accessible to ordinary people; only by reading scripture and reflecting daily about their spiritual condition, he argued, could believers begin to understand the power of God. In 1535, Calvin fled Catholic France and led the Reformation movement from Geneva, Switzerland.

Calvinism emphasized human powerlessness before an omniscient God and stressed the idea of predestination, the belief that God selected a few chosen people for salvation while everyone else was predestined to damnation. Calvinists believed that reading scripture prepared sinners, if they were among the elect, to receive God's grace. In Geneva, Calvin established a Bible commonwealth, a community of believers whose sole source of authority was their interpretation of the Bible, not the authority of any prince or monarch. Soon Calvin's ideas spread to the Netherlands and Scotland.

PROTESTANTISM IN ENGLAND

Protestantism spread beyond the German states and Geneva to England, which had been a Catholic nation for centuries. Luther's idea that scripture should be available in the everyday language of worshippers inspired English scholar William Tyndale to translate the Bible into English in 1526. The seismic break with the Catholic Church in England occurred in the 1530s, when Henry VIII established a new, Protestant state religion.

A devout Catholic, Henry had initially stood in opposition to the Reformation. Pope Leo X even awarded him the title "Defender of the Faith." The tides turned, however, when Henry desired a male heir to the Tudor monarchy. When his Spanish Catholic wife, Catherine (the daughter of Ferdinand and Isabella), did not give birth to a boy, the king sought an annulment to their marriage. When the Pope refused his request, Henry created a new national Protestant church, the Church of England, with himself at its head. This left him free to annul his own marriage and marry Anne Boleyn.

Anne Boleyn also failed to produce a male heir, and when she was accused of adultery, Henry had her executed. His third wife, Jane Seymour, at long last delivered a son, Edward, who ruled for only a short time before dying in 1553 at the age of fifteen. Mary, the daughter of Henry VIII and his discarded first wife Catherine, then came to the throne, committed to restoring Catholicism. She earned the nickname "Bloody Mary" for the many executions of Protestants, often by burning alive, that she ordered during her reign.

Religious turbulence in England was finally quieted when Elizabeth, the Protestant daughter of Henry VIII and Anne Boleyn, ascended the throne in 1558. Under Elizabeth, the Church of England again became the state church, retaining the hierarchical structure and many of the rituals of the Catholic Church. However, by the late 1500s, some English members of the Church began to agitate for more reform. Known as **Puritans**, they worked to erase all vestiges of Catholicism from the Church of England. At the time, the term "puritan" was a pejorative one; many people saw Puritans as holier-than-thou frauds who used religion to swindle their neighbors. Worse still, many in power saw Puritans as a security threat because of their opposition to the national church.

Under Elizabeth, whose long reign lasted from 1558 to 1603, Puritans grew steadily in number. After James I died in 1625 and his son Charles I ascended the throne, Puritans became the target of increasing state pressure to conform. Many crossed the Atlantic in the 1620s and 1630s instead to create a New England, a haven for reformed Protestantism where Puritan was no longer a term of abuse. Thus, the religious upheavals that affected England so much had equally momentous consequences for the Americas.

RELIGIOUS WAR

By the early 1500s, the Protestant Reformation threatened the massive Spanish Catholic empire. As the preeminent Catholic power, Spain would not tolerate any challenge to the Holy Catholic Church. Over the course of the 1500s, it devoted vast amounts of treasure and labor to leading an unsuccessful effort to eradicate Protestantism in Europe.

Spain's main enemies at this time were the runaway Spanish provinces of the North Netherlands. By 1581, these seven northern provinces had declared their independence from Spain and created the Dutch Republic, also called Holland, where Protestantism was tolerated. Determined to deal a death blow to Protestantism in England and Holland, King Philip of Spain assembled a massive force of over thirty thousand men and 130 ships, and in 1588 he sent this navy, the Spanish Armada, north. But English sea power combined with a maritime storm destroyed the fleet.

The defeat of the Spanish Armada in 1588 was but one part of a larger but undeclared war between Protestant England and Catholic Spain. Between 1585 and 1604, the two rivals sparred repeatedly. England launched its own armada in 1589 in an effort to disable the Spanish fleet and capture Spanish treasure. However, the foray ended in disaster for the English, with storms, disease, and the strength of the Spanish Armada combining to bring about defeat.

The conflict between Spain and England dragged on into the early seventeenth century, and the newly Protestant nations, especially England and the Dutch Republic, posed a significant challenge to Spain (and also to Catholic France) as imperial rivalries played out in the Atlantic World. Spain retained its mighty American empire, but by the early 1600s, the nation could no longer keep England and other European rivals—the French and Dutch—from colonizing smaller islands in the Caribbean (Figure 2.9).

FIGURE 2.9 This portrait of Elizabeth I of England, painted by George Gower in about 1588, shows Elizabeth with her hand on a globe, signifying her power over the world. The pictures in the background show the English defeat of the Spanish Armada.

Religious intolerance characterized the sixteenth and seventeenth centuries, an age of powerful state religions with the authority to impose and enforce belief systems on the population. In this climate, religious violence was common. One of the most striking examples is the St. Bartholomew's Day Massacre of 1572, in which French Catholic troops began to kill unarmed French Protestants (Figure 2.10). The murders touched off mob violence that ultimately claimed nine thousand lives, a bloody episode that highlights the degree of religious turmoil that gripped Europe in the aftermath of the Protestant Reformation.

FIGURE 2.10 *Saint Bartholomew's Day Massacre* (1772-84), by François Dubois, shows the horrific violence of the St. Bartholomew's Day Massacre. In this scene, French Catholic troops slaughter French Protestant Calvinists.

2.3 Challenges to Spain's Supremacy

LEARNING OBJECTIVES

By the end of this section, you will be able to:
- Identify regions where the English, French, and Dutch explored and established settlements
- Describe the differences among the early colonies
- Explain the role of the American colonies in European nations' struggles for domination

For Europeans, the discovery of an Atlantic World meant newfound wealth in the form of gold and silver as well as valuable furs. The Americas also provided a new arena for intense imperial rivalry as different European nations jockeyed for preeminence in the New World. The religious motives for colonization spurred European expansion as well, and as the Protestant Reformation gained ground beginning in the 1520s, rivalries between Catholic and Protestant Christians spilled over into the Americas.

ENGLISH EXPLORATION

Disruptions during the Tudor monarchy—especially the creation of the Protestant Church of England by Henry VIII in the 1530s, the return of the nation to Catholicism under Queen Mary in the 1550s, and the restoration of Protestantism under Queen Elizabeth—left England with little energy for overseas projects. More important, England lacked the financial resources for such endeavors. Nonetheless, English monarchs carefully monitored developments in the new Atlantic World and took steps to assert England's claim to the Americas. As early as 1497, Henry VII of England had commissioned John Cabot, an Italian mariner, to explore new lands. Cabot sailed from England that year and made landfall somewhere along the North American coastline. For the next century, English fishermen routinely crossed the Atlantic to fish the rich waters off the North American coast. However, English colonization efforts in the 1500s were closer to home, as England devoted its energy to the colonization of Ireland.

Queen Elizabeth favored England's advance into the Atlantic World, though her main concern was blocking Spain's effort to eliminate Protestantism. Indeed, England could not commit to large-scale colonization in the Americas as long as Spain appeared ready to invade Ireland or Scotland. Nonetheless, Elizabeth approved of English **privateers**, sea captains to whom the home government had given permission to raid the enemy at will. These skilled mariners cruised the Caribbean, plundering Spanish ships whenever they could. Each year the English took more than £100,000 from Spain in this way; English privateer Francis Drake first made a name for himself when, in 1573, he looted silver, gold, and pearls worth £40,000.

Elizabeth did sanction an early attempt at colonization in 1584, when Sir Walter Raleigh, a favorite of the queen's, attempted to establish a colony at **Roanoke**, an island off the coast of present-day North Carolina. The colony was small, consisting of only 117 people, who suffered a poor relationship with the local Croatans, and struggled to survive in their new land (Figure 2.11). Their governor, John White, returned to England in late 1587 to secure more people and supplies, but events conspired to keep him away from Roanoke for three years. By the time he returned in 1590, the entire colony had vanished. The only trace the colonists left behind was the word *Croatoan* carved into a fence surrounding the village. Governor White never knew whether the colonists had decamped for nearby Croatoan Island (now Hatteras) or whether some disaster had befallen them all. Roanoke is still called "the lost colony."

FIGURE 2.11 In 1588, a promoter of English colonization named Thomas Hariot published *A Briefe and True Report of the New Found Land of Virginia*, which contained many engravings of the native peoples who lived on the Carolina coast in the 1580s. This print, "The brovvyllinge of their fishe ouer the flame" (1590) by Theodor de Bry, shows the ingenuity and wisdom of the "savages" of the New World. (credit: UNC Chapel Hill)

English promoters of colonization pushed its commercial advantages and the religious justification that

English colonies would allow the establishment of Protestantism in the Americas. Both arguments struck a chord. In the early 1600s, wealthy English merchants and the landed elite began to pool their resources to form **joint stock companies**. In this novel business arrangement, which was in many ways the precursor to the modern corporation, investors provided the capital for and assumed the risk of a venture in order to reap significant returns. The companies gained the approval of the English crown to establish colonies, and their investors dreamed of reaping great profits from the money they put into overseas colonization.

The first permanent English settlement was established by a joint stock company, the Virginia Company. Named for Elizabeth, the "virgin queen," the company gained royal approval to establish a colony on the east coast of North America, and in 1606, it sent 144 men and boys to the New World. In early 1607, this group sailed up Chesapeake Bay. Finding a river they called the James in honor of their new king, James I, they established a ramshackle settlement and named it Jamestown. Despite serious struggles, the colony survived.

Many of Jamestown's settlers were desperate men; although they came from elite families, they were younger sons who would not inherit their father's estates. The Jamestown adventurers believed they would find instant wealth in the New World and did not actually expect to have to perform work. Henry Percy, the eighth son of the Earl of Northumberland, was among them. His account, excerpted below, illustrates the hardships the English confronted in Virginia in 1607.

MY STORY

George Percy and the First Months at Jamestown

The 144 men and boys who started the Jamestown colony faced many hardships; by the end of the first winter, only 38 had survived. Disease, hunger, and poor relationships with local natives all contributed to the colony's high death toll. George Percy, who served twice as governor of Jamestown, kept records of the colonists' first months in the colony. These records were later published in London in 1608. This excerpt is from his account of August and September of 1607.

"The fourth day of September died Thomas Jacob Sergeant. The fifth day, there died Benjamin Beast. Our men were destroyed with cruel diseases, as Swellings, Fluxes, Burning Fevers, and by wars, and some departed suddenly, but for the most part they died of mere famine. There were never Englishmen left in a foreign Country in such misery as we were in this new discovered Virginia. . . . Our food was but a small Can of Barley sod* in water, to five men a day, our drink cold water taken out of the River, which was at a flood very salty, at a low tide full of slime and filth, which was the destruction of many of our men. Thus we lived for the space of five months in this miserable distress, not having five able men to man our Bulwarks upon any occasion. If it had not pleased God to have put a terror in the Savages' hearts, we had all perished by those wild and cruel Pagans, being in that weak estate as we were; our men night and day groaning in every corner of the Fort most pitiful to hear. If there were any conscience in men, it would make their hearts to bleed to hear the pitiful murmurings and outcries of our sick men without relief, every night and day, for the space of six weeks, some departing out of the World, many times three or four in a night; in the morning, their bodies trailed out of their Cabins like Dogs to be buried. In this sort did I see the mortality of diverse of our people."

"*soaked"

According to George Percy's account, what were the major problems the Jamestown settlers encountered? What kept the colony from complete destruction?

By any measure, England came late to the race to colonize. As Jamestown limped along in the 1610s, the Spanish Empire extended around the globe and grew rich from its global colonial project. Yet the English persisted, and for this reason the Jamestown settlement has a special place in history as the first permanent English colony in what later became the United States.

After Jamestown's founding, English colonization of the New World accelerated. In 1609, a ship bound for Jamestown foundered in a storm and landed on Bermuda. (Some believe this incident helped inspire Shakespeare's 1611 play *The Tempest*.) The admiral of the ship, George Somers, claimed the island for the English crown. The English also began to colonize small islands in the Caribbean, an incursion into the Spanish American empire. They established themselves on small islands such as St. Christopher (1624), Barbados (1627), Nevis (1628), Montserrat (1632), and Antigua (1632).

From the start, the English West Indies had a commercial orientation, for these islands produced cash crops: first tobacco and then sugar. Very quickly, by the mid-1600s, Barbados had become one of the most important English colonies because of the sugar produced there. Barbados was the first English colony dependent on enslaved people, and it became a model for other English slave societies on the American mainland. These differed radically from England itself, where slavery was not practiced.

English Puritans also began to colonize the Americas in the 1620s and 1630s. These intensely religious migrants dreamed of creating communities of reformed Protestantism where the corruption of England would be eliminated. One of the first groups of Puritans to move to North America, known as **Pilgrims** and led by William Bradford, had originally left England to live in the Netherlands. Fearing their children were losing their English identity among the Dutch, however, they sailed for North America in 1620 to settle at Plymouth, the first English settlement in New England. The Pilgrims differed from other Puritans in their insistence on separating from what they saw as the corrupt Church of England. For this reason, Pilgrims are known as **Separatists**.

Like Jamestown, Plymouth occupies an iconic place in American national memory. The tale of the 102 migrants who crossed the Atlantic aboard the *Mayflower* and their struggle for survival is a well-known narrative of the founding of the country. Their story includes the signing of the Mayflower Compact, a written agreement whereby the English voluntarily agreed to help each other. Some interpret this 1620 document as an expression of democratic spirit because of the cooperative and inclusive nature of the agreement to live and work together. In 1630, a much larger contingent of Puritans left England to escape conformity to the Church of England and founded the Massachusetts Bay Colony. In the following years, thousands more arrived to create a new life in the rocky soils and cold climates of New England.

In comparison to Catholic Spain, however, Protestant England remained a very weak imperial player in the early seventeenth century, with only a few infant colonies in the Americas in the early 1600s. The English never found treasure equal to that of the Aztec city of Tenochtitlán, and England did not quickly grow rich from its small American outposts. The English colonies also differed from each other; Barbados and Virginia had a decidedly commercial orientation from the start, while the Puritan colonies of New England were intensely religious at their inception. All English settlements in America, however, marked the increasingly important role of England in the Atlantic World.

FRENCH EXPLORATION

Spanish exploits in the New World whetted the appetite of other would-be imperial powers, including France. Like Spain, France was a Catholic nation and committed to expanding Catholicism around the globe. In the early sixteenth century, it joined the race to explore the New World and exploit the resources of the Western Hemisphere. Navigator Jacques Cartier claimed northern North America for France, naming the area New France. From 1534 to 1541, he made three voyages of discovery on the Gulf of St. Lawrence and the St. Lawrence River. Like other explorers, Cartier made exaggerated claims of mineral wealth in America, but he was unable to send great riches back to France. Due to resistance from the native peoples as well as his own lack of planning, he could not establish a permanent settlement in North America.

Explorer Samuel de Champlain occupies a special place in the history of the Atlantic World for his role in establishing the French presence in the New World. Champlain explored the Caribbean in 1601 and then the coast of New England in 1603 before traveling farther north. In 1608 he founded Quebec, and he made numerous Atlantic crossings as he worked tirelessly to promote New France. Unlike other imperial powers, France—through Champlain's efforts—fostered especially good relationships with native peoples, paving the way for French exploration further into the continent: around the Great Lakes, around Hudson Bay, and eventually to the Mississippi. Champlain made an alliance with the Huron confederacy and the Algonquins and agreed to fight with them against their enemy, the Iroquois (Figure 2.12).

FIGURE 2.12 In this engraving, titled *Defeat of the Iroquois* and based on a drawing by explorer Samuel de Champlain, Champlain is shown fighting on the side of the Huron and Algonquins against the Iroquois. He portrays himself in the middle of the battle, firing a gun, while the native people around him shoot arrows at each other. What does this engraving suggest about the impact of European exploration and settlement on the Americas?

The French were primarily interested in establishing commercially viable colonial outposts, and to that end, they created extensive trading networks in New France. These networks relied on native hunters to harvest furs, especially beaver pelts, and to exchange these items for French glass beads and other trade goods. (French fashion at the time favored broad-brimmed hats trimmed in beaver fur, so French traders had a ready market for their North American goods.) The French also dreamed of replicating the wealth of Spain by colonizing the tropical zones. After Spanish control of the Caribbean began to weaken, the French turned their attention to small islands in the West Indies, and by 1635 they had colonized two, Guadeloupe and Martinique. Though it lagged far behind Spain, France now boasted its own West Indian colonies. Both islands became lucrative sugar plantation sites that turned a profit for French planters by relying on African slave labor.

CLICK AND EXPLORE

To see how cartographers throughout history documented the exploration of the Atlantic World, browse the hundreds of digitized historical maps that make up the collection American Shores: Maps of the Middle Atlantic Region to 1850 (http://openstax.org/l/nypl) at the New York Public Library.

DUTCH COLONIZATION

Dutch entrance into the Atlantic World is part of the larger story of religious and imperial conflict in the early modern era. In the 1500s, Calvinism, one of the major Protestant reform movements, had found adherents in the northern provinces of the Spanish Netherlands. During the sixteenth century, these provinces began a long struggle to achieve independence from Catholic Spain. Established in 1581 but not recognized as independent by Spain until 1648, the Dutch Republic, or Holland, quickly made itself a powerful force in the race for Atlantic colonies and wealth. The Dutch distinguished themselves as commercial leaders in the seventeenth century (Figure 2.13), and their mode of colonization relied on powerful corporations: the Dutch East India Company, chartered in 1602 to trade in Asia, and the Dutch West India Company, established in 1621 to colonize and trade in the Americas.

FIGURE 2.13 Amsterdam was the richest city in the world in the 1600s. In *Courtyard of the Exchange in Amsterdam*, a 1653 painting by Emanuel de Witt, merchants involved in the global trade eagerly attend to news of shipping and the prices of commodities.

While employed by the Dutch East India Company in 1609, the English sea captain Henry Hudson explored New York Harbor and the river that now bears his name. Like many explorers of the time, Hudson was actually seeking a northwest passage to Asia and its wealth, but the ample furs harvested from the region he explored, especially the coveted beaver pelts, provided a reason to claim it for the Netherlands. The Dutch named their colony New Netherlands, and it served as a fur-trading outpost for the expanding and powerful Dutch West India Company. With headquarters in New Amsterdam on the island of Manhattan, the Dutch set up several regional trading posts, including one at Fort Orange—named for the royal Dutch House of Orange-Nassau—in present-day Albany. (The color orange remains significant to the Dutch, having become particularly associated with William of Orange, Protestantism, and the Glorious Revolution of 1688.) A brisk trade in furs with local Algonquian and Iroquois peoples brought the Dutch and native peoples together in a commercial network that extended throughout the Hudson River Valley and beyond.

The Dutch West India Company in turn established colonies on Aruba, Bonaire, and Curaçao, St. Martin, St. Eustatius, and Saba. With their outposts in New Netherlands and the Caribbean, the Dutch had established themselves in the seventeenth century as a commercially powerful rival to Spain. Amsterdam became a trade hub for all the Atlantic World.

2.4 New Worlds in the Americas: Labor, Commerce, and the Columbian Exchange

LEARNING OBJECTIVES

By the end of this section, you will be able to:
- Describe how Europeans solved their labor problems
- Describe the theory of mercantilism and the process of commodification
- Analyze the effects of the Columbian Exchange

European promoters of colonization claimed the Americas overflowed with a wealth of treasures. Burnishing national glory and honor became entwined with carving out colonies, and no nation wanted to be left behind.

However, the realities of life in the Americas—violence, exploitation, and particularly the need for workers—were soon driving the practice of slavery and forced labor. Everywhere in America a stark contrast existed between freedom and slavery. The Columbian Exchange, in which Europeans transported plants, animals, and diseases across the Atlantic in both directions, also left a lasting impression on the Americas.

LABOR SYSTEMS

Physical power—to work the fields, build villages, process raw materials—is a necessity for maintaining a society. During the sixteenth and seventeenth centuries, humans could derive power only from the wind, water, animals, or other humans. Everywhere in the Americas, a crushing demand for labor bedeviled Europeans because there were not enough colonists to perform the work necessary to keep the colonies going. Spain granted **encomiendas**—legal rights to native labor—to conquistadors who could prove their service to the crown. This system reflected the Spanish view of colonization: the king rewarded successful conquistadors who expanded the empire. Some native peoples who had sided with the conquistadors, like the Tlaxcalan, also gained *encomiendas*; Malintzin, the Nahua woman who helped Cortés defeat the Mexica, was granted one.

The Spanish believed native peoples would work for them by right of conquest, and, in return, the Spanish would bring them Catholicism. In theory the relationship consisted of reciprocal obligations, but in practice the Spaniards ruthlessly exploited it, seeing native people as little more than beasts of burden. Convinced of their right to the land and its peoples, they sought both to control native labor and to impose what they viewed as correct religious beliefs upon the land's inhabitants. Native peoples everywhere resisted both the labor obligations and the effort to change their ancient belief systems. Indeed, many retained their religion or incorporated only the parts of Catholicism that made sense to them.

The system of *encomiendas* was accompanied by a great deal of violence (Figure 2.14). One Spaniard, Bartolomé de Las Casas, denounced the brutality of Spanish rule. A Dominican friar, Las Casas had been one of the earliest Spanish settlers in the Spanish West Indies. In his early life in the Americas, he enslaved Native people and was the recipient of an *encomienda*. However, after witnessing the savagery with which *encomenderos* (recipients of *encomiendas*) treated the native people, he reversed his views. In 1515, Las Casas released his enslaved natives, gave up his *encomienda*, and began to advocate for humane treatment of native peoples. He lobbied for new legislation, eventually known as the New Laws, which would eliminate slavery and the *encomienda* system.

FIGURE 2.14 In this startling image from the Kingsborough Codex (a book written and drawn by native Mesoamericans), a well-dressed Spaniard is shown pulling the hair of a bleeding, severely injured Native. The drawing was part of a complaint about Spanish abuses of their *encomiendas*.

Las Casas's writing about the Spaniards' horrific treatment of Native people helped inspire the so-called **Black Legend**, the idea that the Spanish were bloodthirsty conquerors with no regard for human life. Perhaps not surprisingly, those who held this view of the Spanish were Spain's imperial rivals. English writers and others seized on the idea of Spain's ruthlessness to support their own colonization projects. By demonizing the Spanish, they justified their own efforts as more humane. All European colonizers, however, shared a disregard for Native peoples.

MY STORY

Bartolomé de Las Casas on the Mistreatment of Native Peoples

Bartolomé de Las Casas's *A Short Account of the Destruction of the Indies*, written in 1542 and published ten years later, detailed for Prince Philip II of Spain how Spanish colonists had been mistreating natives.

"Into and among these gentle sheep, endowed by their Maker and Creator with all the qualities aforesaid, did creep the Spaniards, who no sooner had knowledge of these people than they became like fierce wolves and tigers and lions who have gone many days without food or nourishment. And no other thing have they done for forty years until this day, and still today see fit to do, but dismember, slay, perturb, afflict, torment, and destroy the Native Americans by all manner of cruelty—new and divers and most singular manners such as never before seen or read or heard of—some few of which shall be recounted below, and they do this to such a degree that on the Island of Hispaniola, of the above three millions souls that we once saw, today there be no more than two hundred of those native people remaining...."

"Two principal and general customs have been employed by those, calling themselves Christians, who have passed this way, in extirpating and striking from the face of the earth those suffering nations. The first being unjust, cruel, bloody, and tyrannical warfare. The other—after having slain all those who might yearn toward or suspire after or think of freedom, or consider escaping from the torments that they are made to suffer, by which I mean all the native-born lords and adult males, for it is the Spaniards' custom in their wars to allow only young boys and females to live—being to oppress them with the hardest, harshest, and most heinous bondage to which men or beasts might ever be bound into."

How might these writings have been used to promote the "black legend" against Spain as well as subsequent English exploration and colonization?

Native peoples were not the only source of cheap labor in the Americas; by the middle of the sixteenth century, Africans formed an important element of the labor landscape, producing the cash crops of sugar and tobacco for European markets. Europeans viewed Africans as non-Christians, which they used as a justification for enslavement. Denied control over their lives, enslaved people endured horrendous conditions. At every opportunity, they resisted enslavement, and their resistance was met with violence. Indeed, physical, mental, and sexual violence formed a key strategy among European slaveholders in their effort to assert mastery and impose their will. The Portuguese led the way in the evolving transport of captive enslaved people across the Atlantic; slave "factories" on the west coast of Africa, like Elmina Castle in Ghana, served as holding pens for enslaved people brought from Africa's interior. In time, other European imperial powers would follow in the footsteps of the Portuguese by constructing similar outposts on the coast of West Africa.

The Portuguese traded or sold enslaved people to Spanish, Dutch, and English colonists in the Americas, particularly in South America and the Caribbean, where sugar was a primary export. Thousands of enslaved Africans found themselves growing, harvesting, and processing **sugarcane** in an arduous routine of physical labor. Enslaved people had to cut the long cane stalks by hand and then bring them to a mill, where the cane juice was extracted. They boiled the extracted cane juice down to a brown, crystalline sugar, which then had to be cured in special curing houses to have the molasses drained from it. The result was refined sugar, while the leftover molasses could be distilled into rum. Every step was labor-intensive and often dangerous.

Las Casas estimated that by 1550, there were fifty thousand enslaved people on Hispaniola. However, it is a mistake to assume that during the very early years of European exploration all Africans came to America as captives; some were free men who took part in expeditions, for example, serving as conquistadors alongside Cortés in his assault on Tenochtitlán. Nonetheless, African slavery was one of the most tragic outcomes in the emerging Atlantic World.

CLICK AND EXPLORE

Browse the PBS collection Africans in America: Part 1 (http://openstax.org/l/afinam) to see information and primary sources for the period 1450 through 1750.

COMMERCE IN THE NEW WORLD

The economic philosophy of **mercantilism** shaped European perceptions of wealth from the 1500s to the late 1700s. Mercantilism held that only a limited amount of wealth, as measured in gold and silver bullion, existed in the world. In order to gain power, nations had to amass wealth by mining these precious raw materials from their colonial possessions. During the age of European exploration, nations employed conquest, colonization, and trade as ways to increase their share of the bounty of the New World. Mercantilists did not believe in free trade, arguing instead that the nation should control trade to create wealth. In this view, colonies existed to strengthen the colonizing nation. Mercantilists argued against allowing their nations to trade freely with other nations.

Spain's mercantilist ideas guided its economic policy. Every year, enslaved laborers or native workers loaded shipments of gold and silver aboard Spanish treasure fleets that sailed from Cuba for Spain. These ships groaned under the sheer weight of bullion, for the Spanish had found huge caches of silver and gold in the New World. In South America, for example, Spaniards discovered rich veins of silver ore in the mountain called Potosí and founded a settlement of the same name there. Throughout the sixteenth century, Potosí was a boom town, attracting settlers from many nations as well as native people from many different cultures.

Colonial mercantilism, which was basically a set of protectionist policies designed to benefit the nation, relied on several factors: colonies rich in raw materials, cheap labor, colonial loyalty to the home government, and control of the shipping trade. Under this system, the colonies sent their raw materials, harvested by enslaved laborers or native workers, back to their mother country. The mother country sent back finished materials of all sorts: textiles, tools, clothing. The colonists could purchase these goods *only* from their mother country; trade with other countries was forbidden.

The 1500s and early 1600s also introduced the process of **commodification** to the New World. American silver, tobacco, and other items, which were used by native peoples for ritual purposes, became European commodities with a monetary value that could be bought and sold. Before the arrival of the Spanish, for example, the Inca people of the Andes consumed *chicha*, a corn beer, for ritual purposes only. When the Spanish discovered chicha, they bought and traded for it, turning it into a commodity instead of a ritual substance. Commodification thus recast native economies and spurred the process of early commercial capitalism. New World resources, from plants to animal pelts, held the promise of wealth for European imperial powers.

THE COLUMBIAN EXCHANGE

As Europeans traversed the Atlantic, they brought with them plants, animals, and diseases that changed lives and landscapes on both sides of the ocean. These two-way exchanges between the Americas and Europe/Africa are known collectively as the **Columbian Exchange** (Figure 2.15).

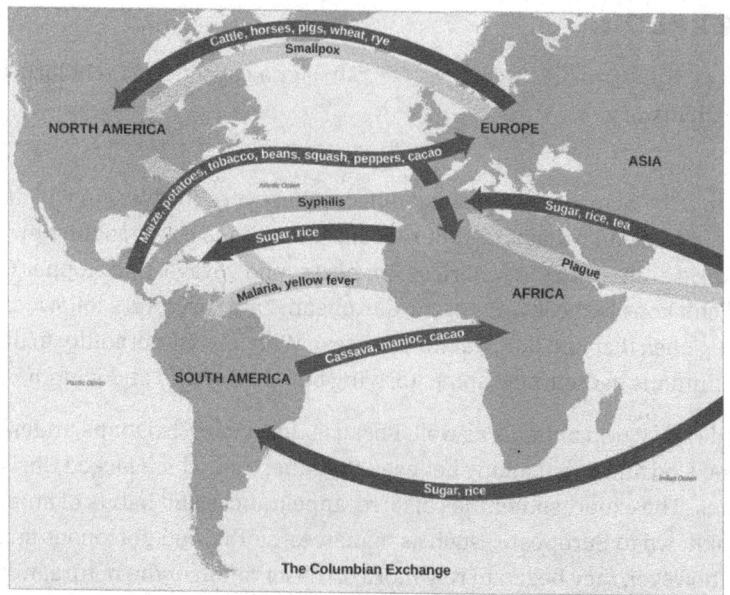

FIGURE 2.15 With European exploration and settlement of the New World, goods and diseases began crossing the Atlantic Ocean in both directions. This "Columbian Exchange" soon had global implications.

Of all the commodities in the Atlantic World, sugar proved to be the most important. Indeed, sugar carried the same economic importance as oil does today. European rivals raced to create sugar plantations in the Americas and fought wars for control of some of the best sugar production areas. Although refined sugar was available in the Old World, Europe's harsher climate made sugarcane difficult to grow, and it was not plentiful. Columbus brought sugar to Hispaniola in 1493, and the new crop was growing there by the end of the 1490s. By the first decades of the 1500s, the Spanish were building sugar mills on the island. Over the next century of colonization, Caribbean islands and most other tropical areas became centers of sugar production.

Though of secondary importance to sugar, tobacco achieved great value for Europeans as a cash crop as well. Native peoples had been growing it for medicinal and ritual purposes for centuries before European contact, smoking it in pipes or powdering it to use as snuff. They believed tobacco could improve concentration and enhance wisdom. To some, its use meant achieving an entranced, altered, or divine state; entering a spiritual place.

Tobacco was unknown in Europe before 1492, and it carried a negative stigma at first. The early Spanish explorers considered natives' use of tobacco to be proof of their savagery and, because of the fire and smoke produced in the consumption of tobacco, evidence of the Devil's sway in the New World. Gradually, however, European colonists became accustomed to and even took up the habit of smoking, and they brought it across the Atlantic. As did the Native Americans, Europeans ascribed medicinal properties to tobacco, claiming that it could cure headaches and skin irritations. Even so, Europeans did not import tobacco in great quantities until the 1590s. At that time, it became the first truly global commodity; English, French, Dutch, Spanish, and Portuguese colonists all grew it for the world market.

Native peoples also introduced Europeans to chocolate, made from cacao seeds and used by the Aztec in Mesoamerica as currency. Mesoamerican Natives consumed unsweetened chocolate in a drink with chili peppers, vanilla, and a spice called achiote. This chocolate drink—*xocolatl*—was part of ritual ceremonies like marriage and an everyday item for those who could afford it. Chocolate contains theobromine, a stimulant, which may be why native people believed it brought them closer to the sacred world.

Spaniards in the New World considered drinking chocolate a vile practice; one called chocolate "the Devil's vomit." In time, however, they introduced the beverage to Spain. At first, chocolate was available only in the Spanish court, where the elite mixed it with sugar and other spices. Later, as its availability spread, chocolate gained a reputation as a love potion.

CLICK AND EXPLORE

Visit Nature Transformed (http://openstax.org/l/naturetrans) for a collection of scholarly essays on the environment in American history.

The crossing of the Atlantic by plants like cacao and tobacco illustrates the ways in which the discovery of the New World changed the habits and behaviors of Europeans. Europeans changed the New World in turn, not least by bringing Old World animals to the Americas. On his second voyage, Christopher Columbus brought pigs, horses, cows, and chickens to the islands of the Caribbean. Later explorers followed suit, introducing new animals or reintroducing ones that had died out (like horses). With less vulnerability to disease, these animals often fared better than humans in their new home, thriving both in the wild and in domestication.

Europeans encountered New World animals as well. Because European Christians understood the world as a place of warfare between God and Satan, many believed the Americas, which lacked Christianity, were home to the Devil and his minions. The exotic, sometimes bizarre, appearances and habits of animals in the Americas that were previously unknown to Europeans, such as manatees, sloths, and poisonous snakes, confirmed this association. Over time, however, they began to rely more on observation of the natural world than solely on scripture. This shift—from seeing the Bible as the source of all received wisdom to trusting observation or empiricism—is one of the major outcomes of the era of early globalization.

Travelers between the Americas, Africa, and Europe also included microbes: silent, invisible life forms that had profound and devastating consequences. Native peoples had no immunity to diseases from across the Atlantic, to which they had never been exposed. European explorers unwittingly brought with them chickenpox, measles, mumps, and **smallpox**, which ravaged native peoples despite their attempts to treat the diseases, decimating some populations and wholly destroying others (Figure 2.16).

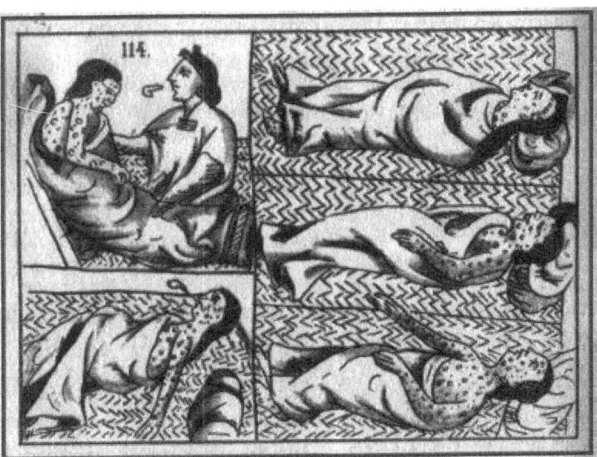

FIGURE 2.16 This sixteenth-century Aztec drawing shows the suffering of a typical victim of smallpox. Smallpox and other contagious diseases brought by European explorers decimated Native populations in the Americas.

In eastern North America, some native peoples interpreted death from disease as a hostile act. Some groups, including the Iroquois, engaged in raids or "**mourning wars**," taking enemy prisoners in order to assuage their grief and replace the departed. In a special ritual, the prisoners were "requickened"—assigned the identity of a dead person—and adopted by the bereaved family to take the place of their dead. As the toll from disease rose, mourning wars intensified and expanded.

Key Terms

Black Legend   Spain's reputation as bloodthirsty conquistadors

Calvinism   a branch of Protestantism started by John Calvin, emphasizing human powerlessness before an omniscient God and stressing the idea of predestination

Columbian Exchange   the movement of plants, animals, and diseases across the Atlantic due to European exploration of the Americas

commodification   the transformation of something—for example, an item of ritual significance—into a commodity with monetary value

encomienda   legal rights to native labor as granted by the Spanish crown

Hispaniola   the island in the Caribbean, present-day Haiti and Dominican Republic, where Columbus landed on his first voyage to the Americas and established a Spanish colony

indulgences   documents for purchase that absolved sinners of their errant behavior

joint stock company   a business entity in which investors provide the capital and assume the risk in order to reap significant returns

mercantilism   the protectionist economic principle that nations should control trade with their colonies to ensure a favorable balance of trade

mourning wars   raids or wars that tribes waged in eastern North America in order to replace members lost to smallpox and other diseases

Pilgrims   Separatists, led by William Bradford, who established the first English settlement in New England

privateers   sea captains to whom the British government had given permission to raid Spanish ships at will

probanza de mérito   proof of merit: a letter written by a Spanish explorer to the crown to gain royal patronage

Protestant Reformation   the schism in Catholicism that began with Martin Luther and John Calvin in the early sixteenth century

Puritans   a group of religious reformers in the sixteenth and seventeenth centuries who wanted to "purify" the Church of England by ridding it of practices associated with the Catholic Church and advocating greater purity of doctrine and worship

Roanoke   the first English colony in Virginia, which mysteriously disappeared sometime between 1587 and 1590

Separatists   a faction of Puritans who advocated complete separation from the Church of England

smallpox   a disease that Europeans accidentally brought to the New World, killing millions of Native Americans, who had no immunity to the disease

sugarcane   one of the primary crops of the Americas, which required a tremendous amount of labor to cultivate

Summary

2.1 Portuguese Exploration and Spanish Conquest

Although Portugal opened the door to exploration of the Atlantic World, Spanish explorers quickly made inroads into the Americas. Spurred by Christopher Columbus's glowing reports of the riches to be found in the New World, throngs of Spanish conquistadors set off to find and conquer new lands. They accomplished this through a combination of military strength and strategic alliances with native peoples. Spanish rulers Ferdinand and Isabella promoted the acquisition of these new lands in order to strengthen and glorify their own empire. As Spain's empire expanded and riches flowed in from the Americas, the Spanish experienced a golden age of art and literature.

2.2 Religious Upheavals in the Developing Atlantic World

The sixteenth century witnessed a new challenge to the powerful Catholic Church. The reformist doctrines of Martin Luther and John Calvin attracted many people dissatisfied with Catholicism, and Protestantism spread across northern Europe, spawning many subgroups with conflicting beliefs. Spain led the charge against Protestantism, leading to decades of undeclared religious wars between Spain and England, and religious intolerance and violence characterized much of the sixteenth and seventeenth centuries. Despite the efforts of the Catholic Church and Catholic nations, however, Protestantism had taken hold by 1600.

2.3 Challenges to Spain's Supremacy

By the beginning of the seventeenth century, Spain's rivals—England, France, and the Dutch Republic—had each established an Atlantic presence, with greater or lesser success, in the race for imperial power. None of the new colonies, all in the eastern part of North America, could match the Spanish possessions for gold and silver resources. Nonetheless, their presence in the New World helped these nations establish claims that they hoped could halt the runaway growth of Spain's Catholic empire. English colonists in Virginia suffered greatly, expecting riches to fall into their hands and finding reality a harsh blow. However, the colony at Jamestown survived, and the output of England's islands in the West Indies soon grew to be an important source of income for the country. New France and New Netherlands were modest colonial holdings in the northeast of the continent, but these colonies' thriving fur trade with native peoples, and their alliances with those peoples, helped to create the foundation for later shifts in the global balance of power.

2.4 New Worlds in the Americas: Labor, Commerce, and the Columbian Exchange

In the minds of European rulers, colonies existed to create wealth for imperial powers. Guided by mercantilist ideas, European rulers and investors hoped to enrich their own nations and themselves, in order to gain the greatest share of what was believed to be a limited amount of wealth. In their own individual quest for riches and preeminence, European colonizers who traveled to the Americas blazed new and disturbing paths, such as the *encomienda* system of forced labor and the enslavement of tens of thousands of Africans.

All Native inhabitants of the Americas who came into contact with Europeans found their worlds turned upside down as the new arrivals introduced their religions and ideas about property and goods. Europeans gained new foods, plants, and animals in the Columbian Exchange, turning whatever they could into a commodity to be bought and sold, and Native peoples were introduced to diseases that nearly destroyed them. At every turn, however, Native Americans placed limits on European colonization and resisted the newcomers' ways.

Review Questions

1. Which country initiated the era of Atlantic exploration?
    A. France
    B. Spain
    C. England
    D. Portugal

2. Which country established the first colonies in the Americas?
    A. England
    B. Portugal
    C. Spain
    D. the Netherlands

3. Where did Christopher Columbus first land?
    A. Hispaniola
    B. the Bahamas
    C. Jamestown
    D. Mexico

4. Why did the authors of *probanzas de méritos* choose to write in the way that they did? What should we consider when we interpret these documents today?

5. Where did the Protestant Reformation begin?
   A. Northern Europe
   B. Spain
   C. England
   D. the American colonies

6. What was the chief goal of the Puritans?
   A. to achieve a lasting peace with the Catholic nations of Spain and France
   B. to eliminate any traces of Catholicism from the Church of England
   C. to assist Henry VIII in his quest for an annulment to his marriage
   D. to create a hierarchy within the Church of England modeled on that of the Catholic Church

7. What reforms to the Catholic Church did Martin Luther and John Calvin call for?

8. Why didn't England make stronger attempts to colonize the New World before the late sixteenth to early seventeenth century?
   A. English attention was turned to internal struggles and the encroaching Catholic menace to Scotland and Ireland.
   B. The English monarchy did not want to declare direct war on Spain by attempting to colonize the Americas.
   C. The English military was occupied in battling for control of New Netherlands.
   D. The English crown refused to fund colonial expeditions.

9. What was the main goal of the French in colonizing the Americas?
   A. establishing a colony with French subjects
   B. trading, especially for furs
   C. gaining control of shipping lanes
   D. spreading Catholicism among native peoples

10. What were some of the main differences among the non-Spanish colonies?

11. How could Spaniards obtain *encomiendas*?
    A. by serving the Spanish crown
    B. by buying them from other Spaniards
    C. by buying them from native chiefs
    D. by inheriting them

12. Which of the following best describes the Columbian Exchange?
    A. the letters Columbus and other conquistadors exchanged with the Spanish crown
    B. an exchange of plants, animals, and diseases between Europe and the Americas
    C. a form of trade between the Spanish and natives
    D. the way in which explorers exchanged information about new lands to conquer

13. Why did diseases like smallpox affect Native Americans so badly?
    A. Native Americans were less robust than Europeans.
    B. Europeans deliberately infected Native Americans.
    C. Native Americans had no immunity to European diseases.
    D. Conditions in the Americas were so harsh that Native Americans and Europeans alike were devastated by disease.

Critical Thinking Questions

14. What were the consequences of the religious upheavals of the sixteenth and seventeenth centuries?

15. What types of labor systems were used in the Americas? Did systems of unfree labor serve more than an economic function?

16. What is meant by the Columbian Exchange? Who was affected the most by the exchange?

17. What were the various goals of the colonial European powers in the expansion of their empires? To what extent were they able to achieve these goals? Where did they fail?

18. On the whole, what was the impact of early European explorations on the New World? What was the impact of the New World on Europeans?

Creating New Social Orders: Colonial Societies, 1500–1700

3

FIGURE 3.1 John Smith's famous map of Virginia (1622) illustrates many geopolitical features of early colonization. In the upper left, Powhatan, who governed a powerful local confederation of Algonquian communities, sits above other local leaders, denoting his authority. Another native figure, Susquehannock, who appears in the upper right, visually reinforces the message that the English did not control the land beyond a few outposts along the Chesapeake.

CHAPTER OUTLINE

3.1 Spanish Exploration and Colonial Society
3.2 Colonial Rivalries: Dutch and French Colonial Ambitions
3.3 English Settlements in America
3.4 The Impact of Colonization

INTRODUCTION By the mid-seventeenth century, the geopolitical map of North America had become a patchwork of imperial designs and ambitions as the Spanish, Dutch, French, and English reinforced their claims to parts of the land. Uneasiness, punctuated by violent clashes, prevailed in the border zones between the Europeans' territorial claims. Meanwhile, still-powerful native peoples waged war to drive the invaders from the continent. In the Chesapeake Bay and New England colonies, conflicts erupted as the English pushed against their native neighbors (Figure 3.1).

The rise of colonial societies in the Americas brought Native Americans, Africans, and Europeans together for the first time, highlighting the radical social, cultural, and religious differences that hampered their ability to understand each other. European settlement affected every aspect of the land and its people, bringing goods, ideas, and diseases that transformed the Americas. Reciprocally, Native American practices, such as the use of tobacco, profoundly altered European habits and tastes.

3.1 Spanish Exploration and Colonial Society

LEARNING OBJECTIVES

By the end of this section, you will be able to:
- Identify the main Spanish American colonial settlements of the 1500s and 1600s
- Discuss economic, political, and demographic similarities and differences between the Spanish colonies

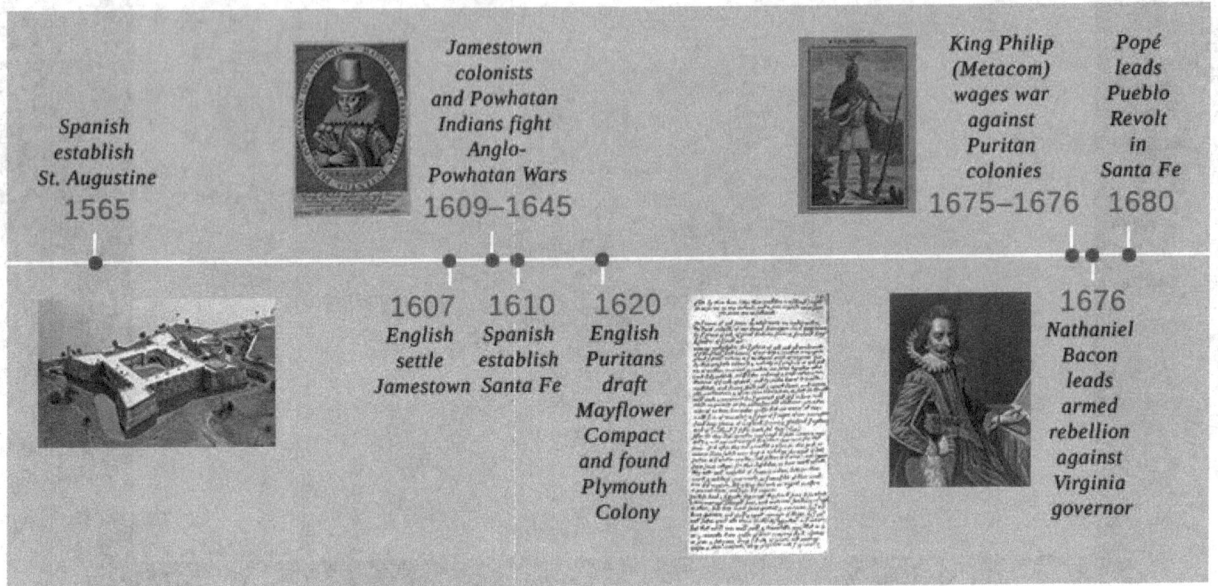

FIGURE 3.2

During the 1500s, Spain expanded its colonial empire to the Philippines in the Far East and to areas in the Americas that later became the United States. The Spanish dreamed of mountains of gold and silver and imagined converting thousands of eager Native Americans to Catholicism. In their vision of colonial society, everyone would know his or her place. Patriarchy (the rule of men over family, society, and government) shaped the Spanish colonial world. Women occupied a lower status. In all matters, the Spanish held themselves to be atop the social pyramid, with Native peoples and Africans beneath them. Both Africans and native peoples, however, contested Spanish claims to dominance. Everywhere the Spanish settled, they brought devastating diseases, such as smallpox, that led to a horrific loss of life among native peoples. European diseases killed far more native inhabitants than did Spanish swords.

The world Native peoples had known before the coming of the Spanish was further upset by Spanish colonial practices. The Spanish imposed the *encomienda* system in the areas they controlled. Under this system, authorities assigned Native workers to mine and plantation owners with the understanding that the recipients would defend the colony and teach the workers the tenets of Christianity. In reality, the *encomienda* system exploited native workers. It was eventually replaced by another colonial labor system, the **repartimiento**, which required Native towns to supply a pool of labor for Spanish overlords.

ST. AUGUSTINE, FLORIDA

Spain gained a foothold in present-day Florida, viewing that area and the lands to the north as a logical extension of their Caribbean empire. In 1513, Juan Ponce de León had claimed the area around today's St. Augustine for the Spanish crown, naming the land Pascua Florida (Feast of Flowers, or Easter) for the nearest feast day. Ponce de León was unable to establish a permanent settlement there, but by 1565, Spain was in need of an outpost to confront the French and English privateers using Florida as a base from which to attack treasure-laden Spanish ships heading from Cuba to Spain. The threat to Spanish interests took a new turn in 1562 when a group of French Protestants (Huguenots) established a small settlement they called Fort Caroline, north of St. Augustine. With the authorization of King Philip II, Spanish nobleman Pedro Menéndez led an attack on Fort Caroline, killing most of the colonists and destroying the fort. Eliminating Fort Caroline served dual purposes for the Spanish—it helped reduce the danger from French privateers and eradicated the French threat to Spain's claim to the area. The contest over Florida illustrates how European rivalries spilled over into the Americas, especially religious conflict between Catholics and Protestants.

In 1565, the victorious Menéndez founded St. Augustine, now the oldest European settlement in the Americas. In the process, the Spanish displaced the local **Timucua** Natives from their ancient town of Seloy, which had stood for thousands of years (Figure 3.3). The Timucua suffered greatly from diseases introduced by the Spanish, shrinking from a population of around 200,000 pre-contact to fifty thousand in 1590. By 1700, only one thousand Timucua remained. As in other areas of Spanish conquest, Catholic priests worked to bring about a spiritual conquest by forcing the surviving Timucua, demoralized and reeling from catastrophic losses of family and community, to convert to Catholicism.

FIGURE 3.3 In this drawing by French artist Jacques le Moyne de Morgues, Timucua flee the Spanish settlers, who arrive by ship. Le Moyne lived at Fort Caroline, the French outpost, before the Spanish destroyed the colony in 1562.

Spanish Florida made an inviting target for Spain's imperial rivals, especially the English, who wanted to gain access to the Caribbean. In 1586, Spanish settlers in St. Augustine discovered their vulnerability to attack when the English pirate Sir Francis Drake destroyed the town with a fleet of twenty ships and one hundred men. Over the next several decades, the Spanish built more wooden forts, all of which were burnt by raiding European rivals. Between 1672 and 1695, the Spanish constructed a stone fort, Castillo de San Marcos (Figure 3.4), to better defend St. Augustine against challengers.

FIGURE 3.4 The Spanish fort of Castillo de San Marcos helped Spanish colonists in St. Augustine fend off marauding privateers from rival European countries.

CLICK AND EXPLORE

Browse the National Park Service's multimedia resources on Castillo de San Marcos (http://openstax.org/l/castillo) to see how the fort and gates have looked throughout history.

SANTA FE, NEW MEXICO

Farther west, the Spanish in Mexico, intent on expanding their empire, looked north to the land of the Pueblo Natives. Under orders from King Philip II, Juan de Oñate explored the American southwest for Spain in the late 1590s. The Spanish hoped that what we know as New Mexico would yield gold and silver, but the land produced little of value to them. In 1610, Spanish settlers established themselves at Santa Fe—originally named La Villa Real de la Santa Fe de San Francisco de Asís, or "Royal City of the Holy Faith of St. Francis of Assisi"—where many Pueblo villages were located. Santa Fe became the capital of the Kingdom of New Mexico, an outpost of the larger Spanish Viceroyalty of New Spain, which had its headquarters in Mexico City.

As they had in other Spanish colonies, Franciscan missionaries labored to bring about a spiritual conquest by converting the Pueblo to Catholicism. At first, the Pueblo adopted the parts of Catholicism that dovetailed with their own long-standing view of the world. However, Spanish priests insisted that natives discard their old ways entirely and angered the Pueblo by focusing on the young, drawing them away from their parents. This deep insult, combined with an extended period of drought and increased attacks by local Apache and Navajo in the 1670s—troubles that the Pueblo came to believe were linked to the Spanish presence—moved the Pueblo to push the Spanish and their religion from the area. Pueblo leader Popé demanded a return to native ways so the hardships his people faced would end. To him and to thousands of others, it seemed obvious that "when Jesus came, the Corn Mothers went away." The expulsion of the Spanish would bring a return to prosperity and a pure, native way of life.

In 1680, the Pueblo launched a coordinated rebellion against the Spanish. The Pueblo Revolt killed over four hundred Spaniards and drove the rest of the settlers, perhaps as many as two thousand, south toward Mexico. However, as droughts and attacks by rival tribes continued, the Spanish sensed an opportunity to regain their foothold. In 1692, they returned and reasserted their control of the area. Some of the Spanish explained the Pueblo success in 1680 as the work of the Devil. Satan, they believed, had stirred up the Pueblo to take arms against God's chosen people—the Spanish—but the Spanish, and their God, had prevailed in the end.

3.2 Colonial Rivalries: Dutch and French Colonial Ambitions

LEARNING OBJECTIVES
By the end of this section, you will be able to:
- Compare and contrast the development and character of the French and Dutch colonies in North America
- Discuss the economies of the French and Dutch colonies in North America

Seventeenth-century French and Dutch colonies in North America were modest in comparison to Spain's colossal global empire. New France and New Netherland remained small commercial operations focused on the fur trade and did not attract an influx of migrants. The Dutch in New Netherland confined their operations to Manhattan Island, Long Island, the Hudson River Valley, and what later became New Jersey. Dutch trade goods circulated widely among the native peoples in these areas and also traveled well into the interior of the continent along preexisting native trade routes. French *habitants*, or farmer-settlers, eked out an existence along the St. Lawrence River. French fur traders and missionaries, however, ranged far into the interior of North America, exploring the Great Lakes region and the Mississippi River. These pioneers gave France somewhat inflated imperial claims to lands that nonetheless remained firmly under the dominion of native peoples.

FUR TRADING IN NEW NETHERLAND

The Dutch Republic emerged as a major commercial center in the 1600s. Its fleets plied the waters of the

Atlantic, while other Dutch ships sailed to the Far East, returning with prized spices like pepper to be sold in the bustling ports at home, especially Amsterdam. In North America, Dutch traders established themselves first on Manhattan Island.

One of the Dutch directors-general of the North American settlement, Peter Stuyvesant, served from 1647 to 1664. He expanded the fledgling outpost of New Netherland east to present-day Long Island, and for many miles north along the Hudson River. The resulting elongated colony served primarily as a fur-trading post, with the powerful Dutch West India Company controlling all commerce. Fort Amsterdam, on the southern tip of Manhattan Island, defended the growing city of New Amsterdam. In 1655, Stuyvesant took over the small outpost of New Sweden along the banks of the Delaware River in present-day New Jersey, Pennsylvania, and Delaware. He also defended New Amsterdam from Native American attacks by ordering enslaved Africans to build a protective wall on the city's northeastern border, giving present-day Wall Street its name (Figure 3.5).

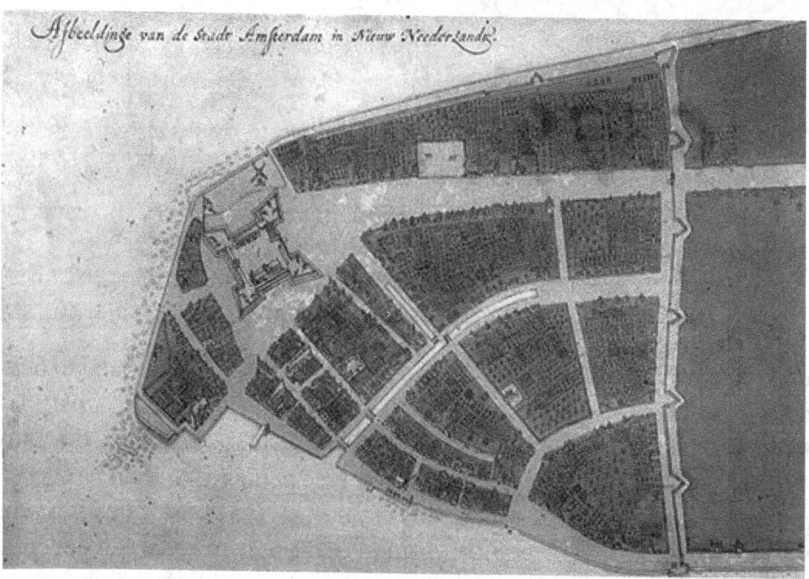

FIGURE 3.5 The Castello Plan is the only extant map of 1660 New Amsterdam (present-day New York City). The line with spikes on the right side of the colony is the northeastern wall for which Wall Street was named.

New Netherland failed to attract many Dutch colonists; by 1664, only nine thousand people were living there. Conflict with Native peoples, as well as dissatisfaction with the Dutch West India Company's trading practices, made the Dutch outpost an undesirable place for many migrants. The small size of the population meant a severe labor shortage, and to complete the arduous tasks of early settlement, the Dutch West India Company imported some 450 enslaved Africans between 1626 and 1664. (The company had involved itself heavily in the slave trade and in 1637 captured Elmina, the slave-trading post on the west coast of Africa, from the Portuguese.) The shortage of labor also meant that New Netherland welcomed non-Dutch immigrants, including Protestants from Germany, Sweden, Denmark, and England, and embraced a degree of religious tolerance, allowing Jewish immigrants to become residents beginning in the 1650s. Thus, a wide variety of people lived in New Netherland from the start. Indeed, one observer claimed eighteen different languages could be heard on the streets of New Amsterdam. As new settlers arrived, the colony of New Netherland stretched farther to the north and the west (Figure 3.6).

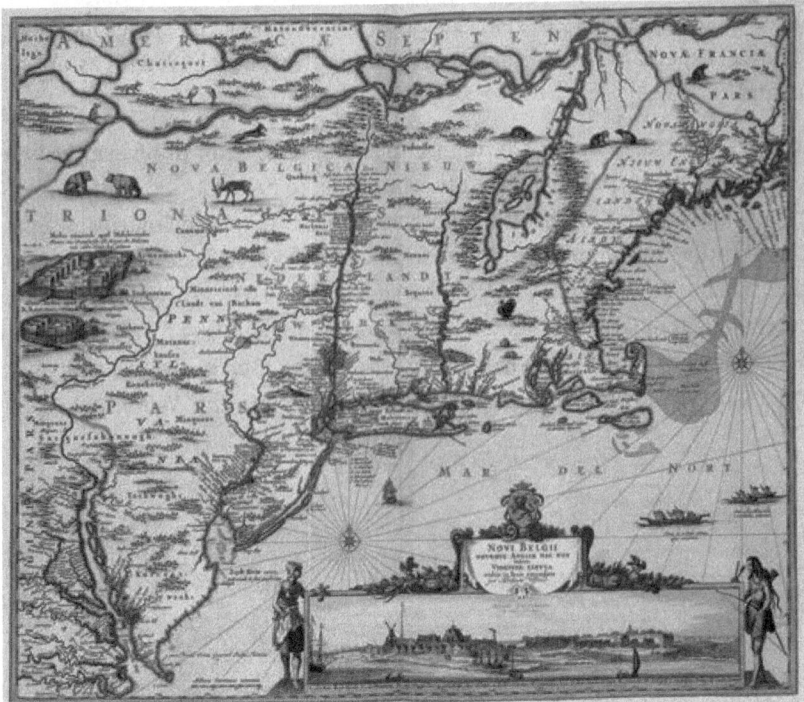

FIGURE 3.6 This 1684 map of New Netherland shows the extent of Dutch settlement.

The Dutch West India Company found the business of colonization in New Netherland to be expensive. To share some of the costs, it granted Dutch merchants who invested heavily in it **patroonships**, or large tracts of land and the right to govern the tenants there. In return, the shareholder who gained the patroonship promised to pay for the passage of at least thirty Dutch farmers to populate the colony. One of the largest patroonships was granted to Kiliaen van Rensselaer, one of the directors of the Dutch West India Company; it covered most of present-day Albany and Rensselaer Counties. This pattern of settlement created a yawning gap in wealth and status between the tenants, who paid rent, and the wealthy patroons.

During the summer trading season, Native Americans gathered at trading posts such as the Dutch site at Beverwijck (present-day Albany), where they exchanged furs for guns, blankets, and alcohol. The furs, especially beaver pelts destined for the lucrative European millinery market, would be sent down the Hudson River to New Amsterdam. There, enslaved laborers or workers would load them aboard ships bound for Amsterdam.

CLICK AND EXPLORE

Explore an interactive map of New Amsterdam in 1660 (http://openstax.org/l/WNET) that shows the city plan and the locations of various structures, including houses, businesses, and public buildings. Rolling over the map reveals relevant historical details, such as street names, the identities of certain buildings and businesses, and the names of residents of the houses (when known).

COMMERCE AND CONVERSION IN NEW FRANCE

After Jacques Cartier's voyages of discovery in the 1530s, France showed little interest in creating permanent colonies in North America until the early 1600s, when Samuel de Champlain established Quebec as a French fur-trading outpost. Although the fur trade was lucrative, the French saw Canada as an inhospitable frozen wasteland, and by 1640, fewer than four hundred settlers had made their home there. The sparse French presence meant that colonists depended on the local native Algonquian people; without them, the French would have perished. French fishermen, explorers, and fur traders made extensive contact with the Algonquian. The Algonquian, in turn, tolerated the French because the colonists supplied them with firearms for their ongoing war with the Iroquois. Thus, the French found themselves escalating native wars and supporting the Algonquian against the Iroquois, who received weapons from their Dutch trading partners. These seventeenth-century conflicts centered on the lucrative trade in beaver pelts, earning them the name of the Beaver Wars. In these wars, fighting between rival native peoples spread throughout the Great Lakes region.

A handful of French Jesuit priests also made their way to Canada, intent on converting the native inhabitants to Catholicism. The **Jesuits** were members of the Society of Jesus, an elite religious order founded in the 1540s to spread Catholicism and combat the spread of Protestantism. The first Jesuits arrived in Quebec in the 1620s, and for the next century, their numbers did not exceed forty priests. Like the Spanish Franciscan missionaries, the Jesuits in the colony called New France labored to convert the native peoples to Catholicism. They wrote detailed annual reports about their progress in bringing the faith to the Algonquian and, beginning in the 1660s, to the Iroquois. These documents are known as the *Jesuit Relations* (Figure 3.7), and they provide a rich source for understanding both the Jesuit view of the Native Americans and the Native response to the colonizers.

One Native convert to Catholicism, a Mohawk woman named Kateri Tekakwitha, so impressed the priests with her piety that a Jesuit named Claude Chauchetière attempted to make her a saint in the Church. However, the effort to canonize Tekakwitha faltered when leaders of the Church balked at elevating a "savage" to such a high status; she was eventually canonized in 2012. French colonizers pressured the native inhabitants of New France to convert, but they virtually never saw Native peoples as their equals.

DEFINING AMERICAN

A Jesuit Priest on Native Healing Traditions

The *Jesuit Relations* (Figure 3.7) provide incredible detail about Native life. For example, the 1636 edition, written by the Catholic priest Jean de Brébeuf, addresses the devastating effects of disease on Native peoples and the efforts made to combat it.

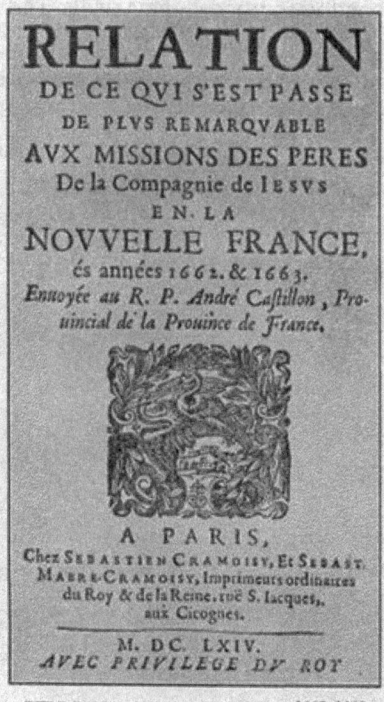

FIGURE 3.7 French Jesuit missionaries to New France kept detailed records of their interactions with—and

observations of—the Algonquian and Iroquois that they converted to Catholicism. (credit: Project Gutenberg).

"Let us return to the feasts. The *Aoutaerohi* is a remedy which is only for one particular kind of disease, which they call also *Aoutaerohi*, from the name of a little Demon as large as the fist, which they say is in the body of the sick man, especially in the part which pains him. They find out that they are sick of this disease, by means of a dream, or by the intervention of some Sorcerer. . . .

Of three kinds of games especially in use among these Peoples,—namely, the games of crosse [lacrosse], dish, and straw,—the first two are, they say, most healing. Is not this worthy of compassion? There is a poor sick man, fevered of body and almost dying, and a miserable Sorcerer will order for him, as a cooling remedy, a game of crosse. Or the sick man himself, sometimes, will have dreamed that he must die unless the whole country shall play crosse for his health; and, no matter how little may be his credit, you will see then in a beautiful field, Village contending against Village, as to who will play crosse the better, and betting against one another Beaver robes and Porcelain collars, so as to excite greater interest."

According to this account, how did Native Americans attempt to cure disease? Why did they prescribe a game of lacrosse? What benefits might these games have for the sick?

3.3 English Settlements in America

LEARNING OBJECTIVES

By the end of this section, you will be able to:
- Identify the first English settlements in America
- Describe the differences between the Chesapeake Bay colonies and the New England colonies
- Compare and contrast the wars between Native inhabitants and English colonists in both the Chesapeake Bay and New England colonies
- Explain the role of Bacon's Rebellion in the rise of chattel slavery in Virginia

At the start of the seventeenth century, the English had not established a permanent settlement in the Americas. Over the next century, however, they outpaced their rivals. The English encouraged emigration far more than the Spanish, French, or Dutch. They established nearly a dozen colonies, sending swarms of immigrants to populate the land. England had experienced a dramatic rise in population in the sixteenth century, and the colonies appeared a welcoming place for those who faced overcrowding and grinding poverty at home. Thousands of English migrants arrived in the Chesapeake Bay colonies of Virginia and Maryland to work in the tobacco fields. Another stream, this one of pious Puritan families, sought to live as they believed scripture demanded and established the Plymouth, Massachusetts Bay, New Haven, Connecticut, and Rhode Island colonies of New England (Figure 3.8).

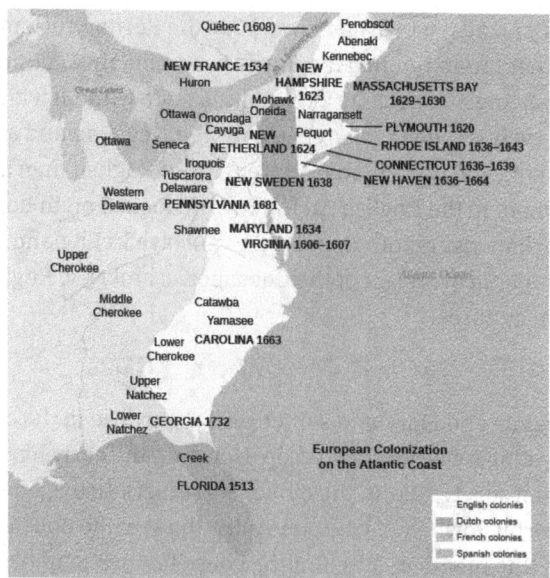

FIGURE 3.8 In the early seventeenth century, thousands of English settlers came to what are now Virginia, Maryland, and the New England states in search of opportunity and a better life.

THE DIVERGING CULTURES OF THE NEW ENGLAND AND CHESAPEAKE COLONIES

Promoters of English colonization in North America, many of whom never ventured across the Atlantic, wrote about the bounty the English would find there. These boosters of colonization hoped to turn a profit—whether by importing raw resources or providing new markets for English goods—and spread Protestantism. The English migrants who actually made the journey, however, had different goals. In Chesapeake Bay, English migrants established Virginia and Maryland with a decidedly commercial orientation. Though the early Virginians at Jamestown hoped to find gold, they and the settlers in Maryland quickly discovered that growing tobacco was the only sure means of making money. Thousands of unmarried, unemployed, and impatient young Englishmen, along with a few Englishwomen, pinned their hopes for a better life on the tobacco fields of these two colonies.

A very different group of English men and women flocked to the cold climate and rocky soil of New England, spurred by religious motives. Many of the Puritans crossing the Atlantic were people who brought families and children. Often they were following their ministers in a migration "beyond the seas," envisioning a new English Israel where reformed Protestantism would grow and thrive, providing a model for the rest of the Christian world and a counter to what they saw as the Catholic menace. While the English in Virginia and Maryland worked on expanding their profitable tobacco fields, the English in New England built towns focused on the church, where each congregation decided what was best for itself. The Congregational Church is the result of the Puritan enterprise in America. Many historians believe the fault lines separating what later became the North and South in the United States originated in the profound differences between the Chesapeake and New England colonies.

The source of those differences lay in England's domestic problems. Increasingly in the early 1600s, the English state church—the Church of England, established in the 1530s—demanded conformity, or compliance with its practices, but Puritans pushed for greater reforms. By the 1620s, the Church of England began to see leading Puritan ministers and their followers as outlaws, a national security threat because of their opposition to its power. As the noose of conformity tightened around them, many Puritans decided to remove to New England. By 1640, New England had a population of twenty-five thousand. Meanwhile, many loyal members of the Church of England, who ridiculed and mocked Puritans both at home and in New England, flocked to Virginia for economic opportunity.

The troubles in England escalated in the 1640s when civil war broke out, pitting Royalist supporters of King

Charles I and the Church of England against Parliamentarians, the Puritan reformers and their supporters in Parliament. In 1649, the Parliamentarians gained the upper hand and, in an unprecedented move, executed Charles I. In the 1650s, therefore, England became a republic, a state without a king. English colonists in America closely followed these events. Indeed, many Puritans left New England and returned home to take part in the struggle against the king and the national church. Other English men and women in the Chesapeake colonies and elsewhere in the English Atlantic World looked on in horror at the mayhem the Parliamentarians, led by the Puritan insurgents, appeared to unleash in England. The turmoil in England made the administration and imperial oversight of the Chesapeake and New England colonies difficult, and the two regions developed divergent cultures.

THE CHESAPEAKE COLONIES: VIRGINIA AND MARYLAND

The Chesapeake colonies of Virginia and Maryland served a vital purpose in the developing seventeenth-century English empire by providing tobacco, a cash crop. However, the early history of Jamestown did not suggest the English outpost would survive. From the outset, its settlers struggled both with each other and with the Native inhabitants, the powerful Powhatan, who controlled the area. Jealousies and infighting among the English destabilized the colony. One member, John Smith, whose famous map begins this chapter, took control and exercised near-dictatorial powers, which furthered aggravated the squabbling. The settlers' inability to grow their own food compounded this unstable situation. They were essentially employees of the Virginia Company of London, an English joint-stock company, in which investors provided the capital and assumed the risk in order to reap the profit, and they had to make a profit for their shareholders as well as for themselves. Most initially devoted themselves to finding gold and silver instead of finding ways to grow their own food.

Early Struggles and the Development of the Tobacco Economy

Poor health, lack of food, and fighting with Native peoples took the lives of many of the original Jamestown settlers. The winter of 1609–1610, which became known as "the starving time," came close to annihilating the colony. By June 1610, the few remaining settlers had decided to abandon the area; only the last-minute arrival of a supply ship from England prevented another failed colonization effort. The supply ship brought new settlers, but only twelve hundred of the seventy-five hundred who came to Virginia between 1607 and 1624 survived.

MY STORY

George Percy on "The Starving Time"
George Percy, the youngest son of an English nobleman, was in the first group of settlers at the Jamestown Colony. He kept a journal describing their experiences; in the excerpt below, he reports on the privations of the colonists' third winter.

"Now all of us at James Town, beginning to feel that sharp prick of hunger which no man truly describe but he which has tasted the bitterness thereof, a world of miseries ensued as the sequel will express unto you, in so much that some to satisfy their hunger have robbed the store for the which I caused them to be executed. Then having fed upon horses and other beasts as long as they lasted, we were glad to make shift with vermin as dogs, cats, rats, and mice. All was fish that came to net to satisfy cruel hunger as to eat boots, shoes, or any other leather some could come by, and, those being spent and devoured, some were enforced to search the woods and to feed upon serpents and snakes and to dig the earth for wild and unknown roots, where many of our men were cut off of and slain by the savages. And now famine beginning to look ghastly and pale in every face that nothing was spared to maintain life and to do those things which seem incredible as to dig up dead corpses out of graves and to eat them, and some have licked up the blood which has fallen from their weak fellows.
—George Percy, "A True Relation of the Proceedings and Occurances of Moment which have happened in Virginia from the Time Sir Thomas Gates shipwrecked upon the Bermudes anno 1609 until my departure out of the

Country which was in anno Domini 1612," London 1624"

What is your reaction to George Percy's story? How do you think Jamestown managed to survive after such an experience? What do you think the Jamestown colonists learned?

By the 1620s, Virginia had weathered the worst and gained a degree of permanence. Political stability came slowly, but by 1619, the fledgling colony was operating under the leadership of a governor, a council, and a House of Burgesses. Economic stability came from the lucrative cultivation of tobacco. Smoking tobacco was a long-standing practice among native peoples, and English and other European consumers soon adopted it. In 1614, the Virginia colony began exporting tobacco back to England, which earned it a sizable profit and saved the colony from ruin. A second tobacco colony, Maryland, was formed in 1634, when King Charles I granted its charter to the Calvert family for their loyal service to England. Cecilius Calvert, the second Lord Baltimore, conceived of Maryland as a refuge for English Catholics.

Growing tobacco proved very labor-intensive (Figure 3.9), and the Chesapeake colonists needed a steady workforce to do the hard work of clearing the land and caring for the tender young plants. The mature leaf of the plant then had to be cured (dried), which necessitated the construction of drying barns. Once cured, the tobacco had to be packaged in hogsheads (large wooden barrels) and loaded aboard ship, which also required considerable labor.

FIGURE 3.9 In this 1670 painting by an unknown artist, enslaved people work in tobacco-drying sheds.

To meet these labor demands, early Virginians relied on indentured servants. An **indenture** is a labor contract that young, impoverished, and often illiterate Englishmen and occasionally Englishwomen signed in England, pledging to work for a number of years (usually between five and seven) growing tobacco in the Chesapeake colonies. In return, indentured servants received paid passage to America and food, clothing, and lodging. At the end of their indenture, servants received "freedom dues," usually food and other provisions, including, in some cases, land provided by the colony. The promise of a new life in America was a strong attraction for members of England's underclass, who had few if any options at home. In the 1600s, some 100,000 indentured servants traveled to the Chesapeake Bay. Most were poor young men in their early twenties.

Life in the colonies proved harsh, however. Indentured servants could not marry, and they were subject to the will of the tobacco planters who bought their labor contracts. Treated much like property, the contracted servants could be essentially sold or traded among those with means to purchase them. Some contract holders did not feed or house their servants well. If an indentured servant committed a crime or disobeyed those who held their contracts, they found their terms of service lengthened, often by several years. Female indentured servants faced special dangers in what was essentially a bachelor colony. Many were exploited by unscrupulous tobacco planters who seduced them with promises of marriage. If the women became pregnant, the planters would then sell them to other tobacco planters to avoid the costs of raising a child.

Nonetheless, those indentured servants who completed their term of service often began new lives as tobacco planters. To entice even more migrants to the New World, the Virginia Company also implemented the **headright system**, in which those who paid their own passage to Virginia received fifty acres plus an additional fifty for each servant or family member they brought with them. The headright system and the promise of a new life for servants acted as powerful incentives for English migrants to hazard the journey to the New World.

CLICK AND EXPLORE

Visit Virtual Jamestown (http://openstax.org/l/jamestown1) to access a database of contracts of indentured servants. Search it by name to find an ancestor or browse by occupation, destination, or county of origin.

The Anglo-Powhatan Wars

By choosing to settle along the rivers on the banks of the Chesapeake, the English unknowingly placed themselves at the center of the Powhatan Empire, a powerful Algonquian confederacy of thirty native groups with perhaps as many as twenty-two thousand people. The territory of the equally impressive Susquehannock people also bordered English settlements at the north end of the Chesapeake Bay.

Tensions ran high between the English and the Powhatan, and near-constant war prevailed. The First Anglo-Powhatan War (1609–1614) resulted not only from the English colonists' intrusion onto Powhatan land, but also from their refusal to follow cultural protocol by giving gifts. English actions infuriated and insulted the Powhatan. In 1613, the settlers captured Pocahontas (also called Matoaka), the daughter of a Powhatan headman named Wahunsonacook, and gave her in marriage to Englishman John Rolfe. Their union, and her choice to remain with the English, helped quell the war in 1614. Pocahontas converted to Christianity, changing her name to Rebecca, and sailed with her husband and several other Powhatan to England where she was introduced to King James I (Figure 3.10). Promoters of colonization publicized Pocahontas as an example of the good work of converting the Powhatan to Christianity.

FIGURE 3.10 This 1616 engraving by Simon van de Passe, completed when Pocahontas and John Rolfe were presented at court in England, is the only known contemporary image of Pocahontas. Note her European garb and pose. What message did the painter likely intend to convey with this portrait of Pocahontas, the daughter of a powerful Native American leader?

CLICK AND EXPLORE

Explore the interactive exhibit Changing Images of Pocahontas (http://openstax.org/l/pocahontas) on PBS's website to see the many ways artists have portrayed Pocahontas over the centuries.

Peace in Virginia did not last long. The Second Anglo-Powhatan War (1620s) broke out because of the expansion of the English settlement nearly one hundred miles into the interior, and because of the continued insults and friction caused by English activities. The Powhatan attacked in 1622 and succeeded in killing almost 350 English, about a third of the settlers. The English responded by annihilating every Powhatan village around Jamestown and from then on became even more intolerant. The Third Anglo-Powhatan War (1644–1646) began with a surprise attack in which the Powhatan killed around five hundred English colonists. However, their ultimate defeat in this conflict forced the Powhatan to acknowledge King Charles I as their sovereign. The Anglo-Powhatan Wars, spanning nearly forty years, illustrate the degree of native resistance that resulted from English intrusion into the Powhatan confederacy.

The Rise of Slavery in the Chesapeake Bay Colonies

The transition from indentured servitude to slavery as the main labor source for some English colonies happened first in the West Indies. On the small island of Barbados, colonized in the 1620s, English planters first grew tobacco as their main export crop, but in the 1640s, they converted to sugarcane and began increasingly to rely on African enslaved people. In 1655, England wrestled control of Jamaica from the Spanish and quickly turned it into a lucrative sugar island, run on forced labor, for its expanding empire. While slavery was slower to take hold in the Chesapeake colonies, by the end of the seventeenth century, both Virginia and Maryland had also adopted chattel slavery—which legally defined Africans as property and not people—as the dominant form of labor to grow tobacco. Chesapeake colonists also enslaved Native people.

When the first Africans arrived in Virginia in 1619, slavery—which did not exist in England—had not yet become an institution in colonial America. Many Africans worked as servants and, like their White counterparts, could acquire land of their own. Some Africans who converted to Christianity became free landowners with White servants. The change in the status of Africans in the Chesapeake to that of enslaved people occurred in the last decades of the seventeenth century.

Bacon's Rebellion, an uprising of both White people and Black people who believed that the Virginia government was impeding their access to land and wealth and seemed to do little to clear the land of Native Americans, hastened the transition to African slavery in the Chesapeake colonies. The rebellion takes its name from Nathaniel Bacon, a wealthy young Englishman who arrived in Virginia in 1674. Despite an early friendship with Virginia's royal governor, William Berkeley, Bacon found himself excluded from the governor's circle of influential friends and councilors. He wanted land on the Virginia frontier, but the governor, fearing war with neighboring tribes, forbade further expansion. Bacon marshaled others, especially former indentured servants who believed the governor was limiting their economic opportunities and denying them the right to own tobacco farms. Bacon's followers believed Berkeley's frontier policy didn't protect English settlers enough. Worse still in their eyes, Governor Berkeley tried to keep peace in Virginia by signing treaties with various local Native peoples. Bacon and his followers, who saw all Native peoples as an obstacle to their access to land, pursued a policy of extermination.

Tensions between the English and the Native peoples in the Chesapeake colonies led to open conflict. In 1675, war broke out when Susquehannock warriors attacked settlements on Virginia's frontier, killing English planters and destroying English plantations, including one owned by Bacon. In 1676, Bacon and other Virginians attacked the Susquehannock without the governor's approval. When Berkeley ordered Bacon's arrest, Bacon led his followers to Jamestown, forced the governor to flee to the safety of Virginia's eastern shore, and then burned the city. The civil war known as Bacon's Rebellion, a vicious struggle between supporters of the governor and those who supported Bacon, ensued. Reports of the rebellion traveled back to

England, leading Charles II to dispatch both royal troops and English commissioners to restore order in the tobacco colonies. By the end of 1676, Virginians loyal to the governor gained the upper hand, executing several leaders of the rebellion. Bacon escaped the hangman's noose, instead dying of dysentery. The rebellion fizzled in 1676, but Virginians remained divided as supporters of Bacon continued to harbor grievances over access to Native land.

Bacon's Rebellion helped to catalyze the creation of a system of racial slavery in the Chesapeake colonies. At the time of the rebellion, indentured servants made up the majority of laborers in the region. Wealthy White people worried over the presence of this large class of laborers and the relative freedom they enjoyed, as well as the alliance that Black and White servants had forged in the course of the rebellion. Replacing indentured servitude with Black slavery diminished these risks, alleviating the reliance on White indentured servants, who were often dissatisfied and troublesome, and creating a caste of racially defined laborers whose movements were strictly controlled. It also lessened the possibility of further alliances between Black and White workers. Racial slavery even served to heal some of the divisions between wealthy and poor White people, who could now unite as members of a "superior" racial group.

While colonial laws in the tobacco colonies had made slavery a legal institution before Bacon's Rebellion, new laws passed in the wake of the rebellion severely curtailed Black freedom and laid the foundation for racial slavery. Virginia passed a law in 1680 prohibiting free Black people and enslaved people from bearing arms, banning Black people from congregating in large numbers, and establishing harsh punishments for enslaved people who assaulted Christians or sought freedom. Two years later, another Virginia law stipulated that all Africans brought to the colony would be enslaved for life. Thus, the increasing reliance on enslaved people in the tobacco colonies—and the draconian laws instituted to control them—not only helped planters meet labor demands, but also served to assuage English fears of further uprisings and alleviate class tensions between rich and poor White people.

DEFINING AMERICAN

Robert Beverley on Servants and Enslaved People

Robert Beverley was a wealthy Jamestown planter and enslaver. This excerpt from his *History and Present State of Virginia*, published in 1705, clearly illustrates the contrast between White servants and enslaved Black people.

"Their Servants, they distinguish by the Names of Slaves for Life, and Servants for a time. Slaves are the Negroes, and their Posterity, following the condition of the Mother, according to the Maxim, partus sequitur ventrem [status follows the womb]. They are call'd Slaves, in respect of the time of their Servitude, because it is for Life. Servants, are those which serve only for a few years, according to the time of their Indenture, or the Custom of the Country. The Custom of the Country takes place upon such as have no Indentures. The Law in this case is, that if such Servants be under Nineteen years of Age, they must be brought into Court, to have their Age adjudged; and from the Age they are judg'd to be of, they must serve until they reach four and twenty: But if they be adjudged upwards of Nineteen, they are then only to be Servants for the term of five Years.

The Male-Servants, and Slaves of both Sexes, are employed together in Tilling and Manuring the Ground, in Sowing and Planting Tobacco, Corn, &c. Some Distinction indeed is made between them in their Cloaths, and Food; but the Work of both, is no other than what the Overseers, the Freemen, and the Planters themselves do. Sufficient Distinction is also made between the Female-Servants, and Slaves; for a White Woman is rarely or never put to work in the Ground, if she be good for any thing else: And to Discourage all Planters from using any Women so, their Law imposes the heaviest Taxes upon Female Servants working in the Ground, while it suffers all other White Women to be absolutely exempted: Whereas on the other hand, it is a common thing to work a Woman Slave out of Doors; nor does the Law make any Distinction in her Taxes, whether her Work be Abroad, or at Home."

According to Robert Beverley, what are the differences between the servants and the enslaved? What protections did servants have that enslaved people did not?

PURITAN NEW ENGLAND

The second major area to be colonized by the English in the first half of the seventeenth century, New England, differed markedly in its founding principles from the commercially oriented Chesapeake tobacco colonies. Settled largely by waves of Puritan families in the 1630s, New England had a religious orientation from the start. In England, reform-minded men and women had been calling for greater changes to the English national church since the 1580s. These reformers, who followed the teachings of John Calvin and other Protestant reformers, were called Puritans because of their insistence on "purifying" the Church of England of what they believed to be un-scriptural, especially Catholic elements that lingered in its institutions and practices.

Many who provided leadership in early New England were learned ministers who had studied at Cambridge or Oxford but who, because they had questioned the practices of the Church of England, had been deprived of careers by the king and his officials in an effort to silence all dissenting voices. Other Puritan leaders, such as the first governor of the Massachusetts Bay Colony, John Winthrop, came from the privileged class of English gentry. These well-to-do Puritans and many thousands more left their English homes not to establish a land of religious freedom, but to practice their own religion without persecution. Puritan New England offered them the opportunity to live as they believed the Bible demanded. In their "New" England, they set out to create a model of reformed Protestantism, a new English Israel.

The conflict generated by Puritanism had divided English society, because the Puritans demanded reforms that undermined the traditional festive culture. For example, they denounced popular pastimes like bear-baiting—letting dogs attack a chained bear—which were often conducted on Sundays when people had a few leisure hours. In the culture where William Shakespeare had produced his masterpieces, Puritans called for an end to the theater, censuring playhouses as places of decadence. Indeed, the Bible itself became part of the struggle between Puritans and James I, who headed the Church of England. Soon after ascending the throne, James commissioned a new version of the Bible in an effort to stifle Puritan reliance on the Geneva Bible, which followed the teachings of John Calvin and placed God's authority above the monarch's. The King James Version, published in 1611, instead emphasized the majesty of kings.

During the 1620s and 1630s, the conflict escalated to the point where the state church prohibited Puritan ministers from preaching. In the Church's view, Puritans represented a national security threat, because their demands for cultural, social, and religious reforms undermined the king's authority. Unwilling to conform to the Church of England, many Puritans found refuge in the New World. Yet those who emigrated to the Americas were not united. Some called for a complete break with the Church of England, while others remained committed to reforming the national church.

Plymouth: The First Puritan Colony

The first group of Puritans to make their way across the Atlantic was a small contingent known as the Pilgrims. Unlike other Puritans, they insisted on a complete separation from the Church of England and had first migrated to the Dutch Republic in Europe seeking religious freedom. Although they found they could worship without hindrance there, they grew concerned that they were losing their Englishness as they saw their children begin to learn the Dutch language and adopt Dutch ways. In addition, the English Pilgrims (and others in Europe) feared another attack on the Dutch Republic by Spain. Therefore, in 1620, they moved on to found the Plymouth Colony in present-day Massachusetts. The governor of Plymouth, William Bradford, was a Separatist, a proponent of complete separation from the English state church. Bradford and the other Pilgrim Separatists represented a major challenge to the prevailing vision of a unified English national church and empire. On board the *Mayflower*, which was bound for Virginia but landed on the tip of Cape Cod, Bradford and forty other adult men signed the Mayflower Compact (Figure 3.11), which presented a religious (rather than an economic) rationale for colonization. The compact expressed a community ideal of working together. When a larger exodus of Puritans established the Massachusetts Bay Colony in the 1630s, the Pilgrims at Plymouth welcomed them and the two colonies cooperated with each other.

> ## AMERICANA
>
> ### The Mayflower Compact and Its Religious Rationale
> The Mayflower Compact, which forty-one Pilgrim men signed on board the *Mayflower* in Plymouth Harbor, has been called the first American governing document, predating the U.S. Constitution by over 150 years. But was the Mayflower Compact a constitution? How much authority did it convey, and to whom? 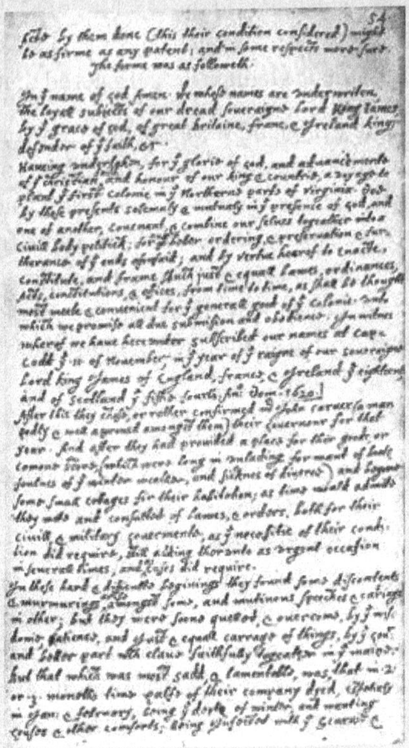
>
> **FIGURE 3.11** The original Mayflower Compact is no longer extant; only copies, such as this ca.1645 transcription by William Bradford, remain.
>
> "In the name of God, Amen. We, whose names are underwritten, the loyal subjects of our dread Sovereign Lord King James, by the Grace of God, of Great Britain, France, and Ireland, King, defender of the Faith, etc. Having undertaken, for the Glory of God, and advancements of the Christian faith and honor of our King and Country, a voyage to plant the first colony in the Northern parts of Virginia, do by these presents, solemnly and mutually, in the presence of God, and one another, covenant and combine ourselves together into a civil body politic; for our better ordering, and preservation and furtherance of the ends aforesaid; and by virtue hereof to enact, constitute, and frame, such just and equal laws, ordinances, acts, constitutions, and offices, from time to time, as shall be thought most meet and convenient for the general good of the colony; unto which we promise all due submission and obedience.
> In witness whereof we have hereunto subscribed our names at Cape Cod the 11th of November, in the year of the reign of our Sovereign Lord King James, of England, France, and Ireland, the eighteenth, and of Scotland the fifty-fourth, 1620"

Different labor systems also distinguished early Puritan New England from the Chesapeake colonies. Puritans expected young people to work diligently at their calling, and all members of their large families, including children, did the bulk of the work necessary to run homes, farms, and businesses. Very few migrants came to

New England as laborers; in fact, New England towns protected their disciplined homegrown workforce by refusing to allow outsiders in, assuring their sons and daughters of steady employment. New England's labor system produced remarkable results, notably a powerful maritime-based economy with scores of oceangoing ships and the crews necessary to sail them. New England mariners sailing New England–made ships transported Virginian tobacco and West Indian sugar throughout the Atlantic World.

"A City upon a Hill"

A much larger group of English Puritans left England in the 1630s, establishing the Massachusetts Bay Colony, the New Haven Colony, the Connecticut Colony, and Rhode Island. Unlike the exodus of young males to the Chesapeake colonies, these migrants were families with young children and their university-trained ministers. Their aim, according to John Winthrop (Figure 3.12), the first governor of Massachusetts Bay, was to create a model of reformed Protestantism—a "city upon a hill," a new English Israel. The idea of a "city upon a hill" made clear the religious orientation of the New England settlement, and the charter of the Massachusetts Bay Colony stated as a goal that the colony's people "may be soe religiously, peaceablie, and civilly governed, as their good Life and orderlie Conversacon, maie wynn and incite the Natives of Country, to the Knowledg and Obedience of the onlie true God and Saulor of Mankinde, and the Christian Fayth." To illustrate this, the seal of the Massachusetts Bay Company (Figure 3.12) shows a Native American who entreats more of the English to "come over and help us."

FIGURE 3.12 In the 1629 seal of the Massachusetts Bay Colony (a), a Native American is shown asking colonists to "Come over and help us." This seal indicates the religious ambitions of John Winthrop (b), the colony's first governor, for his "city upon a hill."

Puritan New England differed in many ways from both England and the rest of Europe. Protestants emphasized literacy so that everyone could read the Bible. This attitude was in stark contrast to that of Catholics, who refused to tolerate private ownership of Bibles in the vernacular. The Puritans, for their part, placed a special emphasis on reading scripture, and their commitment to literacy led to the establishment of the first printing press in English America in 1636. Four years later, in 1640, they published the first book in North America, the Bay Psalm Book. As Calvinists, Puritans adhered to the doctrine of predestination, whereby a few "elect" would be saved and all others damned. No one could be sure whether they were predestined for salvation, but through introspection, guided by scripture, Puritans hoped to find a glimmer of redemptive grace. Church membership was restricted to those Puritans who were willing to provide a conversion narrative telling how they came to understand their spiritual estate by hearing sermons and studying the Bible.

Although many people assume Puritans escaped England to establish religious freedom, they proved to be just as intolerant as the English state church. When dissenters, including Puritan minister Roger Williams and Anne Hutchinson, challenged Governor Winthrop in Massachusetts Bay in the 1630s, they were banished. Roger Williams questioned the Puritans' taking of Native land. Williams also argued for a complete separation from the Church of England, a position other Puritans in Massachusetts rejected, as well as the idea that the state could not punish individuals for their beliefs. Although he did accept that nonbelievers were destined for eternal damnation, Williams did not think the state could compel true orthodoxy. Puritan authorities found him guilty of spreading dangerous ideas, but he went on to found Rhode Island as a colony that sheltered dissenting Puritans from their brethren in Massachusetts. In Rhode Island, Williams wrote favorably about native peoples, contrasting their virtues with Puritan New England's intolerance.

Anne Hutchinson also ran afoul of Puritan authorities for her criticism of the evolving religious practices in the Massachusetts Bay Colony. In particular, she held that Puritan ministers in New England taught a shallow version of Protestantism emphasizing hierarchy and actions—a "covenant of works" rather than a "covenant of grace." Literate Puritan women like Hutchinson presented a challenge to the male ministers' authority. Indeed, her major offense was her claim of direct religious revelation, a type of spiritual experience that negated the role of ministers. Because of Hutchinson's beliefs and her defiance of authority in the colony, especially that of Governor Winthrop, Puritan authorities tried and convicted her of holding false beliefs. In 1638, she was excommunicated and banished from the colony. She went to Rhode Island and later, in 1642, sought safety among the Dutch in New Netherland. The following year, Algonquian warriors killed Hutchinson and her family. In Massachusetts, Governor Winthrop noted her death as the righteous judgment of God against a heretic.

Like many other Europeans, the Puritans believed in the supernatural. Every event appeared to be a sign of God's mercy or judgment, and people believed that witches allied themselves with the Devil to carry out evil deeds and deliberate harm such as the sickness or death of children, the loss of cattle, and other catastrophes. Hundreds were accused of witchcraft in Puritan New England, including townspeople whose habits or appearance bothered their neighbors or who appeared threatening for any reason. Women, seen as more susceptible to the Devil because of their supposedly weaker constitutions, made up the vast majority of suspects and those who were executed. The most notorious cases occurred in Salem Village in 1692. Many of the accusers who prosecuted the suspected witches had been traumatized by the Native wars on the frontier and by unprecedented political and cultural changes in New England. Relying on their belief in witchcraft to help make sense of their changing world, Puritan authorities executed nineteen people and caused the deaths of several others.

CLICK AND EXPLORE

Explore the Salem Witchcraft Trials (http://openstax.org/l/salemwitch) to learn more about the prosecution of witchcraft in seventeenth-century New England.

Puritan Relationships with Native Peoples

Like their Spanish and French Catholic rivals, English Puritans in America took steps to convert native peoples to their version of Christianity. John Eliot, the leading Puritan missionary in New England, urged natives in Massachusetts to live in "praying towns" established by English authorities for converted Native Americans, and to adopt the Puritan emphasis on the centrality of the Bible. In keeping with the Protestant emphasis on reading scripture, he translated the Bible into the local Algonquian language and published his work in 1663. Eliot hoped that as a result of his efforts, some of New England's native inhabitants would become preachers.

Tensions had existed from the beginning between the Puritans and the native people who controlled southern New England (Figure 3.13). Relationships deteriorated as the Puritans continued to expand their settlements aggressively and as European ways increasingly disrupted native life. These strains led to King Philip's War (1675–1676), a massive regional conflict that was nearly successful in pushing the English out of New England.

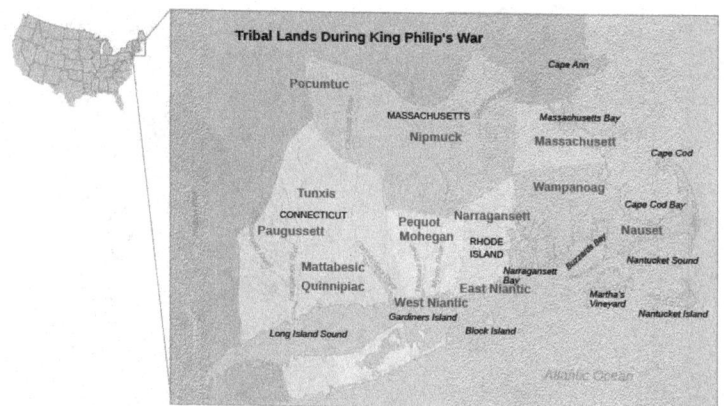

FIGURE 3.13 This map indicates the domains of New England's native inhabitants in 1670, a few years before King Philip's War.

When the Puritans began to arrive in the 1620s and 1630s, local Algonquian peoples had viewed them as potential allies in the conflicts already simmering between rival Native groups. In 1621, the Wampanoag, led by Massasoit, concluded a peace treaty with the Pilgrims at Plymouth. In the 1630s, the Puritans in Massachusetts and Plymouth allied themselves with the Narragansett and Mohegan people against the Pequot, who had recently expanded their claims into southern New England. In May 1637, the Puritans attacked a large group of several hundred Pequot along the Mystic River in Connecticut. To the horror of their Native allies, the Puritans massacred all but a handful of the men, women, and children they found.

By the mid-seventeenth century, the Puritans had pushed their way further into the interior of New England, establishing outposts along the Connecticut River Valley. There seemed no end to their expansion. Wampanoag leader Metacom or Metacomet, also known as King Philip among the English, was determined to stop the encroachment. The Wampanoag, along with the Nipmuck, Pocumtuck, and Narragansett, took up arms to drive the English from the land. In the ensuing conflict, called King Philip's War, Native forces succeeded in destroying half of the frontier Puritan towns; however, in the end, the English (aided by Mohegans and Christian Native Americans) prevailed and sold many captives into slavery in the West Indies. (The severed head of King Philip was publicly displayed in Plymouth.) The war also forever changed the English perception of Native peoples; from then on, Puritan writers took great pains to vilify the Native people as bloodthirsty savages. A new type of racial hatred became a defining feature of Native-English relationships in the Northeast.

MY STORY

Mary Rowlandson's Captivity Narrative

Mary Rowlandson was a Puritan woman whom Native tribes captured and imprisoned for several weeks during King Philip's War. After her release, she wrote *The Narrative of the Captivity and the Restoration of Mrs. Mary Rowlandson*, which was published in 1682 (Figure 3.14). The book was an immediate sensation that was reissued in multiple editions for over a century.

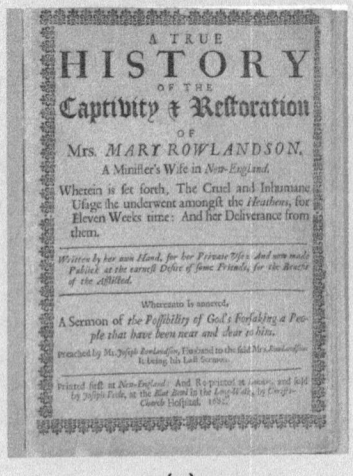

(a) (b)

FIGURE 3.14 Puritan woman Mary Rowlandson wrote her captivity narrative, the front cover of which is shown here (a), after her imprisonment during King Philip's War. In her narrative, she tells of her treatment by the Native Americans holding her as well as of her meetings with the Wampanoag leader Metacom (b), shown in a contemporary portrait.

"But now, the next morning, I must turn my back upon the town, and travel with them into the vast and desolate wilderness, I knew not whither. It is not my tongue, or pen, can express the sorrows of my heart, and bitterness of my spirit that I had at this departure: but God was with me in a wonderful manner, carrying me along, and bearing up my spirit, that it did not quite fail. One of the Indians carried my poor wounded babe upon a horse; it went moaning all along, "I shall die, I shall die." I went on foot after it, with sorrow that cannot be expressed. At length I took it off the horse, and carried it in my arms till my strength failed, and I fell down with it. Then they set me upon a horse with my wounded child in my lap, and there being no furniture upon the horse's back, as we were going down a steep hill we both fell over the horse's head, at which they, like inhumane creatures, laughed, and rejoiced to see it, though I thought we should there have ended our days, as overcome with so many difficulties. But the Lord renewed my strength still, and carried me along, that I might see more of His power; yea, so much that I could never have thought of, had I not experienced it."

What sustains Rowlandson her during her ordeal? How does she characterize her captors? What do you think made her narrative so compelling to readers?

CLICK AND EXPLORE

Access the entire text of Mary Rowlandson's captivity narrative (http://openstax.org/l/captivenarr) at the Gutenberg Project.

3.4 The Impact of Colonization

LEARNING OBJECTIVES

By the end of this section, you will be able to:
- Explain the reasons for the rise of slavery in the American colonies
- Describe changes to Native life, including warfare and hunting
- Contrast European and Native American views on property
- Assess the impact of European settlement on the environment

As Europeans moved beyond exploration and into colonization of the Americas, they brought changes to virtually every aspect of the land and its people, from trade and hunting to warfare and personal property.

European goods, ideas, and diseases shaped the changing continent.

As Europeans established their colonies, their societies also became segmented and divided along religious and racial lines. Most people in these societies were not free; they labored as servants or enslaved people, doing the work required to produce wealth for others. By 1700, the American continent had become a place of stark contrasts between slavery and freedom, between the haves and the have-nots.

THE INSTITUTION OF SLAVERY

Everywhere in the American colonies, a crushing demand for labor existed to grow New World cash crops, especially sugar and tobacco. This need led Europeans to rely increasingly on Africans, and after 1600, the movement of Africans across the Atlantic accelerated. The English crown chartered the Royal African Company in 1672, giving the company a monopoly over the transport of enslaved African people to the English colonies. Over the next four decades, the company transported around 350,000 Africans from their homelands. By 1700, the tiny English sugar island of Barbados had a population of fifty thousand enslaved people, and the English had encoded the institution of chattel slavery into colonial law.

This new system of African slavery came slowly to the English colonists, who did not have slavery at home and preferred to use servant labor. Nevertheless, by the end of the seventeenth century, the English everywhere in America—and particularly in the Chesapeake Bay colonies—had come to rely on enslaved Africans. While Africans had long practiced slavery among their own people, it had not been based on race. Africans enslaved other Africans as war captives, for crimes, and to settle debts; they generally used enslaved people for domestic and small-scale agricultural work, not for growing cash crops on large plantations. Additionally, African slavery was often a temporary condition rather than a lifelong sentence, and, unlike New World slavery, it was typically not heritable (passed from an enslaved mother to her children).

The growing slave trade with Europeans had a profound impact on the people of West Africa, giving prominence to local chieftains and merchants who traded enslaved people for European textiles, alcohol, guns, tobacco, and food. Africans also charged Europeans for the right to trade in enslaved people and imposed taxes on enslaved people purchases. Different African groups and kingdoms even staged large-scale raids on each other to meet the demand for enslaved people.

Once sold to traders, all captured people sent to America endured the hellish **Middle Passage**, the transatlantic crossing, which took one to two months. By 1625, more than 325,800 Africans had been shipped to the New World, though many thousands perished during the voyage. An astonishing number, some four million, were transported to the Caribbean between 1501 and 1830. When they reached their destination in America, Africans found themselves trapped in shockingly brutal slave societies. In the Chesapeake colonies, they faced a lifetime of harvesting and processing tobacco.

Everywhere, Africans resisted slavery, and running away was common. In Jamaica and elsewhere, escaped enslaved people created **maroon communities**, groups that resisted recapture and eked out a living from the land, rebuilding their communities as best they could. When possible, they adhered to traditional ways, following spiritual leaders such as Vodun priests.

CHANGES TO NATIVE LIFE

While the Americas remained firmly under the control of native peoples in the first decades of European settlement, conflict increased as colonization spread and Europeans placed greater demands upon the native populations, including expecting them to convert to Christianity (either Catholicism or Protestantism). Throughout the seventeenth century, the still-powerful native peoples and confederacies that retained control of the land waged war against the invading Europeans, achieving a degree of success in their effort to drive the newcomers from the continent.

At the same time, European goods had begun to change Native life radically. In the 1500s, some of the earliest objects Europeans introduced to Native Americans were glass beads, copper kettles, and metal utensils. Native people often adapted these items for their own use. For example, some cut up copper kettles and refashioned the metal for other uses, including jewelry that conferred status on the wearer, who was seen as connected to the new European source of raw materials.

As European settlements grew throughout the 1600s, European goods flooded Native communities. Soon Native people were using these items for the same purposes as the Europeans. For example, many Native inhabitants abandoned their animal-skin clothing in favor of European textiles. Similarly, clay cookware gave way to metal cooking implements, and Native Americans found that European flint and steel made starting fires much easier (Figure 3.15).

FIGURE 3.15 In this 1681 portrait, the Niantic-Narragansett leader Ninigret wears a combination of European and Native American goods. Which elements of each culture are evident in this portrait?

The abundance of European goods gave rise to new artistic objects. For example, iron awls made the creation of shell beads among the native people of the Eastern Woodlands much easier, and the result was an astonishing increase in the production of **wampum**, shell beads used in ceremonies and as jewelry and currency. Native peoples had always placed goods in the graves of their departed, and this practice escalated with the arrival of European goods. Archaeologists have found enormous caches of European trade goods in the graves of Native Americans on the East Coast.

Native weapons changed dramatically as well, creating an arms race among the peoples living in European colonization zones. Native Americans refashioned European brassware into arrow points and turned axes used for chopping wood into weapons. The most prized piece of European weaponry to obtain was a **musket**, or light, long-barreled European gun. In order to trade with Europeans for these, Native peoples intensified their harvesting of beaver, commercializing their traditional practice.

The influx of European materials made warfare more lethal and changed traditional patterns of authority among tribes. Formerly weaker groups, if they had access to European metal and weapons, suddenly gained the upper hand against once-dominant groups. The Algonquian, for instance, traded with the French for muskets and gained power against their enemies, the Iroquois. Eventually, native peoples also used their new weapons against the European colonizers who had provided them.

CLICK AND EXPLORE

Explore the complexity of Native-European relationships (http://openstax.org/l/NHC) in the series of primary source documents on the National Humanities Center site.

ENVIRONMENTAL CHANGES

The European presence in America spurred countless changes in the environment, setting into motion chains of events that affected native animals as well as people. The popularity of beaver-trimmed hats in Europe, coupled with Native American's desire for European weapons, led to the overhunting of beaver in the Northeast. Soon, beavers were extinct in New England, New York, and other areas. With their loss came the loss of beaver ponds, which had served as habitats for fish as well as water sources for deer, moose, and other animals. Furthermore, Europeans introduced pigs, which they allowed to forage in forests and other wildlands. Pigs consumed the foods on which deer and other indigenous species depended, resulting in scarcity of the game native peoples had traditionally hunted.

European ideas about owning land as private property clashed with natives' understanding of land use. Native peoples did not believe in private ownership of land; instead, they viewed land as a resource to be held in common for the benefit of the group. The European idea of usufruct—the right to common land use and enjoyment—comes close to the native understanding, but colonists did not practice usufruct widely in America. Colonizers established fields, fences, and other means of demarcating private property. Native peoples who moved seasonally to take advantage of natural resources now found areas off limits, claimed by colonizers because of their insistence on private-property rights.

The Introduction of Disease

Perhaps European colonization's single greatest impact on the North American environment was the introduction of disease. Microbes to which native inhabitants had no immunity led to death everywhere Europeans settled. Along the New England coast between 1616 and 1618, epidemics claimed the lives of 75 percent of the native people. In the 1630s, half the Huron and Iroquois around the Great Lakes died of smallpox. As is often the case with disease, the very young and the very old were the most vulnerable and had the highest mortality rates. The loss of the older generation meant the loss of knowledge and tradition, while the death of children only compounded the trauma, creating devastating implications for future generations.

Some native peoples perceived disease as a weapon used by hostile spiritual forces, and they went to war to exorcise the disease from their midst. These "mourning wars" in eastern North America were designed to gain captives who would either be adopted ("requickened" as a replacement for a deceased loved one) or ritually tortured and executed to assuage the anger and grief caused by loss.

The Cultivation of Plants

European expansion in the Americas led to an unprecedented movement of plants across the Atlantic. A prime example is tobacco, which became a valuable export as the habit of smoking, previously unknown in Europe, took hold (Figure 3.16). Another example is sugar. Columbus brought sugarcane to the Caribbean on his second voyage in 1494, and thereafter a wide variety of other herbs, flowers, seeds, and roots made the transatlantic voyage.

FIGURE 3.16 Adriaen van Ostade, a Dutch artist, painted *An Apothecary Smoking in an Interior* in 1646. The large European market for American tobacco strongly influenced the development of some of the American colonies.

Just as pharmaceutical companies today scour the natural world for new drugs, Europeans traveled to America to discover new medicines. The task of cataloging the new plants found there helped give birth to the science of botany. Early botanists included the English naturalist Sir Hans Sloane, who traveled to Jamaica in 1687 and there recorded hundreds of new plants (Figure 3.17). Sloane also helped popularize the drinking of chocolate, made from the cacao bean, in England.

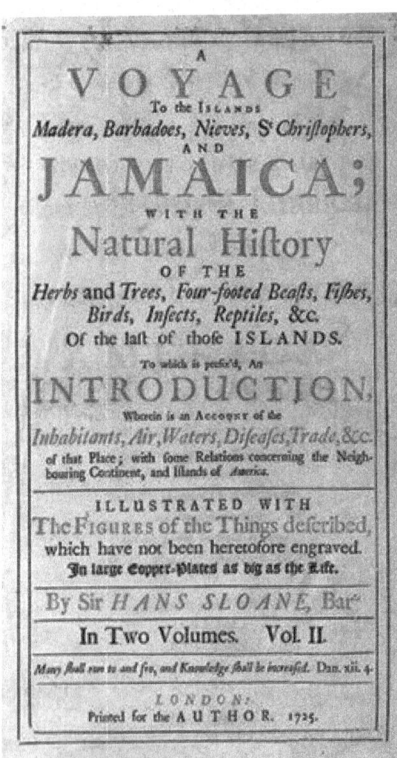

FIGURE 3.17 English naturalist Sir Hans Sloane traveled to Jamaica and other Caribbean islands to catalog the flora of the new world.

Native Americans, who possessed a vast understanding of local New World plants and their properties, would have been a rich source of information for those European botanists seeking to find and catalog potentially useful plants. Enslaved Africans, who had a tradition of the use of medicinal plants in their native land, adapted to their new surroundings by learning the use of New World plants through experimentation or from the native inhabitants. Native peoples and Africans employed their knowledge effectively within their own communities. One notable example was the use of the peacock flower to induce abortions: Native American and enslaved African women living in oppressive colonial regimes are said to have used this herb to prevent the birth of children into slavery. Europeans distrusted medical knowledge that came from African or native sources, however, and thus lost the benefit of this source of information.

Key Terms

headright system   a system in which parcels of land were granted to settlers who could pay their own way to Virginia

indenture   a labor contract that promised young men, and sometimes women, money and land after they worked for a set period of years

Jesuits   members of the Society of Jesus, an elite Catholic religious order founded in the 1540s to spread Catholicism and to combat the spread of Protestantism

maroon communities   groups of escaped enslaved people who resisted recapture and eked a living from the land

Middle Passage   the perilous, often deadly transatlantic crossing of ships carrying captured Africans from the African coast to the New World

musket   a light, long-barreled European gun

patroonships   large tracts of land and governing rights granted to merchants by the Dutch West India Company in order to encourage colonization

repartimiento   a Spanish colonial system requiring Native American towns to supply workers for the colonizers

Timucua   the native people of Florida, whom the Spanish displaced with the founding of St. Augustine, the first Spanish settlement in North America

wampum   shell beads used in ceremonies and as jewelry and currency

Summary

3.1 Spanish Exploration and Colonial Society

In their outposts at St. Augustine and Santa Fe, the Spanish never found the fabled mountains of gold they sought. They did find many native people to convert to Catholicism, but their zeal nearly cost them the colony of Santa Fe, which they lost for twelve years after the Pueblo Revolt. In truth, the grand dreams of wealth, conversion, and a social order based on Spanish control never came to pass as Spain envisioned them.

3.2 Colonial Rivalries: Dutch and French Colonial Ambitions

The French and Dutch established colonies in the northeastern part of North America: the Dutch in present-day New York, and the French in present-day Canada. Both colonies were primarily trading posts for furs. While they failed to attract many colonists from their respective home countries, these outposts nonetheless intensified imperial rivalries in North America. Both the Dutch and the French relied on native peoples to harvest the pelts that proved profitable in Europe.

3.3 English Settlements in America

The English came late to colonization of the Americas, establishing stable settlements in the 1600s after several unsuccessful attempts in the 1500s. After Roanoke Colony failed in 1587, the English found more success with the founding of Jamestown in 1607 and Plymouth in 1620. The two colonies were very different in origin. The Virginia Company of London founded Jamestown with the express purpose of making money for its investors, while Puritans founded Plymouth to practice their own brand of Protestantism without interference.

Both colonies battled difficult circumstances, including poor relationships with neighboring Native American tribes. Conflicts flared repeatedly in the Chesapeake Bay tobacco colonies and in New England, where a massive uprising against the English in 1675 to 1676—King Philip's War—nearly succeeded in driving the intruders back to the sea.

3.4 The Impact of Colonization

The development of the Atlantic slave trade forever changed the course of European settlement in the

Americas. Other transatlantic travelers, including diseases, goods, plants, animals, and even ideas like the concept of private land ownership, further influenced life in America during the sixteenth and seventeenth centuries. The exchange of pelts for European goods including copper kettles, knives, and guns played a significant role in changing the material cultures of native peoples. During the seventeenth century, native peoples grew increasingly dependent on European trade items. At the same time, many native inhabitants died of European diseases, while survivors adopted new ways of living with their new neighbors.

Review Questions

1. Which of the following was a goal of the Spanish in their destruction of Fort Caroline?
   A. establishing a foothold from which to battle the Timucua
   B. claiming a safe place to house the New World treasures that would be shipped back to Spain
   C. reducing the threat of French privateers
   D. locating a site for the establishment of Santa Fe

2. Why did the Spanish build Castillo de San Marcos?
   A. to protect the local Timucua
   B. to defend against imperial challengers
   C. as a seat for visiting Spanish royalty
   D. to house visiting delegates from rival imperial powers

3. How did the Pueblo attempt to maintain their autonomy in the face of Spanish settlement?

4. What was patroonship?
   A. a Dutch ship used for transporting beaver furs
   B. a Dutch system of patronage that encouraged the arts
   C. a Dutch system of granting tracts of land in New Netherland to encourage colonization
   D. a Dutch style of hat trimmed with beaver fur from New Netherland

5. Which religious order joined the French settlement in Canada and tried to convert the natives to Christianity?
   A. Franciscans
   B. Calvinists
   C. Anglicans
   D. Jesuits

6. How did the French and Dutch colonists differ in their religious expectations? How did both compare to Spanish colonists?

7. What was the most lucrative product of the Chesapeake colonies?
   A. corn
   B. tobacco
   C. gold and silver
   D. enslaved people

8. What was the primary cause of Bacon's Rebellion?
   A. former indentured servants wanted more opportunities to expand their territory
   B. Enslaved Africans wanted better treatment
   C. Susquahannock Natives wanted the Jamestown settlers to pay a fair price for their land
   D. Jamestown politicians were jockeying for power

9. The founders of the Plymouth colony were:
    A. Puritans
    B. Catholics
    C. Anglicans
    D. Jesuits

10. Which of the following is *not* true of the Puritan religion?
    A. It required close reading of scripture.
    B. Church membership required a conversion narrative.
    C. Literacy was crucial.
    D. Only men could participate.

11. How did the Chesapeake colonists solve their labor problems?

12. What was the Middle Passage?
    A. the fabled sea route from Europe to the Far East
    B. the land route from Europe to Africa
    C. the transatlantic journey that enslaved Africans made to America
    D. the line between the northern and southern colonies

13. Which of the following is *not* an item Europeans introduced to Native Americans?
    A. wampum
    B. glass beads
    C. copper kettles
    D. metal tools

14. How did European muskets change life for native peoples in the Americas?

15. Compare and contrast European and Native American views on property.

Critical Thinking Questions

16. Compare and contrast life in the Spanish, French, Dutch, and English colonies, differentiating between the Chesapeake Bay and New England colonies. Who were the colonizers? What were their purposes in being there? How did they interact with their environments and the native inhabitants of the lands on which they settled?

17. Describe the attempts of the various European colonists to convert native peoples to their belief systems. How did these attempts compare to one another? What were the results of each effort?

18. How did chattel slavery differ from indentured servitude? How did the former system come to replace the latter? What were the results of this shift?

19. What impact did Europeans have on their New World environments—native peoples and their communities as well as land, plants, and animals? Conversely, what impact did the New World's native inhabitants, land, plants, and animals have on Europeans? How did the interaction of European and Native American societies, together, shape a world that was truly "new"?

Rule Britannia! The English Empire, 1660–1763

4

FIGURE 4.1 Isaac Royall and his family, seen here in a 1741 portrait by Robert Feke (modified), moved to Medford, Massachusetts, from the West Indian island of Antigua, bringing enslaved people with them. They were an affluent British colonial family, proud of their success and the success of the British Empire.

CHAPTER OUTLINE
4.1 Charles II and the Restoration Colonies
4.2 The Glorious Revolution and the English Empire
4.3 An Empire of Slavery and the Consumer Revolution
4.4 Great Awakening and Enlightenment
4.5 Wars for Empire

INTRODUCTION The eighteenth century witnessed the birth of Great Britain (after the union of England and Scotland in 1707) and the expansion of the British Empire. By the mid-1700s, Great Britain had developed into a commercial and military powerhouse; its economic sway ranged from India, where the British East India Company had gained control over both trade and territory, to the West African coast, where British slave traders predominated, and to the British West Indies, whose lucrative sugar plantations, especially in Barbados and Jamaica, provided windfall profits for British planters. Meanwhile, the population rose dramatically in Britain's North American colonies. In the early 1700s the population in the colonies had reached 250,000. By 1750, however, over a million British migrants and enslaved Africans had established a near-continuous zone of settlement on the Atlantic coast from Maine to Georgia.

During this period, the ties between Great Britain and the American colonies only grew stronger. Anglo-American colonists considered themselves part of the British Empire in all ways: politically, militarily, religiously (as Protestants), intellectually, and racially. The portrait of the Royall family (Figure 4.1) exemplifies the colonial American gentry of the eighteenth century. Successful and well-to-do, they display fashions, hairstyles, and furnishings that all speak to their identity as proud and loyal British subjects.

4.1 Charles II and the Restoration Colonies

LEARNING OBJECTIVES

By the end of this section, you will be able to:
- Analyze the causes and consequences of the Restoration
- Identify the Restoration colonies and their role in the expansion of the Empire

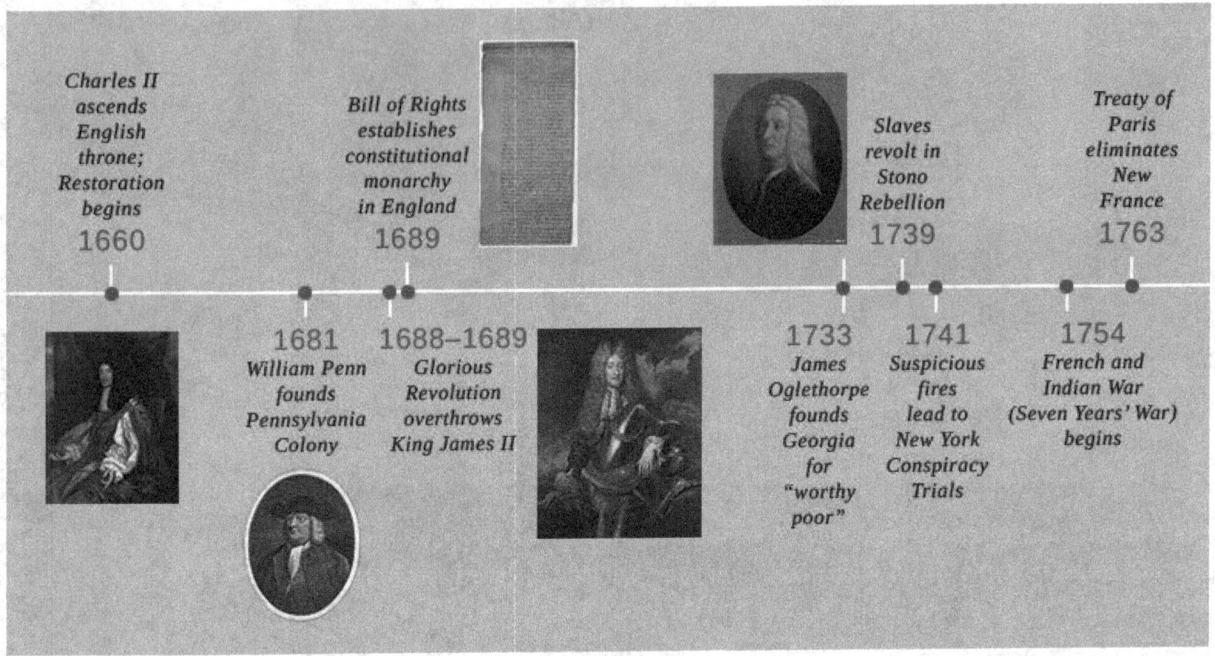

FIGURE 4.2

When Charles II ascended the throne in 1660, English subjects on both sides of the Atlantic celebrated the restoration of the English monarchy after a decade of living without a king as a result of the English Civil Wars. Charles II lost little time in strengthening England's global power. From the 1660s to the 1680s, Charles II added more possessions to England's North American holdings by establishing the Restoration colonies of New York and New Jersey (taking these areas from the Dutch) as well as Pennsylvania and the Carolinas. In order to reap the greatest economic benefit from England's overseas possessions, Charles II enacted the mercantilist Navigation Acts, although many colonial merchants ignored them because enforcement remained lax.

CHARLES II

The chronicle of Charles II begins with his father, Charles I. Charles I ascended the English throne in 1625 and soon married a French Catholic princess, Henrietta Maria, who was not well liked by English Protestants because she openly practiced Catholicism during her husband's reign. The most outspoken Protestants, the Puritans, had a strong voice in Parliament in the 1620s, and they strongly opposed the king's marriage and his ties to Catholicism. When Parliament tried to contest his edicts, including the king's efforts to impose taxes without Parliament's consent, Charles I suspended Parliament in 1629 and ruled without one for the next eleven years.

The ensuing struggle between the king and Parliament led to the outbreak of war. The English Civil War lasted from 1642 to 1649 and pitted the king and his Royalist supporters against Oliver Cromwell and his Parliamentary forces. After years of fighting, the Parliamentary forces gained the upper hand, and in 1649, they charged Charles I with treason and beheaded him. The monarchy was dissolved, and England became a republic: a state without a king. Oliver Cromwell headed the new English Commonwealth, and the period known as the **English interregnum**, or the time between kings, began.

Though Cromwell enjoyed widespread popularity at first, over time he appeared to many in England to be taking on the powers of a military dictator. Dissatisfaction with Cromwell grew. When he died in 1658 and control passed to his son Richard, who lacked the political skills of his father, a majority of the English people feared an alternate hereditary monarchy in the making. They had had enough and asked Charles II to be king. In 1660, they welcomed the son of the executed king Charles I back to the throne to resume the English monarchy and bring the interregnum to an end (Figure 4.3). The return of Charles II is known as the Restoration.

(a) (b)

FIGURE 4.3 The monarchy and Parliament fought for control of England during the seventeenth century. Though Oliver Cromwell (a), shown here in a 1656 portrait by Samuel Cooper, appeared to offer England a better mode of government, he assumed broad powers for himself and disregarded cherished English liberties established under Magna Carta in 1215. As a result, the English people welcomed Charles II (b) back to the throne in 1660. This portrait by John Michael Wright was painted ca. 1660–1665, soon after the new king gained the throne.

Charles II was committed to expanding England's overseas possessions. His policies in the 1660s through the 1680s established and supported the **Restoration colonies**: the Carolinas, New Jersey, New York, and Pennsylvania. All the Restoration colonies started as **proprietary colonies**, that is, the king gave each colony to a trusted individual, family, or group.

THE CAROLINAS

Charles II hoped to establish English control of the area between Virginia and Spanish Florida. To that end, he issued a royal charter in 1663 to eight trusted and loyal supporters, each of whom was to be a feudal-style proprietor of a region of the province of Carolina.

These proprietors did not relocate to the colonies, however. Instead, English plantation owners from the tiny Caribbean island of Barbados, already a well-established English sugar colony fueled by slave labor, migrated to the southern part of Carolina to settle there. In 1670, they established Charles Town (later Charleston), named in honor of Charles II, at the junction of the Ashley and Cooper Rivers (Figure 4.4). As the settlement around Charles Town grew, it began to produce livestock for export to the West Indies. In the northern part of Carolina, settlers used sap from pine trees to create tar and pitch used to waterproof wooden ships. Political disagreements between settlers in the northern and southern parts of Carolina escalated in the 1710s through the 1720s and led to the creation, in 1729, of two colonies, North and South Carolina. The southern part of Carolina had been producing rice and indigo (a plant that yields a dark blue dye used by English royalty) since the 1700s, and South Carolina continued to depend on these main crops. North Carolina continued to produce items for ships, especially turpentine and tar, and its population increased as Virginians moved there to expand their tobacco holdings. Tobacco was the primary export of both Virginia and North Carolina, which also traded in deerskins and captured people from Africa.

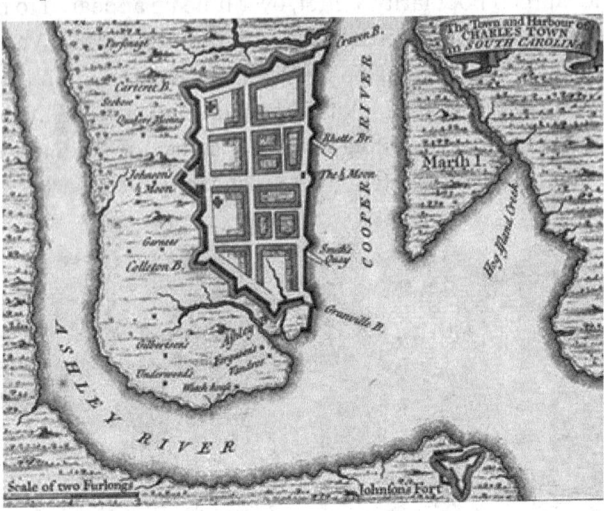

FIGURE 4.4 The port of colonial Charles Towne, depicted here on a 1733 map of North America, was the largest in the South and played a significant role in the Atlantic slave trade.

Slavery developed quickly in the Carolinas, largely because so many of the early migrants came from Barbados, where slavery was well established. By the end of the 1600s, a very wealthy class of rice planters, who relied on enslaved people for labor, had attained dominance in the southern part of the Carolinas, especially around Charles Town. By 1715, South Carolina had a Black majority because of the number of enslaved people in the colony. The legal basis for slavery was established in the early 1700s as the Carolinas began to pass slave laws based on the Barbados slave codes of the late 1600s. These laws reduced Africans to the status of property to be bought and sold as other commodities.

CLICK AND EXPLORE

Visit the Charleston Museum's interactive exhibit The Walled City (http://openstax.org/l/charleston) to learn more about the history of Charleston.

As in other areas of English settlement, native peoples in the Carolinas suffered tremendously from the introduction of European diseases. Despite the effects of disease, Native Americans in the area endured and, following the pattern elsewhere in the colonies, grew dependent on European goods. Local Yamasee and Creek tribes built up a trade deficit with the English, trading deerskins and captive people for European guns. English settlers exacerbated tensions with local Native American tribes, especially the Yamasee, by expanding their rice and tobacco fields into Native American lands. Worse still, English traders took Native women captive as payment for debts.

The outrages committed by traders, combined with the seemingly unstoppable expansion of English settlement onto native land, led to the outbreak of the Yamasee War (1715–1718), an effort by a coalition of local tribes to drive away the European invaders. This native effort to force the newcomers back across the Atlantic nearly succeeded in annihilating the Carolina colonies. Only when the Cherokee allied themselves with the English did the coalition's goal of eliminating the English from the region falter. The Yamasee War demonstrates the key role native peoples played in shaping the outcome of colonial struggles and, perhaps most important, the disunity that existed between different native groups.

NEW YORK AND NEW JERSEY

Charles II also set his sights on the Dutch colony of New Netherland. The English takeover of New Netherland originated in the imperial rivalry between the Dutch and the English. During the Anglo-Dutch wars of the 1650s and 1660s, the two powers attempted to gain commercial advantages in the Atlantic World. During the Second Anglo-Dutch War (1664–1667), English forces gained control of the Dutch fur trading colony of New Netherland, and in 1664, Charles II gave this colony (including present-day New Jersey) to his brother James, Duke of York (later James II). The colony and city were renamed New York in his honor. The Dutch in New York chafed under English rule. In 1673, during the Third Anglo-Dutch War (1672–1674), the Dutch recaptured the colony. However, at the end of the conflict, the English had regained control (Figure 4.5).

FIGURE 4.5 "View of New Amsterdam" (ca. 1665), a watercolor by Johannes Vingboons, was painted during the Anglo-Dutch wars of the 1660s and 1670s. New Amsterdam was officially reincorporated as New York City in 1664, but alternated under Dutch and English rule until 1674.

The Duke of York had no desire to govern locally or listen to the wishes of local colonists. It wasn't until 1683, therefore, almost 20 years after the English took control of the colony, that colonists were able to convene a local representative legislature. The assembly's 1683 Charter of Liberties and Privileges set out the traditional rights of Englishmen, like the right to trial by jury and the right to representative government.

The English continued the Dutch patroonship system, granting large estates to a favored few families. The largest of these estates, at 160,000 acres, was given to Robert Livingston in 1686. The Livingstons and the other manorial families who controlled the Hudson River Valley formed a formidable political and economic force. Eighteenth-century New York City, meanwhile, contained a variety of people and religions—as well as Dutch and English people, it held French Protestants (Huguenots), Jews, Puritans, Quakers, Anglicans, and a large population of enslaved people. As they did in other zones of colonization, native peoples played a key role in shaping the history of colonial New York. After decades of war in the 1600s, the powerful Five Nations of the Iroquois, composed of the Mohawk, Oneida, Onondaga, Cayuga, and Seneca, successfully pursued a policy of neutrality with both the English and, to the north, the French in Canada during the first half of the 1700s. This native policy meant that the Iroquois continued to live in their own villages under their own government while enjoying the benefits of trade with both the French and the English.

PENNSYLVANIA

The Restoration colonies also included Pennsylvania, which became the geographic center of British colonial America. Pennsylvania (which means "Penn's Woods" in Latin) was created in 1681, when Charles II bestowed the largest proprietary colony in the Americas on William Penn (Figure 4.6) to settle the large debt he owed the Penn family. William Penn's father, Admiral William Penn, had served the English crown by helping take Jamaica from the Spanish in 1655. The king personally owed the Admiral money as well.

FIGURE 4.6 Charles II granted William Penn the land that eventually became the Commonwealth of Pennsylvania in order to settle a debt the English crown owed to Penn's father.

Like early settlers of the New England colonies, Pennsylvania's first colonists migrated mostly for religious reasons. William Penn himself was a Quaker, a member of a new Protestant denomination called the Society of Friends. George Fox had founded the Society of Friends in England in the late 1640s, having grown dissatisfied with Puritanism and the idea of predestination. Rather, Fox and his followers stressed that everyone had an "inner light" inside him or her, a spark of divinity. They gained the name Quakers because they were said to quake when the inner light moved them. Quakers rejected the idea of worldly rank, believing instead in a new and radical form of social equality. Their speech reflected this belief in that they addressed all others as equals, using "thee" and "thou" rather than terms like "your lordship" or "my lady" that were customary for privileged individuals of the hereditary elite.

The English crown persecuted Quakers in England, and colonial governments were equally harsh; Massachusetts even executed several early Quakers who had gone to proselytize there. To avoid such persecution, Quakers and their families at first created a community on the sugar island of Barbados. Soon after its founding, however, Pennsylvania became the destination of choice. Quakers flocked to Pennsylvania as well as New Jersey, where they could preach and practice their religion in peace. Unlike New England, whose official religion was Puritanism, Pennsylvania did not establish an official church. Indeed, the colony allowed a degree of religious tolerance found nowhere else in English America. To help encourage immigration to his colony, Penn promised fifty acres of land to people who agreed to come to Pennsylvania and completed their term of service. Not surprisingly, those seeking a better life came in large numbers, so much so that Pennsylvania relied on indentured servants more than any other colony.

One of the primary tenets of Quakerism is pacifism, which led William Penn to establish friendly relationships with local native peoples. He formed a covenant of friendship with the Lenni Lenape (Delaware) tribe, buying their land for a fair price instead of taking it by force. In 1701, he also signed a treaty with the Susquehannocks to avoid war. Unlike other colonies, Pennsylvania did not experience war on the frontier with native peoples during its early history.

As an important port city, Philadelphia grew rapidly. Quaker merchants there established contacts throughout the Atlantic world and participated in the thriving African slave trade. Some Quakers, who were deeply troubled by the contradiction between their belief in the "inner light" and the practice of slavery, rejected the practice and engaged in efforts to abolish it altogether. Philadelphia also acted as a magnet for immigrants, who came not only from England, but from all over Europe by the hundreds of thousands. The city, and indeed all of Pennsylvania, appeared to be the best country for poor men and women, many of whom arrived as servants and dreamed of owning land. A very few, like the fortunate Benjamin Franklin, a runaway from

Puritan Boston, did extraordinarily well. Other immigrant groups in the colony, most notably Germans and Scotch-Irish (families from Scotland and England who had first lived in Ireland before moving to British America), greatly improved their lot in Pennsylvania. Of course, Africans brought into the colony to labor for White enslavers fared far worse.

AMERICANA

John Wilson Offers Reward for Escaped Prisoners

The *American Weekly Mercury*, published by William Bradford, was Philadelphia's first newspaper. This advertisement from "John Wilson, *Goaler*" (jailer) offers a reward for anyone capturing several men who escaped from the jail.

"BROKE out of the Common Goal of Philadelphia, the 15th of this Instant February, 1721, the following Persons: John Palmer, also Plumly, *alias* Paine, *Servant to Joseph Jones, run away and was lately taken up at New-York. He is fully described in the* American Mercury, Novem. 23, 1721. *He has a Cinnamon coloured Coat on, a middle sized fresh coloured Man. His Master will give a Pistole Reward to any who Shall Secure him, besides what is here offered.*

Daniel Oughtopay, *A Dutchman, aged about 24 Years, Servant to Dr. Johnston in Amboy. He is a thin Spare man, grey Drugget Waistcoat and Breeches and a light-coloured Coat on.*

Ebenezor Mallary, *a New-England, aged about 24 Years, is a middle-sized thin Man, having on a Snuff colour'd Coat, and ordinary Ticking Waistcoat and Breeches. He has dark brown strait Hair.*

Matthew Dulany, *an Irish Man, down-look'd Swarthy Complexion, and has on an Olive-coloured Cloth Coat and Waistcoat with Cloth Buttons.*

John Flemming, *an Irish Lad, aged about 18, belonging to Mr. Miranda, Merchant in this City. He has no Coat, a grey Drugget Waistcoat, and a narrow brim'd Hat on.*

John Corbet, *a Shropshire Man, a Runaway Servant from Alexander Faulkner of Maryland, broke out on the 12th Instant. He has got a double-breasted Sailor's Jacket on lined with red Bays, pretends to be a Sailor, and once taught School at Josephs Collings's in the Jerseys.*

Whoever takes up and secures all, or any One of these Felons, shall have a Pistole Reward for each of them and reasonable Charges, paid them by John Wilson, *Goaler*
—Advertisement from the *American Weekly Mercury*, 1722"

What do the descriptions of the men tell you about life in colonial Philadelphia?

CLICK AND EXPLORE

Browse a number of issues of the *American Weekly Mercury* (http://openstax.org/l/philly1) that were digitized by New Jersey's Stockton University. Read through several to get a remarkable flavor of life in early eighteenth-century Philadelphia.

THE NAVIGATION ACTS

Creating wealth for the Empire remained a primary goal, and in the second half of the seventeenth century, especially during the Restoration, England attempted to gain better control of trade with the American colonies. The mercantilist policies by which it tried to achieve this control are known as the **Navigation Acts**.

The 1651 Navigation Ordinance, a product of Cromwell's England, required that only English ships carry goods between England and the colonies, and that the captain and three-fourths of the crew had to be English. The ordinance further listed "enumerated articles" that could be transported only to England or to English colonies, including the most lucrative commodities like sugar and tobacco as well as indigo, rice, molasses, and naval stores such as turpentine. All were valuable goods not produced in England and in demand by the British navy. After ascending the throne, Charles II approved the 1660 Navigation Act, which restated the 1651 act to ensure a monopoly on imports from the colonies.

Other Navigation Acts included the 1663 Staple Act and the 1673 Plantation Duties Act. The Staple Act barred colonists from importing goods that had not been made in England, creating a profitable monopoly for English exporters and manufacturers. The Plantation Duties Act taxed enumerated articles exported from one colony to another, a measure aimed principally at New Englanders, who transported great quantities of molasses from the West Indies, including smuggled molasses from French-held islands, to make into rum.

In 1675, Charles II organized the Lords of Trade and Plantation, commonly known as the Lords of Trade, an administrative body intended to create stronger ties between the colonial governments and the crown. However, the 1696 Navigation Act created the Board of Trade, replacing the Lords of Trade. This act, meant to strengthen enforcement of customs laws, also established vice-admiralty courts where the crown could prosecute customs violators without a jury. Under this act, customs officials were empowered with warrants known as "writs of assistance" to board and search vessels suspected of containing smuggled goods.

Despite the Navigation Acts, however, Great Britain exercised lax control over the English colonies during most of the eighteenth century because of the policies of Prime Minister Robert Walpole. During his long term (1721–1742), Walpole governed according to his belief that commerce flourished best when it was not encumbered with restrictions. Historians have described this lack of strict enforcement of the Navigation Acts as **salutary neglect**. In addition, nothing prevented colonists from building their own fleet of ships to engage in trade. New England especially benefited from both salutary neglect and a vibrant maritime culture made possible by the scores of trading vessels built in the northern colonies. The case of the 1733 Molasses Act illustrates the weaknesses of British mercantilist policy. The 1733 act placed a sixpence-per-gallon duty on raw sugar, rum, and molasses from Britain's competitors, the French and the Dutch, in order to give an advantage to British West Indian producers. Because the British did not enforce the 1733 law, however, New England mariners routinely smuggled these items from the French and Dutch West Indies more cheaply than they could buy them on English islands.

4.2 The Glorious Revolution and the English Empire

LEARNING OBJECTIVES

By the end of this section, you will be able to:
- Identify the causes of the Glorious Revolution
- Explain the outcomes of the Glorious Revolution

During the brief rule of King James II, many in England feared the imposition of a Catholic absolute monarchy by the man who modeled his rule on that of his French Catholic cousin, Louis XIV. Opposition to James II, spearheaded by the English Whig party, overthrew the king in the Glorious Revolution of 1688–1689. This paved the way for the Protestant reign of William of Orange and his wife Mary (James's Protestant daughter).

JAMES II AND THE GLORIOUS REVOLUTION

King James II (Figure 4.7), the second son of Charles I, ascended the English throne in 1685 on the death of his brother, Charles II. James then worked to model his rule on the reign of the French Catholic King Louis XIV, his cousin. This meant centralizing English political strength around the throne, giving the monarchy absolute power. Also like Louis XIV, James II practiced a strict and intolerant form of Roman Catholicism after he converted from Protestantism in the late 1660s. He had a Catholic wife, and when they had a son, the potential for a Catholic heir to the English throne became a threat to English Protestants. James also worked to modernize the English army and navy. The fact that the king kept a standing army in times of peace greatly alarmed the English, who believed that such a force would be used to crush their liberty. As James's strength grew, his opponents feared their king would turn England into a Catholic monarchy with absolute power over her people.

FIGURE 4.7 James II (shown here in a painting ca. 1690) worked to centralize the English government. The Catholic king of France, Louis XIV, provided a template for James's policies.

In 1686, James II applied his concept of a centralized state to the colonies by creating an enormous colony called the **Dominion of New England**. The Dominion included all the New England colonies (Massachusetts, New Hampshire, Plymouth, Connecticut, New Haven, and Rhode Island) and in 1688 was enlarged by the addition of New York and New Jersey. James placed in charge Sir Edmund Andros, a former colonial governor of New York. Loyal to James II and his family, Andros had little sympathy for New Englanders. His regime caused great uneasiness among New England Puritans when it called into question the many land titles that did not acknowledge the king and imposed fees for their reconfirmation. Andros also committed himself to enforcing the Navigation Acts, a move that threatened to disrupt the region's trade, which was based largely on smuggling.

In England, opponents of James II's efforts to create a centralized Catholic state were known as Whigs. The Whigs worked to depose James, and in late 1688 they succeeded, an event they celebrated as the **Glorious Revolution** while James fled to the court of Louis XIV in France. William III (William of Orange) and his wife Mary II ascended the throne in 1689.

The Glorious Revolution spilled over into the colonies. In 1689, Bostonians overthrew the government of the Dominion of New England and jailed Sir Edmund Andros as well as other leaders of the regime (Figure 4.8). The removal of Andros from power illustrates New England's animosity toward the English overlord who had, during his tenure, established Church of England worship in Puritan Boston and vigorously enforced the Navigation Acts, to the chagrin of those in port towns. In New York, the same year that Andros fell from power, Jacob Leisler led a group of Protestant New Yorkers against the dominion government. Acting on his own authority, Leisler assumed the role of King William's governor and organized intercolonial military action independent of British authority. Leisler's actions usurped the crown's prerogative and, as a result, he was tried for treason and executed. In 1691, England restored control over the Province of New York.

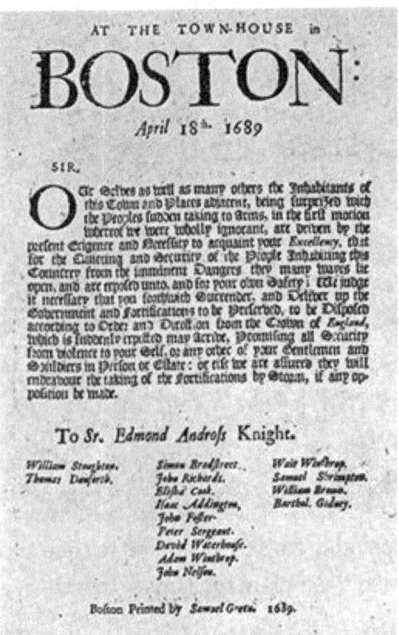

FIGURE 4.8 This broadside, signed by several citizens, demands the surrender of Sir Edmund (spelled here "Edmond") Andros, James II's hand-picked leader of the Dominion of New England.

The Glorious Revolution provided a shared experience for those who lived through the tumult of 1688 and 1689. Subsequent generations kept the memory of the Glorious Revolution alive as a heroic defense of English liberty against a would-be tyrant.

ENGLISH LIBERTY

The Glorious Revolution led to the establishment of an English nation that limited the power of the king and provided protections for English subjects. In October 1689, the same year that William and Mary took the throne, the 1689 Bill of Rights established a constitutional monarchy. It stipulated Parliament's independence from the monarchy and protected certain of Parliament's rights, such as the right to freedom of speech, the right to regular elections, and the right to petition the king. The 1689 Bill of Rights also guaranteed certain rights to all English subjects, including trial by jury and habeas corpus (the requirement that authorities bring an imprisoned person before a court to demonstrate the cause of the imprisonment).

John Locke (1632–1704), a doctor and educator who had lived in exile in Holland during the reign of James II and returned to England after the Glorious Revolution, published his *Two Treatises of Government* in 1690. In it, he argued that government was a form of contract between the leaders and the people, and that representative government existed to protect "life, liberty and property." Locke rejected the divine right of kings and instead advocated for the central role of Parliament with a limited monarchy. Locke's political philosophy had an enormous impact on future generations of colonists and established the paramount importance of representation in government.

CLICK AND EXPLORE

Visit the Digital Locke Project (http://openstax.org/l/jlocke) to read more of John Locke's writings. This digital collection contains over thirty of his philosophical texts.

The Glorious Revolution also led to the English Toleration Act of 1689, a law passed by Parliament that allowed for greater religious diversity in the Empire. This act granted religious tolerance to **nonconformist** Trinitarian Protestants (those who believed in the Holy Trinity of God the Father, Son, and Holy Ghost), such as Baptists (those who advocated adult baptism) and Congregationalists (those who followed the Puritans' lead in creating independent churches). While the Church of England remained the official state religious establishment, the Toleration Act gave much greater religious freedom to nonconformists. However, this tolerance did not extend to Catholics, who were routinely excluded from political power. The 1689 Toleration Act extended to the British colonies, where several colonies—Pennsylvania, Rhode Island, Delaware, and New Jersey—refused to allow the creation of an established colonial church, a major step toward greater religious diversity.

4.3 An Empire of Slavery and the Consumer Revolution

LEARNING OBJECTIVES

By the end of this section, you will be able to:
- Analyze the role slavery played in the history and economy of the British Empire
- Explain the effects of the 1739 Stono Rebellion and the 1741 New York Conspiracy Trials
- Describe the consumer revolution and its effect on the life of the colonial gentry and other settlers

Slavery formed a cornerstone of the British Empire in the eighteenth century. Every colony had enslaved people, from the southern rice plantations in Charles Town, South Carolina, to the northern wharves of Boston. Slavery was more than a labor system; it also influenced every aspect of colonial thought and culture. The uneven relationship it engendered gave White colonists an exaggerated sense of their own status. English liberty gained greater meaning and coherence for White people when they contrasted their status to that of the unfree class of enslaved Black people in British America. African slavery provided White colonists with a shared racial bond and identity.

SLAVERY AND THE STONO REBELLION

The transport of captured Africans to the American colonies accelerated in the second half of the seventeenth century. In 1660, Charles II created the Royal African Company (Figure 4.9) to trade in African goods and enslaved people.. His brother, James II, led the company before ascending the throne. Under both these kings, the Royal African Company had a monopoly on the slave trade to the English colonies. Between 1672 and 1713, the company bought 125,000 captives on the African coast, losing 20 percent of them to death on the Middle Passage, the journey from the African coast to the Americas.

FIGURE 4.9 The 1686 English guinea shows the logo of the Royal African Company, an elephant and castle, beneath a bust of King James II. The coins were commonly called guineas because most British gold came from Guinea in West Africa.

The Royal African Company's monopoly ended in 1689 as a result of the Glorious Revolution. After that date, many more English merchants engaged in the slave trade, greatly increasing the number of captives being transported. Africans who survived the brutal Middle Passage usually arrived in the West Indies, often in Barbados. From there, they were transported to the mainland English colonies on company ships. While merchants in London, Bristol, and Liverpool lined their pockets, Africans trafficked by the company endured a nightmare of misery, privation, and dislocation.

Enslaved Africans strove to adapt to their new lives by forming new communities among themselves, often adhering to traditional African customs and healing techniques. Indeed, the development of families and communities formed the most important response to the trauma of being enslaved. Others dealt with the trauma of their situation by actively resisting their condition, whether by defying their captors or running away. Escaped enslaved people formed what were called "maroon" communities, groups that successfully resisted recapture and formed their own autonomous groups. The most prominent of these communities lived in the interior of Jamaica, controlling the area and keeping the British away.

Enslaved people everywhere resisted their exploitation and attempted to gain freedom. They fully understood that rebellions would bring about massive retaliation from White people and therefore had little chance of success. Even so, rebellions occurred frequently. One notable uprising that became known as the Stono Rebellion took place in South Carolina in September 1739. A literate Angolan named Jemmy led a large group of captive Africans in an armed insurrection against White colonists. The militia suppressed the rebellion after a battle in which both enslaved people and militiamen were killed, and the remaining rebels were executed or sold to enslavers in the West Indies.

Jemmy is believed to have been taken from the Kingdom of Kongo, an area where the Portuguese had introduced Catholicism. Other enslaved people in South Carolina may have had a similar background: Africa-born and familiar with White people. If so, this common background may have made it easier for Jemmy to communicate with the other rebels, enabling them to work together to resist their enslavement even though enslavers labored to keep their captives from forging such communities.

In the wake of the Stono Rebellion, South Carolina passed a new slave code in 1740 called An Act for the Better Ordering and Governing of Negroes and Other Slaves in the Province, also known as the Negro Act of 1740. This law imposed new limits on enslaved people's behavior, prohibiting them from assembling, growing their own food, learning to write, and traveling freely.

THE NEW YORK CONSPIRACY TRIALS OF 1741

Eighteenth-century New York City contained many different ethnic groups, and conflicts among them created strain. In addition, one in five New Yorkers was an enslaved person, and tensions ran high between the enslaved and the free population, especially in the aftermath of the Stono Rebellion. These tensions burst forth in 1741.

That year, thirteen fires broke out in the city, one of which reduced the colony's Fort George to ashes. Ever fearful of an uprising among enslaved New Yorkers, the city's White residents spread rumors that the fires were part of a massive revolt in which enslaved people would murder White people, burn the city, and take over the colony. The Stono Rebellion was only a few years in the past, and throughout British America, fears of similar incidents were still fresh. Searching for solutions, and convinced their captives were the principal danger, nervous British authorities interrogated almost two hundred enslaved people and accused them of conspiracy. Rumors that Roman Catholics had joined the suspected conspiracy and planned to murder Protestant inhabitants of the city only added to the general hysteria. Very quickly, two hundred people were arrested, including a large number of the city's enslaved population.

After a quick series of trials at City Hall, known as the New York Conspiracy Trials of 1741, the government executed seventeen New Yorkers. Thirteen Black men were publicly burned at the stake, while the others (including four White men) were hanged (Figure 4.10). Seventy people were sold to the West Indies. Little evidence exists to prove that an elaborate conspiracy, like the one White New Yorkers imagined, actually existed.

FIGURE 4.10 In the wake of a series of fires throughout New York City, rumors of a slave revolt led authorities to convict and execute thirty people, including thirteen Black men who were publicly burned at the stake.

The events of 1741 in New York City illustrate the racial divide in British America, where panic among White people spurred great violence against and repression of the feared enslaved population. In the end, the Conspiracy Trials furthered White dominance and power over enslaved New Yorkers.

CLICK AND EXPLORE

View the map of New York in the 1740s (http://openstax.org/l/NY1700s) at the New York Public Library's digital gallery, which allows you to zoom in and see specific events. Look closely at numbers 55 and 56 just north of the city limits to see illustrations depicting the executions.

COLONIAL GENTRY AND THE CONSUMER REVOLUTION

British Americans' reliance on indentured servitude and slavery to meet the demand for colonial labor helped give rise to a wealthy colonial class—the gentry—in the Chesapeake tobacco colonies and elsewhere. To be "genteel," that is, a member of the gentry, meant to be refined, free of all rudeness. The British American gentry modeled themselves on the English aristocracy, who embodied the ideal of refinement and gentility. They built elaborate mansions to advertise their status and power. William Byrd II of Westover, Virginia, exemplifies the colonial gentry; a wealthy planter and slaveholder, he is known for founding Richmond and for his diaries documenting the life of a gentleman planter (Figure 4.11).

FIGURE 4.11 This painting by Hans Hysing, ca. 1724, depicts William Byrd II. Byrd was a wealthy gentleman planter in Virginia and a member of the colonial gentry.

MY STORY

William Byrd's Secret Diary

The diary of William Byrd, a Virginia planter, provides a unique way to better understand colonial life on a plantation (Figure 4.12). What does it show about daily life for a "gentleman" planter and enslaver? What does it show about slavery?

"August 27, 1709
I rose at 5 o'clock and read two chapters in Hebrew and some Greek in Josephus. I said my prayers and ate milk for breakfast. I danced my dance. I had like to have whipped my maid Anaka for her laziness but I forgave her. I read a little geometry. I denied my man G-r-l to go to a horse race because there was nothing but swearing and drinking there. I ate roast mutton for dinner. In the afternoon I played at piquet with my own wife and made her out of humor by cheating her. I read some Greek in Homer. Then I walked about the plantation. I lent John H-ch £7 [7 English pounds] in his distress. I said my prayers and had good health, good thoughts, and good humor, thanks be to God Almighty.

September 6, 1709
About one o'clock this morning my wife was happily delivered of a son, thanks be to God Almighty. I was awake in a blink and rose and my cousin Harrison met me on the stairs and told me it was a boy. We drank some French wine and went to bed again and rose at 7 o'clock. I read a chapter in Hebrew and then drank chocolate with the women for breakfast. I returned God humble thanks for so great a blessing and recommended my young son to His divine protection. . . .

September 15, 1710
I rose at 5 o'clock and read two chapters in Hebrew and some Greek in Thucydides. I said my prayers and ate milk and pears for breakfast. About 7 o'clock the negro boy [*or* Betty] that ran away was brought home. My wife against my will caused little Jenny to be burned with a hot iron, for which I quarreled with her. . . ."

FIGURE 4.12 This photograph shows the view down the stairway from the third floor of Westover Plantation, home of William Byrd II. What does this image suggest about the lifestyle of the inhabitants—enslavers and enslaved servants—of this house?

One of the ways in which the gentry set themselves apart from others was through their purchase, consumption, and display of goods. An increased supply of consumer goods from England that became available in the eighteenth century led to a phenomenon called the consumer revolution. These products linked the colonies to Great Britain in real and tangible ways. Indeed, along with the colonial gentry, ordinary settlers in the colonies also participated in the frenzy of consumer spending on goods from Great Britain. Tea, for example, came to be regarded as the drink of the Empire, with or without fashionable tea sets.

The consumer revolution also made printed materials more widely available. Before 1680, for instance, no newspapers had been printed in colonial America. In the eighteenth century, however, a flood of journals, books, pamphlets, and other publications became available to readers on both sides of the Atlantic. This shared trove of printed matter linked members of the Empire by creating a community of shared tastes and ideas.

Cato's Letters, by Englishmen John Trenchard and Thomas Gordon, was one popular series of 144 pamphlets. These Whig circulars were published between 1720 and 1723 and emphasized the glory of England, especially its commitment to liberty. However, the pamphlets cautioned readers to be ever vigilant and on the lookout for attacks upon that liberty. Indeed, *Cato's Letters* suggested that there were constant efforts to undermine and destroy it.

Another very popular publication was the English gentlemen's magazine the *Spectator*, published between 1711 and 1714. In each issue, "Mr. Spectator" observed and commented on the world around him. What made the *Spectator* so wildly popular was its style; the essays were meant to persuade, and to cultivate among readers a refined set of behaviors, rejecting deceit and intolerance and focusing instead on the polishing of genteel taste and manners.

Novels, a new type of literature, made their first appearance in the eighteenth century and proved very popular in the British Atlantic. Daniel Defoe's *Robinson Crusoe* and Samuel Richardson's *Pamela: Or, Virtue Rewarded* found large and receptive audiences. Reading also allowed female readers the opportunity to interpret what they read without depending on a male authority to tell them what to think. Few women beyond the colonial gentry, however, had access to novels.

4.4 Great Awakening and Enlightenment

LEARNING OBJECTIVES

By the end of this section, you will be able to:
- Explain the significance of the Great Awakening
- Describe the genesis, central ideas, and effects of the Enlightenment in British North America

Two major cultural movements further strengthened Anglo-American colonists' connection to Great Britain: the Great Awakening and the Enlightenment. Both movements began in Europe, but they advocated very different ideas: the Great Awakening promoted a fervent, emotional religiosity, while the Enlightenment encouraged the pursuit of reason in all things. On both sides of the Atlantic, British subjects grappled with these new ideas.

THE FIRST GREAT AWAKENING

During the eighteenth century, the British Atlantic experienced an outburst of Protestant revivalism known as the **First Great Awakening**. (A Second Great Awakening would take place in the 1800s.) During the First Great Awakening, evangelists came from the ranks of several Protestant denominations: Congregationalists, Anglicans (members of the Church of England), and Presbyterians. They rejected what appeared to be sterile, formal modes of worship in favor of a vigorous emotional religiosity. Whereas Martin Luther and John Calvin had preached a doctrine of predestination and close reading of scripture, new evangelical ministers spread a message of personal and experiential faith that rose above mere book learning. Individuals could bring about their own salvation by accepting Christ, an especially welcome message for those who had felt excluded by traditional Protestantism: women, the young, and people at the lower end of the social spectrum.

The Great Awakening caused a split between those who followed the evangelical message (the "New Lights") and those who rejected it (the "Old Lights"). The elite ministers in British America were firmly Old Lights, and they censured the new revivalism as chaos. Indeed, the revivals did sometimes lead to excess. In one notorious incident in 1743, an influential New Light minister named James Davenport urged his listeners to burn books. The next day, he told them to burn their clothes as a sign of their casting off the sinful trappings of the world.

He then took off his own pants and threw them into the fire, but a woman saved them and tossed them back to Davenport, telling him he had gone too far.

Another outburst of Protestant revivalism began in New Jersey, led by a minister of the Dutch Reformed Church named Theodorus Frelinghuysen. Frelinghuysen's example inspired other ministers, including Gilbert Tennent, a Presbyterian. Tennent helped to spark a Presbyterian revival in the Middle Colonies (Pennsylvania, New York, and New Jersey), in part by founding a seminary to train other evangelical clergyman. New Lights also founded colleges in Rhode Island and New Hampshire that would later become Brown University and Dartmouth College.

In Northampton, Massachusetts, Jonathan Edwards led still another explosion of evangelical fervor. Edwards had grown frustrated with lack of religious emotion among practicing Christians within his community. He wanted to enliven religious practice. An important component of his approach involved using vivid depictions of the terrors of hell (Figure 4.13). Edward's best-known sermon, "Sinners in the Hands of an Angry God," perfectly exemplifies this terrifying approach. One passage reads: "The wrath of God burns against them [sinners], their damnation don't slumber, the pit is prepared, the fire is made ready, the furnace is now hot, ready to receive them, the flames do now rage and glow. The glittering sword is whet, and held over them, and the pit hath opened her mouth under them." Edwards's revival spread along the Connecticut River Valley, and news of the event spread rapidly through the frequent reprinting of his famous sermon.

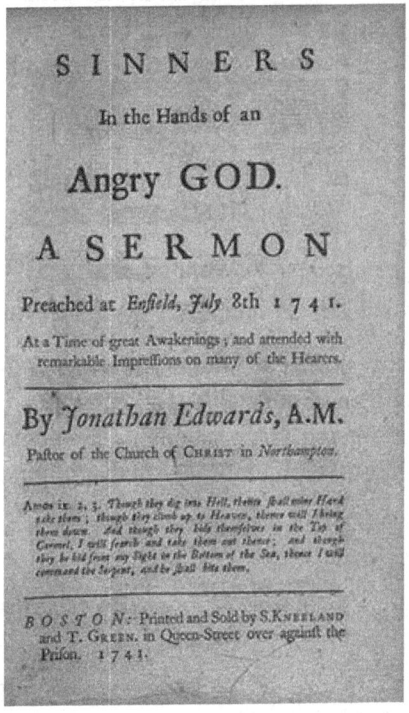

FIGURE 4.13 This image shows the frontispiece of *Sinners in the Hands of an Angry God, A Sermon Preached at Enfield, July 8, 1741* by Jonathan Edwards. Edwards was an evangelical preacher who led a Protestant revival in New England. This was his most famous sermon, the text of which was reprinted often and distributed widely.

The foremost evangelical of the Great Awakening was an Anglican minister named George Whitefield. Like many evangelical ministers, Whitefield was itinerant, traveling the countryside instead of having his own church and congregation. Between 1739 and 1740, he electrified colonial listeners with his brilliant oratory.

AMERICANA

Two Opposing Views of George Whitefield

Not everyone embraced George Whitefield and other New Lights. Many established Old Lights decried the way the new evangelical religions appealed to people's passions, rather than to traditional religious values. The two illustrations below present two very different visions of George Whitefield (Figure 4.14).

(a)

(b)

FIGURE 4.14 In the 1774 portrait of George Whitefield by engraver Elisha Gallaudet (a), Whitefield appears with a gentle expression on his face. Although his hands are raised in exultation or entreaty, he does not look particularly roused or rousing. In the 1763 British political cartoon to the right, "Dr. Squintum's Exaltation or the Reformation" (b), Whitefield's hands are raised in a similar position, but there the similarities end.

Compare the two images above. On the left is an illustration for Whitefield's memoirs, while on the right is a cartoon satirizing the circus-like atmosphere that his preaching seemed to attract (Dr. Squintum was a nickname for Whitefield, who was cross-eyed). How do these two artists portray the same man? What emotions are the illustration for his memoirs intended to evoke? What details can you find in the cartoon that indicate the artist's distaste for the preacher?

The Great Awakening saw the rise of several Protestant denominations, including Methodists, Presbyterians, and Baptists (who emphasized adult baptism of converted Christians rather than infant baptism). These new churches gained converts and competed with older Protestant groups like Anglicans (members of the Church of England), Congregationalists (the heirs of Puritanism in America), and Quakers. The influence of these older Protestant groups, such as the New England Congregationalists, declined because of the Great Awakening. Nonetheless, the Great Awakening touched the lives of thousands on both sides of the Atlantic and provided a shared experience in the eighteenth-century British Empire.

THE ENLIGHTENMENT

The **Enlightenment**, or the Age of Reason, was an intellectual and cultural movement in the eighteenth century that emphasized reason over superstition and science over blind faith. Using the power of the press, Enlightenment thinkers like John Locke, Isaac Newton, and Voltaire questioned accepted knowledge and spread new ideas about openness, investigation, and religious tolerance throughout Europe and the Americas. Many consider the Enlightenment a major turning point in Western civilization, an age of light replacing an age of darkness.

Several ideas dominated Enlightenment thought, including rationalism, empiricism, progressivism, and cosmopolitanism. Rationalism is the idea that humans are capable of using their faculty of reason to gain knowledge. This was a sharp turn away from the prevailing idea that people needed to rely on scripture or church authorities for knowledge. Empiricism promotes the idea that knowledge comes from experience and observation of the world. Progressivism is the belief that through their powers of reason and observation, humans could make unlimited, linear progress over time; this belief was especially important as a response to the carnage and upheaval of the English Civil Wars in the seventeenth century. Finally, cosmopolitanism reflected Enlightenment thinkers' view of themselves as citizens of the world and actively engaged in it, as opposed to being provincial and close-minded. In all, Enlightenment thinkers endeavored to be ruled by reason, not prejudice.

The **Freemasons** were a fraternal society that advocated Enlightenment principles of inquiry and tolerance. Freemasonry originated in London coffeehouses in the early eighteenth century, and Masonic lodges (local units) soon spread throughout Europe and the British colonies. One prominent Freemason, Benjamin Franklin, stands as the embodiment of the Enlightenment in British America (Figure 4.15). Born in Boston in 1706 to a large Puritan family, Franklin loved to read, although he found little beyond religious publications in his father's house. In 1718 he was apprenticed to his brother to work in a print shop, where he learned how to be a good writer by copying the style he found in the *Spectator*, which his brother printed. At the age of seventeen, the independent-minded Franklin ran away, eventually ending up in Quaker Philadelphia. There he began publishing the *Pennsylvania Gazette* in the late 1720s, and in 1732 he started his annual publication *Poor Richard: An Almanack*, in which he gave readers much practical advice, such as "Early to bed, early to rise, makes a man healthy, wealthy, and wise."

FIGURE 4.15 In this 1748 portrait by Robert Feke, a forty-year-old Franklin wears a stylish British wig, as befitted a proud and loyal member of the British Empire.

Franklin subscribed to **deism**, an Enlightenment-era belief in a God who created, but has no continuing involvement in, the world and the events within it. Deists also advanced the belief that personal morality—an individual's moral compass, leading to good works and actions—is more important than strict church doctrines. Franklin's deism guided his many philanthropic projects. In 1731, he established a reading library that became the Library Company of Philadelphia. In 1743, he founded the American Philosophical Society to encourage the spirit of inquiry. In 1749, he provided the foundation for the University of Pennsylvania, and in 1751, he helped found Pennsylvania Hospital.

His career as a printer made Franklin wealthy and well-respected. When he retired in 1748, he devoted himself to politics and scientific experiments. His most famous work, on electricity, exemplified Enlightenment principles. Franklin observed that lightning strikes tended to hit metal objects and reasoned that he could therefore direct lightning through the placement of metal objects during an electrical storm. He used this knowledge to advocate the use of lightning rods: metal poles connected to wires directing lightning's electrical charge into the ground and saving wooden homes in cities like Philadelphia from catastrophic fires. He published his findings in 1751, in *Experiments and Observations on Electricity*.

Franklin also wrote of his "rags to riches" tale, his *Memoir*, in the 1770s and 1780s. This story laid the foundation for the American Dream of upward social mobility.

CLICK AND EXPLORE

Visit the Worldly Ways section (http://openstax.org/l/bfranklin1) of PBS's Benjamin Franklin site to see an interactive map showing Franklin's overseas travels and his influence around the world. His diplomatic, political, scientific, and business achievements had great effects in many countries.

THE FOUNDING OF GEORGIA

The reach of Enlightenment thought was both broad and deep. In the 1730s, it even prompted the founding of a new colony. Having witnessed the terrible conditions of debtors' prison, as well as the results of releasing penniless debtors onto the streets of London, James Oglethorpe, a member of Parliament and advocate of social reform, petitioned King George II for a charter to start a new colony. George II, understanding the strategic advantage of a British colony standing as a buffer between South Carolina and Spanish Florida, granted the charter to Oglethorpe and twenty like-minded proprietors in 1732. Oglethorpe led the settlement of the colony, which was called Georgia in honor of the king. In 1733, he and 113 immigrants arrived on the ship *Anne*. Over the next decade, Parliament funded the migration of twenty-five hundred settlers, making Georgia the only government-funded colonial project.

Oglethorpe's vision for Georgia followed the ideals of the Age of Reason, seeing it as a place for England's "worthy poor" to start anew. To encourage industry, he gave each male immigrant fifty acres of land, tools, and a year's worth of supplies. In Savannah, the Oglethorpe Plan provided for a utopia: "an agrarian model of sustenance while sustaining egalitarian values holding all men as equal."

Oglethorpe's vision called for alcohol and slavery to be banned. However, colonists who relocated from other colonies, especially South Carolina, disregarded these prohibitions. Despite its proprietors' early vision of a colony guided by Enlightenment ideals and free of slavery, by the 1750s, Georgia was producing quantities of rice grown and harvested by the enslaved.

4.5 Wars for Empire

LEARNING OBJECTIVES

By the end of this section, you will be able to:
- Describe the wars for empire
- Analyze the significance of these conflicts

Wars for empire composed a final link connecting the Atlantic sides of the British Empire. Great Britain fought four separate wars against Catholic France from the late 1600s to the mid-1700s. Another war, the War of Jenkins' Ear, pitted Britain against Spain. These conflicts for control of North America also helped colonists forge important alliances with native peoples, as different tribes aligned themselves with different European powers.

GENERATIONS OF WARFARE

Generations of British colonists grew up during a time when much of North America, especially the Northeast, engaged in war. Colonists knew war firsthand. In the eighteenth century, fighting was seasonal. Armies mobilized in the spring, fought in the summer, and retired to winter quarters in the fall. The British army imposed harsh discipline on its soldiers, who were drawn from the poorer classes, to ensure they did not step out of line during engagements. If they did, their officers would kill them. On the battlefield, armies dressed in bright uniforms to advertise their bravery and lack of fear. They stood in tight formation and exchanged volleys with the enemy. They often feared their officers more than the enemy.

CLICK AND EXPLORE

Read the diary of a provincial soldier who fought in the French and Indian War on the Captain David Perry Web Site (http://openstax.org/l/DPerry) hosted by Rootsweb. David Perry's journal, which includes a description of the 1758 campaign, provides a glimpse of warfare in the eighteenth century.

Most imperial conflicts had both American and European fronts, leaving us with two names for each war. For instance, King William's War (1688–1697) is also known as the War of the League of Augsburg. In America, the bulk of the fighting in this conflict took place between New England and New France. The war proved inconclusive, with no clear victor (Figure 4.16).

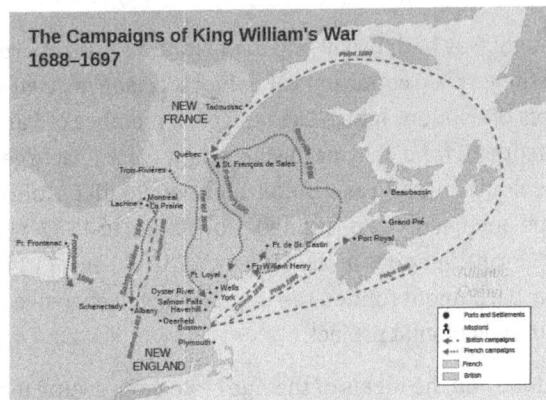

FIGURE 4.16 This map shows the French and British armies' movements during King William's War, in which there was no clear victor.

Queen Anne's War (1702–1713) is also known as the War of Spanish Succession. England fought against both Spain and France over who would ascend the Spanish throne after the last of the Hapsburg rulers died. In North America, fighting took place in Florida, New England, and New France. In Canada, the French prevailed but lost Acadia and Newfoundland; however, the victory was again not decisive because the English failed to take Quebec, which would have given them control of Canada.

This conflict is best remembered in the United States for the French and Native raid against Deerfield, Massachusetts, in 1704. A small French force, combined with a native group made up of Catholic Mohawks and Abenaki (Pocumtucs), attacked the frontier outpost of Deerfield, killing scores and taking 112 prisoners. Among the captives was the seven-year-old daughter of Deerfield's minister John Williams, named Eunice. She was held by the Mohawks for years as her family tried to get her back, and became assimilated into the tribe. To the horror of the Puritan leaders, when she grew up Eunice married a Mohawk and refused to return to New England.

In North America, possession of Georgia and trade with the interior was the focus of the War of Jenkins' Ear (1739–1742), a conflict between Britain and Spain over contested claims to the land occupied by the fledgling colony between South Carolina and Florida. The war got its name from an incident in 1731 in which a Spanish Coast Guard captain severed the ear of British captain Robert Jenkins as punishment for raiding Spanish ships in Panama. Jenkins fueled the growing animosity between England and Spain by presenting his ear to Parliament and stirring up British public outrage. More than anything else, the War of Jenkins' Ear disrupted the Atlantic trade, a situation that hurt both Spain and Britain and was a major reason the war came to a close in 1742. Georgia, founded six years earlier, remained British and a buffer against Spanish Florida.

King George's War (1744–1748), known in Europe as the War of Austrian Succession (1740–1748), was fought in the northern colonies and New France. In 1745, the British took the massive French fortress at Louisbourg on Cape Breton Island, Nova Scotia (Figure 4.17). However, three years later, under the terms of the Treaty of Aix-la-Chapelle, Britain relinquished control of the fortress to the French. Once again, war resulted in an incomplete victory for both Britain and France.

FIGURE 4.17 In this 1747 painting by J. Stevens, *View of the landing of the New England forces in ye expedition against Cape Breton*, British forces land on the island of Cape Breton to capture Fort Louisbourg.

THE FRENCH AND INDIAN WAR

The final imperial war, the **French and Indian War** (1754–1763), known as the Seven Years' War (1756–1763) in Europe, proved to be the decisive contest between Britain and France in America. It began over rival claims along the frontier in present-day western Pennsylvania. Well-connected planters from Virginia faced stagnant tobacco prices and hoped expanding into these western lands would stabilize their wealth and status. Some of them established the Ohio Company of Virginia in 1748, and the British crown granted the company half a million acres in 1749. However, the French also claimed the lands of the Ohio Company, and to protect the region they established Fort Duquesne in 1754, where the Ohio, Monongahela, and Allegheny Rivers met.

The war began in May 1754 because of these competing claims between Britain and France. Twenty-two-year-old Virginian George Washington, a surveyor whose family helped to found the Ohio Company, gave the command to fire on French soldiers near present-day Uniontown, Pennsylvania. This incident on the Pennsylvania frontier proved to be a decisive event that led to imperial war. For the next decade, fighting took place along the frontier of New France and British America from Virginia to Maine. The war also spread to Europe as France and Britain looked to gain supremacy in the Atlantic World.

The British fared poorly in the first years of the war. In 1754, the French and their native allies forced Washington to surrender at Fort Necessity, a hastily built fort constructed after his attack on the French. In 1755, Britain dispatched General Edward Braddock to the colonies to take Fort Duquesne. The French, aided by the Potawotomis, Ottawas, Shawnees, and Delawares, ambushed the fifteen hundred British soldiers and Virginia militia who marched to the fort. The attack sent panic through the British force, and hundreds of British soldiers and militiamen died, including General Braddock. The campaign of 1755 proved to be a disaster for the British. In fact, the only British victory that year was the capture of Nova Scotia. In 1756 and 1757, Britain suffered further defeats with the fall of Fort Oswego and Fort William Henry (Figure 4.18).

FIGURE 4.18 This schematic map depicts the events of the French and Indian War. Note the scarcity of British victories.

The war began to turn in favor of the British in 1758, due in large part to the efforts of William Pitt, a very popular member of Parliament. Pitt pledged huge sums of money and resources to defeating the hated Catholic French, and Great Britain spent part of the money on bounties paid to new young recruits in the colonies, helping invigorate the British forces. In 1758, the Iroquois, Delaware, and Shawnee signed the Treaty of Easton, aligning themselves with the British in return for some contested land around Pennsylvania and Virginia. In 1759, the British took Quebec, and in 1760, Montreal. The French empire in North America had crumbled.

The war continued until 1763, when the French signed the Treaty of Paris. This treaty signaled a dramatic reversal of fortune for France. Indeed, New France, which had been founded in the early 1600s, ceased to exist. The British Empire had now gained mastery over North America. The Empire not only gained New France under the treaty; it also acquired French sugar islands in the West Indies, French trading posts in India, and French-held posts on the west coast of Africa. Great Britain's victory in the French and Indian War meant that it had become a truly global empire. British colonists joyously celebrated, singing the refrain of "Rule, Britannia! / Britannia, rule the waves! / Britons never, never, never shall be slaves!"

In the American colonies, ties with Great Britain were closer than ever. Professional British soldiers had fought alongside Anglo-American militiamen, forging a greater sense of shared identity. With Great Britain's victory, colonial pride ran high as colonists celebrated their identity as British subjects.

This last of the wars for empire, however, also sowed the seeds of trouble. The war led Great Britain deeply into debt, and in the 1760s and 1770s, efforts to deal with the debt through imperial reforms would have the unintended consequence of causing stress and strain that threatened to tear the Empire apart.

Key Terms

deism an Enlightenment-era belief in the existence of a supreme being—specifically, a creator who does not intervene in the universe—representing a rejection of the belief in a supernatural deity who interacts with humankind

Dominion of New England James II's consolidated New England colony, made up of all the colonies from New Haven to Massachusetts and later New York and New Jersey

English interregnum the period from 1649 to 1660 when England had no king

Enlightenment an eighteenth-century intellectual and cultural movement that emphasized reason and science over superstition, religion, and tradition

First Great Awakening an eighteenth-century Protestant revival that emphasized individual, experiential faith over church doctrine and the close study of scripture

Freemasons a fraternal society founded in the early eighteenth century that advocated Enlightenment principles of inquiry and tolerance

French and Indian War the last eighteenth-century imperial struggle between Great Britain and France, leading to a decisive British victory; this war lasted from 1754 to 1763 and was also called the Seven Years' War

Glorious Revolution the overthrow of James II in 1688

Navigation Acts a series of English mercantilist laws enacted between 1651 and 1696 in order to control trade with the colonies

nonconformists Protestants who did not conform to the doctrines or practices of the Church of England

proprietary colonies colonies granted by the king to a trusted individual, family, or group

Restoration colonies the colonies King Charles II established or supported during the Restoration (the Carolinas, New York, New Jersey, and Pennsylvania)

salutary neglect the laxness with which the English crown enforced the Navigation Acts in the eighteenth century

Summary

4.1 Charles II and the Restoration Colonies

After the English Civil War and interregnum, England began to fashion a stronger and larger empire in North America. In addition to wresting control of New York and New Jersey from the Dutch, Charles II established the Carolinas and Pennsylvania as proprietary colonies. Each of these colonies added immensely to the Empire, supplying goods not produced in England, such as rice and indigo. The Restoration colonies also contributed to the rise in population in English America as many thousands of Europeans made their way to the colonies. Their numbers were further augmented by the forced migration of enslaved Africans. Starting in 1651, England pursued mercantilist policies through a series of Navigation Acts designed to make the most of England's overseas possessions. Nonetheless, without proper enforcement of Parliament's acts and with nothing to prevent colonial traders from commanding their own fleets of ships, the Navigation Acts did not control trade as intended.

4.2 The Glorious Revolution and the English Empire

The threat of a Catholic absolute monarchy prompted not only the overthrow of James II but also the adoption of laws and policies that changed English government. The Glorious Revolution restored a Protestant monarchy and at the same time limited its power by means of the 1689 Bill of Rights. Those who lived through the events preserved the memory of the Glorious Revolution and the defense of liberty that it represented. Meanwhile, thinkers such as John Locke provided new models and inspirations for the evolving concept of government.

4.3 An Empire of Slavery and the Consumer Revolution

The seventeenth and eighteenth centuries saw the expansion of slavery in the American colonies from South Carolina to Boston. The institution of slavery created a false sense of superiority in White people, while simultaneously fueling fears of slave revolt. White response to such revolts, or even the threat of them, led to gross overreactions and further constraints on enslaved people's activities. The development of the Atlantic economy also allowed colonists access to more British goods than ever before. The buying habits of both commoners and the rising colonial gentry fueled the consumer revolution, creating even stronger ties with Great Britain by means of a shared community of taste and ideas.

4.4 Great Awakening and Enlightenment

The eighteenth century saw a host of social, religious, and intellectual changes across the British Empire. While the Great Awakening emphasized vigorously emotional religiosity, the Enlightenment promoted the power of reason and scientific observation. Both movements had lasting impacts on the colonies. The beliefs of the New Lights of the First Great Awakening competed with the religions of the first colonists, and the religious fervor in Great Britain and her North American colonies bound the eighteenth-century British Atlantic together in a shared, common experience. The British colonist Benjamin Franklin gained fame on both sides of the Atlantic as a printer, publisher, and scientist. He embodied Enlightenment ideals in the British Atlantic with his scientific experiments and philanthropic endeavors. Enlightenment principles even guided the founding of the colony of Georgia, although those principles could not stand up to the realities of colonial life, and slavery soon took hold in the colony.

4.5 Wars for Empire

From 1688 to 1763, Great Britain engaged in almost continuous power struggles with France and Spain. Most of these conflicts originated in Europe, but their engagements spilled over into the colonies. For almost eighty years, Great Britain and France fought for control of eastern North America. During most of that time, neither force was able to win a decisive victory, though each side saw occasional successes with the crucial help of native peoples. It was not until halfway through the French and Indian War (1754–1763), when Great Britain swelled its troops with more volunteers and native allies, that the balance of power shifted toward the British. With the 1763 Treaty of Paris, New France was eliminated, and Great Britain gained control of all the lands north of Florida and east of the Mississippi. British subjects on both sides of the Atlantic rejoiced.

Review Questions

1. To what does the term "Restoration" refer?
    A. the restoration of New York to English power
    B. the restoration of Catholicism as the official religion of England
    C. the restoration of Charles II to the English throne
    D. the restoration of Parliamentary power in England

2. What was the predominant religion in Pennsylvania?
    A. Quakerism
    B. Puritanism
    C. Catholicism
    D. Protestantism

3. What sorts of labor systems were used in the Restoration colonies?

4. Which of the following represents a concern that those in England and her colonies maintained about James II?
   A. that he would promote the spread of Protestantism
   B. that he would reduce the size of the British army and navy, leaving England and her colonies vulnerable to attack
   C. that he would advocate for Parliament's independence from the monarchy
   D. that he would institute a Catholic absolute monarchy

5. What was the Dominion of New England?
   A. James II's overthrow of the New England colonial governments
   B. the consolidated New England colony James II created
   C. Governor Edmund Andros's colonial government in New York
   D. the excise taxes New England colonists had to pay to James II

6. What was the outcome of the Glorious Revolution?

7. The Negro Act of 1740 was a reaction to _____.
   A. fears of a slave conspiracy in the setting of thirteen fires in New York City
   B. the Stono Rebellion
   C. the Royal African Company's monopoly
   D. the growing power of maroon communities

8. What was the "conspiracy" of the New York Conspiracy Trials of 1741?
   A. American patriots conspiring to overthrow the royal government
   B. indentured servants conspiring to overthrow their contract holders
   C. Enslaved people conspiring to burn down the city and take control
   D. Protestants conspiring to murder Catholics

9. What was the First Great Awakening?
   A. a cultural and intellectual movement that emphasized reason and science over superstition and religion
   B. a Protestant revival that emphasized emotional, experiential faith over book learning
   C. a cultural shift that promoted Christianity among enslaved communities
   D. the birth of an American identity, promoted by Benjamin Franklin

10. Which of the following is not a tenet of the Enlightenment?
    A. atheism
    B. empiricism
    C. progressivism
    D. rationalism

11. Who were the Freemasons, and why were they significant?

12. What was the primary goal of Britain's wars for empire from 1688 to 1763?
    A. control of North America
    B. control of Native Americans
    C. greater power in Europe and the world
    D. defeat of Catholicism

13. Who were the main combatants in the French and Indian War?
    A. France against Native Americans
    B. Great Britain against Native Americans
    C. Great Britain against France
    D. Great Britain against the French and their Native American allies

14. What prompted the French and Indian War?

Critical Thinking Questions

15. How did Pennsylvania's Quaker beginnings distinguish it from other colonies in British America?

16. What were the effects of the consumer revolution on the colonies?

17. How did the ideas of the Enlightenment and the Great Awakening offer opposing outlooks to British Americans? What similarities were there between the two schools of thought?

18. What was the impact of the wars for empire in North America, Europe, and the world?

19. What role did Native Americans play in the wars for empire?

20. What shared experiences, intellectual currents, and cultural elements drew together British subjects on both sides of the Atlantic during this period? How did these experiences, ideas, and goods serve to strengthen those bonds?

Imperial Reforms and Colonial Protests, 1763-1774

5

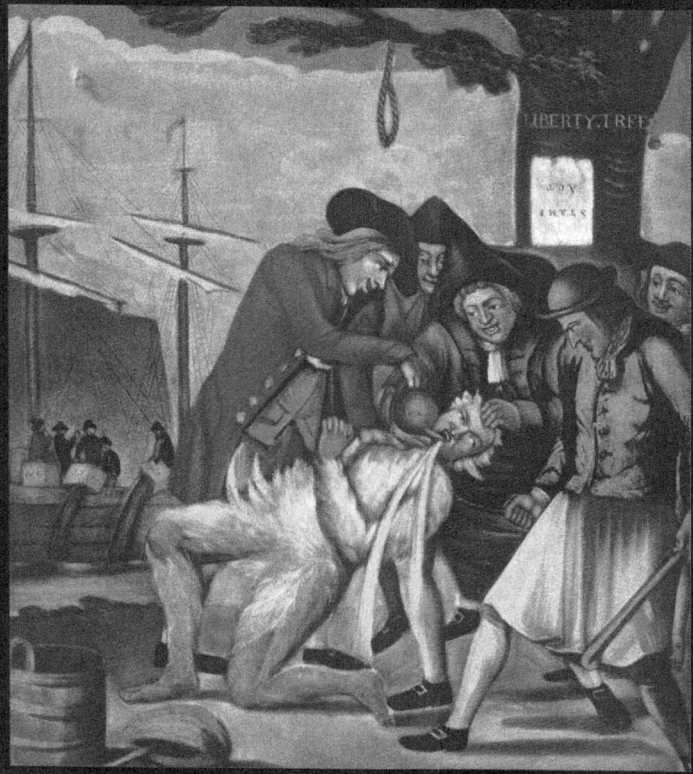

FIGURE 5.1 *The Bostonians Paying the Excise-man, or Tarring and Feathering* (1774), attributed to Philip Dawe (modified), depicts the most publicized tarring and feathering incident of the American Revolution. The victim is John Malcolm, a customs official loyal to the British crown.

CHAPTER OUTLINE

- **5.1** Confronting the National Debt: The Aftermath of the French and Indian War
- **5.2** The Stamp Act and the Sons and Daughters of Liberty
- **5.3** The Townshend Acts and Colonial Protest
- **5.4** The Destruction of the Tea and the Coercive Acts
- **5.5** Disaffection: The First Continental Congress and American Identity

INTRODUCTION *The Bostonians Paying the Excise-man, or Tarring and Feathering* (Figure 5.1), shows five Patriots tarring and feathering the Commissioner of Customs, John Malcolm, a sea captain, army officer, and staunch **Loyalist**. The print shows the Boston Tea Party, a protest against the Tea Act of 1773, and the Liberty Tree, an elm tree near Boston Common that became a rallying point against the Stamp Act of 1765. When the crowd threatened to hang Malcolm if he did not renounce his position as a royal customs officer, he reluctantly agreed and the protestors allowed him to go home. The scene represents the animosity toward those who supported royal authority and illustrates the high tide of unrest in the colonies after the British government imposed a series of imperial reform measures during the years 1763–1774.

The government's formerly lax oversight of the colonies ended as the architects of the British Empire put these new reforms in place. The British hoped to gain greater control over colonial trade and frontier settlement as well as to reduce the administrative cost of the colonies and the enormous debt left by the French and Indian War. Each step the British took, however, generated a backlash. Over time, imperial reforms pushed many colonists toward separation from the British Empire.

5.1 Confronting the National Debt: The Aftermath of the French and Indian War

LEARNING OBJECTIVES

By the end of this section, you will be able to:
- Discuss the status of Great Britain's North American colonies in the years directly following the French and Indian War
- Describe the size and scope of the British debt at the end of the French and Indian War
- Explain how the British Parliament responded to the debt crisis
- Outline the purpose of the Proclamation Line, the Sugar Act, and the Currency Act

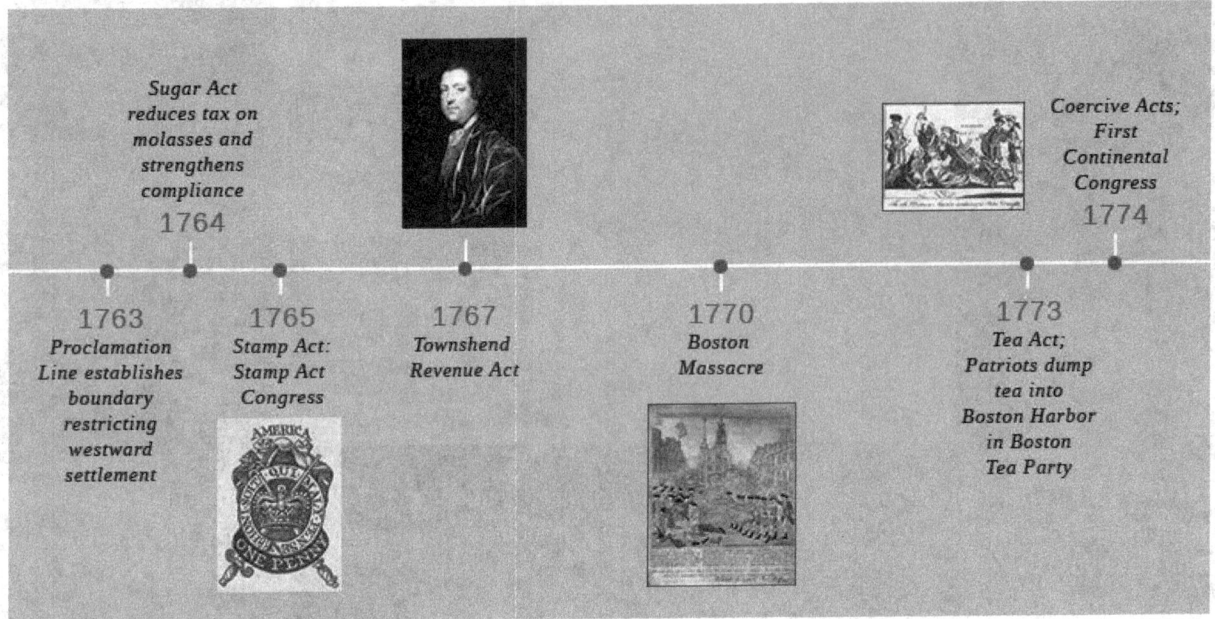

FIGURE 5.2 (credit "1765": modification of work by the United Kingdom Government)

Great Britain had much to celebrate in 1763. The long and costly war with France had finally ended, and Great Britain had emerged victorious. British subjects on both sides of the Atlantic celebrated the strength of the British Empire. Colonial pride ran high; to live under the British Constitution and to have defeated the hated French Catholic menace brought great joy to British Protestants everywhere in the Empire. From Maine to Georgia, British colonists joyously celebrated the victory and sang the refrain of "Rule, Britannia! Britannia, rule the waves! Britons never, never, never shall be slaves!"

Despite the celebratory mood, the victory over France also produced major problems within the British Empire, problems that would have serious consequences for British colonists in the Americas. During the war, many Native American tribes had sided with the French, who supplied them with guns. After the 1763 Treaty of Paris that ended the French and Indian War (or the Seven Years' War), British colonists had to defend the frontier, where French colonists and their tribal allies remained a powerful force. The most organized resistance, Pontiac's Rebellion, highlighted tensions the settlers increasingly interpreted in racial terms.

The massive debt the war generated at home, however, proved to be the most serious issue facing Great Britain. The frontier had to be secure in order to prevent another costly war. Greater enforcement of imperial trade laws had to be put into place. Parliament had to find ways to raise revenue to pay off the crippling debt from the war. Everyone would have to contribute their expected share, including the British subjects across the Atlantic.

PROBLEMS ON THE AMERICAN FRONTIER

With the end of the French and Indian War, Great Britain claimed a vast new expanse of territory, at least on paper. Under the terms of the Treaty of Paris, the French territory known as New France had ceased to exist. British territorial holdings now extended from Canada to Florida, and British military focus shifted to maintaining peace in the king's newly enlarged lands. However, much of the land in the American British Empire remained under the control of powerful native confederacies, which made any claims of British mastery beyond the Atlantic coastal settlements hollow. Great Britain maintained ten thousand troops in North America after the war ended in 1763 to defend the borders and repel any attack by their imperial rivals.

British colonists, eager for fresh land, poured over the Appalachian Mountains to stake claims. The western frontier had long been a "middle ground" where different imperial powers (British, French, Spanish) had interacted and compromised with native peoples. That era of accommodation in the "middle ground" came to an end after the French and Indian War. Virginians (including George Washington) and other land-hungry colonists had already raised tensions in the 1740s with their quest for land. Virginia landowners in particular eagerly looked to diversify their holdings beyond tobacco, which had stagnated in price and exhausted the fertility of the lands along the Chesapeake Bay. They invested heavily in the newly available land. This westward movement brought the settlers into conflict as never before with Native American tribes, such as the Shawnee, Seneca-Cayuga, Wyandot, and Delaware, who increasingly held their ground against any further intrusion by White settlers.

The treaty that ended the war between France and Great Britain proved to be a significant blow to native peoples, who had viewed the conflict as an opportunity to gain additional trade goods from both sides. With the French defeat, many Native Americans who had sided with France lost a valued trading partner as well as bargaining power over the British. Settlers' encroachment on their land, as well as the increased British military presence, changed the situation on the frontier dramatically. After the war, British troops took over the former French forts but failed to court favor with the local tribes by distributing ample gifts, as the French had done. They also significantly reduced the amount of gunpowder and ammunition they sold to the Native Americans, worsening relationships further.

Native Americans' resistance to colonists drew upon the teachings of Delaware (Lenni Lenape) prophet Neolin and the leadership of Ottawa war chief Pontiac. Neolin was a spiritual leader who preached a doctrine of shunning European culture and expelling Europeans from native lands. Neolin's beliefs united Native Americans from many villages. In a broad-based alliance that came to be known as Pontiac's Rebellion, Pontiac led a loose coalition of these native tribes against the colonists and the British army.

Pontiac started bringing his coalition together as early as 1761, urging Native Americans to "drive [the Europeans] out and make war upon them." The conflict began in earnest in 1763, when Pontiac and several hundred Ojibwas, Potawatomis, and Hurons laid siege to Fort Detroit. At the same time, Senecas, Shawnees, and Delawares laid siege to Fort Pitt. Over the next year, the war spread along the backcountry from Virginia to Pennsylvania. Pontiac's Rebellion (also known as Pontiac's War) triggered horrific violence on both sides. Firsthand reports of Native American attacks tell of murder, scalping, dismemberment, and burning at the stake. These stories incited a deep racial hatred among colonists against all Native Americans.

The actions of a group of Scots-Irish settlers from Paxton (or Paxtang), Pennsylvania, in December 1763, illustrates the deadly situation on the frontier. Forming a mob known as the Paxton Boys, these frontiersmen attacked a nearby group of Conestoga of the Susquehannock tribe. The Conestoga had lived peacefully with local settlers, but the Paxton Boys viewed all Native Americans as savages and they brutally murdered the six Conestoga they found at home and burned their houses. When Governor John Penn put the remaining fourteen Conestoga in protective custody in Lancaster, Pennsylvania, the Paxton Boys broke into the building and killed and scalped the Conestoga they found there (Figure 5.3). Although Governor Penn offered a reward for the capture of any Paxton Boys involved in the murders, no one ever identified the attackers. Some colonists reacted to the incident with outrage. Benjamin Franklin described the Paxton Boys as "the barbarous Men who committed the atrocious act, in Defiance of Government, of all Laws human and divine, and to the eternal Disgrace of their Country and Colour," stating that "the Wickedness cannot be covered, the Guilt will lie on the whole Land, till Justice is done on the Murderers. The blood of the innocent will cry to heaven for vengeance." Yet, as the inability to bring the perpetrators to justice clearly indicates, the Paxton Boys had many more supporters than critics.

FIGURE 5.3 This nineteenth-century lithograph depicts the massacre of Conestoga in 1763 at Lancaster, Pennsylvania, where they had been placed in protective custody. None of the attackers, members of the Paxton Boys, were ever identified.

CLICK AND EXPLORE

Visit Explore PAhistory.com (http://openstax.org/l/paxton) to read the full text of Benjamin Franklin's "Benjamin Franklin, An Account of the Paxton Boys' Murder of the Conestoga Indians, 1764."

Pontiac's Rebellion and the Paxton Boys' actions were examples of early American race wars, in which both sides saw themselves as inherently different from the other and believed the other needed to be eradicated. The prophet Neolin's message, which he said he received in a vision from the Master of Life, was: "Wherefore do you suffer the whites to dwell upon your lands? Drive them away; wage war against them." Pontiac echoed this idea in a meeting, exhorting tribes to join together against the British: "It is important for us, my brothers, that we exterminate from our lands this nation which seeks only to destroy us." In his letter suggesting "gifts" to the natives of smallpox-infected blankets, Field Marshal Jeffrey Amherst said, "You will do well to inoculate the Indians by means of blankets, as well as every other method that can serve to extirpate this execrable race." Pontiac's Rebellion came to an end in 1766, when it became clear that the French, whom Pontiac had hoped would side with his forces, would not be returning. The repercussions, however, would last much longer. Race relations between Native Americans and White people remained poisoned on the frontier.

Well aware of the problems on the frontier, the British government took steps to try to prevent bloodshed and another costly war. At the beginning of Pontiac's uprising, the British issued the Proclamation of 1763, which forbade White settlement west of the **Proclamation Line**, a borderline running along the spine of the Appalachian Mountains (Figure 5.4). The Proclamation Line aimed to forestall further conflict on the frontier, the clear flashpoint of tension in British North America. British colonists who had hoped to move west after the war chafed at this restriction, believing the war had been fought and won to ensure the right to settle west. The Proclamation Line therefore came as a setback to their vision of westward expansion.

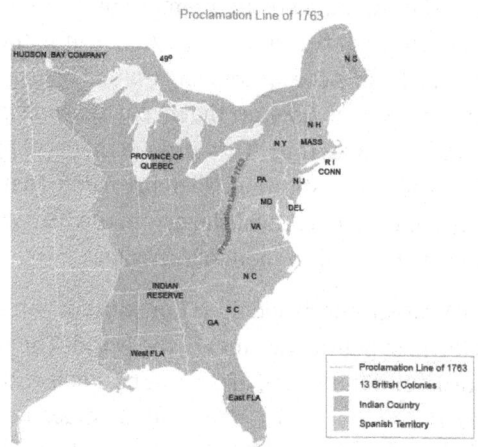

FIGURE 5.4 This map shows the status of the American colonies in 1763, after the end of the French and Indian War. Although Great Britain won control of the territory east of the Mississippi, the Proclamation Line of 1763 prohibited British colonists from settling west of the Appalachian Mountains. (credit: modification of work by the National Atlas of the United States)

THE BRITISH NATIONAL DEBT

Great Britain's newly enlarged empire meant a greater financial burden, and the mushrooming debt from the war was a major cause of concern. The war nearly doubled the British national debt, from £75 million in 1756 to £133 million in 1763. Interest payments alone consumed over half the national budget, and the continuing military presence in North America was a constant drain. The Empire needed more revenue to replenish its dwindling coffers. Those in Great Britain believed that British subjects in North America, as the major beneficiaries of Great Britain's war for global supremacy, should certainly shoulder their share of the financial burden.

The British government began increasing revenues by raising taxes at home, even as various interest groups lobbied to keep their taxes low. Powerful members of the aristocracy, well represented in Parliament, successfully convinced Prime Minister John Stuart, third earl of Bute, to refrain from raising taxes on land. The greater tax burden, therefore, fell on the lower classes in the form of increased import duties, which raised the prices of imported goods such as sugar and tobacco. George Grenville succeeded Bute as prime minister in 1763. Grenville determined to curtail government spending and make sure that, as subjects of the British Empire, the American colonists did their part to pay down the massive debt.

IMPERIAL REFORMS

The new era of greater British interest in the American colonies through imperial reforms picked up in pace in the mid-1760s. In 1764, Prime Minister Grenville introduced the Currency Act of 1764, prohibiting the colonies from printing additional paper money and requiring colonists to pay British merchants in gold and silver instead of the colonial paper money already in circulation. The Currency Act aimed to standardize the currency used in Atlantic trade, a logical reform designed to help stabilize the Empire's economy. This rule brought American economic activity under greater British control. Colonists relied on their own paper currency to conduct trade and, with gold and silver in short supply, they found their finances tight. Not surprisingly, they grumbled about the new imperial currency regulations.

Grenville also pushed Parliament to pass the Sugar Act of 1764, which actually lowered duties on British molasses by half, from six pence per gallon to three. Grenville designed this measure to address the problem of rampant colonial smuggling with the French sugar islands in the West Indies. The act attempted to make it easier for colonial traders, especially New England mariners who routinely engaged in illegal trade, to comply with the imperial law.

To give teeth to the 1764 Sugar Act, the law intensified enforcement provisions. Prior to the 1764 act, colonial violations of the Navigation Acts had been tried in local courts, where sympathetic colonial juries refused to convict merchants on trial. However, the Sugar Act required violators to be tried in **vice-admiralty courts**. These crown-sanctioned tribunals, which settled disputes that occurred at sea, operated without juries. Some colonists saw this feature of the 1764 act as dangerous. They argued that trial by jury had long been honored as a basic right of Englishmen under the British Constitution. To deprive defendants of a jury, they contended, meant reducing liberty-loving British subjects to political slavery. In the British Atlantic world, some colonists perceived this loss of liberty as parallel to the enslavement of Africans.

As loyal British subjects, colonists in America cherished their Constitution, an unwritten system of government that they celebrated as the best political system in the world. The British Constitution prescribed the roles of the King, the House of Lords, and the House of Commons. Each entity provided a check and balance against the worst tendencies of the others. If the King had too much power, the result would be tyranny. If the Lords had too much power, the result would be oligarchy. If the Commons had the balance of power, democracy or mob rule would prevail. The British Constitution promised representation of the will of British subjects, and without such representation, even the **indirect tax** of the Sugar Act was considered a threat to the settlers' rights as British subjects. Furthermore, some American colonists felt the colonies were on equal political footing with Great Britain. The Sugar Act meant they were secondary, mere adjuncts to the Empire. All subjects of the British crown knew they had liberties under the constitution. The Sugar Act suggested that some in Parliament labored to deprive them of what made them uniquely British.

5.2 The Stamp Act and the Sons and Daughters of Liberty

LEARNING OBJECTIVES

By the end of this section, you will be able to:
- Explain the purpose of the 1765 Stamp Act
- Describe the colonial responses to the Stamp Act

In 1765, the British Parliament moved beyond the efforts during the previous two years to better regulate westward expansion and trade by putting in place the Stamp Act. As a **direct tax** on the colonists, the Stamp Act imposed an internal tax on almost every type of printed paper colonists used, including newspapers, legal documents, and playing cards. While the architects of the Stamp Act saw the measure as a way to defray the costs of the British Empire, it nonetheless gave rise to the first major colonial protest against British imperial control as expressed in the famous slogan "no taxation without representation." The Stamp Act reinforced the sense among some colonists that Parliament was not treating them as equals of their peers across the Atlantic.

THE STAMP ACT AND THE QUARTERING ACT

Prime Minister Grenville, author of the Sugar Act of 1764, introduced the Stamp Act in the early spring of 1765. Under this act, anyone who used or purchased anything printed on paper had to buy a revenue stamp (Figure 5.5) for it. In the same year, 1765, Parliament also passed the Quartering Act, a law that attempted to solve the problems of stationing troops in North America. The Parliament understood the Stamp Act and the Quartering Act as an assertion of their power to control colonial policy.

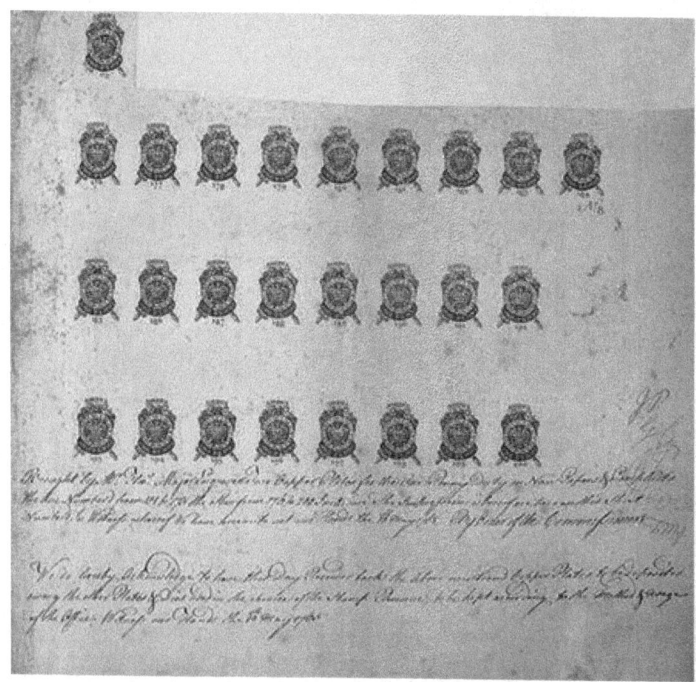 

(a) (b)

FIGURE 5.5 Under the Stamp Act, anyone who used or purchased anything printed on paper had to buy a revenue stamp for it. Image (a) shows a partial proof sheet of one-penny stamps. Image (b) provides a close-up of a one-penny stamp. (credit a: modification of work by the United Kingdom Government; credit b: modification of work by the United Kingdom Government)

The Stamp Act signaled a shift in British policy after the French and Indian War. Before the Stamp Act, the colonists had paid taxes to their colonial governments or indirectly through higher prices, not directly to the Crown's appointed governors. This was a time-honored liberty of representative legislatures of the colonial governments. The passage of the Stamp Act meant that starting on November 1, 1765, the colonists would contribute £60,000 per year—17 percent of the total cost—to the upkeep of the ten thousand British soldiers in North America (Figure 5.6). Because the Stamp Act raised constitutional issues, it triggered the first serious protest against British imperial policy.

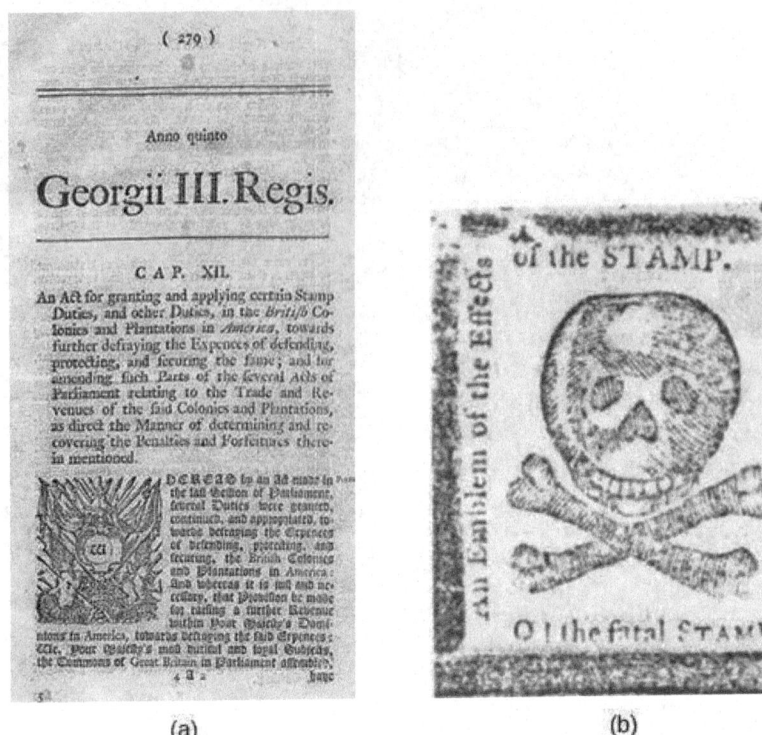

FIGURE 5.6 The announcement of the Stamp Act, seen in this newspaper publication (a), raised numerous concerns among colonists in America. Protests against British imperial policy took many forms, such as this mock stamp (b) whose text reads "An Emblem of the Effects of the STAMP. O! the Fatal STAMP."

Parliament also asserted its prerogative in 1765 with the Quartering Act. The Quartering Act of 1765 addressed the problem of housing British soldiers stationed in the American colonies. It required that they be provided with barracks or places to stay in public houses, and that if extra housing were necessary, then troops could be stationed in barns and other uninhabited private buildings. In addition, the costs of the troops' food and lodging fell to the colonists. Since the time of James II, who ruled from 1685 to 1688, many British subjects had mistrusted the presence of a standing army during peacetime, and having to pay for the soldiers' lodging and food was especially burdensome. Widespread evasion and disregard for the law occurred in almost all the colonies, but the issue was especially contentious in New York, the headquarters of British forces. When fifteen hundred troops arrived in New York in 1766, the New York Assembly refused to follow the Quartering Act.

COLONIAL PROTEST: GENTRY, MERCHANTS, AND THE STAMP ACT CONGRESS

For many British colonists living in America, the Stamp Act raised many concerns. As a direct tax, it appeared to be an unconstitutional measure, one that deprived freeborn British subjects of their liberty, a concept they defined broadly to include various rights and privileges they enjoyed as British subjects, including the right to representation. According to the unwritten British Constitution, only representatives for whom British subjects voted could tax them. Parliament was in charge of taxation, and although it was a representative body, the colonies did not have "actual" (or direct) representation in it. Parliamentary members who supported the Stamp Act argued that the colonists had virtual representation, because the architects of the British Empire knew best how to maximize returns from its possessions overseas. However, this argument did not satisfy the protesters, who viewed themselves as having the same right as all British subjects to avoid taxation without their consent. With no representation in the House of Commons, where bills of taxation originated, they felt themselves deprived of this inherent right.

The British government knew the colonists might object to the Stamp Act's expansion of parliamentary power, but Parliament believed the relationship of the colonies to the Empire was one of dependence, not equality. However, the Stamp Act had the unintended and ironic consequence of drawing colonists from very different areas and viewpoints together in protest. In Massachusetts, for instance, James Otis, a lawyer and defender of British liberty, became the leading voice for the idea that "Taxation without representation is tyranny." In the Virginia House of Burgesses, firebrand and slaveholder Patrick Henry introduced the Virginia Stamp Act Resolutions, which denounced the Stamp Act and the British crown in language so strong that some conservative Virginians accused him of treason (Figure 5.7). Henry replied that Virginians were subject only to taxes that they themselves—or their representatives—imposed. In short, there could be **no taxation without representation**.

FIGURE 5.7 *Patrick Henry Before the Virginia House of Burgesses* (1851), painted by Peter F. Rothermel, offers a romanticized depiction of Henry's speech denouncing the Stamp Act of 1765. Supporters and opponents alike debated the stark language of the speech, which quickly became legendary.

The colonists had never before formed a unified political front, so Grenville and Parliament did not fear true revolt. However, this was to change in 1765. In response to the Stamp Act, the Massachusetts Assembly sent letters to the other colonies, asking them to attend a meeting, or congress, to discuss how to respond to the act. Many American colonists from very different colonies found common cause in their opposition to the Stamp Act. Representatives from nine colonial legislatures met in New York in the fall of 1765 to reach a consensus. Could Parliament impose taxation without representation? The members of this first congress, known as the Stamp Act Congress, said no. These nine representatives had a vested interest in repealing the tax. Not only did it weaken their businesses and the colonial economy, but it also threatened their liberty under the British Constitution. They drafted a rebuttal to the Stamp Act, making clear that they desired only to protect their liberty as loyal subjects of the Crown. The document, called the Declaration of Rights and Grievances, outlined the unconstitutionality of taxation without representation and trials without juries. Meanwhile, popular protest was also gaining force.

CLICK AND EXPLORE

Browse the collection of the Massachusetts Historical Society (http://openstax.org/l/masshist1) to examine digitized primary sources of the documents that paved the way to the fight for liberty.

MOBILIZATION: POPULAR PROTEST AGAINST THE STAMP ACT

The Stamp Act Congress was a gathering of landowning, educated White men who represented the political elite of the colonies and was the colonial equivalent of the British landed aristocracy. While these gentry were drafting their grievances during the Stamp Act Congress, other colonists showed their distaste for the new act by boycotting British goods and protesting in the streets. Two groups, the **Sons of Liberty** and the **Daughters of Liberty**, led the popular resistance to the Stamp Act. Both groups considered themselves British patriots defending their liberty, just as their forebears had done in the time of James II.

Forming in Boston in the summer of 1765, the Sons of Liberty were artisans, shopkeepers, and small-time merchants willing to adopt extralegal means of protest. Before the act had even gone into effect, the Sons of Liberty began protesting. On August 14, they took aim at Andrew Oliver, who had been named the Massachusetts Distributor of Stamps. After hanging Oliver in effigy—that is, using a crudely made figure as a representation of Oliver—the unruly crowd stoned and ransacked his house, finally beheading the effigy and burning the remains. Such a brutal response shocked the royal governmental officials, who hid until the violence had spent itself. Andrew Oliver resigned the next day. By that time, the mob had moved on to the home of Lieutenant Governor Thomas Hutchinson who, because of his support of Parliament's actions, was considered an enemy of English liberty. The Sons of Liberty barricaded Hutchinson in his home and demanded that he renounce the Stamp Act; he refused, and the protesters looted and burned his house. Furthermore, the Sons (also called "True Sons" or "True-born Sons" to make clear their commitment to liberty and distinguish them from the likes of Hutchinson) continued to lead violent protests with the goal of securing the resignation of all appointed stamp collectors (Figure 5.8).

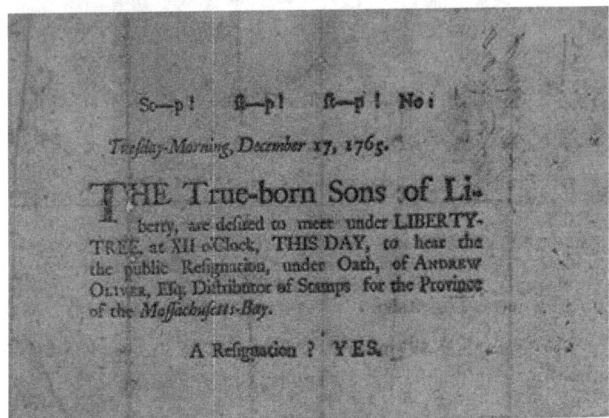

FIGURE 5.8 With this broadside of December 17, 1765, the Sons of Liberty call for the resignation of Andrew Oliver, the Massachusetts Distributor of Stamps.

Starting in early 1766, the Daughters of Liberty protested the Stamp Act by refusing to buy British goods and encouraging others to do the same. They avoided British tea, opting to make their own teas with local herbs and berries. They built a community—and a movement—around creating homespun cloth instead of buying British linen. Well-born women held "spinning bees," at which they competed to see who could spin the most and the finest linen. An entry in *The Boston Chronicle* of April 7, 1766, states that on March 12, in Providence, Rhode Island, "18 Daughters of Liberty, young ladies of good reputation, assembled at the house of Doctor Ephraim Bowen, in this town. . . . There they exhibited a fine example of industry, by spinning from sunrise until dark, and displayed a spirit for saving their sinking country rarely to be found among persons of more age and experience." At dinner, they "cheerfully agreed to omit tea, to render their conduct consistent. Besides this instance of their patriotism, before they separated, they unanimously resolved that the Stamp Act was unconstitutional, that they would purchase no more British manufactures unless it be repealed, and that they would not even admit the addresses of any gentlemen should they have the opportunity, without they determined to oppose its execution to the last extremity, if the occasion required."

The Daughters' **non-importation movement** broadened the protest against the Stamp Act, giving women a new and active role in the political dissent of the time. Women were responsible for purchasing goods for the home, so by exercising the power of the purse, they could wield more power than they had in the past. Although they could not vote, they could mobilize others and make a difference in the political landscape.

From a local movement, the protests of the Sons and Daughters of Liberty soon spread until there was a chapter in every colony. The Daughters of Liberty promoted the boycott on British goods while the Sons enforced it, threatening retaliation against anyone who bought imported goods or used stamped paper. In the protest against the Stamp Act, wealthy, lettered political figures like John Adams supported the goals of the Sons and Daughters of Liberty, even if they did not engage in the Sons' violent actions. These men, who were lawyers, printers, and merchants, ran a propaganda campaign parallel to the Sons' campaign of violence. In newspapers and pamphlets throughout the colonies, they published article after article outlining the reasons the Stamp Act was unconstitutional and urging peaceful protest. They officially condemned violent actions but did not have the protesters arrested; a degree of cooperation prevailed, despite the groups' different economic backgrounds. Certainly, all the protesters saw themselves as acting in the best British tradition, standing up against the corruption (especially the extinguishing of their right to representation) that threatened their liberty (Figure 5.9).

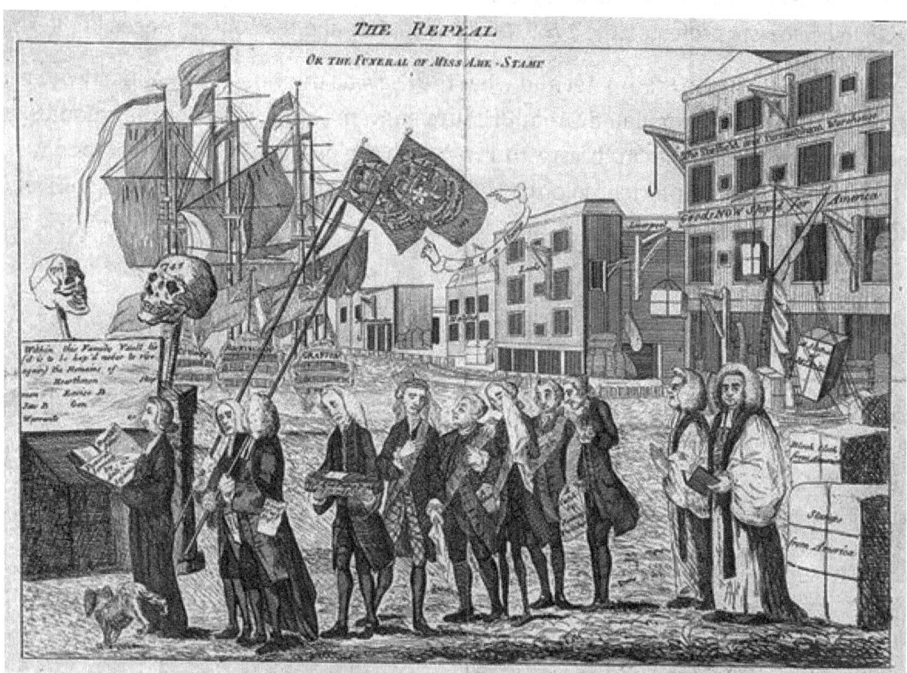

FIGURE 5.9 This 1766 illustration shows a funeral procession for the Stamp Act. Reverend William Scott leads the procession of politicians who had supported the act, while a dog urinates on his leg. George Grenville, pictured fourth in line, carries a small coffin. What point do you think this cartoon is trying to make?

THE DECLARATORY ACT

Back in Great Britain, news of the colonists' reactions worsened an already volatile political situation. Grenville's imperial reforms had brought about increased domestic taxes and his unpopularity led to his dismissal by King George III. While many in Parliament still wanted such reforms, British merchants argued strongly for their repeal. These merchants had no interest in the philosophy behind the colonists' desire for liberty; rather, their motive was that the non-importation of British goods by North American colonists was hurting their business. Many of the British at home were also appalled by the colonists' violent reaction to the Stamp Act. Other Britons cheered what they saw as the manly defense of liberty by their counterparts in the colonies.

In March 1766, the new prime minister, Lord Rockingham, compelled Parliament to repeal the Stamp Act. Colonists celebrated what they saw as a victory for their British liberty; in Boston, merchant John Hancock treated the entire town to drinks. However, to appease opponents of the repeal, who feared that it would weaken parliamentary power over the American colonists, Rockingham also proposed the Declaratory Act. This stated in no uncertain terms that Parliament's power was supreme and that any laws the colonies may have passed to govern and tax themselves were null and void if they ran counter to parliamentary law.

CLICK AND EXPLORE

Visit [Constitution.org (http://www.constitution.org/bcp/decl_act.htm)](http://www.constitution.org/bcp/decl_act.htm) to read the full text of the Declaratory Act, in which Parliament asserted the supremacy of parliamentary power.

5.3 The Townshend Acts and Colonial Protest

LEARNING OBJECTIVES

By the end of this section, you will be able to:
- Describe the purpose of the 1767 Townshend Acts
- Explain why many colonists protested the 1767 Townshend Acts and the consequences of their actions

Colonists' joy over the repeal of the Stamp Act and what they saw as their defense of liberty did not last long. The Declaratory Act of 1766 had articulated Great Britain's supreme authority over the colonies, and Parliament soon began exercising that authority. In 1767, with the passage of the Townshend Acts, a tax on consumer goods in British North America, colonists believed their liberty as loyal British subjects had come under assault for a second time.

THE TOWNSHEND ACTS

Lord Rockingham's tenure as prime minister was not long (1765–1766). Rich landowners feared that if he were not taxing the colonies, Parliament would raise their taxes instead, sacrificing them to the interests of merchants and colonists. George III duly dismissed Rockingham. William Pitt, also sympathetic to the colonists, succeeded him. However, Pitt was old and ill with gout. His chancellor of the exchequer, Charles Townshend (Figure 5.10), whose job was to manage the Empire's finances, took on many of his duties. Primary among these was raising the needed revenue from the colonies.

FIGURE 5.10 Charles Townshend, chancellor of the exchequer, shown here in a 1765 painting by Joshua Reynolds, instituted the Townshend Revenue Act of 1767 in order to raise money to support the British military presence in the colonies.

Townshend's first act was to deal with the unruly New York Assembly, which had voted not to pay for supplies for the garrison of British soldiers that the Quartering Act required. In response, Townshend proposed the Restraining Act of 1767, which disbanded the New York Assembly until it agreed to pay for the garrison's supplies, which it eventually agreed to do.

The Townshend Revenue Act of 1767 placed duties on various consumer items like paper, paint, lead, tea, and glass. These British goods had to be imported, since the colonies did not have the manufacturing base to produce them. Townshend hoped the new duties would not anger the colonists because they were external taxes, not internal ones like the Stamp Act. In 1766, in arguing before Parliament for the repeal of the Stamp Act, Benjamin Franklin had stated, "I never heard any objection to the right of laying duties to regulate commerce; but a right to lay internal taxes was never supposed to be in parliament, as we are not represented there."

The Indemnity Act of 1767 exempted tea produced by the British East India Company from taxation when it was imported into Great Britain. When the tea was re-exported to the colonies, however, the colonists had to pay taxes on it because of the Revenue Act. Some critics of Parliament on both sides of the Atlantic saw this tax policy as an example of corrupt politicians giving preferable treatment to specific corporate interests, creating a monopoly. The sense that corruption had become entrenched in Parliament only increased colonists' alarm.

In fact, the revenue collected from these duties was only nominally intended to support the British army in America. It actually paid the salaries of some royally appointed judges, governors, and other officials whom the colonial assemblies had traditionally paid. Thanks to the Townshend Revenue Act of 1767, however, these officials no longer relied on colonial leadership for payment. This change gave them a measure of independence from the assemblies, so they could implement parliamentary acts without fear that their pay would be withheld in retaliation. The Revenue Act thus appeared to sever the relationship between governors and assemblies, drawing royal officials closer to the British government and further away from the colonial legislatures.

The Revenue Act also gave the customs board greater powers to counteract smuggling. It granted "writs of assistance"—basically, search warrants—to customs commissioners who suspected the presence of contraband goods, which also opened the door to a new level of bribery and trickery on the waterfronts of colonial America. Furthermore, to ensure compliance, Townshend introduced the Commissioners of Customs Act of 1767, which created an American Board of Customs to enforce trade laws. Customs enforcement had been based in Great Britain, but rules were difficult to implement at such a distance, and smuggling was rampant. The new customs board was based in Boston and would severely curtail smuggling in this large colonial seaport.

Townshend also orchestrated the Vice-Admiralty Court Act, which established three more vice-admiralty courts, in Boston, Philadelphia, and Charleston, to try violators of customs regulations without a jury. Before this, the only colonial vice-admiralty court had been in far-off Halifax, Nova Scotia, but with three local courts, smugglers could be tried more efficiently. Since the judges of these courts were paid a percentage of the worth of the goods they recovered, leniency was rare. All told, the Townshend Acts resulted in higher taxes and stronger British power to enforce them. Four years after the end of the French and Indian War, the Empire continued to search for solutions to its debt problem and the growing sense that the colonies needed to be brought under control.

REACTIONS: THE NON-IMPORTATION MOVEMENT

Like the Stamp Act, the Townshend Acts produced controversy and protest in the American colonies. For a second time, many colonists resented what they perceived as an effort to tax them without representation and thus to deprive them of their liberty. The fact that the revenue the Townshend Acts raised would pay royal governors only made the situation worse, because it took control away from colonial legislatures that otherwise had the power to set and withhold a royal governor's salary. The Restraining Act, which had been intended to isolate New York without angering the other colonies, had the opposite effect, showing the rest of the colonies how far beyond the British Constitution some members of Parliament were willing to go.

The Townshend Acts generated a number of protest writings, including "Letters from a Pennsylvania Farmer" by John Dickinson. In this influential pamphlet, which circulated widely in the colonies, Dickinson conceded that the Empire could regulate trade but argued that Parliament could not impose either internal taxes, like stamps, on goods or external taxes, like customs duties, on imports.

AMERICANA

"Address to the Ladies" Verse from *The Boston Post-Boy and Advertiser*

This verse, which ran in a Boston newspaper in November 1767, highlights how women were encouraged to take political action by boycotting British goods. Notice that the writer especially encourages women to avoid British tea (Bohea and Green Hyson) and linen, and to manufacture their own homespun cloth. Building on the protest of the 1765 Stamp Act by the Daughters of Liberty, the non-importation movement of 1767–1768 mobilized women as political actors.

"Young ladies in town, and those that live round,
Let a friend at this season advise you:
Since money's so scarce, and times growing worse
Strange things may soon hap and surprize you:
First then, throw aside your high top knots of pride
Wear none but your own country linnen;
of economy boast, let your pride be the most
What, if homespun they say is not quite so gay
As brocades, yet be not in a passion,
For when once it is known this is much wore in town,
One and all will cry out, 'tis the fashion!
And as one, all agree that you'll not married be
To such as will wear London Fact'ry:
But at first sight refuse, tell'em such you do chuse
As encourage our own Manufact'ry.
No more Ribbons wear, nor in rich dress appear,
Love your country much better than fine things,
Begin without passion, 'twill soon be the fashion
To grace your smooth locks with a twine string.
Throw aside your Bohea, and your Green Hyson Tea,
And all things with a new fashion duty;
Procure a good store of the choice Labradore,
For there'll soon be enough here to suit ye;
These do without fear and to all you'll appear
Fair, charming, true, lovely, and cleaver;
Tho' the times remain darkish, young men may be sparkish.
And love you much stronger than ever. !O!"

In Massachusetts in 1768, Samuel Adams wrote a letter that became known as the **Massachusetts Circular**. Sent by the Massachusetts House of Representatives to the other colonial legislatures, the letter laid out the unconstitutionality of taxation without representation and encouraged the other colonies to again protest the taxes by boycotting British goods. Adams wrote, "It is, moreover, [the Massachusetts House of Representatives] humble opinion, which they express with the greatest deference to the wisdom of the Parliament, that the acts made there, imposing duties on the people of this province, with the sole and express purpose of raising a revenue, are infringements of their natural and constitutional rights; because, as they are not represented in the Parliament, his Majesty's Commons in Britain, by those acts, grant their property without their consent." Note that even in this letter of protest, the humble and submissive tone shows the Massachusetts Assembly's continued deference to parliamentary authority. Even in that hotbed of political protest, it is a clear expression of allegiance and the hope for a restoration of "natural and constitutional rights."

Great Britain's response to this threat of disobedience served only to unite the colonies further. The colonies' initial response to the Massachusetts Circular was lukewarm at best. However, back in Great Britain, the secretary of state for the colonies—Lord Hillsborough—demanded that Massachusetts retract the letter, promising that any colonial assemblies that endorsed it would be dissolved. This threat had the effect of pushing the other colonies to Massachusetts's side. Even the city of Philadelphia, which had originally opposed the Circular, came around.

The Daughters of Liberty once again supported and promoted the boycott of British goods. Women resumed spinning bees and again found substitutes for British tea and other goods. Many colonial merchants signed non-importation agreements, and the Daughters of Liberty urged colonial women to shop only with those merchants. The Sons of Liberty used newspapers and circulars to call out by name those merchants who refused to sign such agreements; sometimes they were threatened by violence. For instance, a broadside from 1769–1770 reads:

"WILLIAM JACKSON,
an IMPORTER;
at the BRAZEN HEAD,
North Side of the TOWN-HOUSE,
and Opposite the Town-Pump, [in]
Corn-hill, BOSTON
It is desired that the SONS
and DAUGHTERS of LIBERTY,
would not buy any one thing of
him, for in so doing they will bring
disgrace upon themselves, and their
Posterity, for ever and ever, AMEN."

The boycott in 1768–1769 turned the purchase of consumer goods into a political gesture. It mattered what you consumed. Indeed, the very clothes you wore indicated whether you were a defender of liberty in homespun or a protector of parliamentary rights in superfine British attire.

CLICK AND EXPLORE

For examples of the types of luxury items that many American colonists favored, visit the National Humanities Center (http://openstax.org/l/britlux) to see pictures and documents relating to home interiors of the wealthy.

TROUBLE IN BOSTON

The Massachusetts Circular got Parliament's attention, and in 1768, Lord Hillsborough sent four thousand British troops to Boston to deal with the unrest and put down any potential rebellion there. The troops were a constant reminder of the assertion of British power over the colonies, an illustration of an unequal relationship between members of the same empire. As an added aggravation, British soldiers moonlighted as dockworkers, creating competition for employment. Boston's labor system had traditionally been closed, privileging native-born laborers over outsiders, and jobs were scarce. Many Bostonians, led by the Sons of Liberty, mounted a campaign of harassment against British troops. The Sons of Liberty also helped protect the smuggling actions of the merchants; smuggling was crucial for the colonists' ability to maintain their boycott of British goods.

John Hancock was one of Boston's most successful merchants and prominent citizens. While he maintained too high a profile to work actively with the Sons of Liberty, he was known to support their aims, if not their means of achieving them. He was also one of the many prominent merchants who had made their fortunes by smuggling, which was rampant in the colonial seaports. In 1768, customs officials seized the *Liberty*, one of his ships, and violence erupted. Led by the Sons of Liberty, Bostonians rioted against customs officials, attacking the customs house and chasing out the officers, who ran to safety at Castle William, a British fort on a Boston harbor island. British soldiers crushed the riots, but over the next few years, clashes between British officials and Bostonians became common.

Conflict turned deadly on March 5, 1770, in a confrontation that came to be known as the **Boston Massacre**. On that night, a crowd of Bostonians from many walks of life started throwing snowballs, rocks, and sticks at the British soldiers guarding the customs house. In the resulting scuffle, some soldiers, goaded by the mob who hectored the soldiers as "lobster backs" (the reference to lobster equated the soldiers with bottom feeders, i.e., aquatic animals that feed on the lowest organisms in the food chain), fired into the crowd, killing five people. Crispus Attucks, the first man killed—and, though no one could have known it then, the first official casualty in the war for independence—was of Wampanoag and African descent. The bloodshed illustrated the level of hostility that had developed as a result of Boston's occupation by British troops, the competition for scarce jobs between Bostonians and the British soldiers stationed in the city, and the larger question of Parliament's efforts to tax the colonies.

The Sons of Liberty immediately seized on the event, characterizing the British soldiers as murderers and their victims as martyrs. Paul Revere, a silversmith and member of the Sons of Liberty, circulated an engraving that showed a line of grim redcoats firing ruthlessly into a crowd of unarmed, fleeing civilians. Among colonists who resisted British power, this view of the "massacre" confirmed their fears of a tyrannous government using its armies to curb the freedom of British subjects. But to others, the attacking mob was equally to blame for pelting the British with rocks and insulting them.

It was not only British Loyalists who condemned the unruly mob. John Adams, one of the city's strongest supporters of peaceful protest against Parliament, represented the British soldiers at their murder trial. Adams argued that the mob's lawlessness required the soldiers' response, and that without law and order, a society was nothing. He argued further that the soldiers were the tools of a much broader program, which transformed a street brawl into the injustice of imperial policy. Of the eight soldiers on trial, the jury acquitted six, convicting the other two of the reduced charge of manslaughter.

Adams argued: "Facts are stubborn things; and whatever may be our wishes, our inclinations, or the dictates of our passions, they cannot alter the state of facts and evidence: nor is the law less stable than the fact; if an assault was made to endanger their lives, the law is clear, they had a right to kill in their own defense; if it was not so severe as to endanger their lives, yet if they were assaulted at all, struck and abused by blows of any sort, by snow-balls, oyster-shells, cinders, clubs, or sticks of any kind; this was a provocation, for which the law reduces the offence of killing, down to manslaughter, in consideration of those passions in our nature, which cannot be eradicated. To your candour and justice I submit the prisoners and their cause."

AMERICANA

Propaganda and the Sons of Liberty

Long after the British soldiers had been tried and punished, the Sons of Liberty maintained a relentless propaganda campaign against British oppression. Many of them were printers or engravers, and they were able to use public media to sway others to their cause. Shortly after the incident outside the customs house, Paul Revere created "The bloody massacre perpetrated in King Street Boston on March 5th 1770 by a party of the 29th Regt." (Figure 5.11), based on an image by engraver Henry Pelham. The picture—which represents only the protesters' point of view—shows the ruthlessness of the British soldiers and the helplessness of the crowd of civilians. Notice the subtle details Revere uses to help convince the viewer of the civilians' innocence and the soldiers' cruelty. Although eyewitnesses said the crowd started the fight by throwing snowballs and rocks, in the engraving they are innocently standing by. Revere also depicts the crowd as well dressed and well-to-do, when in fact they were laborers and probably looked quite a bit rougher.

FIGURE 5.11 The Sons of Liberty circulated this sensationalized version of the events of March 5, 1770, in order to promote the rightness of their cause. The verses below the image begin as follows: "Unhappy Boston! see thy Sons deplore, Thy hallowed Walks besmeared with guiltless Gore."

Newspaper articles and pamphlets that the Sons of Liberty circulated implied that the "massacre" was a planned murder. In the *Boston Gazette* on March 12, 1770, an article describes the soldiers as striking first. It goes on to discuss this version of the events: "On hearing the noise, one Samuel Atwood came up to see what was the matter; and entering the alley from dock square, heard the latter part of the combat; and when the boys had dispersed he met the ten or twelve soldiers aforesaid rushing down the alley towards the square and asked them if they intended to murder people? They answered Yes, by God, root and branch! With that one of them struck Mr. Atwood with a club which was repeated by another; and being unarmed, he turned to go off and received a wound on the left shoulder which reached the bone and gave him much pain."

What do you think most people in the United States think of when they consider the Boston Massacre? How does the propaganda of the Sons of Liberty still affect the way we think of this event?

PARTIAL REPEAL

As it turned out, the Boston Massacre occurred after Parliament had partially repealed the Townshend Acts. By the late 1760s, the American boycott of British goods had drastically reduced British trade. Once again, merchants who lost money because of the boycott strongly pressured Parliament to loosen its restrictions on the colonies and break the non-importation movement. Charles Townshend died suddenly in 1767 and was replaced by Lord North, who was inclined to look for a more workable solution with the colonists. North convinced Parliament to drop all the Townshend duties except the tax on tea. The administrative and enforcement provisions under the Townshend Acts—the American Board of Customs Commissioners and the vice-admiralty courts—remained in place.

To those who had protested the Townshend Acts for several years, the partial repeal appeared to be a major victory. For a second time, colonists had rescued liberty from an unconstitutional parliamentary measure. The hated British troops in Boston departed. The consumption of British goods skyrocketed after the partial repeal, an indication of the American colonists' desire for the items linking them to the Empire.

5.4 The Destruction of the Tea and the Coercive Acts

LEARNING OBJECTIVES

By the end of this section, you will be able to:
- Describe the socio-political environment in the colonies in the early 1770s
- Explain the purpose of the Tea Act of 1773 and discuss colonial reactions to it
- Identify and describe the Coercive Acts

The Tea Act of 1773 triggered a reaction with far more significant consequences than either the 1765 Stamp Act or the 1767 Townshend Acts. Colonists who had joined in protest against those earlier acts renewed their efforts in 1773. They understood that Parliament had again asserted its right to impose taxes without representation, and they feared the Tea Act was designed to seduce them into conceding this important principle by lowering the price of tea to the point that colonists might abandon their scruples. They also deeply resented the East India Company's monopoly on the sale of tea in the American colonies; this resentment sprang from the knowledge that some members of Parliament had invested heavily in the company.

SMOLDERING RESENTMENT

Even after the partial repeal of the Townshend duties, however, suspicion of Parliament's intentions remained high. This was especially true in port cities like Boston and New York, where British customs agents were a daily irritant and reminder of British power. In public houses and squares, people met and discussed politics. Philosopher John Locke's *Two Treatises of Government*, published almost a century earlier, influenced political thought about the role of government to protect life, liberty, and property. The Sons of Liberty issued propaganda ensuring that colonists remained aware when Parliament overreached itself.

Violence continued to break out on occasion, as in 1772, when Rhode Island colonists boarded and burned the British revenue ship *Gaspée* in Narragansett Bay (Figure 5.12). Colonists had attacked or burned British customs ships in the past, but after the Gaspée Affair, the British government convened a Royal Commission of Inquiry. This Commission had the authority to remove the colonists, who were charged with treason, to Great Britain for trial. Some colonial protestors saw this new ability as another example of the overreach of British power.

FIGURE 5.12 This 1883 engraving, which appeared in *Harper's New Monthly Magazine*, depicts the burning of the *Gaspée*. This attack provoked the British government to convene a Royal Commission of Inquiry; some regarded the

Commission as an example of excessive British power and control over the colonies.

Samuel Adams, along with Joseph Warren and James Otis, re-formed the Boston **Committee of Correspondence**, which functioned as a form of shadow government, to address the fear of British overreach. Soon towns all over Massachusetts had formed their own committees, and many other colonies followed suit. These committees, which had between seven and eight thousand members in all, identified enemies of the movement and communicated the news of the day. Sometimes they provided a version of events that differed from royal interpretations, and slowly, the committees began to supplant royal governments as sources of information. They later formed the backbone of communication among the colonies in the rebellion against the Tea Act, and eventually in the revolt against the British crown.

THE TEA ACT OF 1773

Parliament did not enact the Tea Act of 1773 in order to punish the colonists, assert parliamentary power, or even raise revenues. Rather, the act was a straightforward order of economic protectionism for a British tea firm, the East India Company, that was on the verge of bankruptcy. In the colonies, tea was the one remaining consumer good subject to the hated Townshend duties. Protest leaders and their followers still avoided British tea, drinking smuggled Dutch tea as a sign of patriotism.

The Tea Act of 1773 gave the British East India Company the ability to export its tea directly to the colonies without paying import or export duties and without using middlemen in either Great Britain or the colonies. Even with the Townshend tax, the act would allow the East India Company to sell its tea at lower prices than the smuggled Dutch tea, thus undercutting the smuggling trade.

This act was unwelcome to those in British North America who had grown displeased with the pattern of imperial measures. By granting a monopoly to the East India Company, the act not only cut out colonial merchants who would otherwise sell the tea themselves; it also reduced their profits from smuggled foreign tea. These merchants were among the most powerful and influential people in the colonies, so their dissatisfaction carried some weight. Moreover, because the tea tax that the Townshend Acts imposed remained in place, tea had intense power to symbolize the idea of "no taxation without representation."

COLONIAL PROTEST: THE DESTRUCTION OF THE TEA

The 1773 act reignited the worst fears among the colonists. To the Sons and Daughters of Liberty and those who followed them, the act appeared to be proof positive that a handful of corrupt members of Parliament were violating the British Constitution. Veterans of the protest movement had grown accustomed to interpreting British actions in the worst possible light, so the 1773 act appeared to be part of a large conspiracy against liberty.

As they had done to protest earlier acts and taxes, colonists responded to the Tea Act with a boycott. The Committees of Correspondence helped to coordinate resistance in all of the colonial port cities, so up and down the East Coast, British tea-carrying ships were unable to come to shore and unload their wares. In Charlestown, Boston, Philadelphia, and New York, the equivalent of millions of dollars' worth of tea was held hostage, either locked in storage warehouses or rotting in the holds of ships as they were forced to sail back to Great Britain.

In Boston, Thomas Hutchinson, now the royal governor of Massachusetts, vowed that radicals like Samuel Adams would not keep the ships from unloading their cargo. He urged the merchants who would have accepted the tea from the ships to stand their ground and receive the tea once it had been unloaded. When the *Dartmouth* sailed into Boston Harbor in November 1773, it had twenty days to unload its cargo of tea and pay the duty before it had to return to Great Britain. Two more ships, the *Eleanor* and the *Beaver*, followed soon after. Samuel Adams and the Sons of Liberty tried to keep the captains of the ships from paying the duties and posted groups around the ships to make sure the tea would not be unloaded.

On December 16, just as the *Dartmouth*'s deadline approached, townspeople gathered at the Old South

Meeting House determined to take action. From this gathering, a group of Sons of Liberty and their followers approached the three ships. Some were disguised as Mohawks. Protected by a crowd of spectators, they systematically dumped all the tea into the harbor, destroying goods worth almost $1 million in today's dollars, a very significant loss. This act soon inspired further acts of resistance up and down the East Coast. However, not all colonists, and not even all Patriots, supported the dumping of the tea. The wholesale destruction of property shocked people on both sides of the Atlantic.

CLICK AND EXPLORE

To learn more about the Boston Tea Party, explore the extensive resources in the Boston Tea Party Ships and Museum collection (http://openstax.org/l/teapartyship) of articles, photos, and video. At the museum itself, you can board replicas of the *Eleanor* and the *Beaver* and experience a recreation of the dumping of the tea.

PARLIAMENT RESPONDS: THE COERCIVE ACTS

In London, response to the destruction of the tea was swift and strong. The violent destruction of property infuriated King George III and the prime minister, Lord North (Figure 5.13), who insisted the loss be repaid. Though some American merchants put forward a proposal for restitution, the Massachusetts Assembly refused to make payments. Massachusetts's resistance to British authority united different factions in Great Britain against the colonies. North had lost patience with the unruly British subjects in Boston. He declared: "The Americans have tarred and feathered your subjects, plundered your merchants, burnt your ships, denied all obedience to your laws and authority; yet so clement and so long forbearing has our conduct been that it is incumbent on us now to take a different course. Whatever may be the consequences, we must risk something; if we do not, all is over." Both Parliament and the king agreed that Massachusetts should be forced to both pay for the tea and yield to British authority.

FIGURE 5.13 Lord North, seen here in *Portrait of Frederick North, Lord North* (1773–1774), painted by Nathaniel Dance, was prime minister at the time of the destruction of the tea and insisted that Massachusetts make good on the loss.

In early 1774, leaders in Parliament responded with a set of four measures designed to punish Massachusetts, commonly known at the **Coercive Acts**. The Boston Port Act shut down Boston Harbor until the East India Company was repaid. The Massachusetts Government Act placed the colonial government under the direct control of crown officials and made traditional town meetings subject to the governor's approval. The Administration of Justice Act allowed the royal governor to unilaterally move any trial of a crown officer out of Massachusetts, a change designed to prevent hostile Massachusetts juries from deciding these cases. This act was especially infuriating to John Adams and others who emphasized the time-honored rule of law. They saw this part of the Coercive Acts as striking at the heart of fair and equitable justice. Finally, the Quartering Act encompassed all the colonies and allowed British troops to be housed in occupied buildings.

At the same time, Parliament also passed the Quebec Act, which expanded the boundaries of Quebec westward and extended religious tolerance to Roman Catholics in the province. For many Protestant colonists, especially Congregationalists in New England, this forced tolerance of Catholicism was the most objectionable provision of the act. Additionally, expanding the boundaries of Quebec raised troubling questions for many colonists who eyed the West, hoping to expand the boundaries of their provinces. The Quebec Act appeared gratuitous, a slap in the face to colonists already angered by the Coercive Acts.

American Patriots renamed the Coercive and Quebec measures the **Intolerable Acts**. Some in London also thought the acts went too far; see the cartoon "The Able Doctor, or America Swallowing the Bitter Draught" (Figure 5.14) for one British view of what Parliament was doing to the colonies. Meanwhile, punishments designed to hurt only one colony (Massachusetts, in this case) had the effect of mobilizing all the colonies to its side. The Committees of Correspondence had already been active in coordinating an approach to the Tea Act. Now the talk would turn to these new, intolerable assaults on the colonists' rights as British subjects.

FIGURE 5.14 The artist of "The Able Doctor, or America Swallowing the Bitter Draught" (*London Magazine*, May 1, 1774) targets select members of Parliament as the perpetrators of a devilish scheme to overturn the constitution; this is why Mother Britannia weeps. Note that this cartoon came from a British publication; Great Britain was not united in support of Parliament's policies toward the American colonies.

5.5 Disaffection: The First Continental Congress and American Identity

LEARNING OBJECTIVES

By the end of this section, you will be able to:
- Describe the state of affairs between the colonies and the home government in 1774
- Explain the purpose and results of the First Continental Congress

Disaffection—the loss of affection toward the home government—had reached new levels by 1774. Many colonists viewed the Intolerable Acts as a turning point; they now felt they had to take action. The result was the First Continental Congress, a direct challenge to Lord North and British authority in the colonies. Still, it would be a mistake to assume there was a groundswell of support for separating from the British Empire and creating a new, independent nation. Strong ties still bound the Empire together, and colonists did not agree about the proper response. Loyalists tended to be property holders, established residents who feared the loss of their property. To them the protests seemed to promise nothing but mob rule, and the violence and disorder they provoked were shocking. On both sides of the Atlantic, opinions varied.

After the passage of the Intolerable Acts in 1774, the Committees of Correspondence and the Sons of Liberty went straight to work, spreading warnings about how the acts would affect the liberty of all colonists, not just urban merchants and laborers. The Massachusetts Government Act had shut down the colonial government there, but resistance-minded colonists began meeting in extralegal assemblies. One of these assemblies, the Massachusetts Provincial Congress, passed the **Suffolk Resolves** in September 1774, which laid out a plan of resistance to the Intolerable Acts. Meanwhile, the First Continental Congress was convening to discuss how to respond to the acts themselves.

The First Continental Congress was made up of elected representatives of twelve of the thirteen American colonies. (Georgia's royal governor blocked the move to send representatives from that colony, an indication of the continued strength of the royal government despite the crisis.) The representatives met in Philadelphia from September 5 through October 26, 1774, and at first they did not agree at all about the appropriate response to the Intolerable Acts. Joseph Galloway of Pennsylvania argued for a conciliatory approach; he proposed that an elected Grand Council in America, like the Parliament in Great Britain, should be paired with a royally appointed President General, who would represent the authority of the Crown. More radical factions argued for a move toward separation from the Crown.

In the end, Paul Revere rode from Massachusetts to Philadelphia with the Suffolk Resolves, which became the basis of the Declaration and Resolves of the First Continental Congress. In the Declaration and Resolves, adopted on October 14, the colonists demanded the repeal of all repressive acts passed since 1773 and agreed to a non-importation, non-exportation, and non-consumption pact against all British goods until the acts were repealed. In the "Petition of Congress to the King" on October 24, the delegates adopted a further recommendation of the Suffolk Resolves and proposed that the colonies raise and regulate their own militias.

The representatives at the First Continental Congress created a Continental Association to ensure that the full boycott was enforced across all the colonies. The Continental Association served as an umbrella group for colonial and local committees of observation and inspection. By taking these steps, the First Continental Congress established a governing network in opposition to royal authority.

CLICK AND EXPLORE

Visit the Massachusetts Historical Society (http://openstax.org/l/firstcongress) to see a digitized copy and read the transcript of the First Continental Congress's petition to King George.

DEFINING AMERICAN

The First List of Un-American Activities

In her book *Toward A More Perfect Union: Virtue and the Formation of American Republics*, historian Ann Fairfax Withington explores actions the delegates to the First Continental Congress took during the weeks they were together. Along with their efforts to bring about the repeal of the Intolerable Acts, the delegates also banned certain activities they believed would undermine their fight against what they saw as British corruption.

In particular, the delegates prohibited horse races, cockfights, the theater, and elaborate funerals. The reasons for these prohibitions provide insight into the state of affairs in 1774. Both horse races and cockfights encouraged gambling and, for the delegates, gambling threatened to prevent the unity of action and purpose they desired. In addition, cockfighting appeared immoral and corrupt because the roosters were fitted with razors and fought to the death (Figure 5.15).

FIGURE 5.15 Cockfights, as depicted in *The Cockpit* (1759) by British artist and engraver William Hogarth, were among the entertainments the First Continental Congress sought to outlaw, considering them un-American.

The ban on the theater aimed to do away with another corrupt British practice. Critics had long believed that theatrical performances drained money from working people. Moreover, they argued, theatergoers learned to lie and deceive from what they saw on stage. The delegates felt banning the theater would demonstrate their resolve to act honestly and without pretence in their fight against corruption.

Finally, eighteenth-century mourning practices often required lavish spending on luxury items and even the employment of professional mourners who, for a price, would shed tears at the grave. Prohibiting these practices reflected the idea that luxury bred corruption, and the First Continental Congress wanted to demonstrate that the colonists would do without British vices. Congress emphasized the need to be frugal and self-sufficient when confronted with corruption.

The First Continental Congress banned all four activities—horse races, cockfights, the theater, and elaborate funerals—and entrusted the Continental Association with enforcement. Rejecting what they saw as corruption coming from Great Britain, the delegates were also identifying themselves as standing apart from their British relatives. They cast themselves as virtuous defenders of liberty against a corrupt Parliament.

In the Declaration and Resolves and the Petition of Congress to the King, the delegates to the First Continental Congress refer to George III as "Most Gracious Sovereign" and to themselves as "inhabitants of the English colonies in North America" or "inhabitants of British America," indicating that they still considered themselves British subjects of the king, not American citizens. At the same time, however, they were slowly moving away from British authority, creating their own de facto government in the First Continental Congress. One of the provisions of the Congress was that it meet again in one year to mark its progress; the Congress was becoming an elected government.

Key Terms

Boston Massacre   a confrontation between a crowd of Bostonians and British soldiers on March 5, 1770, which resulted in the deaths of five people, including Crispus Attucks, the first official casualty in the war for independence

Coercive Acts   four acts (Administration of Justice Act, Massachusetts Government Act, Port Act, Quartering Act) that Lord North passed to punish Massachusetts for destroying the tea and refusing to pay for the damage

Committees of Correspondence   colonial extralegal shadow governments that convened to coordinate plans of resistance against the British

Daughters of Liberty   well-born British colonial women who led a non-importation movement against British goods

direct tax   a tax that consumers pay directly, rather than through merchants' higher prices

indirect tax   a tax imposed on businesses, rather than directly on consumers

Intolerable Acts   the name American Patriots gave to the Coercive Acts and the Quebec Act

Loyalists   colonists in America who were loyal to Great Britain

Massachusetts Circular   a letter penned by Son of Liberty Samuel Adams that laid out the unconstitutionality of taxation without representation and encouraged the other colonies to boycott British goods

no taxation without representation   the principle, first articulated in the Virginia Stamp Act Resolutions, that the colonists needed to be represented in Parliament if they were to be taxed

non-importation movement   a widespread colonial boycott of British goods

Proclamation Line   a line along the Appalachian Mountains, imposed by the Proclamation of 1763, west of which British colonists could not settle

Sons of Liberty   artisans, shopkeepers, and small-time merchants who opposed the Stamp Act and considered themselves British patriots

Suffolk Resolves   a Massachusetts plan of resistance to the Intolerable Acts that formed the basis of the eventual plan adopted by the First Continental Congress for resisting the British, including the arming of militias and the adoption of a widespread non-importation, non-exportation, and non-consumption agreement

vice-admiralty courts   British royal courts without juries that settled disputes occurring at sea

Summary

5.1 Confronting the National Debt: The Aftermath of the French and Indian War

The British Empire had gained supremacy in North America with its victory over the French in 1763. Almost all of the North American territory east of the Mississippi fell under Great Britain's control, and British leaders took this opportunity to try to create a more coherent and unified empire after decades of lax oversight. Victory over the French had proved very costly, and the British government attempted to better regulate their expanded empire in North America. The initial steps the British took in 1763 and 1764 raised suspicions among some colonists about the intent of the home government. These suspicions would grow and swell over the coming years.

5.2 The Stamp Act and the Sons and Daughters of Liberty

Though Parliament designed the 1765 Stamp Act to deal with the financial crisis in the Empire, it had unintended consequences. Outrage over the act created a degree of unity among otherwise unconnected American colonists, giving them a chance to act together both politically and socially. The crisis of the Stamp Act allowed colonists to loudly proclaim their identity as defenders of British liberty. With the repeal of the Stamp Act in 1766, liberty-loving subjects of the king celebrated what they viewed as a victory.

5.3 The Townshend Acts and Colonial Protest

Like the Stamp Act in 1765, the Townshend Acts led many colonists to work together against what they perceived to be an unconstitutional measure, generating the second major crisis in British Colonial America. The experience of resisting the Townshend Acts provided another shared experience among colonists from diverse regions and backgrounds, while the partial repeal convinced many that liberty had once again been defended. Nonetheless, Great Britain's debt crisis still had not been solved.

5.4 The Destruction of the Tea and the Coercive Acts

The colonial rejection of the Tea Act, especially the destruction of the tea in Boston Harbor, recast the decade-long argument between British colonists and the home government as an intolerable conspiracy against liberty and an excessive overreach of parliamentary power. The Coercive Acts were punitive in nature, awakening the worst fears of otherwise loyal members of the British Empire in America.

5.5 Disaffection: The First Continental Congress and American Identity

The First Continental Congress, which comprised elected representatives from twelve of the thirteen American colonies, represented a direct challenge to British authority. In its Declaration and Resolves, colonists demanded the repeal of all repressive acts passed since 1773. The delegates also recommended that the colonies raise militias, lest the British respond to the Congress's proposed boycott of British goods with force. While the colonists still considered themselves British subjects, they were slowly retreating from British authority, creating their own de facto government via the First Continental Congress.

Review Questions

1. Which of the following was a cause of the British National Debt in 1763?
    A. drought in Great Britain
    B. the French and Indian War
    C. the continued British military presence in the American colonies
    D. both B and C

2. What was the main purpose of the Sugar Act of 1764?
    A. It raised taxes on sugar.
    B. It raised taxes on molasses.
    C. It strengthened enforcement of molasses smuggling laws.
    D. It required colonists to purchase only sugar distilled in Great Britain.

3. What did British colonists find so onerous about the acts that Prime Minister Grenville passed?

4. Which of the following was *not* a goal of the Stamp Act?
    A. to gain control over the colonists
    B. to raise revenue for British troops stationed in the colonies
    C. to raise revenue to pay off British debt from the French and Indian War
    D. to declare null and void any laws the colonies had passed to govern and tax themselves

5. For which of the following activities were the Sons of Liberty responsible?
    A. the Stamp Act Congress
    B. the hanging and beheading of a stamp commissioner in effigy
    C. the massacre of Conestoga in Pennsylvania
    D. the introduction of the Virginia Stamp Act Resolutions

6. Which of the following was *not* one of the goals of the Townshend Acts?
   A. higher taxes
   B. greater colonial unity
   C. greater British control over the colonies
   D. reduced power of the colonial governments

7. Which event was most responsible for the colonies' endorsement of Samuel Adams's Massachusetts Circular?
   A. the Townshend Duties
   B. the Indemnity Act
   C. the Boston Massacre
   D. Lord Hillsborough's threat to dissolve the colonial assemblies that endorsed the letter

8. What factors contributed to the Boston Massacre?

9. Which of the following is true of the Gaspée affair?
   A. Colonists believed that the British response represented an overreach of power.
   B. It was the first time colonists attacked a revenue ship.
   C. It was the occasion of the first official death in the war for independence.
   D. The ship's owner, John Hancock, was a respectable Boston merchant.

10. What was the purpose of the Tea Act of 1773?
    A. to punish the colonists for their boycotting of British tea
    B. to raise revenue to offset the British national debt
    C. to help revive the struggling East India Company
    D. to pay the salaries of royal appointees

11. What was the significance of the Committees of Correspondence?

12. Which of the following was decided at the First Continental Congress?
    A. to declare war on Great Britain
    B. to boycott all British goods and prepare for possible military action
    C. to offer a conciliatory treaty to Great Britain
    D. to pay for the tea that was dumped in Boston Harbor

13. Which colony provided the basis for the Declarations and Resolves?
    A. Massachusetts
    B. Philadelphia
    C. Rhode Island
    D. New York

Critical Thinking Questions

14. Was reconciliation between the American colonies and Great Britain possible in 1774? Why or why not?

15. Look again at the painting that opened this chapter: *The Bostonians Paying the Excise-man, or Tarring and Feathering* (Figure 5.1). How does this painting represent the relationship between Great Britain and the American colonies in the years from 1763 to 1774?

16. Why did the colonists react so much more strongly to the Stamp Act than to the Sugar Act? How did the principles that the Stamp Act raised continue to provide points of contention between colonists and the British government?

17. History is filled with unintended consequences. How do the British government's attempts to control and regulate the colonies during this tumultuous era provide a case in point? How did the aims of the British measure up against the results of their actions?

18. What evidence indicates that colonists continued to think of themselves as British subjects throughout this era? What evidence suggests that colonists were beginning to forge a separate, collective "American" identity? How would you explain this shift?

America's War for Independence, 1775-1783

FIGURE 6.1 This famous 1819 painting by John Trumbull shows members of the committee entrusted with drafting the Declaration of Independence presenting their work to the Continental Congress in 1776. Note the British flags on the wall. Separating from the British Empire proved to be very difficult as the colonies and the Empire were linked with strong cultural, historical, and economic bonds forged over several generations.

CHAPTER OUTLINE
6.1 Britain's Law-and-Order Strategy and Its Consequences
6.2 The Early Years of the Revolution
6.3 War in the South
6.4 Identity during the American Revolution

INTRODUCTION By the 1770s, Great Britain ruled a vast empire, with its American colonies producing useful raw materials and profitably consuming British goods. From Britain's perspective, it was inconceivable that the colonies would wage a successful war for independence; in 1776, they appeared weak and disorganized, no match for the Empire. Yet, although the Revolutionary War did indeed drag on for eight years, in 1783, the thirteen colonies, now the United States, ultimately prevailed against the British.

The Revolution succeeded because colonists from diverse economic and social backgrounds united in their opposition to Great Britain. Although thousands of colonists remained loyal to the crown and many others preferred to remain neutral, a sense of community against a common enemy prevailed among Patriots. The signing of the Declaration of Independence (Figure 6.1) exemplifies the spirit of that common cause.

Representatives asserted: "That these United Colonies are, and of Right ought to be Free and Independent States; that they are Absolved from all Allegiance to the British Crown, . . . And for the support of this Declaration, . . . we mutually pledge to each other our Lives, our Fortunes and our sacred Honor."

6.1 Britain's Law-and-Order Strategy and Its Consequences

LEARNING OBJECTIVES

By the end of this section, you will be able to:
- Explain how Great Britain's response to the destruction of a British shipment of tea in Boston Harbor in 1773 set the stage for the Revolution
- Describe the beginnings of the American Revolution

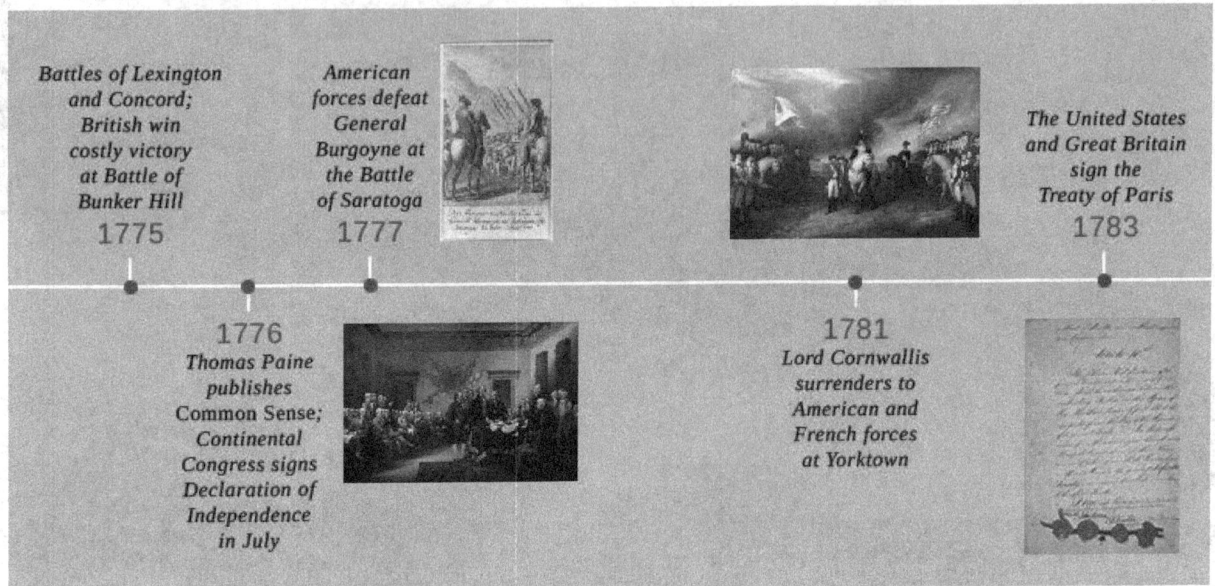

FIGURE 6.2

Great Britain pursued a policy of law and order when dealing with the crises in the colonies in the late 1760s and 1770s. Relations between the British and many American Patriots worsened over the decade, culminating in an unruly mob destroying a fortune in tea by dumping it into Boston Harbor in December 1773 as a protest against British tax laws. The harsh British response to this act in 1774, which included sending British troops to Boston and closing Boston Harbor, caused tensions and resentments to escalate further. The British tried to disarm the insurgents in Massachusetts by confiscating their weapons and ammunition and arresting the leaders of the patriotic movement. However, this effort faltered on April 19, when Massachusetts militias and British troops fired on each other as British troops marched to Lexington and Concord, an event immortalized by poet Ralph Waldo Emerson as the "shot heard round the world." The American Revolution had begun.

ON THE EVE OF REVOLUTION

The decade from 1763 to 1774 was a difficult one for the British Empire. Although Great Britain had defeated the French in the French and Indian War, the debt from that conflict remained a stubborn and seemingly unsolvable problem for both Great Britain and the colonies. Great Britain tried various methods of raising revenue on both sides of the Atlantic to manage the enormous debt, including instituting a tax on tea and other goods sold to the colonies by British companies, but many subjects resisted these taxes. In the colonies, Patriot groups like the Sons of Liberty led boycotts of British goods and took violent measures that stymied British officials.

Boston proved to be the epicenter of protest. In December 1773, a group of Patriots protested the Tea Act passed that year—which, among other provisions, gave the East India Company a monopoly on tea—by boarding British tea ships docked in Boston Harbor and dumping tea worth over $1 million (in current prices) into the water. The destruction of the tea radically escalated the crisis between Great Britain and the American colonies. When the Massachusetts Assembly refused to pay for the tea, Parliament enacted a series of laws called the Coercive Acts, which some colonists called the Intolerable Acts. Parliament designed these laws, which closed the port of Boston, limited the meetings of the colonial assembly, and disbanded all town meetings, to punish Massachusetts and bring the colony into line. However, many British Americans in other colonies were troubled and angered by Parliament's response to Massachusetts. In September and October 1774, all the colonies except Georgia participated in the First Continental Congress in Philadelphia. The Congress advocated a boycott of all British goods and established the Continental Association to enforce local adherence to the boycott. The Association supplanted royal control and shaped resistance to Great Britain.

AMERICANA

Joining the Boycott

Many British colonists in Virginia, as in the other colonies, disapproved of the destruction of the tea in Boston Harbor. However, after the passage of the Coercive Acts, the Virginia House of Burgesses declared its solidarity with Massachusetts by encouraging Virginians to observe a day of fasting and prayer on May 24 in sympathy with the people of Boston. Almost immediately thereafter, Virginia's colonial governor dissolved the House of Burgesses, but many of its members met again in secret on May 30 and adopted a resolution stating that "the Colony of Virginia will concur with the other Colonies in such Measures as shall be judged most effectual for the preservation of the Common Rights and Liberty of British America."

After the First Continental Congress in Philadelphia, Virginia's Committee of Safety ensured that all merchants signed the non-importation agreements that the Congress had proposed. This British cartoon (Figure 6.3) shows a Virginian signing the Continental Association boycott agreement.

FIGURE 6.3 In "The Alternative of Williams-Burg" (1775), a merchant has to sign a non-importation agreement or risk being covered with the tar and feathers suspended behind him.

Note the tar and feathers hanging from the gallows in the background of this image and the demeanor of the people surrounding the signer. What is the message of this engraving? Where are the sympathies of the artist? What is the meaning of the title "The Alternative of Williams-Burg?"

In an effort to restore law and order in Boston, the British dispatched General Thomas Gage to the New England seaport. He arrived in Boston in May 1774 as the new royal governor of the Province of Massachusetts, accompanied by several regiments of British troops. As in 1768, the British again occupied the town.

Massachusetts delegates met in a Provincial Congress and published the Suffolk Resolves, which officially rejected the Coercive Acts and called for the raising of colonial militias to take military action if needed. The Suffolk Resolves signaled the overthrow of the royal government in Massachusetts.

Both the British and the rebels in New England began to prepare for conflict by turning their attention to supplies of weapons and gunpowder. General Gage stationed thirty-five hundred troops in Boston, and from there he ordered periodic raids on towns where guns and gunpowder were stockpiled, hoping to impose law and order by seizing them. As Boston became the headquarters of British military operations, many residents fled the city.

Gage's actions led to the formation of local rebel militias that were able to mobilize in a minute's time. These **minutemen**, many of whom were veterans of the French and Indian War, played an important role in the war for independence. In one instance, General Gage seized munitions in Cambridge and Charlestown, but when he arrived to do the same in Salem, his troops were met by a large crowd of minutemen and had to leave empty-handed. In New Hampshire, minutemen took over Fort William and Mary and confiscated weapons and cannons there. New England readied for war.

THE OUTBREAK OF FIGHTING

Throughout late 1774 and into 1775, tensions in New England continued to mount. General Gage knew that a powder magazine was stored in Concord, Massachusetts, and on April 19, 1775, he ordered troops to seize these munitions. Instructions from London called for the arrest of rebel leaders Samuel Adams and John Hancock. Hoping for secrecy, his troops left Boston under cover of darkness, but riders from Boston let the militias know of the British plans. (Paul Revere was one of these riders, but the British captured him and he never finished his ride. Henry Wadsworth Longfellow memorialized Revere in his 1860 poem, "Paul Revere's Ride," incorrectly implying that he made it all the way to Concord.) Minutemen met the British troops and skirmished with them, first at Lexington and then at Concord (Figure 6.4). The British retreated to Boston, enduring ambushes from several other militias along the way. Over four thousand militiamen took part in these skirmishes with British soldiers. Seventy-three British soldiers and forty-nine Patriots died during the British retreat to Boston. The famous confrontation is the basis for Emerson's "Concord Hymn" (1836), which begins with the description of the "shot heard round the world." Although propagandists on both sides pointed fingers, it remains unclear who fired that shot.

FIGURE 6.4 Amos Doolittle was an American printmaker who volunteered to fight against the British. His engravings of the battles of Lexington and Concord—such as this detail from *The Battle of Lexington, April 19th 1775*—are the only contemporary American visual records of the events there.

After the battles of Lexington and Concord, New England fully mobilized for war. Thousands of militias from towns throughout New England marched to Boston, and soon the city was besieged by a sea of rebel forces (Figure 6.5). In May 1775, Ethan Allen and Colonel Benedict Arnold led a group of rebels against Fort Ticonderoga in New York. They succeeded in capturing the fort, and cannons from Ticonderoga were brought to Massachusetts and used to bolster the Siege of Boston.

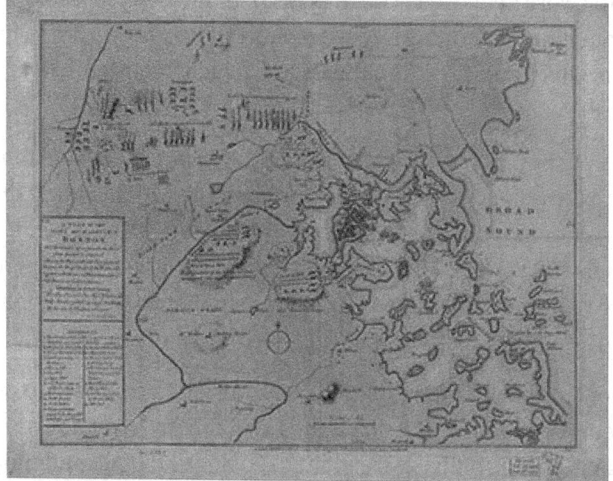

FIGURE 6.5 This 1779 map shows details of the British and Patriot troops in and around Boston, Massachusetts, at the beginning of the war.

In June, General Gage resolved to take Breed's Hill and Bunker Hill, the high ground across the Charles River from Boston, a strategic site that gave the rebel militias an advantage since they could train their cannons on the British. In the Battle of Bunker Hill (Figure 6.6), on June 17, the British launched three assaults on the hills, gaining control only after the rebels ran out of ammunition. British losses were very high—over two hundred were killed and eight hundred wounded—and, despite his victory, General Gage was unable to break the colonial forces' siege of the city. In August, King George III declared the colonies to be in a state of rebellion. Parliament and many in Great Britain agreed with their king. Meanwhile, the British forces in Boston found themselves in a terrible predicament, isolated in the city and with no control over the countryside.

(a)

(b)

FIGURE 6.6 The British cartoon "Bunkers Hill or America's Head Dress" (a) depicts the initial rebellion as an elaborate colonial coiffure. The illustration pokes fun at both the colonial rebellion and the overdone hairstyles for women that had made their way from France and Britain to the American colonies. Despite gaining control of the high ground after the colonial militias ran out of ammunition, General Thomas Gage (b), shown here in a painting made in 1768–1769 by John Singleton Copley, was unable to break the siege of the city.

In the end, General George Washington, commander in chief of the Continental Army since June 15, 1775, used the Fort Ticonderoga cannons to force the evacuation of the British from Boston. Washington had positioned these cannons on the hills overlooking both the fortified positions of the British and Boston Harbor, where the British supply ships were anchored. The British could not return fire on the colonial positions because they could not elevate their cannons. They soon realized that they were in an untenable position and had to withdraw from Boston. On March 17, 1776, the British evacuated their troops to Halifax, Nova Scotia, ending the nearly year-long siege.

By the time the British withdrew from Boston, fighting had broken out in other colonies as well. In May 1775, Mecklenburg County in North Carolina issued the **Mecklenburg Resolves**, stating that a rebellion against Great Britain had begun, that colonists did not owe any further allegiance to Great Britain, and that governing authority had now passed to the Continental Congress. The resolves also called upon the formation of militias to be under the control of the Continental Congress. Loyalists and Patriots clashed in North Carolina in February 1776 at the Battle of Moore's Creek Bridge.

In Virginia, the royal governor, Lord Dunmore, raised Loyalist forces to combat the rebel colonists and also tried to use the large enslaved population to put down the rebellion. In November 1775, he issued a decree, known as **Dunmore's Proclamation**, promising freedom to enslaved people and indentured servants of rebels who remained loyal to the king and who pledged to fight with the Loyalists against the insurgents. Dunmore's Proclamation exposed serious problems for both the Patriot cause and for the British. In order for the British to put down the rebellion, they needed the support of Virginia's landowners, many of whom enslaved people. (While Patriot slaveholders in Virginia and elsewhere proclaimed they acted in defense of liberty, they kept thousands in bondage, a fact the British decided to exploit.) Although a number of enslaved people did join Dunmore's side, the proclamation had the unintended effect of galvanizing Patriot resistance to Britain. From the rebels' point of view, the British looked to deprive them of their enslaved property and incite a race war. Slaveholders feared an uprising and increased their commitment to the cause against Great Britain, calling for independence. Dunmore fled Virginia in 1776.

COMMON SENSE

With the events of 1775 fresh in their minds, many colonists reached the conclusion in 1776 that the time had come to secede from the Empire and declare independence. Over the past ten years, these colonists had argued that they deserved the same rights as Englishmen enjoyed in Great Britain, only to find themselves relegated to an intolerable subservient status in the Empire. The groundswell of support for their cause of independence in 1776 also owed much to the appearance of an anonymous pamphlet, first published in January 1776, entitled *Common Sense*. Thomas Paine, who had emigrated from England to Philadelphia in 1774, was the author. Arguably the most radical pamphlet of the revolutionary era, *Common Sense* made a powerful argument for independence.

Paine's pamphlet rejected the monarchy, calling King George III a "royal brute" and questioning the right of an island (England) to rule over America. In this way, Paine helped to channel colonial discontent toward the king himself and not, as had been the case, toward the British Parliament—a bold move that signaled the desire to create a new political order disavowing monarchy entirely. He argued for the creation of an American republic, a state without a king, and extolled the blessings of **republicanism**, a political philosophy that held that elected representatives, not a hereditary monarch, should govern states. The vision of an American republic put forward by Paine included the idea of **popular sovereignty**: citizens in the republic would determine who would represent them, and decide other issues, on the basis of majority rule. Republicanism also served as a social philosophy guiding the conduct of the Patriots in their struggle against the British Empire. It demanded adherence to a code of virtue, placing the public good and community above narrow self-interest.

Paine wrote *Common Sense* (Figure 6.7) in simple, direct language aimed at ordinary people, not just the learned elite. The pamphlet proved immensely popular and was soon available in all **thirteen colonies**, where it helped convince many to reject monarchy and the British Empire in favor of independence and a republican form of government.

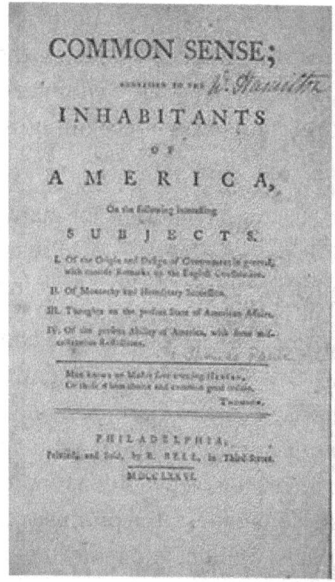 

FIGURE 6.7 Thomas Paine's *Common Sense* (a) helped convince many colonists of the need for independence from Great Britain. Paine, shown here in a portrait by Laurent Dabos (b), was a political activist and revolutionary best known for his writings on both the American and French Revolutions.

THE DECLARATION OF INDEPENDENCE

In the summer of 1776, the Continental Congress met in Philadelphia and agreed to sever ties with Great Britain. Virginian Thomas Jefferson and John Adams of Massachusetts, with the support of the Congress, articulated the justification for liberty in the Declaration of Independence (Figure 6.8). The Declaration, written primarily by Jefferson, included a long list of grievances against King George III and laid out the foundation of American government as a republic in which the consent of the governed would be of paramount importance.

FIGURE 6.8 The Dunlap Broadsides, one of which is shown here, are considered the first published copies of the Declaration of Independence. This one was printed on July 4, 1776.

The preamble to the Declaration began with a statement of Enlightenment principles about universal human rights and values: "We hold these Truths to be self-evident, that all Men are created equal, that they are endowed by their Creator with certain unalienable Rights, that among these are Life, Liberty, and the pursuit of Happiness—That to secure these Rights, Governments are instituted among Men, deriving their just Powers from the Consent of the Governed, that whenever any Form of Government becomes destructive of these Ends, it is the Right of the People to alter or abolish it." In addition to this statement of principles, the document served another purpose: Patriot leaders sent copies to France and Spain in hopes of winning their support and aid in the contest against Great Britain. They understood how important foreign recognition and aid would be to the creation of a new and independent nation.

The Declaration of Independence has since had a global impact, serving as the basis for many subsequent movements to gain independence from other colonial powers. It is part of America's civil religion, and thousands of people each year make pilgrimages to see the original document in Washington, DC.

The Declaration also reveals a fundamental contradiction of the American Revolution: the conflict between the existence of slavery and the idea that "all men are created equal." One-fifth of the population in 1776 was enslaved, and at the time he drafted the Declaration, Jefferson himself owned more than one hundred enslaved individuals. Further, the Declaration framed equality as existing only among White men; women and non-White people were entirely left out of a document that referred to Native peoples as "merciless Indian savages" who indiscriminately killed men, women, and children. Nonetheless, the promise of equality for all planted the seeds for future struggles waged by enslaved individuals, women, and many others to bring about its full realization. Much of American history is the story of the slow realization of the promise of equality expressed in the Declaration of Independence.

CLICK AND EXPLORE

Visit Digital History (http://openstax.org/l/fcombatants) to view "The Female Combatants." In this 1776 engraving by an anonymous artist, Great Britain is depicted on the left as a staid, stern matron, while America, on the right, is shown as a half-dressed Native American. Why do you think the artist depicted the two opposing sides this way?

6.2 The Early Years of the Revolution

LEARNING OBJECTIVES

By the end of this section, you will be able to:
- Explain the British and American strategies of 1776 through 1778
- Identify the key battles of the early years of the Revolution

After the British quit Boston, they slowly adopted a strategy to isolate New England from the rest of the colonies and force the insurgents in that region into submission, believing that doing so would end the conflict. At first, British forces focused on taking the principal colonial centers. They began by easily capturing New York City in 1776. The following year, they took over the American capital of Philadelphia. The larger British effort to isolate New England was implemented in 1777. That effort ultimately failed when the British surrendered a force of over five thousand to the Americans in the fall of 1777 at the Battle of Saratoga.

The major campaigns over the next several years took place in the middle colonies of New York, New Jersey, and Pennsylvania, whose populations were sharply divided between Loyalists and Patriots. Revolutionaries faced many hardships as British superiority on the battlefield became evident and the difficulty of funding the war caused strains.

THE BRITISH STRATEGY IN THE MIDDLE COLONIES

After evacuating Boston in March 1776, British forces sailed to Nova Scotia to regroup. They devised a strategy, successfully implemented in 1776, to take New York City. The following year, they planned to end the rebellion by cutting New England off from the rest of the colonies and starving it into submission. Three British armies were to move simultaneously from New York City, Montreal, and Fort Oswego to converge along the Hudson River; British control of that natural boundary would isolate New England.

General William Howe (Figure 6.9), commander in chief of the British forces in America, amassed thirty-two thousand troops on Staten Island in June and July 1776. His brother, Admiral Richard Howe, controlled New York Harbor. Command of New York City and the Hudson River was their goal. In August 1776, General Howe landed his forces on Long Island and easily routed the American Continental Army there in the Battle of Long Island (August 27). The Americans were outnumbered and lacked both military experience and discipline. Sensing victory, General and Admiral Howe arranged a peace conference in September 1776, where Benjamin Franklin, John Adams, and South Carolinian John Rutledge represented the Continental Congress. Despite the Howes' hopes, however, the Americans demanded recognition of their independence, which the Howes were not authorized to grant, and the conference disbanded.

FIGURE 6.9 General William Howe, shown here in a 1777 portrait by Richard Purcell, led British forces in America in the first years of the war.

On September 16, 1776, George Washington's forces held up against the British at the Battle of Harlem Heights. This important American military achievement, a key reversal after the disaster on Long Island, occurred as most of Washington's forces retreated to New Jersey. A few weeks later, on October 28, General Howe's forces defeated Washington's at the Battle of White Plains and New York City fell to the British. For the next seven years, the British made the city the headquarters for their military efforts to defeat the rebellion, which included raids on surrounding areas. In 1777, the British burned Danbury, Connecticut, and in July 1779, they set fire to homes in Fairfield and Norwalk. They held American prisoners aboard ships in the waters around New York City; the death toll was shocking, with thousands perishing in the holds. Meanwhile, New York City served as a haven for Loyalists who disagreed with the effort to break away from the Empire and establish an American republic.

GEORGE WASHINGTON AND THE CONTINENTAL ARMY

When the Second Continental Congress met in Philadelphia in May 1775, members approved the creation of a professional Continental Army with Washington as commander in chief (Figure 6.10). Although sixteen thousand volunteers enlisted, it took several years for the Continental Army to become a truly professional force. In 1775 and 1776, militias still composed the bulk of the Patriots' armed forces, and these soldiers returned home after the summer fighting season, drastically reducing the army's strength.

FIGURE 6.10 This 1775 etching shows George Washington taking command of the Continental Army at Cambridge, Massachusetts, just two weeks after his appointment by the Continental Congress.

That changed in late 1776 and early 1777, when Washington broke with conventional eighteenth-century military tactics that called for fighting in the summer months only. Intent on raising revolutionary morale after the British captured New York City, he launched surprise strikes against British forces in their winter quarters. In Trenton, New Jersey, he led his soldiers across the Delaware River and surprised an encampment of **Hessians**, German mercenaries hired by Great Britain to put down the American rebellion. Beginning the night of December 25, 1776, and continuing into the early hours of December 26, Washington moved on Trenton where the Hessians were encamped. Maintaining the element of surprise by attacking at Christmastime, he defeated them, taking over nine hundred captive. On January 3, 1777, Washington achieved another much-needed victory at the Battle of Princeton. He again broke with eighteenth-century military protocol by attacking unexpectedly after the fighting season had ended.

DEFINING AMERICAN

Thomas Paine on "The American Crisis"

During the American Revolution, following the publication of *Common Sense* in January 1776, Thomas Paine began a series of sixteen pamphlets known collectively as *The American Crisis* (Figure 6.11). He wrote the first volume in 1776, describing the dire situation facing the revolutionaries at the end of that hard year.

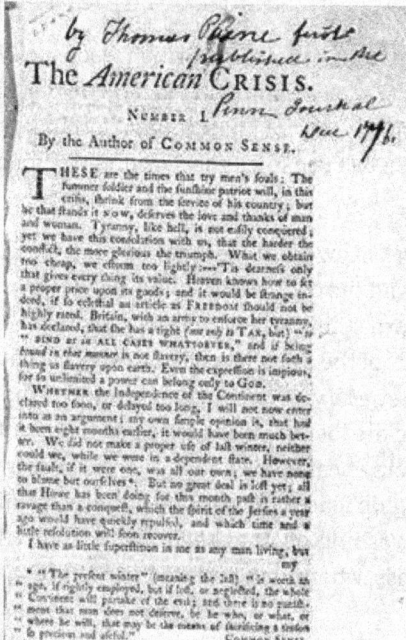

FIGURE 6.11 Thomas Paine wrote the pamphlet *The American Crisis*, the first page of which is shown here, in 1776.

"These are the times that try men's souls. The summer soldier and the sunshine patriot will, in this crisis, shrink from the service of their country; but he that stands it now, deserves the love and thanks of man and woman. . . . Britain, with an army to enforce her tyranny, has declared that she has a right (not only to tax) but "to bind us in all cases whatsoever," and if being bound in that manner, is not slavery, then is there not such a thing as slavery upon earth. Even the expression is impious; for so unlimited a power can belong only to God. . . .

I shall conclude this paper with some miscellaneous remarks on the state of our affairs; and shall begin with asking the following question, Why is it that the enemy have left the New England provinces, and made these middle ones the seat of war? The answer is easy: New England is not infested with Tories, and we are. I have been tender in raising the cry against these men, and used numberless arguments to show them their danger, but it will not do to sacrifice a world either to their folly or their baseness. The period is now arrived, in which either they or we must change our sentiments, or one or both must fall. . . .

By perseverance and fortitude we have the prospect of a glorious issue; by cowardice and submission, the sad choice of a variety of evils—a ravaged country—a depopulated city—habitations without safety, and slavery without hope—our homes turned into barracks and bawdy-houses for Hessians, and a future race to provide for, whose fathers we shall doubt of. Look on this picture and weep over it! and if there yet remains one thoughtless wretch who believes it not, let him suffer it unlamented.

—Thomas Paine, "The American Crisis," December 23, 1776"

What topics does Paine address in this pamphlet? What was his purpose in writing? What does he write about Tories (Loyalists), and why does he consider them a problem?

🔗 CLICK AND EXPLORE

Visit [Wikisource (http://openstax.org/l/amcrisis)](http://openstax.org/l/amcrisis) to read the rest of Thomas Paine's first *American Crisis* pamphlet, as well as the other fifteen in the series.

PHILADELPHIA AND SARATOGA: BRITISH AND AMERICAN VICTORIES

In August 1777, General Howe brought fifteen thousand British troops to Chesapeake Bay as part of his plan to take Philadelphia, where the Continental Congress met. That fall, the British defeated Washington's soldiers in the Battle of Brandywine Creek and took control of Philadelphia, forcing the Continental Congress to flee. During the winter of 1777–1778, the British occupied the city, and Washington's army camped at Valley Forge, Pennsylvania.

Washington's winter at Valley Forge was a low point for the American forces. A lack of supplies weakened the men, and disease took a heavy toll. Amid the cold, hunger, and sickness, soldiers deserted in droves. On February 16, Washington wrote to George Clinton, governor of New York: "For some days past, there has been little less than a famine in camp. A part of the army has been a week without any kind of flesh & the rest three or four days. Naked and starving as they are, we cannot enough admire the incomparable patience and fidelity of the soldiery, that they have not been ere [before] this excited by their sufferings to a general mutiny and dispersion." Of eleven thousand soldiers encamped at Valley Forge, twenty-five hundred died of starvation, malnutrition, and disease. As Washington feared, nearly one hundred soldiers deserted every week. (Desertions continued, and by 1780, Washington was executing recaptured deserters every Saturday.) The low morale extended all the way to Congress, where some wanted to replace Washington with a more seasoned leader.

Assistance came to Washington and his soldiers in February 1778 in the form of the Prussian soldier Friedrich Wilhelm von Steuben (Figure 6.12). Baron von Steuben was an experienced military man, and he implemented a thorough training course for Washington's ragtag troops. By drilling a small corps of soldiers and then having them train others, he finally transformed the Continental Army into a force capable of standing up to the professional British and Hessian soldiers. His drill manual—*Regulations for the Order and Discipline of the Troops of the United States*—informed military practices in the United States for the next several decades.

FIGURE 6.12 Prussian soldier Friedrich Wilhelm von Steuben, shown here in a 1786 portrait by Ralph Earl, was instrumental in transforming Washington's Continental Army into a professional armed force.

CLICK AND EXPLORE

Explore Friedrich Wilhelm von Steuben's Revolutionary War Drill Manual (http://openstax.org/l/steuben) to understand how von Steuben was able to transform the Continental Army into a professional fighting force. Note the tremendous amount of precision and detail in von Steuben's descriptions.

Meanwhile, the campaign to sever New England from the rest of the colonies had taken an unexpected turn during the fall of 1777. The British had attempted to implement the plan, drawn up by Lord George Germain and Prime Minister Lord North, to isolate New England with the combined forces of three armies. One army, led by General John Burgoyne, would march south from Montreal. A second force, led by Colonel Barry St. Leger and made up of British troops and Iroquois, would march east from Fort Oswego on the banks of Lake Ontario. A third force, led by General Sir Henry Clinton, would march north from New York City. The armies would converge at Albany and effectively cut the rebellion in two by isolating New England. This northern campaign fell victim to competing strategies, however, as General Howe had meanwhile decided to take Philadelphia. His decision to capture that city siphoned off troops that would have been vital to the overall success of the campaign in 1777.

The British plan to isolate New England ended in disaster. St. Leger's efforts to bring his force of British regulars, Loyalist fighters, and Iroquois allies east to link up with General Burgoyne failed, and he retreated to Quebec. Burgoyne's forces encountered ever-stiffer resistance as he made his way south from Montreal, down Lake Champlain and the upper Hudson River corridor. Although they did capture Fort Ticonderoga when American forces retreated, Burgoyne's army found themselves surrounded by a sea of colonial militias in Saratoga, New York. In the meantime, the small British force under Clinton that left New York City to aid Burgoyne advanced slowly up the Hudson River, failing to provide the much-needed support for the troops at Saratoga. On October 17, 1777, Burgoyne surrendered his five thousand soldiers to the Continental Army (Figure 6.13).

FIGURE 6.13 This German engraving, created by Daniel Chodowiecki in 1784, shows British soldiers laying down their arms before the American forces.

The American victory at the Battle of Saratoga was the major turning point in the war. This victory convinced the French to recognize American independence and form a military alliance with the new nation, which changed the course of the war by opening the door to badly needed military support from France. Still smarting from their defeat by Britain in the Seven Years' War, the French supplied the United States with gunpowder and money, as well as soldiers and naval forces that proved decisive in the defeat of Great Britain. The French also contributed military leaders, including the Marquis de Lafayette, who arrived in America in 1777 as a volunteer and served as Washington's aide-de-camp.

The war quickly became more difficult for the British, who had to fight the rebels in North America as well as the French in the Caribbean. Following France's lead, Spain joined the war against Great Britain in 1779, though it did not recognize American independence until 1783. The Dutch Republic also began to support the American revolutionaries and signed a treaty of commerce with the United States in 1782.

Great Britain's effort to isolate New England in 1777 failed. In June 1778, the occupying British force in Philadelphia evacuated and returned to New York City in order to better defend that city, and the British then turned their attention to the southern colonies.

6.3 War in the South

LEARNING OBJECTIVES

By the end of this section, you will be able to:
- Outline the British southern strategy and its results
- Describe key American victories and the end of the war
- Identify the main terms of the Treaty of Paris (1783)

By 1778, the war had turned into a stalemate. Although some in Britain, including Prime Minister Lord North, wanted peace, King George III demanded that the colonies be brought to obedience. To break the deadlock, the British revised their strategy and turned their attention to the southern colonies, where they could expect more support from Loyalists. The southern colonies soon became the center of the fighting. The southern strategy brought the British success at first, but thanks to the leadership of George Washington and General Nathanael Greene and the crucial assistance of French forces, the Continental Army defeated the British at Yorktown, effectively ending further large-scale operations during the war.

GEORGIA AND SOUTH CAROLINA

The British architect of the war strategy, Lord George Germain, believed Britain would gain the upper hand with the support of Loyalists, enslaved people, and Native American allies in the South, and indeed, this southern strategy initially achieved great success. The British began their southern campaign by capturing Savannah, the capital of Georgia, in December 1778. In Georgia, they found support from thousands of enslaved individuals who ran to the British side to escape their bondage. As the British regained political control in Georgia, they forced the inhabitants to swear allegiance to the king and formed twenty Loyalist regiments. The Continental Congress had suggested that enslaved people be given freedom if they joined the Patriot army against the British, but revolutionaries in Georgia and South Carolina refused to consider this proposal. Once again, the Revolution served to further divisions over race and slavery.

After taking Georgia, the British turned their attention to South Carolina. Before the Revolution, South Carolina had been starkly divided between the backcountry, which harbored revolutionary partisans, and the coastal regions, where Loyalists remained a powerful force. Waves of violence rocked the backcountry from the late 1770s into the early 1780s. The Revolution provided an opportunity for residents to fight over their local resentments and antagonisms with murderous consequences. Revenge killings and the destruction of property became mainstays in the savage civil war that gripped the South.

In April 1780, a British force of eight thousand soldiers besieged American forces in Charleston (Figure 6.14). After six weeks of the Siege of Charleston, the British triumphed. General Benjamin Lincoln, who led the effort for the revolutionaries, had to surrender his entire force, the largest American loss during the entire war. Many of the defeated Americans were placed in jails or in British prison ships anchored in Charleston Harbor. The British established a military government in Charleston under the command of General Sir Henry Clinton. From this base, Clinton ordered General Charles Cornwallis to subdue the rest of South Carolina.

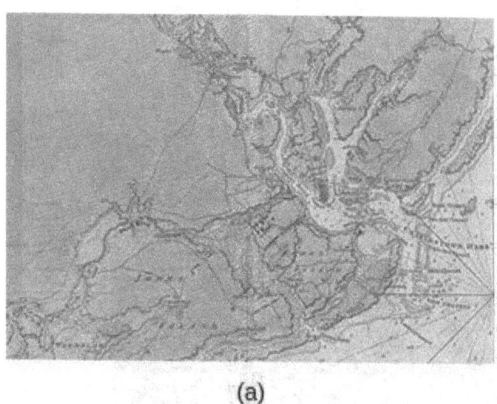 
(a) (b)

FIGURE 6.14 This 1780 map of Charleston (a), which shows details of the Continental defenses, was probably drawn by British engineers in anticipation of the attack on the city. The Siege of Charleston was one of a series of defeats for the Continental forces in the South, which led the Continental Congress to place General Nathanael Greene (b), shown here in a 1783 portrait by Charles Wilson Peale, in command in late 1780. Greene led his troops to two crucial victories.

The disaster at Charleston led the Continental Congress to change leadership by placing General Horatio Gates in charge of American forces in the South. However, General Gates fared no better than General Lincoln; at the Battle of Camden, South Carolina, in August 1780, Cornwallis forced General Gates to retreat into North Carolina. Camden was one of the worst disasters suffered by American armies during the entire Revolutionary War. Congress again changed military leadership, this time by placing General Nathanael Greene (Figure 6.14) in command in December 1780.

As the British had hoped, large numbers of Loyalists helped ensure the success of the southern strategy, and thousands of enslaved individuals seeking freedom arrived to aid Cornwallis's army. However, the war turned in the Americans' favor in 1781. General Greene realized that to defeat Cornwallis, he did not have to win a single battle. So long as he remained in the field, he could continue to destroy isolated British forces. Greene therefore made a strategic decision to divide his own troops to wage war—and the strategy worked. American forces under General Daniel Morgan decisively beat the British at the Battle of Cowpens in South Carolina. General Cornwallis now abandoned his strategy of defeating the backcountry rebels in South Carolina. Determined to destroy Greene's army, he gave chase as Greene strategically retreated north into North Carolina. At the Battle of Guilford Courthouse in March 1781, the British prevailed on the battlefield but suffered extensive losses, an outcome that paralleled the Battle of Bunker Hill nearly six years earlier in June 1775.

YORKTOWN

In the summer of 1781, Cornwallis moved his army to **Yorktown**, Virginia. He expected the Royal Navy to transport his army to New York, where he thought he would join General Sir Henry Clinton. Yorktown was a tobacco port on a peninsula, and Cornwallis believed the British navy would be able to keep the coast clear of rebel ships. Sensing an opportunity, a combined French and American force of sixteen thousand men swarmed the peninsula in September 1781. Washington raced south with his forces, now a disciplined army, as did the Marquis de Lafayette and the Comte de Rochambeau with their French troops. The French Admiral de Grasse sailed his naval force into Chesapeake Bay, preventing Lord Cornwallis from taking a seaward escape route.

In October 1781, the American forces began the battle for Yorktown, and after a siege that lasted eight days, Lord Cornwallis capitulated on October 19 (Figure 6.15). Tradition says that during the surrender of his troops, the British band played "The World Turned Upside Down," a song that befitted the Empire's unexpected reversal of fortune.

FIGURE 6.15 The 1820 painting above, by John Trumbull, is titled *Surrender of Lord Cornwallis*, but Cornwallis actually sent his general, Charles O'Hara, to perform the ceremonial surrendering of the sword. The painting depicts General Benjamin Lincoln holding out his hand to receive the sword. General George Washington is in the background on the brown horse, since he refused to accept the sword from anyone but Cornwallis himself.

DEFINING AMERICAN

"The World Turned Upside Down"

"The World Turned Upside Down," reputedly played during the surrender of the British at Yorktown, was a traditional English ballad from the seventeenth century. It was also the theme of a popular British print that circulated in the 1790s (Figure 6.16).

FIGURE 6.16 In many of the images in this popular print, entitled "The World Turned Upside Down or the Folly of Man," animals and humans have switched places. In one, children take care of their parents, while in another, the sun, moon, and stars appear below the earth.

Why do you think these images were popular in Great Britain in the decade following the Revolutionary War? What would these images imply to Americans?

🔗 CLICK AND EXPLORE

Visit the Public Domain Review (http://openstax.org/l/worldupside) to explore the images in an eighteenth-century British chapbook (a pamphlet for tracts or ballads) titled "The World Turned Upside Down." The chapbook is illustrated with woodcuts similar to those in the popular print mentioned above.

THE TREATY OF PARIS

The British defeat at Yorktown made the outcome of the war all but certain. In light of the American victory, the Parliament of Great Britain voted to end further military operations against the rebels and to begin peace negotiations. Support for the war effort had come to an end, and British military forces began to evacuate the former American colonies in 1782. When hostilities had ended, Washington resigned as commander in chief and returned to his Virginia home.

In April 1782, Benjamin Franklin, John Adams, and John Jay had begun informal peace negotiations in Paris. Officials from Great Britain and the United States finalized the treaty in 1783, signing the Treaty of Paris (Figure 6.17) in September of that year. The treaty recognized the independence of the United States; placed the western, eastern, northern, and southern boundaries of the nation at the Mississippi River, the Atlantic Ocean, Canada, and Florida, respectively; and gave New Englanders fishing rights in the waters off Newfoundland. Under the terms of the treaty, individual states were encouraged to refrain from persecuting Loyalists and to return their confiscated property.

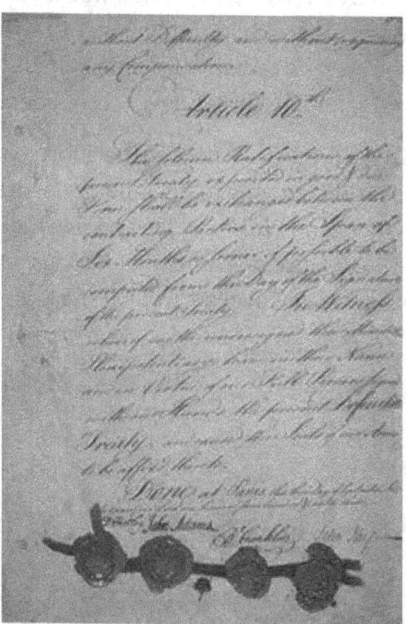

FIGURE 6.17 The last page of the Treaty of Paris, signed on September 3, 1783, contained the signatures and seals of representatives for both the British and the Americans. From right to left, the seals pictured belong to David Hartley, who represented Great Britain, and John Adams, Benjamin Franklin, and John Jay for the Americans.

6.4 Identity during the American Revolution

LEARNING OBJECTIVES

By the end of this section, you will be able to:
- Explain Loyalist and Patriot sentiments
- Identify different groups that participated in the Revolutionary War

The American Revolution in effect created multiple civil wars. Many of the resentments and antagonisms that fed these conflicts predated the Revolution, and the outbreak of war acted as the catalyst they needed to burst forth. In particular, the middle colonies of New York, New Jersey, and Pennsylvania had deeply divided populations. Loyalty to Great Britain came in many forms, from wealthy elites who enjoyed the prewar status quo to escaped enslaved people who desired the freedom that the British offered.

LOYALISTS

Historians disagree on what percentage of colonists were Loyalists; estimates range from 20 percent to over 30 percent. In general, however, of British America's population of 2.5 million, roughly one-third remained loyal to Great Britain, while another third committed themselves to the cause of independence. The remaining third remained apathetic, content to continue with their daily lives as best they could and preferring not to engage in the struggle.

Many Loyalists were royal officials and merchants with extensive business ties to Great Britain, who viewed themselves as the rightful and just defenders of the British constitution. Others simply resented local business and political rivals who supported the Revolution, viewing the rebels as hypocrites and schemers who selfishly used the break with the Empire to increase their fortunes. In New York's Hudson Valley, animosity among the tenants of estates owned by Revolutionary leaders turned them to the cause of King and Empire.

During the war, all the states passed **confiscation acts**, which gave the new revolutionary governments in the former colonies the right to seize Loyalist land and property. To ferret out Loyalists, revolutionary governments also passed laws requiring the male population to take oaths of allegiance to the new states. Those who refused lost their property and were often imprisoned or made to work for the new local revolutionary order.

William Franklin, Benjamin Franklin's only surviving son, remained loyal to Crown and Empire and served as royal governor of New Jersey, a post he secured with his father's help. During the war, revolutionaries imprisoned William in Connecticut; however, he remained steadfast in his allegiance to Great Britain and moved to England after the Revolution. He and his father never reconciled.

As many as nineteen thousand colonists served the British in the effort to put down the rebellion, and after the Revolution, as many as 100,000 colonists left, moving to England or north to Canada rather than staying in the new United States (Figure 6.18). Eight thousand White people and five thousand free Black people went to Britain. Over thirty thousand went to Canada, transforming that nation from predominately French to predominantly British. Another sizable group of Loyalists went to the British West Indies, taking enslaved people with them.

FIGURE 6.18 *The Coming of the Loyalists*, a ca. 1880 work that artist Henry Sandham created at least a century after the Revolution, shows Anglo-American colonists arriving by ship in New Brunswick, Canada.

MY STORY

Hannah Ingraham on Removing to Nova Scotia

Hannah Ingraham was eleven years old in 1783, when her Loyalist family removed from New York to Ste. Anne's Point in the colony of Nova Scotia. Later in life, she compiled her memories of that time.

"[Father] said we were to go to Nova Scotia, that a ship was ready to take us there, so we made all haste to get ready.... Then on Tuesday, suddenly the house was surrounded by rebels and father was taken prisoner and carried away.... When morning came, they said he was free to go.

We had five wagon loads carried down the Hudson in a sloop and then we went on board the transport that was to bring us to Saint John. I was just eleven years old when we left our farm to come here. It was the last transport of the season and had on board all those who could not come sooner. The first transports had come in May so the people had all the summer before them to get settled....

We lived in a tent at St. Anne's until father got a house ready.... There was no floor laid, no windows, no chimney, no door, but we had a roof at least. A good fire was blazing and mother had a big loaf of bread and she boiled a kettle of water and put a good piece of butter in a pewter bowl. We toasted the bread and all sat around the bowl and ate our breakfast that morning and mother said: "Thank God we are no longer in dread of having shots fired through our house. This is the sweetest meal I ever tasted for many a day.""

What do these excerpts tell you about life as a Loyalist in New York or as a transplant to Canada?

ENSLAVED PEOPLE AND NATIVE PEOPLE

While some enslaved people who fought for the Patriot cause received their freedom, revolutionary leaders—unlike the British—did not grant these allies their freedom as a matter of course. Washington, the enslaver of more than two hundred people during the Revolution, refused to let enslaved people serve in the army, although he did allow free Black people to serve. (In his will, Washington did free the people he enslaved.) In the new United States, the Revolution largely reinforced a racial identity based on skin color. Whiteness, now a national identity, denoted freedom and stood as the key to power. Blackness, more than ever before, denoted servile status. Indeed, despite their class and ethnic differences, White revolutionaries stood mostly united in their hostility to both Black and Native Americans.

MY STORY

Boyrereau Brinch and Boston King on the Revolutionary War

In the Revolutionary War, some Black people, both free and enslaved, chose to fight for the Americans (Figure 6.19). Others chose to fight for the British, who offered them freedom for joining their cause. Read the excerpts below for the perspective of a Black veteran from each side of the conflict.

FIGURE 6.19 Jean-Baptiste-Antoine de Verger created this 1781 watercolor, which depicts American soldiers at the Siege of Yorktown. Verger was an officer in Rochambeau's army, and his diary holds firsthand accounts of his experiences in the campaigns of 1780 and 1781. This image contains one of the earliest known representations of a Black Continental soldier.

Boyrereau Brinch was captured in Africa at age sixteen and brought to America. He joined the Patriot forces and was honorably discharged and emancipated after the war. He told his story to Benjamin Prentiss, who published it as *The Blind African Slave* in 1810.

"Finally, I was in the battles at Cambridge, White Plains, Monmouth, Princeton, Newark, Frog's Point, Horseneck where I had a ball pass through my knapsack. All which battels [sic] the reader can obtain a more perfect account of in history, than I can give. At last we returned to West Point and were discharged [1783], as the war was over. Thus was I, a slave for five years fighting for liberty. After we were disbanded, I returned to my old master at Woodbury [Connecticut], with whom I lived one year, my services in the American war, having emancipated me from further slavery, and from being bartered or sold. . . . Here I enjoyed the pleasures of a freeman; my food was sweet, my labor pleasure: and one bright gleam of life seemed to shine upon me."

Boston King was a Charleston-born enslaved man who escaped his captor and joined the Loyalists. He made his way to Nova Scotia and later Sierra Leone, where he published his memoirs in 1792. The excerpt below describes his experience in New York after the war.

"When I arrived at New-York, my friends rejoiced to see me once more restored to liberty, and joined me in praising the Lord for his mercy and goodness. . . . [In 1783] the horrors and devastation of war happily terminated, and peace was restored between America and Great Britain, which diffused universal joy among all parties, except us, who had escaped from slavery and taken refuge in the English army; for a report prevailed at New-York, that all the slaves, in number 2000, were to be delivered up to their masters, altho' some of them had been three or four years among the English. This dreadful rumour filled us all with inexpressible anguish and terror, especially when we saw our old masters coming from Virginia, North-Carolina, and other parts, and seizing upon their slaves in the streets of New-York, or even dragging them out of their beds. Many of the slaves had very cruel masters, so that the thoughts of returning home with them embittered life to us. For some days we lost our appetite for food, and sleep departed from our eyes. The English had compassion upon us in the day of distress, and issued out a Proclamation, importing, That all slaves should be free, who had taken refuge in the British lines, and claimed the sanction and privileges of the Proclamations respecting the security and protection of Negroes. In consequence of this, each of us received a certificate from the commanding officer at New-York, which dispelled all our fears, and filled us with joy and gratitude."

What do these two narratives have in common, and how are they different? How do the two men describe freedom?

For enslaved people willing to run away and join the British, the American Revolution offered a unique occasion to escape bondage. Of the half a million enslaved people in the American colonies during the Revolution, twenty thousand joined the British cause. At Yorktown, for instance, thousands of Black troops fought with Lord Cornwallis. People enslaved by George Washington, Thomas Jefferson, Patrick Henry, and other revolutionaries seized the opportunity for freedom and fled to the British side. Between ten and twenty thousand enslaved people gained their freedom because of the Revolution; arguably, the Revolution created the largest slave uprising and the greatest emancipation until the Civil War. After the Revolution, some of these African Loyalists emigrated to Sierra Leone on the west coast of Africa. Others removed to Canada and England. It is also true that people of color made heroic contributions to the cause of American independence. However, while the British offered freedom, most American revolutionaries clung to notions of Black inferiority.

Powerful Native peoples who had allied themselves with the British, including the Mohawk and the Creek, also remained loyal to the Empire. A Mohawk named Joseph Brant, whose given name was Thayendanegea (Figure 6.20), rose to prominence while fighting for the British during the Revolution. He joined forces with Colonel Barry St. Leger during the 1777 campaign, which ended with the surrender of General Burgoyne at Saratoga. After the war, Brant moved to the Six Nations reserve in Canada. From his home on the shores of Lake Ontario, he remained active in efforts to restrict White encroachment onto Native lands. After their defeat, the British did not keep promises they'd made to help their Native American allies keep their territory; in fact, the Treaty of Paris granted the United States huge amounts of supposedly British-owned regions that were actually Native lands.

(a)

(b)

FIGURE 6.20 What similarities can you see in these two portraits of Joseph Brant, one by Gilbert Stuart in 1786 (a) and one by Charles Wilson Peale in 1797 (b)? What are the differences? Why do you think the artists made the specific choices they did?

PATRIOTS

The American revolutionaries (also called Patriots or Whigs) came from many different backgrounds and included merchants, shoemakers, farmers, and sailors. What is extraordinary is the way in which the struggle for independence brought a vast cross-section of society together, animated by a common cause.

During the war, the revolutionaries faced great difficulties, including massive supply problems; clothing, ammunition, tents, and equipment were all hard to come by. After an initial burst of enthusiasm in 1775 and 1776, the shortage of supplies became acute in 1777 through 1779, as Washington's difficult winter at Valley Forge demonstrates.

Funding the war effort also proved very difficult. Whereas the British could pay in gold and silver, the American forces relied on paper money, backed by loans obtained in Europe. This first American money was called **Continental currency**; unfortunately, it quickly fell in value. "Not worth a Continental" soon became a shorthand term for something of no value. The new revolutionary government printed a great amount of this paper money, resulting in runaway inflation. By 1781, inflation was such that 146 Continental dollars were worth only one dollar in gold. The problem grew worse as each former colony, now a revolutionary state, printed its own currency.

WOMEN

In colonial America, women shouldered enormous domestic and child-rearing responsibilities. The war for independence only increased their workload and, in some ways, solidified their roles. Rebel leaders required women to produce articles for war—everything from clothing to foodstuffs—while also keeping their homesteads going. This was not an easy task when their husbands and sons were away fighting. Women were also expected to provide food and lodging for armies and to nurse wounded soldiers.

The Revolution opened some new doors for women, however, as they took on public roles usually reserved for men. The Daughters of Liberty, an informal organization formed in the mid-1760s to oppose British revenue-raising measures, worked tirelessly to support the war effort. Esther DeBerdt Reed of Philadelphia, wife of Governor Joseph Reed, formed the Ladies Association of Philadelphia and led a fundraising drive to provide sorely needed supplies to the Continental Army. In "The Sentiments of an American Woman" (1780), she wrote to other women, "The time is arrived to display the same sentiments which animated us at the beginning of the Revolution, when we renounced the use of teas, however agreeable to our taste, rather than receive them from our persecutors; when we made it appear to them that we placed former necessaries in the rank of superfluities, when our liberty was interested; when our republican and laborious hands spun the flax, prepared the linen intended for the use of our soldiers; when exiles and fugitives we supported with courage all the evils which are the concomitants of war." Reed and other women in Philadelphia raised almost $300,000 in Continental money for the war.

CLICK AND EXPLORE

Read the entire text of Esther Reed's "The Sentiments of an American Woman" (http://openstax.org/l/estherreed) on a page hosted by the University of Michigan-Dearborn.

Women who did not share Reed's prominent status nevertheless played key economic roles by producing homespun cloth and food. During shortages, some women formed mobs and wrested supplies from those who hoarded them. Crowds of women beset merchants and demanded fair prices for goods; if a merchant refused, a riot would ensue. Still other women accompanied the army as "camp followers," serving as cooks, washerwomen, and nurses. A few also took part in combat and proved their equality with men through violence against the hated British.

Key Terms

confiscation acts state-wide acts that made it legal for state governments to seize Loyalists' property
Continental currency the paper currency that the Continental government printed to fund the Revolution
Dunmore's Proclamation the decree signed by Lord Dunmore, the royal governor of Virginia, which proclaimed that any enslaved or indentured servants who fought on the side of the British would be rewarded with their freedom
Hessians German mercenaries hired by Great Britain to put down the American rebellion
Mecklenburg Resolves North Carolina's declaration of rebellion against Great Britain
minutemen colonial militias prepared to mobilize and fight the British with a minute's notice
popular sovereignty the practice of allowing the citizens of a state or territory to decide issues based on the principle of majority rule
republicanism a political philosophy that holds that states should be governed by representatives, not a monarch; as a social philosophy, republicanism required civic virtue of its citizens
thirteen colonies the British colonies in North America that declared independence from Great Britain in 1776, which included Connecticut, Delaware, Georgia, Maryland, the province of Massachusetts Bay, New Hampshire, New Jersey, New York, North Carolina, Pennsylvania, Rhode Island and Providence Plantations, South Carolina, and Virginia
Yorktown the Virginia port where British General Cornwallis surrendered to American forces

Summary

6.1 Britain's Law-and-Order Strategy and Its Consequences

Until Parliament passed the Coercive Acts in 1774, most colonists still thought of themselves as proud subjects of the strong British Empire. However, the Coercive (or Intolerable) Acts, which Parliament enacted to punish Massachusetts for failing to pay for the destruction of the tea, convinced many colonists that Great Britain was indeed threatening to stifle their liberty. In Massachusetts and other New England colonies, militias like the minutemen prepared for war by stockpiling weapons and ammunition. After the first loss of life at the battles of Lexington and Concord in April 1775, skirmishes continued throughout the colonies. When Congress met in Philadelphia in July 1776, its members signed the Declaration of Independence, officially breaking ties with Great Britain and declaring their intention to be self-governing.

6.2 The Early Years of the Revolution

The British successfully implemented the first part of their strategy to isolate New England when they took New York City in the fall of 1776. For the next seven years, they used New York as a base of operations, expanding their control to Philadelphia in the winter of 1777. After suffering through a terrible winter in 1777–1778 in Valley Forge, Pennsylvania, American forces were revived with help from Baron von Steuben, a Prussian military officer who helped transform the Continental Army into a professional fighting force. The effort to cut off New England from the rest of the colonies failed with the General Burgoyne's surrender at Saratoga in October 1777. After Saratoga, the struggle for independence gained a powerful ally when France agreed to recognize the United States as a new nation and began to send much-needed military support. The entrance of France—Britain's archrival in the contest of global empire—into the American fight helped to turn the tide of the war in favor of the revolutionaries.

6.3 War in the South

The British gained momentum in the war when they turned their military efforts against the southern colonies. They scored repeated victories in the coastal towns, where they found legions of supporters, including people escaping bondage. As in other colonies, however, control of major seaports did not mean the British could control the interior. Fighting in the southern colonies devolved into a merciless civil war as the Revolution opened the floodgates of pent-up anger and resentment between frontier residents and those along the coastal regions. The southern campaign came to an end at Yorktown when Cornwallis surrendered to American forces.

6.4 Identity during the American Revolution

The American Revolution divided the colonists as much as it united them, with Loyalists (or Tories) joining the British forces against the Patriots (or revolutionaries). Both sides included a broad cross-section of the population. However, Great Britain was able to convince many to join its forces by promising them freedom, something the southern revolutionaries would not agree to do. The war provided new opportunities, as well as new challenges, for enslaved and free Black people, women, and Native peoples. After the war, many Loyalists fled the American colonies, heading across the Atlantic to England, north to Canada, or south to the West Indies.

Review Questions

1. How did British General Thomas Gage attempt to deal with the uprising in Massachusetts in 1774?
    A. He offered the rebels land on the Maine frontier in return for loyalty to England.
    B. He allowed for town meetings in an attempt to appease the rebels.
    C. He attempted to seize arms and munitions from the colonial insurgents.
    D. He ordered his troops to burn Boston to the ground to show the determination of Britain.

2. Which of the following was *not* a result of Dunmore's Proclamation?
    A. Enslaved people joined Dunmore to fight for the British.
    B. A majority of enslaved people in the colonies won their freedom.
    C. Patriot forces increased their commitment to independence.
    D. Both slaveholding and non-slaveholding White people feared a rebellion.

3. Which of the following is *not* true of a republic?
    A. A republic has no hereditary ruling class.
    B. A republic relies on the principle of popular sovereignty.
    C. Representatives chosen by the people lead the republic.
    D. A republic is governed by a monarch and the royal officials he or she appoints.

4. What are the main arguments that Thomas Paine makes in his pamphlet *Common Sense*? Why was this pamphlet so popular?

5. Which city served as the base for British operations for most of the war?
    A. Boston
    B. New York
    C. Philadelphia
    D. Saratoga

6. What battle turned the tide of war in favor of the Americans?
    A. the Battle of Saratoga
    B. the Battle of Brandywine Creek
    C. the Battle of White Plains
    D. the Battle of Valley Forge

7. Which term describes German soldiers hired by Great Britain to put down the American rebellion?
   A. Patriots
   B. Royalists
   C. Hessians
   D. Loyalists

8. Describe the British strategy in the early years of the war and explain whether or not it succeeded.

9. How did George Washington's military tactics help him to achieve success?

10. Which American general is responsible for improving the American military position in the South?
    A. John Burgoyne
    B. Nathanael Greene
    C. Wilhelm Frederick von Steuben
    D. Charles Cornwallis

11. Describe the British southern strategy and its results.

12. Which of the following statements best represents the division between Patriots and Loyalists?
    A. Most American colonists were Patriots, with only a few traditionalists remaining loyal to the King and Empire.
    B. Most American colonists were Loyalists, with only a few firebrand revolutionaries leading the charge for independence.
    C. American colonists were divided among those who wanted independence, those who wanted to remain part of the British Empire, and those who were neutral.
    D. The vast majority of American colonists were neutral and didn't take a side between Loyalists and Patriots.

13. Which of the following is *not* one of the tasks women performed during the Revolution?
    A. holding government offices
    B. maintaining their homesteads
    C. feeding, quartering, and nursing soldiers
    D. raising funds for the war effort

Critical Thinking Questions

14. How did the colonists manage to triumph in their battle for independence despite Great Britain's military might? If any of these factors had been different, how might it have affected the outcome of the war?

15. How did the condition of certain groups, such as women, Black people, and Native people, reveal a contradiction in the Declaration of Independence?

16. What was the effect and importance of Great Britain's promise of freedom to enslaved people who joined the British side?

17. How did the Revolutionary War provide both new opportunities and new challenges for enslaved and free Black people in America?

18. Describe the ideology of republicanism. As a political philosophy, how did republicanism compare to the system that prevailed in Great Britain?

19. Describe the backgrounds and philosophies of Patriots and Loyalists. Why did colonists with such diverse individual interests unite in support of their respective causes? What might different groups of Patriots and Loyalists, depending upon their circumstances, have hoped to achieve by winning the war?

Creating Republican Governments, 1776–1790

7

FIGURE 7.1 John Trumbull, Washington's aide-de-camp, painted this wartime image of Washington on a promontory above the Hudson River. Just behind Washington, enslaved William "Billy" Lee has his eyes firmly fixed on his slaveholder. In the far background, British warships fire on an American fort.

CHAPTER OUTLINE

7.1 Common Sense: From Monarchy to an American Republic
7.2 How Much Revolutionary Change?
7.3 Debating Democracy
7.4 The Constitutional Convention and Federal Constitution

INTRODUCTION After the Revolutionary War, the ideology that "all men are created equal" failed to match up with reality, as the revolutionary generation could not solve the contradictions of freedom and slavery in the new United States. Trumbull's 1780 painting of George Washington (Figure 7.1) hints at some of these contradictions. What attitude do you think Trumbull was trying to convey? Why did Trumbull include Billy Lee, a person whom Washington enslaved, and what does Lee represent in this painting?

During the 1770s and 1780s, Americans took bold steps to define American equality. Each state held constitutional conventions and crafted state constitutions that defined how government would operate and who could participate in political life. Many elite revolutionaries recoiled in horror from the idea of majority rule—the basic principle of democracy—fearing that it would effectively create a "mob rule" that would bring about the ruin of the hard-fought struggle for independence. Statesmen everywhere believed that a republic should replace the British monarchy: a government where the important affairs would be entrusted only to representative men of learning and refinement.

7.1 Common Sense: From Monarchy to an American Republic

LEARNING OBJECTIVES

By the end of this section, you will be able to:
- Compare and contrast monarchy and republican government
- Describe the tenets of republicanism

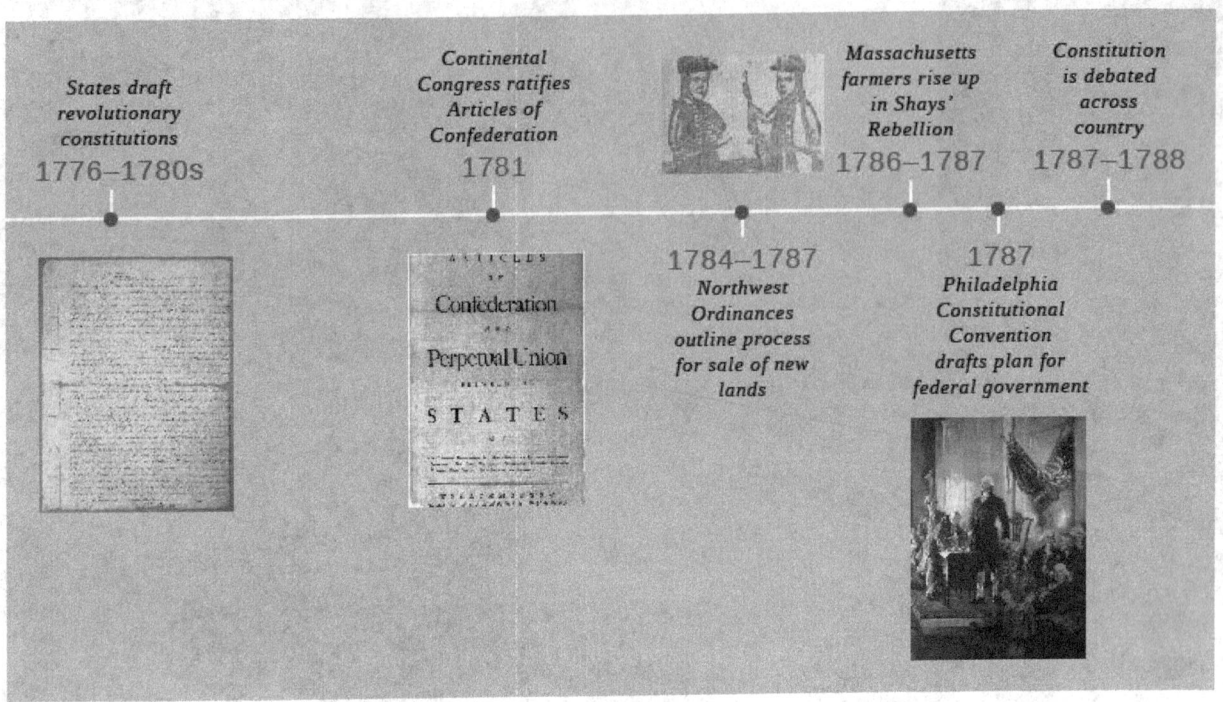

FIGURE 7.2

While monarchies dominated eighteenth-century Europe, American revolutionaries were determined to find an alternative to this method of government. Radical pamphleteer Thomas Paine, whose enormously popular essay *Common Sense* was first published in January 1776, advocated a republic: a state without a king. Six months later, Jefferson's Declaration of Independence affirmed the break with England but did not suggest what form of government should replace monarchy, the only system most English colonists had ever known. In the late eighteenth century, republics were few and far between. Genoa, Venice, and the Dutch Republic provided examples of states without monarchs, but many European Enlightenment thinkers questioned the stability of a republic. Nonetheless, after their break from Great Britain, Americans turned to republicanism for their new government.

REPUBLICANISM AS A POLITICAL PHILOSOPHY

Monarchy rests on the practice of dynastic succession, in which the monarch's child or other relative inherits the throne. Contested dynastic succession produced chronic conflict and warfare in Europe. In the eighteenth century, well-established monarchs ruled most of Europe and, according to tradition, were obligated to protect and guide their subjects. However, by the mid-1770s, many American colonists believed that George III, the king of Great Britain, had failed to do so. Patriots believed the British monarchy under George III had been corrupted and the king turned into a tyrant who cared nothing for the traditional liberties afforded to members of the British Empire. The disaffection from monarchy explains why a republic appeared a better alternative to the revolutionaries.

American revolutionaries looked to the past for inspiration for their break with the British monarchy and their adoption of a republican form of government. The Roman Republic provided guidance. Much like the Americans in their struggle against Britain, Romans had thrown off monarchy and created a republic in which Roman citizens would appoint or select the leaders who would represent them.

CLICK AND EXPLORE

Visit the Metropolitan Museum of Art (http://openstax.org/l/ceracchi) to see a Roman-style bust of George Washington, complete with toga. In 1791, Italian sculptor Giuseppe Ceracchi visited Philadelphia, hoping the government might commission a monument of his creation. He did not succeed, but the bust of Washington, one of the ones he produced to demonstrate his skill, illustrates the connection between the American and Roman republics that revolutionaries made.

While republicanism offered an alternative to monarchy, it was also an alternative to **democracy**, a system of government characterized by **majority rule**, where the majority of citizens have the power to make decisions binding upon the whole. To many revolutionaries, especially wealthy landowners, merchants, and planters, democracy did not offer a good replacement for monarchy. Indeed, **conservative Whigs** defined themselves in opposition to democracy, which they equated with anarchy. In the tenth in a series of essays later known as *The Federalist Papers*, Virginian James Madison wrote: "Democracies have ever been spectacles of turbulence and contention; have ever been found incompatible with personal security or the rights of property; and have in general been as short in their lives as they have been violent in their deaths." Many shared this perspective and worked hard to keep democratic tendencies in check. It is easy to understand why democracy seemed threatening: majority rule can easily overpower minority rights, and the wealthy few had reason to fear that a hostile and envious majority could seize and redistribute their wealth.

While many now assume the United States was founded as a democracy, history, as always, is more complicated. Conservative Whigs believed in government by a patrician class, a ruling group composed of a small number of privileged families. **Radical Whigs** favored broadening the popular participation in political life and pushed for democracy. The great debate after independence was secured centered on this question: Who should rule in the new American republic?

REPUBLICANISM AS A SOCIAL PHILOSOPHY

According to political theory, a republic requires its citizens to cultivate virtuous behavior; if the people are virtuous, the republic will survive. If the people become corrupt, the republic will fall. Whether republicanism succeeded or failed in the United States would depend on civic virtue and an educated citizenry. Revolutionary leaders agreed that the ownership of property provided one way to measure an individual's virtue, arguing that property holders had the greatest stake in society and therefore could be trusted to make decisions for it. By the same token, non-property holders, they believed, should have very little to do with government. In other words, unlike a democracy, in which the mass of non-property holders could exercise the political right to vote, a republic would limit political rights to property holders. In this way, republicanism exhibited a bias toward the elite, a preference that is understandable given the colonial legacy. During colonial times, wealthy planters and merchants in the American colonies had looked to the British ruling class, whose social order demanded deference from those of lower rank, as a model of behavior. Old habits died hard.

DEFINING AMERICAN

Benjamin Franklin's Thirteen Virtues for Character Development

In the 1780s, Benjamin Franklin carefully defined thirteen virtues to help guide his countrymen in maintaining a virtuous republic. His choice of thirteen is telling since he wrote for the citizens of the thirteen new American republics. These virtues were:

"1. Temperance. Eat not to dullness; drink not to elevation.
2. Silence. Speak not but what may benefit others or yourself; avoid trifling conversation.
3. Order. Let all your things have their places; let each part of your business have its time.
4. Resolution. Resolve to perform what you ought; perform without fail what you resolve.
5. Frugality. Make no expense but to do good to others or yourself; i.e., waste nothing.
6. Industry. Lose no time; be always employ'd in something useful; cut off all unnecessary actions.
7. Sincerity. Use no hurtful deceit; think innocently and justly, and, if you speak, speak accordingly.
8. Justice. Wrong none by doing injuries, or omitting the benefits that are your duty.
9. Moderation. Avoid extremes; forbear resenting injuries so much as you think they deserve.
10. Cleanliness. Tolerate no uncleanliness in body, cloaths, or habitation.
11. Tranquillity. Be not disturbed at trifles, or at accidents common or unavoidable.
12. Chastity. Rarely use venery but for health or offspring, never to dullness, weakness, or the injury of your own or another's peace or reputation.
13. Humility. Imitate Jesus and Socrates."

Franklin's thirteen virtues suggest that hard work and good behavior will bring success. What factors does Franklin ignore? How would he likely address a situation in which children inherit great wealth rather than working for it? How do Franklin's values help to define the notion of republican virtue?

CLICK AND EXPLORE

Check how well you are demonstrating all thirteen of Franklin's virtues (http://openstax.org/l/13virtues) on thirteenvirtues.com, where you can register to track your progress.

George Washington served as a role model par excellence for the new republic, embodying the exceptional talent and public virtue prized under the political and social philosophy of republicanism. He did not seek to become the new king of America; instead he retired as commander in chief of the Continental Army and returned to his Virginia estate at Mount Vernon to resume his life among the planter elite. Washington modeled his behavior on that of the Roman aristocrat Cincinnatus, a representative of the patrician or ruling class, who had also retired from public service in the Roman Republic and returned to his estate to pursue agricultural life.

The aristocratic side of republicanism—and the belief that the true custodians of public virtue were those who had served in the military—found expression in the Society of the Cincinnati, of which Washington was the first president general (Figure 7.3). Founded in 1783, the society admitted only officers of the Continental Army and the French forces, not militia members or minutemen. Following the rule of primogeniture, the eldest sons of members inherited their fathers' memberships. The society still exists today and retains the motto *Omnia relinquit servare rempublicam* ("He relinquished everything to save the Republic").

FIGURE 7.3 This membership certificate for the Society of the Cincinnati commemorates "the great Event which gave Independence to North America."

7.2 How Much Revolutionary Change?

LEARNING OBJECTIVES

By the end of this section, you will be able to:
- Describe the status of women in the new republic
- Describe the status of non-White people in the new republic

Elite republican revolutionaries did not envision a completely new society; traditional ideas and categories of race and gender, order and decorum remained firmly entrenched among members of their privileged class. Many Americans rejected the elitist and aristocratic republican order, however, and advocated radical changes. Their efforts represented a groundswell of sentiment for greater equality, a part of the democratic impulse unleashed by the Revolution.

THE STATUS OF WOMEN

In eighteenth-century America, as in Great Britain, the legal status of married women was defined as **coverture**, meaning a married woman (or *feme covert*) had no legal or economic status independent of her husband. She could not conduct business or buy and sell property. Her husband controlled any property she brought to the marriage, although he could not sell it without her agreement. Married women's status as *femes covert* did not change as a result of the Revolution, and wives remained economically dependent on their husbands. The women of the newly independent nation did not call for the right to vote, but some, especially the wives of elite republican statesmen, began to agitate for equality under the law between husbands and wives, and for the same educational opportunities as men.

Some women hoped to overturn coverture. From her home in Braintree, Massachusetts, Abigail Adams (Figure 7.4) wrote to her husband, Whig leader John Adams, in 1776, "In the new code of laws which I suppose it will be necessary for you to make, I desire you would remember the ladies and be more generous and favorable to them than your ancestor. Do not put such unlimited power in the husbands. Remember, all men would be tyrants if they could." Abigail Adams ran the family homestead during the Revolution, but she did not have the ability to conduct business without her husband's consent. Elsewhere in the famous 1776 letter quoted above, she speaks of the difficulties of running the homestead when her husband is away. Her frustration grew when her husband responded in an April 1776 letter: "As to your extraordinary Code of Laws, I cannot but laugh. We have been told that our Struggle has loosened the bands of Government every where. That Children and Apprentices were disobedient—that schools and Colledges were grown turbulent—that Indians slighted their Guardians and Negroes grew insolent to their Masters. But your Letter was the first Intimation that another Tribe more numerous and powerfull than all the rest were grown discontented. . . . Depend on it, We know better than to repeal our Masculine systems."

(a) (b)

FIGURE 7.4 Abigail Adams (a), shown here in a 1766 portrait by Benjamin Blythe, is best remembered for her eloquent letters to her husband, John Adams (b), who would later become the second president of the United States.

Another privileged member of the revolutionary generation, Mercy Otis Warren, also challenged gender assumptions and traditions during the revolutionary era (Figure 7.5). Born in Massachusetts, Warren actively opposed British reform measures before the outbreak of fighting in 1775 by publishing anti-British works. In 1812, she published a three-volume history of the Revolution, a project she had started in the late 1770s. By publishing her work, Warren stepped out of the female sphere and into the otherwise male-dominated sphere of public life.

Inspired by the Revolution, Judith Sargent Murray of Massachusetts advocated women's economic independence and equal educational opportunities for men and women (Figure 7.5). Murray, who came from a well-to-do family in Gloucester, questioned why boys were given access to education as a birthright while girls had very limited educational opportunities. She began to publish her ideas about educational equality beginning in the 1780s, arguing that God had made the minds of women and men equal.

(a) (b)

FIGURE 7.5 John Singleton Copley's 1772 portrait of Judith Sargent Murray (a) and 1763 portrait of Mercy Otis Warren (b) show two of America's earliest advocates for women's rights. Notice how their fine silk dresses telegraph their privileged social status.

Murray's more radical ideas championed woman's economic independence. She argued that a woman's education should be extensive enough to allow her to maintain herself—and her family—if there was no male breadwinner. Indeed, Murray was able to make money of her own from her publications. Her ideas were both radical and traditional, however: Murray also believed that women were much better at raising children and maintaining the morality and virtue of the family than men.

Adams, Murray, and Warren all came from privileged backgrounds. All three were fully literate, while many women in the American republic were not. Their literacy and station allowed them to push for new roles for women in the atmosphere of unique possibility created by the Revolution and its promise of change. Female authors who published their work provide evidence of how women in the era of the American Revolution challenged traditional gender roles.

Overall, the Revolution reconfigured women's roles by undermining the traditional expectations of wives and mothers, including subservience. In the home, the separate domestic sphere assigned to women, women were expected to practice republican virtues, especially frugality and simplicity. Republican motherhood meant that women, more than men, were responsible for raising good children, instilling in them all the virtue necessary to ensure the survival of the republic. The Revolution also opened new doors to educational opportunities for women. Men understood that the republic needed women to play a substantial role in upholding republicanism and ensuring the survival of the new nation. Benjamin Rush, a Whig educator and physician from Philadelphia, strongly advocated for the education of girls and young women as part of the larger effort to ensure that republican virtue and republican motherhood would endure.

THE MEANING OF RACE

By the time of the Revolution, slavery had been firmly in place in America for over one hundred years. In many ways, the Revolution served to reinforce the assumptions about race among White Americans. They viewed the new nation as a White republic; Black people were enslaved, and Native Americans had no place. Racial hatred of Black people increased during the Revolution because many enslaved people fled their enslavers for the freedom offered by the British. The same was true for Native Americans who allied themselves with the British; Jefferson wrote in the Declaration of Independence that separation from the Empire was necessary because George III had incited "the merciless Indian savages" to destroy the White inhabitants on the frontier. Similarly, Thomas Paine argued in *Common Sense* that Great Britain was guilty of inciting "the Indians and Negroes to destroy us." For his part, Benjamin Franklin wrote in the 1780s that, in time, alcoholism would wipe out the Natives, leaving the land free for White settlers.

MY STORY

Phillis Wheatley: "On Being Brought from Africa to America"
Phillis Wheatley (Figure 7.6) was born in Africa in 1753 and sold to the Wheatley family of Boston; her African name is lost to posterity. Although most enslaved people in the eighteenth century had no opportunities to learn to read and write, Wheatley achieved full literacy and went on to become one of the best-known poets of the time, although many doubted her authorship of her poems because of her race.

FIGURE 7.6 This portrait of Phillis Wheatley from the frontispiece of *Poems on various subjects, religious and moral* shows the writer at work. Despite her status as an enslaved person, her poems won great renown in America and in Europe.

Wheatley's poems reflected her deep Christian beliefs. In the poem below, how do her views on Christianity affect her views on slavery?

"Twas mercy brought me from my Pagan land,
Taught my benighted soul to understand
That there's a God, that there's a Saviour too:
Once I redemption neither sought nor knew.
Some view our sable race with scornful eye,
"Their colour is a diabolic dye."
Remember, Christians, Negroes, black as Cain,
May be refin'd, and join th' angelic train.
—Phillis Wheatley, "On Being Brought from Africa to America""

Slavery

Slavery offered the most glaring contradiction between the idea of equality stated in the Declaration of Independence ("all men are created equal") and the reality of race relations in the late eighteenth century.

Racism shaped White views of Black people. Although he penned the Declaration of Independence, Thomas Jefferson enslaved more than one hundred people, of whom he freed only a few either during his lifetime or in his will (Figure 7.7). He thought Black people were inferior to White, dismissing Phillis Wheatley by arguing, "Religion indeed has produced a Phillis Wheatley; but it could not produce a poet." Some White slaveholders raped the people they enslaved, or forced them into long-term sexual relationships, as most historians agree that Jefferson did with Sally Hemings. Together, they had several children.

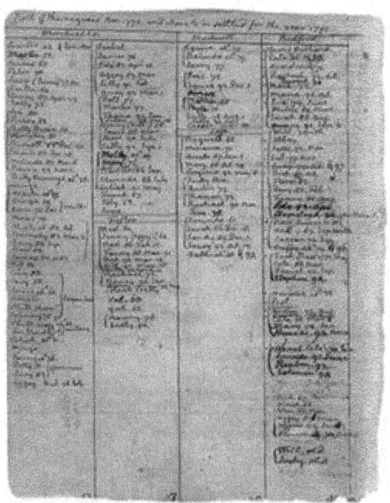

FIGURE 7.7 This page, taken from one of Thomas Jefferson's record books from 1795, lists his the people he held.

CLICK AND EXPLORE

Browse the Thomas Jefferson Papers (http://openstax.org/l/TJefferson) at the Massachusetts Historical Society to examine Jefferson's "farm books," in which he kept records of his land holdings, animal husbandry, and enslaved people, including specific references to Sally Hemings.

Jefferson understood the contradiction fully, and his writings reveal hard-edged racist assumptions. In his *Notes on the State of Virginia* in the 1780s, Jefferson urged the end of slavery in Virginia and the removal of Black people from that state. He wrote: "It will probably be asked, Why not retain and incorporate the blacks into the state, and thus save the expense of supplying, by importation of white settlers, the vacancies they will leave? Deep rooted prejudices entertained by the whites; ten thousand recollections, by the blacks, of the injuries they have sustained; new provocations; the real distinctions which nature has made; and many other circumstances, will divide us into parties, and produce convulsions which will probably never end but in the extermination of the one or the other race. —To these objections, which are political, may be added others, which are physical and moral." Jefferson envisioned an "empire of liberty" for White farmers and relied on the argument of sending Black people out of the United States, even if doing so would completely destroy the slaveholders' wealth in their human property.

Many Southerners strongly objected to Jefferson's views on abolishing slavery and removing Black people from America. When Jefferson was a candidate for president in 1796, an anonymous "Southern Planter" wrote, "If this wild project succeeds, under the auspices of Thomas Jefferson, President of the United States, and three hundred thousand slaves are set free in Virginia, farewell to the safety, prosperity, the importance, perhaps the very existence of the Southern States" (Figure 7.8). Slaveholders and many other Americans protected and defended the institution.

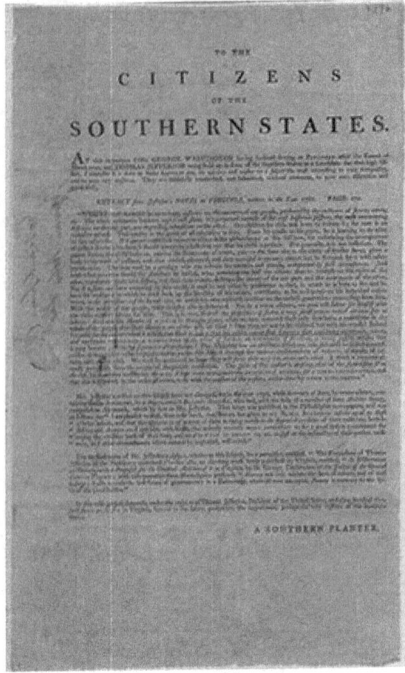

FIGURE 7.8 This 1796 broadside to "the Citizens of the Southern States" by "a Southern Planter" argued that Thomas Jefferson's advocacy of emancipation in his *Notes on the State of Virginia* posed a threat to the safety, the prosperity, and even the existence of the southern states.

Freedom

While racial thinking permeated the new country, and slavery existed in all the new states, the ideals of the Revolution generated a movement toward the abolition of slavery. Private **manumissions**, by which slaveholders freed the enslaved, provided one pathway from bondage. Slaveholders in Virginia freed some ten thousand people. In Massachusetts, the Wheatley family manumitted Phillis in 1773 when she was twenty-one. Other revolutionaries formed societies dedicated to abolishing slavery. One of the earliest efforts began in 1775 in Philadelphia, where Dr. Benjamin Rush and other Philadelphia Quakers formed what became the Pennsylvania Abolition Society. Similarly, wealthy New Yorkers formed the New York Manumission Society in 1785. This society worked to educate Black children and devoted funds to protect free Black people from kidnapping.

Slavery persisted in the North, however, and the example of Massachusetts highlights the complexity of the situation. The 1780 Massachusetts constitution technically freed all enslaved people. Nonetheless, several hundred individuals remained enslaved in the state. In the 1780s, a series of court decisions undermined slavery in Massachusetts when several people, citing assault by their enslavers, successfully sought their freedom in court. These individuals refused to be treated as having slave status in the wake of the American Revolution. Despite these legal victories, about eleven hundred people continued to be held in the New England states in 1800. The contradictions illustrate the difference between the letter and the spirit of the laws abolishing slavery in Massachusetts. In all, over thirty-six thousand people remained enslaved in the North, with the highest concentrations in New Jersey and New York. New York only gradually phased out slavery, with the last individuals emancipated in the late 1820s.

Native Americans

The 1783 Treaty of Paris, which ended the war for independence, did not address Native peoples at all. All lands held by the British east of the Mississippi and south of the Great Lakes (except Spanish Florida) now belonged to the new American republic (Figure 7.9). Though the treaty remained silent on the issue, much of the territory now included in the boundaries of the United States remained under the control of Native peoples. Earlier in the eighteenth century, a "middle ground" had existed between powerful Native groups in the West and British and French imperial zones, a place where the various groups interacted and accommodated each other. As had happened in the French and Indian War and Pontiac's Rebellion, the Revolutionary War turned the middle ground into a battle zone that no one group controlled.

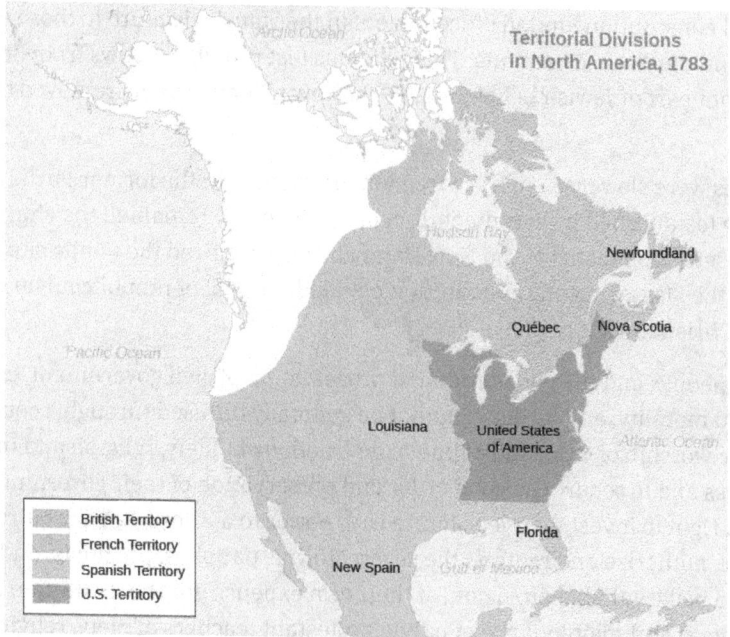

FIGURE 7.9 The 1783 Treaty of Paris divided North America into territories belonging to the United States and several European countries, but it failed to address Native lands at all.

During the Revolution, a complex situation existed among Native groups. Many villages remained neutral. Some native groups, such as the Delaware, split into factions, with some supporting the British while other Delaware maintained their neutrality. The Iroquois Confederacy, a longstanding alliance of tribes, also split up: the Mohawk, Cayuga, Onondaga, and Seneca fought on the British side, while the Oneida and Tuscarora supported the revolutionaries. Ohio River Valley tribes such as the Shawnee, Miami, and Mungo had been fighting for years against colonial expansion west; these groups supported the British. Some native peoples who had previously allied with the French hoped the conflict between the colonies and Great Britain might lead to French intervention and the return of French rule. Few Native Americans sided with the American revolutionaries, because almost all revolutionaries in the middle ground viewed them as an enemy to be destroyed. This racial hatred toward Native peoples found expression in the American massacre of ninety-six Christian Delawares in 1782. Most of the dead were women and children.

After the war, the victorious Americans turned a deaf ear to Native American claims to what the revolutionaries saw as their hard-won land, and they moved aggressively to assert control over western New York and Pennsylvania. In response, Mohawk leader Joseph Brant helped to form the Western Confederacy, an alliance of native peoples who pledged to resist American intrusion into what was then called the Northwest. The Northwest Indian War (1785–1795) ended with the defeat of the Natives and their claims. Under the Treaty of Greenville (1795), the United States gained dominion over land in Ohio.

RELIGION AND THE STATE

Prior to the Revolution, several colonies had official, tax-supported churches. After the Revolution, some questioned the validity of state-authorized churches; the limitation of public office-holding to those of a particular faith; and the payment of taxes to support churches. In other states, especially in New England where the older Puritan heritage cast a long shadow, religion and state remained intertwined.

During the colonial era in Virginia, the established church had been the Church of England, which did not tolerate Catholics, Baptists, or followers or other religions. In 1786, as a revolutionary response against the privileged status of the Church of England, Virginia's lawmakers approved the Virginia Statute for Religious Freedom, which ended the Church of England's hold and allowed religious liberty. Under the statute, no one could be forced to attend or support a specific church or be prosecuted for his or her beliefs.

Pennsylvania's original constitution limited officeholders in the state legislature to those who professed a belief in both the Old and the New Testaments. This religious test prohibited Jews from holding that office, as the New Testament is not part of Jewish belief. In 1790, however, Pennsylvania removed this qualification from its constitution.

The New England states were slower to embrace freedom of religion. In the former Puritan colonies, the Congregational Church (established by seventeenth-century Puritans) remained the church of most inhabitants. Massachusetts, Connecticut, and New Hampshire all required the public support of Christian churches. Article III of the Massachusetts constitution blended the goal of republicanism with the goal of promoting Protestant Christianity. It reads:

"As the happiness of a people, and the good order and preservation of civil government, essentially depend upon piety, religion and morality; and as these cannot be generally diffused through a community, but by the institution of the public worship of GOD, and of public instructions in piety, religion and morality: Therefore, to promote their happiness and to secure the good order and preservation of their government, the people of this Commonwealth have a right to invest their legislature with power to authorize and require, and the legislature shall, from time to time, authorize and require, the several towns, parishes, precincts, and other bodies-politic, or religious societies, to make suitable provision, at their own expense, for the institution of the public worship of GOD, and for the support and maintenance of public protestant teachers of piety, religion and morality, in all cases where such provision shall not be made voluntarily....
And every denomination of Christians, demeaning themselves peaceably, and as good subjects of the Commonwealth, shall be equally under the protection of the law: And no subordination of any one sect or denomination to another shall ever be established by law."

CLICK AND EXPLORE

Read more about religion and state governments at the Religion and the Founding of the American Republic (http://openstax.org/l/farmbook1) exhibition page on the Library of Congress site. What was the meaning of the term "nursing fathers" of the church?

7.3 Debating Democracy

LEARNING OBJECTIVES
By the end of this section, you will be able to:
- Explain the development of state constitutions
- Describe the features of the Articles of Confederation
- Analyze the causes and consequences of Shays' Rebellion

The task of creating republican governments in each of the former colonies, now independent states, presented a new opportunity for American revolutionaries to define themselves anew after casting off British control. On the state and national levels, citizens of the new United States debated who would hold the keys to political power. The states proved to be a laboratory for how much democracy, or majority rule, would be tolerated.

THE STATE CONSTITUTIONS

In 1776, John Adams urged the thirteen independent colonies—soon to be states—to write their own state constitutions. Enlightenment political thought profoundly influenced Adams and other revolutionary leaders seeking to create viable republican governments. The ideas of the French philosopher Montesquieu, who had advocated the separation of powers in government, guided Adams's thinking. Responding to a request for advice on proper government from North Carolina, Adams wrote *Thoughts on Government*, which influenced many state legislatures. Adams did not advocate democracy; rather, he wrote, "there is no good government but what is republican." Fearing the potential for tyranny with only one group in power, he suggested a system of **checks and balances** in which three separate branches of government—executive, legislative, and judicial—would maintain a balance of power. He also proposed that each state remain sovereign, as its own republic. The state constitutions of the new United States illustrate different approaches to addressing the question of how much democracy would prevail in the thirteen republics. Some states embraced democratic practices, while others adopted far more aristocratic and republican ones.

CLICK AND EXPLORE

Visit the Avalon Project (http://openstax.org/l/statecons) to read the constitutions of the seven states (Virginia, New Jersey, North Carolina, Maryland, Connecticut, Pennsylvania, and Delaware) that had written constitutions by the end of 1776.

The 1776 Pennsylvania constitution and the 1784 New Hampshire constitution both provide examples of democratic tendencies. In Pennsylvania, the requirement to own property in order to vote was eliminated, and if a man was twenty-one or older, had paid taxes, and had lived in the same location for one year, he could vote (Figure 7.10). This opened voting to most free White male citizens of Pennsylvania. The 1784 New Hampshire constitution allowed every small town and village to send representatives to the state government, making the lower house of the legislature a model of democratic government.

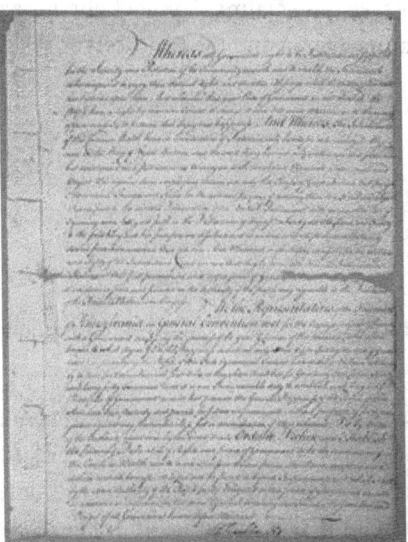

FIGURE 7.10 The 1776 Pennsylvania constitution, the first page of which is shown here, adhered to more democratic principles than some other states' constitutions did initially.

Conservative Whigs, who distrusted the idea of majority rule, recoiled from the abolition of property qualifications for voting and office holding in Pennsylvania. Conservative Whig John Adams reacted with horror to the 1776 Pennsylvania constitution, declaring that it was "so democratical that it must produce confusion and every evil work." In his mind and those of other conservative Whigs, this constitution simply put too much power in the hands of men who had no business exercising the right to vote. Pennsylvania's constitution also eliminated the executive branch (there was no governor) and the upper house. Instead, Pennsylvania had a one-house—a **unicameral**—legislature.

The Maryland and South Carolina constitutions provide examples of efforts to limit the power of a democratic majority. Maryland's, written in 1776, restricted office holding to the wealthy planter class. A man had to own at least £5,000 worth of personal property to be the governor of Maryland, and possess an estate worth £1,000 to be a state senator. This latter qualification excluded over 90 percent of the White males in Maryland from political office. The 1778 South Carolina constitution also sought to protect the interests of the wealthy. Governors and lieutenant governors of the state had to have "a settled plantation or freehold in their and each of their own right of the value of at least ten thousand pounds currency, clear of debt." This provision limited high office in the state to its wealthiest inhabitants. Similarly, South Carolina state senators had to own estates valued at £2,000.

John Adams wrote much of the 1780 Massachusetts constitution, which reflected his fear of too much democracy. It therefore created two legislative chambers, an upper and lower house, and a strong governor with broad veto powers. Like South Carolina, Massachusetts put in place office-holding requirements: To be governor under the new constitution, a candidate had to own an estate worth at least £1,000. To serve in the state senate, a man had to own an estate worth at least £300 and have at least £600 in total wealth. To vote, he had to be worth at least sixty pounds. To further keep democracy in check, judges were appointed, not elected. One final limit was the establishment of the state capitol in the commercial center of Boston, which made it difficult for farmers from the western part of the state to attend legislative sessions.

THE ARTICLES OF CONFEDERATION

Most revolutionaries pledged their greatest loyalty to their individual states. Recalling the experience of British reform efforts imposed in the 1760s and 1770s, they feared a strong national government and took some time to adopt the Articles of Confederation, the first national constitution. In June 1776, the Continental Congress prepared to announce independence and began to think about the creation of a new government to replace royal authority. Reaching agreement on the Articles of Confederation proved difficult as members of the Continental Congress argued over western land claims. Connecticut, for example, used its colonial charter to assert its claim to western lands in Pennsylvania and the Ohio Territory (Figure 7.11).

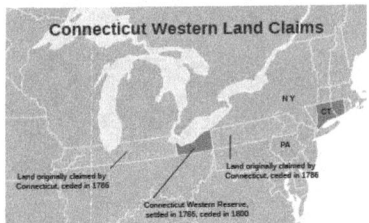

FIGURE 7.11 Connecticut, like many other states, used its state constitution to stake claims to uncharted western lands.

Members of the Continental Congress also debated what type of representation would be best and tried to figure out how to pay the expenses of the new government. In lieu of creating a new federal government, the Articles of Confederation created a "league of friendship" between the states. Congress readied the Articles in 1777 but did not officially approve them until 1781 (Figure 7.12). The delay of four years illustrates the difficulty of getting the thirteen states to agree on a plan of national government. Citizens viewed their respective states as sovereign republics and guarded their prerogatives against other states.

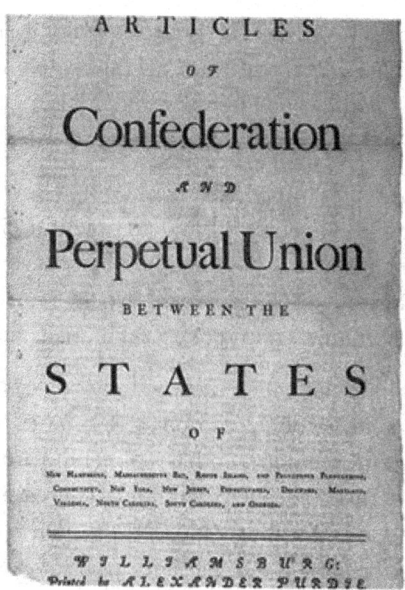

FIGURE 7.12 The first page of the 1777 Articles of Confederation, printed by Alexander Purdie, emphasized the "perpetual union" between the states.

The Articles of Confederation authorized a unicameral legislature, a continuation of the earlier Continental Congress. The people could not vote directly for members of the national Congress; rather, state legislatures decided who would represent the state. In practice, the national Congress was composed of state delegations. There was no president or executive office of any kind, and there was no national judiciary (or Supreme Court) for the United States.

Passage of any law under the Articles of Confederation proved difficult. It took the consensus of nine states for any measure to pass, and amending the Articles required the consent of all the states, also extremely difficult to achieve. Further, any acts put forward by the Congress were non-binding; states had the option to enforce them or not. This meant that while the Congress had power over Native American affairs and foreign policy, individual states could choose whether or not to comply.

The Congress did not have the power to tax citizens of the United States, a fact that would soon have serious consequences for the republic. During the Revolutionary War, the Continental Congress had sent requisitions for funds to the individual former colonies (now revolutionary states). These states already had an enormous financial burden because they had to pay for militias as well as supply them. In the end, the states failed to provide even half the funding requested by the Congress during the war, which led to a national debt in the tens of millions by 1784.

By the 1780s, some members of the Congress were greatly concerned about the financial health of the republic, and they argued that the national government needed greater power, especially the power to tax. This required amending the Articles of Confederation with the consent of all the states. Those who called for a stronger federal government were known as nationalists. The nationalist group that pushed for the power to tax included Washington's chief of staff, Alexander Hamilton; Virginia planter James Madison; Pennsylvania's wealthy merchant Robert Morris (who served under the Confederation government as superintendent of finance in the early 1780s); and Pennsylvania lawyer James Wilson. Two New Yorkers, Gouverneur Morris and James Duane, also joined the effort to address the debt and the weakness of the Confederation government.

These men proposed a 5 percent tax on imports coming into the United States, a measure that would have yielded enough revenue to clear the debt. However, their proposal failed to achieve unanimous support from the states when Rhode Island rejected it. Plans for a national bank also failed to win unanimous support. The lack of support illustrates the Americans' deep suspicion of a powerful national government, a suspicion that originated from the unilateral and heavy-handed reform efforts that the British Parliament imposed on the colonies in the 1760s and 1770s. Without revenue, the Congress could not pay back American creditors who had lent it money. However, it did manage to make interest payments to foreign creditors in France and the Dutch Republic, fearful that defaulting on those payments would destroy the republic's credit and leave it unable to secure loans.

One soldier in the Continental Army, Joseph Plumb Martin, recounted how he received no pay in paper money after 1777 and only one month's payment in specie, or hard currency, in 1781. Like thousands of other soldiers, Martin had fought valiantly against the British and helped secure independence, but had not been paid for his service. In the 1780s and beyond, men like Martin would soon express their profound dissatisfaction with their treatment. Their anger found expression in armed uprisings and political divisions.

Establishing workable foreign and commercial policies under the Articles of Confederation also proved difficult. Each state could decide for itself whether to comply with treaties between the Congress and foreign countries, and there were no means of enforcement. Both Great Britain and Spain understood the weakness of the Confederation Congress, and they refused to make commercial agreements with the United States because they doubted they would be enforced. Without stable commercial policies, American exporters found it difficult to do business, and British goods flooded U.S. markets in the 1780s, in a repetition of the economic imbalance that existed before the Revolutionary War.

The Confederation Congress under the Articles did achieve success through a series of directives called land ordinances, which established rules for the settlement of western lands in the public domain and the admission of new states to the republic. The ordinances were designed to prepare the land for sale to citizens and raise revenue to boost the failing economy of the republic. In the land ordinances, the Confederation Congress created the Mississippi and Southwest Territories and stipulated that slavery would be permitted there. The system of dividing the vast domains of the United States stands as a towering achievement of the era, a blueprint for American western expansion.

The Ordinance of 1784, written by Thomas Jefferson and the first of what were later called the Northwest Ordinances, directed that new states would be formed from a huge area of land below the Great Lakes, and these new states would have equal standing with the original states. The Ordinance of 1785 called for the division of this land into rectangular plots in order to prepare for the government sale of land. Surveyors would divide the land into townships of six square miles, and the townships would be subdivided into thirty-six plots of 640 acres each, which could be further subdivided. The price of an acre of land was set at a minimum of one dollar, and the land was to be sold at public auction under the direction of the Confederation.

The Ordinance of 1787 officially turned the land into an incorporated territory called the Northwest Territory and prohibited slavery north of the Ohio River (Figure 7.13). The map of the 1787 Northwest Territory shows how the public domain was to be divided by the national government for sale. Townships of thirty-six square miles were to be surveyed. Each had land set aside for schools and other civic purposes. Smaller parcels could then be made: a 640-acre section could be divided into quarter-sections of 160 acres, and then again into sixteen sections of 40 acres. The geometric grid pattern established by the ordinance is still evident today on the American landscape. Indeed, much of the western United States, when viewed from an airplane, is composed of an orderly grid system.

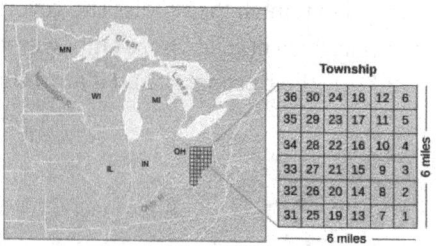

FIGURE 7.13 The Northwest Ordinance of 1787 created territories and an orderly method for the admission of new states.

CLICK AND EXPLORE

Visit [Window Seat (http://openstax.org/l/thescream)](http://openstax.org/l/thescream) to explore aerial views of the grid system established by the Northwest Ordinance of 1787, which is still evident in much of the Midwest.

The land ordinances proved to be the great triumph of the Confederation Congress. The Congress would appoint a governor for the territories, and when the population in the territory reached five thousand free adult settlers, those citizens could create their own legislature and begin the process of moving toward statehood. When the population reached sixty thousand, the territory could become a new state.

SHAYS' REBELLION

Despite Congress's victory in creating an orderly process for organizing new states and territories, land sales failed to produce the revenue necessary to deal with the dire economic problems facing the new country in the 1780s. Each state had issued large amounts of paper money and, in the aftermath of the Revolution, widespread internal devaluation of that currency occurred as many lost confidence in the value of state paper money and the Continental dollar. A period of extreme inflation set in. Added to this dilemma was American citizens' lack of specie (gold and silver currency) to conduct routine business. Meanwhile, demobilized soldiers, many of whom had spent their formative years fighting rather than learning a peacetime trade, searched desperately for work.

The economic crisis came to a head in 1786 and 1787 in western Massachusetts, where farmers were in a difficult position: they faced high taxes and debts, which they found nearly impossible to pay with the worthless state and Continental paper money. For several years after the peace in 1783, these indebted citizens had petitioned the state legislature for redress. Many were veterans of the Revolutionary War who had returned to their farms and families after the fighting ended and now faced losing their homes.

Their petitions to the state legislature raised economic and political issues for citizens of the new state. How could people pay their debts and state taxes when paper money proved unstable? Why was the state government located in Boston, the center of the merchant elite? Why did the 1780 Massachusetts constitution cater to the interests of the wealthy? To the indebted farmers, the situation in the 1780s seemed hauntingly familiar; the revolutionaries had routed the British, but a new form of seemingly corrupt and self-serving government had replaced them.

In 1786, when the state legislature again refused to address the petitioners' requests, Massachusetts citizens took up arms and closed courthouses across the state to prevent foreclosure (seizure of land in lieu of overdue loan payments) on farms in debt. The farmers wanted their debts forgiven, and they demanded that the 1780 constitution be revised to address citizens beyond the wealthy elite who could serve in the legislature.

Many of the rebels were veterans of the war for independence, including Captain Daniel Shays from Pelham (Figure 7.14). Although Shays was only one of many former officers in the Continental Army who took part in the revolt, authorities in Boston singled him out as a ringleader, and the uprising became known as Shays'

Rebellion. The Massachusetts legislature responded to the closing of the courthouses with a flurry of legislation, much of it designed to punish the rebels. The government offered the rebels clemency if they took an oath of allegiance. Otherwise, local officials were empowered to use deadly force against them without fear of prosecution. Rebels would lose their property, and if any militiamen refused to defend the state, they would be executed.

FIGURE 7.14 This woodcut, from Bickerstaff's Boston Almanack of 1787, depicts Daniel Shays and Job Shattuck. Shays and Shattuck were two of the leaders of the rebels who rose up against the Massachusetts government in 1786 to 1787. As Revolutionary War veterans, both men wear the uniform of officers of the Continental Army.

Despite these measures, the rebellion continued. To address the uprising, Governor James Bowdoin raised a private army of forty-four hundred men, funded by wealthy Boston merchants, without the approval of the legislature. The climax of Shays' Rebellion came in January 1787, when the rebels attempted to seize the federal armory in Springfield, Massachusetts. A force loyal to the state defeated them there, although the rebellion continued into February.

Shays' Rebellion resulted in eighteen deaths overall, but the uprising had lasting effects. To men of property, mostly conservative Whigs, Shays' Rebellion strongly suggested the republic was falling into anarchy and chaos. The other twelve states had faced similar economic and political difficulties, and continuing problems seemed to indicate that on a national level, a democratic impulse was driving the population. Shays' Rebellion convinced George Washington to come out of retirement and lead the convention called for by Alexander Hamilton to amend the Articles of Confederation in order to deal with insurgencies like the one in Massachusetts and provide greater stability in the United States.

7.4 The Constitutional Convention and Federal Constitution

LEARNING OBJECTIVES

By the end of this section, you will be able to:
- Identify the central issues of the 1787 Constitutional Convention and their solutions
- Describe the conflicts over the ratification of the federal constitution

The economic problems that plagued the thirteen states of the Confederation set the stage for the creation of a strong central government under a federal constitution. Although the original purpose of the convention was to amend the Articles of Confederation, some—though not all—delegates moved quickly to create a new framework for a more powerful national government. This proved extremely controversial. Those who attended the convention split over the issue of robust, centralized government and questions of how Americans would be represented in the federal government. Those who opposed the proposal for a stronger federal government argued that such a plan betrayed the Revolution by limiting the voice of the American people.

THE CONSTITUTIONAL CONVENTION

There had been earlier efforts to address the Confederation's perilous state. In early 1786, Virginia's James Madison advocated a meeting of states to address the widespread economic problems that plagued the new nation. Heeding Madison's call, the legislature in Virginia invited all thirteen states to meet in Annapolis, Maryland, to work on solutions to the issue of commerce between the states. Eight states responded to the invitation. But the resulting 1786 Annapolis Convention failed to provide any solutions because only five states sent delegates. These delegates did, however, agree to a plan put forward by Alexander Hamilton for a second convention to meet in May 1787 in Philadelphia. Shays' Rebellion gave greater urgency to the planned convention. In February 1787, in the wake of the uprising in western Massachusetts, the Confederation Congress authorized the Philadelphia convention. This time, all the states except Rhode Island sent delegates to Philadelphia to confront the problems of the day.

The stated purpose of the Philadelphia Convention in 1787 was to amend the Articles of Confederation. Very quickly, however, the attendees decided to create a new framework for a national government. That framework became the United States Constitution, and the Philadelphia convention became known as the Constitutional Convention of 1787. Fifty-five men met in Philadelphia in secret; historians know of the proceedings only because James Madison kept careful notes of what transpired. The delegates knew that what they were doing would be controversial; Rhode Island refused to send delegates, and New Hampshire's delegates arrived late. Two delegates from New York, Robert Yates and John Lansing, left the convention when it became clear that the Articles were being put aside and a new plan of national government was being drafted. They did not believe the delegates had the authority to create a strong national government.

CLICK AND EXPLORE

Read "Reasons for Dissent from the Proposed Constitution" (http://openstax.org/l/YatesLansing) in order to understand why Robert Yates and John Lansing, New York's delegates to the 1787 Philadelphia Convention, didn't believe the convention should draft a new plan of national government.

THE QUESTION OF REPRESENTATION

One issue that the delegates in Philadelphia addressed was the way in which representatives to the new national government would be chosen. Would individual citizens be able to elect representatives? Would representatives be chosen by state legislatures? How much representation was appropriate for each state?

James Madison put forward a proposition known as the Virginia Plan, which called for a strong national government that could overturn state laws (Figure 7.15). The plan featured a **bicameral** or two-house legislature, with an upper and a lower house. The people of the states would elect the members of the lower house, whose numbers would be determined by the population of the state. State legislatures would send delegates to the upper house. The number of representatives in the upper chamber would also be based on the state's population. This **proportional representation** gave the more populous states, like Virginia, more political power. The Virginia Plan also called for an executive branch and a judicial branch, both of which were absent under the Articles of Confederation. The lower and upper house together were to appoint members to the executive and judicial branches. Under this plan, Virginia, the most populous state, would dominate national political power and ensure its interests, including slavery, would be safe.

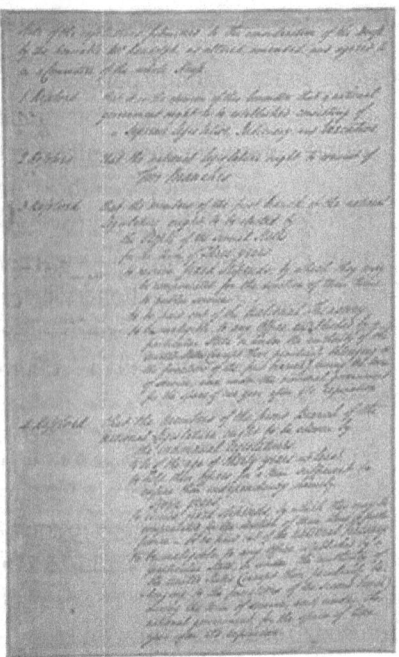

FIGURE 7.15 James Madison's Virginia Plan, shown here, proposed a strong national government with proportional state representation.

The Virginia Plan's call for proportional representation alarmed the representatives of the smaller states. William Paterson introduced a New Jersey Plan to counter Madison's scheme, proposing that all states have equal votes in a unicameral national legislature. He also addressed the economic problems of the day by calling for the Congress to have the power to regulate commerce, to raise revenue though taxes on imports and through postage, and to enforce Congressional requisitions from the states.

Roger Sherman from Connecticut offered a compromise to break the deadlock over the thorny question of representation. His **Connecticut Compromise**, also known as the Great Compromise, outlined a different bicameral legislature in which the upper house, the Senate, would have equal representation for all states; each state would be represented by two senators chosen by the state legislatures. Only the lower house, the House of Representatives, would have proportional representation.

THE QUESTION OF SLAVERY

The question of slavery stood as a major issue at the Constitutional Convention because slaveholders wanted enslaved residents to be counted along with White people, termed "free inhabitants," when determining a state's total population. This, in turn, would augment the number of representatives accorded to those states in the lower house. Some northerners, however, such as New York's Gouverneur Morris, hated slavery and did not even want the term included in the new national plan of government. Slaveholders argued that slavery imposed great burdens upon them and that, because they carried this liability, they deserved special consideration; enslaved people needed to be counted for purposes of representation.

The issue of counting or not counting enslaved people for purposes of representation connected directly to the question of taxation. Beginning in 1775, the Second Continental Congress asked states to pay for war by collecting taxes and sending the tax money to the Congress. The amount each state had to deliver in tax revenue was determined by a state's total population, including both free and enslaved individuals. States routinely fell far short of delivering the money requested by Congress under the plan. In April 1783, the Confederation Congress amended the earlier system of requisition by having the enslaved population count as three-fifths of the White population. In this way, slaveholders gained a significant tax break. The delegates in Philadelphia adopted this same three-fifths formula in the summer of 1787.

Under the **three-fifths compromise** in the 1787 Constitution, three out of every five enslaved people would be counted when determining a state's population. Article 1, Section 2 stipulated that "Representatives and direct Taxes shall be apportioned among the several states . . . according to their respective Number, which shall be determined by adding to the whole number of free Persons, including those bound for service for a Term of Years [White servants], and excluding Indians not taxed, three fifths of all other persons." Since representation in the House of Representatives was based on the population of a state, the three-fifths compromise gave extra political power to slave states, although not as much as if the total population, both free and enslaved, had been used. Significantly, no direct federal income tax was immediately imposed. (The Sixteenth Amendment, ratified in 1913, put in place a federal income tax.) Northerners agreed to the three-fifths compromise because the Northwest Ordinance of 1787, passed by the Confederation Congress, banned slavery in the future states of the northwest. Northern delegates felt this ban balanced political power between states with enslaved people and those without. The three-fifths compromise gave an advantage to slaveholders; they added three-fifths of their human property to their state's population, allowing them to send representatives based in part on the number of people they enslaved.

THE QUESTION OF DEMOCRACY

Many of the delegates to the Constitutional Convention had serious reservations about democracy, which they believed promoted anarchy. To allay these fears, the Constitution blunted democratic tendencies that appeared to undermine the republic. Thus, to avoid giving the people too much direct power, the delegates made certain that senators were chosen by the state legislatures, not elected directly by the people (direct elections of senators came with the Seventeenth Amendment to the Constitution, ratified in 1913). As an additional safeguard, the delegates created the **Electoral College**, the mechanism for choosing the president. Under this plan, each state has a certain number of electors, which is its number of senators (two) plus its number of representatives in the House of Representatives. Critics, then as now, argue that this process prevents the direct election of the president.

THE FIGHT OVER RATIFICATION

The draft constitution was finished in September 1787. The delegates decided that in order for the new national government to be implemented, each state must first hold a special ratifying convention. When nine of the thirteen had approved the plan, the constitution would go into effect.

When the American public learned of the new constitution, opinions were deeply divided, but most people were opposed. To salvage their work in Philadelphia, the architects of the new national government began a campaign to sway public opinion in favor of their blueprint for a strong central government. In the fierce debate that erupted, the two sides articulated contrasting visions of the American republic and of democracy. Supporters of the 1787 Constitution, known as **Federalists**, made the case that a centralized republic provided the best solution for the future. Those who opposed it, known as **Anti-Federalists**, argued that the Constitution would consolidate all power in a national government, robbing the states of the power to make their own decisions. To them, the Constitution appeared to mimic the old corrupt and centralized British regime, under which a far-off government made the laws. Anti-Federalists argued that wealthy aristocrats would run the new national government, and that the elite would not represent ordinary citizens; the rich would monopolize power and use the new government to formulate policies that benefited their class—a development that would also undermine local state elites. They also argued that the Constitution did not contain a bill of rights.

New York's ratifying convention illustrates the divide between the Federalists and Anti-Federalists. When one Anti-Federalist delegate named Melancton Smith took issue with the scheme of representation as being too limited and not reflective of the people, Alexander Hamilton responded:

"It has been observed by an honorable gentleman [Smith], that a pure democracy, if it were practicable, would be the most perfect government. Experience has proven, that no position in politics is more false than this. The ancient democracies, in which the people themselves deliberated, never possessed one feature of good government. Their very character was tyranny; their figure deformity: When they assembled, the field of debate presented an ungovernable mob, not only incapable of deliberation, but prepared for every enormity. In these assemblies, the enemies of the people brought forward their plans of ambition systematically. They were opposed by their enemies of another party; and it became a matter of contingency, whether the people subjected themselves to be led blindly by one tyrant or by another."

The Federalists, particularly John Jay, Alexander Hamilton, and James Madison, put their case to the public in a famous series of essays known as *The Federalist Papers*. These were first published in New York and subsequently republished elsewhere in the United States.

DEFINING AMERICAN

James Madison on the Benefits of Republicanism

The tenth essay in *The Federalist Papers*, often called Federalist No. 10, is one of the most famous. Written by James Madison (Figure 7.16), it addresses the problems of political parties ("factions"). Madison argued that there were two approaches to solving the problem of political parties: a republican government and a democracy. He argued that a large republic provided the best defense against what he viewed as the tumult of direct democracy. Compromises would be reached in a large republic and citizens would be represented by representatives of their own choosing.

FIGURE 7.16 John Vanderlyn's 1816 portrait depicts James Madison, one of the leading Federalists who supported the 1787 Constitution.

"From this view of the subject, it may be concluded, that a pure Democracy, by which I mean a Society consisting of a small number of citizens, who assemble and administer the Government in person, can admit of no cure for the mischiefs of faction. A common passion or interest will, in almost every case, be felt by a majority of the whole; a communication and concert result from the form of Government itself; and there is nothing to check the inducements to sacrifice the weaker party, or an obnoxious individual. Hence it is, that such Democracies have ever been spectacles of turbulence and contention; have ever been found incompatible with personal security, or the rights of property; and have in general been as short in their lives, as they have been violent in their deaths. Theoretic politicians, who have patronized this species of Government, have erroneously supposed, that by reducing mankind to a perfect equality in their political rights, they would, at the same time, be perfectly equalized and assimilated in their possessions, their opinions, and their passions.

A Republic, by which I mean a Government in which the scheme of representation takes place, opens a different prospect, and promises the cure for which we are seeking. Let us examine the points in which it varies from pure Democracy, and we shall comprehend both the nature of the cure, and the efficacy which it must derive from the

Union.

The two great points of difference, between a Democracy and a Republic, are, first, the delegation of the Government, in the latter, to a small number of citizens elected by the rest: Secondly, the greater number of citizens, and greater sphere of country, over which the latter may be extended."

Does Madison recommend republicanism or democracy as the best form of government? What arguments does he use to prove his point?

CLICK AND EXPLORE

Read the full text of Federalist No. 10 (http://openstax.org/l/federalist10) on Wikisource. What do you think are Madison's most and least compelling arguments? How would different members of the new United States view his arguments?

Including all the state ratifying conventions around the country, a total of fewer than two thousand men voted on whether to adopt the new plan of government. In the end, the Constitution only narrowly won approval (Figure 7.17). In New York, the vote was thirty in favor to twenty-seven opposed. In Massachusetts, the vote to approve was 187 to 168, and some claim supporters of the Constitution resorted to bribes in order to ensure approval. Virginia ratified by a vote of eighty-nine to seventy-nine, and Rhode Island by thirty-four to thirty-two. The opposition to the Constitution reflected the fears that a new national government, much like the British monarchy, created too much centralized power and, as a result, deprived citizens in the various states of the ability to make their own decisions.

FIGURE 7.17 The first page of the 1787 United States Constitution, shown here, begins: "We the People of the United States, in Order to form a more perfect Union, establish Justice, insure domestic Tranquility, provide for the common defence, promote the general Welfare, and secure the Blessings of Liberty to ourselves and our Posterity, do ordain and establish this Constitution for the United States of America."

Key Terms

Anti-Federalists   those who opposed the 1787 Constitution and favored stronger individual states

bicameral   having two legislative houses, an upper and a lower house

checks and balances   the system that ensures a balance of power among the branches of government

Connecticut Compromise   also known as the Great Compromise, Roger Sherman's proposal at the Constitutional Convention for a bicameral legislature, with the upper house having equal representation for all states and the lower house having proportional representation

conservative Whigs   the politically and economically elite revolutionary class that wanted to limit political participation to a few powerful families

coverture   the legal status of married women in the United States, which included complete legal and economic dependence on husbands

democracy   a system of government in which the majority rules

Electoral College   the mechanism by which electors, based on the number of representatives from each state, choose the president

Federalists   those who supported the 1787 Constitution and a strong central government; these advocates of the new national government formed the ruling political party in the 1790s

majority rule   a fundamental principle of democracy, providing that the majority should have the power to make decisions binding upon the whole

manumission   the releasing of an enslaved person by his or her owner

monarchy   a form of government with a monarch at its head

proportional representation   representation that gives more populous states greater political power by allowing them more representatives

radical Whigs   revolutionaries who favored broadening participation in the political process

three-fifths compromise   the agreement at the Constitutional Convention that three out of every five enslaved persons would be counted when determining a state's population for purposes of representation

unicameral   having a single house (of legislative government)

Summary

7.1 Common Sense: From Monarchy to an American Republic

The guiding principle of republicanism was that the people themselves would appoint or select the leaders who would represent them. The debate over how much democracy (majority rule) to incorporate in the governing of the new United States raised questions about who was best qualified to participate in government and have the right to vote. Revolutionary leaders argued that property holders had the greatest stake in society and favored a republic that would limit political rights to property holders. In this way, republicanism exhibited a bias toward the elite. George Washington served as a role model for the new republic, embodying the exceptional talent and public virtue prized in its political and social philosophy.

7.2 How Much Revolutionary Change?

After the Revolution, the balance of power between women and men and between White, Black, and Native American people remained largely unchanged. Yet revolutionary principles, including the call for universal equality in the Declaration of Independence, inspired and emboldened many. Abigail Adams and others pressed for greater rights for women, while the Pennsylvania Abolition Society and New York Manumission Society worked toward the abolition of slavery. Nonetheless, for Black people, women, and Native peoples, the revolutionary ideals of equality fell far short of reality. In the new republic, full citizenship—including the right to vote—did not extend to non-White people or to women.

7.3 Debating Democracy

The late 1770s and 1780s witnessed one of the most creative political eras as each state drafted its own constitution. The Articles of Confederation, a weak national league among the states, reflected the dominant view that power should be located in the states and not in a national government. However, neither the state governments nor the Confederation government could solve the enormous economic problems resulting from the long and costly Revolutionary War. The economic crisis led to Shays' Rebellion by residents of western Massachusetts, and to the decision to revise the Confederation government.

7.4 The Constitutional Convention and Federal Constitution

The economic crisis of the 1780s, shortcomings of the Articles of Confederation, and outbreak of Shays' Rebellion spurred delegates from twelve of the thirteen states to gather for the Constitutional Convention of 1787. Although the stated purpose of the convention was to modify the Articles of Confederation, their mission shifted to the building of a new, strong federal government. Federalists like James Madison and Alexander Hamilton led the charge for a new United States Constitution, the document that endures as the oldest written constitution in the world, a testament to the work done in 1787 by the delegates in Philadelphia.

Review Questions

1. To what form of government did the American revolutionaries turn after the war for independence?
    A. republicanism
    B. monarchy
    C. democracy
    D. oligarchy

2. Which of the following was not one of Franklin's thirteen virtues?
    A. sincerity
    B. temperance
    C. mercy
    D. tranquility

3. What defined republicanism as a social philosophy?

4. Which of the following figures did *not* actively challenge the status of women in the early American republic?
    A. Abigail Adams
    B. Phillis Wheatley
    C. Mercy Otis Warren
    D. Judith Sargent Murray

5. Which state had the clearest separation of church and state?
    A. New Hampshire
    B. Pennsylvania
    C. Virginia
    D. New York

6. How would you characterize Thomas Jefferson's ideas on race and slavery?

7. Which of the following states had the most democratic constitution in the 1780s?
    A. Pennsylvania
    B. Massachusetts
    C. South Carolina
    D. Maryland

8. Under the Articles of Confederation, what power did the national Confederation Congress have?
   A. the power to tax
   B. the power to enforce foreign treaties
   C. the power to enforce commercial trade agreements
   D. the power to create land ordinances

9. What were the primary causes of Shays' Rebellion?

10. Which plan resolved the issue of representation for the U.S. Constitution?
    A. the Rhode Island Agreement
    B. the New Jersey Plan
    C. the Connecticut Compromise
    D. the Virginia Plan

11. How was the U.S. Constitution ratified?
    A. by each state at special ratifying conventions
    B. at the Constitutional Convention of 1787
    C. at the Confederation Convention
    D. by popular referendum in each state

12. Explain the argument that led to the three-fifths rule and the consequences of that rule.

Critical Thinking Questions

13. Describe the state constitutions that were more democratic and those that were less so. What effect would these different constitutions have upon those states? Who could participate in government, whether by voting or by holding public office? Whose interests were represented, and whose were compromised?

14. In what ways does the United States Constitution manifest the principles of both republican and democratic forms of government? In what ways does it deviate from those principles?

15. In this chapter's discussion of New York's ratifying convention, Alexander Hamilton takes issue with Anti-Federalist delegate Melancton Smith's assertion that (as Hamilton says) "a pure democracy, if it were practicable, would be the most perfect government." What did Smith—and Hamilton—mean by "a pure democracy"? How does this compare to the type of democracy that represents the modern United States?

16. Describe popular attitudes toward African Americans, women, and Native Americans in the wake of the Revolution. In what ways did the established social and political order depend upon keeping members of these groups in their circumscribed roles? If those roles were to change, how would American society and politics have had to adjust?

17. How did the process of creating and ratifying the Constitution, and the language of the Constitution itself, confirm the positions of African Americans, women, and Native Americans in the new republic? How did these roles compare to the stated goals of the republic?

18. What were the circumstances that led to Shays' Rebellion? What was the government's response? Would this response have confirmed or negated the grievances of the participants in the uprising? Why?

Growing Pains: The New Republic, 1790–1820

FIGURE 8.1 "The happy Effects of the Grand System [sic] of shutting Ports against the English!!" appeared in 1808. Less than a year earlier, Thomas Jefferson had recommended (and Congress had passed) the Embargo Act of 1807, which barred American ships from leaving their ports.

CHAPTER OUTLINE

8.1 Competing Visions: Federalists and Democratic-Republicans
8.2 The New American Republic
8.3 Partisan Politics
8.4 The United States Goes Back to War

INTRODUCTION The partisan political cartoon above (Figure 8.1) lampoons Thomas Jefferson's 1807 Embargo Act, a move that had a devastating effect on American commerce. American farmers and merchants complain to President Jefferson, while the French emperor Napoleon Bonaparte whispers to him, "You shall be King hereafter." This image illustrates one of many political struggles in the years after the fight for ratification of the Constitution. In the nation's first few years, no organized political parties existed. This began to change as U.S. citizens argued bitterly about the proper size and scope of the new national government. As a result, the 1790s witnessed the rise of opposing political parties: the Federalists and the Democratic-Republicans. Federalists saw unchecked democracy as a dire threat to the republic, and they pointed to the excesses of the French Revolution as proof of what awaited. Democratic-Republicans opposed the Federalists' notion that only the wellborn and well educated were able to oversee the republic; they saw it as a pathway to oppression by an aristocracy.

8.1 Competing Visions: Federalists and Democratic-Republicans

LEARNING OBJECTIVES

By the end of this section, you will be able to:
- Describe the competing visions of the Federalists and the Democratic-Republicans
- Identify the protections granted to citizens under the Bill of Rights
- Explain Alexander Hamilton's financial programs as secretary of the treasury

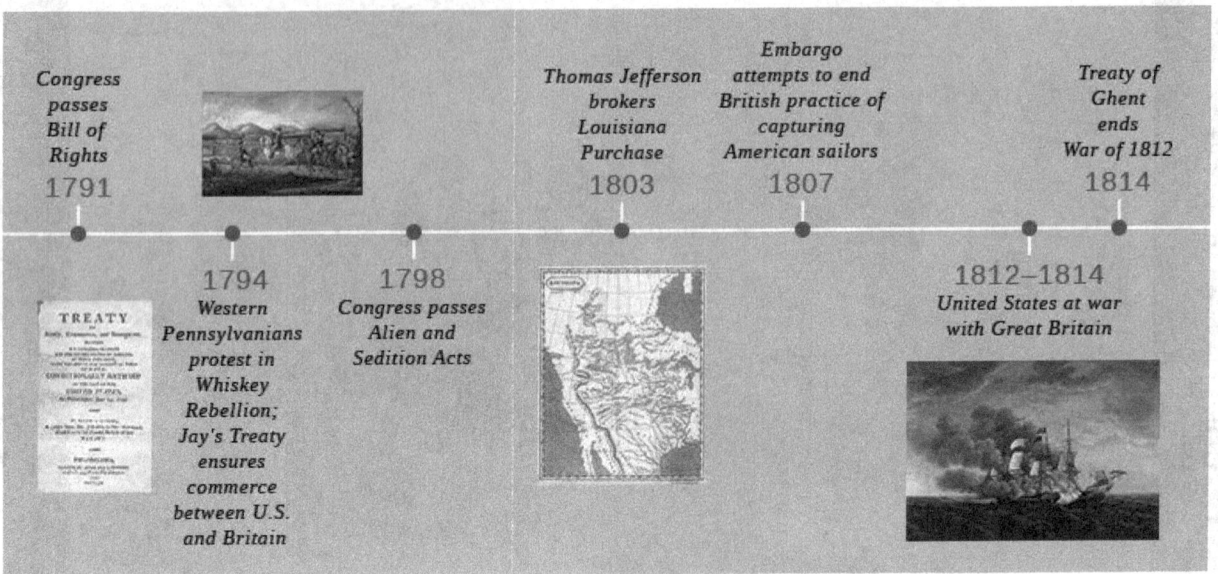

FIGURE 8.2

In June 1788, New Hampshire became the ninth state to ratify the federal Constitution, and the new plan for a strong central government went into effect. Elections for the first U.S. Congress were held in 1788 and 1789, and members took their seats in March 1789. In a reflection of the trust placed in him as the personification of republican virtue, George Washington became the first president in April 1789. John Adams served as his vice president; the pairing of a representative from Virginia (Washington) with one from Massachusetts (Adams) symbolized national unity. Nonetheless, political divisions quickly became apparent. Washington and Adams represented the Federalist Party, which generated a backlash among those who resisted the new government's assertions of federal power.

FEDERALISTS IN POWER

Though the Revolution had overthrown British rule in the United States, supporters of the 1787 federal constitution, known as Federalists, adhered to a decidedly British notion of social hierarchy. The Federalists did not, at first, compose a political party. Instead, Federalists held certain shared assumptions. For them, political participation continued to be linked to property rights, which barred many citizens from voting or holding office. Federalists did not believe the Revolution had changed the traditional social roles between women and men, or between White people and other races. They did believe in clear distinctions in rank and intelligence. To these supporters of the Constitution, the idea that all were equal appeared ludicrous. Women, Black, and Native peoples, they argued, had to know their place as secondary to White male citizens. Attempts to impose equality, they feared, would destroy the republic. The United States was not created to be a democracy.

The architects of the Constitution committed themselves to leading the new republic, and they held a majority among the members of the new national government. Indeed, as expected, many assumed the new executive posts the first Congress created. Washington appointed Alexander Hamilton, a leading Federalist, as secretary of the treasury. For secretary of state, he chose Thomas Jefferson. For secretary of war, he appointed Henry Knox, who had served with him during the Revolutionary War. Edmond Randolph, a Virginia delegate to the

Constitutional Convention, was named attorney general. In July 1789, Congress also passed the Judiciary Act, creating a Supreme Court of six justices headed by those who were committed to the new national government.

Congress passed its first major piece of legislation by placing a duty on imports under the 1789 Tariff Act. Intended to raise revenue to address the country's economic problems, the act was a victory for nationalists, who favored a robust, powerful federal government and had worked unsuccessfully for similar measures during the Confederation Congress in the 1780s. Congress also placed a fifty-cent-per-ton duty (based on materials transported, not the weight of a ship) on foreign ships coming into American ports, a move designed to give the commercial advantage to American ships and goods.

THE BILL OF RIGHTS

Many Americans opposed the 1787 Constitution because it seemed a dangerous concentration of centralized power that threatened the rights and liberties of ordinary U.S. citizens. These opponents, known collectively as Anti-Federalists, did not constitute a political party, but they united in demanding protection for individual rights, and several states made the passing of a bill of rights a condition of their acceptance of the Constitution. Rhode Island and North Carolina rejected the Constitution because it did not already have this specific bill of rights.

Federalists followed through on their promise to add such a bill in 1789, when Virginia Representative James Madison introduced and Congress approved the **Bill of Rights** (Table 8.1). Adopted in 1791, the bill consisted of the first ten amendments to the Constitution and outlined many of the personal rights state constitutions already guaranteed.

Amendment 1	Right to freedoms of religion and speech; right to assemble and to petition the government for redress of grievances
Amendment 2	Right to keep and bear arms to maintain a well-regulated militia
Amendment 3	Right not to house soldiers during time of war
Amendment 4	Right to be secure from unreasonable search and seizure
Amendment 5	Rights in criminal cases, including to due process and indictment by grand jury for capital crimes, as well as the right not to testify against oneself
Amendment 6	Right to a speedy trial by an impartial jury
Amendment 7	Right to a jury trial in civil cases
Amendment 8	Right not to face excessive bail or fines, or cruel and unusual punishment
Amendment 9	Rights retained by the people, even if they are not specifically enumerated by the Constitution
Amendment 10	States' rights to powers not specifically delegated to the federal government

TABLE 8.1 Rights Protected by the First Ten Amendments

The adoption of the Bill of Rights softened the Anti-Federalists' opposition to the Constitution and gave the new federal government greater legitimacy among those who otherwise distrusted the new centralized power created by men of property during the secret 1787 Philadelphia Constitutional Convention.

> **CLICK AND EXPLORE**
>
> Visit the National Archives (http://openstax.org/l/BillRights) to consider the first ten amendments to the Constitution as an expression of the fears many citizens harbored about the powers of the new federal government. What were these fears? How did the Bill of Rights calm them?

ALEXANDER HAMILTON'S PROGRAM

Alexander Hamilton, Washington's secretary of the treasury, was an ardent nationalist who believed a strong federal government could solve many of the new country's financial ills. Born in the West Indies, Hamilton had worked on a St. Croix plantation as a teenager and was in charge of the accounts at a young age. He knew the Atlantic trade very well and used that knowledge in setting policy for the United States. In the early 1790s, he created the foundation for the U.S. financial system. He understood that a robust federal government would provide a solid financial foundation for the country.

The United States began mired in debt. In 1789, when Hamilton took up his post, the federal debt was over $53 million. The states had a combined debt of around $25 million, and the United States had been unable to pay its debts in the 1780s and was therefore considered a credit risk by European countries. Hamilton wrote three reports offering solutions to the economic crisis brought on by these problems. The first addressed public credit, the second addressed banking, and the third addressed raising revenue.

The Report on Public Credit

For the national government to be effective, Hamilton deemed it essential to have the support of those to whom it owed money: the wealthy, domestic creditor class as well as foreign creditors. In January 1790, he delivered his "Report on Public Credit" (Figure 8.3), addressing the pressing need of the new republic to become creditworthy. He recommended that the new federal government honor all its debts, including all paper money issued by the Confederation and the states during the war, at face value. Hamilton especially wanted wealthy American creditors who held large amounts of paper money to be invested, literally, in the future and welfare of the new national government. He also understood the importance of making the new United States financially stable for creditors abroad. To pay these debts, Hamilton proposed that the federal government sell bonds—federal interest-bearing notes—to the public. These bonds would have the backing of the government and yield interest payments. Creditors could exchange their old notes for the new government bonds. Hamilton wanted to give the paper money that states had issued during the war the same status as government bonds; these federal notes would begin to yield interest payments in 1792.

FIGURE 8.3 As the first secretary of the treasury, Alexander Hamilton (a), shown here in a 1792 portrait by John Trumbull, released the "Report on Public Credit" (b) in January 1790.

Hamilton designed his "Report on Public Credit" (later called "First Report on Public Credit") to ensure the survival of the new and shaky American republic. He knew the importance of making the United States financially reliable, secure, and strong, and his plan provided a blueprint to achieve that goal. He argued that his plan would satisfy creditors, citing the goal of "doing justice to the creditors of the nation." At the same time, the plan would work "to promote the increasing respectability of the American name; to answer the calls for justice; to restore landed property to its due value; to furnish new resources both to agriculture and commerce; to cement more closely the union of the states; to add to their security against foreign attack; to establish public order on the basis of upright and liberal policy."

Hamilton's program ignited a heated debate in Congress. A great many of both Confederation and state notes had found their way into the hands of speculators, who had bought them from hard-pressed veterans in the 1780s and paid a fraction of their face value in anticipation of redeeming them at full value at a later date. Because these speculators held so many notes, many in Congress objected that Hamilton's plan would benefit them at the expense of the original note-holders. One of those who opposed Hamilton's 1790 report was James Madison, who questioned the fairness of a plan that seemed to cheat poor soldiers.

Not surprisingly, states with a large debt, like South Carolina, supported Hamilton's plan, while states with less debt, like North Carolina, did not. To gain acceptance of his plan, Hamilton worked out a compromise with Virginians Madison and Jefferson, whereby in return for their support he would give up New York City as the nation's capital and agree on a more southern location, which they preferred. In July 1790, a site along the Potomac River was selected as the new "federal city," which became the District of Columbia.

Hamilton's plan to convert notes to bonds worked extremely well to restore European confidence in the U.S. economy. It also proved a windfall for creditors, especially those who had bought up state and Confederation notes at far less than face value. But it immediately generated controversy about the size and scope of the government. Some saw the plan as an unjust use of federal power, while Hamilton argued that Article 1, Section 8 of the Constitution granted the government "implied powers" that gave the green light to his program.

The Report on a National Bank

As secretary of the treasury, Hamilton hoped to stabilize the American economy further by establishing a national bank. The United States operated with a flurry of different notes from multiple state banks and no coherent regulation. By proposing that the new national bank buy up large volumes of state bank notes and demanding their conversion into gold, Hamilton especially wanted to discipline those state banks that issued paper money irresponsibly. To that end, he delivered his "Report on a National Bank" in December 1790, proposing a Bank of the United States, an institution modeled on the Bank of England. The bank would issue loans to American merchants and bills of credit (federal bank notes that would circulate as money) while serving as a repository of government revenue from the sale of land. Stockholders would own the bank, along with the federal government.

Like the recommendations in his "Report on Public Credit," Hamilton's bank proposal generated opposition. Jefferson, in particular, argued that the Constitution did not permit the creation of a national bank. In response, Hamilton again invoked the Constitution's implied powers. President Washington backed Hamilton's position and signed legislation creating the bank in 1791.

The Report on Manufactures

The third report Hamilton delivered to Congress, known as the "Report on Manufactures," addressed the need to raise revenue to pay the interest on the national debt. Using the power to tax as provided under the Constitution, Hamilton put forth a proposal to tax American-made whiskey. He also knew the importance of promoting domestic manufacturing so the new United States would no longer have to rely on imported manufactured goods. To break from the old colonial system, Hamilton therefore advocated tariffs on all foreign imports to stimulate the production of American-made goods. To promote domestic industry further, he proposed federal subsidies to American industries. Like all of Hamilton's programs, the idea of government involvement in the development of American industries was new.

With the support of Washington, the entire Hamiltonian economic program received the necessary support in Congress to be implemented. In the long run, Hamilton's financial program helped to rescue the United States from its state of near-bankruptcy in the late 1780s. His initiatives marked the beginning of an American capitalism, making the republic creditworthy, promoting commerce, and setting for the nation a solid financial foundation. His policies also facilitated the growth of the stock market, as U.S. citizens bought and sold the federal government's interest-bearing certificates.

THE DEMOCRATIC-REPUBLICAN PARTY AND THE FIRST PARTY SYSTEM

James Madison and Thomas Jefferson felt the federal government had overstepped its authority by adopting the treasury secretary's plan. Madison found Hamilton's scheme immoral and offensive. He argued that it turned the reins of government over to the class of speculators who profited at the expense of hardworking citizens.

Jefferson, who had returned to the United States in 1790 after serving as a diplomat in France, tried unsuccessfully to convince Washington to block the creation of a national bank. He also took issue with what he perceived as favoritism given to commercial classes in the principal American cities. He thought urban life widened the gap between the wealthy few and an underclass of landless poor workers who, because of their oppressed condition, could never be good republican property owners. Rural areas, in contrast, offered far more opportunities for property ownership and virtue. In 1783 Jefferson wrote, "Those who labor in the earth are the chosen people of God, if ever he had a chosen people." Jefferson believed that self-sufficient, property-owning republican citizens or yeoman farmers held the key to the success and longevity of the American republic. (As a creature of his times, he did not envision a similar role for either women or non-White men.) To him, Hamilton's program seemed to encourage economic inequalities and work against the ordinary American yeoman.

Opposition to Hamilton, who had significant power in the new federal government, including the ear of President Washington, began in earnest in the early 1790s. Jefferson turned to his friend Philip Freneau to help organize the effort through the publication of the *National Gazette* as a counter to the Federalist press, especially the *Gazette of the United States* (Figure 8.4). From 1791 until 1793, when it ceased publication, Freneau's partisan paper attacked Hamilton's program and Washington's administration. "Rules for Changing a Republic into a Monarchy," written by Freneau, is an example of the type of attack aimed at the national government, and especially at the elitism of the Federalist Party. Newspapers in the 1790s became enormously important in American culture as partisans like Freneau attempted to sway public opinion. These newspapers did not aim to be objective; instead, they served to broadcast the views of a particular party.

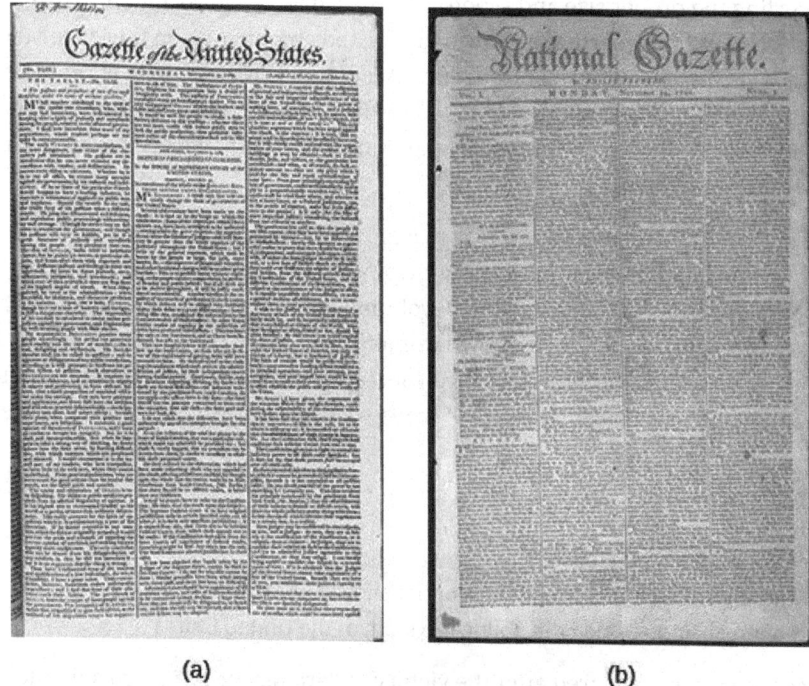

(a)   (b)

FIGURE 8.4 Here, the front page of the Federalist *Gazette of the United States* from September 9, 1789 (a), is shown beside that of the oppositional *National Gazette* from November 14, 1791 (b). The *Gazette of the United States* featured articles, sometimes written pseudonymously or anonymously, from leading Federalists like Alexander Hamilton and John Adams. The *National Gazette* was founded two years later to counter their political influence.

CLICK AND EXPLORE

Visit Lexrex.com (http://openstax.org/l/NatGazette) to read Philip Freneau's essay and others from the *National Gazette*. Can you identify three instances of persuasive writing against the Federalist Party or the government?

Opposition to the Federalists led to the formation of Democratic-Republican societies, composed of men who felt the domestic policies of the Washington administration were designed to enrich the few while ignoring everyone else. **Democratic-Republicans** championed limited government. Their fear of centralized power originated in the experience of the 1760s and 1770s when the distant, overbearing, and seemingly corrupt British Parliament attempted to impose its will on the colonies. The 1787 federal constitution, written in secret by fifty-five wealthy men of property and standing, ignited fears of a similar menacing plot. To opponents, the Federalists promoted aristocracy and a monarchical government—a betrayal of what many believed to be the goal of the American Revolution.

While wealthy merchants and planters formed the core of the Federalist leadership, members of the Democratic-Republican societies in cities like Philadelphia and New York came from the ranks of artisans. These citizens saw themselves as acting in the spirit of 1776, this time not against the haughty British but by what they believed to have replaced them—a commercial class with no interest in the public good. Their political efforts against the Federalists were a battle to preserve republicanism, to promote the public good against private self-interest. They published their views, held meetings to voice their opposition, and sponsored festivals and parades. In their strident newspapers attacks, they also worked to undermine the traditional forms of deference and subordination to aristocrats, in this case the Federalist elites. Some members of northern Democratic-Republican clubs denounced slavery as well.

DEFINING CITIZENSHIP

While questions regarding the proper size and scope of the new national government created a divide among Americans and gave rise to political parties, a consensus existed among men on the issue of who qualified and who did not qualify as a citizen. The 1790 Naturalization Act defined citizenship in stark racial terms. To be a citizen of the American republic, an immigrant had to be a "free White person" of "good character." By excluding enslaved, free Black, Native, and Asian people from citizenship, the act laid the foundation for the United States as a republic of White men.

Full citizenship that included the right to vote was restricted as well. Many state constitutions directed that only male property owners or taxpayers could vote. For women, the right to vote remained out of reach except in the state of New Jersey. In 1776, the fervor of the Revolution led New Jersey revolutionaries to write a constitution extending the right to vote to unmarried women who owned property worth £50. Federalists and Democratic-Republicans competed for the votes of New Jersey women who met the requirements to cast ballots. This radical innovation continued until 1807, when New Jersey restricted voting to free White males.

8.2 The New American Republic

LEARNING OBJECTIVES

By the end of this section, you will be able to:
- Identify the major foreign and domestic uprisings of the early 1790s
- Explain the effect of these uprisings on the political system of the United States

The colonies' alliance with France, secured after the victory at Saratoga in 1777, proved crucial in their victory against the British, and during the 1780s France and the new United States enjoyed a special relationship. Together they had defeated their common enemy, Great Britain. But despite this shared experience, American opinions regarding France diverged sharply in the 1790s when France underwent its own revolution. Democratic-Republicans seized on the French revolutionaries' struggle against monarchy as the welcome harbinger of a larger republican movement around the world. To the Federalists, however, the French Revolution represented pure anarchy, especially after the execution of the French king in 1793. Along with other foreign and domestic uprisings, the French Revolution helped harden the political divide in the United States in the early 1790s.

THE FRENCH REVOLUTION

The French Revolution, which began in 1789, further split American thinkers into different ideological camps, deepening the political divide between Federalists and their Democratic-Republican foes. At first, in 1789 and 1790, the revolution in France appeared to most in the United States as part of a new chapter in the rejection of corrupt monarchy, a trend inspired by the American Revolution. A constitutional monarchy replaced the absolute monarchy of Louis XVI in 1791, and in 1792, France was declared a republic. Republican liberty, the creed of the United States, seemed to be ushering in a new era in France. Indeed, the American Revolution served as an inspiration for French revolutionaries.

The events of 1793 and 1794 challenged the simple interpretation of the French Revolution as a happy chapter in the unfolding triumph of republican government over monarchy. The French king was executed in January 1793 (Figure 8.5), and the next two years became known as **the Terror**, a period of extreme violence against perceived enemies of the revolutionary government. Revolutionaries advocated direct representative democracy, dismantled Catholicism, replaced that religion with a new philosophy known as the Cult of the Supreme Being, renamed the months of the year, and relentlessly employed the guillotine against their enemies. Federalists viewed these excesses with growing alarm, fearing that the radicalism of the French Revolution might infect the minds of citizens at home. Democratic-Republicans interpreted the same events with greater optimism, seeing them as a necessary evil of eliminating the monarchy and aristocratic culture that supported the privileges of a hereditary class of rulers.

FIGURE 8.5 An image from a 1791 Hungarian journal depicts the beheading of Louis XVI during the French Revolution. The violence of the revolutionary French horrified many in the United States—especially Federalists, who saw it as an example of what could happen when the mob gained political control and instituted direct democracy.

The controversy in the United States intensified when France declared war on Great Britain and Holland in February 1793. France requested that the United States make a large repayment of the money it had borrowed from France to fund the Revolutionary War. However, Great Britain would judge any aid given to France as a hostile act. Washington declared the United States neutral in 1793, but Democratic-Republican groups denounced neutrality and declared their support of the French republicans. The Federalists used the violence of the French revolutionaries as a reason to attack Democratic-Republicanism in the United States, arguing that Jefferson and Madison would lead the country down a similarly disastrous path.

CLICK AND EXPLORE

Visit Liberty, Equality, Fraternity (http://openstax.org/l/revolution) for images, texts, and songs relating to the French Revolution. This momentous event's impact extended far beyond Europe, influencing politics in the United States and elsewhere in the Atlantic World.

THE CITIZEN GENÊT AFFAIR AND JAY'S TREATY

In 1793, the revolutionary French government sent Edmond-Charles Genêt to the United States to negotiate an alliance with the U.S. government. France authorized Genêt to issue **letters of marque**—documents authorizing ships and their crews to engage in piracy—to allow him to arm captured British ships in American ports with U.S. soldiers. Genêt arrived in Charleston, South Carolina, amid great Democratic-Republican fanfare. He immediately began commissioning American privateer ships and organizing volunteer American militias to attack Spanish holdings in the Americas, then traveled to Philadelphia, gathering support for the French cause along the way. President Washington and Hamilton denounced Genêt, knowing his actions threatened to pull the United States into a war with Great Britain. The **Citizen Genêt affair**, as it became known, spurred Great Britain to instruct its naval commanders in the West Indies to seize all ships trading with the French. The British captured hundreds of American ships and their cargoes, increasing the possibility of war between the two countries.

In this tense situation, Great Britain worked to prevent a wider conflict by ending its seizure of American ships and offered to pay for captured cargoes. Hamilton saw an opportunity and recommended to Washington that the United States negotiate. Supreme Court Justice John Jay was sent to Britain, instructed by Hamilton to secure compensation for captured American ships; ensure the British leave the Northwest outposts they still occupied despite the 1783 Treaty of Paris; and gain an agreement for American trade in the West Indies. Even though Jay personally disliked slavery, his mission also required him to seek compensation from the British for self-emancipated enslaved people who left with the British at the end of the Revolutionary War.

The resulting 1794 agreement, known as Jay's Treaty, fulfilled most of his original goals. The British would turn over the frontier posts in the Northwest, American ships would be allowed to trade freely in the West Indies, and the United States agreed to assemble a commission charged with settling colonial debts U.S. citizens owed British merchants. The treaty did not address the important issue of **impressment**, however—the British navy's practice of forcing or "impressing" American sailors to work and fight on British warships. Jay's Treaty led the Spanish, who worried that it signaled an alliance between the United States and Great Britain, to negotiate a treaty of their own—Pinckney's Treaty—that allowed American commerce to flow through the Spanish port of New Orleans. Pinckney's Treaty allowed American farmers, who were moving in greater numbers to the Ohio River Valley, to ship their products down the Ohio and Mississippi Rivers to New Orleans, where they could be transported to East Coast markets.

Jay's Treaty confirmed the fears of Democratic-Republicans, who saw it as a betrayal of republican France, cementing the idea that the Federalists favored aristocracy and monarchy. Partisan American newspapers tried to sway public opinion, while the skillful writing of Hamilton, who published a number of essays on the subject, explained the benefits of commerce with Great Britain.

THE FRENCH REVOLUTION'S CARIBBEAN LEGACY

Unlike the American Revolution, which ultimately strengthened the institution of slavery and the powers of American slaveholders, the French Revolution inspired slave rebellions in the Caribbean, including a 1791 uprising in the French colony of Saint-Domingue (modern-day Haiti). Thousands of enslaved people joined together to overthrow the brutal system of slavery. They took control of a large section of the island, burning sugar plantations and killing the White people who had forced them to labor under the lash.

In 1794, French revolutionaries abolished slavery in the French empire, and both Spain and England attacked Saint-Domingue, hoping to add the colony to their own empires. Toussaint L'Ouverture, who had been born with slave status was later freed, emerged as the leader in the fight against Spain and England to secure a Haiti free of slavery and further European colonialism. Because revolutionary France had abolished slavery, Toussaint aligned himself with France, hoping to keep Spain and England at bay (Figure 8.6).

FIGURE 8.6 An 1802 portrait shows Toussaint L'Ouverture, *"Chef des Noirs Insurgés de Saint Domingue"* ("Leader of the Black Insurgents of Saint Domingue"), mounted and armed in an elaborate uniform.

Events in Haiti further complicated the partisan wrangling in the United States. White refugee planters from Haiti and other French West Indian islands, along with enslaved and free people of color, left the Caribbean for the United States and for Louisiana, which at the time was held by Spain. The presence of these French migrants raised fears, especially among Federalists, that they would bring the contagion of French radicalism to the United States. In addition, the idea that the French Revolution could inspire a successful slave uprising just off the American coastline filled southern White people and slaveholders with horror.

THE WHISKEY REBELLION

While the wars in France and the Caribbean divided American citizens, a major domestic test of the new national government came in 1794 over the issue of a tax on whiskey, an important part of Hamilton's financial program. In 1791, Congress had authorized a tax of 7.5 cents per gallon of whiskey and rum. Although most citizens paid without incident, trouble erupted in four western Pennsylvania counties in an uprising known as the Whiskey Rebellion.

Farmers in the western counties of Pennsylvania produced whiskey from their grain for economic reasons. Without adequate roads or other means to transport a bulky grain harvest, these farmers distilled their grains into gin and whiskey, which were more cost-effective to transport. Since these farmers depended on the sale of whiskey, some citizens in western Pennsylvania (and elsewhere) viewed the new tax as further proof that the new national government favored the commercial classes on the eastern seaboard at the expense of farmers in the West. On the other hand, supporters of the tax argued that it helped stabilize the economy and its cost could easily be passed on to the consumer, not the farmer-distiller. However, in the spring and summer months of 1794, angry citizens rebelled against the federal officials in charge of enforcing the federal excise law. Like the Sons of Liberty before the American Revolution, the whiskey rebels used violence and intimidation to protest policies they saw as unfair. They tarred and feathered federal officials, intercepted the federal mail, and intimidated wealthy citizens. The extent of their discontent found expression in their plan to form an independent western commonwealth, and they even began negotiations with British and Spanish representatives, hoping to secure their support for independence from the United States. The rebels also contacted their backcountry neighbors in Kentucky and South Carolina, circulating the idea of secession.

With their emphasis on personal freedoms, the whiskey rebels aligned themselves with the Democratic-Republican Party. They saw the tax as part of a larger Federalist plot to destroy their republican liberty and, in its most extreme interpretation, turn the United States into a monarchy. The federal government lowered the tax, but when federal officials tried to subpoena those distillers who remained intractable, trouble escalated. Washington responded by creating a thirteen-thousand-man militia, drawn from several states, to put down the rebellion (Figure 8.7). This force made it known, both domestically and to the European powers that looked on in anticipation of the new republic's collapse, that the national government would do everything in its power to ensure the survival of the United States.

FIGURE 8.7 This painting, attributed to Frederick Kemmelmeyer ca. 1795, depicts the massive force George Washington led to put down the Whiskey Rebellion of the previous year. Federalists made clear they would not

tolerate mob action.

DEFINING AMERICAN

Alexander Hamilton: "Shall the majority govern or be governed?"

Alexander Hamilton frequently wrote persuasive essays under pseudonyms, like "Tully," as he does here. In this 1794 essay, Hamilton denounces the whiskey rebels and majority rule.

"It has been observed that the means most likely to be employed to turn the insurrection in the western country to the detriment of the government, would be artfully calculated among other things 'to divert your attention from the true question to be decided.'

Let us see then what is this question. It is plainly this—shall the majority govern or be governed? shall the nation rule, or be ruled? shall the general will prevail, or the will of a faction? shall there be government, or no government? . . .

The Constitution *you* have ordained for yourselves and your posterity contains this express clause, 'The Congress *shall have power* to lay and collect taxes, duties, imposts, and *Excises*, to pay the debts, and provide for the common defence and general welfare of the United States.' You have then, by a solemn and deliberate act, the most important and sacred that a nation can perform, pronounced and decreed, that your Representatives in Congress shall have power to lay Excises. You have done nothing since to reverse or impair that decree. . . .

But the four western counties of Pennsylvania, undertake to rejudge and reverse your decrees, you have said, 'The Congress *shall have power* to lay *Excises*.' They say, 'The Congress *shall not have* this power.' . . .

There is no road to *despotism* more sure or more to be dreaded than that which begins at *anarchy*."

—Alexander Hamilton's "Tully No. II" for the *American Daily Advertiser*, Philadelphia, August 26, 1794"

What are the major arguments put forward by Hamilton in this document? Who do you think his audience is?

WASHINGTON'S NATIVE AMERICAN POLICY

Relationships with Native Americans were a significant problem for Washington's administration, but one on which White citizens agreed: Native Americans stood in the way of White settlement and, as the 1790 Naturalization Act made clear, were not citizens. After the War of Independence, White settlers poured into lands west of the Appalachian Mountains. As a result, from 1785 to 1795, a state of war existed on the frontier between these settlers and the Native Americans who lived in the Ohio territory. In both 1790 and 1791, the Shawnee and Miami had defended their lands against the White settlers who arrived in greater and greater numbers from the East. In response, Washington appointed General Anthony Wayne to bring the Western Confederacy—a loose alliance of tribes—to heel. In 1794, at the Battle of Fallen Timbers, Wayne was victorious. With the 1795 Treaty of Greenville (Figure 8.8), the Western Confederacy gave up their claims to Ohio.

FIGURE 8.8 Notice the contrasts between the depictions of federal and Native representatives in this painting of the signing of the Treaty of Greenville in 1795. What message or messages did the artist intend to convey?

8.3 Partisan Politics

LEARNING OBJECTIVES

By the end of this section, you will be able to:
- Identify key examples of partisan wrangling between the Federalists and Democratic-Republicans
- Describe how foreign relations affected American politics
- Assess the importance of the Louisiana Purchase

George Washington, who had been reelected in 1792 by an overwhelming majority, refused to run for a third term, thus setting a precedent for future presidents. In the presidential election of 1796, the two parties—Federalist and Democratic-Republican—competed for the first time. Partisan rancor over the French Revolution and the Whiskey Rebellion fueled the divide between them, and Federalist John Adams defeated his Democratic-Republican rival Thomas Jefferson by a narrow margin of only three electoral votes. In 1800, another close election swung the other way, and Jefferson began a long period of Democratic-Republican government.

THE PRESIDENCY OF JOHN ADAMS

The war between Great Britain and France in the 1790s shaped U.S. foreign policy. As a new and, in comparison to the European powers, extremely weak nation, the American republic had no control over European events, and no real leverage to obtain its goals of trading freely in the Atlantic. To Federalist president John Adams, relations with France posed the biggest problem. After the Terror, the French Directory ruled France from 1795 to 1799. During this time, Napoleon rose to power.

AMERICANA

The Art of Ralph Earl

Ralph Earl was an eighteenth-century American artist, born in Massachusetts, who remained loyal to the British during the Revolutionary War. He fled to England in 1778, but he returned to New England in the mid-1780s and began painting portraits of leading Federalists.

His portrait of Connecticut Federalist Oliver Ellsworth and his wife Abigail conveys the world as Federalists liked to view it: an orderly landscape administered by men of property and learning. His portrait of dry goods merchant Elijah Boardman shows Boardman as well-to-do and highly cultivated; his books include the works of Shakespeare and Milton (Figure 8.9).

(a) (b)

FIGURE 8.9 Ralph Earl's portraits are known for placing their subjects in an orderly world, as seen here in the 1801 portrait of Oliver and Abigail Wolcott Ellsworth (a) and the 1789 portrait of Elijah Boardman (b).

What similarities do you see in the two portraits by Ralph Earl? What do the details of each portrait reveal about the sitters? About the artist and the 1790s?

Because France and Great Britain were at war, the French Directory issued decrees stating that any ship carrying British goods could be seized on the high seas. In practice, this meant the French would target American ships, especially those in the West Indies, where the United States conducted a brisk trade with the British. France declared its 1778 treaty with the United States null and void, and as a result, France and the United States waged an undeclared war—or what historians refer to as the Quasi-War—from 1796 to 1800. Between 1797 and 1799, the French seized 834 American ships, and Adams urged the buildup of the U.S. Navy, which consisted of only a single vessel at the time of his election in 1796 (Figure 8.10).

FIGURE 8.10 This 1799 print, entitled "Preparation for WAR to defend Commerce," shows the construction of a naval ship, part of the effort to ensure the United States had access to free trade in the Atlantic world.

In 1797, Adams sought a diplomatic solution to the conflict with France and dispatched envoys to negotiate terms. The French foreign minister, Charles-Maurice de Talleyrand, sent emissaries who told the American envoys that the United States must repay all outstanding debts owed to France, lend France 32 million guilders

(Dutch currency), and pay a £50,000 bribe before any negotiations could take place. News of the attempt to extract a bribe, known as the **XYZ affair** because the French emissaries were referred to as X, Y, and Z in letters that President Adams released to Congress, outraged the American public and turned public opinion decidedly against France (Figure 8.11). In the court of public opinion, Federalists appeared to have been correct in their interpretation of France, while the pro-French Democratic-Republicans had been misled.

FIGURE 8.11 This anonymous 1798 cartoon, *Property Protected à la Françoise*, satirizes the XYZ affair. Five Frenchmen are shown plundering the treasures of a woman representing the United States. One man holds a sword labeled "French Argument" and a sack of gold and riches labeled "National Sack and Diplomatic Perquisites," while the others collect her valuables. A group of other Europeans look on and commiserate that France treated them the same way.

CLICK AND EXPLORE

Read the "transcript" of the above cartoon in the America in Caricature, 1765–1865 (http://openstax.org/l/cartoon) collection at Indiana University's Lilly Library.

The complicated situation in Haiti, which remained a French colony in the late 1790s, also came to the attention of President Adams. The president, with the support of Congress, had created a U.S. Navy that now included scores of vessels. Most of the American ships cruised the Caribbean, giving the United States the edge over France in the region. In Haiti, the rebellion leader Toussaint, who had to contend with various domestic rivals seeking to displace him, looked to end U.S. embargo on France and its colonies, put in place in 1798, so that his forces would receive help to deal with the civil unrest. In early 1799, in order to capitalize upon trade in the lucrative West Indies and undermine France's hold on the island, Congress ended the ban on trade with Haiti—a move that acknowledged Toussaint's leadership, to the horror of American slaveholders. Toussaint was able to secure an independent Black republic in Haiti by 1804.

THE ALIEN AND SEDITION ACTS

The surge of animosity against France during the Quasi-War led Congress to pass several measures that in time undermined Federalist power. These 1798 war measures, known as the Alien and Sedition Acts, aimed to increase national security against what most had come to regard as the French menace. The Alien Act and the Alien Enemies Act took particular aim at French immigrants fleeing the West Indies by giving the president the power to deport new arrivals who appeared to be a threat to national security. The act expired in 1800 with no immigrants having been deported. The Sedition Act imposed harsh penalties—up to five years' imprisonment and a massive fine of $5,000 in 1790 dollars—on those convicted of speaking or writing "in a scandalous or malicious" manner against the government of the United States. Twenty-five men, all Democratic-Republicans, were indicted under the act, and ten were convicted. One of these was Congressman Matthew Lyon (Figure 8.12), representative from Vermont, who had launched his own newspaper, *The Scourge Of Aristocracy and Repository of Important Political Truth*.

FIGURE 8.12 This 1798 cartoon, "Congressional Pugilists," shows partisan chaos in the U.S. House of Representatives as Matthew Lyon, a Democratic-Republican from Vermont, holds forth against his opponent, Federalist Roger Griswold.

The Alien and Sedition Acts raised constitutional questions about the freedom of the press provided under the First Amendment. Democratic-Republicans argued that the acts were evidence of the Federalists' intent to squash individual liberties and, by enlarging the powers of the national government, crush states' rights. Jefferson and Madison mobilized the response to the acts in the form of statements known as the Virginia and Kentucky Resolutions, which argued that the acts were illegal and unconstitutional. The resolutions introduced the idea of nullification, the right of states to nullify acts of Congress, and advanced the argument of states' rights. The resolutions failed to rally support in other states, however. Indeed, most other states rejected them, citing the necessity of a strong national government.

The Quasi-War with France came to an end in 1800, when President Adams was able to secure the Treaty of Mortefontaine. His willingness to open talks with France divided the Federalist Party, but the treaty reopened trade between the two countries and ended the French practice of taking American ships on the high seas.

THE REVOLUTION OF 1800 AND THE PRESIDENCY OF THOMAS JEFFERSON

The **Revolution of 1800** refers to the first transfer of power from one party to another in American history, when the presidency passed to Democratic-Republican Thomas Jefferson (Figure 8.13) in the 1800 election. The peaceful transition calmed contemporary fears about possible violent reactions to a new party's taking the reins of government. The passing of political power from one political party to another without bloodshed also set an important precedent.

FIGURE 8.13 Thomas Jefferson's victory in 1800 signaled the ascendency of the Democratic-Republicans and the decline of Federalist power.

The election did prove even more divisive than the 1796 election, however, as both the Federalist and Democratic-Republican Parties waged a mudslinging campaign unlike any seen before. Because the Federalists were badly divided, the Democratic-Republicans gained political ground. Alexander Hamilton, who disagreed with President Adams's approach to France, wrote a lengthy letter, meant for people within his party, attacking his fellow Federalist's character and judgment and ridiculing his handling of foreign affairs. Democratic-Republicans got hold of and happily reprinted the letter.

Jefferson viewed participatory democracy as a positive force for the republic, a direct departure from Federalist views. His version of participatory democracy only extended, however, to the White yeoman farmers in whom Jefferson placed great trust. While Federalist statesmen, like the architects of the 1787 federal constitution, feared a pure democracy, Jefferson was far more optimistic that the common American farmer could be trusted to make good decisions. He believed in majority rule, that is, that the majority of yeoman should have the power to make decisions binding upon the whole. Jefferson had cheered the French Revolution, even when the French republic instituted the Terror to ensure the monarchy would not return. By 1799, however, he had rejected the cause of France because of his opposition to Napoleon's seizure of power and creation of a dictatorship.

Over the course of his two terms as president—he was reelected in 1804—Jefferson reversed the policies of the Federalist Party by turning away from urban commercial development. Instead, he promoted agriculture through the sale of western public lands in small and affordable lots. Perhaps Jefferson's most lasting legacy is his vision of an "empire of liberty." He distrusted cities and instead envisioned a rural republic of land-owning White men, or yeoman republican farmers. He wanted the United States to be the breadbasket of the world, exporting its agricultural commodities without suffering the ills of urbanization and industrialization. Since American yeomen would own their own land, they could stand up against those who might try to buy their votes with promises of property. Jefferson championed the rights of states and insisted on limited federal government as well as limited taxes. This stood in stark contrast to the Federalists' insistence on a strong, active federal government. Jefferson also believed in fiscal austerity. He pushed for—and Congress approved—the end of all internal taxes, such as those on whiskey and rum. The most significant trimming of the federal budget came at the expense of the military; Jefferson did not believe in maintaining a costly military, and he slashed the size of the navy Adams had worked to build up. Nonetheless, Jefferson responded to the capture of American ships and sailors by pirates off the coast of North Africa by leading the United States into war against the Muslim Barbary States in 1801, the first conflict fought by Americans overseas.

The slow decline of the Federalists, which began under Jefferson, led to a period of one-party rule in national politics. Historians call the years between 1815 and 1828 the "Era of Good Feelings" and highlight the

"Virginia dynasty" of the time, since the two presidents who followed Jefferson—James Madison and James Monroe—both hailed from his home state. Like him, they were slaveholders and represented the Democratic-Republican Party. Though Federalists continued to enjoy popularity, especially in the Northeast, their days of prominence in setting foreign and domestic policy had ended.

PARTISAN ACRIMONY

The earliest years of the nineteenth century were hardly free of problems between the two political parties. Early in Jefferson's term, controversy swirled over President Adams's judicial appointments of many Federalists during his final days in office. When Jefferson took the oath of office, he refused to have the commissions for these Federalist justices delivered to the appointed officials.

One of Adams's appointees, William Marbury, had been selected to be a justice of the peace in the District of Columbia, and when his commission did not arrive, he petitioned the Supreme Court for an explanation from Jefferson's secretary of state, James Madison. In deciding the case, **Marbury v. Madison**, in 1803, Chief Justice John Marshall agreed that Marbury had the right to a legal remedy, establishing that individuals had rights even the president of the United States could not abridge. However, Marshall also found that Congress's Judicial Act of 1789, which would have given the Supreme Court the power to grant Marbury remedy, was unconstitutional because the Constitution did not allow for cases like Marbury's to come directly before the Supreme Court. Thus, Marshall established the principle of judicial review, which strengthened the court by asserting its power to review (and possibly nullify) the actions of Congress and the president. Jefferson was not pleased, but neither did Marbury get his commission.

The animosity between the political parties exploded into open violence in 1804, when Aaron Burr, Jefferson's first vice president, and Alexander Hamilton engaged in a duel. When Democratic-Republican Burr lost his bid for the office of governor of New York, he was quick to blame Hamilton, who had long hated him and had done everything in his power to discredit him. On July 11, the two antagonists met in Weehawken, New Jersey, to exchange bullets in a duel in which Burr shot and mortally wounded Hamilton.

THE LOUISIANA PURCHASE

Jefferson, who wanted to expand the United States to bring about his "empire of liberty," realized his greatest triumph in 1803 when the United States bought the Louisiana territory from France. For $15 million—a bargain price, considering the amount of land involved—the United States doubled in size. Perhaps the greatest real estate deal in American history, the **Louisiana Purchase** greatly enhanced the Jeffersonian vision of the United States as an agrarian republic in which yeomen farmers worked the land. Jefferson also wanted to bolster trade in the West, seeing the port of New Orleans and the Mississippi River (then the western boundary of the United States) as crucial to American agricultural commerce. In his mind, farmers would send their produce down the Mississippi River to New Orleans, where it would be sold to European traders.

The purchase of Louisiana came about largely because of circumstances beyond Jefferson's control, though he certainly recognized the implications of the transaction. Until 1801, Spain had controlled New Orleans and had given the United States the right to traffic goods in the port without paying customs duties. That year, however, the Spanish had ceded Louisiana (and New Orleans) to France. In 1802, the United States lost its right to deposit goods free in the port, causing outrage among many, some of whom called for war with France.

Jefferson instructed Robert Livingston, the American envoy to France, to secure access to New Orleans, sending James Monroe to France to add additional pressure. The timing proved advantageous. Because enslaved Black people in the French colony of Haiti had successfully overthrown the brutal plantation regime, Napoleon could no longer hope to restore the empire lost with France's defeat in the French and Indian War (1754–1763). His vision of Louisiana and the Mississippi Valley as the source for food for Haiti, the most profitable sugar island in the world, had failed. The emperor therefore agreed to the sale in early 1803.

CLICK AND EXPLORE

Explore the collected maps and documents relating to the Louisiana Purchase and its history at the Library of Congress (http://openstax.org/l/LaPurchase) site.

The true extent of the United States' new territory remained unknown (Figure 8.14). Would it provide the long-sought quick access to Asian markets? Geographical knowledge was limited; indeed, no one knew precisely what lay to the west or how long it took to travel from the Mississippi to the Pacific. Jefferson selected two fellow Virginians, Meriwether Lewis and William Clark, to lead an expedition to the new western lands. Their purpose was to discover the commercial possibilities of the new land and, most importantly, potential trade routes. From 1804 to 1806, Lewis and Clark traversed the West.

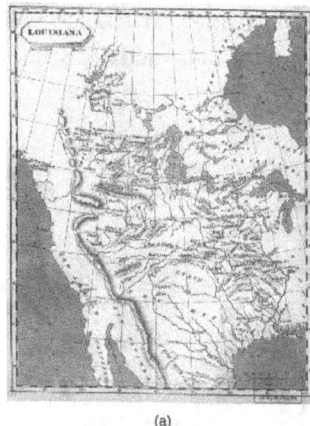
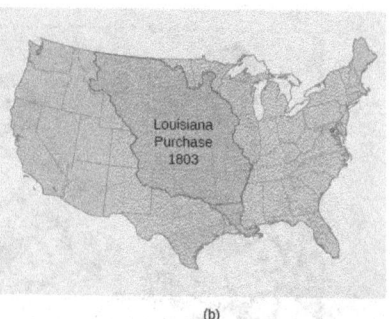

(a) (b)

FIGURE 8.14 This 1804 map (a) shows the territory added to the United States in the Louisiana Purchase of 1803. Compare this depiction to the contemporary map (b). How does the 1804 version differ from what you know of the geography of the United States?

The Louisiana Purchase helped Jefferson win reelection in 1804 by a landslide. Of 176 electoral votes cast, all but 14 were in his favor. The great expansion of the United States did have its critics, however, especially northerners who feared the addition of more slave states and a corresponding lack of representation of their interests in the North. And under a strict interpretation of the Constitution, it remained unclear whether the president had the power to add territory in this fashion. But the vast majority of citizens cheered the increase in the size of the republic. For slaveholders, new western lands would be a boon; for their captives, the Louisiana Purchase threatened to entrench their suffering further.

8.4 The United States Goes Back to War

LEARNING OBJECTIVES
By the end of this section, you will be able to:
- Describe the causes and consequences of the War of 1812
- Identify the important events of the War of 1812 and explain their significance

The origins of the War of 1812, often called the Second War of American Independence, are found in the unresolved issues between the United States and Great Britain. One major cause was the British practice of impressment, whereby American sailors were taken at sea and forced to fight on British warships; this issue was left unresolved by Jay's Treaty in 1794. In addition, the British in Canada supported Native Americans in their fight against further U.S. expansion in the Great Lakes region. Though Jefferson wanted to avoid what he called "entangling alliances," staying neutral proved impossible.

THE EMBARGO OF 1807

France and England, engaged in the Napoleonic Wars, which raged between 1803 and 1815, both declared open season on American ships, which they seized on the high seas. England was the major offender, since the Royal Navy, following a time-honored practice, "impressed" American sailors by forcing them into its service. The issue came to a head in 1807 when the HMS *Leopard*, a British warship, fired on a U.S. naval ship, the *Chesapeake*, off the coast of Norfolk, Virginia. The British then boarded the ship and took four sailors. Jefferson chose what he thought was the best of his limited options and responded to the crisis through the economic means of a sweeping ban on trade, the Embargo Act of 1807. This law prohibited American ships from leaving their ports until Britain and France stopped seizing them on the high seas. As a result of the embargo, American commerce came to a near-total halt.

The logic behind the embargo was that cutting off all trade would so severely hurt Britain and France that the seizures at sea would end. However, while the embargo did have some effect on the British economy, it was American commerce that actually felt the brunt of the impact (Figure 8.15). The embargo hurt American farmers, who could no longer sell their goods overseas, and seaport cities experienced a huge increase in unemployment and an uptick in bankruptcies. All told, American business activity declined by 75 percent from 1808 to 1809.

FIGURE 8.15 In this political cartoon from 1807, a snapping turtle (holding a shipping license) grabs a smuggler in the act of sneaking a barrel of sugar to a British ship. The smuggler cries, "Oh, this cursed Ograbme!" ("Ograbme" is "embargo" spelled backwards.)

Enforcement of the embargo proved very difficult, especially in the states bordering British Canada. Smuggling was widespread; Smugglers' Notch in Vermont, for example, earned its name from illegal trade with British Canada. Jefferson attributed the problems with the embargo to lax enforcement.

At the very end of his second term, Jefferson signed the Non-Intercourse Act of 1808, lifting the unpopular embargoes on trade except with Britain and France. In the election of 1808, American voters elected another Democratic-Republican, James Madison. Madison inherited Jefferson's foreign policy issues involving Britain and France. Most people in the United States, especially those in the West, saw Great Britain as the major problem.

TECUMSEH AND THE WESTERN CONFEDERACY

Another underlying cause of the War of 1812 was British support for native resistance to U.S. western expansion. For many years, White settlers in the American western territories had besieged the Native Americans living there. Under Jefferson, two policies existed: forcing Native Americans to adopt American ways of agricultural life, or aggressively driving them into debt in order to force them to sell their lands.

In 1809, Tecumseh, a Shawnee war chief, rejuvenated the Western Confederacy. His brother, Tenskwatawa, was a prophet among the Shawnee who urged a revival of native ways and rejection of Anglo-American culture, including alcohol. In 1811, William Henry Harrison, the governor of the Indiana Territory, attempted to eliminate the native presence by attacking Prophetstown, a Shawnee settlement named in honor of

Tenskwatawa. In the ensuing Battle of Tippecanoe, U.S. forces led by Harrison destroyed the settlement (Figure 8.16). They also found ample evidence that the British had supplied the Western Confederacy with weapons, despite the stipulations of earlier treaties.

(a) (b)

FIGURE 8.16 Portrait (a), painted by Charles Bird King in 1820, is a depiction of Shawnee prophet Tenskwatawa. Portrait (b) is Rembrandt Peele's 1813 depiction of William Henry Harrison. What are the significant similarities and differences between the portraits? What was each artist trying to convey?

THE WAR OF 1812

The seizure of American ships and sailors, combined with the British support of Native American resistance, led to strident calls for war against Great Britain. The loudest came from the "war hawks," led by Henry Clay from Kentucky and John C. Calhoun from South Carolina, who would not tolerate British insults to American honor. Opposition to the war came from Federalists, especially those in the Northeast, who knew war would disrupt the maritime trade on which they depended. In a narrow vote, Congress authorized the president to declare war against Britain in June 1812.

The war went very badly for the United States at first. In August 1812, the United States lost Detroit to the British and their Native allies, including a force of one thousand men led by Tecumseh. By the end of the year, the British controlled half the Northwest. The following year, however, U.S. forces scored several victories. Captain Oliver Hazard Perry and his naval force defeated the British on Lake Erie. At the Battle of the Thames in Ontario, the United States defeated the British and their native allies, and Tecumseh was counted among the dead. Native American resistance began to ebb, opening the Indiana and Michigan territories for White settlement.

These victories could not turn the tide of the war, however. With the British gaining the upper hand during the Napoleonic Wars and Napoleon's French army on the run, Great Britain now could divert skilled combat troops from Europe to fight in the United States. In July 1814, forty-five hundred hardened British soldiers sailed up the Chesapeake Bay and burned Washington, DC, to the ground, forcing President Madison and his wife to run for their lives (Figure 8.17). According to one report, they left behind a dinner the British officers ate. That summer, the British shelled Baltimore, hoping for another victory. However, they failed to dislodge the U.S. forces, whose survival of the bombardment inspired Francis Scott Key to write "The Star-Spangled Banner."

FIGURE 8.17 George Munger painted *The President's House* shortly after the War of 1812, ca. 1814–1815. The painting shows the result of the British burning of Washington, DC.

AMERICANA

Francis Scott Key's "In Defense of Fort McHenry"

After the British bombed Baltimore's Fort McHenry in 1814 but failed to overcome the U.S. forces there, Francis Scott Key was inspired by the sight of the American flag, which remained hanging proudly in the aftermath. He wrote the poem "In Defense of Fort McHenry," which was later set to the tune of a British song called "The Anacreontic Song" and eventually became the U.S. national anthem, "The Star-Spangled Banner."

"Oh, say, can you see, by the dawn's early light,
What so proudly we hailed at the twilight's last gleaming?
Whose broad stripes and bright stars, thru the perilous fight,
O'er the ramparts we watched, were so gallantly streaming?
And the rockets' red glare, the bombs bursting in air,
Gave proof through the night that our flag was still there.
O say, does that star-spangled banner yet wave
O'er the land of the free and the home of the brave?

On the shore dimly seen through the mists of the deep,
Where the foe's haughty host in dread silence reposes,
What is that which the breeze, o'er the towering steep,
As it fitfully blows, half conceals, half discloses?
Now it catches the gleam of the morning's first beam,
In full glory reflected, now shines on the stream:
Tis the star-spangled banner: O, long may it wave
O'er the land of the free and the home of the brave!

And where is that band who so vauntingly swore
That the havoc of war and the battle's confusion
A home and a country should leave us no more?
Their blood has washed out their foul footsteps' pollution.
No refuge could save the hireling and slave
From the terror of flight or the gloom of the grave:
And the star-spangled banner in triumph doth wave
O'er the land of the free and the home of the brave.

O, thus be it ever when freemen shall stand,

Between their loved home and the war's desolation!
Blest with victory and peace, may the heav'n-rescued land
Praise the Power that hath made and preserved us a nation!
Then conquer we must, when our cause it is just,
And this be our motto: "In God is our trust"
And the star-spangled banner in triumph shall wave
O'er the land of the free and the home of the brave!
—Francis Scott Key, "In Defense of Fort McHenry," 1814
"

What images does Key use to describe the American spirit? Most people are familiar with only the first verse of the song; what do you think the last three verses add?

CLICK AND EXPLORE

Visit the Smithsonian Institute (http://openstax.org/l/flag) to explore an interactive feature on the flag that inspired "The Star-Spangled Banner," where clickable "hot spots" on the flag reveal elements of its history.

With the end of the war in Europe, Britain was eager to end the conflict in the Americas as well. In 1814, British and U.S. diplomats met in Flanders, in northern Belgium, to negotiate the Treaty of Ghent, signed in December. The boundaries between the United States and British Canada remained as they were before the war, an outcome welcome to those in the United States who feared a rupture in the country's otherwise steady expansion into the West.

The War of 1812 was very unpopular in New England because it inflicted further economic harm on a region dependent on maritime commerce. This unpopularity caused a resurgence of the Federalist Party in New England. Many Federalists deeply resented the power of the slaveholding Virginians (Jefferson and then Madison), who appeared indifferent to their region. The depth of the Federalists' discontent is illustrated by the proceedings of the December 1814 Hartford Convention, a meeting of twenty-six Federalists in Connecticut, where some attendees issued calls for New England to secede from the United States. These arguments for disunion during wartime, combined with the convention's condemnation of the government, made Federalists appear unpatriotic. The convention forever discredited the Federalist Party and led to its downfall.

EPILOGUE: THE BATTLE OF NEW ORLEANS

Due to slow communication, the last battle in the War of 1812 happened after the Treaty of Ghent had been signed ending the war. Andrew Jackson had distinguished himself in the war by defeating the Creek Natives in March 1814 before invading Florida in May of that year. After taking Pensacola, he moved his force of Tennessee fighters to New Orleans to defend the strategic port against British attack.

On January 8, 1815 (despite the official end of the war), a force of battle-tested British veterans of the Napoleonic Wars attempted to take the port. Jackson's forces devastated the British, killing over two thousand. New Orleans and the vast Mississippi River Valley had been successfully defended, ensuring the future of American settlement and commerce. The Battle of New Orleans immediately catapulted Jackson to national prominence as a war hero, and in the 1820s, he emerged as the head of the new Democratic Party.

Key Terms

Bill of Rights   the first ten amendments to the United States Constitution, which guarantee individual rights

Citizen Genêt affair   the controversy over the French representative who tried to involve the United States in France's war against Great Britain

Democratic-Republicans   advocates of limited government who were troubled by the expansive domestic policies of Washington's administration and opposed the Federalists

impressment   the practice of capturing sailors and forcing them into military service

letters of marque   French warrants allowing ships and their crews to engage in piracy

Louisiana Purchase   the U.S. purchase of the large territory of Louisiana from France in 1803

Marbury v. Madison   the landmark 1803 case establishing the Supreme Court's powers of judicial review, specifically the power to review and possibly nullify actions of Congress and the president

Revolution of 1800   the peaceful transfer of power from the Federalists to the Democratic-Republicans with the election of 1800

the Terror   a period during the French Revolution characterized by extreme violence and the execution of numerous enemies of the revolutionary government, from 1793 through 1794

XYZ affair   the French attempt to extract a bribe from the United States during the Quasi-War of 1798–1800

Summary

8.1 Competing Visions: Federalists and Democratic-Republicans

While they did not yet constitute distinct political parties, Federalists and Anti-Federalists, shortly after the Revolution, found themselves at odds over the Constitution and the power that it concentrated in the federal government. While many of the Anti-Federalists' fears were assuaged by the adoption of the Bill of Rights in 1791, the early 1790s nevertheless witnessed the rise of two political parties: the Federalists and the Democratic-Republicans. These rival political factions began by defining themselves in relationship to Hamilton's financial program, a debate that exposed contrasting views of the proper role of the federal government. By championing Hamilton's bold financial program, Federalists, including President Washington, made clear their intent to use the federal government to stabilize the national economy and overcome the financial problems that had plagued it since the 1780s. Members of the Democratic-Republican opposition, however, deplored the expanded role of the new national government. They argued that the Constitution did not permit the treasury secretary's expansive program and worried that the new national government had assumed powers it did not rightfully possess. Only on the question of citizenship was there broad agreement: only free, White males who met taxpayer or property qualifications could cast ballots as full citizens of the republic.

8.2 The New American Republic

Federalists and Democratic-Republicans interpreted the execution of the French monarch and the violent establishment of a French republic in very different ways. Revolutionaries' excesses in France and the slave revolt in the French colony of Haiti raised fears among Federalists of similar radicalism and slave uprisings on American shores. They looked to better relationships with Great Britain through Jay's Treaty. Pinckney's Treaty, which came about as a result of Jay's Treaty, improved U.S. relations with the Spanish and opened the Spanish port of New Orleans to American commerce. Democratic-Republicans took a more positive view of the French Revolution and grew suspicious of the Federalists when they brokered Jay's Treaty. Domestically, the partisan divide came to a dramatic head in western Pennsylvania when distillers of whiskey, many aligned with the Democratic-Republicans, took action against the federal tax on their product. Washington led a massive force to put down the uprising, demonstrating Federalist intolerance of mob action. Though divided on many issues, the majority of White citizens agreed on the necessity of eradicating the Native presence on the frontier.

8.3 Partisan Politics

Partisan politics dominated the American political scene at the close of the eighteenth century. The Federalists' and Democratic-Republicans' views of the role of government were in direct opposition to each other, and the close elections of 1796 and 1801 show how the nation grappled with these opposing visions. The high tide of the Federalist Party came after the election of 1796, when the United States engaged in the Quasi-War with France. The issues arising from the Quasi-War gave Adams and the Federalists license to expand the powers of the federal government. However, the tide turned with the close election of 1800, when Jefferson began an administration based on Democratic-Republican ideals. A major success of Jefferson's administration was the Louisiana Purchase of 1803, which helped to fulfill his vision of the United States as an agrarian republic.

8.4 The United States Goes Back to War

The United States was drawn into its "Second War of Independence" against Great Britain when the British, engaged in the Napoleonic Wars against France, took liberties with the fledgling nation by impressing (capturing) its sailors on the high seas and arming its Native enemies. The War of 1812 ended with the boundaries of the United States remaining as they were before the war. The Native peoples in the Western Confederacy suffered a significant defeat, losing both their leader Tecumseh and their fight for contested land in the Northwest. The War of 1812 proved to be of great importance because it generated a surge of national pride, with expressions of American identity such as the poem by Francis Scott Key. The United States was unequivocally separate from Britain and could now turn as never before to expansion in the West.

Review Questions

1. Which of the following is *not* one of the rights the Bill of Rights guarantees?
    A. the right to freedom of speech
    B. the right to an education
    C. the right to bear arms
    D. the right to a trial by jury

2. Which of Alexander Hamilton's financial policies and programs seemed to benefit speculators at the expense of poor soldiers?
    A. the creation of a national bank
    B. the public credit plan
    C. the tax on whiskey
    D. the "Report on Manufactures"

3. What were the fundamental differences between the Federalist and Democratic-Republican visions?

4. Which of the following was *not* true of Jay's Treaty of 1794?
    A. It gave the United States land rights in the West Indies.
    B. It gave American ships the right to trade in the West Indies.
    C. It hardened differences between the political parties of the United States.
    D. It stipulated that U.S. citizens would repay their debts from the Revolutionary War.

5. What was the primary complaint of the rebels in the Whiskey Rebellion?
    A. the ban on alcohol
    B. the lack of political representation for farmers
    C. the need to fight Native Americans for more land
    D. the tax on whiskey and rum

6. How did the French Revolution in the early 1790s influence the evolution of the American political system?

7. What was the primary issue of Adams's presidency?
    A. war with Spain
    B. relations with the native population
    C. infighting within the Federalist Party
    D. relations with France

8. Which of the following events is *not* an example of partisan acrimony?
    A. the jailing of Matthew Lyon
    B. the XYZ affair
    C. the *Marbury v. Madison* case
    D. the Hamilton-Burr duel

9. What was the importance of the Louisiana Purchase?
    A. It gave the United States control of the port of New Orleans for trade.
    B. It opened up the possibility of quick trade routes to Asia.
    C. It gave the United States political leverage against the Spanish.
    D. It provided Napoleon with an impetus to restore France's empire.

10. How did U.S. relations with France influence events at the end of the eighteenth century?

11. Why do historians refer to the election of Thomas Jefferson as the Revolution of 1800?

12. What prompted the Embargo of 1807?
    A. British soldiers burned the U.S. capitol.
    B. The British supplied arms to Native fighters.
    C. The British navy captured American ships on the high seas and impressed their sailors into service for the British.
    D. The British hadn't abandoned their posts in the Northwest Territory as required by Jay's Treaty.

13. What event inspired "The Star-Spangled Banner"?
    A. Betsy Ross sewing the first American flag raised during a time of war
    B. the British bombardment of Baltimore
    C. the British burning of Washington, DC
    D. the naval battle between the *Leopard* and the *Chesapeake*

Critical Thinking Questions

14. Describe Alexander Hamilton's plans to address the nation's financial woes. Which aspects proved most controversial, and why? What elements of the foundation Hamilton laid can still be found in the system today?

15. Describe the growth of the first party system in the United States. How did these parties come to develop? How did they define themselves, both independently and in opposition to one another? Where did they find themselves in agreement?

16. What led to the passage of the Alien and Sedition Acts? What made them so controversial?

17. What was the most significant impact of the War of 1812?

18. In what ways did the events of this era pose challenges to the U.S. Constitution? What constitutional issues were raised, and how were they addressed?

Industrial Transformation in the North, 1800–1850

9

FIGURE 9.1 *Five Points* (1827), by George Catlin, depicts the infamous Five Points neighborhood of New York City, so called because it was centered at the intersection of five streets. Five Points was home to a polyglot mix of recent immigrants, formerly enslaved people, and other members of the working class.

CHAPTER OUTLINE

9.1 Early Industrialization in the Northeast
9.2 A Vibrant Capitalist Republic
9.3 On the Move: The Transportation Revolution
9.4 A New Social Order: Class Divisions

INTRODUCTION By the 1830s, the United States had developed a thriving industrial and commercial sector in the Northeast. Farmers embraced regional and distant markets as the primary destination for their products. Artisans witnessed the methodical division of the labor process in factories. Wage labor became an increasingly common experience. These industrial and market revolutions, combined with advances in transportation, transformed the economic and social landscape. Americans could now quickly produce larger amounts of goods for a nationwide, and sometimes an international, market and rely less on foreign imports than in colonial times.

As American economic life shifted rapidly and modes of production changed, new class divisions emerged and solidified, resulting in previously unknown economic and social inequalities. This image of the Five Points district in New York City captures the turbulence of the time (Figure 9.1). Five Points began as a settlement for freed formerly enslaved people, but it soon became a crowded urban world of American day laborers and low-wage workers who lived a precarious existence that the economic benefits of the new economy largely bypassed. An influx of immigrant workers swelled and diversified an already crowded urban population. By the 1830s, the area had become a slum, home to widespread poverty, crime, and disease. Advances in industrialization and the market revolution came at a human price.

9.1 Early Industrialization in the Northeast

LEARNING OBJECTIVES

By the end of this section, you will be able to:

- Explain the role of the putting-out system in the rise of industrialization
- Understand industrialization's impact on the nature of production and work
- Describe the effect of industrialization on consumption
- Identify the goals of workers' organizations like the Working Men's Party

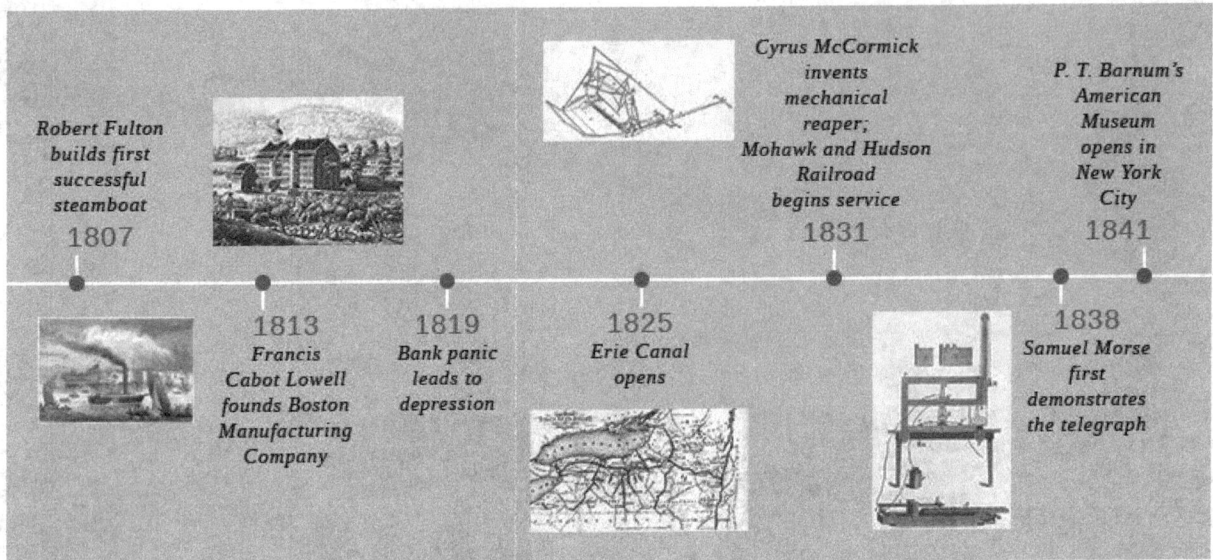

FIGURE 9.2 (credit "1807 photo": Project Gutenberg Archives)

Northern industrialization expanded rapidly following the War of 1812. Industrialized manufacturing began in New England, where wealthy merchants built water-powered textile mills (and mill towns to support them) along the rivers of the Northeast. These mills introduced new modes of production centralized within the confines of the mill itself. As never before, production relied on mechanized sources with water power, and later steam, to provide the force necessary to drive machines. In addition to the mechanization and centralization of work in the mills, specialized, repetitive tasks assigned to wage laborers replaced earlier modes of handicraft production done by artisans at home. The operations of these mills irrevocably changed the nature of work by deskilling tasks, breaking down the process of production to its most basic, elemental parts. In return for their labor, the workers, who at first were young women from rural New England farming families, received wages. From its origin in New England, manufacturing soon spread to other regions of the United States.

FROM ARTISANS TO WAGE WORKERS

During the seventeenth and eighteenth centuries, **artisans**—skilled, experienced craft workers—produced goods by hand. The production of shoes provides a good example. In colonial times, people bought their shoes from master shoemakers, who achieved their status by living and working as apprentices under the rule of an older master artisan. An apprenticeship would be followed by work as a journeyman (a skilled worker without his own shop). After sufficient time as a journeyman, a shoemaker could at last set up his own shop as a master artisan. People came to the shop, usually attached to the back of the master artisan's house, and there the shoemaker measured their feet in order to cut and stitch together an individualized product for each customer.

In the late eighteenth and early nineteenth century, merchants in the Northeast and elsewhere turned their attention as never before to the benefits of using unskilled wage labor to make a greater profit by reducing labor costs. They used the **putting-out system**, which the British had employed at the beginning of their own Industrial Revolution, whereby they hired farming families to perform specific tasks in the production process for a set wage. In the case of shoes, for instance, American merchants hired one group of workers to cut soles into standardized sizes. A different group of families cut pieces of leather for the uppers, while still another was employed to stitch the standardized parts together.

This process proved attractive because it whittled production costs. The families who participated in the putting-out system were not skilled artisans. They had not spent years learning and perfecting their craft and did not have ambitious journeymen to pay. Therefore, they could not demand—and did not receive—high wages. Most of the year they tended fields and orchards, ate the food that they produced, and sold the surplus. Putting-out work proved a welcome source of extra income for New England farm families who saw their profits dwindle from new competition from midwestern farms with higher-yield lands.

Much of this part-time production was done under contract to merchants. Some farming families engaged in shoemaking (or shoe assemblage), as noted above. Many made brooms, plaited hats from straw or palm leaves (which merchants imported from Cuba and the West Indies), crafted furniture, made pottery, or wove baskets. Some, especially those who lived in Connecticut, made parts for clocks. The most common part-time occupation, however, was the manufacture of textiles. Farm women spun woolen thread and wove fabric. They also wove blankets, made rugs, and knit stockings. All this manufacturing took place on the farm, giving farmers and their wives control over the timing and pace of their labor. Their domestic productivity increased the quantity of goods available for sale in country towns and nearby cities.

THE RISE OF MANUFACTURING

In the late 1790s and early 1800s, Great Britain boasted the most advanced textile mills and machines in the world, and the United States continued to rely on Great Britain for finished goods. Great Britain hoped to maintain its economic advantage over its former colonies in North America. So, in an effort to prevent the knowledge of advanced manufacturing from leaving the Empire, the British banned the emigration of mechanics, skilled workers who knew how to build and repair the latest textile machines.

Some skilled British mechanics, including Samuel Slater, managed to travel to the United States in the hopes of profiting from their knowledge and experience with advanced textile manufacturing. Slater ([Figure 9.3](#)) understood the workings of the latest water-powered textile mills, which British industrialist Richard Arkwright had pioneered. In the 1790s in Pawtucket, Rhode Island, Slater convinced several American merchants, including the wealthy Providence industrialist Moses Brown, to finance and build a water-powered cotton mill based on the British models. Slater's knowledge of both technology and mill organization made him the founder of the first truly successful cotton mill in the United States.

(a) (b)

FIGURE 9.3 Samuel Slater (a) was a British migrant who brought plans for English textile mills to the United States and built the nation's first successful water-powered mill in Pawtucket, Massachusetts (b).

The success of Slater and his partners Smith Brown and William Almy, relatives of Moses Brown, inspired others to build additional mills in Rhode Island and Massachusetts. By 1807, thirteen more mills had been established. President Jefferson's embargo on British manufactured goods from late 1807 to early 1809 (discussed in a previous chapter) spurred more New England merchants to invest in industrial enterprises. By 1812, seventy-eight new textile mills had been built in rural New England towns. More than half turned out woolen goods, while the rest produced cotton cloth.

Slater's mills and those built in imitation of his were fairly small, employing only seventy people on average. Workers were organized the way that they had been in English factories, in family units. Under the "Rhode Island system," families were hired. The father was placed in charge of the family unit, and he directed the labor of his wife and children. Instead of being paid in cash, the father was given "credit" equal to the extent of his family's labor that could be redeemed in the form of rent (of company-owned housing) or goods from the company-owned store.

The Embargo of 1807 and the War of 1812 played a pivotal role in spurring industrial development in the United States. Jefferson's embargo prevented American merchants from engaging in the Atlantic trade, severely cutting into their profits. The War of 1812 further compounded the financial woes of American merchants. The acute economic problems led some New England merchants, including Francis Cabot Lowell, to cast their gaze on manufacturing. Lowell had toured English mills during a stay in Great Britain. He returned to Massachusetts having memorized the designs for the advanced textile machines he had seen in his travels, especially the power loom, which replaced individual hand weavers. Lowell convinced other wealthy merchant families to invest in the creation of new mill towns. In 1813, Lowell and these wealthy investors, known as the Boston Associates, created the Boston Manufacturing Company. Together they raised $400,000 and, in 1814, established a textile mill in Waltham and a second one in the same town shortly thereafter (Figure 9.4).

FIGURE 9.4 The Boston Manufacturing Company, shown in this engraving made in 1813–1816, was headquartered in Waltham, Massachusetts. The company started the northeastern textile industry by building water-powered textile mills along suitable rivers and developing mill towns around them.

At Waltham, cotton was carded and drawn into coarse strands of cotton fibers called rovings. The rovings were then spun into yarn, and the yarn woven into cotton cloth. Yarn no longer had to be put out to farm families for further processing. All the work was now performed at a central location—the factory.

The work in Lowell's mills was both mechanized and specialized. Specialization meant the work was broken down into specific tasks, and workers repeatedly did the one task assigned to them in the course of a day. As machines took over labor from humans and people increasingly found themselves confined to the same repetitive step, the process of **deskilling** began.

The Boston Associates' mills, which each employed hundreds of workers, were located in company towns, where the factories and worker housing were owned by a single company. This gave the owners and their agents control over their workers. The most famous of these company towns was Lowell, Massachusetts. The new town was built on land the Boston Associates purchased in 1821 from the village of East Chelmsford at the falls of the Merrimack River, north of Boston. The mill buildings themselves were constructed of red brick with large windows to let in light. Company-owned boarding houses to shelter employees were constructed near the mills. The mill owners planted flowers and trees to maintain the appearance of a rural New England town and to forestall arguments, made by many, that factory work was unnatural and unwholesome.

In contrast to many smaller mills, the Boston Associates' enterprises avoided the Rhode Island system, preferring individual workers to families. These employees were not difficult to find. The competition New England farmers faced from farmers now settling in the West, and the growing scarcity of land in population-dense New England, had important implications for farmers' children. Realizing their chances of inheriting a large farm or receiving a substantial dowry were remote, these teenagers sought other employment opportunities, often at the urging of their parents. While young men could work at a variety of occupations, young women had more limited options. The textile mills provided suitable employment for the daughters of Yankee farm families.

Needing to reassure anxious parents that their daughters' virtue would be protected and hoping to avoid what they viewed as the problems of industrialization—filth and vice—the Boston Associates established strict rules governing the lives of these young workers. The women lived in company-owned boarding houses to which they paid a portion of their wages. They woke early at the sound of a bell and worked a twelve-hour day during which talking was forbidden. They could not swear or drink alcohol, and they were required to attend church on Sunday. Overseers at the mills and boarding-house keepers kept a close eye on the young women's behavior; workers who associated with people of questionable reputation or acted in ways that called their virtue into question lost their jobs and were evicted.

DEFINING AMERICAN

Michel Chevalier on Mill Worker Rules and Wages

In the 1830s, the French government sent engineer and economist Michel Chevalier to study industrial and financial affairs in Mexico and the United States. In 1839, he published *Society, Manners, and Politics in the United States*, in which he recorded his impressions of the Lowell textile mills. In the excerpt below, Chevalier describes the rules and wages of the Lawrence Company in 1833.

"All persons employed by the Company must devote themselves assiduously to their duty during working-hours. They must be capable of doing the work which they undertake, or use all their efforts to this effect. They must on all occasions, both in their words and in their actions, show that they are penetrated by a laudable love of temperance and virtue, and animated by a sense of their moral and social obligations. The Agent of the Company shall endeavour to set to all a good example in this respect. Every individual who shall be notoriously dissolute, idle, dishonest, or intemperate, who shall be in the practice of absenting himself from divine service, or shall violate the Sabbath, or shall be addicted to gaming, shall be dismissed from the service of the Company. . . . All ardent spirits are banished from the Company's grounds, except when prescribed by a physician. All games of hazard and cards are prohibited within their limits and in the boarding-houses.

Weekly wages were as follows:
For picking and carding, $2.78 to $3.10
For spinning, $3.00
For weaving, $3.10 to $3.12
For warping and sizing, $3.45 to $4.00
For measuring and folding, $3.12"

What kind of world were the factory owners trying to create with these rules? How do you think those who believed all White people were born free and equal would react to them?

CLICK AND EXPLORE

Visit the Textile Industry History (https://sites.textiles.ncsu.edu/history/) site to explore the mills of New England through its collection of history, images, and ephemera.

The mechanization of formerly handcrafted goods, and the removal of production from the home to the factory, dramatically increased output of goods. For example, in one nine-month period, the numerous Rhode Island women who spun yarn into cloth on hand looms in their homes produced a total of thirty-four thousand yards of fabrics of different types. In 1855, the women working in just one of Lowell's mechanized mills produced more than forty-three thousand yards.

The Boston Associates' cotton mills quickly gained a competitive edge over the smaller mills established by Samuel Slater and those who had imitated him. Their success prompted the Boston Associates to expand. In Massachusetts, in addition to Lowell, they built new mill towns in Chicopee, Lawrence, and Holyoke. In New Hampshire, they built them in Manchester, Dover, and Nashua. And in Maine, they built a large mill in Saco on the Saco River. Other entrepreneurs copied them. By the time of the Civil War, 878 textile factories had been built in New England. All together, these factories employed more than 100,000 people and produced more than 940 million yards of cloth.

Success in New England was repeated elsewhere. Small mills, more like those in Rhode Island than those in northern Massachusetts, New Hampshire, and Maine, were built in New York, Delaware, and Pennsylvania. By midcentury, three hundred textile mills were located in and near Philadelphia. Many produced specialty goods, such as silks and printed fabrics, and employed skilled workers, including people working in their own homes. Even in the South, the region that otherwise relied on slave labor to produce the very cotton that fed the northern factory movement, more than two hundred textile mills were built. Most textiles, however, continued to be produced in New England before the Civil War.

Alongside the production of cotton and woolen cloth, which formed the backbone of the Industrial Revolution in the United States as in Britain, other crafts increasingly became mechanized and centralized in factories in the first half of the nineteenth century. Shoe making, leather tanning, papermaking, hat making, clock making, and gun making had all become mechanized to one degree or another by the time of the Civil War. Flour milling, because of the inventions of Oliver Evans (Figure 9.5), had become almost completely automated and centralized by the early decades of the nineteenth century. So efficient were Evans-style mills that two employees were able to do work that had originally required five, and mills using Evans's system spread throughout the mid-Atlantic states.

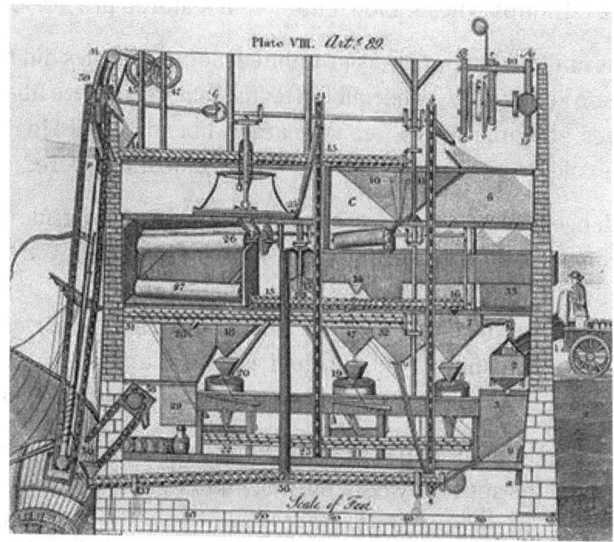

FIGURE 9.5 Oliver Evans was an American engineer and inventor, best known for developing ways to automate the flour milling process, which is illustrated here in a drawing from a 1785 instructional book called *The Young Mill-Wright & Miller's Guide*.

THE RISE OF CONSUMERISM

At the end of the eighteenth century, most American families lived in candlelit homes with bare floors and unadorned walls, cooked and warmed themselves over fireplaces, and owned few changes of clothing. All manufactured goods were made by hand and, as a result, were usually scarce and fairly expensive.

The automation of the manufacturing process changed that, making consumer goods that had once been thought of as luxury items widely available for the first time. Now all but the very poor could afford the necessities and some of the small luxuries of life. Rooms were lit by oil lamps, which gave brighter light than candles. Homes were heated by parlor stoves, which allowed for more privacy; people no longer needed to huddle together around the hearth. Iron cookstoves with multiple burners made it possible for housewives to prepare more elaborate meals. Many people could afford carpets and upholstered furniture, and even farmers could decorate their homes with curtains and wallpaper. Clocks, which had once been quite expensive, were now within the reach of most ordinary people.

THE WORK EXPERIENCE TRANSFORMED

As production became mechanized and relocated to factories, the experience of workers underwent significant changes. Farmers and artisans had controlled the pace of their labor and the order in which things were done. If an artisan wanted to take the afternoon off, he could. If a farmer wished to rebuild his fence on Thursday instead of on Wednesday, he could. They conversed and often drank during the workday. Indeed, journeymen were often promised alcohol as part of their wages. One member of the group might be asked to read a book or a newspaper aloud to the others. In the warm weather, doors and windows might be opened to the outside, and work stopped when it was too dark to see.

Work in factories proved to be quite different. Employees were expected to report at a certain time, usually early in the morning, and to work all day. They could not leave when they were tired or take breaks other than at designated times. Those who arrived late found their pay docked; five minutes' tardiness could result in several hours' worth of lost pay, and repeated tardiness could result in dismissal. The monotony of repetitive tasks made days particularly long. Hours varied according to the factory, but most factory employees toiled ten to twelve hours a day, six days a week. In the winter, when the sun set early, oil lamps were used to light the factory floor, and employees strained their eyes to see their work and coughed as the rooms filled with smoke from the lamps. In the spring, as the days began to grow longer, factories held "blowing-out" celebrations to mark the extinguishing of the oil lamps. These "blow-outs" often featured processions and dancing.

Freedom within factories was limited. Drinking was prohibited. Some factories did not allow employees to sit down. Doors and windows were kept closed, especially in textile factories where fibers could be easily disturbed by incoming breezes, and mills were often unbearably hot and humid in the summer. In the winter, workers often shivered in the cold. In such environments, workers' health suffered.

The workplace posed other dangers as well. The presence of cotton bales alongside the oil used to lubricate machines made fire a common problem in textile factories. Workplace injuries were also common. Workers' hands and fingers were maimed or severed when they were caught in machines; in some cases, their limbs or entire bodies were crushed. Workers who didn't die from such injuries almost certainly lost their jobs, and with them, their income. Corporal punishment of both children and adults was common in factories; where abuse was most extreme, children sometimes died as a result of injuries suffered at the hands of an overseer.

As the decades passed, working conditions deteriorated in many mills. Workers were assigned more machines to tend, and the owners increased the speed at which the machines operated. Wages were cut in many factories, and employees who had once labored for an hourly wage now found themselves reduced to piecework, paid for the amount they produced and not for the hours they toiled. Owners also reduced compensation for piecework. Low wages combined with regular periods of unemployment to make the lives of workers difficult, especially for those with families to support. In New York City in 1850, for example, the average male worker earned $300 a year; it cost approximately $600 a year to support a family of five.

WORKERS AND THE LABOR MOVEMENT

Many workers undoubtedly enjoyed some of the new wage opportunities factory work presented. For many of the young New England women who ran the machines in Waltham, Lowell, and elsewhere, the experience of being away from the family was exhilarating and provided a sense of solidarity among them. Though most sent a large portion of their wages home, having even a small amount of money of their own was a liberating experience, and many used their earnings to purchase clothes, ribbons, and other consumer goods for themselves.

The long hours, strict discipline, and low wages, however, soon led workers to organize to protest their working conditions and pay. In 1821, the young women employed by the Boston Manufacturing Company in Waltham went on strike for two days when their wages were cut. In 1824, workers in Pawtucket struck to protest reduced pay rates and longer hours, the latter of which had been achieved by cutting back the amount of time allowed for meals. Similar strikes occurred at Lowell and in other mill towns like Dover, New Hampshire, where the women employed by the Cocheco Manufacturing Company ceased working in December 1828 after their wages were reduced. In the 1830s, female mill operatives in Lowell formed the Lowell Factory Girls Association to organize strike activities in the face of wage cuts (Figure 9.6) and, later, established the Lowell Female Labor Reform Association to protest the twelve-hour workday. Even though strikes were rarely successful and workers usually were forced to accept reduced wages and increased hours, work stoppages as a form of labor protest represented the beginnings of the labor movement in the United States.

(a) (b)

FIGURE 9.6 New England mill workers were often young women, as seen in this early tintype made ca. 1870 (a). When management proposed rent increases for those living in company boarding houses, female textile workers in Lowell responded by forming the Lowell Factory Girls Association—its constitution is shown in image (b)—in 1836 and organizing a "turn-out" or strike.

Critics of industrialization blamed it for the increased concentration of wealth in the hands of the few: the factory owners made vast profits while the workers received only a small fraction of the revenue from what they produced. Under the **labor theory of value**, said critics, the value of a product should accurately reflect the labor needed to produce it. Profits from the sale of goods produced by workers should be distributed so laborers recovered in the form of wages the value their effort had added to the finished product. While factory owners, who contributed the workspace, the machinery, and the raw materials needed to create a product, should receive a share of the profits, their share should not be greater than the value of their contribution. Workers should thus receive a much larger portion of the profits than they currently did, and factory owners should receive less.

In Philadelphia, New York, and Boston—all cities that experienced dizzying industrial growth during the nineteenth century—workers united to form political parties. Thomas Skidmore, from Connecticut, was the outspoken organizer of the **Working Men's Party**, which lodged a radical protest against the exploitation of workers that accompanied industrialization. Skidmore took his cue from Thomas Paine and the American Revolution to challenge the growing inequity in the United States. He argued that inequality originated in the unequal distribution of property through inheritance laws. In his 1829 treatise, *The Rights of Man to Property*, Skidmore called for the abolition of inheritance and the redistribution of property. The Working Men's Party also advocated the end of imprisonment for debt, a common practice whereby the debtor who could not pay was put in jail and his tools and property, if any, were confiscated. Skidmore's vision of radical equality extended to all; women and men, no matter their race, should be allowed to vote and receive property, he believed. Skidmore died in 1832 when a cholera epidemic swept New York City, but the state of New York did away with imprisonment for debt in the same year.

Worker activism became less common in the late 1840s and 1850s. As German and Irish immigrants poured into the United States in the decades preceding the Civil War, native-born laborers found themselves competing for jobs with new arrivals who were willing to work longer hours for less pay. In Lowell, Massachusetts, for example, the daughters of New England farmers encountered competition from the daughters of Irish farmers suffering the effects of the potato famine; these immigrant women were willing to work for far less and endure worse conditions than native-born women. Many of these native-born "daughters of freemen," as they referred to themselves, left the factories and returned to their families. Not all wage workers had this luxury, however. Widows with children to support and girls from destitute families had no choice but to stay and accept the faster pace and lower pay. Male German and Irish immigrants competed with native-born men. Germans, many of whom were skilled workers, took jobs in furniture making. The Irish provided a ready source of unskilled labor needed to lay railroad track and dig canals. American men with families to support grudgingly accepted low wages in order to keep their jobs. As work became increasingly deskilled, no worker was irreplaceable, and no one's job was safe.

9.2 A Vibrant Capitalist Republic

LEARNING OBJECTIVES

By the end of this section, you will be able to:
- Explain the process of selling western land
- Discuss the causes of the Panic of 1819
- Identify key American innovators and inventors

By the 1840s, the United States economy bore little resemblance to the import-and-export economy of colonial days. It was now a market economy, one in which the production of goods, and their prices, were unregulated by the government. Commercial centers, to which job seekers flocked, mushroomed. New York City's population skyrocketed. In 1790, it was 33,000; by 1820, it had reached 200,000; and by 1825, it had swelled to 270,000. New opportunities for wealth appeared to be available to anyone.

However, the expansion of the American economy made it prone to the boom-and-bust cycle. Market economies involve fluctuating prices for labor, raw materials, and consumer goods and depend on credit and financial instruments—any one of which can be the source of an imbalance and an economic downturn in which businesses and farmers default, wage workers lose their employment, and investors lose their assets. This happened for the first time in the United States in 1819, when waves of enthusiastic speculation (expectations of rapidly rising prices) in land and commodities gave way to drops in prices.

THE LAND OFFICE BUSINESS

In the early nineteenth century, people poured into the territories west of the long-settled eastern seaboard. Among them were speculators seeking to buy cheap parcels from the federal government in anticipation of a rise in prices. The Ohio Country in the Northwest Territory appeared to offer the best prospects for many in the East, especially New Englanders. The result was "Ohio fever," as thousands traveled there to reap the benefits of settling in this newly available territory (Figure 9.7).

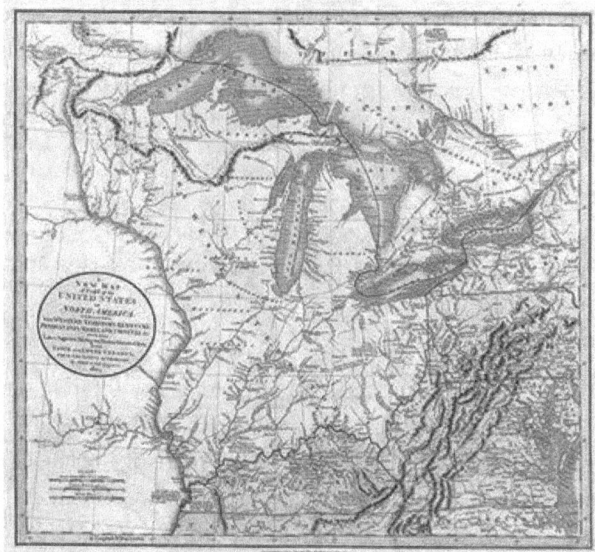

FIGURE 9.7 Cartographer John Cary drew this map "exhibiting The Western Territory, Kentucky, Pennsylvania, Maryland, Virginia &c" for his 1808 atlas; it depicted the huge western territory that fascinated settlers in the early nineteenth century.

The federal government oversaw the orderly transfer of public land to citizens at public auctions. The Land Law of 1796 applied to the territory of Ohio after it had been wrested from Native people. Under this law, the United States would sell a minimum parcel of 640 acres for $2 an acre. The Land Law of 1800 further encouraged land sales in the Northwest Territory by reducing the minimum parcel size by half and enabling sales on credit, with the goal of stimulating settlement by ordinary farmers. The government created **land offices** to handle these sales and established them in the West within easy reach of prospective landowners. They could thus purchase land directly from the government, at the price the government had set. Buyers were given low interest rates, with payments that could be spread over four years. Surveyors marked off the parcels in straight lines, creating a landscape of checkerboard squares.

The future looked bright for those who turned their gaze on the land in the West. Surveying, settling, and farming, turning the wilderness into a profitable commodity, gave purchasers a sense of progress. A uniquely American story of settling the land developed: hardy individuals wielding an axe cleared it, built a log cabin, and turned the frontier into a farm that paved the way for mills and towns (Figure 9.8).

FIGURE 9.8 Thomas Cole, who painted *Home in the Woods* in 1847, was an American artist. Cole founded the

Hudson River School, a style renowned for portrayals of landscapes and wilderness influenced by the emotional aesthetic known as romanticism. In what ways is this image realistic, and how is it idealized or romanticized?

MY STORY

A New Englander Heads West

A native of Vermont, Gershom Flagg was one of thousands of New Englanders who caught "Ohio fever." In this letter to his brother, Azariah Flagg, dated August 3, 1817, he describes the hustle and bustle of the emerging commercial town of Cincinnati.

"DEAR BROTHER,
Cincinnati is an incorporated City. It contained in 1815, 1,100 buildings of different descriptions among which are above 20 of Stone 250 of brick & 800 of Wood. The population in 1815 was 6,500. There are about 60 Mercantile stores several of which are wholesale. Here are a great share of Mechanics of all kinds.
Here is one Woolen Factory four Cotton factories but not now in operation. A most stupendously large building of Stone is likewise erected immediately on the bank of the River for a steam Mill. It is nine stories high at the Waters edge & is 87 by 62 feet. It drives four pair of Stones besides various other Machinery as Wool carding &c &c. There is also a valuable Steam Saw Mill driving four saws also an inclined Wheel ox Saw Mill with two saws, one Glass Factory. The town is Rapidly increasing in Wealth & population. Here is a Branch of the United States Bank and three other banks & two Printing offices. The country around is rich. . . .
That you may all be prospered in the world is the anxious wish of your affectionate Brother
GERSHOM FLAGG"

What caught Flagg's attention? From your reading of this letter and study of the engraving below (Figure 9.9), what impression can you take away of Cincinnati in 1817?

FIGURE 9.9 This engraving from *A Topographical Description of the State of Ohio, Indiana Territory, and Louisiana* (1812), by Jervis Cutler, presents a view of Cincinnati as it may have looked to Gershom Flagg.

CLICK AND EXPLORE

Learn more about settlement of and immigration to the Northwest Territory by exploring the National Park Service's Historic Resource Study (http://openstax.org/l/15LincMemorial) related to the Lincoln Boyhood National Memorial. According to the guide's maps, what lands were available for purchase?

THE PANIC OF 1819

The first major economic crisis in the United States after the War of 1812 was due, in large measure, to factors in the larger Atlantic economy. It was made worse, however, by land speculation and poor banking practices at home. British textile mills voraciously consumed American cotton, and the devastation of the Napoleonic Wars made Europe reliant on other American agricultural commodities such as wheat. This drove up both the price of American agricultural products and the value of the land on which staples such as cotton, wheat, corn, and tobacco were grown.

Many Americans were struck with "land fever." Farmers strove to expand their acreage, and those who lived in areas where unoccupied land was scarce sought holdings in the West. They needed money to purchase this land, however. Small merchants and factory owners, hoping to take advantage of this boom time, also sought to borrow money to expand their businesses. When existing banks refused to lend money to small farmers and others without a credit history, state legislatures chartered new banks to meet the demand. In one legislative session, Kentucky chartered forty-six. As loans increased, paper money from new state banks flooded the country, creating inflation that drove the price of land and goods still higher. This, in turn, encouraged even more people to borrow money with which to purchase land or to expand or start their own businesses. Speculators took advantage of this boom in the sale of land by purchasing property not to live on, but to buy cheaply and resell at exorbitant prices.

During the War of 1812, the Bank of the United States had suspended payments in **specie**, "hard money" usually in the form of gold and silver coins. When the war ended, the bank continued to issue only paper banknotes and to redeem notes issued by state banks with paper only. The newly chartered banks also adopted this practice, issuing banknotes in excess of the amount of specie in their vaults. This shaky economic scheme worked only so long as people were content to conduct business with paper money and refrain from demanding that banks instead give them the gold and silver that was supposed to back it. If large numbers of people, or banks that had loaned money to other banks, began to demand specie payments, the banking system would collapse, because there was no longer enough specie to support the amount of paper money the banks had put into circulation. So terrified were bankers that customers would demand gold and silver that an irate bank employee in Ohio stabbed a customer who had the audacity to ask for specie in exchange for the banknotes he held.

In an effort to bring stability to the nation's banking system, Congress chartered the Second Bank of the United States (a revival of Alexander Hamilton's national bank) in 1816. But this new institution only compounded the problem by making risky loans, opening branches in the South and West where land fever was highest, and issuing a steady stream of Bank of the United States notes, a move that increased inflation and speculation.

The inflated economic bubble burst in 1819, resulting in a prolonged economic depression or severe downturn in the economy called the Panic of 1819. It was the first economic depression experienced by the American public, who panicked as they saw the prices of agricultural products fall and businesses fail. Prices had already begun falling in 1815, at the end of the Napoleonic Wars, when Britain began to "dump" its surplus manufactured goods, the result of wartime overproduction, in American ports, where they were sold for low prices and competed with American-manufactured goods. In 1818, to make the economic situation worse, prices for American agricultural products began to fall both in the United States and in Europe; the overproduction of staples such as wheat and cotton coincided with the recovery of European agriculture, which reduced demand for American crops. Crop prices tumbled by as much 75 percent.

This dramatic decrease in the value of agricultural goods left farmers unable to pay their debts. As they defaulted on their loans, banks seized their property. However, because the drastic fall in agricultural prices had greatly reduced the value of land, the banks were left with farms they were unable to sell. Land speculators lost the value of their investments. As the countryside suffered, hard-hit farmers ceased to purchase manufactured goods. Factories responded by cutting wages or firing employees.

In 1818, the Second Bank of the United States needed specie to pay foreign investors who had loaned money to the United States to enable the country to purchase Louisiana. The bank began to call in the loans it had made and required that state banks pay their debts in gold and silver. State banks that could not collect loan payments from hard-pressed farmers could not, in turn, meet their obligations to the Second Bank of the United States. Severe consequences followed as banks closed their doors and businesses failed. Three-quarters of the work force in Philadelphia was unemployed, and charities were swamped by thousands of newly destitute people needing assistance. In states with imprisonment for debt, the prison population swelled. As a result, many states drafted laws to provide relief for debtors. Even those at the top of the social ladder were affected by the Panic of 1819. Thomas Jefferson, who had cosigned a loan for a friend, nearly lost Monticello when his acquaintance defaulted, leaving Jefferson responsible for the debt.

In an effort to stimulate the economy in the midst of the economic depression, Congress passed several acts modifying land sales. The Land Law of 1820 lowered the price of land to $1.25 per acre and allowed small parcels of eighty acres to be sold. The Relief Act of 1821 allowed Ohioans to return land to the government if they could not afford to keep it. The money they received in return was credited toward their debt. The act also extended the credit period to eight years. States, too, attempted to aid those faced with economic hard times by passing laws to prevent mortgage foreclosures so buyers could keep their homes. Americans made the best of the opportunities presented in business, in farming, or on the frontier, and by 1823 the Panic of 1819 had ended. The recovery provided ample evidence of the vibrant and resilient nature of the American people.

ENTREPRENEURS AND INVENTORS

The volatility of the U.S. economy did nothing to dampen the creative energies of its citizens in the years before the Civil War. In the 1800s, a frenzy of entrepreneurship and invention yielded many new products and machines. The republic seemed to be a laboratory of innovation, and technological advances appeared unlimited.

One of the most influential advancements of the early nineteenth century was the cotton engine or gin, invented by Eli Whitney and patented in 1794. Whitney, who was born in Massachusetts, had spent time in the South and knew that a device to speed up the production of cotton was desperately needed so cotton farmers could meet the growing demand for their crop. He hoped the cotton gin would render slavery obsolete. Whitney's seemingly simple invention cleaned the seeds from the raw cotton far more quickly and efficiently than could enslaved workers by hand (Figure 9.10). The raw cotton with seeds was placed in the cotton gin, and with the use of a hand crank, the seeds were extracted through a carding device that aligned the cotton fibers in strands for spinning.

FIGURE 9.10 *The First Cotton-Gin*, an 1869 drawing by William L. Sheppard, shows the first use of a cotton gin "at the close of the last century." Enslaved African Americans handle the gin while White men conduct business in the

background. What do you think the artist was trying to convey with this image? (credit: Library of Congress)

Whitney also worked on **machine tools**, devices that cut and shaped metal to make standardized, interchangeable parts for other mechanical devices like clocks and guns. Whitney's machine tools to manufacture parts for muskets enabled guns to be manufactured and repaired by people other than skilled gunsmiths. His creative genius served as a source of inspiration for many other American inventors.

Another influential new technology of the early 1800s was the steamship engine, invented by Robert Fulton in 1807. Fulton's first steamship, the *Clermont*, used paddle wheels to travel the 150 miles from New York City to Albany in a record time of only thirty-two hours (Figure 9.11). Soon, a fleet of steamboats was traversing the Hudson River and New York Harbor, later expanding to travel every major American river including the mighty Mississippi. By the 1830s there were over one thousand of these vessels, radically changing water transportation by ending its dependence on the wind. Steamboats could travel faster and more cheaply than sailing vessels or keelboats, which floated downriver and had to be poled or towed upriver on the return voyage. Steamboats also arrived with much greater dependability. The steamboat facilitated the rapid economic development of the massive Mississippi River Valley and the settlement of the West.

FIGURE 9.11 Fulton's steamboat the *Clermont* transformed the speed, cost, and dependability of water transportation in the United States. (credit: Project Gutenberg Archives)

Virginia-born Cyrus McCormick wanted to replace the laborious process of using a scythe to cut and gather wheat for harvest. In 1831, he and the enslaved workers on his family's plantation tested a horse-drawn mechanical reaper, and over the next several decades, he made constant improvements to it (Figure 9.12). More farmers began using it in the 1840s, and greater demand for the McCormick reaper led McCormick and his brother to establish the McCormick Harvesting Machine Company in Chicago, where labor was more readily available. By the 1850s, McCormick's mechanical reaper had enabled farmers to vastly increase their output. McCormick—and also John Deere, who improved on the design of plows—opened the prairies to agriculture. McCormick's bigger machine could harvest grain faster, and Deere's plow could cut through the thick prairie sod. Agriculture north of the Ohio River became the pantry that would lower food prices and feed the major cities in the East. In short order, Ohio, Indiana, and Illinois all become major agricultural states.

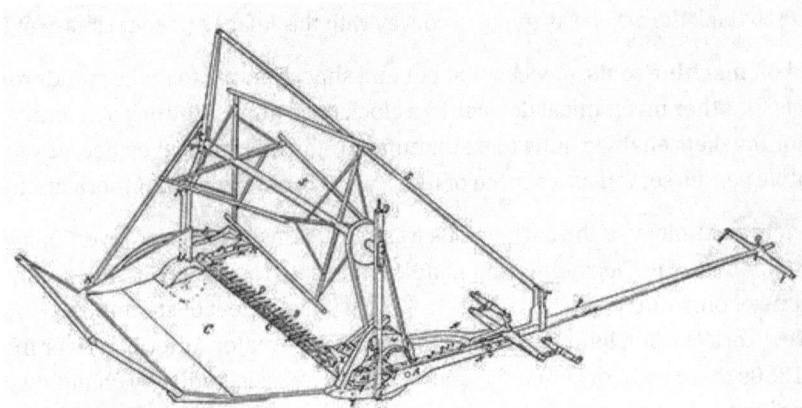

FIGURE 9.12 This sketch is from the 1845 patent for an improved grain reaper invented by Cyrus Hall McCormick. The reaper mechanized the labor-intensive use of scythes to harvest wheat.

Samuel Morse added the telegraph to the list of American innovations introduced in the years before the Civil War. Born in Massachusetts in 1791, Morse first gained renown as a painter before turning his attention to the development of a method of rapid communication in the 1830s. In 1838, he gave the first public demonstration of his method of conveying electric pulses over a wire, using the basis of what became known as Morse code. In 1843, Congress agreed to help fund the new technology by allocating $30,000 for a telegraph line to connect Washington, DC, and Baltimore along the route of the Baltimore and Ohio Railroad. In 1844, Morse sent the first telegraph message on the new link. Improved communication systems fostered the development of business, economics, and politics by allowing for dissemination of news at a speed previously unknown.

9.3 On the Move: The Transportation Revolution

LEARNING OBJECTIVES

By the end of this section, you will be able to:
- Describe the development of improved methods of nineteenth-century domestic transportation
- Identify the ways in which roads, canals, and railroads impacted Americans' lives in the nineteenth century

Americans in the early 1800s were a people on the move, as thousands left the eastern coastal states for opportunities in the West. Unlike their predecessors, who traveled by foot or wagon train, these settlers had new transport options. Their trek was made possible by the construction of roads, canals, and railroads, projects that required the funding of the federal government and the states.

New technologies, like the steamship and railroad lines, had brought about what historians call the transportation revolution. States competed for the honor of having the most advanced transport systems. People celebrated the transformation of the wilderness into an orderly world of improvement demonstrating the steady march of progress and the greatness of the republic. In 1817, John C. Calhoun of South Carolina looked to a future of rapid internal improvements, declaring, "Let us . . . bind the Republic together with a perfect system of roads and canals." Americans agreed that internal transportation routes would promote progress. By the eve of the Civil War, the United States had moved beyond roads and canals to a well-established and extensive system of railroads.

ROADS AND CANALS

One key part of the transportation revolution was the widespread building of roads and turnpikes. In 1811, construction began on the **Cumberland Road**, a national highway that provided thousands with a route from Maryland to Illinois. The federal government funded this important artery to the West, beginning the creation of a transportation infrastructure for the benefit of settlers and farmers. Other entities built turnpikes, which (as today) charged fees for use. New York State, for instance, chartered turnpike companies that dramatically increased the miles of state roads from one thousand in 1810 to four thousand by 1820. New York led the way in building turnpikes.

Canal mania swept the United States in the first half of the nineteenth century. Promoters knew these artificial rivers could save travelers immense amounts of time and money. Even short waterways, such as the two-and-a-half-mile canal going around the rapids of the Ohio River near Louisville, Kentucky, proved a huge leap forward, in this case by opening a water route from Pittsburgh to New Orleans. The preeminent example was the **Erie Canal** (Figure 9.13), which linked the Hudson River, and thus New York City and the Atlantic seaboard, to the Great Lakes and the Mississippi River Valley.

With its central location, large harbor, and access to the hinterland via the Hudson River, New York City already commanded the lion's share of commerce. Still, the city's merchants worried about losing ground to their competitors in Philadelphia and Baltimore. Their search for commercial advantage led to the dream of creating a water highway connecting the city's Hudson River to Lake Erie and markets in the West. The result was the Erie Canal. Chartered in 1817 by the state of New York, the canal took seven years to complete. When it opened in 1825, it dramatically decreased the cost of shipping while reducing the time to travel to the West. Soon $15 million worth of goods (more than $200 million in today's money) was being transported on the 363-mile waterway every year.

FIGURE 9.13 Although the Erie Canal was primarily used for commerce and trade, in *Pittsford on the Erie Canal* (1837), George Harvey portrays it in a pastoral, natural setting. Why do you think the painter chose to portray the canal this way?

🔗 CLICK AND EXPLORE

Explore the Erie Canal on ErieCanal.org (http://openstax.org/l/15ErieCanal) via an interactive map. Click throughout the map for images of and artifacts from this historic waterway.

The success of the Erie Canal led to other, similar projects. The Wabash and Erie Canal, which opened in the early 1840s, stretched over 450 miles, making it the longest canal in North America (Figure 9.14). Canals added immensely to the country's sense of progress. Indeed, they appeared to be the logical next step in the process of transforming wilderness into civilization.

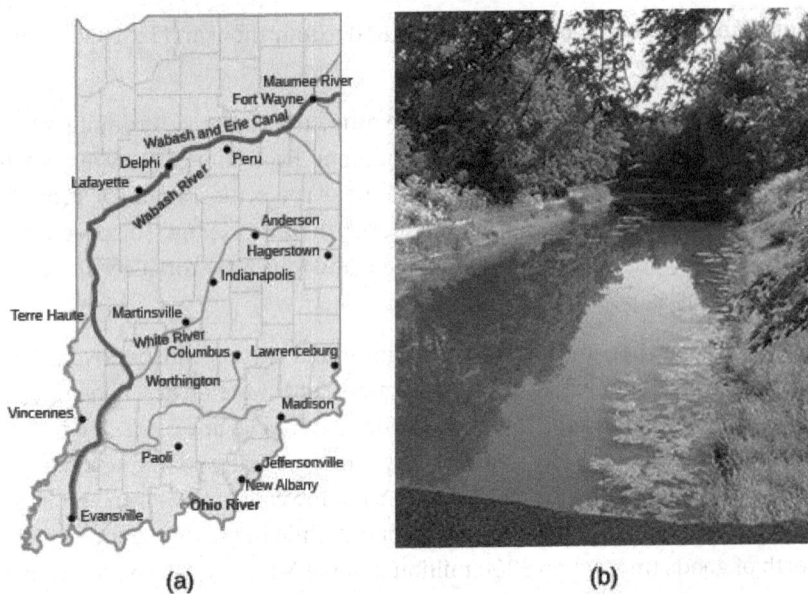

FIGURE 9.14 This map (a) shows the route taken by the Wabash and Erie Canal through the state of Indiana. The canal began operation in 1843 and boats operated on it until the 1870s. Sections have since been restored, as shown in this 2007 photo (b) from Delphi, Indiana.

CLICK AND EXPLORE

Visit Southern Indiana Trails (http://openstax.org/l/15WabashEire) to see historic photographs of the Wabash and Erie Canal:

As with highway projects such as the Cumberland Road, many canals were federally sponsored, especially during the presidency of John Quincy Adams in the late 1820s. Adams, along with Secretary of State Henry Clay, championed what was known as the American System, part of which included plans for a broad range of internal transportation improvements. Adams endorsed the creation of roads and canals to facilitate commerce and develop markets for agriculture as well as to advance settlement in the West.

RAILROADS

Starting in the late 1820s, steam locomotives began to compete with horse-drawn locomotives. The railroads with steam locomotives offered a new mode of transportation that fascinated citizens, buoying their optimistic view of the possibilities of technological progress. The **Mohawk and Hudson Railroad** was the first to begin service with a steam locomotive. Its inaugural train ran in 1831 on a track outside Albany and covered twelve miles in twenty-five minutes. Soon it was traveling regularly between Albany and Schenectady.

Toward the middle of the century, railroad construction kicked into high gear, and eager investors quickly formed a number of railroad companies. As a railroad grid began to take shape, it stimulated a greater demand for coal, iron, and steel. Soon, both railroads and canals crisscrossed the states (Figure 9.15), providing a transportation infrastructure that fueled the growth of American commerce. Indeed, the transportation revolution led to development in the coal, iron, and steel industries, providing many Americans with new job opportunities.

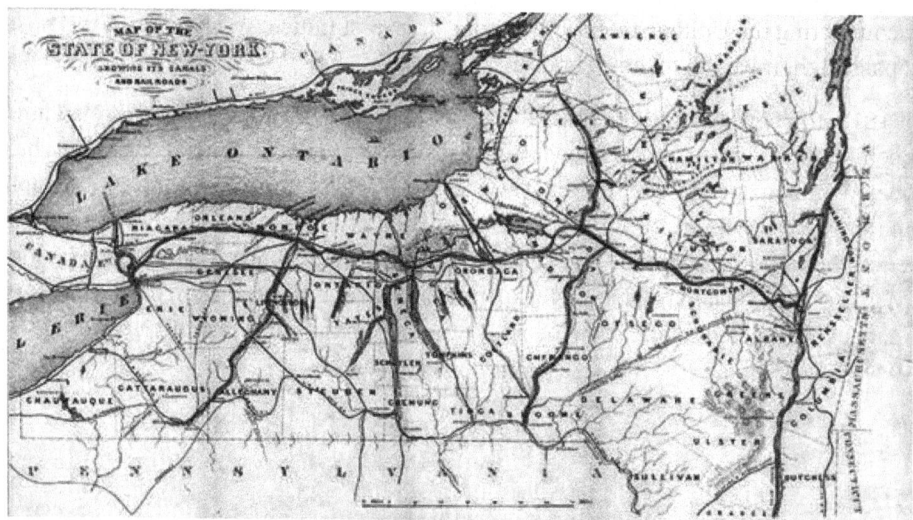

FIGURE 9.15 This 1853 map of the "Empire State" shows the extent of New York's canal and railroad networks. The entire country's transportation infrastructure grew dramatically during the first half of the nineteenth century.

AMERICANS ON THE MOVE

The expansion of roads, canals, and railroads changed people's lives. In 1786, it had taken a minimum of four days to travel from Boston, Massachusetts, to Providence, Rhode Island. By 1840, the trip took half a day on a train. In the twenty-first century, this may seem intolerably slow, but people at the time were amazed by the railroad's speed. Its average of twenty miles per hour was twice as fast as other available modes of transportation.

By 1840, more than three thousand miles of canals had been dug in the United States, and thirty thousand miles of railroad track had been laid by the beginning of the Civil War. Together with the hundreds of steamboats that plied American rivers, these advances in transportation made it easier and less expensive to ship agricultural products from the West to feed people in eastern cities, and to send manufactured goods from the East to people in the West. Without this ability to transport goods, the market revolution would not have been possible. Rural families also became less isolated as a result of the transportation revolution. Traveling circuses, menageries, peddlers, and itinerant painters could now more easily make their way into rural districts, and people in search of work found cities and mill towns within their reach.

9.4 A New Social Order: Class Divisions

LEARNING OBJECTIVES

By the end of this section, you will be able to:
- Identify the shared perceptions and ideals of each social class
- Assess different social classes' views of slavery

The profound economic changes sweeping the United States led to equally important social and cultural transformations. The formation of distinct classes, especially in the rapidly industrializing North, was one of the most striking developments. The unequal distribution of newly created wealth spurred new divisions along class lines. Each class had its own specific culture and views on the issue of slavery.

THE ECONOMIC ELITE

Economic elites gained further social and political ascendance in the United States due to a fast-growing economy that enhanced their wealth and allowed distinctive social and cultural characteristics to develop among different economic groups. In the major northern cities of Boston, New York, and Philadelphia, leading merchants formed an industrial capitalist elite. Many came from families that had been deeply engaged in colonial trade in tea, sugar, pepper, enslaved Africans, and other commodities and that were familiar with trade networks connecting the United States with Europe, the West Indies, and the Far East. These colonial merchants had passed their wealth to their children.

After the War of 1812, the new generation of merchants expanded their economic activities. They began to specialize in specific types of industry, spearheading the development of industrial capitalism based on factories they owned and on specific commercial services such as banking, insurance, and shipping. Junius Spencer Morgan (Figure 9.16), for example, rose to prominence as a banker. His success began in Boston, where he worked in the import business in the 1830s. He then formed a partnership with a London banker, George Peabody, and created Peabody, Morgan & Co. In 1864, he renamed the enterprise J. S. Morgan & Co. His son, J. P. Morgan, became a noted financier in the later nineteenth and early twentieth century.

FIGURE 9.16 Junius Spencer Morgan of Boston was one of the fathers of the American private banking system. (credit: Project Gutenberg Archives)

CLICK AND EXPLORE

Visit the Internet Archive (http://openstax.org/l/15Hunts) to see scanned pages from *Hunt's Merchant's Magazine and Commercial Review*. This monthly business review provided the business elite with important information about issues pertaining to trade and finance: commodity prices, new laws affecting business, statistics regarding imports and exports, and similar content. Choose three articles and decide how they might have been important to the northern business elite.

Members of the northern business elite forged close ties with each other to protect and expand their economic interests. Marriages between leading families formed a crucial strategy to advance economic advantage, and the homes of the northern elite became important venues for solidifying social bonds. Exclusive neighborhoods started to develop as the wealthy distanced themselves from the poorer urban residents, and cities soon became segregated by class.

Industrial elites created chambers of commerce to advance their interests; by 1858 there were ten in the United States. These networking organizations allowed top bankers and merchants to stay current on the economic activities of their peers and further strengthen the bonds among themselves. The elite also established social clubs to forge and maintain ties. The first of these, the Philadelphia Club, came into being in 1834. Similar clubs soon formed in other cities and hosted a range of social activities designed to further bind together the leading economic families. Many northern elites worked hard to ensure the transmission of their inherited wealth from one generation to the next. Politically, they exercised considerable power in local and state elections. Most also had ties to the cotton trade, so they were strong supporters of slavery.

The Industrial Revolution led some former artisans to reinvent themselves as manufacturers. These enterprising leaders of manufacturing differed from the established commercial elite in the North and South because they did not inherit wealth. Instead, many came from very humble working-class origins and embodied the dream of achieving upward social mobility through hard work and discipline. As the beneficiaries of the economic transformations sweeping the republic, these newly established manufacturers formed a new economic elite that thrived in the cities and cultivated its own distinct sensibilities. They created a culture that celebrated hard work, a position that put them at odds with southern planter elites who prized leisure and with other elite northerners who had largely inherited their wealth and status.

Peter Cooper provides one example of the new northern manufacturing class. Ever inventive, Cooper dabbled in many different moneymaking enterprises before gaining success in the glue business. He opened his Manhattan glue factory in the 1820s and was soon using his profits to expand into a host of other activities, including iron production. One of his innovations was the steam locomotive, which he invented in 1827 (Figure 9.17). Despite becoming one of the wealthiest men in New York City, Cooper lived simply. Rather than buying an ornate bed, for example, he built his own. He believed respectability came through hard work, not family pedigree.

FIGURE 9.17 Peter Cooper, who would go on to found the Cooper Union for the Advancement of Science and Art in New York City, designed and built the Tom Thumb, the first American-built steam locomotive, a replica of which is shown here.

Those who had inherited their wealth derided self-made men like Cooper, and he and others like him were excluded from the social clubs established by the merchant and financial elite of New York City. Self-made northern manufacturers, however, created their own organizations that aimed to promote upward mobility. The Providence Association of Mechanics and Manufacturers was formed in 1789 and promoted both industrial arts and education as a pathway to economic success. In 1859, Peter Cooper established the Cooper Union for the Advancement of Science and Art, a school in New York City dedicated to providing education in technology. Merit, not wealth, mattered most according to Cooper, and admission to the school was based solely on ability; race, sex, and family connections had no place. The best and brightest could attend Cooper Union tuition-free, a policy that remained in place until 2014.

THE MIDDLE CLASS

Not all enterprising artisans were so successful that they could rise to the level of the elite. However, many artisans and small merchants, who owned small factories and stores, did manage to achieve and maintain respectability in an emerging middle class. Lacking the protection of great wealth, members of the middle class agonized over the fear that they might slip into the ranks of wage laborers; thus they strove to maintain or improve their middle-class status and that of their children.

To this end, the middle class valued cleanliness, discipline, morality, hard work, education, and good manners. Hard work and education enabled them to rise in life. Middle-class children, therefore, did not work in factories. Instead they attended school and in their free time engaged in "self-improving" activities, such as reading or playing the piano, or they played with toys and games that would teach them the skills and values they needed to succeed in life. In the early nineteenth century, members of the middle class began to limit the number of children they had. Children no longer contributed economically to the household, and raising them "correctly" required money and attention. It therefore made sense to have fewer of them.

Middle-class women did not work for wages. Their job was to care for the children and to keep the house in a state of order and cleanliness, often with the help of a servant. They also performed the important tasks of cultivating good manners among their children and their husbands and of purchasing consumer goods; both activities proclaimed to neighbors and prospective business partners that their families were educated, cultured, and financially successful.

Northern business elites, many of whom owned or had invested in businesses like cotton mills that profited from slave labor, often viewed the institution of slavery with ambivalence. Most members of the middle class took a dim view of it, however, since it promoted a culture of leisure. Slavery stood as the antithesis of the middle-class view that dignity and respectability were achieved through work, and many members of this class became active in efforts to end it.

This class of upwardly mobile citizens promoted temperance, or abstinence from alcohol. They also gave their support to Protestant ministers like Charles Grandison Finney, who preached that all people possessed **free moral agency**, meaning they could change their lives and bring about their own salvation, a message that resonated with members of the middle class, who already believed their worldly efforts had led to their economic success.

THE WORKING CLASS

The Industrial Revolution in the United States created a new class of wage workers, and this working class also developed its own culture. They formed their own neighborhoods, living away from the oversight of bosses and managers. While industrialization and the market revolution brought some improvements to the lives of the working class, these sweeping changes did not benefit laborers as much as they did the middle class and the elites. The working class continued to live an often precarious existence. They suffered greatly during economic slumps, such as the Panic of 1819.

Although most working-class men sought to emulate the middle class by keeping their wives and children out of the work force, their economic situation often necessitated that others besides the male head of the family contribute to its support. Thus, working-class children might attend school for a few years or learn to read and write at Sunday school, but education was sacrificed when income was needed, and many working-class children went to work in factories. While the wives of wage laborers usually did not work for wages outside the home, many took in laundry or did piecework at home to supplement the family's income.

Although the urban working class could not afford the consumer goods that the middle class could, its members did exercise a great deal of influence over popular culture. Theirs was a festive public culture of release and escape from the drudgery of factory work, catered to by the likes of Phineas Taylor Barnum, the celebrated circus promoter and showman. Taverns also served an important function as places to forget the long hours and uncertain wages of the factories. Alcohol consumption was high among the working class, although many workers did take part in the temperance movement. It is little wonder that middle-class manufacturers attempted to abolish alcohol.

AMERICANA

P. T. Barnum and the Feejee Mermaid

The Connecticut native P. T. Barnum catered to the demand for escape and cheap amusements among the working class. His American Museum in New York City opened in 1841 and achieved great success. Millions flocked to see Barnum's exhibits, which included a number of fantastic human and animal oddities, almost all of which were hoaxes. One exhibit in the 1840s featured the "Feejee Mermaid," which Barnum presented as proof of the existence of the mythical mermaids of the deep (Figure 9.18). In truth, the mermaid was a half-monkey, half-fish stitched together.

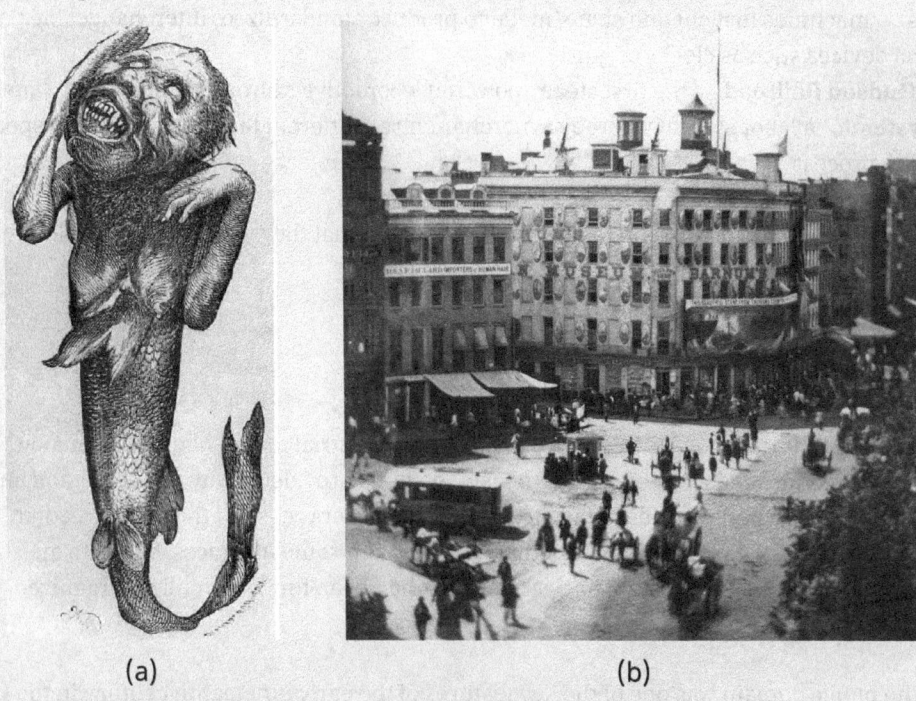

(a) (b)

FIGURE 9.18 Spurious though they were, attractions such as the Feejee mermaid (a) from P. T. Barnum's American Museum in New York City (b) drew throngs of working-class wage earners in the middle of the nineteenth century.

CLICK AND EXPLORE

Visit The Lost Museum (http://openstax.org/l/15LostMuseum) to take a virtual tour of P. T. Barnum's incredible museum.

Wage workers in the North were largely hostile to the abolition of slavery, fearing it would unleash more competition for jobs from free Black people. Many were also hostile to immigration. The pace of immigration to the United States accelerated in the 1840s and 1850s as Europeans were drawn to the promise of employment and land in the United States. Many new members of the working class came from the ranks of these immigrants, who brought new foods, customs, and religions. The Roman Catholic population of the United States, fairly small before this period, began to swell with the arrival of the Irish and the Germans.

Key Terms

artisan   skilled, experienced worker who produces specialized goods by hand

Cumberland Road   a national highway that provided thousands with a route from Maryland to Illinois

deskilling   breaking an artisanal production process into smaller steps that unskilled workers can perform

Erie Canal   a canal that connected the Hudson River to Lake Erie and markets in the West

free moral agency   the freedom to change one's own life and bring about one's own salvation

labor theory of value   an economic theory holding that profits from the sale of the goods produced by workers should be equitably distributed to those workers

land offices   sites where prospective landowners could buy public land from the government

machine tools   machines that cut and shape metal to produce standardized, interchangeable parts for mechanical devices such as clocks or guns

Mohawk and Hudson Railroad   the first steam-powered locomotive railroad in the United States

putting-out system   a labor system whereby a merchant hired different families to perform specific tasks in a production process

specie   "hard" money, usually in the form of gold and silver coins

Working Men's Party   a political group that radically opposed what they viewed as the exploitation of workers

Summary

9.1 Early Industrialization in the Northeast

Industrialization led to radical changes in American life. New industrial towns, like Waltham, Lowell, and countless others, dotted the landscape of the Northeast. The mills provided many young women an opportunity to experience a new and liberating life, and these workers relished their new freedom. Workers also gained a greater appreciation of the value of their work and, in some instances, began to question the basic fairness of the new industrial order. The world of work had been fundamentally reorganized.

9.2 A Vibrant Capitalist Republic

The selling of the public domain was one of the key features of the early nineteenth century in the United States. Thousands rushed west to take part in the bounty. In the wild frenzy of land purchases and speculation in land, state banks advanced risky loans and created unstable paper money not backed by gold or silver, ultimately leading to the Panic of 1819. The ensuing economic depression was the first in U.S. history. Recovery came in the 1820s, followed by a period of robust growth. In this age of entrepreneurship, in which those who invested their money wisely in land, business ventures, or technological improvements reaped vast profits, inventors produced new wonders that transformed American life.

9.3 On the Move: The Transportation Revolution

A transportation infrastructure rapidly took shape in the 1800s as American investors and the government began building roads, turnpikes, canals, and railroads. The time required to travel shrank vastly, and people marveled at their ability to conquer great distances, enhancing their sense of the steady advance of progress. The transportation revolution also made it possible to ship agricultural and manufactured goods throughout the country and enabled rural people to travel to towns and cities for employment opportunities.

9.4 A New Social Order: Class Divisions

The creation of distinctive classes in the North drove striking new cultural developments. Even among the wealthy elites, northern business families, who had mainly inherited their money, distanced themselves from the newly wealthy manufacturing leaders. Regardless of how they had earned their money, however, the elite lived and socialized apart from members of the growing middle class. The middle class valued work, consumption, and education and dedicated their energies to maintaining or advancing their social status. Wage workers formed their own society in industrial cities and mill villages, though lack of money and long working hours effectively prevented the working class from consuming the fruits of their labor, educating their children, or advancing up the economic ladder.

Review Questions

1. How were the New England textile mills planned and built?
    A. Experienced British builders traveled to the United States to advise American merchants.
    B. New England merchants paid French and German mechanics to design factories for them.
    C. New England merchants and British migrants memorized plans from British mills.
    D. Textile mills were a purely American creation, invented by Francis Cabot Lowell in 1813.

2. Which is the best characterization of textile mill workers in the early nineteenth century?
    A. male and female indentured servants from Great Britain who worked hard to win their freedom
    B. young men who found freedom in the rowdy lifestyle of mill work
    C. experienced artisans who shared their knowledge in exchange for part ownership in the company
    D. young farm women whose behavior was closely monitored

3. What effect did industrialization have on consumers?

4. Most people who migrated within the United States in the early nineteenth century went _____.
    A. north toward Canada
    B. west toward Ohio
    C. south toward Georgia
    D. east across the Mississippi River

5. Which of the following was *not* a cause of the Panic of 1819?
    A. The Second Bank of the United States made risky loans.
    B. States chartered too many banks.
    C. Prices for American commodities dropped.
    D. Banks hoarded gold and silver.

6. Robert Fulton is known for inventing _____.
    A. the cotton gin
    B. the mechanical reaper
    C. the steamship engine
    D. machine tools

7. What did federal and state governments do to help people who were hurt in the Panic of 1819?

8. Which of the following was *not* a factor in the transportation revolution?
    A. the steam-powered locomotive
    B. the canal system
    C. the combustion engine
    D. the government-funded road system

9. What was the significance of the Cumberland Road?
    A. It gave settlers a quicker way to move west.
    B. It reduced the time it took to move goods from New York Harbor to Lake Erie.
    C. It improved trade from the Port of New Orleans.
    D. It was the first paved road.

10. What were the benefits of the transportation revolution?

11. Which of the following groups supported the abolition of slavery?
    A. northern business elites
    B. southern planter elites
    C. wage workers
    D. middle-class northerners

12. Which social class was most drawn to amusements like P. T. Barnum's museum?
    A. wage workers
    B. middle-class northerners
    C. southern planter elites
    D. northern business elites

13. What did Peter Cooper envision for the United States, and how did he work to bring his vision to life?

Critical Thinking Questions

14. Industrialization in the Northeast produced great benefits and also major problems. What were they? Who benefited and who suffered? Did the benefits outweigh the problems, or vice versa?

15. What factors led to the Panic of 1819? What government regulations might have prevented it?

16. Would the Industrial Revolution have been possible without the use of slave labor? Why or why not?

17. What might have been the advantages and disadvantages of railroads for the people who lived along the routes or near the stations?

18. What were the values of the middle class? How did they differ from the values of those above and below them on the socioeconomic ladder? In what ways are these values similar to or different from those held by the middle class today?

Jacksonian Democracy, 1820–1840

FIGURE 10.1 In *President's Levee, or all Creation going to the White House, Washington* (1841), by Robert Cruikshank, the artist depicts Andrew Jackson's inauguration in 1829, with crowds surging into the White House to join the celebrations. Rowdy revelers destroyed many White House furnishings in their merriment. A new political era of democracy had begun, one characterized by the rule of the majority.

CHAPTER OUTLINE

- 10.1 A New Political Style: From John Quincy Adams to Andrew Jackson
- 10.2 The Rise of American Democracy
- 10.3 The Nullification Crisis and the Bank War
- 10.4 Indian Removal
- 10.5 The Tyranny and Triumph of the Majority

INTRODUCTION The most extraordinary political development in the years before the Civil War was the rise of American democracy. Whereas the founders envisioned the United States as a republic, not a democracy, and had placed safeguards such as the Electoral College in the 1787 Constitution to prevent simple majority rule, the early 1820s saw many Americans embracing majority rule and rejecting old forms of deference that were based on elite ideas of virtue, learning, and family lineage.

A new breed of politicians learned to harness the magic of the many by appealing to the resentments, fears, and passions of ordinary citizens to win elections. The charismatic Andrew Jackson gained a reputation as a fighter and defender of American expansion, emerging as the quintessential figure leading the rise of American democracy. In the image above (Figure 10.1), crowds flock to the White House to celebrate his inauguration as president. While earlier inaugurations had been reserved for Washington's political elite, Jackson's was an event for the people, so much so that the pushing throngs caused thousands of dollars of damage to White House property. Characteristics of modern American democracy, including the turbulent nature of majority rule, first appeared during the Age of Jackson.

10.1 A New Political Style: From John Quincy Adams to Andrew Jackson

LEARNING OBJECTIVES

By the end of this section, you will be able to:
- Explain and illustrate the new style of American politics in the 1820s
- Describe the policies of John Quincy Adams's presidency and explain the political divisions that resulted

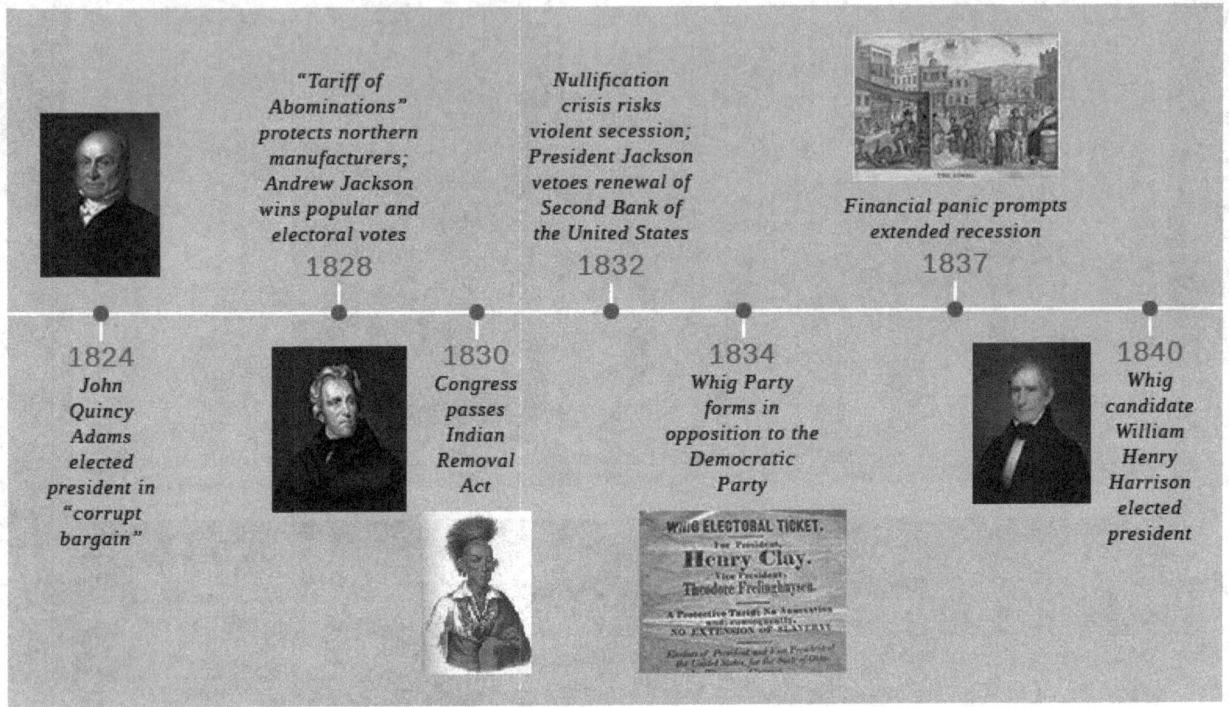

FIGURE 10.2

In the 1820s, American political culture gave way to the democratic urges of the citizenry. Political leaders and parties rose to popularity by championing the will of the people, pushing the country toward a future in which a wider swath of citizens gained a political voice. However, this expansion of political power was limited to White men; women, free Black people, and Native Americans remained—or grew increasingly—disenfranchised by the American political system.

THE DECLINE OF FEDERALISM

The first party system in the United States shaped the political contest between the Federalists and the Democratic-Republicans. The Federalists, led by Washington, Hamilton, and Adams, dominated American politics in the 1790s. After the election of Thomas Jefferson—the Revolution of 1800—the Democratic-Republicans gained ascendance. The gradual decline of the Federalist Party is evident in its losses in the presidential contests that occurred between 1800 and 1820. After 1816, in which Democratic-Republican James Monroe defeated his Federalist rival Rufus King, the Federalists never ran another presidential candidate.

Before the 1820s, a **code of deference** had underwritten the republic's political order. Deference was the practice of showing respect for individuals who had distinguished themselves through military accomplishments, educational attainment, business success, or family pedigree. Such individuals were members of what many Americans in the early republic agreed was a natural aristocracy. Deference shown to them dovetailed with republicanism and its emphasis on virtue, the ideal of placing the common good above narrow self-interest. Republican statesmen in the 1780s and 1790s expected and routinely received deferential treatment from others, and ordinary Americans deferred to their "social betters" as a matter of course.

For the generation who lived through the American Revolution, for instance, George Washington epitomized republican virtue, entitling him to great deference from his countrymen. His judgment and decisions were considered beyond reproach. An Anglican minister named Mason Locke Weems wrote the classic tale of Washington's unimpeachable virtue in his 1800 book, *The Life of Washington*. Generations of nineteenth-century American children read its fictional story of a youthful Washington chopping down one of his father's cherry trees and, when confronted by his father, confessing: "I cannot tell a lie" (Figure 10.3). The story spoke to Washington's unflinching honesty and integrity, encouraging readers to remember the deference owed to such towering national figures.

FIGURE 10.3 "*Father, I Can Not Tell a Lie: I Cut the Tree*" (1867) by John McRae, after a painting by George Gorgas White, illustrates Mason Locke Weems's tale of Washington's honesty and integrity as revealed in the incident of the cherry tree. Although it was fiction, this story about Washington taught generations of children about the importance of virtue.

Washington and those who celebrated his role as president established a standard for elite, virtuous leadership that cast a long shadow over subsequent presidential administrations. The presidents who followed Washington shared the first president's pedigree. With the exception of John Adams, who was from Massachusetts, all the early presidents—Thomas Jefferson, James Madison, and James Monroe—were members of Virginia's elite slaveholder aristocracy.

DEMOCRATIC REFORMS

In the early 1820s, deference to pedigree began to wane in American society. A new type of deference—to the will of the majority and not to a ruling class—took hold. The spirit of democratic reform became most evident in the widespread belief that all White men, regardless of whether they owned property, had the right to participate in elections.

Before the 1820s, many state constitutions had imposed property qualifications for voting as a means to keep democratic tendencies in check. However, as Federalist ideals fell out of favor, ordinary men from the middle and lower classes increasingly questioned the idea that property ownership was an indication of virtue. They argued for **universal manhood suffrage**, or voting rights for all White male adults.

New states adopted constitutions that did not contain property qualifications for voting, a move designed to stimulate migration across their borders. Vermont and Kentucky, admitted to the Union in 1791 and 1792 respectively, granted the right to vote to all White men regardless of whether they owned property or paid taxes. Ohio's state constitution placed a minor taxpaying requirement on voters but otherwise allowed for expansive White male suffrage. Alabama, admitted to the Union in 1819, eliminated property qualifications for voting in its state constitution. Two other new states, Indiana (1816) and Illinois (1818), also extended the right to vote to White men regardless of property. Initially, the new state of Mississippi (1817) restricted voting to White male property holders, but in 1832 it eliminated this provision.

In Connecticut, Federalist power largely collapsed in 1818 when the state held a constitutional convention. The new constitution granted the right to vote to all White men who paid taxes or served in the militia. Similarly, New York amended its state constitution in 1821–1822 and removed the property qualifications for voting.

Expanded voting rights did not extend to women, Native, or free Black people in the North. Indeed, race replaced property qualifications as the criterion for voting rights. American democracy had a decidedly racist orientation; a White majority limited the rights of Black minorities. New Jersey explicitly restricted the right to vote to White men only. Connecticut passed a law in 1814 taking the right to vote away from free Black men and restricting suffrage to White men only. By the 1820s, 80 percent of the White male population could vote in New York State elections. No other state had expanded suffrage so dramatically. At the same time, however, New York effectively disenfranchised free Black men in 1822 (Black men had had the right to vote under the 1777 constitution) by requiring that "men of color" must possess property over the value of $250.

PARTY POLITICS AND THE ELECTION OF 1824

In addition to expanding White men's right to vote, democratic currents also led to a new style of political party organization, most evident in New York State in the years after the War of 1812. Under the leadership of Martin Van Buren, New York's "Bucktail" Republican faction (so named because members wore a deer's tail on their hats, a symbol of membership in the Tammany Society) gained political power by cultivating loyalty to the will of the majority, not to an elite family or renowned figure. The Bucktails emphasized a pragmatic approach. For example, at first they opposed the Erie Canal project, but when the popularity of the massive transportation venture became clear, they supported it.

One of the Bucktails' greatest achievements in New York came in the form of revisions to the state constitution in the 1820s. Under the original constitution, a Council of Appointments selected local officials such as sheriffs and county clerks. The Bucktails replaced this process with a system of direct elections, which meant thousands of jobs immediately became available to candidates who had the support of the majority. In practice, Van Buren's party could nominate and support their own candidates based on their loyalty to the party. In this way, Van Buren helped create a political machine of disciplined party members who prized loyalty above all else, a harbinger of future patronage politics in the United States. This system of rewarding party loyalists is known as the **spoils system** (from the expression, "To the victor belong the spoils"). Van Buren's political machine helped radically transform New York politics.

Party politics also transformed the national political landscape, and the election of 1824 proved a turning point in American politics. With tens of thousands of new voters, the older system of having members of Congress form congressional caucuses to determine who would run no longer worked. The new voters had regional interests and voted on them. For the first time, the popular vote mattered in a presidential election. Electors were chosen by popular vote in eighteen states, while the six remaining states used the older system in which state legislatures chose electors.

With the caucus system defunct, the presidential election of 1824 featured five candidates, all of whom ran as Democratic-Republicans (the Federalists having ceased to be a national political force). The crowded field included John Quincy Adams, the son of the second president, John Adams. Candidate Adams had broken with the Federalists in the early 1800s and served on various diplomatic missions, including the mission to secure peace with Great Britain in 1814. He represented New England. A second candidate, John C. Calhoun from South Carolina, had served as secretary of war and represented the slaveholding South. He dropped out of the presidential race to run for vice president. A third candidate, Henry Clay, the Speaker of the House of Representatives, hailed from Kentucky and represented the western states. He favored an active federal government committed to internal improvements, such as roads and canals, to bolster national economic development and settlement of the West. William H. Crawford, a slaveholder from Georgia, suffered a stroke in 1823 that left him largely incapacitated, but he ran nonetheless and had the backing of the New York machine headed by Van Buren. Andrew Jackson, the famed "hero of New Orleans," rounded out the field. Jackson had very little formal education, but he was popular for his military victories in the War of 1812 and in wars against the Creek and the Seminole. He had been elected to the Senate in 1823, and his popularity soared as pro-Jackson newspapers sang the praises of the courage and daring of the Tennessee slaveholder (Figure 10.4).

FIGURE 10.4 The two most popular presidential candidates in the election of 1824 were Andrew Jackson (a), who won the popular vote but failed to secure the requisite number of votes in the Electoral College, and John Quincy Adams (b), who emerged victorious after a contentious vote in the U.S. House of Representatives.

Results from the eighteen states where the popular vote determined the electoral vote gave Jackson the election, with 152,901 votes to Adams's 114,023, Clay's 47,217, and Crawford's 46,979. The Electoral College, however, was another matter. Of the 261 electoral votes, Jackson needed 131 or better to win but secured only 99. Adams won 84, Crawford 41, and Clay 37. Because Jackson did not receive a majority vote from the Electoral College, the election was decided following the terms of the Twelfth Amendment, which stipulated that when a candidate did not receive a majority of electoral votes, the election went to the House of Representatives, where each state would provide one vote. House Speaker Clay did not want to see his rival, Jackson, become president and therefore worked within the House to secure the presidency for Adams, convincing many to cast their vote for the New Englander. Clay's efforts paid off; despite not having won the popular vote, John Quincy Adams was certified by the House as the next president. Once in office, he elevated Henry Clay to the post of secretary of state.

Jackson and his supporters cried foul. To them, the election of Adams reeked of anti-democratic corruption. So too did the appointment of Clay as secretary of state. John C. Calhoun labeled the whole affair a **"corrupt bargain"** (Figure 10.5). Everywhere, Jackson supporters vowed revenge against the anti-majoritarian result of 1824.

(a) (b)

FIGURE 10.5 John C. Calhoun (a) believed that the assistance Henry Clay (b) gave to John Quincy Adams in the U.S. House of Representatives' vote to decide the presidential election of 1824 indicated that a "corrupt bargain" had been made.

THE PRESIDENCY OF JOHN QUINCY ADAMS

Secretary of State Clay championed what was known as the **American System** of high tariffs, a national bank, and federally sponsored internal improvements of canals and roads. Once in office, President Adams embraced Clay's American System and proposed a national university and naval academy to train future leaders of the republic. The president's opponents smelled elitism in these proposals and pounced on what they viewed as the administration's catering to a small privileged class at the expense of ordinary citizens.

Clay also envisioned a broad range of internal transportation improvements. Using the proceeds from land sales in the West, Adams endorsed the creation of roads and canals to facilitate commerce and the advance of settlement in the West. Many in Congress vigorously opposed federal funding of internal improvements, citing among other reasons that the Constitution did not give the federal government the power to fund these projects. However, in the end, Adams succeeded in extending the Cumberland Road into Ohio (a federal highway project). He also broke ground for the Chesapeake and Ohio Canal on July 4, 1828.

CLICK AND EXPLORE

Visit the Cumberland Road Project (http://openstax.org/l/15cumberland) and the Chesapeake and Ohio Canal National Historic Park (http://openstax.org/l/15OandCcanal) to learn more about transportation developments in the first half of the nineteenth century. How were these two projects important for westward expansion?

Tariffs, which both Clay and Adams promoted, were not a novel idea; since the birth of the republic they had been seen as a way to advance domestic manufacturing by making imports more expensive. Congress had approved a tariff in 1789, for instance, and Alexander Hamilton had proposed a protective tariff in 1790. Congress also passed tariffs in 1816 and 1824. Clay spearheaded the drive for the federal government to impose high tariffs to help bolster domestic manufacturing. If imported goods were more expensive than domestic goods, then people would buy American-made goods.

President Adams wished to promote manufacturing, especially in his home region of New England. To that end, in 1828 he proposed a high tariff on imported goods, amounting to 50 percent of their value. The tariff raised questions about how power should be distributed, causing a fiery debate between those who supported states' rights and those who supported the expanded power of the federal government (Figure 10.6). Those who championed states' rights denounced the 1828 measure as the **Tariff of Abominations**, clear evidence that the federal government favored one region, in this case the North, over another, the South. They made their case by pointing out that the North had an expanding manufacturing base while the South did not. Therefore, the South imported far more manufactured goods than the North, causing the tariff to fall most heavily on the southern states.

FIGURE 10.6 *The Monkey System or 'Every one for himself at the expense of his neighbor!!!!!!!!'* (1831) critiqued Henry Clay's proposed tariff and system of internal improvements. In this political cartoon by Edward Williams Clay, four caged monkeys labeled "Home," "Consumption," "Internal," and "Improv" (improvements)—different parts of the nation's economy—steal each other's food while Henry Clay, in the foreground, extols the virtues of his "grand original American System." (credit: Project Gutenberg Archives)

The 1828 tariff generated additional fears among southerners. In particular, it suggested to them that the federal government would unilaterally take steps that hurt the South. This line of reasoning led some southerners to fear that the very foundation of the South—slavery—could come under attack from a hostile northern majority in Congress. The spokesman for this southern view was President Adams's vice president, John C. Calhoun.

DEFINING AMERICAN

John C. Calhoun on the Tariff of 1828

Vice President John C. Calhoun, angry about the passage of the Tariff of 1828, anonymously wrote a report titled "South Carolina Exposition and Protest" (later known as "Calhoun's Exposition") for the South Carolina legislature. As a native of South Carolina, Calhoun articulated the fear among many southerners that the federal government could exercise undue power over the states.

" If it be conceded, as it must be by every one who is the least conversant with our institutions, that the sovereign powers delegated are divided between the General and State Governments, and that the latter hold their portion by the same tenure as the former, it would seem impossible to deny to the States the right of deciding on the infractions of their powers, and the proper remedy to be applied for their correction. The right of judging, in such cases, is an essential attribute of sovereignty, of which the States cannot be divested without losing their sovereignty itself, and being reduced to a subordinate corporate condition. In fact, to divide power, and to give to one of the parties the exclusive right of judging of the portion allotted to each, is, in reality, not to divide it at all; and to reserve such exclusive right to the General Government (it matters not by what department) to be exercised, is to convert it, in fact, into a great consolidated government, with unlimited powers, and to divest the States, in reality, of all their rights, It is impossible to understand the force of terms, and to deny so plain a conclusion.
—John C. Calhoun, "South Carolina Exposition and Protest," 1828 "

What is Calhoun's main point of protest? What does he say about the sovereignty of the states?

10.2 The Rise of American Democracy

LEARNING OBJECTIVES

By the end of this section, you will be able to:
- Describe the key points of the election of 1828
- Explain the scandals of Andrew Jackson's first term in office

A turning point in American political history occurred in 1828, which witnessed the election of Andrew Jackson over the incumbent John Quincy Adams. While democratic practices had been in ascendance since 1800, the year also saw the further unfolding of a democratic spirit in the United States. Supporters of Jackson called themselves Democrats or the Democracy, giving birth to the Democratic Party. Political authority appeared to rest with the majority as never before.

THE CAMPAIGN AND ELECTION OF 1828

During the 1800s, democratic reforms made steady progress with the abolition of property qualifications for voting and the birth of new forms of political party organization. The 1828 campaign pushed new democratic practices even further and highlighted the difference between the Jacksonian expanded electorate and the older, exclusive Adams style. A slogan of the day, "Adams who can write/Jackson who can fight," captured the contrast between Adams the aristocrat and Jackson the frontiersman.

The 1828 campaign differed significantly from earlier presidential contests because of the party organization that promoted Andrew Jackson. Jackson and his supporters reminded voters of the "corrupt bargain" of 1824. They framed it as the work of a small group of political elites deciding who would lead the nation, acting in a self-serving manner and ignoring the will of the majority (Figure 10.7). From Nashville, Tennessee, the Jackson campaign organized supporters around the nation through editorials in partisan newspapers and other publications. Pro-Jackson newspapers heralded the "hero of New Orleans" while denouncing Adams. Though he did not wage an election campaign filled with public appearances, Jackson did give one major campaign speech in New Orleans on January 8, the anniversary of the defeat of the British in 1815. He also engaged in rounds of discussion with politicians who came to his home, the Hermitage, in Nashville.

FIGURE 10.7 The bitter rivalry between Andrew Jackson and Henry Clay was exacerbated by the "corrupt bargain" of 1824, which Jackson made much of during his successful presidential campaign in 1828. This drawing, published in the 1830s during the debates over the future of the Second Bank of the United States, shows Clay sewing up

Jackson's mouth while the "cure for calumny [slander]" protrudes from his pocket.

At the local level, Jackson's supporters worked to bring in as many new voters as possible. Rallies, parades, and other rituals further broadcast the message that Jackson stood for the common man against the corrupt elite backing Adams and Clay. Democratic organizations called Hickory Clubs, a tribute to Jackson's nickname, Old Hickory, also worked tirelessly to ensure his election.

In November 1828, Jackson won an overwhelming victory over Adams, capturing 56 percent of the popular vote and 68 percent of the electoral vote. As in 1800, when Jefferson had won over the Federalist incumbent John Adams, the presidency passed to a new political party, the Democrats. The election was the climax of several decades of expanding democracy in the United States and the end of the older politics of deference.

CLICK AND EXPLORE

Visit The Hermitage (http://openstax.org/l/15Hermitage) to explore a timeline of Andrew Jackson's life and career. How do you think the events of his younger life affected the trajectory of his political career?

SCANDAL IN THE PRESIDENCY

Amid revelations of widespread fraud, including the disclosure that some $300,000 was missing from the Treasury Department, Jackson removed almost 50 percent of appointed civil officers, which allowed him to handpick their replacements. This replacement of appointed federal officials is called **rotation in office**. Lucrative posts, such as postmaster and deputy postmaster, went to party loyalists, especially in places where Jackson's support had been weakest, such as New England. Some Democratic newspaper editors who had supported Jackson during the campaign also gained public jobs.

Jackson's opponents were angered and took to calling the practice the spoils system, after the policies of Van Buren's Bucktail Republican Party. The rewarding of party loyalists with government jobs resulted in spectacular instances of corruption. Perhaps the most notorious occurred in New York City, where a Jackson appointee made off with over $1 million. Such examples seemed proof positive that the Democrats were disregarding merit, education, and respectability in decisions about the governing of the nation.

In addition to dealing with rancor over rotation in office, the Jackson administration became embroiled in a personal scandal known as the Petticoat affair. This incident exacerbated the division between the president's team and the insider class in the nation's capital, who found the new arrivals from Tennessee lacking in decorum and propriety. At the center of the storm was Margaret ("Peggy") O'Neal, a well-known socialite in Washington, DC (Figure 10.8). O'Neal had connections to the republic's most powerful men. She married John Timberlake, a naval officer, and they had three children. Rumors abounded, however, about her involvement with John Eaton, a U.S. senator from Tennessee who had come to Washington in 1818.

FIGURE 10.8 Peggy O'Neal was so well known that advertisers used her image to sell products to the public. In this

anonymous nineteenth-century cigar-box lid, her portrait is flanked by vignettes showing her scandalous past. On the left, President Andrew Jackson presents her with flowers. On the right, two men fight a duel for her.

Timberlake committed suicide in 1828, setting off a flurry of rumors that he had been distraught over his wife's reputed infidelities. Eaton and Mrs. Timberlake married soon after, with the full approval of President Jackson. The so-called Petticoat affair divided Washington society. Many Washington socialites snubbed the new Mrs. Eaton as a woman of low moral character. Among those who would have nothing to do with her was Vice President John C. Calhoun's wife, Floride. Calhoun fell out of favor with President Jackson, who defended Peggy Eaton and derided those who would not socialize with her, declaring she was "as chaste as a virgin." (Jackson had personal reasons for defending Eaton: he drew a parallel between Eaton's treatment and that of his late wife, Rachel, who had been subjected to attacks on her reputation related to her first marriage, which had ended in divorce.) Martin Van Buren, who defended the Eatons and organized social gatherings with them, became close to Jackson, who came to rely on a group of informal advisers that included Van Buren and was dubbed the **Kitchen Cabinet**. This select group of presidential supporters highlights the importance of party loyalty to Jackson and the Democratic Party.

10.3 The Nullification Crisis and the Bank War

LEARNING OBJECTIVES
By the end of this section, you will be able to:
- Explain the factors that contributed to the Nullification Crisis
- Discuss the origins and creation of the Whig Party

The crisis over the Tariff of 1828 continued into the 1830s and highlighted one of the currents of democracy in the Age of Jackson: namely, that many southerners believed a democratic majority could be harmful to their interests. These southerners saw themselves as an embattled minority and claimed the right of states to nullify federal laws that appeared to threaten state sovereignty. Another undercurrent was the resentment and anger of the majority against symbols of elite privilege, especially powerful financial institutions like the Second Bank of the United States.

THE NULLIFICATION CRISIS

The Tariff of 1828 had driven Vice President Calhoun to pen his "South Carolina Exposition and Protest," in which he argued that if a national majority acted against the interest of a regional minority, then individual states could void—or nullify—federal law. By the early 1830s, the battle over the tariff took on new urgency as the price of cotton continued to fall. In 1818, cotton had been thirty-one cents per pound. By 1831, it had sunk to eight cents per pound. While production of cotton had soared during this time and this increase contributed to the decline in prices, many southerners blamed their economic problems squarely on the tariff for raising the prices they had to pay for imported goods while their own income shrank.

Resentment of the tariff was linked directly to the issue of slavery, because the tariff demonstrated the use of federal power. Some southerners feared the federal government would next take additional action against the South, including the abolition of slavery. The theory of **nullification**, or the voiding of unwelcome federal laws, provided wealthy slaveholders, who were a minority in the United States, with an argument for resisting the national government if it acted contrary to their interests. James Hamilton, who served as governor of South Carolina in the early 1830s, denounced the "despotic majority that oppresses us." Nullification also raised the specter of secession; aggrieved states at the mercy of an aggressive majority would be forced to leave the Union.

On the issue of nullification, South Carolina stood alone. Other southern states backed away from what they saw as the extremism behind the idea. President Jackson did not make the repeal of the 1828 tariff a priority and denied the nullifiers' arguments. He and others, including former President Madison, argued that Article 1, Section 8 of the Constitution gave Congress the power to "lay and collect taxes, duties, imposts, and excises." Jackson pledged to protect the Union against those who would try to tear it apart over the tariff issue. "The union shall be preserved," he declared in 1830.

To deal with the crisis, Jackson advocated a reduction in tariff rates. The Tariff of 1832, passed in the summer, lowered the rates on some products like imported goods, a move designed to calm southerners. It did not have the desired effect, however, and Calhoun's nullifiers still claimed their right to override federal law. In November, South Carolina passed the Ordinance of Nullification, declaring the 1828 and 1832 tariffs null and void in the Palmetto State. Jackson responded, however, by declaring in the December 1832 Nullification Proclamation that a state did not have the power to void a federal law.

With the states and the federal government at an impasse, civil war seemed a real possibility. The next governor of South Carolina, Robert Hayne, called for a force of ten thousand volunteers (Figure 10.9) to defend the state against any federal action. At the same time, South Carolinians who opposed the nullifiers told Jackson that eight thousand men stood ready to defend the Union. Congress passed the Force Bill of 1833, which gave the federal government the right to use federal troops to ensure compliance with federal law. The crisis—or at least the prospect of armed conflict in South Carolina—was defused by the Compromise Tariff of 1833, which reduced tariff rates considerably. Nullifiers in South Carolina accepted it, but in a move that demonstrated their inflexibility, they nullified the Force Bill.

FIGURE 10.9 The governor of South Carolina, Robert Hayne, elected in 1832, was a strong proponent of states' rights and the theory of nullification.

The Nullification Crisis illustrated the growing tensions in American democracy: an aggrieved minority of elite, wealthy slaveholders taking a stand against the will of a democratic majority; an emerging sectional divide between South and North over slavery; and a clash between those who believed in free trade and those who believed in protective tariffs to encourage the nation's economic growth. These tensions would color the next three decades of politics in the United States.

THE BANK WAR

Congress established the Bank of the United States in 1791 as a key pillar of Alexander Hamilton's financial program, but its twenty-year charter expired in 1811. Congress, swayed by the majority's hostility to the bank as an institution catering to the wealthy elite, did not renew the charter at that time. In its place, Congress approved a new national bank—the Second Bank of the United States—in 1816. It too had a twenty-year charter, set to expire in 1836.

The Second Bank of the United States was created to stabilize the banking system. More than two hundred banks existed in the United States in 1816, and almost all of them issued paper money. In other words, citizens faced a bewildering welter of paper money with no standard value. In fact, the problem of paper money had contributed significantly to the Panic of 1819.

In the 1820s, the national bank moved into a magnificent new building in Philadelphia. However, despite Congress's approval of the Second Bank of the United States, a great many people continued to view it as tool of the wealthy, an anti-democratic force. President Jackson was among them; he had faced economic crises of his own during his days speculating in land, an experience that had made him uneasy about paper money. To Jackson, hard currency—that is, gold or silver—was the far better alternative. The president also personally disliked the bank's director, Nicholas Biddle.

A large part of the allure of mass democracy for politicians was the opportunity to capture the anger and resentment of ordinary Americans against what they saw as the privileges of a few. One of the leading opponents of the bank was Thomas Hart Benton, a senator from Missouri, who declared that the bank served "to make the rich richer, and the poor poorer." The self-important statements of Biddle, who claimed to have more power than President Jackson, helped fuel sentiments like Benton's.

In the reelection campaign of 1832, Jackson's opponents in Congress, including Henry Clay, hoped to use their support of the bank to their advantage. In January 1832, they pushed for legislation that would re-charter it, even though its charter was not scheduled to expire until 1836. When the bill for re-chartering passed and came to President Jackson, he used his executive authority to veto the measure.

The defeat of the Second Bank of the United States demonstrates Jackson's ability to focus on the specific issues that aroused the democratic majority. Jackson understood people's anger and distrust toward the bank, which stood as an emblem of special privilege and big government. He skillfully used that perception to his advantage, presenting the bank issue as a struggle of ordinary people against a rapacious elite class who cared nothing for the public and pursued only their own selfish ends. As Jackson portrayed it, his was a battle for small government and ordinary Americans. His stand against what bank opponents called the "**monster bank**" proved very popular, and the Democratic press lionized him for it (Figure 10.10). In the election of 1832, Jackson received nearly 53 percent of the popular vote against his opponent Henry Clay.

FIGURE 10.10 In *General Jackson Slaying the Many Headed Monster* (1836), the artist, Henry R. Robinson, depicts President Jackson using a cane marked "Veto" to battle a many-headed snake representing state banks, which supported the national bank. Battling alongside Martin Van Buren and Jack Downing, Jackson addresses the largest head, that of Nicholas Biddle, the director of the national bank: "Biddle thou Monster Avaunt [go away]!! . . ."

Jackson's veto was only one part of the war on the "monster bank." In 1833, the president removed the deposits from the national bank and placed them in state banks. Biddle, the bank's director, retaliated by restricting loans to the state banks, resulting in a reduction of the money supply. The financial turmoil only increased when Jackson issued an executive order known as the Specie Circular, which required that western land sales be conducted using gold or silver only. Unfortunately, this policy proved a disaster when the Bank of England, the source of much of the hard currency borrowed by American businesses, dramatically cut back on loans to the United States. Without the flow of hard currency from England, American depositors drained the gold and silver from their own domestic banks, making hard currency scarce. Adding to the economic distress of the late 1830s, cotton prices plummeted, contributing to a financial crisis called the Panic of 1837. This economic panic would prove politically useful for Jackson's opponents in the coming years and Van Buren, elected president in 1836, would pay the price for Jackson's hard-currency preferences.

WHIGS

Jackson's veto of the bank and his Specie Circular helped galvanize opposition forces into a new political party, the **Whigs**, a faction that began to form in 1834. The name was significant; opponents of Jackson saw him as exercising tyrannical power, so they chose the name Whig after the eighteenth-century political party that resisted the monarchical power of King George III. One political cartoon dubbed the president "King Andrew the First" and displayed Jackson standing on the Constitution, which has been ripped to shreds (Figure 10.11).

FIGURE 10.11 This anonymous 1833 political caricature (a) represents President Andrew Jackson as a despotic ruler, holding a scepter in one hand and a veto in the other. Contrast the image of "King Andrew" with a political cartoon from 1831 (b) of Jackson overseeing a scene of uncontrollable chaos as he falls from a hickory chair "coming to pieces at last."

Whigs championed an active federal government committed to internal improvements, including a national bank. They made their first national appearance in the presidential election of 1836, a contest that pitted Jackson's handpicked successor, Martin Van Buren, against a field of several Whig candidates. Indeed, the large field of Whig candidates indicated the new party's lack of organization compared to the Democrats. This helped Van Buren, who carried the day in the Electoral College. As the effects of the Panic of 1837 continued to be felt for years afterward, the Whig press pinned the blame for the economic crisis on Van Buren and the Democrats.

CLICK AND EXPLORE

Explore a Library of Congress (http://openstax.org/l/15PolPrints) collection of 1830s political cartoons from the pages of *Harper's Weekly* to learn more about how Andrew Jackson was viewed by the public in that era.

10.4 Indian Removal

LEARNING OBJECTIVES

By the end of this section, you will be able to:
- Explain the legal wrangling that surrounded the Indian Removal Act
- Describe how depictions of Native peoples in popular culture helped lead to Native removal
- Describe the Indian Removal Act's effect on Native American people, and their responses to it.

Pro-Jackson newspapers touted the president as a champion of opening land for White settlement and moving native inhabitants beyond the boundaries of "American civilization." In this effort, Jackson reflected majority opinion: most Americans believed Native peoples had no place in the White republic. Jackson's animosity toward Native Americans ran deep. He had fought against the Creek in 1813 and against the Seminole in 1817, and his reputation and popularity rested in large measure on his firm commitment to remove Native residents from states in the South. The 1830 Indian Removal Act and subsequent displacement of the Creek, Choctaw, Chickasaw, Seminole, and Cherokee tribes of the Southeast fulfilled the vision of a White nation and became one of the identifying characteristics of the Age of Jackson.

NATIVE AMERICANS IN POPULAR CULTURE

Popular culture in the first half of the nineteenth century reflected the aversion to Native Americans that was pervasive during the Age of Jackson. Jackson skillfully played upon this racial hatred to engage the United States in a policy of ethnic cleansing, eradicating the Native presence from the land to make way for White civilization.

In an age of mass democracy, powerful anti-Native sentiments found expression in mass culture, shaping popular perceptions. James Fenimore Cooper's very popular historical novel, *The Last of the Mohicans*, published in 1826 as part of his Leatherstocking series, told the tale of Nathaniel "Natty" Bumppo (aka Hawkeye), who lived among Native Americans but had been born to White parents. Cooper provides a romantic version of the French and Indian War in which Natty helps the British against the French and the feral, bloodthirsty Huron. Natty endures even as his Native American friends die, including the noble Uncas, the last Mohican, in a narrative that dovetailed with most people's approval of Native removal.

Native Americans also made frequent appearances in art. George Catlin produced many paintings of Native peoples, which he offered as true representations despite routinely emphasizing their supposed "savage" nature. *The Cutting Scene, Mandan O-kee-pa Ceremony* (Figure 10.12) is one example. Scholars have long questioned the accuracy of this portrayal of a rite of passage among the Mandan people. Accuracy aside, the painting captured the imaginations of White viewers, reinforcing their disgust at the savagery of Native Americans.

FIGURE 10.12 *The Cutting Scene, Mandan O-kee-pa Ceremony*, an 1832 painting by George Catlin, depicts a rite-of-passage ceremony that Catlin said he witnessed. It featured wooden splints inserted into the chest and back muscles of young men. Such paintings increased Native Americans' reputation as savages.

AMERICANA

The Paintings of George Catlin

George Catlin seized upon the public fascination with the supposedly exotic and savage Native American, seeing an opportunity to make money by painting them in a way that conformed to popular White stereotypes (Figure 10.13). In the late 1830s, he toured major cities with his Indian Gallery, a collection of paintings of Native peoples. Though he hoped his exhibition would be profitable, it did not bring him financial security.

(a)

(b)

FIGURE 10.13 In *Attacking the Grizzly Bear* (a), painted in 1844, Catlin focused on the Natives' own vanishing culture, while in *Wi-jún-jon, Pigeon's Egg Head (The Light) Going To and Returning From Washington* (b), painted in 1837–1839, he contrasted their ways with those of White people by showing an Assiniboine leader transformed by a visit to Washington, DC.

Catlin routinely painted Native Americans in a supposedly aboriginal state. In *Attacking the Grizzly Bear*, the hunters do not have rifles and instead rely on spears. Such a portrayal stretches credibility as Native peoples had long been exposed to and adopted European weapons. Indeed, the painting's depiction of Native people riding horses, which were introduced by the Spanish, makes clear that, as much as Catlin and White viewers wanted to believe in the primitive and savage Native, the reality was otherwise.

In *Wi-jún-jon, Pigeon's Egg Head (The Light) Going To and Returning From Washington,* the viewer is shown a before and after portrait of Wi-jún-jon, who tried to emulate White dress and manners after going to Washington, DC. What differences do you see between these two representations of Wi-jún-jon? Do you think his attempt to imitate White people was successful? Why or why not? What do you think Catlin was trying to convey with this depiction of Wi-jún-jon's assimilation?

THE INDIAN REMOVAL ACT

In his first message to Congress, Jackson had proclaimed that Native American groups living independently within states, as sovereign entities, presented a major problem for state sovereignty. This message referred directly to the situation in Georgia, Mississippi, and Alabama, where the Creek, Choctaw, Chickasaw, Seminole, and Cherokee peoples stood as obstacles to White settlement. These groups were known as the **Five Civilized Tribes**, because they had largely adopted Anglo-American culture, speaking English and practicing Christianity. Some held enslaved people like their White counterparts.

White people especially resented the Cherokee in Georgia, coveting the tribe's rich agricultural lands in the northern part of the state. The impulse to remove the Cherokee only increased when gold was discovered on their lands. Ironically, while White people insisted the Cherokee and other Native peoples could never be good citizens because of their savage ways, the Cherokee had arguably gone farther than any other indigenous group in adopting White culture. The *Cherokee Phoenix*, the newspaper of the Cherokee, began publication in 1828 (Figure 10.14) in English and the Cherokee language. Although the Cherokee followed the lead of their White neighbors by farming and owning property, as well as embracing Christianity and enslaving people, this proved of little consequence in an era when White people perceived all Native Americans as incapable of becoming full citizens of the republic.

FIGURE 10.14 This image depicts the front page of the *Cherokee Phoenix* newspaper from May 21, 1828. The paper was published in both English and the Cherokee language.

Jackson's anti-Native stance struck a chord with a majority of White citizens, many of whom shared a hatred of non-White people that spurred Congress to pass the 1830 Indian Removal Act. The act called for the removal of the Five Civilized Tribes from their home in the southeastern United States to land in the West, in present-day Oklahoma. Jackson declared in December 1830, "It gives me pleasure to announce to Congress that the benevolent policy of the Government, steadily pursued for nearly thirty years, in relation to the removal of the Native Americans beyond the White settlements is approaching to a happy consummation. Two important tribes have accepted the provision made for their removal at the last session of Congress, and it is believed that their example will induce the remaining tribes also to seek the same obvious advantages."

The Cherokee decided to fight the federal law, however, and took their case to the Supreme Court. Their legal fight had the support of anti-Jackson members of Congress, including Henry Clay and Daniel Webster, and they retained the legal services of former attorney general William Wirt. In *Cherokee Nation v. Georgia*, Wirt argued that the Cherokee constituted an independent foreign nation, and that an injunction (a stop) should be placed on Georgia laws aimed at eradicating them. In 1831, the Supreme Court found the Cherokee did not meet the criteria for being a foreign nation.

Another case involving the Cherokee also found its way to the highest court in the land. This legal struggle—*Worcester v. Georgia*—asserted the rights of non-natives to live on Native American lands. Samuel Worcester was a Christian missionary and federal postmaster of New Echota, the capital of the Cherokee nation. A Congregationalist, he had gone to live among the Cherokee in Georgia to further the spread of Christianity, and he strongly opposed Native American removal.

By living among the Cherokee, Worcester had violated a Georgia law forbidding White people, unless they were agents of the federal government, to live in Native American territory. Worcester was arrested, but because his federal job as postmaster gave him the right to live there, he was released. Jackson supporters then succeeded in taking away Worcester's job, and he was re-arrested. This time, a court sentenced him and nine others for violating the Georgia state law banning White people from living on Native land. Worcester was sentenced to four years of hard labor. When the case of *Worcester v. Georgia* came before the Supreme Court in 1832, Chief Justice John Marshall ruled in favor of Worcester, finding that the Cherokee constituted "distinct political communities" with sovereign rights to their own territory.

DEFINING AMERICAN

Chief Justice John Marshall's Ruling in *Worcester v. Georgia*

In 1832, Chief Justice of the Supreme Court John Marshall ruled in favor of Samuel Worcester in *Worcester v. Georgia*. In doing so, he established the principle of tribal sovereignty. Although this judgment contradicted *Cherokee Nation v. Georgia*, it failed to halt the Indian Removal Act. In his opinion, Marshall wrote the following:

"From the commencement of our government Congress has passed acts to regulate trade and intercourse with the Indians; which treat them as nations, respect their rights, and manifest a firm purpose to afford that protection which treaties stipulate. All these acts, and especially that of 1802, which is still in force, manifestly consider the several Indian nations as distinct political communities, having territorial boundaries, within which their authority is exclusive, and having a right to all the lands within those boundaries, which is not only acknowledged, but guaranteed by the United States. . . .

The Cherokee Nation, then, is a distinct community, occupying its own territory, with boundaries accurately described, in which the laws of Georgia can have no force, and which the citizens of Georgia have no right to enter but with the assent of the Cherokees themselves or in conformity with treaties and with the acts of Congress. The whole intercourse between the United States and this nation is, by our Constitution and laws, vested in the government of the United States.

The act of the State of Georgia under which the plaintiff in error was prosecuted is consequently void, and the judgment a nullity. . . . The Acts of Georgia are repugnant to the Constitution, laws, and treaties of the United States. "

How does this opinion differ from the outcome of *Cherokee Nation v. Georgia* just one year earlier? Why do you think the two outcomes were different?

The Supreme Court did not have the power to enforce its ruling in *Worcester v. Georgia*, however, and it became clear that the Cherokee would be compelled to move. Those who understood that the only option was removal traveled west, but the majority stayed on their land. In order to remove them, the president relied on the U.S. military. In a series of forced marches, some fifteen thousand Cherokee were finally relocated to Oklahoma. This forced migration, known as the **Trail of Tears**, caused the deaths of as many as four thousand Cherokee (Figure 10.15). The Creek, Choctaw, Chickasaw, and Seminole peoples were also compelled to go. The removal of the Five Civilized Tribes provides an example of the power of majority opinion in a democracy.

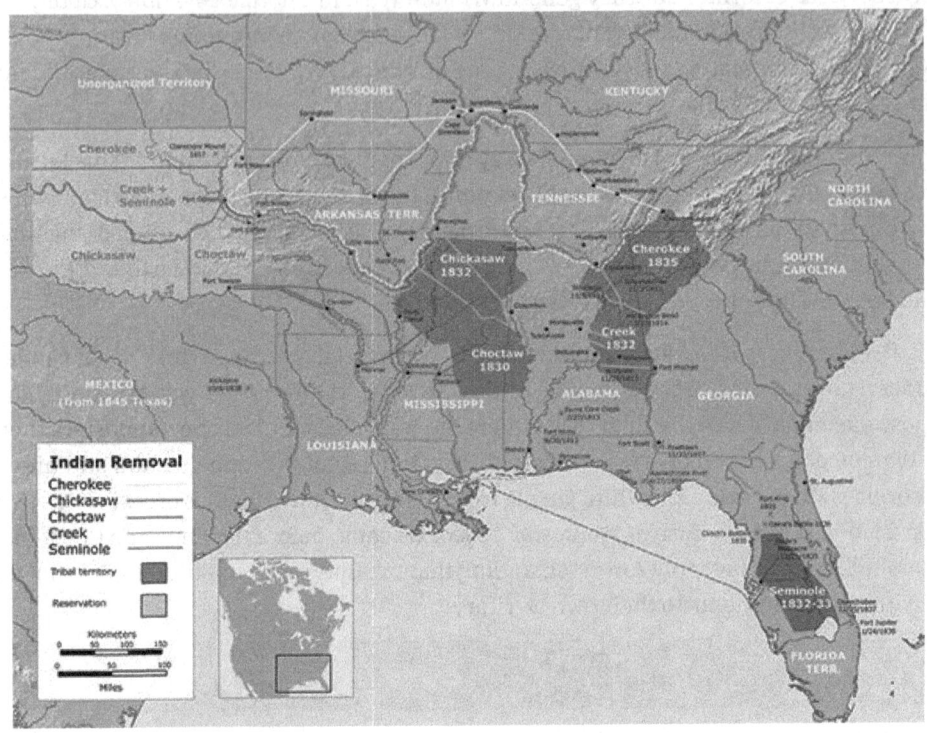

FIGURE 10.15 After the passage of the Indian Removal Act, the U.S. military forced the Cherokee, Creek, Choctaw, Chickasaw, and Seminole to relocate from the Southeast to an area in the western territory (now Oklahoma), marching them along the routes shown here.

CLICK AND EXPLORE

Explore the interactive Trail of Tears map (http://openstax.org/l/15NativeAm) at PBS.org to see the routes the Five Civilized Tribes traveled when they were expelled from their lands. Then listen to a collection of Cherokee oral histories (http://openstax.org/l/15NativeAm2) including verses of a Cherokee-language song about the Trail of Tears. What do you think is the importance of oral history in documenting the Cherokee experience?

BLACK HAWK'S WAR

The policy of removal led some Native Americans to actively resist. In 1832, the Fox and the Sauk, led by Sauk chief Black Hawk (Makataimeshekiakiah), moved back across the Mississippi River to reclaim their ancestral home in northern Illinois. A brief war in 1832, Black Hawk's War, ensued. White settlers panicked at the return of the Sauk, and militias and federal troops quickly mobilized. At the Bad Axe Massacre, they killed over two hundred men, women, and children. Some seventy White settlers and soldiers also lost their lives in the conflict (Figure 10.16). The war, which lasted only a matter of weeks, illustrates how much White people on the frontier hated and feared Native Americans during the Age of Jackson.

FIGURE 10.16 Charles Bird King's 1837 portrait *Sauk Chief Makataimeshekiakiah, or Black Hawk* (a), depicts the Sauk chief who led the Fox and Sauk peoples in an ill-fated effort to return to their native lands in northern Illinois. This engraving depicting the Bad Axe Massacre (b) shows U.S. soldiers on a steamer firing on Native Americans aboard a raft. (credit b: modification of work by Library of Congress)

10.5 The Tyranny and Triumph of the Majority

LEARNING OBJECTIVES

By the end of this section, you will be able to:
- Explain Alexis de Tocqueville's analysis of American democracy
- Describe the election of 1840 and its outcome

To some observers, the rise of democracy in the United States raised troubling questions about the new power of the majority to silence minority opinion. As the will of the majority became the rule of the day, everyone outside of mainstream, White American opinion, especially Native American and Black people, were vulnerable to the wrath of the majority. Some worried that the rights of those who opposed the will of the majority would never be safe. Mass democracy also shaped political campaigns as never before. The 1840 presidential election marked a significant turning point in the evolving style of American democratic politics.

ALEXIS DE TOCQUEVILLE

Perhaps the most insightful commentator on American democracy was the young French aristocrat Alexis de Tocqueville, whom the French government sent to the United States to report on American prison reforms (Figure 10.17). Tocqueville marveled at the spirit of democracy that pervaded American life. Given his place in French society, however, much of what he saw of American democracy caused him concern.

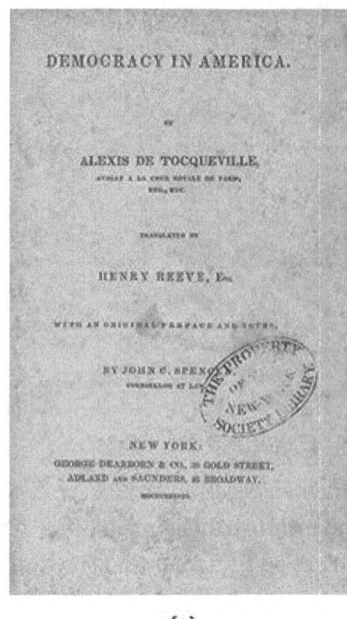 

(a) (b)

FIGURE 10.17 Alexis de Tocqueville is best known for his insightful commentary on American democracy found in *De la démocratie en Amérique*. The first volume of Tocqueville's two-volume work was immediately popular throughout Europe. The first English translation, by Henry Reeve and titled *Democracy in America* (a), was published in New York in 1838. Théodore Chassériau painted this portrait of Alexis de Tocqueville in 1850 (b).

Tocqueville's experience led him to believe that democracy was an unstoppable force that would one day overthrow monarchy around the world. He wrote and published his findings in 1835 and 1840 in a two-part work entitled *Democracy in America*. In analyzing the democratic revolution in the United States, he wrote that the major benefit of democracy came in the form of equality before the law. A great deal of the social revolution of democracy, however, carried negative consequences. Indeed, Tocqueville described a new type of tyranny, the **tyranny of the majority**, which overpowers the will of minorities and individuals and was, in his view, unleashed by democracy in the United States.

In this excerpt from *Democracy in America*, Alexis de Tocqueville warns of the dangers of democracy when the majority will can turn to tyranny:

" When an individual or a party is wronged in the United States, to whom can he apply for redress? If to public opinion, public opinion constitutes the majority; if to the legislature, it represents the majority, and implicitly obeys its injunctions; if to the executive power, it is appointed by the majority, and remains a passive tool in its hands; the public troops consist of the majority under arms; the jury is the majority invested with the right of hearing judicial cases; and in certain States even the judges are elected by the majority. However iniquitous or absurd the evil of which you complain may be, you must submit to it as well as you can.

The authority of a king is purely physical, and it controls the actions of the subject without subduing his private will; but the majority possesses a power which is physical and moral at the same time; it acts upon the will as well as upon the actions of men, and it represses not only all contest, but all controversy. I know no country in which there is so little true independence of mind and freedom of discussion as in America."

CLICK AND EXPLORE

Take the Alexis de Tocqueville Tour (http://openstax.org/l/15Tocqueville) to experience nineteenth-century America as Tocqueville did, by reading his journal entries about the states and territories he visited with fellow countryman Gustave de Beaumont. What regional differences can you draw from his descriptions?

THE 1840 ELECTION

The presidential election contest of 1840 marked the culmination of the democratic revolution that swept the United States. By this time, the **second party system** had taken hold, a system whereby the older Federalist and Democratic-Republican Parties had been replaced by the new Democratic and Whig Parties. Both Whigs and Democrats jockeyed for election victories and commanded the steady loyalty of political partisans. Large-scale presidential campaign rallies and emotional propaganda became the order of the day. Voter turnout increased dramatically under the second party system. Roughly 25 percent of eligible voters had cast ballots in 1828. In 1840, voter participation surged to nearly 80 percent.

The differences between the parties were largely about economic policies. Whigs advocated accelerated economic growth, often endorsing federal government projects to achieve that goal. Democrats did not view the federal government as an engine promoting economic growth and advocated a smaller role for the national government. The membership of the parties also differed: Whigs tended to be wealthier; they were prominent planters in the South and wealthy urban northerners—in other words, the beneficiaries of the market revolution. Democrats presented themselves as defenders of the common people against the elite.

In the 1840 presidential campaign, taking their cue from the Democrats who had lionized Jackson's military accomplishments, the Whigs promoted William Henry Harrison as a war hero based on his 1811 military service against the Shawnee chief Tecumseh at the Battle of Tippecanoe. John Tyler of Virginia ran as the vice presidential candidate, leading the Whigs to trumpet, "Tippecanoe and Tyler too!" as a campaign slogan.

The campaign thrust Harrison into the national spotlight. Democrats tried to discredit him by declaring, "Give him a barrel of hard [alcoholic] cider and settle a pension of two thousand a year on him, and take my word for it, he will sit the remainder of his days in his log cabin." The Whigs turned the slur to their advantage by presenting Harrison as a man of the people who had been born in a log cabin (in fact, he came from a privileged background in Virginia), and the contest became known as the **log cabin campaign** (Figure 10.18). At Whig political rallies, the faithful were treated to whiskey made by the E. C. Booz Company, leading to the introduction of the word "booze" into the American lexicon. Tippecanoe Clubs, where booze flowed freely, helped in the marketing of the Whig candidate.

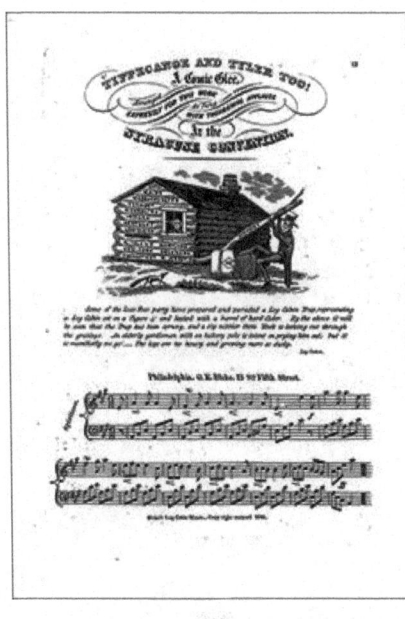
(a)

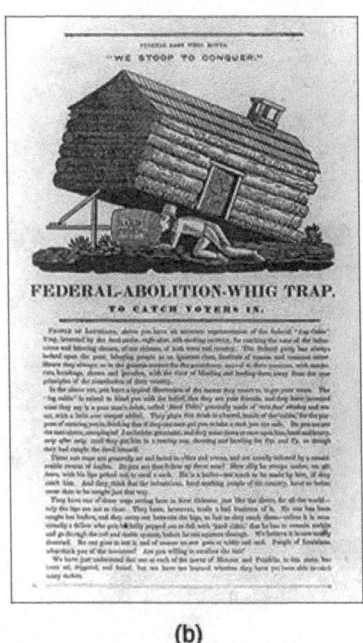
(b)

FIGURE 10.18 The Whig campaign song "Tippecanoe and Tyler Too!" (a) and the anti-Whig flyers (b) that were circulated in response to the "log cabin campaign" illustrate the partisan fervor of the 1840 election.

The Whigs' efforts, combined with their strategy of blaming Democrats for the lingering economic collapse that began with the hard-currency Panic of 1837, succeeded in carrying the day. A mass campaign with political rallies and party mobilization had molded a candidate to fit an ideal palatable to a majority of American voters, and in 1840 Harrison won what many consider the first modern election.

Key Terms

American System   the program of federally sponsored roads and canals, protective tariffs, and a national bank advocated by Henry Clay and enacted by President Adams

code of deference   the practice of showing respect for individuals who had distinguished themselves through accomplishments or birth

corrupt bargain   the term that Andrew Jackson's supporters applied to John Quincy Adams's 1824 election, which had occurred through the machinations of Henry Clay in the U.S. House of Representatives

Five Civilized Tribes   the five tribes—Cherokee, Seminole, Creek, Choctaw, and Chickasaw—who had most thoroughly adopted Anglo-American culture; they also happened to be the tribes that were believed to stand in the way of western settlement in the South

Kitchen Cabinet   a nickname for Andrew Jackson's informal group of loyal advisers

log cabin campaign   the 1840 election, in which the Whigs painted William Henry Harrison as a man of the people

monster bank   the term Democratic opponents used to denounce the Second Bank of the United States as an emblem of special privilege and big government

nullification   the theory, advocated in response to the Tariff of 1828, that states could void federal law at their discretion

rotation in office   originally, simply the system of having term limits on political appointments; in the Jackson era, this came to mean the replacement of officials with party loyalists

second party system   the system in which the Democratic and Whig Parties were the two main political parties after the decline of the Federalist and Democratic-Republican Parties

spoils system   the political system of rewarding friends and supporters with political appointments

Tariff of Abominations   a federal tariff introduced in 1828 that placed a high duty on imported goods in order to help American manufacturers, which southerners viewed as unfair and harmful to their region

Trail of Tears   the route of the forced removal of the Cherokee and other tribes from the southeastern United States to the territory that is now Oklahoma

tyranny of the majority   Alexis de Tocqueville's phrase warning of the dangers of American democracy

universal manhood suffrage   voting rights for all male adults

Whigs   a political party that emerged in the early 1830s to oppose what members saw as President Andrew Jackson's abuses of power

Summary

10.1 A New Political Style: From John Quincy Adams to Andrew Jackson

The early 1800s saw an age of deference give way to universal manhood suffrage and a new type of political organization based on loyalty to the party. The election of 1824 was a fight among Democratic-Republicans that ended up pitting southerner Andrew Jackson against northerner John Quincy Adams. When Adams won through political negotiations in the House of Representatives, Jackson's supporters derided the election as a "corrupt bargain." The Tariff of 1828 further stirred southern sentiment, this time against a perceived bias in the federal government toward northeastern manufacturers. At the same time, the tariff stirred deeper fears that the federal government might take steps that could undermine the system of slavery.

10.2 The Rise of American Democracy

The Democratic-Republicans' "corrupt bargain" that brought John Quincy Adams and Henry Clay to office in 1824 also helped to push them out of office in 1828. Jackson used it to highlight the cronyism of Washington politics. Supporters presented him as a true man of the people fighting against the elitism of Clay and Adams. Jackson rode a wave of populist fervor all the way to the White House, ushering in the ascendency of a new political party: the Democrats. Although Jackson ran on a platform of clearing the corruption out of Washington, he rewarded his own loyal followers with plum government jobs, thus continuing and intensifying the cycle of favoritism and corruption.

10.3 The Nullification Crisis and the Bank War

Andrew Jackson's election in 1832 signaled the rise of the Democratic Party and a new style of American politics. Jackson understood the views of the majority, and he skillfully used the popular will to his advantage. He adroitly navigated through the Nullification Crisis and made headlines with what his supporters viewed as his righteous war against the bastion of money, power, and entrenched insider interests, the Second Bank of the United States. His actions, however, stimulated opponents to fashion an opposition party, the Whigs.

10.4 Indian Removal

Popular culture in the Age of Jackson emphasized the perceived savagery of the Native peoples and shaped domestic policy. Popular animosity found expression in the Indian Removal Act. Even the U.S. Supreme Court's ruling in favor of the Cherokee in Georgia offered no protection against the forced removal of the Five Civilized Tribes from the Southeast, mandated by the 1830 Indian Removal Act and carried out by the U.S. military.

10.5 The Tyranny and Triumph of the Majority

American culture of the 1830s reflected the rise of democracy. The majority exercised a new type of power that went well beyond politics, leading Alexis de Tocqueville to write about the "tyranny of the majority." Very quickly, politicians among the Whigs and Democrats learned to master the magic of the many by presenting candidates and policies that catered to the will of the majority. In the 1840 "log cabin campaign," both sides engaged in the new democratic electioneering. The uninhibited expression during the campaign inaugurated a new political style.

Review Questions

1. Which group saw an expansion of their voting rights in the early nineteenth century?
    A. free Black people
    B. non-property-owning men
    C. women
    D. Native Americans

2. What was the lasting impact of the Bucktail Republican Party in New York?
    A. They implemented universal suffrage.
    B. They pushed for the expansion of the canal system.
    C. They elevated Martin Van Buren to the national political stage.
    D. They changed state election laws from an appointee system to a system of open elections.

3. Who won the popular vote in the election of 1824?
    A. Andrew Jackson
    B. Martin Van Buren
    C. Henry Clay
    D. John Quincy Adams

4. Why did Andrew Jackson and his supporters consider the election of John Quincy Adams to be a "corrupt bargain"?

5. Who stood to gain from the Tariff of Abominations, and who expected to lose by it?

6. What was the actual result of Jackson's policy of "rotation in office"?
   A. an end to corruption in Washington
   B. a replacement of Adams's political loyalists with Jackson's political loyalists
   C. the filling of government posts with officials the people chose themselves
   D. the creation of the Kitchen Cabinet

7. The election of 1828 brought in the first presidency of which political party?
   A. the Democrats
   B. the Democratic-Republicans
   C. the Republicans
   D. the Bucktails

8. What were the planks of Andrew Jackson's campaign platform in 1828?

9. What was the significance of the Petticoat affair?

10. South Carolina threatened to nullify which federal act?
    A. the abolition of slavery
    B. the expansion of the transportation infrastructure
    C. the protective tariff on imported goods
    D. the rotation in office that expelled several federal officers

11. How did President Jackson respond to Congress's re-chartering of the Second Bank of the United States?
    A. He vetoed it.
    B. He gave states the right to implement it or not.
    C. He signed it into law.
    D. He wrote a counterproposal.

12. Why did the Second Bank of the United States make such an inviting target for President Jackson?

13. What were the philosophies and policies of the new Whig Party?

14. How did most White people in the United States view Native Americans in the 1820s?
    A. as savages
    B. as being in touch with nature
    C. as enslaved people
    D. as shamans

15. The 1830 Indian Removal Act is best understood as _____.
    A. an example of President Jackson forcing Congress to pursue an unpopular policy
    B. an illustration of the widespread hatred of Native Americans during the Age of Jackson
    C. an example of laws designed to integrate Native Americans into American life
    D. an effort to deprive the Cherokee of their enslaved property

16. What was the Trail of Tears?

17. The winner of the 1840 election was _____.
    A. a Democrat
    B. a Democratic-Republican
    C. an Anti-Federalist
    D. a Whig

18. Which of the following did *not* characterize political changes in the 1830s?
    A. higher voter participation
    B. increasing political power of free Black voters
    C. stronger partisan ties
    D. political battles between Whigs and Democrats

19. How did Alexis de Tocqueville react to his visit to the United States? What impressed and what worried him?

Critical Thinking Questions

20. What were some of the social and cultural beliefs that became widespread during the Age of Jackson? What lay behind these beliefs, and do you observe any of them in American culture today?

21. Were the political changes of the early nineteenth century positive or negative? Explain your opinion.

22. If you were defending the Cherokee and other native nations before the U.S. Supreme Court in the 1830s, what arguments would you make? If you were supporting Native American removal, what arguments would you make?

23. How did depictions of Native Americans in popular culture help to sway popular opinion? Does modern popular culture continue to wield this kind of power over us? Why or why not?

24. Does Alexis de Tocqueville's argument about the tyranny of the majority reflect American democracy today? Provide examples to support your answer.

A Nation on the Move: Westward Expansion, 1800–1860

11

FIGURE 11.1 In the first half of the nineteenth century, settlers began to move west of the Mississippi River in large numbers. In John Gast's *American Progress* (ca. 1872), the figure of Columbia, representing the United States and the spirit of democracy, makes her way westward, literally bringing light to the darkness as she advances.

CHAPTER OUTLINE

11.1 Lewis and Clark
11.2 The Missouri Crisis
11.3 Independence for Texas
11.4 The Mexican-American War, 1846–1848
11.5 Free or Slave Soil? The Dilemma of the West

INTRODUCTION After 1800, the United States militantly expanded westward across North America, confident of its right and duty to gain control of the continent and spread the benefits of its "superior" culture. In John Gast's *American Progress* (Figure 11.1), the White, blonde figure of Columbia—a historical personification of the United States—strides triumphantly westward with the Star of Empire on her head. She brings education, symbolized by the schoolbook, and modern technology, represented by the telegraph wire. White settlers follow her lead, driving the Native peoples away and bringing successive waves of technological progress in their wake. In the first half of the nineteenth century, the quest for control of the West led to the Louisiana Purchase, the annexation of Texas, and the Mexican-American War. Efforts to seize western territories from Native peoples and expand the republic by warring with Mexico succeeded beyond expectations. Few nations ever expanded so quickly. Yet, this expansion led to debates about the fate of slavery in the West, creating tensions between North and South that ultimately led to the collapse of American democracy and a brutal civil war.

11.1 Lewis and Clark

LEARNING OBJECTIVES

By the end of this section, you will be able to:
- Explain the significance of the Louisiana Purchase
- Describe the terms of the Adams-Onís Treaty
- Describe the role played by the filibuster in American expansion

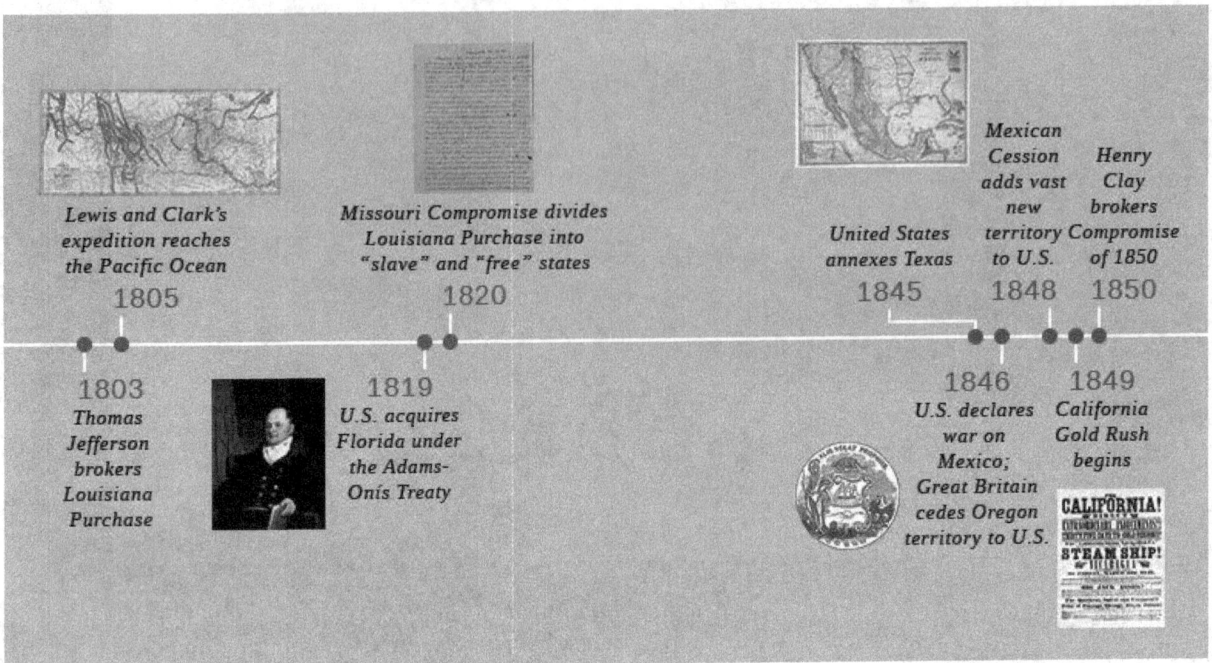

FIGURE 11.2

For centuries Europeans had mistakenly believed an all-water route across the North American continent existed. This "**Northwest Passage**" would afford the country that controlled it not only access to the interior of North America but also—more importantly—a relatively quick route to the Pacific Ocean and to trade with Asia. The Spanish, French, and British searched for years before American explorers took up the challenge of finding it. Indeed, shortly before Lewis and Clark set out on their expedition for the U.S. government, Alexander Mackenzie, an officer of the British North West Company, a fur trading outfit, had attempted to discover the route. Mackenzie made it to the Pacific and even believed (erroneously) he had discovered the headwaters of the Columbia River, but he could not find an easy water route with a minimum of difficult portages, that is, spots where boats must be carried overland.

Many Americans also dreamed of finding a Northwest Passage and opening the Pacific to American commerce and influence, including President Thomas Jefferson. In April 1803, Jefferson achieved his goal of purchasing the Louisiana Territory from France, effectively doubling the size of the United States. The purchase was made possible due to events outside the nation's control. With the success of the Haitian Revolution, an uprising of enslaved people against the French, France's Napoleon abandoned his quest to re-establish an extensive French Empire in America. As a result, he was amenable to selling off the vast Louisiana territory. President Jefferson quickly set out to learn precisely what he had bought and to assess its potential for commercial exploitation. Above all else, Jefferson wanted to exert U.S. control over the territory, an area already well known to French and British explorers. It was therefore vital for the United States to explore and map the land to pave the way for future White settlement.

JEFFERSON'S CORPS OF DISCOVERY HEADS WEST

To head the expedition into the Louisiana territory, Jefferson appointed his friend and personal secretary, twenty-nine-year-old army captain Meriwether Lewis, who was instructed to form a **Corps of Discovery**. Lewis in turn selected William Clark, who had once been his commanding officer, to help him lead the group (Figure 11.3).

(a) (b)

FIGURE 11.3 Charles Willson Peale, celebrated portraitist of the American Revolution, painted both William Clark (a) and Meriwether Lewis (b) in 1810 and 1807, respectively, after they returned from their expedition west.

Jefferson wanted to improve the ability of American merchants to access the ports of China. Establishing a river route from St. Louis to the Pacific Ocean was crucial to capturing a portion of the fur trade that had proven so profitable to Great Britain. He also wanted to legitimize American claims to the land against rivals, such as Great Britain and Spain. Lewis and Clark were thus instructed to map the territory through which they would pass and to explore all tributaries of the Missouri River. This part of the expedition struck fear into Spanish officials, who believed that Lewis and Clark would encroach on New Mexico, the northern part of New Spain. Spain dispatched four unsuccessful expeditions from Santa Fe to intercept the explorers. Jefferson also tasked Lewis and Clark with paving the way for American trade among the western tribes. Establishing an overland route to the Pacific would bolster U.S. claims to the Pacific Northwest, first established in 1792 when Captain Robert Gray sailed his ship *Columbia* into the mouth of the river that now bears his vessel's name and forms the present-day border between Oregon and Washington. Finally, Jefferson, who had a keen interest in science and nature, ordered Lewis and Clark to take extensive notes on the geography, plant life, animals, and natural resources of the region into which they would journey.

After spending the winter of 1803–1804 encamped at the mouth of the Missouri River while the men prepared for their expedition, the corps set off in May 1804. Although the thirty-three frontiersmen, boatmen, and hunters took with them Alexander Mackenzie's account of his explorations and the best maps they could find, they did not have any real understanding of the difficulties they would face. Fierce storms left them drenched and freezing. Enormous clouds of gnats and mosquitos swarmed about their heads as they made their way up the Missouri River. Along the way they encountered (and killed) a variety of animals including elk, buffalo, and grizzly bears. One member of the expedition survived a rattlesnake bite. As the men collected minerals and specimens of plants and animals, the overly curious Lewis sampled minerals by tasting them and became seriously ill at one point. What they did not collect, they sketched and documented in the journals they kept. They also noted the customs of the tribes who controlled the land and attempted to establish peaceful relationships with them in order to ensure that future White settlement would not be impeded.

CLICK AND EXPLORE

Read the journals of Lewis and Clark on the University of Virginia (http://openstax.org/l/15LandClark) website or on the University of Nebraska–Lincoln (http://openstax.org/l/15LandClark1) website, which also has footnotes, maps, and commentary. According to their writings, what challenges did the explorers confront?

The corps spent their first winter in the wilderness, 1804–1805, in a Mandan village in what is now North Dakota. There they encountered a reminder of France's former vast North American empire when they met a French fur trapper named Toussaint Charbonneau. When the corps left in the spring of 1805, Charbonneau accompanied them as a guide and interpreter, bringing Sacagawea—who had been kidnapped and sold to Charbonneau, who made her his wife—and their newborn son. Charbonneau knew the land better than the Americans, and Sacagawea proved invaluable as an interpreter and diplomat to the Shoshone people. The presence of a young woman and her infant convinced many groups that the expedition was not a war party and meant no harm (Figure 11.4).

FIGURE 11.4 In this idealized image, Sacagawea leads Lewis and Clark through the Montana wilderness. In reality, she was still a teenager at the time. Although she served important roles as an interpreter and diplomat, she did not actually guide the party. Kidnapped as a child, she would not likely have retained detailed memories about the place where she grew up.

The corps set about making friends with Native tribes while simultaneously attempting to assert American power over the territory. Hoping to overawe the people of the land, Lewis would let out a blast of his air rifle, a relatively new piece of technology the Native Americans had never seen. The corps also followed native custom by distributing gifts, including shirts, ribbons, and kettles, as a sign of goodwill. The explorers presented native leaders with medallions, many of which bore Jefferson's image, and invited them to visit their new "ruler" in the East. These medallions or peace medals were meant to allow future explorers to identify friendly native groups. Not all efforts to assert U.S. control went peacefully; some Indians rejected the explorers' intrusion onto their land. Lewis unintentionally created tension with the Blackfeet by discussing trade deals made with their traditional enemies. The encounter turned hostile, and members of the corps killed two Blackfeet men.

After spending eighteen long months on the trail and nearly starving to death in the Bitterroot Mountains of Montana, the Corps of Discovery finally reached the Pacific Ocean in 1805 and spent the winter of 1805–1806 in Oregon. They returned to St. Louis later in 1806 having lost only one man, who had died of appendicitis. Upon their return, Meriwether Lewis was named governor of the Louisiana Territory. Unfortunately, he died only three years later in circumstances that are still disputed, before he could write a complete account of what the expedition had discovered.

Although the Corps of Discovery failed to find an all-water route to the Pacific Ocean (for none existed), it nevertheless accomplished many of the goals Jefferson had set. The men traveled across the North American continent and established relationships with many Native American tribes, paving the way for fur traders like John Jacob Astor who later established trading posts solidifying U.S. claims to Oregon. Delegates of several tribes did go to Washington to meet the president. Hundreds of plant and animal specimens were collected, several of which were named for Lewis and Clark in recognition of their efforts. And the territory was now more accurately mapped and legally claimed by the United States. Nonetheless, most of the vast territory, home to a variety of native peoples, remained unknown to Americans (Figure 11.5).

FIGURE 11.5 This 1814 map of Lewis and Clark's path across North America from the Missouri River to the Pacific Ocean was based on maps and notes made by William Clark. Although most of the West still remained unknown, the expedition added greatly to knowledge of what lay west of the Mississippi. Most important, it allowed the United States to solidify its claim to the immense territory.

AMERICANA

A Selection of Hats for the Fashionable Gentleman

Beaver hats (Figure 11.6) were popular apparel in the eighteenth and nineteenth centuries in both Europe and the United States because they were naturally waterproof and bore a glossy sheen. Demand for beaver pelts (and for the pelts of sea otters, foxes, and martens) by hat makers, dressmakers, and tailors led many fur trappers into the wilderness in pursuit of riches and encouraged trade and relationships with Native American nations. Beaver hats fell out of fashion in the 1850s when silk hats became the rage and beaver became harder to find. In some parts of the West, the animals had been hunted nearly to extinction.

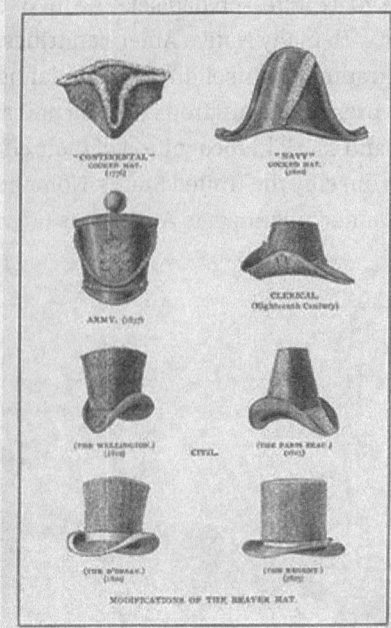

FIGURE 11.6 This illustration from *Castrologia, Or, The History and Traditions of the Canadian Beaver* shows a variety of beaver hat styles. Beaver pelts were also used to trim women's bonnets.

Are there any contemporary fashions or fads that likewise promise to alter the natural world?

SPANISH FLORIDA AND THE ADAMS-ONÍS TREATY

Despite the Lewis and Clark expedition, the boundaries of the Louisiana Purchase remained contested. Expansionists chose to believe the purchase included vast stretches of land, including all of Spanish Texas. The Spanish government disagreed, however. The first attempt to resolve this issue took place in February 1819 with the signing of the Adams-Onís Treaty, which was actually intended to settle the problem of Florida.

Spanish Florida had presented difficulties for its neighbors since the settlement of the original North American colonies, first for England and then for the United States. By 1819, American settlers no longer feared attack by Spanish troops garrisoned in Florida, but militant groups within the Creek and Seminole Nations raided Georgia and then retreated to the relative safety of the Florida wilderness. These tribes also sheltered self-emancipated enslaved people, often intermarrying with them and making them members of their tribes. Sparsely populated by Spanish colonists and far from both Mexico City and Madrid, the frontier in Florida proved next to impossible for the Spanish government to control.

In March 1818, General Andrew Jackson, frustrated by his inability to punish Creek and Seminole raiders, pursued them across the international border into Spanish Florida. Under Jackson's command, U.S. troops aided by Cherokees and Creeks defeated the Creek and Seminole militants, occupied several Florida settlements, and executed two British citizens accused of acting against the United States. Outraged by the U.S. invasion of its territory, the Spanish government demanded that Jackson and his troops withdraw. In agreeing to the withdrawal, however, U.S. Secretary of State John Quincy Adams also offered to purchase the colony. Realizing that conflict between the United States and the Creek and Seminole fighters would continue, Spain opted to cede the Spanish colony to its northern neighbor. The Adams-Onís Treaty, named for Adams and the Spanish ambassador, Luís de Onís, made the cession of Florida official while also setting the boundary between the United States and Mexico at the Sabine River (Figure 11.7). In exchange, Adams gave up U.S. claims to lands west of the Sabine and forgave Spain's $5 million debt to the United States.

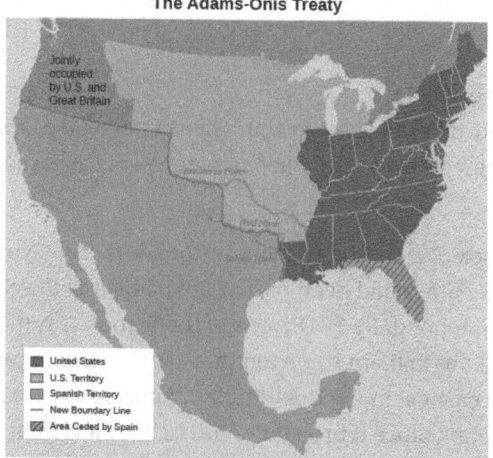

FIGURE 11.7 The red line indicates the border between U.S. and Spanish territory established by the Adams-Onís Treaty of 1819.

The Adams-Onís Treaty upset many American expansionists, who criticized Adams for not laying claim to all of Texas, which they believed had been included in the Louisiana Purchase. In the summer of 1819, James Long, a planter from Natchez, Mississippi, became a **filibuster**, or a private, unauthorized military adventurer, when he led three hundred men on an expedition across the Sabine River to take control of Texas. Long's men succeeded in capturing Nacogdoches, writing a Declaration of Independence (see below), and setting up a republican government. Spanish troops drove them out a month later. Returning in 1820 with a much smaller force, Long was arrested by the Spanish authorities, imprisoned, and killed. Long was but one of many nineteenth-century American filibusters who aimed at seizing territory in the Caribbean and Central America.

DEFINING AMERICAN

The Long Expedition's Declaration of Independence

The Long Expedition's short-lived Republic of Texas was announced with the drafting of a Declaration of Independence in 1819. The declaration named settlers' grievances against the limits put on expansion by the Adams-Onís treaty and expressed their fears of Spain:

"The citizens of Texas have long indulged the hope, that in the adjustment of the boundaries of the Spanish possessions in America, and of the territories of the United States, that they should be included within the limits of the latter. The claims of the United States, long and strenuously urged, encouraged the hope. The recent [Adams-Onís] treaty between Spain and the United States of America has dissipated an illusion too long fondly cherished, and has roused the citizens of Texas . . . They have seen themselves . . . literally abandoned to the dominion of the crown of Spain and left a prey . . . to all those exactions which Spanish rapacity is fertile in devising. The citizens of Texas would have proved themselves unworthy of the age . . . unworthy of their ancestry, of the kindred of the republics of the American continent, could they have hesitated in this emergency . . . Spurning the fetters of colonial vassalage, disdaining to submit to the most atrocious despotism that ever disgraced the annals of Europe, they have resolved under the blessing of God to be free."

How did the filibusters view Spain? What do their actions say about the nature of American society and of U.S. expansion?

11.2 The Missouri Crisis

LEARNING OBJECTIVES

By the end of this section, you will be able to:
- Explain why the North and South differed over the admission of Missouri as a state
- Explain how the admission of new states to the Union threatened to upset the balance between free and slave states in Congress

Another stage of U.S. expansion took place when inhabitants of Missouri began petitioning for statehood beginning in 1817. The Missouri territory had been part of the Louisiana Purchase and was the first part of that vast acquisition to apply for statehood. By 1818, tens of thousands of settlers had flocked to Missouri, including slaveholders who brought with them some ten thousand enslaved people. When the status of the Missouri territory was taken up in earnest in the U.S. House of Representatives in early 1819, its admission to the Union proved to be no easy matter, since it brought to the surface a violent debate over whether slavery would be allowed in the new state.

Politicians had sought to avoid the issue of slavery ever since the 1787 Constitutional Convention arrived at an uneasy compromise in the form of the "three-fifths clause." This provision stated that the entirety of a state's free population and 60 percent of its enslaved population would be counted in establishing the number of that state's members in the House of Representatives and the size of its federal tax bill. Although slavery existed in several northern states at the time, the compromise had angered many northern politicians because, they argued, the "extra" population of enslaved people would give southern states more votes than they deserved in both the House and the Electoral College. Admitting Missouri as a slave state also threatened the tenuous balance between free and slave states in the Senate by giving slave states a two-vote advantage.

The debate about representation shifted to the morality of slavery itself when New York representative James Tallmadge, an opponent of slavery, attempted to amend the statehood bill in the House of Representatives. Tallmadge proposed that Missouri be admitted as a free state, that no more enslaved people be allowed to enter Missouri after it achieved statehood, and that all enslaved children born there after its admission be freed at age twenty-five. The amendment shifted the terms of debate by presenting slavery as an evil to be stopped.

Northern representatives supported the **Tallmadge Amendment**, denouncing slavery as immoral and opposed to the nation's founding principles of equality and liberty. Southerners in Congress rejected the amendment as an attempt to gradually abolish slavery—not just in Missouri but throughout the Union—by violating the property rights of slaveholders and their freedom to take their property wherever they wished. Slavery's apologists, who had long argued that slavery was a necessary evil, now began to perpetuate the idea that slavery was a positive good for the United States. They asserted that it generated wealth and left White men free to exercise their true talents instead of toiling in the soil, as the descendants of Africans were better suited to do. Enslaved people were cared for, supporters argued, and were better off exposed to the teachings of Christianity as enslaved than living as free heathens in uncivilized Africa. Above all, the United States had a destiny, they argued, to create an empire of slavery throughout the Americas. These proslavery arguments were to be made repeatedly and forcefully as expansion to the West proceeded.

Most disturbing for the unity of the young nation, however, was that debaters divided along sectional lines, not party lines. With only a few exceptions, northerners supported the Tallmadge Amendment regardless of party affiliation, and southerners opposed it despite having party differences on other matters. It did not pass, and the crisis over Missouri led to strident calls of disunion and threats of civil war.

Congress finally came to an agreement, called the **Missouri Compromise**, in 1820. Missouri and Maine (which had been part of Massachusetts) would enter the Union at the same time, Maine as a free state, Missouri as a slave state. The Tallmadge Amendment was narrowly rejected, the balance between free and slave states was maintained in the Senate, and southerners did not have to fear that Missouri slaveholders would be deprived of their human property. To prevent similar conflicts each time a territory applied for statehood, a line coinciding with the southern border of Missouri (at latitude 36° 30') was drawn across the remainder of the Louisiana Territory (Figure 11.8). Slavery could exist south of this line but was forbidden north of it, with the obvious exception of Missouri.

FIGURE 11.8 The Missouri Compromise resulted in the District of Maine, which had originally been settled in 1607 by the Plymouth Company and was a part of Massachusetts, being admitted to the Union as a free state and Missouri being admitted as a slave state.

MY STORY

Thomas Jefferson on the Missouri Crisis

On April 22, 1820, Thomas Jefferson wrote to John Holmes to express his reaction to the Missouri Crisis, especially the open threat of disunion and war:

"I thank you, Dear Sir, for the copy you have been so kind as to send me of the letter to your constituents on the Missouri question. it is a perfect justification to them. I had for a long time ceased to read the newspapers or pay any attention to public affairs, confident they were in good hands, and content to be a passenger in our bark to the shore from which I am not distant. but this momentous question [over slavery in Missouri], like a fire bell in the night, awakened and filled me with terror. I considered it at once as the knell of the Union. it is hushed indeed for the moment. but this is a reprieve only, not a final sentence. a geographical line, coinciding with a marked principle, moral and political, once concieved [sic] and held up to the angry passions of men, will never be obliterated; and every new irritation will mark it deeper and deeper. I can say with conscious truth that there is not a man on earth who would sacrifice more than I would, to relieve us from this heavy reproach, in any practicable way. . . .

I regret that I am now to die in the belief that the useless sacrifice of themselves, by the generation of 76. to acquire self government and happiness to their country, is to be thrown away by the unwise and unworthy passions of their sons, and that my only consolation is to be that I live not to weep over it. if they would but dispassionately weigh the blessings they will throw away against an abstract principle more likely to be effected by union than by scission, they would pause before they would perpetuate this act of suicide themselves and of treason against the hopes of the world. to yourself as the faithful advocate of union I tender the offering of my high esteem and respect.
Th. Jefferson "

How would you characterize the former president's reaction? What do you think he means by writing that the Missouri Compromise line "is a reprieve only, not a final sentence"?

CLICK AND EXPLORE

Access a collection of primary documents relating to the Missouri Compromise, including Missouri's application for admission into the Union and Jefferson's correspondence on the Missouri question, at the Library of Congress (http://openstax.org/l/15MOComp) website.

11.3 Independence for Texas

LEARNING OBJECTIVES

By the end of this section, you will be able to:
- Explain why American settlers in Texas sought independence from Mexico
- Discuss early attempts to make Texas independent of Mexico
- Describe the relationship between Anglo-Americans and Tejanos in Texas before and after independence

As the incursions of the earlier filibusters into Texas demonstrated, American expansionists had desired this area of Spain's empire in America for many years. After the 1819 Adams-Onís treaty established the boundary between Mexico and the United States, more American expansionists began to move into the northern portion of Mexico's province of Coahuila y Texas. Following Mexico's independence from Spain in 1821, American settlers immigrated to Texas in even larger numbers, intent on taking the land from the new and vulnerable Mexican nation in order to create a new American slave state.

AMERICAN SETTLERS MOVE TO TEXAS

After the 1819 Adams-Onís Treaty defined the U.S.-Mexico boundary, the Spanish Mexican government began actively encouraging Americans to settle their northern province. Texas was sparsely settled, and the few Mexican farmers and ranchers who lived there were under constant threat of attack by tribes, especially the Comanche Empire, which supplemented its hunting with raids in pursuit of horses and cattle.

To increase the non-Native population in Texas, provide a buffer zone between its tribes and the rest of Mexico, and provide a bulwark against potential American expansion, Spain began to recruit *empresarios*. An **empresario** was someone who brought settlers to the region in exchange for generous grants of land. Moses Austin, a once-prosperous entrepreneur reduced to poverty by the Panic of 1819, requested permission to settle three hundred English-speaking American residents in Texas. Spain agreed on the condition that the resettled people convert to Roman Catholicism.

On his deathbed in 1821, Austin asked his son Stephen to carry out his plans, and Mexico, which had won independence from Spain the same year, allowed Stephen to take control of his father's grant. Like Spain, Mexico also wished to encourage settlement in the state of Coahuila y Texas and passed colonization laws to encourage immigration. Thousands of Americans, primarily from slave states, flocked to Texas and quickly came to outnumber the **Tejanos**, the Mexican residents of the region. The soil and climate offered good opportunities to expand slavery and the cotton kingdom. Land was plentiful and offered at generous terms. Unlike the U.S. government, Mexico allowed buyers to pay for their land in installments and did not require a minimum purchase. Furthermore, to many White people, it seemed not only their God-given right but also their patriotic duty to populate the lands beyond the Mississippi River, bringing with them American slavery, culture, laws, and political traditions (Figure 11.9).

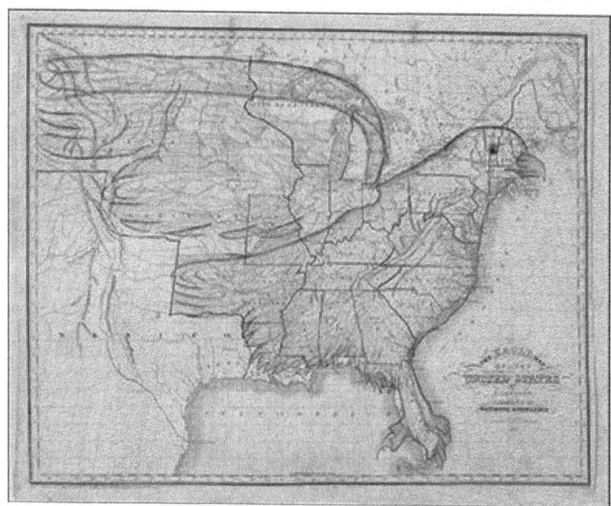

FIGURE 11.9 By the early 1830s, all the lands east of the Mississippi River had been settled and admitted to the Union as states. The land west of the river, though in this contemporary map united with the settled areas in the body of an eagle symbolizing the territorial ambitions of the United States, remained largely unsettled by White Americans. Texas (just southwest of the bird's tail feathers) remained outside the U.S. border.

THE TEXAS WAR FOR INDEPENDENCE

Many Americans who migrated to Texas at the invitation of the Mexican government did not completely shed their identity or loyalty to the United States. They brought American traditions and expectations with them (including, for many, the right to enslave individuals). For instance, the majority of these new settlers were Protestant, and though they were not required to attend the Catholic mass, Mexico's prohibition on the public practice of other religions upset them and they routinely ignored it.

Accustomed to representative democracy, jury trials, and the defendant's right to appear before a judge, the Anglo-American settlers in Texas also disliked the Mexican legal system, which provided for an initial hearing by an **alcalde**, an administrator who often combined the duties of mayor, judge, and law enforcement officer. The *alcalde* sent a written record of the proceeding to a judge in Saltillo, the state capital, who decided the outcome. Settlers also resented that at most two Texas representatives were allowed in the state legislature.

Their greatest source of discontent, though, was the Mexican government's 1829 abolition of slavery. Most American settlers were from southern states, and many had brought enslaved people with them. Mexico tried to accommodate them by maintaining the fiction that the enslaved workers were indentured servants. But American slaveholders in Texas distrusted the Mexican government and wanted Texas to be a new U.S. slave state. The dislike of most for Roman Catholicism (the prevailing religion of Mexico) and a widely held belief in American racial superiority led them generally to regard Mexicans as dishonest, ignorant, and backward.

Belief in their own superiority inspired some Texans to try to undermine the power of the Mexican government. When *empresario* Haden Edwards attempted to evict people who had settled his land grant before he gained title to it, the Mexican government nullified its agreement with him. Outraged, Edwards and a small party of men took prisoner the *alcalde* of Nacogdoches. The Mexican army marched to the town, and Edwards and his troop then declared the formation of the Republic of Fredonia between the Sabine and Rio Grande Rivers. To demonstrate loyalty to their adopted country, a force led by Stephen Austin hastened to Nacogdoches to support the Mexican army. Edwards's revolt collapsed, and the revolutionaries fled Texas.

The growing presence of American settlers in Texas, their reluctance to abide by Mexican law, and their desire for independence caused the Mexican government to grow wary. In 1830, it forbade future U.S. immigration and increased its military presence in Texas. Settlers continued to stream illegally across the long border; by 1835, after immigration resumed, there were twenty thousand Anglo-Americans in Texas (Figure 11.10).

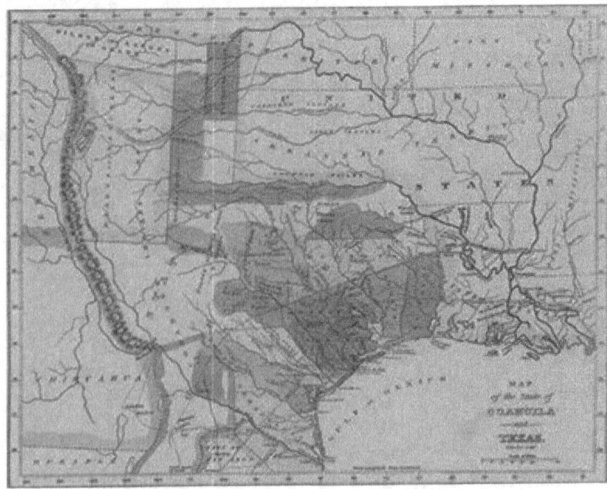

FIGURE 11.10 This 1833 map shows the extent of land grants made by Mexico to American settlers in Texas. Nearly all are in the eastern portion of the state, one factor that led to war with Mexico in 1846.

Fifty-five delegates from the Anglo-American settlements gathered in 1832 to demand the suspension of customs duties, the resumption of immigration from the United States, the granting of promised land titles, and the creation of an independent state of Texas separate from Coahuila. Ordered to disband, the delegates reconvened in early April 1833 to write a constitution for an independent Texas. Surprisingly, General Antonio Lopez de Santa Anna, Mexico's new president, agreed to all demands, except the call for statehood (Figure 11.11). Coahuila y Texas made provisions for jury trials, increased Texas's representation in the state legislature, and removed restrictions on commerce.

FIGURE 11.11 This portrait of General Antonio Lopez de Santa Anna depicts the Mexican president and general in full military regalia.

Texans' hopes for independence were quashed in 1834, however, when Santa Anna dismissed the Mexican Congress and abolished all state governments, including that of Coahuila y Texas. In January 1835, reneging on earlier promises, he dispatched troops to the town of Anahuac to collect customs duties. Lawyer and soldier William B. Travis and a small force marched on Anahuac in June, and the fort surrendered. On October 2, Anglo-American forces met Mexican troops at the town of Gonzales; the Mexican troops fled and the Americans moved on to take San Antonio. Now more cautious, delegates to the Consultation of 1835 at San Felipe de Austin voted against declaring independence, instead drafting a statement, which became known as the Declaration of Causes, promising continued loyalty if Mexico returned to a constitutional form of government. They selected Henry Smith, leader of the Independence Party, as governor of Texas and placed Sam Houston, a former soldier who had been a congressman and governor of Tennessee, in charge of its small military force.

The Consultation delegates met again in March 1836. They declared their independence from Mexico and drafted a constitution calling for an American-style judicial system and an elected president and legislature. Significantly, they also established that slavery would not be prohibited in Texas. Many wealthy Tejanos supported the push for independence, hoping for liberal governmental reforms and economic benefits.

REMEMBER THE ALAMO!

Mexico had no intention of losing its northern province. Santa Anna and his army of four thousand had besieged San Antonio in February 1836. Hopelessly outnumbered, its two hundred defenders, under Travis, fought fiercely from their refuge in an old mission known as the Alamo (Figure 11.12). After ten days, however, the mission was taken and all but a few of the defenders were dead, including Travis and James Bowie, the famed frontiersman who was also a land speculator and slave trader. A few male survivors, possibly including the frontier legend and former Tennessee congressman Davy Crockett, were led outside the walls and executed. The few women and children inside the mission were allowed to leave with the only adult male survivor, a person enslaved by Travis, who was then freed by the Mexican Army. Terrified, they fled.

FIGURE 11.12 The *Fall of the Alamo*, painted by Theodore Gentilz fewer than ten years after this pivotal moment in the Texas Revolution, depicts the 1836 assault on the Alamo complex.

Although hungry for revenge, the Texas forces under Sam Houston nevertheless withdrew across Texas, gathering recruits as they went. Coming upon Santa Anna's encampment on the banks of San Jacinto River on April 21, 1836, they waited as the Mexican troops settled for an afternoon nap. Assured by Houston that "Victory is certain!" and told to "Trust in God and fear not!" the seven hundred men descended on a sleeping force nearly twice their number with cries of "Remember the Alamo!" Within fifteen minutes the Battle of San Jacinto was over. Approximately half the Mexican troops were killed, and the survivors, including Santa Anna, taken prisoner.

Santa Anna grudgingly signed a peace treaty and was sent to Washington, where he met with President Andrew Jackson and, under pressure, agreed to recognize an independent Texas with the Rio Grande River as its southwestern border. By the time the agreement had been signed, however, Santa Anna had been removed from power in Mexico. For that reason, the Mexican Congress refused to be bound by Santa Anna's promises and continued to insist that the renegade territory still belonged to Mexico.

CLICK AND EXPLORE

Visit the official Alamo (http://openstax.org/l/15Alamo) website to learn more about the battle of the Alamo and take a virtual tour of the old mission.

THE LONE STAR REPUBLIC

In September 1836, military hero Sam Houston was elected president of Texas, and, following the relentless logic of U.S. expansion, Texans voted in favor of annexation to the United States. This had been the dream of many settlers in Texas all along. They wanted to expand the United States west and saw Texas as the next logical step. Slaveholders there, such as Sam Houston, William B. Travis and James Bowie (the latter two of whom died at the Alamo), believed too in the destiny of slavery. Mindful of the vicious debates over Missouri that had led to talk of disunion and war, American politicians were reluctant to annex Texas or, indeed, even to recognize it as a sovereign nation. Annexation would almost certainly mean war with Mexico, and the admission of a state with a large enslaved population, though permissible under the Missouri Compromise, would bring the issue of slavery once again to the fore. Texas had no choice but to organize itself as the independent Lone Star Republic. To protect itself from Mexican attempts to reclaim it, Texas sought and received recognition from France, Great Britain, Belgium, and the Netherlands. The United States did not officially recognize Texas as an independent nation until March 1837, nearly a year after the final victory over the Mexican army at San Jacinto.

Uncertainty about its future did not discourage Americans committed to expansion, especially slaveholders, from rushing to settle in the Lone Star Republic, however. Between 1836 and 1846, its population nearly tripled. By 1840, nearly twelve thousand enslaved Africans had been brought to Texas by American slaveholders. Many new settlers had suffered financial losses in the severe financial depression of 1837 and hoped for a new start in the new nation. According to folklore, across the United States, homes and farms were deserted overnight, and curious neighbors found notes reading only "GTT" ("Gone to Texas"). Many Europeans, especially Germans, also immigrated to Texas during this period.

Americans in Texas generally treated both Tejano and Native American residents with utter contempt, eager to displace and dispossess them. Anglo-American leaders failed to return the support their Tejano neighbors had extended during the rebellion and repaid them by seizing their lands. In 1839, Mireau B. Lamar, the second president of the Lone Star Republic, instituted a program of ethnic cleansing aimed at pushing all Native American tribes out of Texas.

The impulse to expand did not lay dormant, and Anglo-American settlers and leaders in the newly formed Texas republic soon cast their gaze on the Mexican province of New Mexico as well. Repeating the tactics of earlier filibusters, a Texas force set out in 1841 intent on taking Santa Fe. Its members encountered an army of New Mexicans and were taken prisoner and sent to Mexico City. On Christmas Day, 1842, Texans avenged a Mexican assault on San Antonio by attacking the Mexican town of Mier. In August, another Texas army was sent to attack Santa Fe, but Mexican troops forced them to retreat. Clearly, hostilities between Texas and Mexico had not ended simply because Texas had declared its independence.

11.4 The Mexican-American War, 1846–1848

LEARNING OBJECTIVES

By the end of this section, you will be able to:
- Identify the causes of the Mexican-American War
- Describe the outcomes of the war in 1848, especially the Mexican Cession
- Describe the effect of the California Gold Rush on westward expansion

Tensions between the United States and Mexico rapidly deteriorated in the 1840s as American expansionists eagerly eyed Mexican land to the west, including the lush northern Mexican province of California. Indeed, in 1842, a U.S. naval fleet, incorrectly believing war had broken out, seized Monterey, California, a part of Mexico. Monterey was returned the next day, but the episode only added to the uneasiness with which Mexico viewed its northern neighbor. The forces of expansion, however, could not be contained, and American voters elected

James Polk in 1844 because he promised to deliver more lands. President Polk fulfilled his promise by gaining Oregon and, most spectacularly, provoking a war with Mexico that ultimately fulfilled the wildest fantasies of expansionists. By 1848, the United States encompassed much of North America, a republic that stretched from the Atlantic to the Pacific.

JAMES K. POLK AND THE TRIUMPH OF EXPANSION

A fervent belief in expansion gripped the United States in the 1840s. In 1845, a New York newspaper editor, John O'Sullivan, introduced the concept of "manifest destiny" to describe the very popular idea of the special role of the United States in overspreading the continent—the divine right and duty of White Americans to seize and settle the American West, thus spreading Protestant, democratic values. In this climate of opinion, voters in 1844 elected James K. Polk, a slaveholder from Tennessee, because he vowed to annex Texas as a new slave state and take Oregon.

Annexing Oregon was an important objective for U.S. foreign policy because it appeared to be an area rich in commercial possibilities. Northerners favored U.S. control of Oregon because ports in the Pacific Northwest would be gateways for trade with Asia. Southerners hoped that, in exchange for their support of expansion into the northwest, northerners would not oppose plans for expansion into the southwest.

President Polk—whose campaign slogan in 1844 had been "Fifty-four forty or fight!"—asserted the United States' right to gain full control of what was known as Oregon Country, from its southern border at 42° latitude (the current boundary with California) to its northern border at 54° 40' latitude. According to an 1818 agreement, Great Britain and the United States held joint ownership of this territory, but the 1827 Treaty of Joint Occupation opened the land to settlement by both countries. Realizing that the British were not willing to cede all claims to the territory, Polk proposed the land be divided at 49° latitude (the current border between Washington and Canada). The British, however, denied U.S. claims to land north of the Columbia River (Oregon's current northern border) (Figure 11.13). Indeed, the British foreign secretary refused even to relay Polk's proposal to London. However, reports of the difficulty Great Britain would face defending Oregon in the event of a U.S. attack, combined with concerns over affairs at home and elsewhere in its empire, quickly changed the minds of the British, and in June 1846, Queen Victoria's government agreed to a division at the forty-ninth parallel.

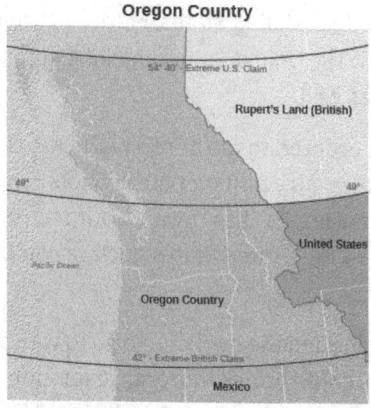

FIGURE 11.13 This map of the Oregon territory during the period of joint occupation by the United States and Great Britain shows the area whose ownership was contested by the two powers.

In contrast to the diplomatic solution with Great Britain over Oregon, when it came to Mexico, Polk and the American people proved willing to use force to wrest more land for the United States. In keeping with voters' expectations, President Polk set his sights on the Mexican state of California. After the mistaken capture of Monterey, negotiations about purchasing the port of San Francisco from Mexico broke off until September 1845. Then, following a revolt in California that left it divided in two, Polk attempted to purchase Upper California and New Mexico as well. These efforts went nowhere. The Mexican government, angered by U.S.

actions, refused to recognize the independence of Texas.

Finally, after nearly a decade of public clamoring for the annexation of Texas, in December 1845 Polk officially agreed to the annexation of the former Mexican state, making the Lone Star Republic an additional slave state. Incensed that the United States had annexed Texas, however, the Mexican government refused to discuss the matter of selling land to the United States. Indeed, Mexico refused even to acknowledge Polk's emissary, John Slidell, who had been sent to Mexico City to negotiate. Not to be deterred, Polk encouraged Thomas O. Larkin, the U.S. consul in Monterey, to assist any American settlers and any **Californios**, the Mexican residents of the state, who wished to proclaim their independence from Mexico. By the end of 1845, having broken diplomatic ties with the United States over Texas and having grown alarmed by American actions in California, the Mexican government warily anticipated the next move. It did not have long to wait.

WAR WITH MEXICO, 1846–1848

Expansionistic fervor propelled the United States to war against Mexico in 1846. The United States had long argued that the Rio Grande was the border between Mexico and the United States, and at the end of the Texas war for independence Santa Anna had been pressured to agree. Mexico, however, refused to be bound by Santa Anna's promises and insisted the border lay farther north, at the Nueces River (Figure 11.14). To set it at the Rio Grande would, in effect, allow the United States to control land it had never occupied. In Mexico's eyes, therefore, President Polk violated its sovereign territory when he ordered U.S. troops into the disputed lands in 1846. From the Mexican perspective, it appeared the United States had invaded their nation.

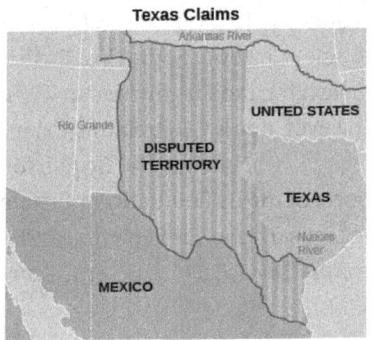

FIGURE 11.14 In 1845, when Texas joined the United States, Mexico insisted the United States had a right only to the territory northeast of the Nueces River. The United States argued in turn that it should have title to all land between the Nueces and the Rio Grande as well.

In January 1846, the U.S. force that was ordered to the banks of the Rio Grande to build a fort on the "American" side encountered a Mexican cavalry unit on patrol. Shots rang out, and sixteen U.S. soldiers were killed or wounded. Angrily declaring that Mexico "has invaded our territory and shed American blood upon American soil," President Polk demanded the United States declare war on Mexico. On May 12, Congress obliged.

The small but vocal antislavery faction decried the decision to go to war, arguing that Polk had deliberately provoked hostilities so the United States could annex more slave territory. Illinois representative Abraham Lincoln and other members of Congress issued the "Spot Resolutions" in which they demanded to know the precise spot on U.S. soil where American blood had been spilled. Many Whigs also denounced the war. Democrats, however, supported Polk's decision, and volunteers for the army came forward in droves from every part of the country except New England, the seat of abolitionist activity. Enthusiasm for the war was aided by the widely held belief that Mexico was a weak, impoverished country and that the Mexican people, perceived as ignorant, lazy, and controlled by a corrupt Roman Catholic clergy, would be easy to defeat. (Figure 11.15).

FIGURE 11.15 Anti-Catholic sentiment played an important role in the Mexican-American War. The American public widely regarded Roman Catholics as cowardly and vice-ridden, like the clergy in this ca. 1846 lithograph who are shown fleeing the Mexican town of Matamoros accompanied by pretty women and baskets full of alcohol. (credit: Library of Congress)

U.S. military strategy had three main objectives: 1) Take control of northern Mexico, including New Mexico; 2) seize California; and 3) capture Mexico City. General Zachary Taylor and his Army of the Center were assigned to accomplish the first goal, and with superior weapons they soon captured the Mexican city of Monterrey. Taylor quickly became a hero in the eyes of the American people, and Polk appointed him commander of all U.S. forces.

General Stephen Watts Kearny, commander of the Army of the West, accepted the surrender of Santa Fe, New Mexico, and moved on to take control of California, leaving Colonel Sterling Price in command. Despite Kearny's assurances that New Mexicans need not fear for their lives or their property, the region's residents rose in revolt in January 1847 in an effort to drive the Americans away. Although Price managed to put an end to the rebellion, tensions remained high.

Kearny, meanwhile, arrived in California to find it already in American hands through the joint efforts of California settlers, U.S. naval commander John D. Sloat, and John C. Fremont, a former army captain and son-in-law of Missouri senator Thomas Benton. Sloat, at anchor off the coast of Mazatlan, learned that war had begun and quickly set sail for California. He seized the town of Monterey in July 1846, less than a month after a group of American settlers led by William B. Ide had taken control of Sonoma and declared California a republic. A week after the fall of Monterey, the navy took San Francisco with no resistance. Although some Californios staged a short-lived rebellion in September 1846, many others submitted to the U.S. takeover. Thus Kearny had little to do other than take command of California as its governor.

Leading the Army of the South was General Winfield Scott. Both Taylor and Scott were potential competitors for the presidency, and believing—correctly—that whoever seized Mexico City would become a hero, Polk assigned Scott the campaign to avoid elevating the more popular Taylor, who was affectionately known as "Old Rough and Ready."

Scott captured Veracruz in March 1847, and moving in a northwesterly direction from there (much as Spanish conquistador Hernán Cortés had done in 1519), he slowly closed in on the capital. Every step of the way was a hard-fought victory, however, and Mexican soldiers and civilians both fought bravely to save their land from the American invaders. Mexico City's defenders, including young military cadets, fought to the end. According to legend, cadet Juan Escutia's last act was to save the Mexican flag, and he leapt from the city's walls with it wrapped around his body. On September 14, 1847, Scott entered Mexico City's central plaza; the city had fallen (Figure 11.16). While Polk and other expansionists called for "all Mexico," the Mexican government and the

United States negotiated for peace in 1848, resulting in the Treaty of Guadalupe Hidalgo.

FIGURE 11.16 In *General Scott's Entrance into Mexico* (1851), Carl Nebel depicts General Winfield Scott on a white horse entering Mexico City's Plaza de la Constitución as anxious residents of the city watch. One woman peers furtively from behind the curtain of an upstairs window. On the left, a man bends down to pick up a paving stone to throw at the invaders.

The Treaty of Guadalupe Hidalgo, signed in February 1848, was a triumph for American expansion under which Mexico ceded nearly half its land to the United States. The **Mexican Cession**, as the conquest of land west of the Rio Grande was called, included the current states of California, New Mexico, Arizona, Nevada, Utah, and portions of Colorado and Wyoming. Mexico also recognized the Rio Grande as the border with the United States. The United States promised to grant Mexican citizens in the ceded territory U.S. citizenship in the future when the territories they were living in became states, and promised to recognize the Spanish land grants to the Pueblos in New Mexico. In exchange, the United States agreed to assume $3.35 million worth of Mexican debts owed to U.S. citizens, paid Mexico $15 million for the loss of its land, and promised to guard the residents of the Mexican Cession from Native American raids.

As extensive as the Mexican Cession was, some argued the United States should not be satisfied until it had taken all of Mexico. Many who were opposed to this idea were southerners who, while desiring the annexation of more slave territory, did not want to make Mexico's large mestizo (people of mixed Native American and European ancestry) population part of the United States. Others did not want to absorb a large group of Roman Catholics. These expansionists could not accept the idea of new U.S. territory filled with mixed-race, Catholic populations.

CLICK AND EXPLORE

Explore the U.S.-Mexican War (http://openstax.org/l/15MexAmWar) at PBS to read about life in the Mexican and U.S. armies during the war and to learn more about the various battles.

CALIFORNIA AND THE GOLD RUSH

The United States had no way of knowing that part of the land about to be ceded by Mexico had just become far more valuable than anyone could have imagined. On January 24, 1848, James Marshall discovered gold in the millrace of the sawmill he had built with his partner John Sutter on the south fork of California's American River. Word quickly spread, and within a few weeks all of Sutter's employees had left to search for gold. When the news reached San Francisco, most of its inhabitants abandoned the town and headed for the American River. By the end of the year, thousands of California's residents had gone north to the gold fields with visions of wealth dancing in their heads, and in 1849 thousands of people from around the world followed them (Figure 11.17). The Gold Rush had begun.

FIGURE 11.17 Word about the discovery of gold in California in 1848 quickly spread and thousands soon made their way to the West Coast in search of quick riches.

The fantasy of instant wealth induced a mass exodus to California. Settlers in Oregon and Utah rushed to the American River. Easterners sailed around the southern tip of South America or to Panama's Atlantic coast, where they crossed the Isthmus of Panama to the Pacific and booked ship's passage for San Francisco. As California-bound vessels stopped in South American ports to take on food and fresh water, hundreds of Peruvians and Chileans streamed aboard. Easterners who could not afford to sail to California crossed the continent on foot, on horseback, or in wagons. Others journeyed from as far away as Hawaii and Europe. Chinese people came as well, adding to the polyglot population in the California boomtowns (Figure 11.18).

FIGURE 11.18 This Currier & Ives lithograph from 1849 imagines the extreme lengths that people might go to in order to be part of the California Gold Rush. In addition to the men with picks and shovels trying to reach the ship from the dock, airships and rocket are shown flying overhead. (credit: Library of Congress)

Once in California, gathered in camps with names like Drunkard's Bar, Angel's Camp, Gouge Eye, and Whiskeytown, the "**forty-niners**" did not find wealth so easy to come by as they had first imagined. Although some were able to find gold by panning for it or shoveling soil from river bottoms into sieve-like contraptions called rockers, most did not. The placer gold, the gold that had been washed down the mountains into streams and rivers, was quickly exhausted, and what remained was deep below ground. Independent miners were supplanted by companies that could afford not only to purchase hydraulic mining technology but also to hire laborers to work the hills. The frustration of many a miner was expressed in the words of Sullivan Osborne. In 1857, Osborne wrote that he had arrived in California "full of high hopes and bright anticipations of the future" only to find his dreams "have long since perished." Although $550 million worth of gold was found in California between 1849 and 1850, very little of it went to individuals.

Observers in the gold fields also reported abuse of Native Americans by miners. Some miners forced Native Americans to work their claims for them; others drove them off their lands, stole from them, and even murdered them as part of a systemic campaign of extermination. Some scholars view the resulting loss of Native American life as a clear example of genocide in the United States. Foreigners were generally disliked, especially those from South America. The most despised, however, were the thousands of Chinese migrants. Eager to earn money to send to their families in Hong Kong and southern China, they quickly earned a reputation as frugal men and hard workers who routinely took over diggings others had abandoned as worthless and worked them until every scrap of gold had been found. Many American miners, often spendthrifts, resented their presence and discriminated against them, believing the Chinese, who represented about 8 percent of the nearly 300,000 who arrived, were depriving them of the opportunity to make a living.

CLICK AND EXPLORE

Visit The Chinese in California (http://openstax.org/l/15ChinaCA) to learn more about the experience of Chinese migrants who came to California in the Gold Rush era.

In 1850, California imposed a tax on foreign miners, and in 1858 it prohibited all immigration from China. Those Chinese who remained in the face of the growing hostility were often beaten and killed, and some Westerners made a sport of cutting off Chinese men's queues, the long braids of hair worn down their backs (Figure 11.19). In 1882, Congress took up the power to restrict immigration by banning the further immigration of Chinese.

FIGURE 11.19 "Pacific Chivalry: Encouragement to Chinese Immigration," which appeared in *Harper's Weekly* in 1869, depicts a White man attacking a Chinese man with a whip as he holds him by the queue. Americans sometimes forcefully cut off the queues of Chinese immigrants. This could have serious consequences for the victim. Until 1911, all Chinese men were required by their nation's law to wear the queue as a sign of loyalty. Miners returning to China without it could be put to death. (credit: Library of Congress)

As people flocked to California in 1849, the population of the new territory swelled from a few thousand to about 100,000. The new arrivals quickly organized themselves into communities, and the trappings of "civilized" life—stores, saloons, libraries, stage lines, and fraternal lodges—began to appear. Newspapers were established, and musicians, singers, and acting companies arrived to entertain the gold seekers. The epitome of these Gold Rush boomtowns was San Francisco, which counted only a few hundred residents in 1846 but by 1850 had reached a population of thirty-four thousand (Figure 11.20). So quickly did the territory grow that by

1850 California was ready to enter the Union as a state. When it sought admission, however, the issue of slavery expansion and sectional tensions emerged once again.

FIGURE 11.20 This daguerreotype shows the bustling port of San Francisco in January 1851, just a few months after San Francisco became part of the new U.S. state of California. (credit: Library of Congress)

11.5 Free or Slave Soil? The Dilemma of the West

LEARNING OBJECTIVES

By the end of this section, you will be able to:
- Describe the terms of the Wilmot Proviso
- Discuss why the Free-Soil Party objected to the westward expansion of slavery
- Explain why sectional and political divisions in the United States grew
- Describe the terms of the Compromise of 1850

The 1848 treaty with Mexico did not bring the United States domestic peace. Instead, the acquisition of new territory revived and intensified the debate over the future of slavery in the western territories, widening the growing division between North and South and leading to the creation of new single-issue parties. Increasingly, the South came to regard itself as under attack by radical northern abolitionists, and many northerners began to speak ominously of a southern drive to dominate American politics for the purpose of protecting slaveholders' human property. As tensions mounted and both sides hurled accusations, national unity frayed. Compromise became nearly impossible and antagonistic sectional rivalries replaced the idea of a unified, democratic republic.

THE LIBERTY PARTY, THE WILMOT PROVISO, AND THE ANTISLAVERY MOVEMENT

Committed to protecting White workers by keeping slavery out of the lands taken from Mexico, Pennsylvania congressman David Wilmot attached to an 1846 revenue bill an amendment that would prohibit slavery in the new territory. The **Wilmot Proviso** was not entirely new. Other congressmen had drafted similar legislation, and Wilmot's language was largely copied from the 1787 Northwest Ordinance that had banned slavery in that territory. His ideas were very controversial in the 1840s, however, because his proposals would prevent American slaveholders from bringing what they viewed as their lawful property, enslaved people, into the western lands. The measure passed the House but was defeated in the Senate. When Polk tried again to raise revenue the following year (to pay for lands taken from Mexico), the Wilmot Proviso was reintroduced, this time calling for the prohibition of slavery not only in the Mexican Cession but in all U.S. territories. The revenue bill passed, but without the proviso.

That Wilmot, a loyal Democrat, should attempt to counter the actions of a Democratic president hinted at the party divisions that were to come. The 1840s were a particularly active time in the creation and reorganization of political parties and constituencies, mainly because of discontent with the positions of the mainstream Whig and Democratic Parties in regard to slavery and its extension into the territories. The first new party, the small and politically weak **Liberty Party** founded in 1840, was a single-issue party, as were many of those that followed it. Its members were abolitionists who fervently believed slavery was evil and should be ended, and that this was best accomplished by political means.

The Wilmot Proviso captured the "antislavery" sentiments during and after the Mexican War. Antislavery advocates differed from the abolitionists. While abolitionists called for the end of slavery everywhere, antislavery advocates, for various reasons, did not challenge the presence of slavery in the states where it already existed. Those who supported antislavery fervently opposed its expansion westward because, they argued, slavery would degrade White labor and reduce its value, cast a stigma upon hard-working White people, and deprive them of a chance to advance economically. The western lands, they argued, should be open to White men only—small farmers and urban workers for whom the West held the promise of economic advancement. Where slavery was entrenched, according to antislavery advocates, there was little land left for small farmers to purchase, and such men could not compete fairly with slaveholders who held large farms and gangs of enslaved people. Ordinary laborers suffered also; no one would pay a White man a decent wage when an enslaved person worked for nothing. When labor was associated with loss of freedom, antislavery supporters argued, all White workers carried a stigma that marked them as little better than the enslaved.

Wilmot opposed the extension of slavery into the Mexican Cession not because of his concern for African Americans, but because of his belief that slavery hurt White workers, and that lands acquired by the government should be used to better the position of White small farmers and laborers. Work was not simply something that people did; it gave them dignity, but in a slave society, labor had no dignity. In response to these arguments, southerners maintained that laborers in northern factories were treated worse than enslaved people. Their work was tedious and low paid. Their meager income was spent on inadequate food, clothing, and shelter. There was no dignity in such a life. In contrast, they argued, southern enslaved people were provided with a home, the necessities of life, and the protection of their slaveholders. Factory owners did not care for or protect their employees in the same way.

THE FREE-SOIL PARTY AND THE ELECTION OF 1848

The Wilmot Proviso was an issue of great importance to the Democrats. Would they pledge to support it? At the party's New York State convention in Buffalo, Martin Van Buren's antislavery supporters—called **Barnburners** because they were likened to farmers who were willing to burn down their own barn to get rid of a rat infestation—spoke in favor of the proviso. Their opponents, known as Hunkers, refused to support it. Angered, the Barnburners organized their own convention, where they chose antislavery, pro–Wilmot Proviso delegates to send to the Democrats' national convention in Baltimore. In this way, the controversy over the expansion of slavery divided the Democratic Party.

At the national convention, both sets of delegates were seated—the pro-proviso ones chosen by the Barnburners and the anti-proviso ones chosen by the Hunkers. When it came time to vote for the party's presidential nominee, the majority of votes were for Lewis Cass, an advocate of popular sovereignty. Popular sovereignty was the belief that citizens should be able to decide issues based on the principle of majority rule; in this case, residents of a territory should have the right to decide whether slavery would be allowed in it. Theoretically, this doctrine would allow slavery to become established in any U.S. territory, including those from which it had been banned by earlier laws.

Disgusted by the result, the Barnburners united with antislavery Whigs and former members of the Liberty Party to form a new political party—the **Free-Soil Party**, which took as its slogan "Free Soil, Free Speech, Free Labor, and Free Men." The party had one real goal—to oppose the extension of slavery into the territories (Figure 11.21). In the minds of its members and many other northerners of the time, southern slaveholders had marshaled their wealth and power to control national politics for the purpose of protecting the institution of slavery and extending it into the territories. Many in the Free-Soil Party believed in this far-reaching conspiracy of the slaveholding elite to control both foreign affairs and domestic policies for their own ends, a cabal that came to be known as the **Slave Power**.

FIGURE 11.21 This political cartoon depicts Martin Van Buren and his son John, both Barnburners, forcing the slavery issue within the Democratic Party by "smoking out" fellow Democrat Lewis Cass on the roof. Their support of the Wilmot Proviso and the new Free-Soil Party is demonstrated by John's declaration, "That's you Dad! more 'Free-Soil.' We'll rat 'em out yet. Long life to Davy Wilmot." (credit: Library of Congress)

In the wake of the Mexican War, antislavery sentiment entered mainstream American politics when the new Free-Soil party promptly selected Martin Van Buren as its presidential candidate. For the first time, a national political party committed itself to the goal of stopping the expansion of slavery. The Democrats chose Lewis Cass, and the Whigs nominated General Zachary Taylor, as Polk had assumed they would. On Election Day, Democrats split their votes between Van Buren and Cass. With the strength of the Democratic vote diluted, Taylor won. His popularity with the American people served him well, and his status as a slaveholder helped him win the South.

CLICK AND EXPLORE

Visit the archives of the Gilder Lehrman Institute (http://openstax.org/l/15GerritSmith) to read an August 1848 letter from Gerrit Smith, a staunch abolitionist, regarding the Free-Soil candidate, Martin Van Buren. Smith played a major role in the Liberty Party and was their presidential candidate in 1848.

THE COMPROMISE OF 1850

The election of 1848 did nothing to quell the controversy over whether slavery would advance into the Mexican Cession. Some slaveholders, like President Taylor, considered the question a moot point because the lands acquired from Mexico were far too dry for growing cotton and therefore, they thought, no slaveholder would want to move there. Other southerners, however, argued that the question was not whether slaveholders *would* want to move to the lands of the Mexican Cession, but whether they *could* and still retain control of their enslaved property. Denying them the right to freely relocate with their lawful property was, they maintained, unfair and unconstitutional. Northerners argued, just as fervidly, that because Mexico had abolished slavery, no enslaved people currently lived in the Mexican Cession, and to introduce slavery there would extend it to a new territory, thus furthering the institution and giving the Slave Power more control over the United States. The strong current of antislavery sentiment—that is, the desire to protect White labor—only increased the opposition to the expansion of slavery into the West.

Most northerners, except members of the Free-Soil Party, favored popular sovereignty for California and the New Mexico territory. Many southerners opposed this position, however, for they feared residents of these regions might choose to outlaw slavery. Some southern politicians spoke ominously of secession from the United States. Free-Soilers rejected popular sovereignty and demanded that slavery be permanently excluded from the territories.

Beginning in January 1850, Congress worked for eight months on a compromise that might quiet the growing sectional conflict. Led by the aged Henry Clay, members finally agreed to the following:

"1. California, which was ready to enter the Union, was admitted as a free state in accordance with its state constitution.
2. Popular sovereignty was to determine the status of slavery in New Mexico and Utah, even though Utah and part of New Mexico were north of the Missouri Compromise line.
3. The slave trade was banned in the nation's capital. Slavery, however, was allowed to remain.
4. Under a new fugitive slave law, those who helped escaped enslaved individuals or refused to assist in their return would be fined and possibly imprisoned.
5. The border between Texas and New Mexico was established. "

The **Compromise of 1850** brought temporary relief. It resolved the issue of slavery in the territories for the moment and prevented secession. The peace would not last, however. Instead of relieving tensions between North and South, it had actually made them worse.

Key Terms

alcalde   a Mexican official who often served as combined civil administrator, judge, and law enforcement officer

Barnburners   northern Democrats loyal to Martin Van Buren who opposed the extension of slavery into the territories and broke away from the main party when it nominated a pro-popular sovereignty candidate

Californios   Mexican residents of California

Compromise of 1850   five separate laws passed by Congress in September 1850 to resolve issues stemming from the Mexican Cession and the sectional crisis

Corps of Discovery   the group led by Meriwether Lewis and William Clark on the expedition to explore and map the territory acquired in the Louisiana Purchase

empresario   a person who brought new settlers to Texas in exchange for a grant of land

filibuster   a person who engages in an unofficial military operation intended to seize land from foreign countries or foment revolution there

forty-niners   the nickname for those who traveled to California in 1849 in hopes of finding gold

Free-Soil Party   a political party that sought to exclude slavery from the western territories, leaving these areas open for settlement by White farmers and ensuring that White laborers would not have to compete with enslaved labor

Liberty Party   a political party formed in 1840 by those who believed political measures were the best means by which abolition could be accomplished

Mexican Cession   the lands west of the Rio Grande ceded to the United States by Mexico in 1848, including California, Arizona, New Mexico, Nevada, Utah, and parts of Wyoming and Colorado

Missouri Compromise   an agreement reached in Congress in 1820 that allowed Missouri to enter the Union as a slave state, brought Maine into the Union as a free state, and prohibited slavery north of 36° 30' latitude

Northwest Passage   the nonexistent all-water route across the North American continent sought by European and American explorers

Slave Power   a term northerners used to describe the disproportionate influence that they felt elite southern slaveholders wielded in both domestic and international affairs

Tallmadge Amendment   an amendment (which did not pass) proposed by representative James Tallmadge in 1819 that called for Missouri to be admitted as a free state and for all enslaved people there to be gradually emancipated

Tejanos   Mexican residents of Texas

Wilmot Proviso   an amendment to a revenue bill that would have barred slavery from all the territory acquired from Mexico

Summary

11.1 Lewis and Clark

In 1803, Thomas Jefferson appointed Meriwether Lewis to organize an expedition into the Louisiana Territory to explore and map the area but also to find an all-water route from the Missouri River to the Pacific Coast. The Louisiana Purchase and the journey of Lewis and Clark's Corps of Discovery captured the imagination of many, who dedicated themselves to the economic exploitation of the western lands and the expansion of American influence and power. In the South, the Adams-Onís treaty legally secured Florida for the United States, though it did nothing to end the resistance of the Seminoles against American expansionists. At the same time, the treaty frustrated those Americans who considered Texas a part of the Louisiana Purchase. Taking matters into their own hands, some American settlers tried to take Texas by force.

11.2 The Missouri Crisis

The Missouri Crisis created a division over slavery that profoundly and ominously shaped sectional identities and rivalries as never before. Conflict over the uneasy balance between slave and free states in Congress came to a head when Missouri petitioned to join the Union as a slave state in 1819, and the debate broadened from simple issues of representation to a critique of the morality of slavery. The debates also raised the specter of disunion and civil war, leading many, including Thomas Jefferson, to fear for the future of the republic. Under the Missouri Compromise, Missouri and Maine entered the Union at the same time, Maine as a free state, Missouri as a slave state, and a line was drawn across the remainder of the Louisiana territory north of which slavery was forbidden.

11.3 Independence for Texas

The establishment of the Lone Star Republic formed a new chapter in the history of U.S. westward expansion. In contrast to the addition of the Louisiana Territory through diplomacy with France, Americans in Texas employed violence against Mexico to achieve their goals. Orchestrated largely by slaveholders, the acquisition of Texas appeared the next logical step in creating an American empire that included slavery. Nonetheless, with the Missouri Crisis in mind, the United States refused the Texans' request to enter the United States as a slave state in 1836. Instead, Texas formed an independent republic where slavery was legal. But American settlers there continued to press for more land. The strained relationship between expansionists in Texas and Mexico in the early 1840s hinted of things to come.

11.4 The Mexican-American War, 1846–1848

President James K. Polk's administration was a period of intensive expansion for the United States. After overseeing the final details regarding the annexation of Texas from Mexico, Polk negotiated a peaceful settlement with Great Britain regarding ownership of the Oregon Country, which brought the United States what are now the states of Washington and Oregon. The acquisition of additional lands from Mexico, a country many in the United States perceived as weak and inferior, was not so bloodless. The Mexican Cession added nearly half of Mexico's territory to the United States, including New Mexico and California, and established the U.S.-Mexico border at the Rio Grande. The California Gold Rush rapidly expanded the population of the new territory, but also prompted concerns over immigration, especially from China, and led to a massive loss of Native American life in the state.

11.5 Free or Slave Soil? The Dilemma of the West

The acquisition of lands from Mexico in 1848 reawakened debates regarding slavery. The suggestion that slavery be barred from the Mexican Cession caused rancorous debate between North and South and split the Democratic Party when many northern members left to create the Free-Soil Party. Although the Compromise of 1850 resolved the question of whether slavery would be allowed in the new territories, the solution pleased no one. The peace brought by the compromise was short-lived, and the debate over slavery continued.

Review Questions

1. As a result of the Adams-Onís Treaty, the United States gained which territory from Spain?
    A. Florida
    B. New Mexico
    C. California
    D. Nevada

2. The Long Expedition established a short-lived republic in Texas known as _____.
    A. the Lone Star Republic
    B. the Republic of Texas
    C. Columbiana
    D. the Republic of Fredonia

3. For what purposes did Thomas Jefferson send Lewis and Clark to explore the Louisiana Territory? What did he want them to accomplish?

4. A proposal to prohibit the importation of enslaved people to Missouri following its admission to the United States was made by _____.
   A. John C. Calhoun
   B. Henry Clay
   C. James Tallmadge
   D. John Quincy Adams

5. To balance votes in the Senate, _____ was admitted to the Union as a free state at the same time that Missouri was admitted as a slave state.
   A. Florida
   B. Maine
   C. New York
   D. Arkansas

6. Why did the Missouri Crisis trigger threats of disunion and war? Identify the positions of both southern slaveholders and northern opponents of the spread of slavery.

7. Texas won its independence from Mexico in _____.
   A. 1821
   B. 1830
   C. 1836
   D. 1845

8. Texans defeated the army of General Antonio Lopez de Santa Anna at the battle of _____.
   A. the Alamo
   B. San Jacinto
   C. Nacogdoches
   D. Austin

9. How did Texas settlers' view of Mexico and its people contribute to the history of Texas in the 1830s?

10. Which of the following was *not* a reason the United States was reluctant to annex Texas?
    A. The United States did not want to fight a war with Mexico.
    B. Annexing Texas would add more slave territory to the United States and anger abolitionists.
    C. Texans considered U.S. citizens inferior and did not want to be part of their country.
    D. Adding Texas would upset the balance between free and slave states in Congress.

11. According to treaties signed in 1818 and 1827, with which country did the United States jointly occupy Oregon?
    A. Great Britain
    B. Spain
    C. Mexico
    D. France

12. During the war between the United States and Mexico, revolts against U.S. control broke out in _____.
    A. Florida and Texas
    B. New Mexico and California
    C. California and Texas
    D. Florida and California

13. Why did White people in California dislike the Chinese so much?

14. The practice of allowing residents of territories to decide whether their land should be slave or free was called _____.
    A. the democratic process
    B. the Wilmot Proviso
    C. popular sovereignty
    D. the Free Soil solution

15. Which of the following was not a provision of the Compromise of 1850?
    A. California was admitted as a free state.
    B. Slavery was abolished in Washington, DC.
    C. A stronger fugitive slave law was passed.
    D. Residents of New Mexico and Utah were to decide for themselves whether their territories would be slave or free.

16. Describe the events leading up to the formation of the Free-Soil Party.

Critical Thinking Questions

17. Consider the role of filibusters in American expansion. What are some arguments in favor of filibustering? What are some arguments against it?

18. What are the economic and political issues raised by having an imbalance between free and slave states? Why did the balance of free and slave states matter?

19. How did Anglo-American settlers in Texas see themselves? Did they adopt a Mexican identity because they were living in Mexican territory? Why or why not?

20. Consider the annexation of Texas and the Mexican-American War from a Mexican perspective. What would you find objectionable about American actions, foreign policy, and attitudes in the 1840s?

21. Describe the place of Texas in the history of American westward expansion by comparing Texas's early history to the Missouri Crisis in 1819–1820. What are the similarities and what are the differences?

22. Consider the arguments over the expansion of slavery made by both northerners and southerners in the aftermath of the U.S. victory over Mexico. Who had the more compelling case? Or did each side make equally significant arguments?

Cotton is King: The Antebellum South, 1800–1860

12

FIGURE 12.1 *Bateaux à Vapeur Géant, la Nouvelle-Orléans 1853* (*Giant Steamboats at New Orleans, 1853*), by Hippolyte Sebron, shows how New Orleans, at the mouth of the Mississippi River, was the primary trading hub for the cotton that fueled the growth of the southern economy.

CHAPTER OUTLINE

12.1 The Economics of Cotton
12.2 African Americans in the Antebellum United States
12.3 Wealth and Culture in the South
12.4 The Filibuster and the Quest for New Slave States

INTRODUCTION Nine new slave states entered the Union between 1789 and 1860, rapidly expanding and transforming the South into a region of economic growth built on slave labor. In the image above (Figure 12.1), innumerable enslaved workers load cargo onto a steamship in the Port of New Orleans, the commercial center of the antebellum South, while two well-dressed White men stand by talking. Commercial activity extends as far as the eye can see.

By the mid-nineteenth century, southern commercial centers like New Orleans had become home to the greatest concentration of wealth in the United States. While most White southerners did not own hold, they aspired to join the ranks of elite slaveholders, who played a key role in the politics of both the South and the nation. Meanwhile, slavery shaped the culture and society of the South, which rested on a racial ideology of White supremacy and a vision of the United States as a White man's republic. Enslaved people endured the traumas of slavery by creating their own culture and using the Christian message of redemption to find hope for a world of freedom without violence.

12.1 The Economics of Cotton

LEARNING OBJECTIVES

By the end of this section, you will be able to:
- Explain the labor-intensive processes of cotton production
- Describe the importance of cotton to the Atlantic and American antebellum economy

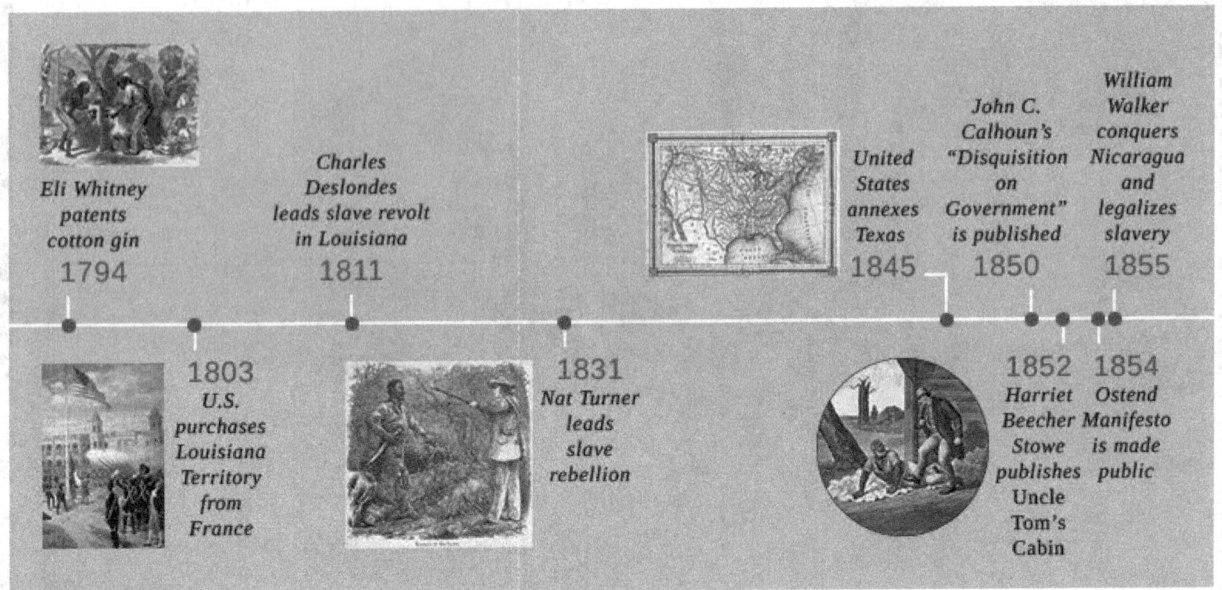

FIGURE 12.2

In the **antebellum** era—that is, in the years before the Civil War—American planters in the South continued to grow Chesapeake tobacco and Carolina rice as they had in the colonial era. Cotton, however, emerged as the antebellum South's major commercial crop, eclipsing tobacco, rice, and sugar in economic importance. By 1860, the region was producing two-thirds of the world's cotton. In 1793, Eli Whitney revolutionized the production of cotton when he developed the **cotton gin**, likely influenced by suggestions from enslaved people. It was a device that separated the seeds from raw cotton. Suddenly, a process that was extraordinarily labor-intensive when done by hand could be completed quickly and easily. American plantation owners, who were searching for a successful staple crop to compete on the world market, found it in cotton.

As a commodity, cotton had the advantage of being easily stored and transported. A demand for it already existed in the industrial textile mills in Great Britain, and in time, a steady stream of slave-grown American cotton would also supply northern textile mills. Southern cotton, picked and processed by enslaved labor, helped fuel the nineteenth-century Industrial Revolution in both the United States and Great Britain.

KING COTTON

Almost no cotton was grown in the United States in 1787, the year the federal constitution was written. However, following the War of 1812, a huge increase in production resulted in the so-called **cotton boom**, and by midcentury, cotton became the key **cash crop** (a crop grown to sell rather than for the farmer's sole use) of the southern economy and the most important American commodity. By 1850, of the 3.2 million enslaved people in the country's fifteen slave states, 1.8 million were producing cotton; by 1860, enslaved labor was producing over two billion pounds of cotton per year. Indeed, American cotton soon made up two-thirds of the global supply, and production continued to soar. By the time of the Civil War, South Carolina politician James Hammond confidently proclaimed that the North could never threaten the South because "cotton is king."

The crop grown in the South was a hybrid: *Gossypium barbadense*, known as Petit Gulf cotton, a mix of

Mexican, Georgia, and Siamese strains. Petit Gulf cotton grew extremely well in different soils and climates. It dominated cotton production in the Mississippi River Valley—home of the new slave states of Louisiana, Mississippi, Arkansas, Tennessee, Kentucky, and Missouri—as well as in other states like Texas. Whenever new slave states entered the Union, White slaveholders sent armies of the enslaved to clear the land in order to grow and pick the lucrative crop. The phrase "to be sold down the river," used by Harriet Beecher Stowe in her 1852 novel *Uncle Tom's Cabin*, refers to this forced migration from the upper southern states to the Deep South, lower on the Mississippi, to grow cotton.

The enslaved people who built this cotton kingdom with their forced labor started by clearing the land. Although the Jeffersonian vision of the settlement of new U.S. territories entailed White yeoman farmers single-handedly carving out small independent farms, the reality proved quite different. Entire old-growth forests and cypress swamps fell to the axe as enslaved people labored to strip the vegetation to make way for cotton. With the land cleared, they readied the earth by plowing and planting. To ambitious White planters, the extent of new land available for cotton production seemed almost limitless, and many planters simply leapfrogged from one area to the next, abandoning their fields every ten to fifteen years after the soil became exhausted. As a result, enslaved people composed the vanguard of this American expansion to the West.

Cotton planting took place in March and April, when enslaved people planted seeds in rows around three to five feet apart. Over the next several months, from April to August, they carefully tended the plants. Weeding the cotton rows took significant energy and time. In August, after the cotton plants had flowered and the flowers had begun to give way to cotton bolls (the seed-bearing capsule that contains the cotton fiber), all the plantation's enslaved men, women, and children worked together to pick the crop (Figure 12.3). On each day of cotton picking, enslaved workers went to the fields with sacks, which they would fill as many times as they could. The effort was laborious, and a White "driver" employed the lash to make the enslaved people work as quickly as possible.

FIGURE 12.3 In the late nineteenth century, J. N. Wilson captured this image of harvest time at a southern plantation. While the workers in this photograph are not enslaved laborers, the process of cotton harvesting shown here had changed little from antebellum times.

Cotton planters projected the amount of cotton they could harvest based on the number of enslaved people under their control. In general, planters expected a good "hand," or enslaved laborer, to work ten acres of land and pick two hundred pounds of cotton a day. An overseer or "master" measured each enslaved individual's daily yield. Great pressure existed to meet the expected daily amount, and some overseers whipped enslaved people who picked less than expected.

Cotton picking occurred as many as seven times a season as the plant grew and continued to produce bolls through the fall and early winter. During the picking season, enslaved people worked from sunrise to sunset with a ten-minute break at lunch; many slaveholders tended to give them little to eat, since spending on food would cut into their profits. Other slaveholders knew that feeding the enslaved could increase productivity and therefore provided what they thought would help ensure a profitable crop. Enslaved people's day didn't end after they picked the cotton; once they had brought it to the gin house to be weighed, they then had to care for the animals and perform other chores. Indeed, they often maintained their own gardens and livestock, which they tended after working the cotton fields, in order to supplement their supply of food.

Sometimes the cotton was dried before it was ginned (put through the process of separating the seeds from the cotton fiber). The cotton gin allowed an enslaved laborer to remove the seeds from fifty pounds of cotton a day, compared to one pound if done by hand. After the seeds had been removed, the cotton was pressed into bales. These bales, weighing about four hundred to five hundred pounds, were wrapped in burlap cloth and sent down the Mississippi River.

CLICK AND EXPLORE

Visit the Internet Archive (http://openstax.org/l/15LoadCotton) to watch a 1937 WPA film showing cotton bales being loaded onto a steamboat.

As the cotton industry boomed in the South, the Mississippi River quickly became the essential water highway in the United States. Steamboats, a crucial part of the transportation revolution thanks to their enormous freight-carrying capacity and ability to navigate shallow waterways, became a defining component of the cotton kingdom. Steamboats also illustrated the class and social distinctions of the antebellum age. While the decks carried precious cargo, ornate rooms graced the interior. In these spaces, White people socialized in the ship's saloons and dining halls while enslaved Black people served them (Figure 12.4).

FIGURE 12.4 As in this depiction of the saloon of the Mississippi River steamboat *Princess*, elegant and luxurious rooms often occupied the interiors of antebellum steamships, whose decks were filled with cargo.

Investors poured huge sums into steamships. In 1817, only seventeen plied the waters of western rivers, but by 1837, there were over seven hundred steamships in operation. Major new ports developed at St. Louis, Missouri; Memphis, Tennessee; and other locations. By 1860, some thirty-five hundred vessels were steaming in and out of New Orleans, carrying an annual cargo made up primarily of cotton that amounted to $220 million worth of goods (approximately $6.5 billion in 2014 dollars).

New Orleans had been part of the French empire before the United States purchased it, along with the rest of the Louisiana Territory, in 1803. In the first half of the nineteenth century, it rose in prominence and importance largely because of the cotton boom, steam-powered river traffic, and its strategic position near the mouth of the Mississippi River. Steamboats moved down the river transporting cotton grown on plantations along the river and throughout the South to the port at New Orleans. From there, the bulk of American cotton

..., England, where it was sold to British manufacturers who ran the cotton mills in Manchester ...ewhere. This lucrative international trade brought new wealth and new residents to the city. By 1840, New Orleans alone had 12 percent of the nation's total banking capital, and visitors often commented on the great cultural diversity of the city. In 1835, Joseph Holt Ingraham wrote: "Truly does New-Orleans represent every other city and nation upon earth. I know of none where is congregated so great a variety of the human species." Slave labor, cotton, and the steamship transformed the city from a relatively isolated corner of North America in the eighteenth century to a thriving metropolis that rivaled New York in importance (Figure 12.5).

FIGURE 12.5 This print of *The Levee - New Orleans* (1884) shows the bustling port of New Orleans with bales of cotton waiting to be shipped. The sheer volume of cotton indicates its economic importance throughout the century.

THE DOMESTIC SLAVE TRADE

The South's dependence on cotton was matched by its dependence on stolen labor from enslaved people to harvest the cotton. Despite the rhetoric of the Revolution that "all men are created equal," slavery not only endured in the American republic but formed the very foundation of the country's economic success. Cotton and slavery occupied a central—and intertwined—place in the nineteenth-century economy.

In 1807, the U.S. Congress abolished the foreign slave trade, a ban that went into effect on January 1, 1808. After this date, importing captives from Africa became illegal in the United States. While smuggling continued to occur, the end of the international slave trade meant that enslaved domestic people were in very high demand. Fortunately for Americans whose wealth depended upon the exploitation of slave labor, a fall in the price of tobacco had caused landowners in the Upper South to reduce their production of this crop and use more of their land to grow wheat, which was far more profitable. While tobacco was a labor-intensive crop that required many people to cultivate it, wheat was not. Former tobacco farmers in the older states of Virginia and Maryland found themselves with "surplus" enslaved people whom they were obligated to feed, clothe, and shelter. Some slaveholders responded to this situation by releasing enslaved people; far more decided to sell their excess bondsmen. Virginia and Maryland therefore took the lead in the **domestic slave trade**, the trading of enslaved people within the borders of the United States.

The domestic slave trade offered many economic opportunities for White men. Those who sold the enslaved could realize great profits, as could the slave brokers who served as middlemen between sellers and buyers. Other White men could benefit from the trade as owners of warehouses and pens in which the enslaved were held, or as suppliers of clothing and food for enslaved people on the move. Between 1790 and 1859, slaveholders in Virginia sold more than half a million people. In the early part of this period, many were sold to people living in Kentucky, Tennessee, and North and South Carolina. By the 1820s, however, people in Kentucky and the Carolinas had begun to sell many of the people they held in bondage. Maryland slave dealers sold at least 185,000 people. Kentucky slaveholders sold some seventy-one thousand individuals. Most of the slave traders forced these enslaved people south to Alabama, Louisiana, and Mississippi. New Orleans, the hub of commerce, boasted the largest slave market in the United States and grew to become the nation's fourth-largest city as a result. Natchez, Mississippi, had the second-largest market. In Virginia, Maryland, Carolinas, and elsewhere in the South, slave auctions happened every day.

All told, the movement of enslaved people in the South made up one of the largest forced internal migrations in the United States. In each of the decades between 1820 and 1860, about 200,000 people were sold and relocated. The 1800 census recorded over one million African Americans, of which nearly 900,000 had slave status. By 1860, the total number of African Americans increased to 4.4 million, and of that number, 3.95 million were held in bondage. For many of the enslaved, the domestic slave trade incited the terror of being sold away from family and friends.

MY STORY

Solomon Northup Remembers the New Orleans Slave Market

Solomon Northup was a free Black man living in Saratoga, New York, when he was kidnapped and sold into slavery in 1841. He later escaped and wrote a book about his experiences: *Twelve Years a Slave. Narrative of Solomon Northup, a Citizen of New-York, Kidnapped in Washington City in 1841 and Rescued in 1853* (the basis of a 2013 Academy Award–winning film). This excerpt derives from Northup's description of being sold in New Orleans, along with fellow slave Eliza and her children Randall and Emily.

"One old gentleman, who said he wanted a coachman, appeared to take a fancy to me. . . . The same man also purchased Randall. The little fellow was made to jump, and run across the floor, and perform many other feats, exhibiting his activity and condition. All the time the trade was going on, Eliza was crying aloud, and wringing her hands. She besought the man not to buy him, unless he also bought her self and Emily. . . . Freeman turned round to her, savagely, with his whip in his uplifted hand, ordering her to stop her noise, or he would flog her. He would not have such work—such snivelling; and unless she ceased that minute, he would take her to the yard and give her a hundred lashes. . . . Eliza shrunk before him, and tried to wipe away her tears, but it was all in vain. She wanted to be with her children, she said, the little time she had to live. All the frowns and threats of Freeman, could not wholly silence the afflicted mother."

What does Northup's narrative tell you about the experience of being enslaved? How does he characterize Freeman, the slave trader? How does he characterize Eliza?

THE SOUTH IN THE AMERICAN AND WORLD MARKETS

The first half of the nineteenth century saw a market revolution in the United States, one in which industrialization brought changes to both the production and the consumption of goods. Some southerners of the time believed that their region's reliance on a single cash crop and its use of stolen labor to produce it gave the South economic independence and made it immune from the effects of these changes, but this was far from the truth. Indeed, the production of cotton brought the South more firmly into the larger American and Atlantic markets. Northern mills depended on the South for supplies of raw cotton that was then converted into textiles. But this domestic cotton market paled in comparison to the Atlantic market. About 75 percent of the cotton produced in the United States was eventually exported abroad. Exporting at such high volumes made the United States the undisputed world leader in cotton production. Between the years 1820 and 1860, approximately 80 percent of the global cotton supply was produced in the United States. Nearly all the exported cotton was shipped to Great Britain, fueling its burgeoning textile industry and making the powerful British Empire increasingly dependent on American cotton and southern slavery.

The power of cotton on the world market may have brought wealth to the South, but it also increased its economic dependence on other countries and other parts of the United States. Much of the corn and pork that enslaved people consumed came from farms in the West. Some of the inexpensive clothing, called "slops," and shoes worn by enslaved people were manufactured in the North. The North also supplied the furnishings found in the homes of both wealthy planters and members of the middle class. Many of the trappings of domestic life, such as carpets, lamps, dinnerware, upholstered furniture, books, and musical instruments—all the accoutrements of comfortable living for southern White people—were made in either the North or Europe. Southern planters also borrowed money from banks in northern cities, and in the southern summers, took advantage of the developments in transportation to travel to resorts at Saratoga, New York; Litchfield, Connecticut; and Newport, Rhode Island.

12.2 African Americans in the Antebellum United States

LEARNING OBJECTIVES

By the end of this section, you will be able to:
- Discuss the similarities and differences in the lives of enslaved and free Black people
- Describe the independent culture and customs that enslaved people developed

In addition to cotton, the great commodity of the antebellum South was human chattel. Slavery was the cornerstone of the southern economy. By 1850, about 3.2 million enslaved people labored in the United States, 1.8 million of whom worked in the cotton fields. They faced arbitrary power abuses from White people; they coped by creating family and community networks. Storytelling, song, and Christianity also provided solace and allowed enslaved individuals to develop their own interpretations of their condition.

LIFE AS AN ENSLAVED PERSON

Southern White people frequently relied upon the idea of **paternalism**—the premise that White slaveholders acted in the best interests of those they enslaved, taking responsibility for their care, feeding, discipline, and even their Christian morality—to justify the existence of slavery. This grossly misrepresented the reality of slavery, which was, by any measure, a dehumanizing, traumatizing, and horrifying human disaster and crime against humanity. Nevertheless, the enslaved were hardly passive victims of their conditions; they sought and found myriad ways to resist their shackles and develop their own communities and cultures.

Enslaved people often used the notion of paternalism to their advantage, finding opportunities within this system to engage in acts of resistance and win a degree of freedom and autonomy. For example, some played into their enslavers' racism by hiding their intelligence and feigning childishness and ignorance. The enslaved could then slow down the workday and sabotage the system in small ways by "accidentally" breaking tools, for example; the slaveholder, seeing the enslaved as unsophisticated and childlike, would believe these incidents were accidents rather than rebellions. Some enslaved individuals engaged in more dramatic forms of resistance, such as poisoning their captors slowly. Other enslaved people reported their fellow captives to their slaveholders, hoping to gain preferential treatment. Those who informed their holders about planned slave rebellions could often expect the slaveholder's gratitude and, perhaps, more lenient treatment. Such expectations were always tempered by the individual personality and caprice of the slaveholder.

Slaveholders used both psychological coercion and physical violence to prevent enslaved people from disobeying their wishes. Often, the most efficient way to discipline people was to threaten to sell them. The lash, while the most common form of punishment, was effective but not efficient; whippings sometimes left the victims incapacitated or even dead. Slaveholders and overseers also used punishment gear like neck braces, balls and chains, leg irons, and paddles with holes to produce blood blisters. The enslaved lived in constant terror of both physical violence and separation from family and friends (Figure 12.6).

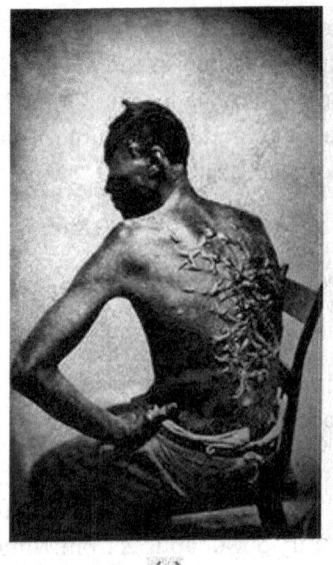 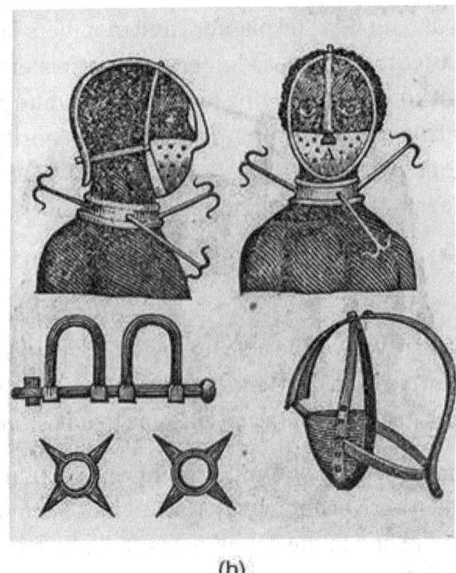

FIGURE 12.6 The original caption of this photograph of an enslaved victim's scarred back (a), taken in Baton Rouge, Louisiana, in 1863, reads as follows: "*Overseer Artayou Carrier whipped me. I was two months in bed sore from the whipping. My master come after I was whipped; he discharged the overseer. The very words of poor Peter, taken as he sat for his picture.*" Images like this one helped bolster the northern abolitionist message of the inhumanity of slavery. The drawing of an iron mask, collar, leg shackles, and spurs (b) demonstrates the various cruel and painful instruments used to restrain enslaved people.

Under southern law, enslaved people could not marry. Nonetheless, some slaveholders allowed marriages to promote the birth of children and to foster harmony on plantations. Some slaveholders even forced certain individuals to form unions, anticipating the birth of more children (and consequently greater profits) from them. Slaveholders sometimes allowed enslaved people to choose their own partners, but they could also veto a match. Enslaved couples always faced the prospect of being sold away from each other, and, once they had children, the horrifying reality that their children could be sold and sent away at any time.

CLICK AND EXPLORE

Browse a collection of first-hand narratives of enslaved and former enslaved people at the National Humanities Center (http://openstax.org/l/15Enslavement) to learn more about the experience of slavery.

Enslaved parents had to show their children the best way to survive under slavery. This meant teaching them to be discreet, submissive, and guarded around White people. Parents also taught their children through the stories they told. Popular stories among the enslaved included tales of tricksters, sly captives, or animals like **Brer Rabbit**, who outwitted their antagonists (Figure 12.7). Such stories provided comfort in humor and conveyed the sense of the wrongs of slavery. Enslaved people's work songs commented on the harshness of their life and often had double meanings—a literal meaning that White people would not find offensive and a deeper meaning for the enslaved.

FIGURE 12.7 Brer Rabbit, depicted here in an illustration from *Uncle Remus, His Songs and His Sayings: The Folk-Lore of the Old Plantation* (1881) by Joel Chandler Harris, was a trickster who outwitted his opponents.

African beliefs, including ideas about the spiritual world and the importance of African healers, survived in the South as well. White people who became aware of non-Christian rituals among the enslaved labeled such practices as witchcraft. Among Africans, however, the rituals and use of various plants by respected enslaved healers created connections between the African past and the American South while also providing a sense of community and identity for enslaved individuals. Other African customs, including traditional naming patterns, the making of baskets, and the cultivation of certain native African plants that had been brought to the New World, also endured.

AMERICANA

African Americans and Christian Spirituals

Many of the enslaved embraced Christianity. Their holders emphasized a scriptural message of obedience to White people and a better day awaiting them in heaven, but enslaved people focused on the uplifting message of being freed from bondage.

The styles of worship in the Methodist and Baptist churches, which emphasized emotional responses to scripture, attracted the enslaved to those traditions and inspired some to become preachers. Spiritual songs that referenced the Exodus (the biblical account of the Hebrews' escape from slavery in Egypt), such as "Roll, Jordan, Roll," allowed enslaved individuals to freely express messages of hope, struggle, and overcoming adversity (Figure 12.8).

FIGURE 12.8 This version of "Roll, Jordan, Roll" was included in *Slave Songs of the United States*, the first published collection of African American music, which appeared in 1867.

What imagery might the Jordan River suggest to enslaved people working in the Deep South? What lyrics in this song suggest redemption and a better world ahead?

CLICK AND EXPLORE

Listen to a rendition of "Roll, Jordan, Roll" (http://openstax.org/l/15RollJordan) from the movie based on Solomon Northup's memoir and life.

THE FREE BLACK POPULATION

Complicating the picture of the antebellum South was the existence of a large free Black population. In fact, more free Black people lived in the South than in the North; roughly 261,000 lived in slave states, while 226,000 lived in northern states without slavery. Most free Black people did not live in the Lower, or Deep South: the states of Alabama, Arkansas, Florida, Georgia, Louisiana, Mississippi, South Carolina, and Texas. Instead, the largest number lived in the upper southern states of Delaware, Maryland, Virginia, North Carolina, and later Kentucky, Missouri, Tennessee, and the District of Columbia.

Part of the reason for the large number of free Black people living in slave states were the many instances of manumission—the formal granting of freedom to enslaved people—that occurred as a result of the Revolution, when many slaveholders put into action the ideal that "all men are created equal" and released the people they enslaved. The transition in the Upper South to the staple crop of wheat, which did not require large numbers of enslaved laborers to produce, also spurred manumissions. Another large group of free Black people in the South had been free residents of Louisiana before the 1803 Louisiana Purchase, while still other free Black people came from Cuba and Haiti.

Most free Black people in the South lived in cities, and a majority of free Black people were lighter-skinned women, a reflection of the interracial unions that formed between White men and Black women. Everywhere in the United States Blackness had come to be associated with slavery, the station at the bottom of the social ladder. Both White people and those with African ancestry tended to delineate varying degrees of lightness in skin color in a social hierarchy. In the slaveholding South, different names described one's distance from Blackness or Whiteness: mulattos (those with one Black and one White parent), quadroons (those with one Black grandparent), and octoroons (those with one Black great-grandparent) (Figure 12.9). Lighter-skinned Black people often looked down on their darker counterparts, an indication of the ways in which both White and Black people internalized the racism of the age.

FIGURE 12.9 In this late eighteenth-century painting, a free woman of color stands with her quadroon daughter in New Orleans. Families with members that had widely varying ethnic characteristics were not uncommon at the time,

especially in the larger cities.

Some free Black people in the South owned enslaved people themselves. Andrew Durnford, for example, was born in New Orleans in 1800, three years before the Louisiana Purchase. His father was White, and his mother was a free Black woman. Durnford became an American citizen after the Louisiana Purchase, rising to prominence as a Louisiana sugar planter and slaveholder. William Ellison, another free Black person who amassed great wealth and power in the South, was born with a slave status in 1790 in South Carolina. After buying his freedom and that of his wife and daughter, he proceeded to purchase his own enslaved people, whom he then put to work manufacturing cotton gins. By the eve of the Civil War, Ellison had become one of the richest and largest slaveholders in the entire state.

The phenomenon of free Black people amassing large fortunes within a slave society predicated on racial difference, however, was exceedingly rare. Most free Black people in the South lived under the specter of slavery and faced many obstacles. Beginning in the early nineteenth century, southern states increasingly made manumission illegal. They also devised laws that divested free Black people of their rights, such as the right to testify against White people in court or the right to seek employment where they pleased. Interestingly, it was in the upper southern states that such laws were the harshest. In Virginia, for example, legislators made efforts to require free Black people to leave the state. In parts of the Deep South, free Black people were able to maintain their rights more easily. The difference in treatment between free Black people in the Deep South and those in the Upper South, historians have surmised, came down to economics. In the Deep South, slavery as an institution was strong and profitable. In the Upper South, the opposite was true. The anxiety of this economic uncertainty manifested in the form of harsh laws that targeted free Black people.

SLAVE REVOLTS

Captives resisted their enslavement in small ways every day, but this resistance did not usually translate into mass uprisings. The enslaved understood that the chances of ending slavery through rebellion were slim and would likely result in massive retaliation; many also feared the risk that participating in such actions would pose to themselves and their families. White slaveholders, however, constantly feared uprisings and took drastic steps, including torture and mutilation, whenever they believed that rebellions might be simmering. Gripped by the fear of insurrection, White people often imagined revolts to be in the works even when no uprising actually happened.

At least two major slave uprisings did occur in the antebellum South. In 1811, a major rebellion broke out in the sugar parishes of the booming territory of Louisiana. Inspired by the successful overthrow of the White planter class in Haiti, a group of people enslaved in Louisiana took up arms against slaveholders. Perhaps as many five hundred joined the rebellion, led by Charles Deslondes, a mixed-race slave driver on a sugar plantation owned by Manuel Andry.

The revolt began in January 1811 on Andry's plantation. Deslondes and others attacked the Andry household, where they killed the slaveholder's son (although Andry himself escaped). The rebels then began traveling toward New Orleans, armed with weapons gathered at Andry's plantation. Militias mobilized to stop the rebellion, but not before Deslondes and the other enslaved people set fire to three plantations and killed numerous White people. A small force led by Andry ultimately captured Deslondes, whose body was mutilated and burned following his execution. Other rebels were beheaded, and their heads placed on pikes along the Mississippi River.

The second rebellion, led by the enslaved Nat Turner, occurred in 1831 in Southampton County, Virginia. Turner had suffered not only from personal enslavement, but also from the additional trauma of having his wife sold away from him. Bolstered by Christianity, Turner became convinced that like Christ, he should lay down his life to end slavery. Mustering his relatives and friends, he began the rebellion August 22, killing scores of White people in the county. White people mobilized quickly and within forty-eight hours had brought the rebellion to an end. Shocked by Nat Turner's Rebellion, Virginia's state legislature considered ending slavery in the state in order to provide greater security. In the end, legislators decided slavery would remain and that their state would continue to play a key role in the domestic slave trade.

SLAVE MARKETS

As discussed above, after centuries of slave trade with West Africa, Congress banned the further importation of enslaved Africans beginning in 1808. The domestic slave trade then expanded rapidly. As the cotton trade grew in size and importance, so did the domestic slave trade; the cultivation of cotton gave new life and importance to slavery, increasing the value of enslaved individuals. To meet the South's fierce demand for labor, American smugglers illegally transferred captives through Florida and later through Texas. Many more enslaved Africans arrived illegally from Cuba; indeed, Cubans relied on the smuggling of enslaved people to prop up their finances. The largest number of enslaved people after 1808, however, came from the massive, legal internal slave market in which slave states in the Upper South sold enslaved men, women, and children to states in the Lower South. For the enslaved, the domestic trade presented the full horrors of slavery as children were ripped from their mothers and fathers and families destroyed, creating heartbreak and alienation.

Some slaveholders sought to increase the number of enslaved children by placing enslaved males with fertile enslaved females, and slaveholders routinely raped enslaved females. The resulting births played an important role in slavery's expansion in the first half of the nineteenth century, as many enslaved children were born as a result of rape. One account written by an enslaved person named William J. Anderson captures the horror of sexual exploitation in the antebellum South. Anderson wrote about how a Mississippi slaveholder

"divested a poor female slave of all wearing apparel, tied her down to stakes, and whipped her with a handsaw until he broke it over her naked body. In process of time he ravished [raped] her person, and became the father of a child by her. Besides, he always kept a colored Miss in the house with him. This is another curse of Slavery—concubinage and illegitimate connections—which is carried on to an alarming extent in the far South. A poor slave man who lives close by his wife, is permitted to visit her but very seldom, and other men, both white and colored, cohabit with her. It is undoubtedly the worst place of incest and bigamy in the world. A white man thinks nothing of putting a colored man out to carry the fore row [front row in field work], and carry on the same sport with the colored man's wife at the same time."

Anderson, a devout Christian, recognized and explains in his narrative that one of the evils of slavery is the way it undermines the family. Anderson was not the only critic of slavery to emphasize this point. Frederick Douglass, an enslaved person from Maryland who escaped to the North in 1838, elaborated on this dimension of slavery in his 1845 narrative. He recounted how enslavers had to sell their own children whom they had with enslaved women to appease the White wives who despised their offspring.

The selling of enslaved people was a major business enterprise in the antebellum South, representing a key part of the economy. White men invested substantial sums in enslaved people, carefully calculating the annual returns they could expect from each enslaved person as well as the possibility of greater profits through natural increase. The domestic slave trade was highly visible, and like the infamous Middle Passage that brought captive Africans to the Americas, it constituted an equally disruptive and horrifying journey now called the **second middle passage**. Between 1820 and 1860, White American traders sold a million or more captives in the domestic slave market. Groups of enslaved people were transported by ship from places like Virginia, a state that specialized in raising enslaved people for sale, to New Orleans, where they were sold to planters in the Mississippi Valley. Others made the overland trek from older states like North Carolina to new and booming Deep South states like Alabama.

New Orleans had the largest slave market in the United States (Figure 12.10). Slaveholders brought the people they enslaved there from the East (Virginia, Maryland, and the Carolinas) and the West (Tennessee and Kentucky) to be sold for work in the Mississippi Valley. The slave trade benefited White people in the Chesapeake and Carolinas, providing them with extra income: A healthy young enslaved male in the 1850s could be sold for $1,000 (approximately $30,000 in 2014 dollars), and a planter who could sell ten such enslaved people collected a windfall.

FIGURE 12.10 In *Sale of Estates, Pictures and Slaves in the Rotunda, New Orleans* (1853) by J. M. Starling, it is clear that people are considered property to be auctioned off, just like pictures or other items.

In fact, by the 1850s, the demand for enslaved people reached an all-time high, and prices therefore doubled. An enslaved person who would have sold for $400 in the 1820s could command a price of $800 in the 1850s. The high price of enslaved people in the 1850s and the inability of natural increase to satisfy demands led some southerners to demand the reopening of the international slave trade, a movement that caused a rift between the Upper South and the Lower South. White people in the Upper South who sold enslaved people to their counterparts in the Lower South worried that reopening the trade would lower prices and therefore hurt their profits.

MY STORY

John Brown on Slave Life in Georgia

An enslaved person named John Brown lived in Virginia, North Carolina, and Georgia before he escaped and moved to England. While there, he dictated his autobiography to someone at the British and Foreign Anti-Slavery Society, who published it in 1855.

"I really thought my mother would have died of grief at being obliged to leave her two children, her mother, and her relations behind. But it was of no use lamenting, the few things we had were put together that night, and we completed our preparations for being parted for life by kissing one another over and over again, and saying good bye till some of us little ones fell asleep. . . . And here I may as well tell what kind of man our new master was. He was of small stature, and thin, but very strong. He had sandy hair, a very red face, and chewed tobacco. His countenance had a very cruel expression, and his disposition was a match for it. He was, indeed, a very bad man, and used to flog us dreadfully. He would make his slaves work on one meal a day, until quite night, and after supper, set them to burn brush or spin cotton. We worked from four in the morning till twelve before we broke our fast, and from that time till eleven or twelve at night . . . we labored eighteen hours a day.
—John Brown, *Slave Life in Georgia: A Narrative of the Life, Sufferings, and Escape of John Brown, A Fugitive Slave, Now in England*, 1855"

What features of the domestic slave trade does Brown's narrative illuminate? Why do you think he brought his story to an antislavery society? How do you think people responded to this narrative?

CLICK AND EXPLORE

Read through several narratives at "Born in Slavery," part of the American Memory (http://openstax.org/l/15BornSlavery) collection at the Library of Congress. Do these narratives have anything in common? What differences can you find between them?

12.3 Wealth and Culture in the South

LEARNING OBJECTIVES

By the end of this section, you will be able to:
- Assess the distribution of wealth in the antebellum South
- Describe the southern culture of honor
- Identify the main proslavery arguments in the years prior to the Civil War

During the antebellum years, wealthy southern planters formed an elite class that wielded most of the economic and political power of the region. They created their own standards of gentility and honor, defining ideals of southern White manhood and womanhood and shaping the culture of the South. To defend the system of forced labor on which their economic survival and genteel lifestyles depended, elite southerners developed several proslavery arguments that they levied at those who would see the institution dismantled.

SLAVERY AND THE WHITE CLASS STRUCTURE

The South prospered, but its wealth was very unequally distributed. Upward social mobility did not exist for the millions of enslaved people who produced a good portion of the nation's wealth, while poor southern White people envisioned a day when they might rise enough in the world to own enslaved people of their own. Because of the cotton boom, there were more millionaires per capita in the Mississippi River Valley by 1860 than anywhere else in the United States. However, in that same year, only 3 percent of White people enslaved more than fifty people, and two-thirds of White households in the South did not enslave any people at all (Figure 12.11). Distribution of wealth in the South became less democratic over time; fewer White people enslaved people in 1860 than in 1840.

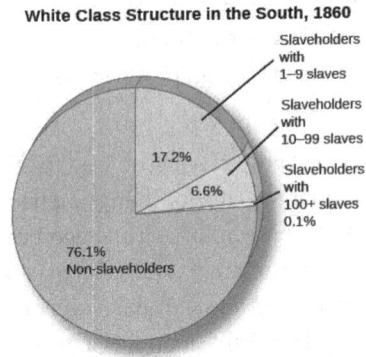

FIGURE 12.11 As the wealth of the antebellum South increased, it also became more unequally distributed, and an ever-smaller percentage of slaveholders held a substantial number of enslaved people.

At the top of southern White society stood the planter elite, which comprised two groups. In the Upper South, an aristocratic gentry, generation upon generation of whom had grown up with slavery, held a privileged place. In the Deep South, an elite group of slaveholders gained new wealth from cotton. Some members of this group hailed from established families in the eastern states (Virginia and the Carolinas), while others came from humbler backgrounds. South Carolinian Nathaniel Heyward, a wealthy rice planter and member of the aristocratic gentry, came from an established family and sat atop the pyramid of southern slaveholders. He amassed an enormous estate; in 1850, he enslaved more than eighteen hundred people. When he died in 1851, he left an estate worth more than $2 million (approximately $63 million in 2014 dollars).

...on production increased, new wealth flowed to the cotton planters. These planters became the staunchest defenders of slavery, and as their wealth grew, they gained considerable political power.

One member of the planter elite was Edward Lloyd V, who came from an established and wealthy family of Talbot County, Maryland. Lloyd had inherited his position rather than rising to it through his own labors. His hundreds of enslaved people formed a crucial part of his wealth. Like many of the planter elite, Lloyd's plantation was a masterpiece of elegant architecture and gardens (Figure 12.12).

FIGURE 12.12 The grand house of Edward Lloyd V advertised the status and wealth of its owner. In its heyday, the Lloyd family's plantation boasted holdings of forty-two thousand acres and one thousand enslaved people.

One of the people enslaved on Lloyd's plantation was Frederick Douglass, who escaped in 1838 and became an abolitionist leader, writer, statesman, and orator in the North. In his autobiography, Douglass described the plantation's elaborate gardens and racehorses, but also its underfed and brutalized enslaved population. Lloyd provided employment opportunities to other White people in Talbot County, many of whom served as slave traders and the "slave breakers" entrusted with beating and overworking unruly enslaved people into submission. Like other members of the planter elite, Lloyd himself served in a variety of local and national political offices. He was governor of Maryland from 1809 to 1811, a member of the House of Representatives from 1807 to 1809, and a senator from 1819 to 1826. As a representative and a senator, Lloyd defended slavery as the foundation of the American economy.

Wealthy plantation owners like Lloyd came close to forming an American ruling class in the years before the Civil War. They helped shape foreign and domestic policy with one goal in view: to expand the power and reach of the cotton kingdom of the South. Socially, they cultivated a refined manner and believed White people, especially members of their class, should not perform manual labor. Rather, they created an identity for themselves based on a world of leisure in which horse racing and entertainment mattered greatly, and where the enslavement of others was the bedrock of civilization.

Below the wealthy planters were the yeoman farmers, or small landowners (Figure 12.13). Below yeomen were poor, landless White people, who made up the majority of White people in the South. These landless White men dreamed of owning land and enslaving people and served as slave overseers, drivers, and traders in the southern economy. In fact, owning land and enslaved people provided one of the only opportunities for upward social and economic mobility. In the South, living the American dream meant enslaving people, producing cotton, and owning land.

FIGURE 12.13 In this painting by Felix Octavius Carr Darley, a yeoman farmer carrying a scythe follows his livestock down the road.

Despite this unequal distribution of wealth, non-slaveholding White people shared with White slaveholders a common set of values, most notably a belief in White supremacy. White people, whether rich or poor, were bound together by racism. Slavery defused class tensions among them, because no matter how poor they were, White southerners had race in common with the mighty plantation owners. Non-slaveholders accepted the rule of the planters as defenders of their shared interest in maintaining a racial hierarchy. Significantly, all White people were also bound together by the constant, prevailing fear of slave uprisings.

MY STORY

D. R. Hundley on the Southern Yeoman

Daniel Robinson Hundley was a well-educated lawyer who was born into a slaveholding family from Alabama. He earned a degree from Harvard and resided in the North, where he began working on a book meant to counter the common northern assumption, including that the South was made up exclusively of two tiers of White residents: the very wealthy planter class and the very poor landless White people. In his 1860 book, *Social Relations in Our Southern States*, Hundley describes what he calls the "Southern Yeomen," a social group he insists is roughly equivalent to the middle-class farmers of the North.

"*But you have no Yeomen in the South, my dear Sir?* Beg your pardon, our dear Sir, but we have—hosts of them. *I thought you had only poor White Trash?* Yes, we dare say as much—and that the moon is made of green cheese! . . . Know, then, that the Poor Whites of the South constitute a separate class to themselves; the Southern Yeomen are as distinct from them as the Southern Gentleman is from the Cotton Snob. Certainly the Southern Yeomen are nearly always poor, at least so far as this world's goods are to be taken into account. As a general thing they own no slaves; and even in case they do, the wealthiest of them rarely possess more than from ten to fifteen. . . . The Southern Yeoman much resembles in his speech, religious opinions, household arrangements, indoor sports, and family traditions, the middle class farmers of the Northern States. He is fully as intelligent as the latter, and is on the whole much better versed in the lore of politics and the provisions of our Federal and State Constitutions. . . . [A]lthough not as a class pecuniarily interested in slave property, the Southern Yeomanry are almost unanimously pro-slavery in sentiment. Nor do we see how any honest, thoughtful person can reasonably find fault with them on this account.
—D. R. Hundley, *Social Relations in Our Southern States*, 1860"

What elements of social relations in the South is Hundley attempting to emphasize for his readers? In what respects might his position as an educated person born into a relatively wealthy family influence his understanding of social relations in the South?

Non-slaveholding White people took part in civil duties. They served on juries and voted. They also engaged in the daily rounds of maintaining slavery by serving on neighborhood patrols to ensure that enslaved people did not escape and that rebellions did not occur. The practical consequence of such activities was that the institution of slavery, and its perpetuation, became a source of commonality among different economic and social tiers that otherwise were separated by a gulf of difference.

Southern planters exerted a powerful influence on the federal government. Seven of the first eleven presidents were enslavers, and more than half of the Supreme Court justices who served on the court from its inception to the Civil War came from slaveholding states. However, southern White yeoman farmers generally did not support an active federal government. They were suspicious of the state bank and supported President Jackson's dismantling of the Second Bank of the United States. They also did not support taxes to create internal improvements such as canals and railroads; to them, government involvement in the economic life of the nation disrupted what they perceived as the natural workings of the economy. They also feared a strong national government might tamper with slavery.

Planters operated within a larger capitalist society, but the labor system they used to produce goods—that is, slavery—was similar to systems that existed before capitalism, such as feudalism and serfdom. Under capitalism, free workers are paid for their labor (by owners of capital) to produce commodities; the money from the sale of the goods is used to pay for the work performed. As enslaved people did not reap any earnings from their forced labor, some economic historians consider the antebellum plantation system a "pre-capitalist" system.

HONOR IN THE SOUTH

A complicated code of honor among privileged White southerners, dictating the beliefs and behavior of "gentlemen" and "ladies," developed in the antebellum years. Maintaining appearances and reputation was supremely important. It can be argued that, as in many societies, the concept of honor in the antebellum South had much to do with control over dependents, whether enslaved people, wives, or relatives. Defending their honor and ensuring that they received proper respect became preoccupations of White people in the slaveholding South. To question another man's assertions was to call his honor and reputation into question. Insults in the form of words or behavior, such as calling someone a coward, could trigger a rupture that might well end on the dueling ground (Figure 12.14). Dueling had largely disappeared in the antebellum North by the early nineteenth century, but it remained an important part of the southern code of honor through the Civil War years. Southern White men, especially those of high social status, settled their differences with duels, before which antagonists usually attempted reconciliation, often through the exchange of letters addressing the alleged insult. If the challenger was not satisfied by the exchange, a duel would often result.

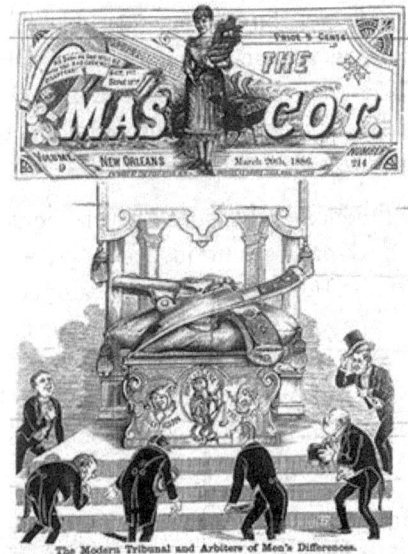

FIGURE 12.14 "The Modern Tribunal and Arbiter of Men's Differences," an illustration that appeared on the cover of *The Mascot*, a newspaper published in nineteenth-century New Orleans, reveals the importance of dueling in southern culture; it shows men bowing before an altar on which are laid a pistol and knife.

The dispute between South Carolina's James Hammond and his erstwhile friend (and brother-in-law) Wade Hampton II illustrates the southern culture of honor and the place of the duel in that culture. A strong friendship bound Hammond and Hampton together. Both stood at the top of South Carolina's society as successful, married plantation owners involved in state politics. Prior to his election as governor of the state in 1842, Hammond became sexually involved with each of Hampton's four teenage daughters, who were his nieces by marriage. Hampton found out about these acts, and in keeping with the code of honor, could have demanded a duel with Hammond. However, Hampton instead tried to use the liaisons to destroy his former friend politically. This effort proved disastrous for Hampton, because it represented a violation of the southern code of honor. "As matters now stand," Hammond wrote, "he [Hampton] is a convicted dastard who, not having nerve to redress his own wrongs, put forward bullies to do it for him. . . . To challenge me [to a duel] would be to throw himself upon my mercy for he knows I am not bound to meet him [for a duel]." Because Hampton's behavior marked him as a man who lacked honor, Hammond was no longer bound to meet Hampton in a duel even if Hampton were to demand one. Hammond's reputation, though tarnished, remained high in the esteem of South Carolinians, and the governor went on to serve as a U.S. senator from 1857 to 1860. As for the four Hampton daughters, they never married; their names were disgraced, not only by the whispered-about scandal but by their father's actions in response to it; and no man of honor in South Carolina would stoop so low as to marry them.

GENDER AND THE SOUTHERN HOUSEHOLD

The antebellum South was an especially male-dominated society. Far more than in the North, southern men, particularly wealthy planters, were patriarchs and sovereigns of their own household. Among the White members of the household, labor and daily ritual conformed to rigid gender delineations. Men represented their household in the larger world of politics, business, and war. Within the family, the patriarchal male was the ultimate authority. White women were relegated to the household and lived under the thumb and protection of the male patriarch. The ideal southern lady conformed to her prescribed gender role, a role that was largely domestic and subservient. While responsibilities and experiences varied across different social tiers, women's subordinate state in relation to the male patriarch remained the same.

Writers in the antebellum period were fond of celebrating the image of the ideal southern woman (Figure 12.15). One such writer, Thomas Roderick Dew, president of Virginia's College of William and Mary in the mid-nineteenth century, wrote approvingly of the virtue of southern women, a virtue he concluded derived from natural weakness, piety, grace, and modesty. In his *Dissertation on the Characteristic Differences Between the Sexes*, he writes that southern women derive their power not by

"leading armies to combat, or of enabling her to bring into more formidable action the physical power which nature has conferred on her. No! It is but the better to perfect all those feminine graces, all those fascinating attributes, which render her the center of attraction, and which delight and charm all those who breathe the atmosphere in which she moves; and, in the language of Mr. Burke, would make ten thousand swords leap from their scabbards to avenge the insult that might be offered to her. By her very meekness and beauty does she subdue all around her."

Such popular idealizations of elite southern White women, however, are difficult to reconcile with their lived experience: in their own words, these women frequently described the trauma of childbirth, the loss of children, and the loneliness of the plantation.

FIGURE 12.15 This cover illustration from *Harper's Weekly* in 1861 shows the ideal of southern womanhood.

MY STORY

Louisa Cheves McCord's "Woman's Progress"

Louisa Cheves McCord was born in Charleston, South Carolina, in 1810. A child of some privilege in the South, she received an excellent education and became a prolific writer. As the excerpt from her poem "Woman's Progress" indicates, some southern women also contributed to the idealization of southern White womanhood.

"Sweet Sister! stoop not thou to be a man!
Man has his place as woman hers; and she
As made to comfort, minister and help;
Moulded for gentler duties, ill fulfils
His jarring destinies. Her mission is
To labour and to pray; to help, to heal,
To soothe, to bear; patient, with smiles, to suffer;
And with self-abnegation noble lose
Her private interest in the dearer weal
Of those she loves and lives for. Call not this—
(The all-fulfilling of her destiny;
She the world's soothing mother)—call it not,
With scorn and mocking sneer, a drudgery.
The ribald tongue profanes Heaven's holiest things,

> But holy still they are. The lowliest tasks
> Are sanctified in nobly acting them.
> Christ washed the apostles' feet, not thus cast shame
> Upon the God-like in him. Woman lives
> Man's constant prophet. If her life be true
> And based upon the instincts of her being,
> She is a living sermon of that truth
> Which ever through her gentle actions speaks,
> That life is given to labour and to love.
> —Louisa Susanna Cheves McCord, "Woman's Progress," 1853"
>
> What womanly virtues does Louisa Cheves McCord emphasize? How might her social status, as an educated southern woman of great privilege, influence her understanding of gender relations in the South?

For White slaveholders, the male-dominated household operated to protect gendered divisions and prevalent gender norms; for enslaved women, however, the same system exposed them to brutality and frequent sexual domination. The demands on the labor of enslaved women made it impossible for them to perform the role of domestic caretaker that was so idealized by southern men. That slaveholders put them out into the fields, where they frequently performed work traditionally thought of as male, reflected little the ideal image of gentleness and delicacy reserved for White women. Nor did the enslaved woman's role as daughter, wife, or mother garner any patriarchal protection. Each of these roles and the relationships they defined was subject to the prerogative of a slaveholder, who could freely violate enslaved women's persons, sell off their children, or separate them from their families.

DEFENDING SLAVERY

With the rise of democracy during the Jacksonian era in the 1830s, slaveholders worried about the power of the majority. If political power went to a majority that was hostile to slavery, the South—and the honor of White southerners—would be imperiled. White southerners keen on preserving the institution of slavery bristled at what they perceived to be northern attempts to deprive them of their livelihood. Powerful southerners like South Carolinian John C. Calhoun (Figure 12.16) highlighted laws like the Tariff of 1828 as evidence of the North's desire to destroy the southern economy and, by extension, its culture. Such a tariff, he and others concluded, would disproportionately harm the South, which relied heavily on imports, and benefit the North, which would receive protections for its manufacturing centers. The tariff appeared to open the door for other federal initiatives, including the abolition of slavery. Because of this perceived threat to southern society, Calhoun argued that states could nullify federal laws. This belief illustrated the importance of the states' rights argument to the southern states. It also showed slaveholders' willingness to unite against the federal government when they believed it acted unjustly against their interests.

FIGURE 12.16 John C. Calhoun, shown here in a ca. 1845 portrait by George Alexander Healy, defended states' rights, especially the right of the southern states to protect slavery from a hostile northern majority.

As the nation expanded in the 1830s and 1840s, the writings of abolitionists—a small but vocal group of northerners committed to ending slavery—reached a larger national audience. White southerners responded by putting forth arguments in defense of slavery, their way of life, and their honor. Calhoun became a leading political theorist defending slavery and the rights of the South, which he saw as containing an increasingly embattled minority. He advanced the idea of a **concurrent majority**, a majority of a separate region (that would otherwise be in the minority of the nation) with the power to veto or disallow legislation put forward by a hostile majority.

Calhoun's idea of the concurrent majority found full expression in his 1850 essay "Disquisition on Government." In this treatise, he wrote about government as a necessary means to ensure the preservation of society, since society existed to "preserve and protect our race." If government grew hostile to society, then a concurrent majority had to take action, including forming a new government. "Disquisition on Government" advanced a profoundly anti-democratic argument. It illustrates southern leaders' intense suspicion of democratic majorities and their ability to effect legislation that would challenge southern interests.

CLICK AND EXPLORE

Go to the Internet Archive (http://openstax.org/l/15Disquisition) to read John C. Calhoun's "Disquisition on Government." Why do you think he proposed the creation of a concurrent majority?

White southerners reacted strongly to abolitionists' attacks on slavery. In making their defense of slavery, they critiqued wage labor in the North. They argued that the Industrial Revolution had brought about a new type of slavery—wage slavery—and that this form of "slavery" was far worse than the slave labor used on southern plantations. Defenders of the institution also lashed out directly at abolitionists such as William Lloyd Garrison for daring to call into question their way of life. Indeed, Virginians cited Garrison as the instigator of Nat Turner's 1831 rebellion.

The Virginian George Fitzhugh contributed to the defense of slavery with his book *Sociology for the South, or the Failure of Free Society* (1854). Fitzhugh argued that laissez-faire capitalism, as celebrated by Adam Smith, benefited only the quick-witted and intelligent, leaving the ignorant at a huge disadvantage. Slaveholders, he argued, took care of the ignorant—in Fitzhugh's argument, the enslaved people of the South. Southerners provided the enslaved with care from birth to death, he asserted; this offered a stark contrast to the wage slavery of the North, where workers were at the mercy of economic forces beyond their control. Fitzhugh's ideas exemplified southern notions of paternalism.

DEFINING AMERICAN

George Fitzhugh's Defense of Slavery

George Fitzhugh, a southern writer of social treatises, was a staunch supporter of slavery, not as a necessary evil but as what he argued was a necessary good, a way to take care of enslaved people and keep them from being a burden on society. He published *Sociology for the South, or the Failure of Free Society* in 1854, in which he laid out what he believed to be the benefits of slavery to both the enslaved and society as a whole. According to Fitzhugh:

"[I]t is clear the Athenian democracy would not suit a negro nation, nor will the government of mere law suffice for the individual negro. He is but a grown up child and must be governed as a child . . . The master occupies towards him the place of parent or guardian. . . . The negro is improvident; will not lay up in summer for the wants of winter; will not accumulate in youth for the exigencies of age. He would become an insufferable burden to society. Society has the right to prevent this, and can only do so by subjecting him to domestic slavery. In the last place, the negro race is inferior to the white race, and living in their midst, they would be far outstripped or outwitted in the chase of free competition. . . . Our negroes are not only better off as to physical comfort than free laborers, but their moral condition is better."

What arguments does Fitzhugh use to promote slavery? What basic premise underlies his ideas? Can you think of a modern parallel to Fitzhugh's argument?

The North also produced defenders of slavery, including Louis Agassiz, a Harvard professor of zoology and geology. Agassiz helped to popularize **polygenism**, the idea that different human races came from separate origins. According to this formulation, no single human family origin existed, and Black people made up a race wholly separate from the White race. Agassiz's notion gained widespread popularity in the 1850s with the 1854 publication of George Gliddon and Josiah Nott's *Types of Mankind* and other books. The theory of polygenism codified racism, giving the notion of Black inferiority the lofty mantle of science. One popular advocate of the idea posited that Black people occupied a place in evolution between the Greeks and chimpanzees (Figure 12.17).

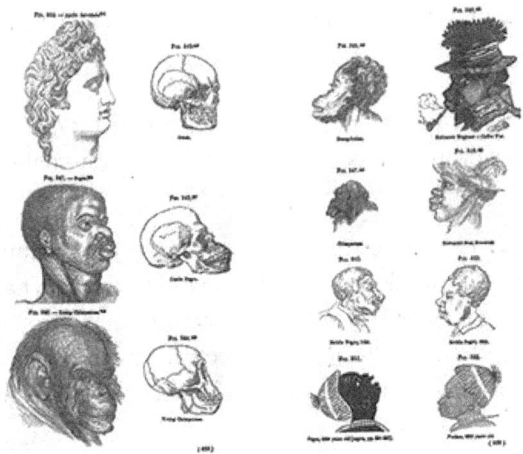

FIGURE 12.17 This 1857 illustration by an advocate of polygenism indicates that the "Negro" occupies a place between the Greeks and chimpanzees. What does this image reveal about the methods of those who advocated polygenism?

The Filibuster and the Quest for New Slave States

LEARNING OBJECTIVES

By the end of this section, you will be able to:
- Explain the expansionist goals of advocates of slavery
- Describe the filibuster expeditions undertaken during the antebellum era

Southern expansionists had spearheaded the drive to add more territory to the United States. They applauded the Louisiana Purchase and fervently supported Native American removal, the annexation of Texas, and the Mexican-American War. Drawing inspiration from the annexation of Texas, proslavery expansionists hoped to replicate that feat by bringing Cuba and other territories into the United States and thereby enlarging the American empire of slavery.

In the 1850s, the expansionist drive among White southerners intensified. Among southern imperialists, one way to push for the creation of an American empire of slavery was through the actions of filibusters—men who led unofficial military operations intended to seize land from foreign countries or foment revolution there. These unsanctioned military adventures were not part of the official foreign policy of the United States; American citizens simply formed themselves into private armies to forcefully annex new land without the government's approval.

An 1818 federal law made it a crime to undertake such adventures, which was an indication of both the reality of efforts at expansion through these illegal expeditions and the government's effort to create a U.S. foreign policy. Nonetheless, Americans continued to filibuster throughout the nineteenth century. In 1819, an expedition of two hundred Americans invaded Spanish Texas, intent on creating a republic modeled on the United States, only to be driven out by Spanish forces. Using force, taking action, and asserting White supremacy in these militaristic drives were seen by many as an ideal of American male vigor. President Jackson epitomized this military prowess as an officer in the Tennessee militia, where earlier in the century he had played a leading role in ending the Red Stick War and forcing the Creek Nation to cede millions of acres in Alabama and Georgia. His reputation helped him to win the presidency in 1828 and again in 1832.

Filibustering plots picked up pace in the 1850s as the drive for expansion continued. Slaveholders looked south to the Caribbean, Mexico, and Central America, hoping to add new slave states. Spanish Cuba became the objective of many American slaveholders in the 1850s, as debate over the island dominated the national conversation. Many who urged its annexation believed Cuba had to be made part of the United States to prevent it from going the route of Haiti, with enslaved Black people overthrowing their captors and creating another Black republic, a prospect horrifying to many in the United States. Americans also feared that the British, who had an interest in the sugar island, would make the first move and snatch Cuba from the United States. Since Britain had outlawed slavery in its colonies in 1833, Black people on the island of Cuba would then be free.

Narciso López, a Venezuelan who wanted to end Spanish control of the island, gained American support. He tried five times to take the island, with his last effort occurring in the summer of 1851 when he led an armed group from New Orleans. Thousands came out to cheer his small force as they set off to wrest Cuba from the Spanish. Unfortunately for López and his supporters, however, the effort to take Cuba did not produce the hoped-for spontaneous uprising of the Cuban people. Spanish authorities in Cuba captured and executed López and the American filibusters.

Efforts to take Cuba continued under President Franklin Pierce, who had announced at his inauguration in 1853 his intention to pursue expansion. In 1854, American diplomats met in Ostend, Belgium, to find a way to gain Cuba. They wrote a secret memo, known as the **Ostend Manifesto** (thought to be penned by James Buchanan, who was elected president two years later), stating that if Spain refused to sell Cuba to the United States, the United States was justified in taking the island as a national security measure.

The contents of this memo were supposed to remain secret, but details were leaked to the public, leading the

House of Representatives to demand a copy. Many in the North were outraged over what appeared to be a southern scheme, orchestrated by what they perceived as the Slave Power—a term they used to describe the disproportionate influence that elite slaveholders wielded—to expand slavery. European powers also reacted with anger. Southern annexationists, however, applauded the effort to take Cuba. The Louisiana legislature in 1854 asked the federal government to take decisive action, and John Quitman, a former Mississippi governor, raised money from slaveholders to fund efforts to take the island.

CLICK AND EXPLORE

Read an 1860 editorial titled Annexation of Cuba Made Easy (http://openstax.org/l/15AnnexCuba) from the online archives of *The New York Times*. Does the author support annexation? Why or why not?

Controversy around the Ostend Manifesto caused President Pierce to step back from the plan to take Cuba. After his election, President Buchanan, despite his earlier expansionist efforts, denounced filibustering as the action of pirates. Filibustering caused an even wider gulf between the North and the South (Figure 12.18).

FIGURE 12.18 The *"Ostend Doctrine"* (1856), by artist Louis Maurer and lithographer Nathaniel Currier, mocks James Buchanan by depicting him being robbed, just as many northerners believed slaveholders were attempting to rob Spain. The thugs robbing Buchanan use specific phrases from the Ostend Manifesto as they relieve him of his belongings.

Cuba was not the only territory in slaveholders' expansionist sights: some focused on Mexico and Central America. In 1855, Tennessee-born William Walker, along with an army of no more than sixty mercenaries, gained control of the Central American nation of Nicaragua. Previously, Walker had launched a successful invasion of Mexico, dubbing his conquered land the Republic of Sonora. In a relatively short period of time, Walker was dislodged from Sonora by Mexican authorities and forced to retreat back to the United States. His conquest of Nicaragua garnered far more attention, catapulting him into national popularity as the heroic embodiment of White supremacy (Figure 12.19).

(a)   (b)

FIGURE 12.19 Famed Civil War photographer Mathew Brady took this photograph (a) of "General" William Walker circa 1855–1860. Walker led a filibuster expedition and briefly conquered Nicaragua, fulfilling a dream of many pro-expansionist southern slaveholders. Cornelius Vanderbilt (b), the shipping tycoon who controlled much of the traffic across Nicaragua between the Atlantic and the Pacific, clashed with Walker and ultimately supported Costa Rica in its war against him.

Why Nicaragua? Nicaragua presented a tempting target because it provided a quick route from the Caribbean to the Pacific: Only twelve miles of land stood between the Pacific Ocean, the inland Lake Nicaragua, and the river that drained into the Atlantic. Shipping from the East Coast to the West Coast of the United States had to travel either by land across the continent, south around the entire continent of South America, or through Nicaragua. Previously, American tycoon Cornelius Vanderbilt (Figure 12.19) had recognized the strategic importance of Nicaragua and worked with the Nicaraguan government to control shipping there. The filibustering of William Walker may have excited expansionist-minded southerners, but it greatly upset Vanderbilt's business interests in the region.

Walker clung to the racist, expansionist philosophies of the proslavery South. In 1856, Walker made slavery legal in Nicaragua—it had been illegal there for thirty years—in a move to gain the support of the South. He also reopened the slave trade. In 1856, he was elected president of Nicaragua, but in 1857, he was chased from the country. When he returned to Central America in 1860, he was captured by the British and released to Honduran authorities, who executed him by firing squad.

Key Terms

antebellum   a term meaning "before the war" and used to describe the decades before the American Civil War began in 1861

cash crop   a crop grown to be sold for profit instead of consumption by the farmer's family

concurrent majority   a majority of a separate region (that would otherwise be in the minority of the nation) with the power to veto or disallow legislation put forward by a hostile majority

cotton boom   the upswing in American cotton production during the nineteenth century

cotton gin   a device, patented by Eli Whitney in 1794, that separated the seeds from raw cotton quickly and easily

domestic slave trade   the trading of enslaved people within the borders of the United States

Ostend Manifesto   the secret diplomatic memo stating that if Spain refused to sell Cuba to the United States, the United States was justified in taking the island as a national security measure

paternalism   the premise that southern White slaveholders acted in the best interests of those they enslaved

polygenism   the idea that Black and White people come from different origins

second middle passage   the internal forced migration of enslaved people to the South and West in the United States

Summary

12.1 The Economics of Cotton

In the years before the Civil War, the South produced the bulk of the world's supply of cotton. The Mississippi River Valley slave states became the epicenter of cotton production, an area of frantic economic activity where the landscape changed dramatically as land was transformed from pinewoods and swamps into cotton fields. Cotton's profitability relied on the institution of slavery, which generated the product that fueled cotton mill profits in the North. When the international slave trade was outlawed in 1808, the domestic slave trade exploded, providing economic opportunities for White people involved in many aspects of the trade and increasing the possibility of enslaved people's dislocation and separation from kin and friends. Although the larger American and Atlantic markets relied on southern cotton in this era, the South depended on these other markets for food, manufactured goods, and loans. Thus, the market revolution transformed the South just as it had other regions.

12.2 African Americans in the Antebellum United States

Slave labor in the antebellum South generated great wealth for plantation owners. Enslaved people, in contrast, endured daily traumas as human property. Enslaved people resisted their condition in a variety of ways, and many found some solace in Christianity and the communities they created in the slave quarters. While some free Black people achieved economic prosperity and even became slaveholders themselves, the vast majority found themselves restricted by the same White-supremacist assumptions upon which the institution of slavery was based.

12.3 Wealth and Culture in the South

Although a small White elite owned the vast majority of enslaved people in the South, and most other White people could only aspire to slaveholders' wealth and status, slavery shaped the social life of all White southerners in profound ways. Southern culture valued a behavioral code in which men's honor, based on the domination of others and the protection of southern White womanhood, stood as the highest good. Slavery also decreased class tensions, binding White people together on the basis of race despite their inequalities of wealth. Several defenses of slavery were prevalent in the antebellum era, including Calhoun's argument that the South's "concurrent majority" could overrule federal legislation deemed hostile to southern interests; the notion that slaveholders' care of their chattel made the enslaved better off than wage workers in the North; and the profoundly racist ideas underlying polygenism.

Filibuster and the Quest for New Slave States

The decade of the 1850s witnessed various schemes to expand the American empire of slavery. The Ostend Manifesto articulated the right of the United States to forcefully seize Cuba if Spain would not sell it, while filibuster expeditions attempted to annex new slave states without the benefit of governmental approval. Those who pursued the goal of expanding American slavery believed they embodied the true spirit of White racial superiority.

Review Questions

1. Which of the following was *not* one of the effects of the cotton boom?
   A. U.S. trade increased with France and Spain.
   B. Northern manufacturing expanded.
   C. The need for slave labor grew.
   D. Port cities like New Orleans expanded.

2. The abolition of the foreign slave trade in 1807 led to _____.
   A. a dramatic decrease in the price and demand for enslaved people
   B. the rise of a thriving domestic slave trade
   C. a reform movement calling for the complete end to slavery in the United States
   D. the decline of cotton production

3. Why did some southerners believe their region was immune to the effects of the market revolution? Why was this thinking misguided?

4. Under the law in the antebellum South, enslaved people were _____.
   A. servants
   B. animals
   C. property
   D. indentures

5. How did both slaveholders and enslaved people use the concept of paternalism to their advantage?

6. The largest group of White people in the South _____.
   A. enslaved no one
   B. enslaved between one and nine people each
   C. enslaved between ten and ninety-nine people each
   D. enslaved over one hundred people each

7. John C. Calhoun argued for greater rights for southerners with which idea?
   A. polygenism
   B. nullification
   C. concurrent majority
   D. paternalism

8. How did defenders of slavery use the concept of paternalism to structure their ideas?

9. Why did southern expansionists conduct filibuster expeditions?
   A. to gain political advantage
   B. to annex new slave states
   C. to prove they could raise an army
   D. to map unknown territories

10. The controversy at the heart of the Ostend Manifesto centered on the fate of:
    A. Ostend, Belgium
    B. Nicaragua
    C. Cuba
    D. Louisiana

11. Why did expansionists set their sights on the annexation of Spanish Cuba?

Critical Thinking Questions

12. Compare and contrast the steamboats of the antebellum years with technologies today. In your estimation, what modern technology compares to steamboats in its transformative power?

13. Does the history of the cotton kingdom support or undermine the Jeffersonian vision of White farmers on self-sufficient farms? Explain your answer.

14. Based on your reading of William J. Anderson's and John Brown's accounts, what types of traumas did enslaved people experience? How were the experiences of Black women and men similar and different?

15. What strategies did enslaved people employ to resist, revolt, and sustain their own independent communities and cultures? How did enslaved individuals use White southerners' own philosophies—paternalism and Christianity, for example—to their advantage in these efforts?

16. What are the major arguments put forward by proslavery advocates? How would you argue against their statements?

17. Consider filibustering from the point of view of the Cuban or Nicaraguan people. If you lived in Cuba or Nicaragua, would you support filibustering? Why or why not?

Antebellum Idealism and Reform Impulses, 1820–1860

13

FIGURE 13.1 The masthead of *The Liberator*, by Hammatt Billings in 1850, highlights the religious aspect of antislavery crusades. *The Liberator* was an abolitionist newspaper published by William Lloyd Garrison, one of the leaders of the abolitionist movement in the United States.

CHAPTER OUTLINE

13.1 An Awakening of Religion and Individualism
13.2 Antebellum Communal Experiments
13.3 Reforms to Human Health
13.4 Addressing Slavery
13.5 Women's Rights

INTRODUCTION This masthead for the abolitionist newspaper *The Liberator* shows two Americas (Figure 13.1). On the left is the southern version where enslaved people are being sold; on the right, free Black people enjoy the blessing of liberty. Reflecting the role of evangelical Protestantism in reforms such as abolition, the image features Jesus as the central figure. The caption reads, "I come to break the bonds of the oppressor," and below the masthead, "Our country is the World, our Countrymen are all Mankind."

The reform efforts of the antebellum years, including abolitionism, aimed to perfect the national destiny and redeem the souls of individual Americans. A great deal of optimism, fueled by evangelical Protestantism revivalism, underwrote the moral crusades of the first half of the nineteenth century. Some reformers targeted what they perceived as the shallow, materialistic, and democratic market culture of the United States and advocated a stronger sense of individualism and self-reliance. Others dreamed of a more equal society and established their own idealistic communities. Still others, who viewed slavery as the most serious flaw in American life, labored to end the institution. Women's rights, temperance, health reforms, and a host of other efforts also came to the forefront during the heyday of reform in the 1830s and 1840s.

13.1 An Awakening of Religion and Individualism

LEARNING OBJECTIVES

By the end of this section, you will be able to:
- Explain the connection between evangelical Protestantism and the Second Great Awakening
- Describe the message of the transcendentalists

FIGURE 13.2

Protestantism shaped the views of the vast majority of Americans in the antebellum years. The influence of religion only intensified during the decades before the Civil War, as religious camp meetings spread the word that people could bring about their own salvation, a direct contradiction to the Calvinist doctrine of predestination. Alongside this religious fervor, transcendentalists advocated a more direct knowledge of the self and an emphasis on individualism. The writers and thinkers devoted to transcendentalism, as well as the reactions against it, created a trove of writings, an outpouring that has been termed the American Renaissance.

THE SECOND GREAT AWAKENING

The reform efforts of the antebellum era sprang from the Protestant revival fervor that found expression in what historians refer to as the **Second Great Awakening**. (The First Great Awakening of evangelical Protestantism had taken place in the 1730s and 1740s.) The Second Great Awakening emphasized an emotional religious style in which sinners grappled with their unworthy nature before concluding that they were born again, that is, turning away from their sinful past and devoting themselves to living a righteous, Christ-centered life. This emphasis on personal salvation, with its rejection of predestination (the Calvinist concept that God selected only a chosen few for salvation), was the religious embodiment of the Jacksonian celebration of the individual. Itinerant ministers preached the message of the awakening to hundreds of listeners at outdoors revival meetings (Figure 13.3).

FIGURE 13.3 This 1819 engraving by Jacques Gerard shows a Methodist camp meeting. Revivalist camp meetings held by itinerant Protestant ministers became a feature of nineteenth-century American life.

The burst of religious enthusiasm that began in Kentucky and Tennessee in the 1790s and early 1800s among Baptists, Methodists, and Presbyterians owed much to the uniqueness of the early decades of the republic. These years saw swift population growth, broad western expansion, and the rise of participatory democracy. These political and social changes made many people anxious, and the more egalitarian, emotional, and individualistic religious practices of the Second Great Awakening provided relief and comfort for Americans experiencing rapid change. The awakening soon spread to the East, where it had a profound impact on Congregationalists and Presbyterians. The thousands swept up in the movement believed in the possibility of creating a much better world. Many adopted **millennialism**, the fervent belief that the Kingdom of God would be established on earth and that God would reign on earth for a thousand years, characterized by harmony and Christian morality. Those drawn to the message of the Second Great Awakening yearned for stability, decency, and goodness in the new and turbulent American republic.

The Second Great Awakening also brought significant changes to American culture. Church membership doubled in the years between 1800 and 1835. Several new groups formed to promote and strengthen the message of religious revival. The American Bible Society, founded in 1816, distributed Bibles in an effort to ensure that every family had access to the sacred text, while the American Sunday School Union, established in 1824, focused on the religious education of children and published religious materials specifically for young readers. In 1825, the American Tract Society formed with the goal of disseminating the Protestant revival message in a flurry of publications.

Missionaries and circuit riders (ministers without a fixed congregation) brought the message of the awakening across the United States, including into the lives of the enslaved. The revival spurred many slaveholders to begin encouraging the people they enslaved to become Christians. Previously, many slaveholders feared allowing the enslaved to convert, due to a belief that Christians could not be enslaved and because of the fear that enslaved people might use Christian principles to oppose their enslavement. However, by the 1800s, Americans established a legal foundation for the enslavement of Christians. Also, by this time, slaveholders had come to believe that if enslaved people learned the "right" (that is, White) form of Christianity, then they would be more obedient and hardworking. Allowing enslaved people access to Christianity also served to ease the consciences of Christian slaveholders, who argued that slavery was divinely ordained, yet it was a faith that also required slaveholders to bring enslaved people to the "truth." Also important to this era was the creation of African American forms of worship as well as African American churches such as the African Methodist Episcopal Church, the first independent Black Protestant church in the United States. Formed in the 1790s by Richard Allen, the African Methodist Episcopal Church advanced the African American effort to express their faith apart from White Methodists (Figure 13.4).

FIGURE 13.4 Charles Grandison Finney (a) was one of the best-known ministers of the Second Great Awakening. Richard Allen (b) created the first separate African American church, the African Methodist Episcopal Church, in the 1790s.

In the Northeast, Presbyterian minister Charles Grandison Finney rose to prominence as one of the most important evangelicals in the movement (Figure 13.4). Born in 1792 in western New York, Finney studied to be a lawyer until 1821, when he experienced a religious conversion and thereafter devoted himself to revivals. He led revival meetings in New York and Pennsylvania, but his greatest success occurred after he accepted a ministry in Rochester, New York, in 1830. At the time, Rochester was a boomtown because the Erie Canal had brought a lively shipping business.

The new middle class—an outgrowth of the Industrial Revolution—embraced Finney's message. It fit perfectly with their understanding of themselves as people shaping their own destiny. Workers also latched onto the message that they too could control their salvation, spiritually and perhaps financially as well. Western New York gained a reputation as the "burned over district," a reference to the intense flames of religious fervor that swept the area during the Second Great Awakening.

TRANSCENDENTALISM

Beginning in the 1820s, a new intellectual movement known as **transcendentalism** began to grow in the Northeast. In this context, to transcend means to go beyond the ordinary sensory world to grasp personal insights and gain appreciation of a deeper reality, and transcendentalists believed that all people could attain an understanding of the world that surpassed rational, sensory experience. Transcendentalists were critical of mainstream American culture. They reacted against the age of mass democracy in Jacksonian America—what Tocqueville called the "tyranny of majority"—by arguing for greater individualism against conformity. European romanticism, a movement in literature and art that stressed emotion over cold, calculating reason, also influenced transcendentalists in the United States, especially the transcendentalists' celebration of the uniqueness of individual feelings.

Ralph Waldo Emerson emerged as the leading figure of this movement (Figure 13.5). Born in Boston in 1803, Emerson came from a religious family. His father served as a Unitarian minister and, after graduating from Harvard Divinity School in the 1820s, Emerson followed in his father's footsteps. However, after his wife died in 1831, he left the clergy. On a trip to Europe in 1832, he met leading figures of romanticism who rejected the hyper-rationalism of the Enlightenment, emphasizing instead emotion and the sublime.

 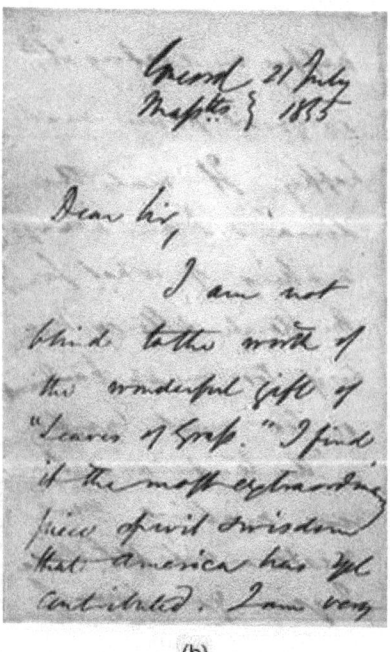

FIGURE 13.5 Ralph Waldo Emerson (a), shown here circa 1857, is considered the father of transcendentalism. This letter (b) from Emerson to Walt Whitman, another brilliant writer of the transcendentalist movement, demonstrates the closeness of a number of these writers.

When Emerson returned home the following year, he began giving lectures on his romanticism-influenced ideas. In 1836, he published "Nature," an essay arguing that humans can find their true spirituality in nature, not in the everyday bustling working world of Jacksonian democracy and industrial transformation. In 1841, Emerson published his essay "Self-Reliance," which urged readers to think for themselves and reject the mass conformity and mediocrity he believed had taken root in American life. In this essay, he wrote, "Whoso would be a man must be a nonconformist," demanding that his readers be true to themselves and not blindly follow a herd mentality. Emerson's ideas dovetailed with those of the French aristocrat, Alexis de Tocqueville, who wrote about the "tyranny of the majority" in his *Democracy in America*. Tocqueville, like Emerson, expressed concern that a powerful majority could overpower the will of individuals.

CLICK AND EXPLORE

Visit Emerson Central (http://openstax.org/l/15SelfReliance) to read the full text of "Self Reliance" by Ralph Waldo Emerson. How have Emerson's ideas influenced American society?

Emerson's ideas struck a chord with a class of literate adults who also were dissatisfied with mainstream American life and searching for greater spiritual meaning. Many writers were drawn to transcendentalism, and they started to express its ideas through new stories, poems, essays, and articles. The ideas of transcendentalism were able to permeate American thought and culture through a prolific print culture, which allowed magazines and journals to be widely disseminated.

Among those attracted to Emerson's ideas was his friend Henry David Thoreau, whom he encouraged to write about his own ideas. Thoreau placed a special emphasis on the role of nature as a gateway to the transcendentalist goal of greater individualism. In 1848, Thoreau gave a lecture in which he argued that individuals must stand up to governmental injustice, a topic he chose because of his disgust over the Mexican-American War and slavery. In 1849, he published his lecture "Civil Disobedience" and urged readers to refuse to support a government that was immoral. In 1854, he published *Walden; Or, Life in the Woods*, a book about the two years he spent in a small cabin on Walden Pond near Concord, Massachusetts (Figure 13.6). Thoreau had lived there as an experiment in living apart, but not too far apart, from his conformist neighbors.

 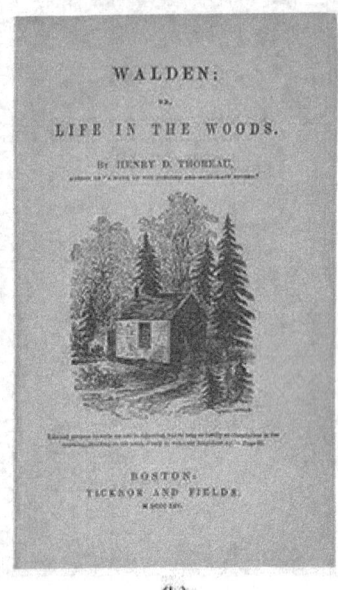

(a) (b)

FIGURE 13.6 Henry David Thoreau (a) argued that men had the right to resist authority if they deemed it unjust. "All men recognize the right of revolution; that is, the right to refuse allegiance to, and to resist, the government, when its tyranny or its inefficiency are great and unendurable." Thoreau's *Walden; or, Life in the Woods* (b) articulated his emphasis on the importance of nature as a gateway to greater individuality.

Margaret Fuller also came to prominence as a leading transcendentalist and advocate for women's equality. Fuller was a friend of Emerson and Thoreau, and other intellectuals of her day. Because she was a woman, she could not attend Harvard, as it was a male-only institution for undergraduate students until 1973. However, she was later granted the use of the library there because of her towering intellect. In 1840, she became the editor of *The Dial*, a transcendentalist journal, and she later found employment as a book reviewer for the *New York Tribune* newspaper. Tragically, in 1850, she died at the age of forty in a shipwreck off Fire Island, New York.

Walt Whitman also added to the transcendentalist movement, most notably with his 1855 publication of twelve poems, entitled *Leaves of Grass*, which celebrated the subjective experience of the individual. One of the poems, "Song of Myself," amplified the message of individualism, but by uniting the individual with all other people through a transcendent bond.

AMERICANA

Walt Whitman's "Song of Myself"
Walt Whitman (Figure 13.7) was a poet associated with the transcendentalists. His 1855 poem, "Song of Myself," shocked many when it was first published, but it has been called one of the most influential poems in American literature.

FIGURE 13.7 This steel engraving of Walt Whitman by Samuel Hollyer is from a lost daguerreotype by Gabriel Harrison, taken in 1854.

"I CELEBRATE myself, and sing myself,
And what I assume you shall assume,
For every atom belonging to me as good belongs to you.
I loafe and invite my soul,
I lean and loafe at my ease observing a spear of summer grass.
My tongue, every atom of my blood, form'd from this soil, this air,
Born here of parents born here from parents the same, and their parents the same,
I, now thirty-seven years old in perfect health begin,
Hoping to cease not till death. . . .
And I say to mankind, Be not curious about God,
For I who am curious about each am not curious about God,
(No array of terms can say how much I am at peace about God and about death.)
I hear and behold God in every object, yet understand God not in the least,
Nor do I understand who there can be more wonderful than myself. . . .
I too am not a bit tamed, I too am untranslatable,
I sound my barbaric yawp over the roofs of the world. . . .
You will hardly know who I am or what I mean,
But I shall be good health to you nevertheless,
And filter and fibre your blood.
Failing to fetch me at first keep encouraged,
Missing me one place search another,
I stop somewhere waiting for you."

What images does Whitman use to describe himself and the world around him? What might have been shocking about this poem in 1855? Why do you think it has endured?

Some critics took issue with transcendentalism's emphasis on rampant individualism by pointing out the destructive consequences of compulsive human behavior. Herman Melville's novel *Moby Dick; or, The Whale* emphasized the perils of individual obsession by telling the tale of Captain Ahab's single-minded quest to kill a white whale, Moby Dick, which had destroyed Ahab's original ship and caused him to lose one of his legs. Edgar Allan Poe, a popular author, critic, and poet, decried "the so-called poetry of the so-called transcendentalists."

These American writers who questioned transcendentalism illustrate the underlying tension between individualism and conformity in American life.

13.2 Antebellum Communal Experiments

LEARNING OBJECTIVES

By the end of this section, you will be able to:
- Identify similarities and differences among utopian groups of the antebellum era
- Explain how religious utopian communities differed from nonreligious ones

Prior to 1815, in the years before the market and Industrial Revolution, most Americans lived on farms where they produced much of the foods and goods they used. This largely pre-capitalist culture centered on large family units whose members all lived in the same towns, counties, and parishes.

Economic forces unleashed after 1815, however, forever altered that world. More and more people now bought their food and goods in the thriving market economy, a shift that opened the door to a new way of life. These economic transformations generated various reactions; some people were nostalgic for what they viewed as simpler, earlier times, whereas others were willing to try new ways of living and working. In the early nineteenth century, experimental communities sprang up, created by men and women who hoped not just to create a better way of life but to recast American civilization, so that greater equality and harmony would prevail. Indeed, some of these reformers envisioned the creation of alternative ways of living, where people could attain perfection in human relations. The exact number of these societies is unknown because many of them were so short-lived, but the movement reached its apex in the 1840s.

RELIGIOUS UTOPIAN SOCIETIES

Most of those attracted to utopian communities had been profoundly influenced by evangelical Protestantism, especially the Second Great Awakening. However, their experience of revivalism had left them wanting to further reform society. The communities they formed and joined adhered to various socialist ideas and were considered radical, because members wanted to create a new social order, not reform the old.

German Protestant migrants formed several **pietistic** societies: communities that stressed transformative individual religious experience or piety over religious rituals and formality. One of the earliest of these, the Ephrata Cloister in Pennsylvania, was founded by a charismatic leader named Conrad Beissel in the 1730s. By the antebellum era, it was the oldest communal experiment in the United States. Its members devoted themselves to spiritual contemplation and a disciplined work regime while they awaited the millennium. They wore homespun rather than buying cloth or premade clothing, and encouraged celibacy. Although the Ephrata Cloister remained small, it served as an early example of the type of community that antebellum reformers hoped to create.

In 1805, a second German religious society, led by George Rapp, took root in Pennsylvania with several hundred members called Rappites who encouraged celibacy and adhered to the socialist principle of holding all goods in common (as opposed to allowing individual ownership). They not only built the town of Harmony but also produced surplus goods to sell to the outside world. In 1815, the group sold its Pennsylvanian holdings and moved to Indiana, establishing New Harmony on a twenty-thousand-acre plot along the Wabash River. In 1825, members returned to Pennsylvania, and established themselves in the town called Economy.

The **Shakers** provide another example of a community established with a religious mission. The Shakers started in England as an outgrowth of the Quaker religion in the middle of the eighteenth century. Ann Lee, a leader of the group in England, emigrated to New York in the 1770s, having experienced a profound religious awakening that convinced her that she was "mother in Christ." She taught that God was both male and female; Jesus embodied the male side, while Mother Ann (as she came to be known by her followers) represented the female side. To Shakers in both England and the United States, Mother Ann represented the completion of divine revelation and the beginning of the millennium of heaven on earth.

In practice, men and women in Shaker communities were held as equals—a radical departure at the time—and women often outnumbered men. Equality extended to the possession of material goods as well; no one could hold private property. Shaker communities aimed for self-sufficiency, raising food and making all that was necessary, including furniture that emphasized excellent workmanship as a substitute for worldly pleasure.

The defining features of the Shakers were their spiritual mysticism and their prohibition of sexual intercourse, which they held as an example of a lesser spiritual life and a source of conflict between women and men. Rapturous Shaker dances, for which the group gained notoriety, allowed for emotional release (Figure 13.8). The high point of the Shaker movement came in the 1830s, when about six thousand members populated communities in New England, New York, Ohio, Indiana, and Kentucky.

FIGURE 13.8 In this image of a Shaker dance from 1840, note the raised arms, indicating emotional expression.

CLICK AND EXPLORE

Learn more about the musical heritage (http://openstax.org/l/15ShakerMusic) of the Shakers, including the well-known song "Simple Gifts," which has become part of American culture.

Another religious utopian experiment, the Oneida Community, began with the teachings of John Humphrey Noyes, a Vermonter who had graduated from Dartmouth, Andover Theological Seminary, and Yale. The Second Great Awakening exerted a powerful effect on him, and he came to believe in perfectionism, the idea that it is possible to be perfect and free of sin. Noyes claimed to have achieved this state of perfection in 1834.

Noyes applied his idea of perfection to relationships between men and women, earning notoriety for his unorthodox views on marriage and sexuality. Beginning in his home town of Putney, Vermont, he began to advocate what he called "complex marriage:" a form of communal marriage in which women and men who had achieved perfection could engage in sexual intercourse without sin. Noyes also promoted "male continence," whereby men would not ejaculate, thereby freeing women from pregnancy and the difficulty of determining paternity when they had many partners. Intercourse became fused with spiritual power among Noyes and his followers.

The concept of complex marriage scandalized the townspeople in Putney, so Noyes and his followers removed to Oneida, New York. Individuals who wanted to join the Oneida Community underwent a tough screening process to weed out those who had not reached a state of perfection, which Noyes believed promoted self-control, not out-of-control behavior. The goal was a balance between individuals in a community of love and respect. The perfectionist community Noyes envisioned ultimately dissolved in 1881, although the Oneida Community itself continues to this day (Figure 13.9).

FIGURE 13.9 The Oneida Community was a utopian experiment located in Oneida, New York, from **1848** to **1881**.

The most successful religious utopian community to arise in the antebellum years was begun by Joseph Smith. Smith came from a large Vermont family that had not prospered in the new market economy and moved to the town of Palmyra, in the "burned over district" of western New York. In 1823, Smith indicated that he had been visited by the angel Moroni, who told him the location of a trove of golden plates or tablets. During the late 1820s, Smith translated the writing on the golden plates, and in 1830, he published his finding as *The Book of Mormon*. That same year, he organized the Church of Christ, the progenitor of the Church of Jesus Christ of Latter-day Saints then popularly known as **Mormons**. He presented himself as a prophet and aimed to recapture what he viewed as the purity of the primitive Christian church, purity that had been lost over the centuries.

Smith emphasized the importance of families being led by fathers. His vision of a reinvigorated patriarchy resonated with men and women who had not thrived during the market revolution, and his claims attracted those who hoped for a better future. Smith's new church placed great stress on work and discipline. He aimed to create a New Jerusalem where the church exercised oversight of its members.

Smith's claims of translating the golden plates antagonized his neighbors in New York. Difficulties with anti-Mormons led him and his followers to move to Kirtland, Ohio, in 1831. By 1838, as the United States experienced continued economic turbulence following the Panic of 1837, Smith and his followers were facing financial collapse after a series of efforts in banking and money-making ended in disaster. They moved to Missouri, but trouble soon developed there as well, as citizens reacted against the Church members' beliefs. Actual fighting broke out in 1838, and the ten thousand or so members of the Church of Jesus Christ removed to Nauvoo, Illinois, where they founded a new center of Mormonism.

By the 1840s, Nauvoo boasted a population of thirty thousand, making it the largest utopian community in the United States. Thanks to some important conversions among powerful citizens in Illinois, the Church members had virtual autonomy in Nauvoo, which they used to create the largest armed force in the state. Smith also received further revelations there, including one that allowed male church leaders to practice polygamy. He also declared that all of North and South America would be the new Zion and announced that he would run for president in the 1844 election.

Smith and the Church members' convictions and practices generated a great deal of opposition from neighbors in surrounding towns. Smith was arrested for treason (for his role in the destruction of the printing press of a newspaper that criticized Mormonism), and while he was in prison, an anti-Mormon mob stormed into his cell and killed him. Brigham Young (Figure 13.10) then assumed leadership of the group, which he led to a permanent home in what is now Salt Lake City, Utah.

FIGURE 13.10 Carl Christian Anton Christensen depicts *The angel Moroni delivering the plates of the Book of Mormon to Joseph Smith*, circa 1886 (a). On the basis of these plates, Joseph Smith (b) founded the Church of Latter-Day Saints. Following Smith's death at the hands of a mob in Illinois, Brigham Young took control of the church and led them west to the Salt Lake Valley, which at that time was still part of Mexico.

SECULAR UTOPIAN SOCIETIES

Not all utopian communities were prompted by the religious fervor of the Second Great Awakening; some were outgrowths of the intellectual ideas of the time, such as romanticism with its emphasis on the importance of individualism over conformity. One of these, Brook Farm, took shape in West Roxbury, Massachusetts, in the 1840s. It was founded by George Ripley, a transcendentalist from Massachusetts. In the summer of 1841, this utopian community gained support from Boston-area thinkers and writers, an intellectual group that included many important transcendentalists. Brook Farm is best characterized as a community of intensely individualistic personalities who combined manual labor, such as the growing and harvesting food, with intellectual pursuits. They opened a school that specialized in the liberal arts rather than rote memorization and published a weekly journal called *The Harbinger*, which was "Devoted to Social and Political Progress" (Figure 13.11). Members of Brook Farm never totaled more than one hundred, but it won renown largely because of the luminaries, such as Emerson and Thoreau, whose names were attached to it. Nathaniel Hawthorne, a Massachusetts writer who took issue with some of the transcendentalists' claims, was a founding member of Brook Farm, and he fictionalized some of his experiences in his novel *The Blithedale Romance*. In 1846, a fire destroyed the main building of Brook Farm, and already hampered by financial problems, the Brook Farm experiment came to an end in 1847.

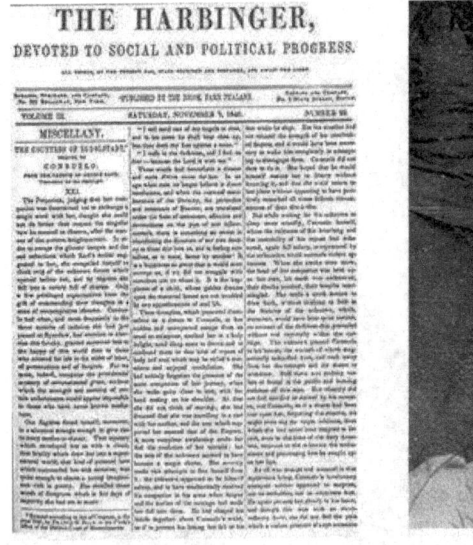

FIGURE 13.11 Brook Farm printed *The Harbinger* (a) to share its ideals more widely. George Ripley (b), who founded the farm, was burdened with a huge debt several years later when the community collapsed.

Robert Owen, a British industrialist, helped inspire those who dreamed of a more equitable world in the face of the changes brought about by industrialization. Owen had risen to prominence before he turned thirty by running cotton mills in New Lanark, Scotland; these were considered the most successful cotton mills in Great Britain. Owen was very uneasy about the conditions of workers, and he devoted both his life and his fortune to trying to create cooperative societies where workers would lead meaningful, fulfilled lives. Unlike the founders of many utopian communities, he did not gain inspiration from religion; his vision derived instead from his faith in human reason to make the world better.

When the Rappite community in Harmony, Indiana, decided to sell its holdings and relocate to Pennsylvania, Owen seized the opportunity to put his ideas into action. In 1825, he bought the twenty-thousand-acre parcel in Indiana and renamed it New Harmony (Figure 13.12). After only a few years, however, a series of bad decisions by Owen and infighting over issues like the elimination of private property led to the dissolution of the community. But Owen's ideas of cooperation and support inspired other "Owenite" communities in the United States, Canada, and Great Britain.

FIGURE 13.12 This 1838 engraving of New Harmony shows the ideal collective community that Robert Owen hoped to build.

A French philosopher who advocated the creation of a new type of utopian community, Charles Fourier also inspired American readers, notably Arthur Brisbane, who popularized Fourier's ideas in the United States. Fourier emphasized collective effort by groups of people or "associations." Members of the association would be housed in large buildings or "phalanxes," a type of communal living arrangement. Converts to Fourier's ideas about a new science of living published and lectured vigorously. They believed labor was a type of capital, and the more unpleasant the job, the higher the wages should be. Fourierists in the United States created some twenty-eight communities between 1841 and 1858, but by the late 1850s, the movement had run its course in the United States.

13.3 Reforms to Human Health

LEARNING OBJECTIVES

By the end of this section, you will be able to:
- Explain the different reforms aimed at improving the health of the human body
- Describe the various factions and concerns within the temperance movement

Antebellum reform efforts aimed at perfecting the spiritual and social worlds of individuals, and as an outgrowth of those concerns, some reformers moved in the direction of ensuring the health of American citizens. Many Americans viewed drunkenness as a major national problem, and the battle against alcohol and the many problems associated with it led many to join the temperance movement. Other reformers offered plans to increase physical well-being, instituting plans designed to restore vigor. Still others celebrated new sciences that would unlock the mysteries of human behavior and, by doing so, advance American civilization.

TEMPERANCE

According to many antebellum reformers, intemperance (drunkenness) stood as the most troubling problem in the United States, one that eroded morality, Christianity, and played a starring role in corrupting American democracy. Americans consumed huge quantities of liquor in the early 1800s, including gin, whiskey, rum, and brandy. Indeed, scholars agree that the rate of consumption of these drinks during the first three decades of the 1800s reached levels that have never been equaled in American history.

A variety of reformers created organizations devoted to **temperance**, that is, moderation or self-restraint. Each of these organizations had its own distinct orientation and target audience. The earliest ones were formed in the 1810s in New England. The Massachusetts Society for the Suppression of Intemperance and the Connecticut Society for the Reformation of Morals were both formed in 1813. Protestant ministers led both organizations, which enjoyed support from New Englanders who clung to the ideals of the Federalist Party and later the Whigs. These early temperance societies called on individuals to lead pious lives and avoid sin, including the sin of overindulging in alcohol. They called not for the eradication of drinking but for a more restrained and genteel style of imbibing.

AMERICANA

The Drunkard's Progress

This 1840 temperance illustration (Figure 13.13) charts the path of destruction for those who drink. The step-by-step progression reads:

" Step 1. A glass with a friend.
Step 2. A glass to keep the cold out.
Step 3. A glass too much.
Step 4. Drunk and riotous.
Step 5. The summit attained. Jolly companions. A confirmed drunkard.
Step 6. Poverty and disease.
Step 7. Forsaken by Friends.
Step 8. Desperation and crime.
Step 9. Death by suicide."

FIGURE 13.13 This 1846 image, *The Drunkards Progress. From the First Glass to the Grave*, by Nathaniel Currier, shows the destruction that prohibitionists thought could result from drinking alcoholic beverages.

Who do you think was the intended audience for this engraving? How do you think different audiences (children, drinkers, nondrinkers) would react to the story it tells? Do you think it is an effective piece of propaganda? Why or why not?

In the 1820s, temperance gained ground largely through the work of Presbyterian minister Lyman Beecher. In 1825, Beecher delivered six sermons on temperance that were published the follow year as *Six Sermons on the Nature, Occasions, Signs, Evils, and Remedy of Intemperance*. He urged total abstinence from hard liquor and called for the formation of voluntary associations to bring forth a new day without spirits (whiskey, rum, gin, brandy). Lyman's work enjoyed a wide readership and support from leading Protestant ministers as well as the emerging middle class; temperance fit well with the middle-class ethic of encouraging hard work and a sober workforce.

In 1826, the American Temperance Society was formed, and by the early 1830s, thousands of similar societies had sprouted across the country. Members originally pledged to shun only hard liquor. By 1836, however, leaders of the temperance movement, including Beecher, called for a more comprehensive approach. Thereafter, most temperance societies advocated total abstinence; no longer would beer and wine be tolerated. Such total abstinence from alcohol is known as **teetotalism**.

Teetotalism led to disagreement within the movement and a loss of momentum for reform after 1836. However, temperance enjoyed a revival in the 1840s, as a new type of reformer took up the cause against alcohol. The engine driving the new burst of enthusiastic temperance reform was the Washington Temperance Society (named in deference to George Washington), which organized in 1840. The leaders of the Washingtonians came not from the ranks of Protestant ministers but from the working class. They aimed their efforts at confirmed alcoholics, unlike the early temperance advocates who mostly targeted the middle class.

Washingtonians welcomed the participation of women and children, as they cast alcohol as the destroyer of families, and those who joined the group took a public pledge of teetotalism. Americans flocked to the Washingtonians; as many as 600,000 had taken the pledge by 1844. The huge surge in membership had much to do with the style of this reform effort. The Washingtonians turned temperance into theater by dramatizing the plight of those who fell into the habit of drunkenness. Perhaps the most famous fictional drama put forward by the temperance movement was *Ten Nights in a Bar-Room* (1853), a novel that became the basis for popular theatrical productions. The Washingtonians also sponsored picnics and parades that drew whole families into the movement. The group's popularity quickly waned in the late 1840s and early 1850s, when questions arose about the effectiveness of merely taking a pledge. Many who had done so soon relapsed into alcoholism.

Still, by that time, temperance had risen to a major political issue. Reformers lobbied for laws limiting or prohibiting alcohol, and states began to pass the first temperance laws. The earliest, an 1838 law in Massachusetts, prohibited the sale of liquor in quantities less than fifteen gallons, a move designed to make it difficult for ordinary workmen of modest means to buy spirits. The law was repealed in 1840, but Massachusetts towns then took the initiative by passing local laws banning alcohol. In 1845, close to one hundred towns in the state went "dry."

An 1839 Mississippi law, similar to Massachusetts' original law, outlawed the sale of less than a gallon of liquor. Mississippi's law illustrates the national popularity of temperance; regional differences notwithstanding, citizens in northern and southern states agreed on the issue of alcohol. Nonetheless, northern states pushed hardest for outlawing alcohol. Maine enacted the first statewide prohibition law in 1851. New England, New York, and states in the Midwest passed local laws in the 1850s, prohibiting the sale and manufacture of intoxicating beverages.

REFORMS FOR THE BODY AND THE MIND

Beyond temperance, other reformers looked to ways to maintain and improve health in a rapidly changing world. Without professional medical organizations or standards, health reform went in many different directions; although the American Medical Association was formed in 1847, it did not have much power to oversee medical practices. Too often, quack doctors prescribed regimens and medicines that did far more harm that good.

Sylvester Graham stands out as a leading light among the health reformers in the antebellum years. A Presbyterian minister, Graham began his career as a reformer, lecturing against the evils of strong drink. He combined an interest in temperance with vegetarianism and sexuality into what he called a "Science of Human Life," calling for a regimented diet of more vegetables, fruits, and grain, and no alcohol, meat, or spices.

Graham advocated baths and cleanliness in general to preserve health; hydropathy, or water cures for various ailments, became popular in the United States in the 1840s and 1850s. He also viewed masturbation and excessive sex as a cause of disease and debility. His ideas led him to create what he believed to be a perfect food that would maintain health: the Graham cracker, which he invented in 1829. Followers of Graham, known as Grahamites, established boardinghouses where lodgers followed the recommended strict diet and sexual regimen.

During the early nineteenth century, reformers also interested themselves in the workings of the mind in an effort to better understand the effects of a rapidly changing world awash with religious revivals and democratic movements. **Phrenology**—the mapping of the cranium to specific human attributes—stands as an early type of science, related to what would become psychology and devoted to understanding how the mind worked. Although their theories would ultimately be proven wrong, phrenologists believed that the mind contained thirty-seven "faculties," the strengths or weaknesses of which could be determined by a close examination of the size and shape of the cranium (Figure 13.14).

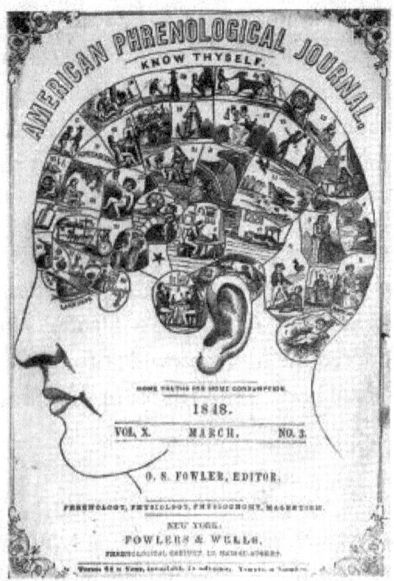

FIGURE 13.14 This March 1848 cover of the *American Phrenological Journal* illustrates the different faculties of the mind as envisioned by phrenologists.

Initially developed in Europe by Franz Joseph Gall, a German doctor, phrenology first came to the United States in the 1820s. In the 1830s and 1840s, it grew in popularity as lecturers crisscrossed the republic. It was sometimes used as an educational test, and like temperance, it also became a form of popular entertainment. While phrenology is now considered pseudoscience, Gall's assertion that different parts of the brain were responsible for different functions is viewed as an important scientific advance.

CLICK AND EXPLORE

Map the brain! Check out all thirty-seven of phrenology's purported faculties (http://openstax.org/l/15Phrenology) of the mind.

The popularity of phrenology offers us some insight into the emotional world of the antebellum United States. Its popularity speaks to the desire of those living in a rapidly changing society, where older ties to community and family were being challenged, to understand one another. It appeared to offer a way to quickly recognize an otherwise-unknown individual as a readily understood set of human faculties.

13.4 Addressing Slavery

LEARNING OBJECTIVES
By the end of this section, you will be able to:
- Identify the different approaches to reforming the institution of slavery
- Describe the abolitionist movement in the early to mid-nineteenth century

The issue of slavery proved especially combustible in the reform-minded antebellum United States. Those who hoped to end slavery had different ideas about how to do it. Some could not envision a biracial society and advocated sending Black people to Africa or the Caribbean. Others promoted the use of violence as the best method to bring American slavery to an end. Abolitionists, by contrast, worked to end slavery and to create a multiracial society of equals using moral arguments—moral suasion—to highlight the immorality of slavery. In keeping with the religious fervor of the era, abolitionists hoped to bring about a mass conversion in public opinion to end slavery.

"REFORMS" TO SLAVERY

An early and popular "reform" to slavery was **colonization**, or a movement advocating the displacement of

African Americans out of the country, usually to Africa. In 1816, the Society for the Colonization of Free People of Color of America (also called the American Colonization Society or ACS) was founded with this goal. Leading statesmen including Thomas Jefferson endorsed the idea of colonization.

Members of the ACS did not believe that Black and White people could live as equals, so they targeted the roughly 200,000 free Black people in the United States for relocation to Africa. For several years after the ACS's founding, they raised money and pushed Congress for funds. In 1819, they succeeded in getting $100,000 from the federal government to further the colonization project. The ACS played a major role in the creation of the colony of Liberia, on the west coast of Africa. The country's capital, Monrovia, was named in honor of President James Monroe. The ACS stands as an example of how White reformers, especially men of property and standing, addressed the issue of slavery. Their efforts stand in stark contrast with other reformers' efforts to deal with slavery in the United States.

Although rebellion stretches the definition of reform, another potential solution to slavery was its violent overthrow. Nat Turner's Rebellion, one of the largest slave uprisings in American history, took place in 1831, in Southampton County, Virginia. Like many enslaved people, Nat Turner was inspired by the evangelical Protestant fervor sweeping the republic. He preached to other enslaved people in Southampton County, gaining a reputation among them as a prophet. He organized them for rebellion, awaiting a sign to begin, until an eclipse in August signaled that the appointed time had come.

Turner and as many as seventy other enslaved people killed their enslavers and their families, a total of around sixty-five people (Figure 13.15). Turner eluded capture until late October, when he was tried, hanged, and then beheaded and quartered. Virginia put to death fifty-six others whom they believed to have taken part in the rebellion. White vigilantes and organized militias killed two hundred more as panic swept through Virginia and the rest of the South.

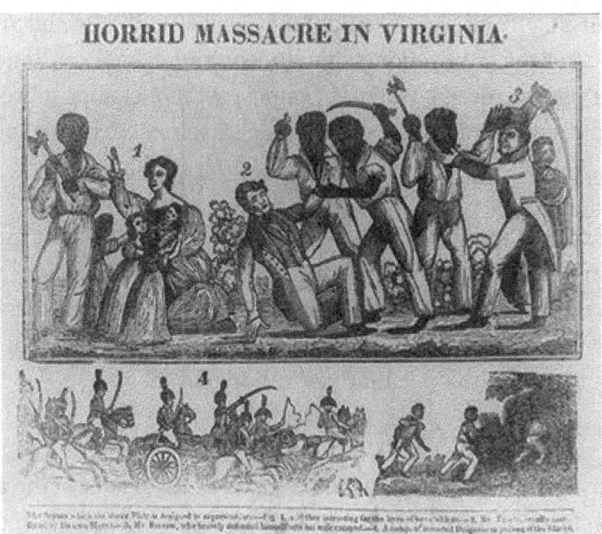

FIGURE 13.15 In *Horrid Massacre in Virginia*, circa 1831, the text on the bottom reads, "The Scenes which the above plate is designed to represent are Fig 1. a mother intreating for the lives of her children. -2. Mr. Travis, cruelly murdered by his own Slaves. -3. Mr. Barrow, who bravely defended himself until his wife escaped. -4. A comp. of mounted Dragoons in pursuit of the Blacks." From whose side do you think the illustrator is telling this story?

MY STORY

Nat Turner on His Battle against Slavery

Thomas R. Gray was a lawyer in Southampton, Virginia, where he visited Nat Turner in jail. He published *The Confessions of Nat Turner, the leader of the late insurrection in Southampton, Va., as fully and voluntarily made* to Thomas R. Gray in November 1831, after Turner had been executed.

"For as the blood of Christ had been shed on this earth, and had ascended to heaven for the salvation of sinners, and was now returning to earth again in the form of dew . . . it was plain to me that the Saviour was about to lay down the yoke he had borne for the sins of men, and the great day of judgment was at hand. . . . And on the 12th of May, 1828, I heard a loud noise in the heavens, and the Spirit instantly appeared to me and said the Serpent was loosened, and Christ had laid down the yoke he had borne for the sins of men, and that I should take it on and fight against the Serpent, . . . *Ques.* Do you not find yourself mistaken now? *Ans.* Was not Christ crucified. And by signs in the heavens that it would make known to me when I should commence the great work—and on the appearance of the sign, (the eclipse of the sun last February) I should arise and prepare myself, and slay my enemies with their own weapons."

How did Turner interpret his fight against slavery? What did he mean by the "serpent?"

Nat Turner's Rebellion provoked a heated discussion in Virginia over slavery. The Virginia legislature was already in the process of revising the state constitution, and some delegates advocated for an easier manumission process. The rebellion, however, rendered that reform impossible. Virginia and other slave states recommitted themselves to the institution of slavery, and defenders of slavery in the South increasingly blamed northerners for provoking the enslaved to rebel.

Literate, educated Black people, including David Walker, also favored rebellion. Walker was born a free Black man in North Carolina in 1796. He moved to Boston in the 1820s, lectured on slavery, and promoted the first African American newspaper, *Freedom's Journal*. He called for Black people to actively resist slavery and to use violence if needed. He published *An Appeal to the Colored Citizens of the World* in 1829, denouncing the scheme of colonization and urging Black people to fight for equality in the United States, to take action against racism. Walker died months after the publication of his *Appeal*, and debate continues to this day over the cause of his death. Many believe he was murdered. Walker became a symbol of hope to free people in the North and a symbol of the terrors of literate, educated Black people to the slaveholders of the South.

ABOLITIONISM

Abolitionists took a far more radical approach to the issue of the slavery by using moral arguments to advocate its immediate elimination. They publicized the atrocities committed under slavery and aimed to create a society characterized by equality of Black and White people. In a world of intense religious fervor, they hoped to bring about a mass awakening in the United States of the sin of slavery, confident that they could transform the national conscience against the South's peculiar institution.

William Lloyd Garrison and Antislavery Societies

William Lloyd Garrison of Massachusetts distinguished himself as the leader of the **abolitionist** movement. Although he had once been in favor of colonization, he came to believe that such a scheme only deepened racism and perpetuated the sinful practices of his fellow Americans. In 1831, he founded the abolitionist newspaper *The Liberator*, whose first edition declared:

> I am aware that many object to the severity of my language; but is there not cause for severity? I will be as harsh as truth, and as uncompromising as justice. On this subject, I do not wish to think, or speak, or write, with moderation. No! No! Tell a man whose house is on fire to give a moderate alarm; tell him to moderately rescue his wife from the hands of the ravisher; tell the mother to gradually extricate her babe from the fire into which it has fallen;—but urge me not to use moderation in a cause like the present. I am in earnest—I will not equivocate—I will not excuse—I will not retreat a single inch—AND I WILL BE HEARD.

White Virginians blamed Garrison for stirring up enslaved people and instigating slave rebellions like Nat

Turner's.

Garrison founded the New England Anti-Slavery Society in 1831, and the American Anti-Slavery Society (AASS) in 1833. By 1838, the AASS had 250,000 members, sometimes called Garrisonians. They rejected colonization as a racist scheme and opposed the use of violence to end slavery. Influenced by evangelical Protestantism, Garrison and other abolitionists believed in **moral suasion**, a technique of appealing to the conscience of the public, especially slaveholders. Moral suasion relied on dramatic narratives, often from formerly enslaved people, about the horrors of slavery, arguing that slavery destroyed families, as children were sold and taken away from their mothers and fathers (Figure 13.16). Moral suasion resonated with many women, who condemned the sexual violence against enslaved women and the victimization of southern White women by adulterous husbands.

(a)　　　　(b)

FIGURE 13.16 These woodcuts of a chained and pleading enslaved person, *Am I Not a Man and a Brother?* (a) and *Am I Not a Woman and a Sister?*, accompanied abolitionist John Greenleaf Whittier's antislavery poem, "Our Countrymen in Chains." Such images exemplified moral suasion: showing with pathos and humanity the moral wrongness of slavery.

CLICK AND EXPLORE

Read the full text of John Greenleaf Whittier's antislavery poem (http://openstax.org/l/15AmericasLost) "Our Countrymen in Chains."

What imagery and rhetoric does Whittier use to advance the cause of abolitionism?

Garrison also preached **immediatism**: the moral demand to take immediate action to end slavery. He wrote of equal rights and demanded that Black people be treated as equal to White people. He appealed to women and men, Black and White, to join the fight. The abolition press, which produced hundreds of tracts, helped to circulate moral suasion. Garrison and other abolitionists also used the power of petitions, sending hundreds of petitions to Congress in the early 1830s, demanding an end to slavery. Since most newspapers published congressional proceedings, the debate over abolition petitions reached readers throughout the nation.

Although Garrison rejected the U.S. political system as a tool of slaveholders, other abolitionists believed mainstream politics could bring about their goal, and they helped create the Liberty Party in 1840. Its first candidate was James G. Birney, who ran for president that year. Birney epitomized the ideal and goals of the abolitionist movement. Born in Kentucky in 1792, Birney was an enslaver and, searching for a solution to what he eventually condemned as the immorality of slavery, initially endorsed colonization. In the 1830s, however, he rejected colonization, released the people he enslaved, and began to advocate the immediate end of slavery. The Liberty Party did not generate much support and remained a fringe third party. Many of its supporters turned to the Free-Soil Party in the aftermath of the Mexican Cession.

The vast majority of northerners rejected abolition entirely. Indeed, abolition generated a fierce backlash in the United States, especially during the Age of Jackson, when racism saturated American culture. Anti-abolitionists in the North saw Garrison and other abolitionists as the worst of the worst, a threat to the republic that might destroy all decency and order by upending time-honored distinctions between Black and White people, and between women and men. Northern anti-abolitionists feared that if slavery ended, the North would be flooded with Black people who would take jobs from White people.

Opponents made clear their resistance to Garrison and others of his ilk; Garrison nearly lost his life in 1835, when a Boston anti-abolitionist mob dragged him through the city streets. Anti-abolitionists tried to pass federal laws that made the distribution of abolitionist literature a criminal offense, fearing that such literature, with its engravings and simple language, could spark rebellious Black people to action. Their sympathizers in Congress passed a "gag rule" that forbade the consideration of the many hundreds of petitions sent to Washington by abolitionists. A mob in Illinois killed an abolitionist named Elijah Lovejoy in 1837, and the following year, ten thousand protestors destroyed the abolitionists' newly built Pennsylvania Hall in Philadelphia, burning it to the ground.

Frederick Douglass

Many escaped enslaved people joined the abolitionist movement, including Frederick Douglass. Douglass was born in Maryland in 1818, escaping to New York in 1838. He later moved to New Bedford, Massachusetts, with his wife. Douglass's commanding presence and powerful speaking skills electrified his listeners when he began to provide public lectures on slavery. He came to the attention of Garrison and others, who encouraged him to publish his story. In 1845, Douglass published *Narrative of the Life of Frederick Douglass, An American Slave Written by Himself*, in which he told about his life of slavery in Maryland (Figure 13.17). He identified by name the White people who had brutalized him, and for that reason, along with the mere act of publishing his story, Douglass had to flee the United States to avoid being murdered.

(a)

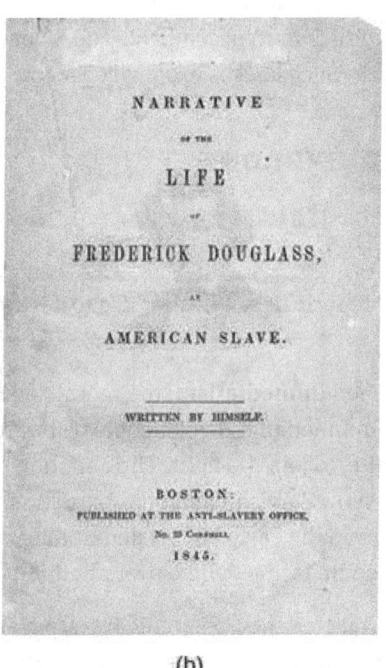
(b)

FIGURE 13.17 This 1856 ambrotype of Frederick Douglass (a) demonstrates an early type of photography developed on glass. Douglass was an escaped enslaved person who was instrumental in the abolitionism movement. His slave narrative, told in *Narrative of the Life of Frederick Douglass, An American Slave Written by Himself* (b), followed a long line of similar narratives that demonstrated the brutality of slavery for northerners unfamiliar with the institution.

British abolitionist friends bought his freedom from his Maryland owner, and Douglass returned to the United

States. He began to publish his own abolitionist newspaper, *North Star*, in Rochester, New York. During the 1840s and 1850s, Douglass labored to bring about the end of slavery by telling the story of his life and highlighting how slavery destroyed families, both Black and White.

MY STORY

Frederick Douglass on Slavery

Most White slaveholders frequently raped enslaved girls and women. In this excerpt, Douglass explains the consequences for the children fathered by White men and enslaved women.

"Slaveholders have ordained, and by law established, that the children of slave women shall in all cases follow the condition of their mothers . . . this is done too obviously to administer to their own lusts, and make a gratification of their wicked desires profitable as well as pleasurable . . . the slaveholder, in cases not a few, sustains to his slaves the double relation of master and father. . . .

Such slaves [born of white masters] invariably suffer greater hardships . . . They are . . . a constant offence to their mistress . . . she is never better pleased than when she sees them under the lash, . . . The master is frequently compelled to sell this class of his slaves, out of deference to the feelings of his white wife; and, cruel as the deed may strike any one to be, for a man to sell his own children to human flesh-mongers, . . . for, unless he does this, he must not only whip them himself, but must stand by and see one white son tie up his brother, of but few shades darker . . . and ply the gory lash to his naked back.
—Frederick Douglass, *Narrative of the Life of Frederick Douglass, An American Slave Written by Himself* (1845)"

What moral complications did slavery unleash upon White slaveholders in the South, according to Douglass? What imagery does he use?

13.5 Women's Rights

LEARNING OBJECTIVES

By the end of this section, you will be able to:
- Explain the connections between abolition, reform, and antebellum feminism
- Describe the ways antebellum women's movements were both traditional and revolutionary

Women took part in all the antebellum reforms, from transcendentalism to temperance to abolition. In many ways, traditional views of women as nurturers played a role in encouraging their participation. Women who joined the cause of temperance, for example, amplified their accepted role as moral guardians of the home. Some women advocated a much more expansive role for themselves and their peers by educating children and men in solid republican principles. But it was their work in antislavery efforts that served as a springboard for women to take action against gender inequality. Many, especially northern women, came to the conclusion that they, like enslaved people, were held in shackles in a society dominated by men. Even men who were progressive on some issues, such as abolition, adhered to traditional gender roles, and demanded that their families did as well. Women also had very limited rights regarding property ownership and legal authority. Until states began passing property laws in the 1840s, husbands often fully controlled women's earnings, collection of debts, and rights regarding inheritance. The laws gave women some additional power, but that power was far from universal.

Despite the radical nature of their effort to end slavery and create a biracial society, most abolitionist men clung to traditional notions of proper gender roles. White and Black women, as well as free Black men, were forbidden from occupying leadership positions in the AASS. Because women were not allowed to join the men in playing leading roles in the organization, they formed separate societies, such as the Boston Female Anti-Slavery Society, the Philadelphia Female Anti-Slavery Society, and similar groups.

THE GRIMKÉ SISTERS

Two leading abolitionist women, Sarah and Angelina Grimké, played major roles in combining the fight to end slavery with the struggle to achieve female equality. The sisters had been born into a prosperous slaveholding family in South Carolina. Both were caught up in the religious fervor of the Second Great Awakening, and they moved to the North and converted to Quakerism.

In the mid-1830s, the sisters joined the abolitionist movement, and in 1837, they embarked on a public lecture tour, speaking about immediate abolition to "promiscuous assemblies," that is, to audiences of women and men. This public action thoroughly scandalized respectable society, where it was unheard of for women to lecture to men. William Lloyd Garrison endorsed the Grimké sisters' public lectures, but other abolitionists did not. Their lecture tour served as a turning point; the reaction against them propelled the question of women's proper sphere in society to the forefront of public debate.

THE DECLARATION OF RIGHTS AND SENTIMENTS

Participation in the abolitionist movement led some women to embrace feminism, the advocacy of women's rights. Lydia Maria Child, an abolitionist and feminist, observed, "The comparison between women and the colored race is striking . . . both have been kept in subjection by physical force." Other women, including Elizabeth Cady Stanton, Lucy Stone, and Susan B. Anthony, agreed (Figure 13.18).

(a) (b)

FIGURE 13.18 Elizabeth Cady Stanton (a) and Lucretia Mott (b) both emerged from the abolitionist movement as strong advocates of women's rights.

In 1848, about three hundred male and female feminists, many of them veterans of the abolition campaign, gathered at the **Seneca Falls** Convention in New York for a conference on women's rights that was organized by Lucretia Mott and Elizabeth Cady Stanton. It was the first of what became annual meetings that have continued to the present day. Attendees agreed to a "Declaration of Rights and Sentiments" based on the Declaration of Independence; it declared, "We hold these truths to be self-evident: that all men and women are created equal; that they are endowed by their Creator with certain inalienable rights; that among these are life, liberty, and the pursuit of happiness." "The history of mankind," the document continued, "is a history of repeated injuries and usurpations on the part of man toward woman, having in direct object the establishment of an absolute tyranny over her."

CLICK AND EXPLORE

Read the entire text of the Declaration of Rights and Sentiments (http://openstax.org/l/15SenecaFalls) in the Internet Modern History Sourcebook at Fordham University.

REPUBLICAN MOTHERHOOD IN THE ANTEBELLUM YEARS

Some northern female reformers saw new and vital roles for their sex in the realm of education. They believed in traditional gender roles, viewing women as inherently more moral and nurturing than men. Because of these attributes, the feminists argued, women were uniquely qualified to take up the roles of educators of children.

Catharine Beecher, the daughter of Lyman Beecher, pushed for women's roles as educators. In her 1845 book, *The Duty of American Women to Their Country*, she argued that the United States had lost its moral compass due to democratic excess. Both "intelligence and virtue" were imperiled in an age of riots and disorder. Women, she argued, could restore the moral center by instilling in children a sense of right and wrong. Beecher represented a northern, middle-class female sensibility. The home, especially the parlor, became the site of northern female authority.

DEFINING AMERICAN

Sojourner Truth, "Ain't I A Woman?"

Born into slavery with the name Isabella Baumfree, Sojourner Truth gained her freedom in 1826 and devoted much of the rest of her life to championing the causes of abolition and women's rights. She became the first Black woman to win a lawsuit against a White person when she sued to gain the freedom of her son. Supported by leaders such as Frederick Douglass and William Lloyd Garrison, Truth became a powerful voice in the abolition movement. But she was not afraid to challenge the prevailing notions about the rights and priorities of men and women within the abolition movement, nor did she avoid challenging the notions about Black people's priority within the women's rights movement. While some advocated with a step-by-step approach—first White women's suffrage, then Black women's suffrage—Truth disagreed.

In 1851, Truth delivered a speech at the Women's Rights Convention in Akron, Ohio. Ultimately, it came to be titled "Ain't I a Woman." One of the most famous transcriptions of this speech was published in an 1851 edition of the *Anti-Slavery Bugle* by Reverend Marius Robinson, an Ohio abolitionist who had worked with Truth. Another was published in an 1863 edition of the *Anti-Slavery Standard* by Frances Dana Gage, an abolitionist and feminist who presided over the convention at which Truth spoke.

"I have as much muscle as any man, and can do as much work as any man. I have plowed and reaped and husked and chopped and mowed, and can any man do more than that? I have heard much about the sexes being equal; I can carry as much as any man, and can eat as much too, if I can get it. I am strong as any man that is now."

"As for intellect, all I can say is, if woman have a pint and man a quart—why can't she have her little pint full? You need not be afraid to give us our rights for fear we will take too much—for we won't take more than our pint'll hold."

"The poor men seem to be all in confusion and don't know what to do. Why children, if you have woman's rights give it to her and you will feel better. You will have your own rights, and they won't be so much trouble."

"I can't read, but I can hear. I have heard the Bible and have learned that Eve caused man to sin. Well if woman upset the world, do give her a chance to set it right side up again."

What might be the reasons for the different versions of Truth's speech? Could the different publishers have had different motivations?

What is Truth's theme in this speech?

Key Terms

abolitionist   a believer in the complete elimination of slavery

colonization   the strategy of moving African Americans out of the United States, usually to Africa

immediatism   the moral demand to take immediate action against slavery to bring about its end

millennialism   the belief that the Kingdom of God would be established on earth and that God would reign on earth for a thousand years characterized by harmony and Christian morality

moral suasion   an abolitionist technique of appealing to the consciences of the public, especially slaveholders

Mormons   members of an American denomination of The Church of Jesus Christ of Latter-day Saints that emphasized patriarchal leadership

phrenology   the mapping of the mind to specific human attributes, later considered pseudoscience

pietistic   the stressing of stressed transformative individual religious experience or piety over religious rituals and formality

Second Great Awakening   a revival of evangelical Protestantism in the early nineteenth century

Seneca Falls   the location of the first American conference on women's rights and the signing of the "Declaration of Rights and Sentiments" in 1848

Shakers   a religious sect that emphasized communal living and celibacy

teetotalism   complete abstinence from all alcohol

temperance   a social movement encouraging moderation or self-restraint in the consumption of alcoholic beverages

transcendentalism   the belief that all people can attain an understanding of the world that transcends rational, sensory experience

Summary

13.1 An Awakening of Religion and Individualism

Evangelical Protestantism pervaded American culture in the antebellum era and fueled a belief in the possibility of changing society for the better. Leaders of the Second Great Awakening like Charles G. Finney urged listeners to take charge of their own salvation. This religious message dovetailed with the new economic possibilities created by the market and Industrial Revolution, making the Protestantism of the Second Great Awakening, with its emphasis on individual spiritual success, a reflection of the individualistic, capitalist spirit of the age. Transcendentalists took a different approach, but like their religiously oriented brethren, they too looked to create a better existence. These authors, most notably Emerson, identified a major tension in American life between the effort to be part of the democratic majority and the need to remain true to oneself as an individual.

13.2 Antebellum Communal Experiments

Reformers who engaged in communal experiments aimed to recast economic and social relationships by introducing innovations designed to create a more stable and equitable society. Their ideas found many expressions, from early socialist experiments (such as by the Fourierists and the Owenites) to the dreams of the New England intellectual elite (such as Brook Farm). The Second Great Awakening also prompted many religious utopias, like those of the Rappites and Shakers. By any measure, the Mormons emerged as the most successful of these.

13.3 Reforms to Human Health

Reformers targeted vices that corrupted the human body and society: the individual and the national soul. For many, alcohol appeared to be the most destructive and widespread. Indeed, in the years before the Civil War, the United States appeared to be a republic of drunkenness to many. To combat this national substance abuse problem, reformers created a host of temperance organizations that first targeted the middle and upper classes, and then the working classes. Thanks to Sylvester Graham and other health reformers, exercise and fresh air, combined with a good diet, became fashionable. Phrenologists focused on revealing the secrets of the mind and personality. In a fast-paced world, phrenology offered the possibility of knowing different human characteristics.

13.4 Addressing Slavery

Contrasting proposals were put forth to deal with slavery. Reformers in the antebellum United States addressed the thorny issue of slavery through contrasting proposals that offered profoundly different solutions to the dilemma of the institution. Many leading American statesmen, including slaveholders, favored colonization, relocating Black Americans to Africa, which abolitionists scorned. Slave rebellions sought the end of the institution through its violent overthrow, a tactic that horrified many in the North and the South. Abolitionists, especially those who followed William Lloyd Garrison, provoked equally strong reactions by envisioning a new United States without slavery, where Black people and White people stood on equal footing. Opponents saw abolition as the worst possible reform, a threat to all order and decency. Slaveholders, in particular, saw slavery as a positive aspect of American society, one that reformed the lives of enslaved people by exposing them to civilization and religion.

13.5 Women's Rights

The spirit of religious awakening and reform in the antebellum era impacted women lives by allowing them to think about their lives and their society in new and empowering ways. Of all the various antebellum reforms, however, abolition played a significant role in generating the early feminist movement in the United States. Although this early phase of American feminism did not lead to political rights for women, it began the long process of overcoming gender inequalities in the republic.

Review Questions

1. Which of the following is *not* a characteristic of the Second Great Awakening?
    A. greater emphasis on nature
    B. greater emphasis on religious education of children
    C. greater church attendance
    D. belief in the possibility of a better world

2. Transcendentalists were most concerned with _____.
    A. the afterlife
    B. predestination
    C. the individual
    D. democracy

3. What do the Second Great Awakening and transcendentalism have in common?

4. Which religious community focused on the power of patriarchy?
    A. Shakers
    B. Mormons
    C. Owenites
    D. Rappites

5. Which community or movement is associated with transcendentalism?
    A. the Oneida Community
    B. the Ephrata Cloister
    C. Brook Farm
    D. Fourierism

6. How were the reform communities of the antebellum era treated by the general population?

7. The first temperance laws were enacted by _____.
   A. state governments
   B. local governments
   C. the federal government
   D. temperance organizations

8. Sylvester Graham's reformers targeted _____.
   A. the human body
   B. nutrition
   C. sexuality
   D. all of the above

9. Whom did temperance reformers target?

10. In the context of the antebellum era, what does colonization refer to?
    A. Great Britain's colonization of North America
    B. the relocation of African Americans to Africa
    C. American colonization of the Caribbean
    D. American colonization of Africa

11. Which of the following did William Lloyd Garrison *not* employ in his abolitionist efforts?
    A. moral suasion
    B. immediatism
    C. political involvement
    D. pamphleteering

12. Why did William Lloyd Garrison's endorsement of the Grimké sisters divide the abolitionist movement?
    A. They advocated equal rights for women.
    B. They supported colonization.
    C. They attended the Seneca Falls Convention.
    D. They lectured to co-ed audiences.

13. Which female reformer focused on women's roles as the educators of children?
    A. Lydia Maria Child
    B. Sarah Grimké
    C. Catherine Beecher
    D. Susan B. Anthony

14. How did the abolitionist movement impact the women's movement?

Critical Thinking Questions

15. In what ways did the Second Great Awakening and transcendentalism reflect and react to the changes in antebellum American thought and culture?

16. What did the antebellum communal projects have in common? How did the ones most influenced by religion differ from those that had other influences?

17. In what ways do temperance, health reforms, and phrenology offer reflections on the changes in the United States before the Civil War? What needs did these reforms fill in the lives of antebellum Americans?

18. Of the various approaches to the problem of slavery, which one do you find to be the most effective and why?

19. In what ways were antebellum feminists radical? In what ways were they traditional?

Troubled Times: the Tumultuous 1850s

14

FIGURE 14.1 In *Southern Chivalry: Argument versus Club's* (1856), by John Magee, South Carolinian Preston Brooks attacks Massachusetts senator Charles Sumner after his speech denouncing "border ruffians" pouring into Kansas from Missouri. For southerners, defending slavery meant defending southern honor.

CHAPTER OUTLINE

14.1 The Compromise of 1850
14.2 The Kansas-Nebraska Act and the Republican Party
14.3 The Dred Scott Decision and Sectional Strife
14.4 John Brown and the Election of 1860

INTRODUCTION The heated sectional controversy between the North and the South reached new levels of intensity in the 1850s. Southerners and northerners grew ever more antagonistic as they debated the expansion of slavery in the West. The notorious confrontation between Representative Preston Brooks of South Carolina and Massachusetts senator Charles Sumner depicted in the image above (Figure 14.1), illustrates the contempt between extremists on both sides. The "Caning of Sumner" in May 1856 followed upon a speech given by Sumner two days earlier in which he condemned slavery in no uncertain terms, declaring: "[Admitting Kansas as a slave state] is the rape of a virgin territory, compelling it to the hateful embrace of slavery; and it may be clearly traced to a depraved longing for a new slave state, the hideous offspring of such a crime, in the hope of adding to the power of slavery in the national government." Sumner criticized proslavery legislators, particularly attacking a fellow senator and relative of Preston Brooks. Brooks responded by beating Sumner with a cane, a thrashing that southerners celebrated as a manly defense of gentlemanly honor and their way of life. The episode highlights the violent clash between pro- and antislavery factions in the 1850s, a conflict that would eventually lead to the traumatic unraveling of American democracy and civil war.

14.1 The Compromise of 1850

LEARNING OBJECTIVES

By the end of this section, you will be able to:
- Explain the contested issues that led to the Compromise of 1850
- Describe and analyze the reactions to the 1850 Fugitive Slave Act

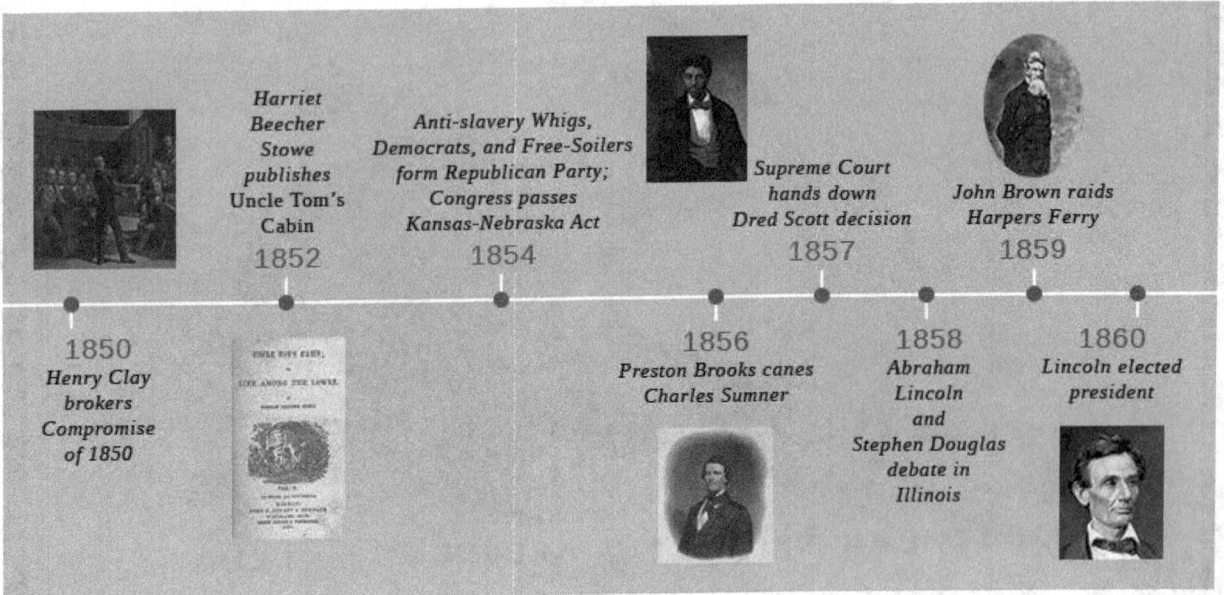

FIGURE 14.2

At the end of the Mexican-American War, the United States gained a large expanse of western territory known as the Mexican Cession. The disposition of this new territory was in question; would the new states be slave states or free-soil states? In the long run, the Mexican-American War achieved what abolitionism alone had failed to do: it mobilized many in the North against slavery.

Antislavery northerners clung to the idea expressed in the 1846 Wilmot Proviso: slavery would not expand into the areas taken, and later bought, from Mexico. Though the proviso remained a proposal and never became a law, it defined the sectional division. The Free-Soil Party, which formed at the conclusion of the Mexican-American War in 1848 and included many members of the failed Liberty Party, made this position the centerpiece of all its political activities, ensuring that the issue of slavery and its expansion remained at the front and center of American political debate. Supporters of the Wilmot Proviso and members of the new Free-Soil Party did not want to abolish slavery in the states where it already existed; rather, Free-Soil advocates demanded that the western territories be kept free of slavery for the benefit of White laborers who might settle there. They wanted to protect White workers from having to compete with slave labor in the West. (Abolitionists, in contrast, looked to destroy slavery everywhere in the United States.) Southern extremists, especially wealthy slaveholders, reacted with outrage at this effort to limit slavery's expansion. They argued for the right to bring their enslaved property west, and they vowed to leave the Union if necessary to protect their way of life—meaning the right to enslave people—and ensure that the American empire of slavery would continue to grow.

BROKERING THE COMPROMISE

The issue of what to do with the western territories added to the republic by the Mexican Cession consumed Congress in 1850. Other controversial matters, which had been simmering over time, complicated the problem further. Chief among these issues were the slave trade in the District of Columbia, which antislavery advocates hoped to end, and the fugitive slave laws, which southerners wanted to strengthen. The border between Texas and New Mexico remained contested because many Texans hoped to enlarge their state further, and, finally, the issue of California had not been resolved. California was the crown jewel of the Mexican Cession, and following the discovery of gold, it was flush with thousands of emigrants. By most estimates, however, it would be a free state, since the former Mexican ban on slavery still remained in force and slavery had not taken root in California. The map below (Figure 14.3) shows the disposition of land before the 1850 compromise.

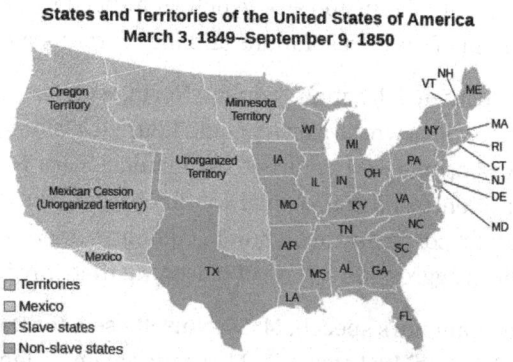

FIGURE 14.3 This map shows the states and territories of the United States as they were in 1849–1850. (credit "User:Golbez"/Wikimedia Commons)

The presidential election of 1848 did little to solve the problems resulting from the Mexican Cession. Both the Whigs and the Democrats attempted to avoid addressing the issue of slavery publicly as much as possible. The Democrats nominated Lewis Cass of Michigan, a supporter of the idea of popular sovereignty, or letting the people in the territories decide the issue of whether or not to permit slavery based on majority rule. The Whigs nominated General Zachary Taylor, a slaveholder from Louisiana, who had achieved national prominence as a military hero in the Mexican-American War. Taylor did not take a personal stand on any issue and remained silent throughout the campaign. The fledgling Free-Soil Party put forward former president Martin Van Buren as their candidate. The Free-Soil Party attracted northern Democrats who supported the Wilmot Proviso, northern Whigs who rejected Taylor because he was a slaveholder, former members of the Liberty Party, and other abolitionists.

Both the Whigs and the Democrats ran different campaigns in the North and South. In the North, all three parties attempted to win voters with promises of keeping the territories free of slavery, while in the South, Whigs and Democrats promised to protect slavery in the territories. For southern voters, the slaveholder Taylor appeared the natural choice. In the North, the Free-Soil Party took votes away from Whigs and Democrats and helped to ensure Taylor's election in 1848.

As president, Taylor sought to defuse the sectional controversy as much as possible, and, above all else, to preserve the Union. Although Taylor was born in Virginia before relocating to Kentucky and enslaved more than one hundred people by the late 1840s, he did not push for slavery's expansion into the Mexican Cession. However, the California Gold Rush made California's statehood into an issue demanding immediate attention. In 1849, after California residents adopted a state constitution prohibiting slavery, President Taylor called on Congress to admit California and New Mexico as free states, a move that infuriated southern defenders of slavery who argued for the right to bring their enslaved property wherever they chose. Taylor, who did not believe slavery could flourish in the arid lands of the Mexican Cession because the climate prohibited plantation-style farming, proposed that the Wilmot Proviso be applied to the entire area.

In Congress, Kentucky senator Henry Clay, a veteran of congressional conflicts, offered a series of resolutions addressing the list of issues related to slavery and its expansion. Clay's resolutions called for the admission of California as a free state; no restrictions on slavery in the rest of the Mexican Cession (a rejection of the Wilmot Proviso and the Free-Soil Party's position); a boundary between New Mexico and Texas that did not expand

Texas (an important matter, since Texas allowed slavery and a larger Texas meant more opportunities for the expansion of slavery); payment of outstanding Texas debts from the Lone Star Republic days; and the end of the slave trade (but not of slavery) in the nation's capital, coupled with a more robust federal fugitive slave law. Clay presented these proposals as an omnibus bill, that is, one that would be voted on its totality.

Clay's proposals ignited a spirited and angry debate that lasted for eight months. The resolution calling for California to be admitted as a free state aroused the wrath of the aged and deathly ill John C. Calhoun, the elder statesman for the proslavery position. Calhoun, too sick to deliver a speech, had his friend Virginia senator James Mason present his assessment of Clay's resolutions and the current state of sectional strife.

In Calhoun's eyes, blame for the stalemate fell squarely on the North, which stood in the way of southern and American prosperity by limiting the zones where slavery could flourish. Calhoun called for a vigorous federal law to ensure that escaped enslaved people were returned to their enslavers. He also proposed a constitutional amendment specifying a dual presidency—one office that would represent the South and another for the North—a suggestion that hinted at the possibility of disunion. Calhoun's argument portrayed an embattled South faced with continued northern aggression—a line of reasoning that only furthered the sectional divide.

Several days after Mason delivered Calhoun's speech, Massachusetts senator Daniel Webster countered Calhoun in his "Seventh of March" speech. Webster called for national unity, famously declaring that he spoke "not as a Massachusetts man, not as a Northern man, but as an American." Webster asked southerners to end threats of disunion and requested that the North stop antagonizing the South by harping on the Wilmot Proviso. Like Calhoun, Webster also called for a new federal law to ensure the return of escaped enslaved people.

Webster's efforts to compromise led many abolitionist sympathizers to roundly denounce him as a traitor. Whig senator William H. Seward, who aspired to be president, declared that slavery—which he characterized as incompatible with the assertion in the Declaration of Independence that "all men are created equal"—would one day be extinguished in the United States. Seward's speech, in which he invoked the idea of a higher moral law than the Constitution, secured his reputation in the Senate as an advocate of abolition.

The speeches made in Congress were published in the nation's newspapers, and the American public followed the debates with great interest, anxious to learn how the issues of the day, especially the potential advance of slavery, would be resolved. Colorful reports of wrangling in Congress further piqued public interest. Indeed, it was not uncommon for arguments to devolve into fistfights or worse. One of the most astonishing episodes of the debate occurred in April 1850, when a quarrel erupted between Missouri Democratic senator Thomas Hart Benton, who by the time of the debate had become a critic of slavery (despite being an enslaver), and Mississippi Democratic senator Henry S. Foote. When the burly Benton appeared ready to assault Foote, the Mississippi senator drew his pistol (Figure 14.4).

FIGURE 14.4 This 1850 print, *Scene in Uncle Sam's Senate*, depicts Mississippi senator Henry S. Foote taking aim at Missouri senator Thomas Hart Benton. In the print, Benton declares: "Get out of the way, and let the assassin fire! let the scoundrel use his weapon! I have no arm's! I did not come here to assassinate!" Foote responds, "I only

meant to defend myself!" (credit: Library of Congress)

President Taylor and Henry Clay, whose resolutions had begun the verbal fireworks in the Senate, had no patience for each other. Clay had long harbored ambitions for the White House, and, for his part, Taylor resented Clay and disapproved of his resolutions. With neither side willing to budge, the government stalled on how to resolve the disposition of the Mexican Cession and the other issues of slavery. The drama only increased when on July 4, 1850, President Taylor became gravely ill, reportedly after eating an excessive amount of fruit washed down with milk. He died five days later, and Vice President Millard Fillmore became president. Unlike his predecessor, who many believed would be opposed to a compromise, Fillmore worked with Congress to achieve a solution to the crisis of 1850.

In the end, Clay stepped down as leader of the compromise effort in frustration, and Illinois senator Stephen Douglas pushed five separate bills through Congress, collectively composing the Compromise of 1850. First, as advocated by the South, Congress passed the Fugitive Slave Act, a law that provided federal money—or "bounties"—to slave-catchers. Second, to balance this concession to the South, Congress admitted California as a free state, a move that cheered antislavery advocates and abolitionists in the North. Third, Congress settled the contested boundary between New Mexico and Texas by favoring New Mexico and not allowing for an enlarged Texas, another outcome pleasing to the North. In return, the federal government paid the debts Texas had incurred as an independent republic. Fourth, antislavery advocates welcomed Congress's ban on the slave trade in Washington, DC, although slavery continued to thrive in the nation's capital. Finally, on the thorny issue of whether slavery would expand into the territories, Congress avoided making a direct decision and instead relied on the principle of popular sovereignty. This put the onus on residents of the territories to decide for themselves whether to allow slavery. Popular sovereignty followed the logic of American democracy; majorities in each territory would decide the territory's laws. The compromise, however, further exposed the sectional divide as votes on the bills divided along strict regional lines.

Most Americans breathed a sigh of relief over the deal brokered in 1850, choosing to believe it had saved the Union. Rather than resolving divisions between the North and the South, however, the compromise stood as a truce in an otherwise white-hot sectional conflict. Tensions in the nation remained extremely high; indeed, southerners held several conventions after the compromise to discuss ways to protect the South. At these meetings, extremists who called for secession found themselves in the minority, since most southerners committed themselves to staying in the Union—but only if slavery remained in the states where it already existed, and if no effort was made to block its expansion into areas where citizens wanted it, thereby applying the idea of popular sovereignty (Figure 14.5).

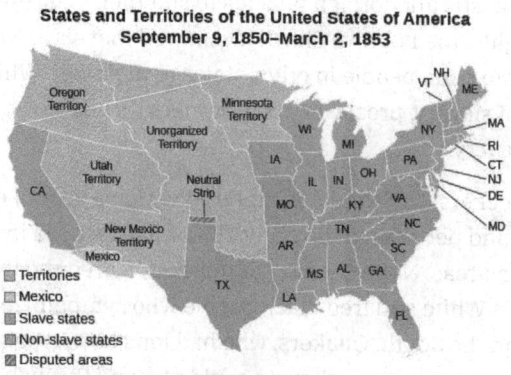

FIGURE 14.5 This map shows the states and territories of the United States as they were from 1850 to March 1853. (credit "User:Golbez"/Wikimedia Commons)

THE FUGITIVE SLAVE ACT AND ITS CONSEQUENCES

The hope that the Compromise of 1850 would resolve the sectional crisis proved short-lived when the Fugitive

Slave Act turned into a major source of conflict. The federal law imposed heavy fines and prison sentences on northerners and midwesterners who aided those who had escaped their captivity or refused to join posses to catch freedom-seekers. Many northerners felt the law forced them to act as slave-catchers against their will.

The law also established a new group of federal commissioners who would decide the fate of freedom-seekers brought before them. In some instances, slave-catchers even brought in free northern Black people, prompting abolitionist societies to step up their efforts to prevent kidnappings (Figure 14.6). The commissioners had a financial incentive to send recaptured enslaved and free Black people to the slaveholding South, since they received ten dollars for every African American sent to the South and only five if they decided the person who came before them was actually free. The commissioners used no juries, and the alleged runaways could not testify in their own defense.

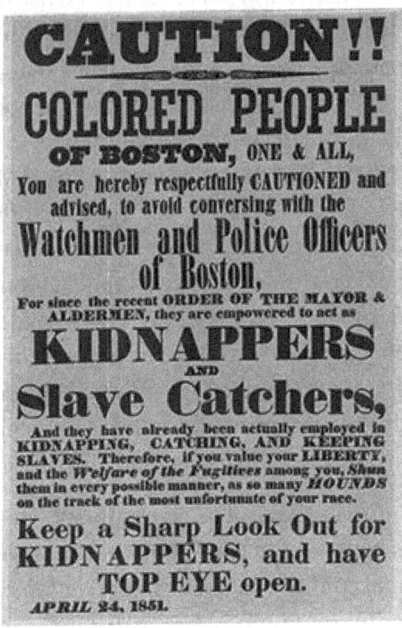

FIGURE 14.6 This 1851 poster, written by Boston abolitionist Theodore Parker, warned that any Black person, free or enslaved, risked kidnapping by slave-catchers.

The operation of the law further alarmed northerners and confirmed for many the existence of a "Slave Power"—that is, a minority of elite slaveholders who wielded a disproportionate amount of power over the federal government, shaping domestic and foreign policies to suit their interests. Despite southerners' repeated insistence on states' rights, the Fugitive Slave Act showed that slaveholders were willing to use the power of the federal government to bend people in other states to their will. While rejecting the use of federal power to restrict the expansion of slavery, proslavery southerners turned to the federal government to protect and promote the institution of slavery.

The actual number of freedom-seekers who were not captured within a year of escaping remained very low, perhaps no more than one thousand per year in the early 1850s. Most stayed in the South, hiding in plain sight among free Black people in urban areas. Nonetheless, southerners feared the influence of a vast **Underground Railroad**: the network of northern White and free Black people who sympathized with escapees and provided safe houses and safe passage from the South. Quakers, who had long been troubled by slavery, were especially active in this network. It is unclear how many enslaved people escaped through the Underground Railroad, but historians believe that between 50,000 and 100,000 used the network in their bids for freedom. Meanwhile, the 1850 Fugitive Slave Act greatly increased the perils of being captured. For many thousands of freedom-seekers, escaping the United States completely by going to southern Ontario, Canada, where slavery had been abolished, offered the best chance of a better life beyond the reach of slaveholders.

Harriet Tubman, one of the thousands of enslaved people who made their escape through the Underground

Railroad, distinguished herself for her efforts in helping other enslaved men and women escape. Born a slave in Maryland around 1822, Tubman, who suffered greatly under slavery but found solace in Christianity, made her escape in the late 1840s. She returned to the South more than a dozen times to lead other enslaved people, including her family and friends, along the Underground Railroad to freedom.

DEFINING AMERICAN

Harriet Tubman: An American Moses?

Harriet Tubman (Figure 14.7) was a legendary figure in her own time and beyond. An escaped enslaved person herself, she returned to the South thirteen times to help over three hundred other freedom-seekers through the Underground Railroad to liberty in the North. In 1869, printer William J. Moses published Sarah H. Bradford's *Scenes in the Life of Harriet Tubman*. Bradford was a writer and biographer who had known Tubman's family for years. The excerpt below is from the beginning of her book, which she updated in 1886 under the title *Harriet, the Moses of Her People*.

FIGURE 14.7 This full-length portrait of Harriet Tubman hangs in the National Portrait Gallery of the Smithsonian.

"It is proposed in this little book to give a plain and unvarnished account of some scenes and adventures in the life of a woman who, though one of earth's lowly ones, and of dark-hued skin, has shown an amount of heroism in her character rarely possessed by those of any station in life. Her name (we say it advisedly and without exaggeration) deserves to be handed down to posterity side by side with the names of Joan of Arc, Grace Darling, and Florence Nightingale; for not one of these women has shown more courage and power of endurance in facing danger and death to relieve human suffering, than has this woman in her heroic and successful endeavors to reach and save all whom she might of her oppressed and suffering race, and to pilot them from the land of Bondage to the promised land of Liberty. Well has she been called "Moses," for she has been a leader and deliverer unto hundreds of her people.
—Sarah H. Bradford, *Scenes in the Life of Harriet Tubman*"

How does Bradford characterize Tubman? What language does Bradford use to tie religion into the fight for freedom?

The Fugitive Slave Act provoked widespread reactions in the North. Some abolitionists, such as Frederick Douglass, believed that standing up against the law necessitated violence. In Boston and elsewhere, abolitionists tried to protect fugitives from federal authorities. One case involved Anthony Burns, who had escaped slavery in Virginia in 1853 and made his way to Boston (Figure 14.8). When federal officials arrested Burns in 1854, abolitionists staged a series of mass demonstrations and a confrontation at the courthouse. Despite their best efforts, however, Burns was returned to Virginia when President Franklin Pierce supported the Fugitive Slave Act with federal troops. Boston abolitionists eventually bought Burns's freedom. For many northerners, however, the Burns incident, combined with Pierce's response, only amplified their sense of a conspiracy of southern power.

FIGURE 14.8 *Anthony Burns*, drawn ca. 1855 by an artist identified only as "Barry," shows a portrait of the freedom-seeker surrounded by scenes from his life, including his escape from Virginia, his arrest in Boston, and his address to the court.

The most consequential reaction against the Fugitive Slave Act came in the form of a novel, *Uncle Tom's Cabin*. In it, author Harriet Beecher Stowe, born in Connecticut, made use of enslaved people's stories she had heard firsthand after marrying and moving to Ohio, then on the country's western frontier. Her novel first appeared as a series of stories in a Free-Soil newspaper, the *National Era*, in 1851 and was published as a book the following year. Stowe told the tale of enslaved people who were sold by their Kentucky enslaver. While Uncle Tom is indeed sold down the river, young Eliza escapes with her baby (Figure 14.9). The story highlighted the idea that slavery was a sin because it destroyed families, ripping children from their parents and husbands and wives from one another. Stowe also emphasized the ways in which slavery corrupted White citizens. The cruelty of some of the novel's White slaveholders (who genuinely believe that enslaved people don't feel things the way that White people do) and the brutality of the slave dealer Simon Legree, who beats enslaved people and sexually exploits an enslaved woman, demonstrate the dehumanizing effect of the institution even on those who benefit from it.

FIGURE 14.9 This drawing from *Uncle Tom's Cabin*, captioned "Eliza comes to tell Uncle Tom that he is sold, and that she is running away to save her child," illustrates the ways in which Harriet Beecher Stowe's antislavery novel bolstered abolitionists' arguments against slavery.

Stowe's novel proved a runaway bestseller and was the most-read novel of the nineteenth century, inspiring multiple theatrical productions and musical compositions. It was translated into sixty languages and remains in print to this day. Its message about the evils of slavery helped convince many northerners of the righteousness of the cause of abolition. The novel also demonstrated the power of women to shape public opinion. Stowe and other American women believed they had a moral obligation to mold the conscience of the United States, even though they could not vote (Figure 14.10).

FIGURE 14.10 This photograph shows Harriet Beecher Stowe, the author of *Uncle Tom's Cabin*, in 1852. Stowe's work was an inspiration not only to abolitionists, but also to those who believed that women could play a significant role in upholding the nation's morality and shaping public opinion.

CLICK AND EXPLORE

Visit the Documenting the American South (http://openstax.org/l/15LeviCoffin) collection on the University of North Carolina at Chapel Hill website to read the memoirs of Levi Coffin, a prominent Quaker abolitionist who was known as the "president" of the Underground Railroad for his active role in helping enslaved people to freedom. The memoirs include the story of Eliza Harris, which inspired Harriet Beecher Stowe's famous character.

The backlash against the Fugitive Slave Act, fueled by *Uncle Tom's Cabin* and well-publicized cases like that of

Anthony Burns, also found expression in personal liberty laws passed by eight northern state legislatures. These laws emphasized that the state would provide legal protection to any arrested freedom seekers (including the right to trial by jury). The personal liberty laws stood as a clear-cut example of the North's use of states' rights in opposition to federal power while providing further evidence to southerners that northerners had no respect for the Fugitive Slave Act or slaveholders' property rights.

CLICK AND EXPLORE

Go to an archived page from the Michigan Department of Natural Resources (http://openstax.org/l/15MIPFreedom) site to read the original text of Michigan's 1855 personal liberty laws. How do these laws refute the provisions of the federal Fugitive Slave Act of 1850?

14.2 The Kansas-Nebraska Act and the Republican Party

LEARNING OBJECTIVES

By the end of this section, you will be able to:
- Explain the political ramifications of the Kansas-Nebraska Act
- Describe the founding of the Republican Party

In the early 1850s, the United States' sectional crisis had abated somewhat, cooled by the Compromise of 1850 and the nation's general prosperity. In 1852, voters went to the polls in a presidential contest between Whig candidate Winfield Scott and Democratic candidate Franklin Pierce. Both men endorsed the Compromise of 1850. Though it was considered unseemly to hit the campaign trail, Scott did so—much to the benefit of Pierce, as Scott's speeches focused on forty-year-old battles during the War of 1812 and the weather. In New York, Scott, known as "Old Fuss and Feathers," talked about a thunderstorm that did not occur and greatly confused the crowd. In Ohio, a cannon firing to herald Scott's arrival killed a spectator.

Pierce was a supporter of the "Young America" movement of the Democratic Party, which enthusiastically anticipated extending democracy around the world and annexing additional territory for the United States. Pierce did not take a stance on the slavery issue. Helped by Scott's blunders and the fact that he had played no role in the bruising political battles of the past five years, Pierce won the election. The brief period of tranquility between the North and South did not last long, however; it came to an end in 1854 with the passage of the Kansas-Nebraska Act. This act led to the formation of a new political party, the Republican Party, that committed itself to ending the further expansion of slavery.

THE KANSAS-NEBRASKA ACT

The relative calm over the sectional issue was broken in 1854 over the issue of slavery in the territory of Kansas. Pressure had been building among northerners to organize the territory west of Missouri and Iowa, which had been admitted to the Union as a free state in 1846. This pressure came primarily from northern farmers, who wanted the federal government to survey the land and put it up for sale. Promoters of a transcontinental railroad were also pushing for this westward expansion.

Southerners, however, had long opposed the Wilmot Proviso's stipulation that slavery should not expand into the West. By the 1850s, many in the South were also growing resentful of the Missouri Compromise of 1820, which established the 36° 30' parallel as the geographical boundary of slavery on the north-south axis. Proslavery southerners now contended that popular sovereignty should apply to all territories, not just Utah and New Mexico. They argued for the right to bring their enslaved property wherever they chose.

Attitudes toward slavery in the 1850s were represented by a variety of regional factions. For three decades, the abolitionists remained a minority, but they had a significant effect on American society by bringing the evils of slavery into the public consciousness. In 1840, the Liberty Party was the first political organization to campaign for abolition. This group sought to work within the existing political system, a strategy Garrison and others rejected. Meanwhile, the Free-Soil Party committed itself to ensuring that White laborers would find work in newly acquired territories and not have to compete with unpaid enslaved people. By the 1850s, some abolitionists advocated the use of violence against slaveholders.

It is important to note that, even among those who opposed the expansion of slavery in the West, very different attitudes toward slavery existed. Some antislavery northerners wanted the West to be the best country for poor White people to go and seek opportunity. They did not want White workers to have to compete with slave labor, a contest that they believed demeaned White labor. Radical abolitionists, in contrast, envisioned the end of all slavery, and a society of equality between Black and White people. Others opposed slavery in principle, but believed that the best approach was colonization; that is, settling freed enslaved people in a colony in Africa.

The growing political movement to address the issue of slavery stiffened the resolve of southern slaveholders to defend themselves and their society at all costs. Prohibiting slavery's expansion, they argued, ran counter to basic American property rights. As abolitionists fanned the flames of antislavery sentiment, southerners solidified their defense of their enormous investment in human chattel. Across the country, people of all political stripes worried that the nation's arguments would cause irreparable rifts in the country (Figure 14.11).

FIGURE 14.11 In this 1850 political cartoon, the artist takes aim at abolitionists, the Free-Soil Party, Southern states' rights activists, and others he believes risk the health of the Union.

As these different factions were agitating for the settlement of Kansas and Nebraska, leaders of the Democratic Party in 1853 and 1854 sought to bind their party together in the aftermath of intraparty fights over the distribution of patronage jobs. Illinois Democratic senator Stephen Douglas believed he had found a solution—the Kansas-Nebraska bill—that would promote party unity and also satisfy his colleagues from the South, who detested the Missouri Compromise line. In January 1854, Douglas introduced the bill (Figure 14.12). The act created two territories: Kansas, directly west of Missouri; and Nebraska, west of Iowa. The act also applied the principle of popular sovereignty, dictating that the people of these territories would decide for themselves whether to adopt slavery. In a concession crucial to many southerners, the proposed bill would also repeal the 36° 30' line from the Missouri Compromise. Douglas hoped his bill would increase his political capital and provide a step forward on his quest for the presidency. Douglas also wanted the territory organized in hopes of placing the eastern terminus of a transcontinental railroad in Chicago, rather than St. Louis or New Orleans.

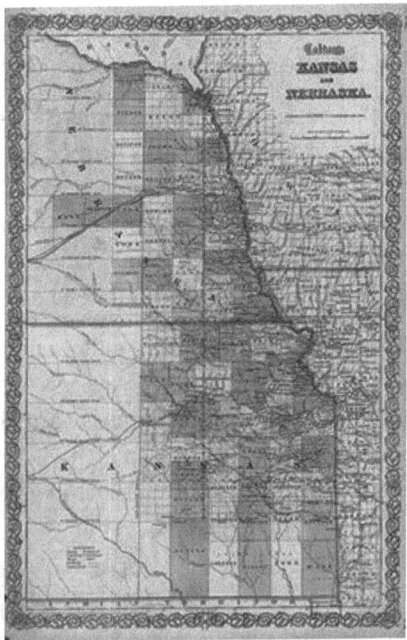

FIGURE 14.12 This 1855 map shows the new territories of Kansas and Nebraska, complete with proposed routes of the transcontinental railroad.

After heated debates, Congress narrowly passed the Kansas-Nebraska Act. (In the House of Representatives, the bill passed by a mere three votes: 113 to 110.) This move had major political consequences. The Democrats divided along sectional lines as a result of the bill, and the Whig party, in decline in the early 1850s, found its political power slipping further. Most important, the Kansas-Nebraska Act gave rise to the **Republican Party**, a new political party that attracted northern Whigs, Democrats who shunned the Kansas-Nebraska Act, members of the Free-Soil Party, and assorted abolitionists. Indeed, with the formation of the Republican Party, the Free-Soil Party ceased to exist.

The new Republican Party pledged itself to preventing the spread of slavery into the territories and railed against the Slave Power, infuriating the South. As a result, the party became a solidly northern political organization. As never before, the U.S. political system was polarized along sectional fault lines.

BLEEDING KANSAS

In 1855 and 1856, pro- and antislavery activists flooded Kansas with the intention of influencing the popular-sovereignty rule of the territories. Proslavery Missourians who crossed the border to vote in Kansas became known as **border ruffians**; these gained the advantage by winning the territorial elections, most likely through voter fraud and illegal vote counting. (By some estimates, up to 60 percent of the votes cast in Kansas were fraudulent.) Once in power, the proslavery legislature, meeting at Lecompton, Kansas, drafted a proslavery constitution known as the Lecompton Constitution. It was supported by President Buchanan, but opposed by Democratic Senator Stephen A. Douglas of Illinois.

DEFINING AMERICAN

The Lecompton Constitution

Kansas was home to no fewer than four state constitutions in its early years. Its first constitution, the Topeka Constitution, would have made Kansas a free-soil state. A proslavery legislature, however, created the 1857 Lecompton Constitution to enshrine the institution of slavery in the new Kansas-Nebraska territories. In January 1858, Kansas voters defeated the proposed Lecompton Constitution, excerpted below, with an overwhelming margin of 10,226 to 138.

"ARTICLE VII.—SLAVERY

SECTION 1. The right of property is before and higher than any constitutional sanction, and the right of the owner of a slave to such slave and its increase is the same and as inviolable as the right of the owner of any property whatever.

SEC. 2. The Legislature shall have no power to pass laws for the emancipation of slaves without the consent of the owners, or without paying the owners previous to their emancipation a full equivalent in money for the slaves so emancipated. They shall have no power to prevent immigrants to the State from bringing with them such persons as are deemed slaves by the laws of any one of the United States or Territories, so long as any person of the same age or description shall be continued in slavery by the laws of this State: Provided, That such person or slave be the bona fide property of such immigrants."

How are "slaves" defined in the 1857 Kansas constitution? How does this constitution safeguard the rights of slaveholders?

The majority in Kansas, however, were Free-Soilers who seethed at the border ruffians' co-opting of the democratic process (Figure 14.13). Many had come from New England to ensure a numerical advantage over the border ruffians. The New England Emigrant Aid Society, a northern antislavery group, helped fund these efforts to halt the expansion of slavery into Kansas and beyond.

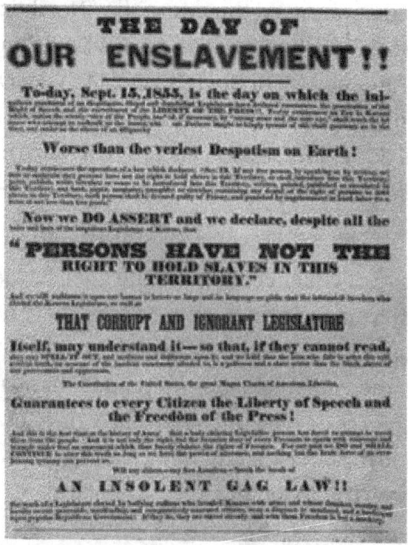

FIGURE 14.13 This full-page editorial ran in the Free-Soiler *Kansas Tribune* on September 15, 1855, the day Kansas' Act to Punish Offences against Slave Property of 1855 went into effect. This law made it punishable by death to aid or abet a fugitive slave, and it called for punishment of no less than two years for anyone who might: "print, publish, write, circulate, or cause to be introduced into this Territory . . . [any materials] . . . containing any denial of the right of persons to hold slaves in this Territory."

CLICK AND EXPLORE

Go to the Kansas Historical Society's Kansapedia (http://openstax.org/l/15KSConst) to read the four different state constitutions that Kansas had during its early years as a United States Territory. What can you deduce about the authors of each constitution?

In 1856, clashes between antislavery Free-Soilers and border ruffians came to a head in Lawrence, Kansas. The town had been founded by the New England Emigrant Aid Society, which funded antislavery settlement in the territory and were determined that Kansas should be a free-soil state. Proslavery emigrants from Missouri were equally determined that no "abolitionist tyrants" or "negro thieves" would control the territory. In the spring of 1856, several of Lawrence's leading antislavery citizens were indicted for treason, and federal marshal Israel Donaldson called for a posse to help make arrests. He did not have trouble finding volunteers from Missouri. When the posse, which included Douglas County sheriff Samuel Jones, arrived outside Lawrence, the antislavery town's "committee of safety" agreed on a policy of nonresistance. Most of those who were indicted fled. Donaldson arrested two men without incident and dismissed the posse.

However, Jones, who had been shot during an earlier confrontation in the town, did not leave. On May 21, falsely claiming that he had a court order to do so, Jones took command of the posse and rode into town armed with rifles, revolvers, cutlasses and bowie knives. At the head of the procession, two flags flew: an American flag and a flag with a crouching tiger. Other banners followed, bearing the words "Southern rights" and "The Superiority of the White Race." In the rear were five artillery pieces, which were dragged to the center of town. The posse smashed the presses of the two newspapers, *Herald of Freedom* and the *Kansas Free State*, and burned down the deserted Free State Hotel (Figure 14.14). When the posse finally left, Lawrence residents found themselves unharmed but terrified.

The next morning, a man named John Brown and his sons, who were on their way to provide Lawrence with reinforcements, heard the news of the attack. Brown, a strict, God-fearing Calvinist and staunch abolitionist, once remarked that "God had raised him up on purpose to break the jaws of the wicked." Disappointed that the citizens of Lawrence did not resist the "slave hounds" of Missouri, Brown opted not to go to Lawrence, but to the homes of proslavery settlers near Pottawatomie Creek in Kansas. The group of seven, including Brown's four sons, arrived on May 24, 1856, and announced they were the "Northern Army" that had come to serve justice. They burst into the cabin of proslavery Tennessean James Doyle and marched him and two of his sons off, sparing the youngest at the desperate request of Doyle's wife, Mahala. One hundred yards down the road, Owen and Salmon Brown hacked their captives to death with broadswords and John Brown shot a bullet into Doyle's forehead. Before the night was done, the Browns visited two more cabins and brutally executed two other proslavery settlers. None of those executed enslaved any people or had had anything to do with the raid on Lawrence.

Brown's actions precipitated a new wave of violence. All told, the guerilla warfare between proslavery "border ruffians" and antislavery forces, which would continue and even escalate during the Civil War, resulted in over 150 deaths and significant property loss. The events in Kansas served as an extreme reply to Douglas's proposition of popular sovereignty. As the violent clashes increased, Kansas became known as "**Bleeding Kansas**." Antislavery advocates' use of force carved out a new direction for some who opposed slavery. Distancing themselves from William Lloyd Garrison and other pacifists, Brown and fellow abolitionists believed the time had come to fight slavery with violence.

FIGURE 14.14 This undated image shows the aftermath of the sacking of Lawrence, Kansas, by border ruffians. Shown are the ruins of the Free State Hotel.

The violent hostilities associated with Bleeding Kansas were not limited to Kansas itself. It was the controversy over Kansas that prompted the caning of Charles Sumner, introduced at the beginning of this chapter with the political cartoon *Southern Chivalry: Argument versus Club's* (Figure 14.1). Note the title of the cartoon; it lampoons the southern ideal of chivalry, the code of behavior that Preston Brooks believed he was following in his attack on Sumner. In Sumner's "Crime against Kansas" speech he went much further than politics, filling his verbal attack with allusions to sexuality by singling out fellow senator Andrew Butler from South Carolina, a zealous supporter of slavery and Brooks's uncle. Sumner insulted Butler by comparing slavery to prostitution, declaring, "Of course he [Butler] has chosen a mistress to whom he has made his vows, and who, though ugly to others, is always lovely to him; though polluted in the sight of the world, is chaste in his sight. I mean the harlot Slavery." Because Butler was aged, it was his nephew, Brooks, who sought satisfaction for Sumner's attack on his family and southern honor. Brooks did not challenge Sumner to a duel; by choosing to beat him with a cane instead, he made it clear that he did not consider Sumner a gentleman. Many in the South rejoiced over Brooks's defense of slavery, southern society, and family honor, sending him hundreds of canes to replace the one he had broken assaulting Sumner. The attack by Brooks left Sumner incapacitated physically and mentally for a long period of time. Despite his injuries, the people of Massachusetts reelected him.

THE PRESIDENTIAL ELECTION OF 1856

The electoral contest in 1856 took place in a transformed political landscape. A third political party appeared: the anti-immigrant **American Party**, a formerly secretive organization with the nickname "the Know-Nothing Party" because its members denied knowing anything about it. By 1856, the American or Know-Nothing Party had evolved into a national force committed to halting further immigration. Its members were especially opposed to the immigration of Irish Catholics, whose loyalty to the Pope, they believed, precluded their loyalty to the United States. On the West Coast, they opposed the entry of immigrant laborers from China, who were thought to be too foreign to ever assimilate into a White America.

The election also featured the new Republican Party, which offered John C. Fremont as its candidate. Republicans accused the Democrats of trying to nationalize slavery through the use of popular sovereignty in the West, a view captured in the 1856 political cartoon *Forcing Slavery Down the Throat of a Free Soiler* (Figure 14.15). The cartoon features the image of a Free-Soiler settler tied to the Democratic Party platform while Senator Douglas (author of the Kansas-Nebraska Act) and President Pierce force an enslaved person down his throat. Note that the enslaved person cries out "Murder!!! Help—neighbors help, O my poor Wife and Children," a reference to the abolitionists' argument that slavery destroyed families.

FIGURE 14.15 This 1856 political cartoon, *Forcing Slavery Down the Throat of a Free Soiler*, by John Magee, shows Republican resentment of the Democratic platform—here represented as an actual platform—of expanding slavery into new western territories.

The Democrats offered James Buchanan as their candidate. Buchanan did not take a stand on either side of the issue of slavery; rather, he attempted to please both sides. His qualification, in the minds of many, was that he was out of the country when the Kansas-Nebraska Act was passed. In the above political cartoon, Buchanan, along with Democratic senator Lewis Cass, holds down the Free-Soil advocate. Buchanan won the election, but Fremont garnered more than 33 percent of the popular vote, an impressive return for a new party. The Whigs had ceased to exist and had been replaced by the Republican Party. Know-Nothings also transferred their allegiance to the Republicans because the new party also took an anti-immigrant stance, a move that further boosted the new party's standing. (The Democrats courted the Catholic immigrant vote.) The Republican Party was a thoroughly northern party; no southern delegate voted for Fremont.

14.3 The Dred Scott Decision and Sectional Strife

LEARNING OBJECTIVES

By the end of this section, you will be able to:
- Explain the importance of the Supreme Court's Dred Scott ruling
- Discuss the principles of the Republican Party as expressed by Abraham Lincoln in 1858

As president, Buchanan confronted a difficult and volatile situation. The nation needed a strong personality to lead it, and Buchanan did not possess this trait. The violence in Kansas demonstrated that applying popular sovereignty—the democratic principle of majority rule—to the territory offered no solution to the national battle over slavery. A decision by the Supreme Court in 1857, which concerned the enslaved Dred Scott, only deepened the crisis.

DRED SCOTT

In 1857, several months after President Buchanan took the oath of office, the Supreme Court ruled in ***Dred Scott v. Sandford***. Dred Scott (Figure 14.16), born with slave status in Virginia in 1795, had been one of the thousands forced to relocate as a result of the massive internal slave trade and taken to Missouri, where slavery had been adopted as part of the Missouri Compromise. In 1820, Scott's owner took him first to Illinois and then to the Wisconsin territory. However, both of those regions were part of the Northwest Territory, where the 1787 Northwest Ordinance had prohibited slavery. When Scott returned to Missouri, he attempted to buy his freedom. After his owner refused, he sought relief in the state courts, arguing that by virtue of having lived in areas where slavery was banned, he should be free.

FIGURE 14.16 This 1888 portrait by Louis Schultze shows Dred Scott, who fought for his freedom through the American court system.

In a complicated set of legal decisions, a jury found that Scott, along with his wife and two children, were free. However, on appeal from Scott's owner, the state Superior Court reversed the decision, and the Scotts remained enslaved. Scott then became the property of John Sanford (his name was misspelled as "Sandford" in later court documents), who lived in New York. He continued his legal battle, and because the issue involved Missouri and New York, the case fell under the jurisdiction of the federal court. In 1854, Scott lost in federal court and appealed to the United States Supreme Court.

In 1857, the Supreme Court—led by Chief Justice Roger Taney, a former slaveholder who had freed his those he had enslaved—handed down its decision. On the question of whether Scott was free, the Supreme Court decided he remained enslaved. The court then went beyond the specific issue of Scott's freedom to make a sweeping and momentous judgment about the status of Black people, both free and enslaved. Per the court, Black people could never be citizens of the United States. Further, the court ruled that Congress had no authority to stop or limit the spread of slavery into American territories. This proslavery ruling explicitly made the Missouri Compromise unconstitutional; implicitly, it made Douglas's popular sovereignty unconstitutional.

DEFINING AMERICAN

Roger Taney on *Dred Scott v. Sandford*

In 1857, the United States Supreme Court ended years of legal battles when it ruled that Dred Scott, an enslaved person who had resided in several free states, should remain enslaved. The decision, written by Chief Justice Roger Taney, also stated that Black people could not be citizens and that Congress had no power to limit the spread of slavery. The excerpt below is from Taney's decision.

"A free negro of the African race, whose ancestors were brought to this country and sold as slaves, is not a "citizen" within the meaning of the Constitution of the United States. . . .
The only two clauses in the Constitution which point to this race treat them as persons whom it was morally lawfully to deal in as articles of property and to hold as slaves. . . .
Every citizen has a right to take with him into the Territory any article of property which the Constitution of the United States recognises as property. . . .
The Constitution of the United States recognises slaves as property, and pledges the Federal Government to protect it. And Congress cannot exercise any more authority over property of that description than it may constitutionally exercise over property of any other kind. . . .
Prohibiting a citizen of the United States from taking with him his slaves when he removes to the Territory . . . is an exercise of authority over private property which is not warranted by the Constitution, and the removal of the plaintiff [Dred Scott] by his owner to that Territory gave him no title to freedom."

How did the Supreme Court define Dred Scott? How did the court interpret the Constitution on this score?

The Dred Scott decision infuriated Republicans by rendering their goal—to prevent slavery's spread into the territories—unconstitutional. To Republicans, the decision offered further proof of the reach of the South's Slave Power, which now apparently extended even to the Supreme Court. The decision also complicated life for northern Democrats, especially Stephen Douglas, who could no longer sell popular sovereignty as a symbolic concession to southerners from northern voters. Few northerners favored slavery's expansion westward.

THE LINCOLN-DOUGLAS DEBATES

The turmoil in Kansas, combined with the furor over the Dred Scott decision, provided the background for the 1858 senatorial contest in Illinois between Democratic senator Stephen Douglas and Republican hopeful Abraham Lincoln (Figure 14.17). Lincoln and Douglas engaged in seven debates before huge crowds that met to hear the two men argue the central issue of slavery and its expansion. Newspapers throughout the United States published their speeches. Whereas Douglas already enjoyed national recognition, Lincoln remained largely unknown before the debates. These appearances provided an opportunity for him to raise his profile with both northerners and southerners.

(a) (b)

FIGURE 14.17 In 1858, Abraham Lincoln (a) debated Stephen Douglas (b) seven times in the Illinois race for the U.S. Senate. Although Douglas won the seat, the debates propelled Lincoln into the national political spotlight.

Douglas portrayed the Republican Party as an abolitionist effort—one that aimed to bring about **miscegenation**, or race-mixing through sexual relations or marriage. The "Black Republicans," Douglas declared, posed a dangerous threat to the Constitution. Indeed, because Lincoln declared the nation could not survive if the slave state–free state division continued, Douglas claimed the Republicans aimed to destroy what the founders had created.

For his part, Lincoln said: "A house divided against itself cannot stand. I believe this government cannot endure permanently half Slave and half Free. I do not expect the Union to be dissolved—I do not expect the house to fall—but I do expect it will cease to be divided. It will become all one thing, or all the other. Either the opponents of slavery will arrest the further spread of it, and place it where the public mind shall rest in the belief that it is in the course of ultimate extinction: or its advocates will push it forward till it shall became alike lawful in all the States—old as well as new, North as well as South." Lincoln interpreted the Dred Scott decision and the Kansas-Nebraska Act as efforts to nationalize slavery: that is, to make it legal everywhere from New England to the Midwest and beyond.

DEFINING AMERICAN

The Lincoln-Douglas Debates

On August 21, 1858, Abraham Lincoln and Stephen Douglas met in Ottawa, Illinois, for the first of seven debates. People streamed into Ottawa from neighboring counties and from as far away as Chicago. Reporting on the event was strictly partisan, with each of the candidates' supporters claiming victory for their candidate. In this excerpt, Lincoln addresses the issues of equality between Black and White people.

"[A]nything that argues me into his idea of perfect social and political equality with the negro, is but a specious and fantastic arrangement of words, . . . I have no purpose, directly or indirectly, to interfere with the institution of slavery in the States where it exists. I believe I have no lawful right to do so, and I have no inclination to do so. I have no purpose to introduce political and social equality between the white and the black races. There is a physical difference between the two, which, in my judgment, will probably forever forbid their living together upon the footing of perfect equality, . . . I, as well as Judge Douglas, am in favor of the race to which I belong having the superior position. . . . [N]otwithstanding all this, there is no reason in the world why the negro is not entitled to all the natural rights enumerated in the Declaration of Independence, the right to life, liberty, and the pursuit of happiness. I hold that he is as much entitled to these as the White man. . . . [I]n the right to eat the bread, without the leave of anybody else, which his own hand earns, he is my equal and the equal of Judge Douglas, and the equal of every living man.

—Lincoln's speech on August 21, 1858, in Ottawa, Illinois"

How would you characterize Lincoln's position on equality between Black and White people? What types of equality exist, according to Lincoln?

CLICK AND EXPLORE

Go to the Lincoln Home National Historic Site (http://openstax.org/l/15LincDoug) on the National Park Service's website to read excerpts from and full texts of the debates. Then, visit The Lincoln/Douglas Debates of 1858 (http://openstax.org/l/15LincDoug2) on the Northern Illinois University website to read different newspaper accounts of the debates. Do you see any major differences in the way the newspapers reported the debates? How does the commentary vary, and why?

During the debates, Lincoln demanded that Douglas explain whether or not he believed that the 1857 Supreme Court decision in the Dred Scott case trumped the right of a majority to prevent the expansion of slavery under the principle of popular sovereignty. Douglas responded to Lincoln during the second debate at Freeport, Illinois. In what became known as the **Freeport Doctrine**, Douglas adamantly upheld popular sovereignty, declaring: "It matters not what way the Supreme Court may hereafter decide as to the abstract question whether slavery may or may not go into a territory under the Constitution, the people have the lawful means to introduce it or exclude it as they please." The Freeport Doctrine antagonized southerners who supported slavery, and caused a major rift in the Democratic Party. The doctrine did help Douglas in Illinois, however, where most voters opposed the further expansion of slavery. The Illinois legislature selected Douglas over Lincoln for the senate, but the debates had the effect of launching Lincoln into the national spotlight. Lincoln had argued that slavery was morally wrong, even as he accepted the racism inherent in slavery. He warned that Douglas and the Democrats would nationalize slavery through the policy of popular sovereignty. Though Douglas had survived the senate election challenge from Lincoln, his Freeport Doctrine damaged the political support he needed from the Southern Democrats. This helped him to lose the following presidential election, undermining the Democratic Party as a national force.

14.4 John Brown and the Election of 1860

LEARNING OBJECTIVES
By the end of this section, you will be able to:
- Describe John Brown's raid on Harpers Ferry and its results
- Analyze the results of the election of 1860

Events in the late 1850s did nothing to quell the country's sectional unrest, and compromise on the issue of slavery appeared impossible. Lincoln's 1858 speeches during his debates with Douglas made the Republican Party's position well known; Republicans opposed the extension of slavery and believed a Slave Power conspiracy sought to nationalize the institution. They quickly gained political momentum and took control of the House of Representatives in 1858. Southern leaders were divided on how to respond to Republican success. Southern extremists, known as **"Fire-Eaters,"** openly called for secession. Others, like Mississippi senator Jefferson Davis, put forward a more moderate approach by demanding constitutional protection of slavery.

JOHN BROWN

In October 1859, the radical abolitionist John Brown and eighteen armed men, both Black and White, attacked the federal arsenal in **Harpers Ferry**, Virginia. They hoped to capture the weapons there and distribute them among enslaved people to begin a massive uprising that would bring an end to slavery. Brown had already demonstrated during the 1856 Pottawatomie attack in Kansas that he had no patience for the nonviolent approach preached by pacifist abolitionists like William Lloyd Garrison. Born in Connecticut in 1800, Brown

(Figure 14.18) spent much of his life in the North, moving from Ohio to Pennsylvania and then upstate New York as his various business ventures failed. To him, slavery appeared an unacceptable evil that must be purged from the land, and like his Puritan forebears, he believed in using the sword to defeat the ungodly.

FIGURE 14.18 John Brown, shown here in a photograph from 1859, was a radical abolitionist who advocated the violent overthrow of slavery.

Brown had gone to Kansas in the 1850s in an effort to stop slavery, and there, he had perpetrated the killings at Pottawatomie. He told other abolitionists of his plan to take Harpers Ferry Armory and initiate a massive slave uprising. Some abolitionists provided financial support, while others, including Frederick Douglass, found the plot suicidal and refused to join. On October 16, 1859, Brown's force easily took control of the federal armory, which was unguarded (Figure 14.19). However, his vision of a mass uprising failed completely. Very few enslaved people lived in the area to rally to Brown's side, and the group found themselves holed up in the armory's engine house with townspeople taking shots at them. Federal troops, commanded by Colonel Robert E. Lee, soon captured Brown and his followers. On December 2, Brown was hanged by the state of Virginia for treason.

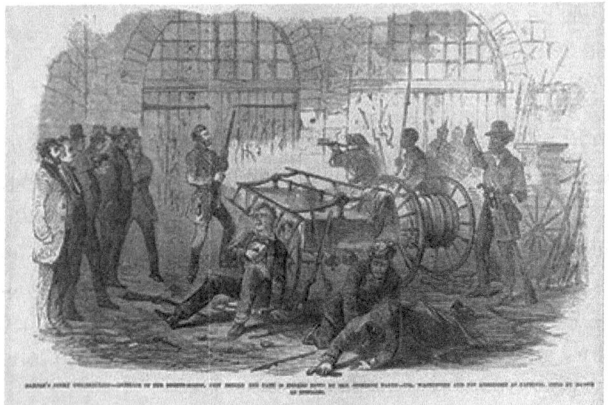

FIGURE 14.19 John Brown's raid on Harpers Ferry represented the radical abolitionist's attempt to start a revolt that would ultimately end slavery. This 1859 illustration, captioned "Harper's Ferry insurrection—Interior of the Engine-House, just before the gate is broken down by the storming party—Col. Washington and his associates as captives, held by Brown as hostages," is from *Frank Leslie's Illustrated Magazine*. Do you think this image represents a southern or northern version of the raid? How are the characters in the scene depicted?

CLICK AND EXPLORE

Visit the Avalon Project (http://openstax.org/l/15JohnBrown) on Yale Law School's website to read the impassioned speech that Henry David Thoreau delivered on October 30, 1859, arguing against the execution of John Brown. How does Thoreau characterize Brown? What does he ask of his fellow citizens?

John Brown's raid on Harpers Ferry generated intense reactions in both the South and the North. Southerners grew especially apprehensive of the possibility of other violent plots. They viewed Brown as a terrorist bent on destroying their civilization, and support for secession grew. Their anxiety led several southern states to pass laws designed to prevent rebellions by the enslaved. It seemed that the worst fears of the South had come true: A hostile majority would stop at nothing to destroy slavery. Was it possible, one resident of Maryland asked, to "live under a government, a majority of whose subjects or citizens regard John Brown as a martyr and Christian hero?" Many antislavery northerners did in fact consider Brown a martyr to the cause, and those who viewed slavery as a sin saw easy comparisons between him and Jesus Christ.

THE ELECTION OF 1860

The election of 1860 threatened American democracy when the elevation of Abraham Lincoln to the presidency inspired secessionists in the South to withdraw their states from the Union.

Lincoln's election owed much to the disarray in the Democratic Party. The Dred Scott decision and the Freeport Doctrine had opened up huge sectional divisions among Democrats. Though Brown did not intend it, his raid had furthered the split between northern and southern Democrats. Fire-Eaters vowed to prevent a northern Democrat, especially Illinois's Stephen Douglas, from becoming their presidential candidate. These proslavery zealots insisted on a southern Democrat.

The Democratic nominating convention met in April 1860 in Charleston, South Carolina. However, it broke up after northern Democrats, who made up a majority of delegates, rejected Jefferson Davis's efforts to protect slavery in the territories. These northern Democratic delegates knew that supporting Davis on this issue would be very unpopular among the people in their states. A second conference, held in Baltimore, further illustrated the divide within the Democratic Party. Northern Democrats nominated Stephen Douglas, while southern Democrats, who met separately, put forward Vice President John Breckinridge from Kentucky. The Democratic Party had fractured into two competing sectional factions.

By offering two candidates for president, the Democrats gave the Republicans an enormous advantage. Also hoping to prevent a Republican victory, pro-Unionists from the border states organized the Constitutional Union Party and put up a fourth candidate, John Bell, for president, who pledged to end slavery agitation and preserve the Union but never fully explained how he'd accomplish this objective. In a pro-Lincoln political cartoon of the time (Figure 14.20), the presidential election is presented as a baseball game. Lincoln stands on home plate. A skunk raises its tail at the other candidates. Holding his nose, southern Democrat John Breckinridge holds a bat labeled "Slavery Extension" and declares "I guess I'd better leave for Kentucky, for I smell something strong around here, and begin to think, that we are completely skunk'd."

FIGURE 14.20 *The national game. Three "outs" and one "run"* (1860), by Currier and Ives, shows the two Democratic candidates and one Constitutional Union candidate who lost the 1860 election to Republican Lincoln, shown at right.

The Republicans nominated Lincoln, and in the November election, he garnered a mere 40 percent of the popular vote, though he won every northern state except New Jersey. (Lincoln's name was blocked from even appearing on many southern states' ballots by southern Democrats.) More importantly, Lincoln did gain a majority in the Electoral College (Figure 14.21). The Fire-Eaters, however, refused to accept the results. With South Carolina leading the way, Fire-Eaters in southern states began to withdraw formally from the United States in 1860. South Carolinian Mary Boykin Chesnut wrote in her diary about the reaction to the Lincoln's election. "Now that the Black radical Republicans have the power," she wrote, "I suppose they will Brown us all." Her statement revealed many southerners' fear that with Lincoln as President, the South could expect more mayhem like the John Brown raid.

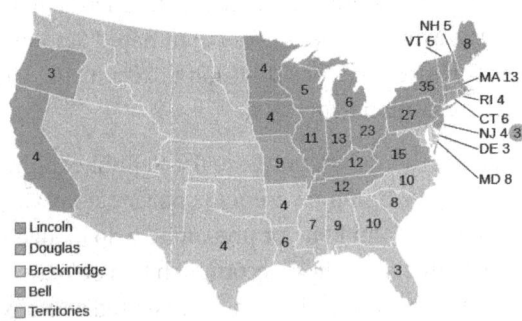

FIGURE 14.21 This map shows the disposition of electoral votes for the election of 1860. The votes were divided along almost perfect sectional lines.

Key Terms

American Party   also called the Know-Nothing Party, a political party that emerged in 1856 with an anti-immigration platform

Bleeding Kansas   a reference to the violent clashes in Kansas between Free-Soilers and slavery supporters

border ruffians   proslavery Missourians who crossed the border into Kansas to influence the legislature

Compromise of 1850   five laws passed by Congress to resolve issues stemming from the Mexican Cession and the sectional crisis

Dred Scott v. Sandford   an 1857 case in which the Supreme Court ruled that Black people could not be citizens and Congress had no jurisdiction to impede the expansion of slavery

Fire-Eaters   radical southern secessionists

Free-Soil Party   a political party committed to ensuring that White laborers would not have to compete with unpaid enslaved people in newly acquired territories

Freeport Doctrine   a doctrine that emerged during the Lincoln-Douglas debates in which Douglas reaffirmed his commitment to popular sovereignty, including the right to halt the spread of slavery, despite the 1857 Dred Scott decision affirming slaveholders' right to bring their property wherever they wished

Harpers Ferry   the site of a federal arsenal in Virginia, where radical abolitionist John Brown staged an ill-fated effort to end slavery by instigating a mass uprising among enslaved people

miscegenation   race-mixing through sexual relations or marriage

popular sovereignty   the principle of letting the people residing in a territory decide whether or not to permit slavery in that area based on majority rule

Republican Party   an antislavery political party formed in 1854 in response to Stephen Douglas's Kansas-Nebraska Act

Underground Railroad   a network of free Black and northern White people who helped enslaved people escape bondage through a series of designated routes and safe houses

Summary

14.1 The Compromise of 1850

The difficult process of reaching a compromise on slavery in 1850 exposed the sectional fault lines in the United States. After several months of rancorous debate, Congress passed five laws—known collectively as the Compromise of 1850—that people on both sides of the divide hoped had solved the nation's problems. However, many northerners feared the impact of the Fugitive Slave Act, which made it a crime not only to help enslaved people escape, but also to fail to help capture them. Many Americans, both Black and White, flouted the Fugitive Slave Act by participating in the Underground Railroad, providing safe houses for freedom-seekers on the run from the South. Eight northern states passed personal liberty laws to counteract the effects of the Fugitive Slave Act.

14.2 The Kansas-Nebraska Act and the Republican Party

The application of popular sovereignty to the organization of the Kansas and Nebraska territories ended the sectional truce that had prevailed since the Compromise of 1850. Senator Douglas's Kansas-Nebraska Act opened the door to chaos in Kansas as proslavery and Free-Soil forces waged war against each other, and radical abolitionists, notably John Brown, committed themselves to violence to end slavery. The act also upended the second party system of Whigs and Democrats by inspiring the formation of the new Republican Party, committed to arresting the further spread of slavery. Many voters approved its platform in the 1856 presidential election, though the Democrats won the race because they remained a national, rather than a sectional, political force.

14.3 The Dred Scott Decision and Sectional Strife

The Dred Scott decision of 1857 went well beyond the question of whether or not Dred Scott gained his freedom. Instead, the Supreme Court delivered a far-reaching pronouncement about African Americans in the United States, finding they could never be citizens and that Congress could not interfere with the expansion of slavery into the territories. Republicans erupted in anger at this decision, which rendered their party's central platform unconstitutional. Abraham Lincoln fully articulated the Republican position on the issue of slavery in his 1858 debates with Senator Stephen Douglas. By the end of that year, Lincoln had become a nationally known Republican icon. For the Democrats' part, unity within their party frayed over both the Dred Scott case and the Freeport Doctrine, undermining the Democrats' future ability to retain control of the presidency.

14.4 John Brown and the Election of 1860

A new level of animosity and distrust emerged in 1859 in the aftermath of John Brown's raid. The South exploded in rage at the northern celebration of Brown as a heroic freedom fighter. Fire-Eaters called openly for disunion. Poisoned relations split the Democrats into northern and southern factions, a boon to the Republican candidate Lincoln. His election triggered the downfall of the American experiment with democracy as southern states began to leave the Union.

Review Questions

1. What was President Zachary Taylor's top priority as president?
    A. preserving the Union
    B. ensuring the recapture of escaped enslaved people
    C. expanding slavery
    D. enlarging the state of Texas

2. Which of the following was *not* a component of the Compromise of 1850?
    A. the passage of the Fugitive Slave Act
    B. the admission of Kansas as a free state
    C. the admission of California as a free state
    D. a ban on the slave trade in Washington, DC

3. Why did many in the North resist the Fugitive Slave Act?

4. Which of the following was a focus of the new Republican Party?
    A. supporting Irish Catholic immigration
    B. encouraging the use of popular sovereignty to determine where slavery could exist
    C. promoting states' rights
    D. halting the spread of slavery

5. Border ruffians helped to _____.
    A. chase abolitionists out of Missouri
    B. elect a proslavery legislature in Kansas
    C. capture escaped enslaved people
    D. disseminate abolitionist literature in Kansas

6. How did the "Bleeding Kansas" incident change the face of antislavery advocacy?

7. On what grounds did Dred Scott sue for freedom?
   A. the inherent inhumanity of slavery
   B. the cruelty of his enslaver
   C. the fact that he had lived in free states
   D. the fact that his family would be torn apart

8. Which of the following was *not* a result of the Lincoln-Douglas debates?
   A. Douglas was elected senator of Illinois.
   B. Lincoln's national profile was raised.
   C. Citizens in both the North and South followed the debates closely.
   D. Lincoln successfully defended the principle of popular sovereignty.

9. What are the main points of the Dred Scott decision?

10. Why did John Brown attack the armory at Harpers Ferry?
    A. to seize weapons to distribute to enslaved people for a massive uprising
    B. to hold as a military base against proslavery forces
    C. in revenge after the sacking of Lawrence
    D. to prevent southern states from seceding

11. Which of the following did *not* contribute to Lincoln's victory in the election of 1860?
    A. the split between northern and southern democrats
    B. the defeat of the Whig party
    C. Lincoln's improved national standing after his senatorial debates with Stephen Douglas
    D. the Constitutional Union party's further splintering the vote

12. What were southerners' and northerners' views of John Brown?

Critical Thinking Questions

13. Why would Americans view the Compromise of 1850 as a final solution to the sectional controversy that began with the Wilmot Proviso in 1846?

14. If you were a proslavery advocate, how would you feel about the platform of the newly formed Republican Party?

15. Based on the text of the Lincoln-Douglas debates, what was the position of the Republican Party in 1858? Was the Republican Party an abolitionist party? Why or why not?

16. John Brown is often described as a terrorist. Do you agree with this description? Why or why not? What attributes might make him fit this profile?

17. Was it possible to save American democracy in 1860? What steps might have been taken to maintain unity? Why do you think these steps were not taken?

The Civil War, 1860–1865   15

FIGURE 15.1 This photograph by John Reekie, entitled, "A burial party on the battle-field of Cold Harbor," drives home the brutality and devastation wrought by the Civil War. Here, in April 1865, African Americans collect the bones of soldiers killed in Virginia during General Ulysses S. Grant's Wilderness Campaign of May–June 1864.

CHAPTER OUTLINE
15.1 The Origins and Outbreak of the Civil War
15.2 Early Mobilization and War
15.3 1863: The Changing Nature of the War
15.4 The Union Triumphant

INTRODUCTION In May 1864, General Ulysses S. Grant ordered the Union's Army of the Potomac to cross the Rapidan River in Virginia. Grant knew that Confederate general Robert E. Lee would defend the Confederate capital at Richmond at all costs, committing troops that might otherwise be sent to the Shenandoah or the Deep South to stop Union general William Tecumseh Sherman from capturing Atlanta, a key Confederate city. For two days, the Army of the Potomac fought Lee's troops in the Wilderness, a wooded area along the Rapidan River. Nearly ten thousand Confederate soldiers were killed or wounded, as were more than seventeen thousand Union troops. A few weeks later, the armies would meet again at the Battle of Cold Harbor, where another fifteen thousand men would be wounded or killed. As in many battles, the bodies of those who died were left on the field where they fell. A year later, African Americans, who were often called upon to perform menial labor for the Union army (Figure 15.1), collected the skeletal remains of the dead for a proper burial. The state of the graves of many Civil War soldiers partly inspired the creation of Memorial Day, a day set aside for visiting and decorating the graves of the dead.

15.1 The Origins and Outbreak of the Civil War

LEARNING OBJECTIVES

By the end of this section, you will be able to:
- Explain the major events that occurred during the Secession Crisis
- Describe the creation and founding principles of the Confederate States of America

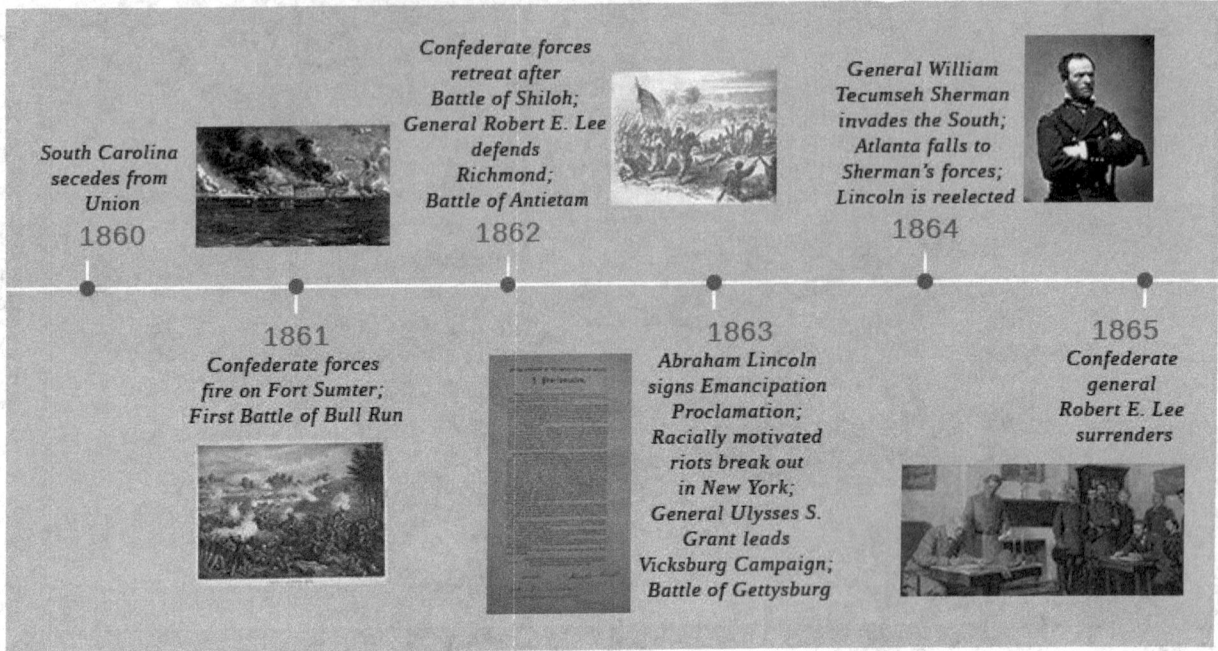

FIGURE 15.2 (credit "1865": modification of work by "Alaskan Dude"/Wikimedia Commons)

The 1860 election of Abraham Lincoln was a turning point for the United States. Throughout the tumultuous 1850s, the Fire-Eaters of the southern states had been threatening to leave the Union. With Lincoln's election, they prepared to make good on their threats. Indeed, the Republican president-elect appeared to be their worst nightmare. The Republican Party committed itself to keeping slavery out of the territories as the country expanded westward, a position that shocked southern sensibilities. Meanwhile, southern leaders suspected that Republican abolitionists would employ the violent tactics of John Brown to deprive southerners of their enslaved property. The threat posed by the Republican victory in the election of 1860 spurred eleven southern states to leave the Union to form the Confederate States of America, a new republic dedicated to maintaining and expanding slavery. The Union, led by President Lincoln, was unwilling to accept the departure of these states and committed itself to restoring the country. Beginning in 1861 and continuing until 1865, the United States engaged in a brutal Civil War that claimed the lives of over 600,000 soldiers. By 1863, the conflict had become not only a war to save the Union, but also a war to end slavery in the United States. Only after four years of fighting did the North prevail. The Union was preserved, and the institution of slavery had been destroyed in the nation.

THE CAUSES OF THE CIVIL WAR

Lincoln's election sparked the southern secession fever into flame, but it did not cause the Civil War. For decades before Lincoln took office, the sectional divisions in the country had been widening. Both the Northern and southern states engaged in inflammatory rhetoric and agitation, and violent emotions ran strong on both sides. Several factors played into the ultimate split between the North and the South.

One key irritant was the question of slavery's expansion westward. The debate over whether new states would be slave or free reached back to the controversy over statehood for Missouri beginning in 1819 and Texas in the 1830s and early 1840s. This question arose again after the Mexican-American War (1846–1848), when the government debated whether slavery would be permitted in the territories taken from Mexico. Efforts in Congress to reach a compromise in 1850 fell back on the principle of popular sovereignty—letting the people in the new territories south of the 1820 Missouri Compromise line decide whether to allow slavery. This same principle came to be applied to the Kansas-Nebraska territories in 1854, a move that added fuel to the fire of sectional conflict by destroying the Missouri Compromise boundary and leading to the birth of the Republican Party. In the end, popular sovereignty proved to be no solution at all. This was especially true in "Bleeding Kansas" in the mid-1850s, as pro- and antislavery forces battled each another in an effort to gain the upper hand.

The small but very vocal abolitionist movement further contributed to the escalating tensions between the North and the South. Since the 1830s, abolitionists, led by journalist and reformer William Lloyd Garrison, had cast slavery as a national sin and called for its immediate end. For three decades, the abolitionists—a minority even within the antislavery movement—had had a significant effect on American society by bringing the evils of slavery into the public consciousness. By the 1850s, some of the most radical abolitionists, such as John Brown, had resorted to violence in their efforts to destroy the institution of slavery.

The formation of the Liberty Party (1840), the Free-Soil Party (1848), and the Republican Party (1854), all of which strongly opposed the spread of slavery to the West, brought the question solidly into the political arena. Although not all those who opposed the westward expansion of slavery had a strong abolitionist bent, the attempt to limit slaveholders' control of their human property stiffened the resolve of southern leaders to defend their society at all costs. Prohibiting slavery's expansion, they argued, ran counter to fundamental American property rights. Across the country, people of all political stripes worried that the nation's arguments would cause irreparable rifts in the country.

Despite the ruptures and tensions, by the 1860s, some hope of healing the nation still existed. Before Lincoln took office, John Crittenden, a senator from Kentucky who had helped form the Constitutional Union Party during the 1860 presidential election, attempted to defuse the explosive situation by offering six constitutional amendments and a series of resolutions, known as the **Crittenden Compromise**. Crittenden's goal was to keep the South from seceding, and his strategy was to transform the Constitution to explicitly protect slavery forever. Specifically, Crittenden proposed an amendment that would restore the 36°30′ line from the Missouri Compromise and extend it all the way to the Pacific Ocean, protecting and ensuring slavery south of the line while prohibiting it north of the line (Figure 15.3). He further proposed an amendment that would prohibit Congress from abolishing slavery anywhere it already existed or from interfering with the interstate slave trade.

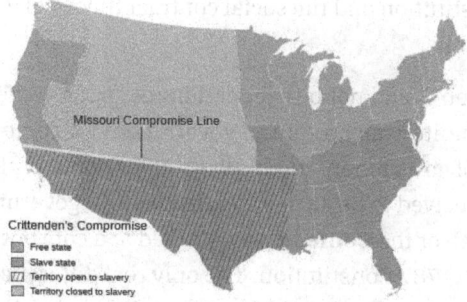

FIGURE 15.3 Crittenden's Compromise would protect slavery in all states where it already existed. More importantly, however, it proposed to allow the western expansion of slavery into states below the Missouri Compromise line.

Republicans, including President-elect Lincoln, rejected Crittenden's proposals because they ran counter to the party's goal of keeping slavery out of the territories. The southern states also rejected Crittenden's attempts at compromise, because it would prevent slaveholders from taking their human chattel north of the 36°30′

line. On December 20, 1860, only a few days after Crittenden's proposal was introduced in Congress, South Carolina began the march towards war when it seceded from the United States. Three more states of the Deep South—Mississippi, Florida, and Alabama—seceded before the U.S. Senate rejected Crittenden's proposal on January 16, 1861. Georgia, Louisiana, and Texas joined them in rapid succession on January 19, January 26, and February 1, respectively (Figure 15.4). In many cases, these secessions occurred after extremely divided conventions and popular votes. A lack of unanimity prevailed in much of the South.

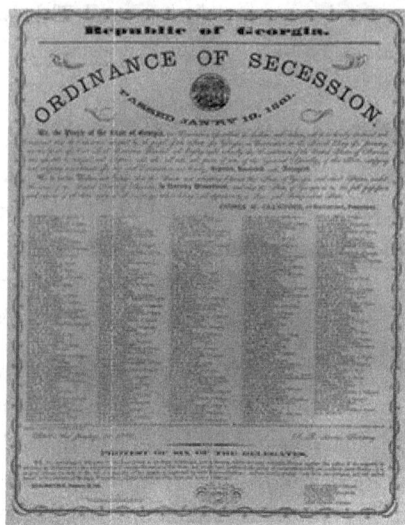

FIGURE 15.4 Georgia's Ordinance of Secession and those of the other Deep South states were all based on that of South Carolina, which was drafted just a month after Abraham Lincoln was elected.

CLICK AND EXPLORE

Explore the causes, battles, and aftermath of the Civil War at the interactive website (http://openstax.org/l/15Causes) offered by the National Parks Service.

THE CREATION OF THE CONFEDERATE STATES OF AMERICA

The seven Deep South states that seceded quickly formed a new government. In the opinion of many Southern politicians, the federal Constitution that united the states as one nation was a contract by which individual states had agreed to be bound. However, they maintained, the states had not sacrificed their autonomy and could withdraw their consent to be controlled by the federal government. In their eyes, their actions were in keeping with the nature of the Constitution and the social contract theory of government that had influenced the founders of the American Republic.

The new nation formed by these men would not be a federal union, but a confederation. In a confederation, individual member states agree to unite under a central government for some purposes, such as defense, but to retain autonomy in other areas of government. In this way, states could protect themselves, and slavery, from interference by what they perceived to be an overbearing central government. The constitution of the Confederate States of America (CSA), or the **Confederacy**, drafted at a convention in Montgomery, Alabama, in February 1861, closely followed the 1787 Constitution. The only real difference between the two documents centered on slavery. The Confederate Constitution declared that the new nation existed to defend and perpetuate racial slavery, and the leadership of the slaveholding class. Specifically, the constitution protected the interstate slave trade, guaranteed that slavery would exist in any new territory gained by the Confederacy, and, perhaps most importantly, in Article One, Section Nine, declared that "No . . . law impairing or denying the right of property in negro slaves shall be passed." Beyond its focus on slavery, the Confederate Constitution resembled the 1787 U.S. Constitution. It allowed for a Congress composed of two chambers, a judicial branch, and an executive branch with a president to serve for six years.

The convention delegates chose Jefferson Davis of Mississippi to lead the new provisional government as president and Alexander Stephens of Georgia to serve as vice president until elections could be held in the spring and fall of 1861. By that time, four new states—Virginia, Arkansas, Tennessee, and North Carolina—had joined the CSA. As 1861 progressed, the Confederacy claimed Missouri and Kentucky, even though no ordinance of secession had been approved in those states. Southern nationalism ran high, and the Confederacy, buoyed by its sense of purpose, hoped that their new nation would achieve eminence in the world.

By the time Lincoln reached Washington, DC, in February 1861, the CSA had already been established. The new president confronted an unprecedented crisis. A conference held that month with delegates from the Southern states failed to secure a promise of peace or to restore the Union. On inauguration day, March 4, 1861, the new president repeated his views on slavery: "I have no purpose, directly or indirectly, to interfere with the institution of slavery in the States where it exists. I believe I have no lawful right to do so, and I have no inclination to do so." His recognition of slavery in the South did nothing to mollify slaveholders, however, because Lincoln also pledged to keep slavery from expanding into the new western territories. Furthermore, in his inaugural address, Lincoln made clear his commitment to maintaining federal power against the secessionists working to destroy it. Lincoln declared that the Union could not be dissolved by individual state actions, and, therefore, secession was unconstitutional.

CLICK AND EXPLORE

Read Lincoln's entire inaugural address (http://openstax.org/l/15LincAddress) at the Yale Avalon project's website. How would Lincoln's audience have responded to this speech?

FORT SUMTER

President Lincoln made it clear to Southern secessionists that he would fight to maintain federal property and to keep the Union intact. Other politicians, however, still hoped to avoid the use of force to resolve the crisis. In February 1861, in an effort to entice the rebellious states to return to the Union without resorting to force, Thomas Corwin, a representative from Ohio, introduced a proposal to amend the Constitution in the House of Representatives. His was but one of several measures proposed in January and February 1861, to head off the impending conflict and save the United States. The proposed amendment would have made it impossible for Congress to pass any law abolishing slavery. The proposal passed the House on February 28, 1861, and the Senate passed the proposal on March 2, 1861. It was then sent to the states to be ratified. Once ratified by three-quarters of state legislatures, it would become law. In his inaugural address, Lincoln stated that he had no objection to the amendment, and his predecessor James Buchanan had supported it. By the time of Lincoln's inauguration, however, seven states had already left the Union. Of the remaining states, Ohio ratified the amendment in 1861, and Maryland and Illinois did so in 1862. Despite this effort at reconciliation, the Confederate states did not return to the Union.

Indeed, by the time of the Corwin amendment's passage through Congress, Confederate forces in the Deep South had already begun to take over federal forts. The loss of **Fort Sumter**, in the harbor of Charleston, South Carolina, proved to be the flashpoint in the contest between the new Confederacy and the federal government. A small Union garrison of fewer than one hundred soldiers and officers held the fort, making it a vulnerable target for the Confederacy. Fire-Eaters pressured Jefferson Davis to take Fort Sumter and thereby demonstrate the Confederate government's resolve. Some also hoped that the Confederacy would gain foreign recognition, especially from Great Britain, by taking the fort in the South's most important Atlantic port. The situation grew dire as local merchants refused to sell food to the fort's Union soldiers, and by mid-April, the garrison's supplies began to run out. President Lincoln let it be known to Confederate leaders that he planned to resupply the Union forces. His strategy was clear: The decision to start the war would rest squarely on the Confederates, not on the Union. On April 12, 1861, Confederate forces in Charleston began a bombardment of Fort Sumter (Figure 15.5). Two days later, the Union soldiers there surrendered.

FIGURE 15.5 The Confederacy's attack on Fort Sumter, depicted here in an 1861 lithograph by Currier and Ives, stoked pro-war sentiment on both sides of the conflict.

The attack on Fort Sumter meant war had come, and on April 15, 1861, Lincoln called upon loyal states to supply armed forces to defeat the rebellion and regain Fort Sumter. Faced with the need to choose between the Confederacy and the Union, border states and those of the Upper South, which earlier had been reluctant to dissolve their ties with the United States, were inspired to take action. They quickly voted for secession. A convention in Virginia that had been assembled earlier to consider the question of secession voted to join the Confederacy on April 17, two days after Lincoln called for troops. Arkansas left the Union on May 6 along with Tennessee one day later. North Carolina followed on May 20.

Not all residents of the border states and the Upper South wished to join the Confederacy, however. Pro-Union feelings remained strong in Tennessee, especially in the eastern part of the state where the enslaved population was small and consisted largely of house servants owned by the wealthy. The state of Virginia—home of revolutionary leaders and presidents such as George Washington, Thomas Jefferson, James Madison, and James Monroe—literally was split on the issue of secession. Residents in the north and west of the state, where few slaveholders resided, rejected secession. These counties subsequently united to form "West Virginia," which entered the Union as a free state in 1863. The rest of Virginia, including the historic lands along the Chesapeake Bay that were home to such early American settlements as Jamestown and Williamsburg, joined the Confederacy. The addition of this area gave the Confederacy even greater hope and brought General Robert E. Lee, arguably the best military commander of the day, to their side. In addition, the secession of Virginia brought Washington, DC, perilously close to the Confederacy, and fears that the border state of Maryland would also join the CSA, thus trapping the U.S. capital within Confederate territories, plagued Lincoln.

The Confederacy also gained the backing of the Five Civilized Tribes, as they were called, in the Indian Territory. The Five Civilized Tribes comprised the Choctaws, Chickasaws, Creeks, Seminoles, and Cherokees. The tribes supported slavery and many members were enslavers. These Native American slaveholders, who had been forced from their lands in Georgia and elsewhere in the Deep South during the presidency of Andrew Jackson, now found unprecedented common cause with White slaveholders. The CSA even allowed them to send delegates to the Confederate Congress.

While most slaveholding states joined the Confederacy, four crucial slave states remained in the Union (Figure 15.6). Delaware, which was technically a slave state despite its tiny enslaved population, never voted to secede. Maryland, despite deep divisions, remained in the Union as well. Missouri became the site of vicious fighting and the home of pro-Confederate guerilla but never joined the Confederacy. Kentucky declared itself neutral, although that did little to stop the fighting that occurred within the state. In all, these four states deprived the Confederacy of key resources and soldiers.

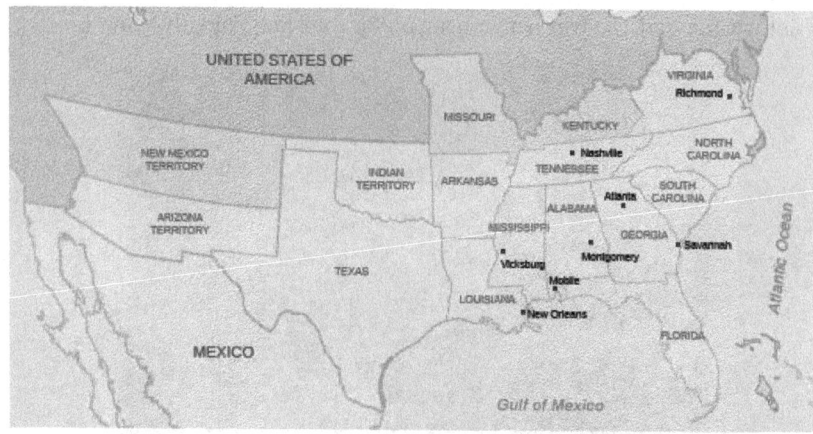

FIGURE 15.6 This map illustrates the southern states that seceded from the Union and formed the Confederacy in 1861, at the outset of the Civil War.

15.2 Early Mobilization and War

LEARNING OBJECTIVES

By the end of this section, you will be able to:
- Assess the strengths and weaknesses of the Confederacy and the Union
- Explain the strategic importance of the Battle of Bull Run and the Battle of Shiloh

In 1861, enthusiasm for war ran high on both sides. The North fought to restore the Union, which Lincoln declared could never be broken. The Confederacy, which by the summer of 1861 consisted of eleven states, fought for its independence from the United States. The continuation of slavery was a central issue in the war, of course, although abolitionism and western expansion also played roles, and Northerners and Southerners alike flocked eagerly to the conflict. Both sides thought it would be over quickly. Militarily, however, the North and South were more equally matched than Lincoln had realized, and it soon became clear that the war effort would be neither brief nor painless. In 1861, Americans in both the North and South romanticized war as noble and positive. Soon the carnage and slaughter would awaken them to the horrors of war.

THE FIRST BATTLE OF BULL RUN

After the fall of Fort Sumter on April 15, 1861, Lincoln called for seventy-five thousand volunteers from state militias to join federal forces. His goal was a ninety-day campaign to put down the Southern rebellion. The response from state militias was overwhelming, and the number of Northern troops exceeded the requisition. Also in April, Lincoln put in place a naval blockade of the South, a move that gave tacit recognition of the Confederacy while providing a legal excuse for the British and the French to trade with Southerners. The Confederacy responded to the blockade by declaring that a state of war existed with the United States. This official pronouncement confirmed the beginning of the Civil War. Men rushed to enlist, and the Confederacy turned away tens of thousands who hoped to defend the new nation.

Many believed that a single, heroic battle would decide the contest. Some questioned how committed Southerners really were to their cause. Northerners hoped that most Southerners would not actually fire on the American flag. Meanwhile, Lincoln and military leaders in the North hoped a quick blow to the South, especially if they could capture the Confederacy's new capital of Richmond, Virginia, would end the rebellion before it went any further. On July 21, 1861, the two armies met near Manassas, Virginia, along Bull Run Creek, only thirty miles from Washington, DC. So great was the belief that this would be a climactic Union victory that many Washington socialites and politicians brought picnic lunches to a nearby area, hoping to witness history unfolding before them. At the First Battle of Bull Run, also known as First Manassas, some sixty thousand troops assembled, most of whom had never seen combat, and each side sent eighteen thousand into the fray. The Union forces attacked first, only to be pushed back. The Confederate forces then carried the day, sending the Union soldiers and Washington, DC, onlookers scrambling back from Virginia and destroying Union hopes of a quick, decisive victory. Instead, the war would drag on for four long, deadly years (Figure 15.7).

FIGURE 15.7 The First Battle of Bull Run, which many Northerners thought would put a quick and decisive end to the South's rebellion, ended with a Confederate victory.

BALANCE SHEET: THE UNION AND THE CONFEDERACY

As it became clearer that the Union would not be dealing with an easily quashed rebellion, the two sides assessed their strengths and weaknesses. At the onset on the war, in 1861 and 1862, they stood as relatively equal combatants.

The Confederates had the advantage of being able to wage a defensive war, rather than an offensive one. They had to protect and preserve their new boundaries, but they did not have to be the aggressors against the Union. The war would be fought primarily in the South, which gave the Confederates the advantages of the knowledge of the terrain and the support of the civilian population. Further, the vast coastline from Texas to Virginia offered ample opportunities to evade the Union blockade. And with the addition of the Upper South states, especially Virginia, North Carolina, Tennessee, and Arkansas, the Confederacy gained a much larger share of natural resources and industrial might than the Deep South states could muster.

Still, the Confederacy had disadvantages. The South's economy depended heavily on the export of cotton, but with the naval blockade, the flow of cotton to England, the region's primary importer, came to an end. The blockade also made it difficult to import manufactured goods. Although the secession of the Upper South added some industrial assets to the Confederacy, overall, the South lacked substantive industry or an extensive railroad infrastructure to move men and supplies. To deal with the lack of commerce and the resulting lack of funds, the Confederate government began printing paper money, leading to runaway inflation (Figure 15.8). The advantage that came from fighting on home territory quickly turned to a disadvantage when Confederate armies were defeated and Union forces destroyed Southern farms and towns, and forced Southern civilians to take to the road as refugees. Finally, the population of the South stood at fewer than nine million people, of whom nearly four million were enslaved Black people, compared to over twenty million residents in the North. These limited numbers became a major factor as the war dragged on and the death toll rose.

FIGURE 15.8 The Confederacy started printing paper money at an accelerated rate, causing runaway inflation and an economy in which formerly well-off people were unable to purchase food.

The Union side held many advantages as well. Its larger population, bolstered by continued immigration from Europe throughout the 1860s, gave it greater manpower reserves to draw upon. The North's greater industrial capabilities and extensive railroad grid made it far better able to mobilize men and supplies for the war effort. The Industrial Revolution and the transportation revolution, beginning in the 1820s and continuing over the next several decades, had transformed the North. Throughout the war, the North was able to produce more war materials and move goods more quickly than the South. Furthermore, the farms of New England, the Mid-Atlantic, the Old Northwest, and the prairie states supplied Northern civilians and Union troops with abundant food throughout the war. Food shortages and hungry civilians were common in the South, where the best land was devoted to raising cotton, but not in the North.

Unlike the South, however, which could hunker down to defend itself and needed to maintain relatively short supply lines, the North had to go forth and conquer. Union armies had to establish long supply lines, and Union soldiers had to fight on unfamiliar ground and contend with a hostile civilian population off the battlefield. Furthermore, to restore the Union—Lincoln's overriding goal, in 1861—the United States, after defeating the Southern forces, would then need to pacify a conquered Confederacy, an area of over half a million square miles with nearly nine million residents. In short, although it had better resources and a larger population, the Union faced a daunting task against the well-positioned Confederacy.

MILITARY STALEMATE

The military forces of the Confederacy and the Union battled in 1861 and early 1862 without either side gaining the upper hand. The majority of military leaders on both sides had received the same military education and often knew one another personally, either from their time as students at West Point or as commanding officers in the Mexican-American War. This familiarity allowed them to anticipate each other's strategies. Both sides believed in the use of concentrated armies charged with taking the capital city of the enemy. For the Union, this meant the capture of the Confederate capital in Richmond, Virginia, whereas Washington, DC, stood as the prize for Confederate forces. After hopes of a quick victory faded at Bull Run, the months dragged on without any major movement on either side (Figure 15.9).

FIGURE 15.9 As this cartoon indicates, the fighting strategy at the beginning of the war included watchful waiting by the leaders of the North and South.

General George B. McClellan, the **general in chief** of the army, responsible for overall control of Union land forces, proved especially reluctant to engage in battle with the Confederates. In direct command of the **Army of the Potomac**, the Union fighting force operating outside Washington, DC, McClellan believed, incorrectly, that Confederate forces were too strong to defeat and was reluctant to risk his troops in battle. His cautious nature made him popular with his men but not with the president or Congress. By 1862, however, both President Lincoln and the new Secretary of War Edwin Stanton had tired of waiting. The Union put forward a new effort to bolster troop strength, enlisting one million men to serve for three-year stints in the Army of the Potomac. In January 1862, Lincoln and Stanton ordered McClellan to invade the Confederacy with the goal of capturing Richmond.

To that end, General McClellan slowly moved 100,000 soldiers of the Army of the Potomac toward Richmond but stopped a few miles outside the city. As he did so, a Confederate force led by Thomas "Stonewall" Jackson moved north to take Washington, DC. To fend off Jackson's attack, somewhere between one-quarter and one-third of McClellan's soldiers, led by Major General Irvin McDowell, returned to defend the nation's capital, a move that Jackson hoped would leave the remaining troops near Richmond more vulnerable. Having succeeding in drawing off a sizable portion of the Union force, he joined General Lee to launch an attack on McClellan's remaining soldiers near Richmond. From June 25 to July 1, 1862, the two sides engaged in the brutal Seven Days Battles that killed or wounded almost twenty thousand Confederate and ten thousand Union soldiers. McClellan's army finally returned north, having failed to take Richmond.

General Lee, flush from his success at keeping McClellan out of Richmond, tried to capitalize on the Union's failure by taking the fighting northward. He moved his forces into northern Virginia, where, at the Second Battle of Bull Run, the Confederates again defeated the Union forces. Lee then pressed into Maryland, where his troops met the much larger Union forces near Sharpsburg, at Antietam Creek. The ensuing one-day battle on September 17, 1862, led to a tremendous loss of life. Although there are varying opinions about the total number of deaths, eight thousand soldiers were killed or wounded, more than on any other single day of combat. Once again, McClellan, mistakenly believing that the Confederate troops outnumbered his own, held back a significant portion of his forces. Lee withdrew from the field first, but McClellan, fearing he was outnumbered, refused to pursue him.

The Union army's inability to destroy Lee's army at Antietam made it clear to Lincoln that McClellan would never win the war, and the president was forced to seek a replacement. Lincoln wanted someone who could deliver a decisive Union victory. He also personally disliked McClellan, who referred to the president as a "baboon" and a "gorilla," and constantly criticized his decisions. Lincoln chose General Ambrose E. Burnside to replace McClellan as commander of the Army of the Potomac, but Burnside's efforts to push into Virginia failed in December 1862, as Confederates held their position at Fredericksburg and devastated Burnside's forces with heavy artillery fire. The Union's defeat at Fredericksburg harmed morale in the North but bolstered Confederate spirits. By the end of 1862, the Confederates were still holding their ground in Virginia. Burnside's failure led Lincoln to make another change in leadership, and Joseph "Fighting Joe" Hooker took over command of the Army of the Potomac in January 1863.

General Ulysses S. Grant's **Army of the West**, operating in Kentucky, Tennessee, and the Mississippi River Valley, had been more successful. In the western campaign, the goal of both the Union and the Confederacy was to gain control of the major rivers in the west, especially the Mississippi. If the Union could control the Mississippi, the Confederacy would be split in two. The fighting in this campaign initially centered in Tennessee, where Union forces commanded by Grant pushed Confederate troops back and gained control of the state. The major battle in the western theater took place at Pittsburgh Landing, Tennessee, on April 6 and 7, 1862. Grant's army was camped on the west side of the Tennessee River near a small log church called Shiloh, which gave the battle its name. On Sunday morning, April 6, Confederate forces under General Albert Sidney Johnston attacked Grant's encampment with the goal of separating them from their supply line on the Tennessee River and driving them into the swamps on the river's western side, where they could be destroyed. Union general William Tecumseh Sherman tried to rally the Union forces as Grant, who had been convalescing from an injured leg when the attack began and was unable to walk without crutches, called for reinforcements and tried to mount a defense. Many of Union troops fled in terror.

Unfortunately for the Confederates, Johnston was killed on the afternoon of the first day. Leadership of the Southern forces fell to General P. G. T. Beauregard, who ordered an assault at the end of that day. This assault was so desperate that one of the two attacking columns did not even have ammunition. Heavily reinforced Union forces counterattacked the next day, and the Confederate forces were routed. Grant had maintained the Union foothold in the western part of the Confederacy. The North could now concentrate on its efforts to gain control of the Mississippi River, splitting the Confederacy in two and depriving it of its most important water route.

CLICK AND EXPLORE

Read a first-hand account (http://www.pbs.org/wgbh/americanexperience/features/grant-stanley/) from a Confederate soldier at the Battle at Shiloh, followed by the perspective of a Union soldier (http://www.pbs.org/wgbh/americanexperience/features/grant-boyd/) at the same battle.

In the spring and summer of 1862, the Union was successful in gaining control of part of the Mississippi River. In April 1862, the Union navy under Admiral David Farragut fought its way past the forts that guarded New Orleans and fired naval guns upon the below-sea-level city. When it became obvious that New Orleans could no longer be defended, Confederate major general Marshall Lovell sent his artillery upriver to Vicksburg, Mississippi. Armed civilians in New Orleans fought the Union forces that entered the city. They also destroyed ships and military supplies that might be used by the Union. Upriver, Union naval forces also bombarded Fort Pillow, forty miles from Memphis, Tennessee, a Southern industrial center and one of the largest cities in the Confederacy. On June 4, 1862, the Confederate defenders abandoned the fort. On June 6, Memphis fell to the Union after the ships defending it were destroyed.

15.3 1863: The Changing Nature of the War

LEARNING OBJECTIVES

By the end of this section, you will be able to:
- Explain what is meant by the term "total war" and provide examples
- Describe mobilization efforts in the North and the South
- Explain why 1863 was a pivotal year in the war
- Summarize the purpose and effect of the Emancipation Proclamation

Wars have their own logic; they last far longer than anyone anticipates at the beginning of hostilities. As they drag on, the energy and zeal that marked the entry into warfare often wane, as losses increase and people on both sides suffer the tolls of war. The American Civil War is a case study of this characteristic of modern war.

Although Northerners and Southerners both anticipated that the battle between the Confederacy and the Union would be settled quickly, it soon became clear to all that there was no resolution in sight. The longer the war continued, the more it began to affect life in both the North and the South. Increased need for manpower, the issue of slavery, and the ongoing challenges of keeping the war effort going changed the way life on both sides as the conflict progressed.

MASS MOBILIZATION

By late 1862, the course of the war had changed to take on the characteristics of **total war**, in which armies attempt to demoralize the enemy by both striking military targets and disrupting their opponent's ability to wage war through destruction of their resources. In this type of war, armies often make no distinction between civilian and military targets. Both the Union and Confederate forces moved toward total war, although neither side ever entirely abolished the distinction between military and civilian. Total war also requires governments to mobilize all resources, extending their reach into their citizens' lives as never before. Another reality of war that became apparent in 1862 and beyond was the influence of combat on the size and scope of government. Both the Confederacy and the Union governments had to continue to grow in order to manage the logistics of recruiting men and maintaining, feeding, and equipping an army.

Confederate Mobilization

The Confederate government in Richmond, Virginia, exercised sweeping powers to ensure victory, in stark contradiction to the states' rights sentiments held by many Southern leaders. The initial emotional outburst of enthusiasm for war in the Confederacy waned, and the Confederate government instituted a military draft in April 1862. Under the terms of the draft, all men between the ages of eighteen and thirty-five would serve three years. The draft had a different effect on men of different socioeconomic classes. One loophole permitted men to hire substitutes instead of serving in the Confederate army. This provision favored the wealthy over the poor, and led to much resentment and resistance. Exercising its power over the states, the Confederate Congress denied state efforts to circumvent the draft.

In order to fund the war, the Confederate government also took over the South's economy. The government ran Southern industry and built substantial transportation and industrial infrastructure to make the weapons of war. Over the objections of slaveholders, it impressed enslaved people, seizing these enslaved workers from their owners and forcing them to work on fortifications and rail lines. Concerned about the resistance to and unhappiness with the government measures, in 1862, the Confederate Congress gave President Davis the power to suspend the writ of **habeas corpus**, the right of those arrested to be brought before a judge or court to determine whether there is cause to hold the prisoner. With a stated goal of bolstering national security in the fledgling republic, this change meant that the Confederacy could arrest and detain indefinitely any suspected enemy without giving a reason. This growth of the Confederate central government stood as a glaring contradiction to the earlier states' rights argument of pro-Confederate advocates.

The war efforts were costing the new nation dearly. Nevertheless, the Confederate Congress heeded the pleas of wealthy plantation owners and refused to place a tax on enslaved people or cotton, despite the Confederacy's desperate need for the revenue that such a tax would have raised. Instead, the Confederacy drafted a taxation plan that kept the Southern elite happy but in no way met the needs of the war. The government also resorted to printing immense amounts of paper money, which quickly led to runaway inflation. Food prices soared, and poor, White Southerners faced starvation. In April 1863, thousands of hungry people rioted in Richmond, Virginia (Figure 15.10). Many of the rioters were mothers who could not feed their children. The riot ended when President Davis threatened to have Confederate forces open fire on the crowds.

FIGURE 15.10 Rampant inflation in the 1860s made food too expensive for many Southerners, leading to widespread starvation.

One of the reasons that the Confederacy was so economically devastated was its ill-advised gamble that cotton sales would continue during the war. The government had high hopes that Great Britain and France, which both used cotton as the raw material in their textile mills, would ensure the South's economic strength—and therefore victory in the war—by continuing to buy. Furthermore, the Confederate government hoped that Great Britain and France would make loans to their new nation in order to ensure the continued flow of raw materials. These hopes were never realized. Great Britain in particular did not wish to risk war with the United States, which would have meant the invasion of Canada. The United States was also a major source of grain for Britain and an important purchaser of British goods. Furthermore, the blockade made Southern trade with Europe difficult. Instead, Great Britain, the major consumer of American cotton, found alternate sources in India and Egypt, leaving the South without the income or alliance it had anticipated.

Dissent within the Confederacy also affected the South's ability to fight the war. Confederate politicians disagreed over the amount of power that the central government should be allowed to exercise. Many states' rights advocates, who favored a weak central government and supported the sovereignty of individual states, resented President Davis's efforts to conscript troops, impose taxation to pay for the war, and requisition necessary resources. Governors in the Confederate states often proved reluctant to provide supplies or troops for the use of the Confederate government. Even Jefferson Davis's vice president Alexander Stephens opposed conscription, the seizure of enslaved property to work for the Confederacy, and suspension of habeas corpus. Class divisions also divided Confederates. Poor White people resented the ability of wealthy slaveholders to excuse themselves from military service. Racial tensions plagued the South as well. On those occasions when free Black people volunteered to serve in the Confederate army, they were turned away, and enslaved African Americans were regarded with fear and suspicion, as White people whispered among themselves about the possibility of insurrections by enslaved people.

Union Mobilization

Mobilization for war proved to be easier in the North than it was in the South. During the war, the federal government in Washington, DC, like its Southern counterpart, undertook a wide range of efforts to ensure its victory over the Confederacy. To fund the war effort and finance the expansion of Union infrastructure, Republicans in Congress drastically expanded government activism, impacting citizens' everyday lives through measures such as new types of taxation. The government also contracted with major suppliers of food, weapons, and other needed materials. Virtually every sector of the Northern economy became linked to the war effort.

In keeping with their longstanding objective of keeping slavery out of the newly settled western territories, the Republicans in Congress (the dominant party) passed several measures in 1862. First, the Homestead Act provided generous inducements for Northerners to relocate and farm in the West. Settlers could lay claim to 160 acres of federal land by residing on the property for five years and improving it. The act not only motivated free-labor farmers to move west, but it also aimed to increase agricultural output for the war effort. The federal government also turned its attention to creating a transcontinental railroad to facilitate the movement of people and goods across the country. Congress chartered two companies, the Union Pacific and the Central Pacific, and provided generous funds for these two businesses to connect the country by rail.

The Republican emphasis on free labor, rather than enslaved labor, also influenced the 1862 Land Grant College Act, commonly known as the Morrill Act after its author, Vermont Republican senator Justin Smith Morrill. The measure provided for the creation of agricultural colleges, funded through federal grants, to teach the latest agricultural techniques. Each state in the Union would be granted thirty thousand acres of federal land for the use of these institutions of higher education.

Congress paid for the war using several strategies. They levied a tax on the income of the wealthy, as well as a tax on all inheritances. They also put high tariffs in place. Finally, they passed two National Bank Acts, one in 1863 and one in 1864, calling on the U.S. Treasury to issue war bonds and on Union banks to buy the bonds. A Union campaign to convince individuals to buy the bonds helped increase sales. The Republicans also passed the Legal Tender Act of 1862, calling for paper money—known as **greenbacks**—to be printed Figure 15.11). Some $150 million worth of greenbacks became legal tender, and the Northern economy boomed, although high inflation also resulted.

FIGURE 15.11 The Union began printing these paper "greenbacks" to use as legal tender as one of its strategies for funding the war effort.

Like the Confederacy, the Union turned to conscription to provide the troops needed for the war. In March 1863, Congress passed the Enrollment Act, requiring all unmarried men between the ages of twenty and twenty-five, and all married men between the ages of thirty-five and forty-five—including immigrants who had filed for citizenship—to register with the Union to fight in the Civil War. All who registered were subject to military service, and draftees were selected by a lottery system (Figure 15.12). As in the South, a loophole in the law allowed individuals to hire substitutes if they could afford it. Others could avoid enlistment by paying $300 to the federal government. In keeping with the Supreme Court decision in *Dred Scott v. Sandford*, African Americans were not citizens and were therefore exempt from the draft.

FIGURE 15.12 The Union tried to provide additional incentives for soldiers, in the form of bounties, to enlist without waiting for the draft, as shown in recruitment posters (a) and (b).

Like the Confederacy, the Union also took the step of suspending habeas corpus rights, so those suspected of pro-Confederate sympathies could be arrested and held without being given the reason. Lincoln had selectively suspended the writ of habeas corpus in the slave state of Maryland, home to many Confederate sympathizers, in 1861 and 1862, in an effort to ensure that the Union capital would be safe. In March 1863, he signed into law the Habeas Corpus Suspension Act, giving him the power to detain suspected Confederate operatives throughout the Union. The Lincoln administration also closed down three hundred newspapers as a national security measure during the war.

In both the North and the South, the Civil War dramatically increased the power of the belligerent governments. Breaking all past precedents in American history, both the Confederacy and the Union employed the power of their central governments to mobilize resources and citizens.

Women's Mobilization

As men on both sides mobilized for the war, so did women. In both the North and the South, women were forced to take over farms and businesses abandoned by their husbands as they left for war. Women organized themselves into ladies' aid societies to sew uniforms, knit socks, and raise money to purchase necessities for the troops. In the South, women took wounded soldiers into their homes to nurse. In the North, women volunteered for the United States Sanitary Commission, which formed in June 1861. They inspected military camps with the goal of improving cleanliness and reducing the number of soldiers who died from disease, the most common cause of death in the war. They also raised money to buy medical supplies and helped with the injured. Other women found jobs in the Union army as cooks and laundresses. Thousands volunteered to care for the sick and wounded in response to a call by reformer Dorothea Dix, who was placed in charge of the Union army's nurses. According to rumor, Dix sought respectable women over the age of thirty who were "plain almost to repulsion in dress" and thus could be trusted not to form romantic liaisons with soldiers. Women on both sides also acted as spies and, disguised as men, engaged in combat.

EMANCIPATION

Early in the war, President Lincoln approached the issue of slavery cautiously. While he disapproved of slavery personally, he did not believe that he had the authority to abolish it. Furthermore, he feared that making the abolition of slavery an objective of the war would cause the border slave states to join the Confederacy. His one objective in 1861 and 1862 was to restore the Union.

DEFINING AMERICAN

Lincoln's Evolving Thoughts on Slavery

President Lincoln wrote the following letter to newspaper editor Horace Greeley on August 22, 1862. In it, Lincoln states his position on slavery, which is notable for being a middle-of-the-road stance. Lincoln's later public speeches on the issue take the more strident antislavery tone for which he is remembered.

"I would save the Union. I would save it the shortest way under the Constitution. The sooner the national authority can be restored the nearer the Union will be "the Union as it was." If there be those who would not save the Union unless they could at the same time save Slavery, I do not agree with them. If there be those who would not save the Union unless they could at the same time destroy Slavery, I do not agree with them. My paramount object in this struggle is to save the Union, and is not either to save or destroy Slavery. If I could save the Union without freeing any slave, I would do it, and if I could save it by freeing all the slaves, I would do it, and if I could save it by freeing some and leaving others alone, I would also do that. What I do about Slavery and the colored race, I do because I believe it helps to save this Union, and what I forbear, I forbear because I do not believe it would help to save the Union. I shall do less whenever I shall believe what I am doing hurts the cause, and I shall do more whenever I shall believe doing more will help the cause. I shall try to correct errors when shown to be errors; and I shall adopt new views so fast as they shall appear to be true views. I have here stated my purpose according to my view of official duty, and I intend no modification of my oft-expressed personal wish that all men, everywhere, could be free. Yours, A. LINCOLN."

How would you characterize Lincoln's public position in August 1862? What was he prepared to do for enslaved people, and under what conditions?

Since the beginning of the war, thousands of enslaved people had fled to the safety of Union lines. In May 1861, Union general Benjamin Butler and others labeled these refugees from slavery **contrabands**. Butler reasoned that since Southern states had left the United States, he was not obliged to follow federal fugitive slave laws. Escaped enslaved people who made it through the Union lines were shielded by the U.S. military and not returned to slavery. The intent was not only to assist them but also to deprive the South of a valuable source of manpower.

Congress began to define the status of formerly enslaved people in 1861 and 1862. In August 1861, legislators approved the Confiscation Act of 1861, empowering the Union to seize property, including the enslaved, used by the Confederacy. The Republican-dominated Congress took additional steps, abolishing slavery in Washington, DC, in April 1862. Congress passed a second Confiscation Act in July 1862, which extended freedom to escaped enslaved people and those captured by Union armies. In that month, Congress also addressed the issue of slavery in the West, banning the practice in the territories. This federal law made the 1846 Wilmot Proviso and the dreams of the Free-Soil Party a reality. However, even as the Union government took steps to aid enslaved individuals and to limit the practice of slavery, it passed no measure to address the institution of slavery as a whole.

Lincoln moved slowly and cautiously on the issue of abolition. His primary concern was the cohesion of the Union and the bringing of the Southern states back into the fold. However, as the war dragged on and many thousands of contrabands made their way north, Republicans in Congress continued to call for the end of slavery. Throughout his political career, Lincoln's plans for formerly enslaved people had been to send them to Liberia. As late as August 1862, he had hoped to interest African Americans in building a colony for formerly enslaved people in Central America, an idea that found favor neither with Black leaders nor with abolitionists, and thus was abandoned by Lincoln. Responding to Congressional demands for an end to slavery, Lincoln presented an ultimatum to the Confederates on September 22, 1862, shortly after the Confederate retreat at Antietam. He gave the Confederate states until January 1, 1863, to rejoin the Union. If they did, slavery would the slave states. If they refused to rejoin, however, the war would continue and all of the enslaved would be freed at its conclusion. The Confederacy took no action. It had committed itself to maintaining its independence and had no interest in the president's ultimatum.

On January 1, 1863, Lincoln made good on his promise and signed the **Emancipation Proclamation**. It stated "That on the first day of January, in the year of our Lord one thousand eight hundred and sixty-three, all persons held as slaves within any State or designated part of a State, the people whereof shall then be in rebellion against the United States, shall be then, thenceforward, and forever free." The proclamation did not immediately free the those enslaved in the Confederate states. Although they were in rebellion against the United States, the lack of the Union army's presence in such areas meant that the president's directive could not be enforced. The proclamation also did not free those enslaved in the border states, because these states were not, by definition, in rebellion. Lincoln relied on his powers as commander-in-chief in issuing the Emancipation Proclamation. He knew the proclamation could be easily challenged in court, but by excluding the territories still outside his control, slaveholders and slave governments could not sue him. Moreover, slave states in the Union, such as Kentucky, could not sue because the proclamation did not apply to them. Slaveholders in Kentucky knew full well that if the institution were abolished throughout the South, it would not survive in a handful of border territories. Despite the limits of the proclamation, Lincoln dramatically shifted the objective of the war increasingly toward ending slavery. The Emancipation Proclamation became a monumental step forward on the road to changing the character of the United States.

CLICK AND EXPLORE

Read through the full text of the Emancipation Proclamation (http://openstax.org/l/15Emancipation) at the National Archives website.

The proclamation generated quick and dramatic reactions. The news created euphoria among enslaved people, as it signaled the eventual end of their bondage. Predictably, Confederate leaders raged against the proclamation, reinforcing their commitment to fight to maintain slavery, the foundation of the Confederacy. In the North, opinions split widely on the issue. Abolitionists praised Lincoln's actions, which they saw as the fulfillment of their long campaign to strike down an immoral institution. But other Northerners, especially Irish, working-class, urban dwellers loyal to the Democratic Party and others with racist beliefs, hated the new goal of emancipation and found the idea of freed formerly enslaved people repugnant. At its core, much of this racism had an economic foundation: Many Northerners feared competing with emancipated people for scarce jobs.

In New York City, the Emancipation Proclamation, combined with unhappiness over the Union draft, which began in March 1863, fanned the flames of White racism. Many New Yorkers supported the Confederacy for business reasons, and, in 1861, the city's mayor actually suggested that New York City leave the Union. On July 13, 1863, two days after the first draft lottery took place, this racial hatred erupted into violence. A volunteer fire company whose commander had been drafted initiated a riot, and the violence spread quickly across the city. The rioters chose targets associated either with the Union army or with African Americans. An armory was destroyed, as was a Brooks Brothers' store, which supplied uniforms to the army. White mobs attacked and killed Black New Yorkers and destroyed an African American orphanage (Figure 15.13). On the fourth day of the riots, federal troops dispatched by Lincoln arrived in the city and ended the violence. Millions of dollars in property had been destroyed. More than one hundred people died, approximately one thousand were left injured, and about one-fifth of the city's African American population fled New York in fear.

FIGURE 15.13 The race riots in New York showed just how divided the North was on the issue of equality, even as the North went to war with the South over the issue of slavery.

UNION ADVANCES

The war in the west continued in favor of the North in 1863. At the start of the year, Union forces controlled much of the Mississippi River. In the spring and summer of 1862, they had captured New Orleans—the most important port in the Confederacy, through which cotton harvested from all the Southern states was exported—and Memphis. Grant had then attempted to capture Vicksburg, Mississippi, a commercial center on the bluffs above the Mississippi River. Once Vicksburg fell, the Union would have won complete control over the river. A military bombardment that summer failed to force a Confederate surrender. An assault by land forces also failed in December 1862.

In April 1863, the Union began a final attempt to capture Vicksburg. On July 3, after more than a month of a Union siege, during which Vicksburg's residents hid in caves to protect themselves from the bombardment and ate their pets to stay alive, Grant finally achieved his objective. The trapped Confederate forces surrendered. The Union had succeeded in capturing Vicksburg and splitting the Confederacy (Figure 15.14). This victory inflicted a serious blow to the Southern war effort.

FIGURE 15.14 In this illustration, Union gun boats fire on Vicksburg in the campaign that helped the Union take control of the Mississippi River.

As Grant and his forces pounded Vicksburg, Confederate strategists, at the urging of General Lee, who had defeated a larger Union army at Chancellorsville, Virginia, in May 1863, decided on a bold plan to invade the North. Leaders hoped this invasion would force the Union to send troops engaged in the Vicksburg campaign east, thus weakening their power over the Mississippi. Further, they hoped the aggressive action of pushing north would weaken the Union's resolve to fight. Lee also hoped that a significant Confederate victory in the North would convince Great Britain and France to extend support to Jefferson Davis's government and encourage the North to negotiate peace.

Beginning in June 1863, General Lee began to move the Army of Northern Virginia north through Maryland. The Union army—the Army of the Potomac—traveled east to end up alongside the Confederate forces. The two armies met at Gettysburg, Pennsylvania, where Confederate forces had gone to secure supplies. The resulting battle lasted three days, July 1–3 (Figure 15.15) and remains the biggest and costliest battle ever fought in North America. The climax of the Battle of Gettysburg occurred on the third day. In the morning, after a fight lasting several hours, Union forces fought back a Confederate attack on Culp's Hill, one of the Union's defensive positions. To regain a perceived advantage and secure victory, Lee ordered a frontal assault, known as Pickett's Charge (for Confederate general George Pickett), against the center of the Union lines on Cemetery Ridge. Approximately fifteen thousand Confederate soldiers took part, and more than half lost their lives, as they advanced nearly a mile across an open field to attack the entrenched Union forces. In all, more than a third of the Army of Northern Virginia had been lost, and on the evening of July 4, Lee and his men slipped away in the rain. General George Meade did not pursue them. Both sides suffered staggering losses. Total casualties numbered around twenty-three thousand for the Union and some twenty-eight thousand among the Confederates. With its defeats at Gettysburg and Vicksburg, both on the same day, the Confederacy lost its momentum. The tide had turned in favor of the Union in both the east and the west.

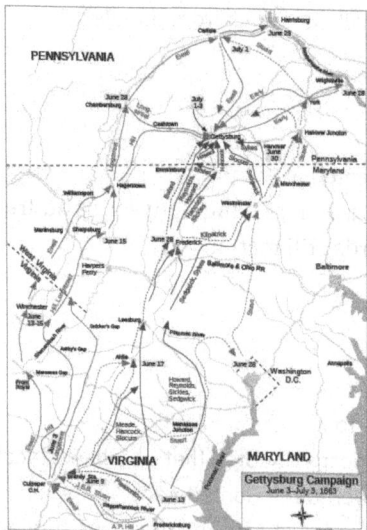

FIGURE 15.15 As this map indicates, the battlefield at Gettysburg was the farthest north that the Confederate army advanced. (credit: Hal Jesperson)

Following the Battle of Gettysburg, the bodies of those who had fallen were hastily buried. Attorney David Wills, a resident of Gettysburg, campaigned for the creation of a national cemetery on the site of the battlefield, and the governor of Pennsylvania tasked him with creating it. President Lincoln was invited to attend the cemetery's dedication. After the featured orator had delivered a two-hour speech, Lincoln addressed the crowd for several minutes. In his speech, known as the **Gettysburg Address**, which he had finished writing while a guest in David Wills' home the day before the dedication, Lincoln invoked the Founding Fathers and the spirit of the American Revolution. The Union soldiers who had died at Gettysburg, he proclaimed, had died not only to preserve the Union, but also to guarantee freedom and equality for all.

DEFINING AMERICAN

Lincoln's Gettysburg Address

Several months after the battle at Gettysburg, Lincoln traveled to Pennsylvania and, speaking to an audience at the dedication of the new Soldiers' National Ceremony near the site of the battle, he delivered his now-famous Gettysburg Address to commemorate the turning point of the war and the soldiers whose sacrifices had made it possible. The two-minute speech was politely received at the time, although press reactions split along party lines. Upon receiving a letter of congratulations from Massachusetts politician and orator William Everett, whose speech at the ceremony had lasted for two hours, Lincoln said he was glad to know that his brief address, now virtually immortal, was not "a total failure."

"Four score and seven years ago our fathers brought forth on this continent, a new nation, conceived in Liberty, and dedicated to the proposition that all men are created equal." "Now we are engaged in a great civil war, testing whether that nation, or any nation so conceived and so dedicated, can long endure. We are met on a great battle-field of that war. We have come to dedicate a portion of that field, as a final resting place for those who here gave their lives that that nation might live. It is altogether fitting and proper that we should do this." "It is for us the living . . . to be here dedicated to the great task remaining before us—that from these honored dead we take increased devotion to that cause for which they gave the last full measure of devotion—that we here highly resolve that these dead shall not have died in vain—that this nation, under God, shall have a new birth of freedom—and that government of the people, by the people, for the people, shall not perish from the earth.
—Abraham Lincoln, Gettysburg Address, November 19, 1863"

What did Lincoln mean by "a new birth of freedom"? What did he mean when he said "a government of the people, by the people, for the people, shall not perish from the earth"?

CLICK AND EXPLORE

Acclaimed filmmaker Ken Burns has created a documentary (http://openstax.org/l/15Address) about a small boys' school in Vermont where students memorize the Gettysburg Address. It explores the value the address has in these boys' lives, and why the words still matter.

15.4 The Union Triumphant

LEARNING OBJECTIVES

By the end of this section, you will be able to:
- Describe the reasons why many Americans doubted that Abraham Lincoln would be reelected
- Explain how the Union forces overpowered the Confederacy
- Describe the contributions and experiences of African Americans serving in the Civil War

By the outset of 1864, after three years of war, the Union had mobilized its resources for the ongoing struggle on a massive scale. The government had overseen the construction of new railroad lines and for the first time used standardized rail tracks that allowed the North to move men and materials with greater ease. The North's economy had shifted to a wartime model. The Confederacy also mobilized, perhaps to a greater degree than the Union, its efforts to secure independence and maintain slavery. Yet the Confederacy experienced ever-greater hardships after years of war. Without the population of the North, it faced a shortage of manpower. The lack of industry, compared to the North, undercut the ability to sustain and wage war. Rampant inflation as well as food shortages in the South lowered morale.

THE RELATIONSHIP WITH EUROPE

From the beginning of the war, the Confederacy placed great hope in being recognized and supported by Great Britain and France. European intervention in the conflict remained a strong possibility, but when it did occur, it was not in a way anticipated by either the Confederacy or the Union.

Napoleon III of France believed the Civil War presented an opportunity for him to restore a French empire in the Americas. With the United States preoccupied, the time seemed ripe for action. Napoleon's target was Mexico, and in 1861, a large French fleet took Veracruz. The French then moved to capture Mexico City, but the advance came to an end when Mexican forces defeated the French in 1862. Despite this setback, France eventually did conquer Mexico, establishing a regime that lasted until 1867. Rather than coming to the aid of

...federacy, France used the Civil War to provide a pretext for efforts to reestablish its former eighteenth-century colonial holdings.

Still, the Confederacy had great confidence that it would find an ally in Great Britain despite the antislavery sentiment there. Southerners hoped Britain's dependence on cotton for its textile mills would keep the country on their side. The fact that the British proved willing to build and sell ironclad ships intended to smash through the Union naval blockade further raised Southern hopes. The Confederacy purchased two of these armored blockade runners, the CSS *Florida* and the CSS *Alabama*. Both were destroyed during the war.

The Confederacy's staunch commitment to slavery eventually worked against British recognition and support, since Great Britain had abolished slavery in 1833. The 1863 Emancipation Proclamation ended any doubts the British had about the goals of the Union cause. In the aftermath of the proclamation, many in Great Britain cheered for a Union victory. Ultimately, Great Britain, like France, disappointed the Confederacy's hope of an alliance, leaving the outnumbered and out-resourced states that had left the Union to fend for themselves.

AFRICAN AMERICAN SOLDIERS

At the beginning of the war, in 1861 and 1862, Union forces had used contrabands, or escaped enslaved people, for manual labor. The Emancipation Proclamation, however, led to the enrollment of African American men as Union soldiers. Huge numbers of formerly enslaved as well as free Black people from the North enlisted, and by the end of the war in 1865, their numbers had swelled to over 190,000. Racism among White people in the Union army ran deep, however, fueling the belief that Black soldiers could never be effective or trustworthy. The Union also feared for the fate of captured Black soldiers. Although many Black soldiers saw combat duty, these factors affected the types of tasks assigned to them. Many Black regiments were limited to hauling supplies, serving as cooks, digging trenches, and doing other types of labor, rather than serving on the battlefield (Figure 15.16).

FIGURE 15.16 This 1865 daguerreotype illustrates three of the Union's distinct advantages: African American soldiers, a stream of cannons and supplies, and an extensive railroad grid. (credit: Library of Congress)

African American soldiers also received lower wages than their White counterparts: ten dollars per month, with three dollars deducted for clothing. White soldiers, in contrast, received thirteen dollars monthly, with no deductions. Abolitionists and their Republican supporters in Congress worked to correct this discriminatory practice, and in 1864, Black soldiers began to receive the same pay as White soldiers plus retroactive pay to 1863 (Figure 15.17).

FIGURE 15.17 African American and White soldiers of the Union army pose together in this photograph, although in reality, Black soldiers were often kept separate and given only menial jobs.

For their part, African American soldiers welcomed the opportunity to prove themselves. Some 85 percent were formerly enslaved people who were fighting for the liberation of all of the enslaved and the end of slavery. When given the opportunity to serve, many Black regiments did so heroically. One such regiment, the Fifty-Fourth Regiment of Massachusetts Volunteers, distinguished itself at Fort Wagner in South Carolina by fighting valiantly against an entrenched Confederate position. They willingly gave their lives for the cause.

The Confederacy, not surprisingly, showed no mercy to African American troops. In April 1864, Southern forces attempted to take Fort Pillow in Tennessee from the Union forces that had captured it in 1862. Confederate troops under Major General Nathan Bedford Forrest, the future founder of the Ku Klux Klan, quickly overran the fort, and the Union defenders surrendered. Instead of taking the African American soldiers prisoner, as they did the White soldiers, the Confederates executed them. The massacre outraged the North, and the Union refused to engage in any future exchanges of prisoners with the Confederacy.

THE CAMPAIGNS OF 1864 AND 1865

In the final years of the war, the Union continued its efforts on both the eastern and western fronts while bringing the war into the Deep South. Union forces increasingly engaged in total war, not distinguishing between military and civilian targets. They destroyed everything that lay in their path, committed to breaking the will of the Confederacy and forcing an end to the war. General Grant, mastermind of the Vicksburg campaign, took charge of the war effort. He understood the advantage of having large numbers of soldiers at his disposal and recognized that Union soldiers could be replaced, whereas the Confederates, whose smaller population was feeling the strain of the years of war, could not. Grant thus pushed forward relentlessly, despite huge losses of men. In 1864, Grant committed his forces to destroying Lee's army in Virginia.

In the Virginia campaign, Grant hoped to use his larger army to his advantage. But at the Battle of the Wilderness, fought from May 5 to May 7, Confederate forces stopped Grant's advance. Rather than retreating, he pushed forward. At the Battle of Spotsylvania on May 8 through 12, Grant again faced determined Confederate resistance, and again his advance was halted. As before, he renewed the Union campaign. At the Battle of Cold Harbor in early June, Grant had between 100,000 and 110,000 soldiers, whereas the Confederates had slightly more than half that number. Again, the Union advance was halted, if only momentarily, as Grant awaited reinforcements. An attack on the Confederate position on June 3 resulted in heavy casualties for the Union, and nine days later, Grant led his army away from Cold Harbor to Petersburg, Virginia, a rail center that supplied Richmond. The immense losses that Grant's forces suffered severely hurt

Union morale. The war seemed unending, and with the tremendous loss of life, many in the North began to question the war and desire peace. Undaunted by the changing opinion in the North and hoping to destroy the Confederate rail network in the Upper South, however, Grant laid siege to Petersburg for nine months. As the months wore on, both sides dug in, creating miles of trenches and gun emplacements.

The other major Union campaigns of 1864 were more successful and gave President Lincoln the advantage that he needed to win reelection in November. In August 1864, the Union navy captured Mobile Bay. General Sherman invaded the Deep South, advancing slowly from Tennessee into Georgia, confronted at every turn by the Confederates, who were commanded by Johnston. When President Davis replaced Johnston with General John B. Hood, the Confederates made a daring but ultimately costly direct attack on the Union army that failed to drive out the invaders. Atlanta fell to Union forces on September 2, 1864. The fall of Atlanta held tremendous significance for the war-weary Union and helped to reverse the North's sinking morale. In keeping with the logic of total war, Sherman's forces cut a swath of destruction to Savannah. On **Sherman's March to the Sea**, the Union army, seeking to demoralize the South, destroyed everything in its path, despite strict instructions regarding the preservation of civilian property. Although towns were left standing, houses and barns were burned. Homes were looted, food was stolen, crops were destroyed, orchards were burned, and livestock was killed or confiscated. Savannah fell on December 21, 1864—a Christmas gift for Lincoln, Sherman proclaimed. In 1865, Sherman's forces invaded South Carolina, capturing Charleston and Columbia. In Columbia, the state capital, the Union army burned slaveholders' homes and destroyed much of the city. From South Carolina, Sherman's force moved north in an effort to join Grant and destroy Lee's army.

MY STORY

Dolly Sumner Lunt on Sherman's March to the Sea

The following account is by Dolly Sumner Lunt, a widow who ran her Georgia cotton plantation after the death of her husband. She describes General Sherman's march to Savannah, where he enacted the policy of total war by burning and plundering the landscape to inhibit the Confederates' ability to keep fighting.

"Alas! little did I think while trying to save my house from plunder and fire that they were forcing my boys [slaves] from home at the point of the bayonet. One, Newton, jumped into bed in his cabin, and declared himself sick. Another crawled under the floor,—a lame boy he was,—but they pulled him out, placed him on a horse, and drove him off. Mid, poor Mid! The last I saw of him, a man had him going around the garden, looking, as I thought, for my sheep, as he was my shepherd. Jack came crying to me, the big tears coursing down his cheeks, saying they were making him go. I said: 'Stay in my room.'" "But a man followed in, cursing him and threatening to shoot him if he did not go; so poor Jack had to yield. . . ." "Sherman himself and a greater portion of his army passed my house that day. All day, as the sad moments rolled on, were they passing not only in front of my house, but from behind; they tore down my garden palings, made a road through my back-yard and lot field, driving their stock and riding through, tearing down my fences and desolating my home—wantonly doing it when there was no necessity for it. . . ." "About ten o'clock they had all passed save one, who came in and wanted coffee made, which was done, and he, too, went on. A few minutes elapsed, and two couriers riding rapidly passed back. Then, presently, more soldiers came by, and this ended the passing of Sherman's army by my place, leaving me poorer by thirty thousand dollars than I was yesterday morning. And a much stronger Rebel!"

According to this account, what was the reaction of enslaved people to the arrival of the Union forces? What did the Union forces do with the enslaved? For Lunt, did the strategy of total war work as planned?

THE ELECTION OF 1864

Despite the military successes for the Union army in 1863, in 1864, Lincoln's status among many Northern voters plummeted. Citing the suspension of the writ of habeas corpus, many saw him as a dictator, bent on grabbing power while senselessly and uncaringly drafting more young men into combat. Arguably, his greatest liability, however, was the Emancipation Proclamation and the enlistment of African American soldiers. Many White people in the North found this deeply offensive, since they still believed in racial inequality. The 1863 New York City Draft Riots illustrated the depth of White anger.

Northern Democrats railed against Lincoln and the war. Republicans labeled these vocal opponents of the President **Copperheads**, a term that many antiwar Democrats accepted. As the anti-Lincoln poster below illustrates, his enemies tried to paint him as an untrustworthy and suspect leader (Figure 15.18). It seemed to most in the North that the Democratic candidate, General George B. McClellan, who did not support abolition and was replaced with another commander by Lincoln, would win the election.

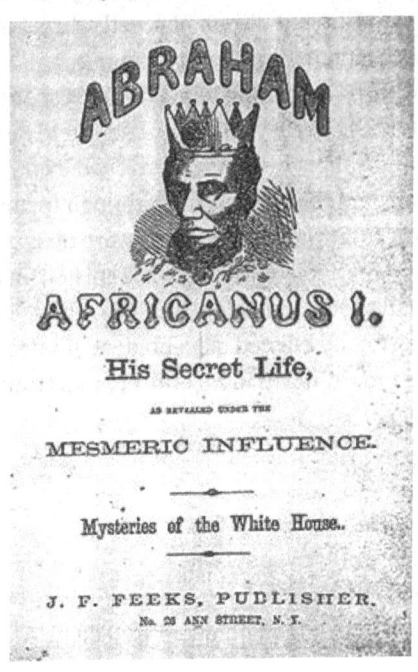

FIGURE 15.18 Anti-Lincoln sentiment in the North ran high in 1864, and many believed he would not be reelected president that year.

The Republican Party also split over the issue of reelecting Lincoln. Those who found him timid and indecisive, and favored extending full rights to African Americans, as well as completely refashioning the South after its defeat, earned the name Radicals. A moderate faction of Republicans opposed the Radicals. For his part, Lincoln did not align himself with either group.

The tide of the election campaign turned in favor of Lincoln, however, in the fall of 1864. Above all else, Union victories, including the fall of Atlanta in September and General Philip Sheridan's successes in the Shenandoah Valley of Virginia, bolstered Lincoln's popularity and his reelection bid. In November 1864, despite earlier forecasts to the contrary, Lincoln was reelected. Lincoln won all but three states—New Jersey and the border states of Delaware and Kentucky. To the chagrin of his opponent, McClellan, even Union army troops voted overwhelmingly for the incumbent President.

THE WAR ENDS

By the spring of 1865, it had become clear to both sides that the Confederacy could not last much longer. Most of its major cities, ports, and industrial centers—Atlanta, Savannah, Charleston, Columbia, Mobile, New Orleans, and Memphis—had been captured. In April 1865, Lee had abandoned both Petersburg and Richmond. His goal in doing so was to unite his depleted army with Confederate forces commanded by General Johnston. Grant effectively cut him off. On April 9, 1865, Lee surrendered to Grant at Appomattox Court House in Virginia (Figure 15.19). By that time, he had fewer than 35,000 soldiers, while Grant had some 100,000. Meanwhile, Sherman's army proceeded to North Carolina, where General Johnston surrendered on April 19, 1865. The Civil War had come to an end. The war had cost the lives of more than 600,000 soldiers. Many more been wounded. Thousands of women were left widowed. Children were left without fathers, and many parents were deprived of a source of support in their old age. In some areas, where local volunteer units had marched off to battle, never to return, an entire generation of young women was left without marriage partners. Millions of dollars' worth of property had been destroyed, and towns and cities were laid to waste. With the conflict finally over, the very difficult work of reconciling North and South and reestablishing the United States lay ahead.

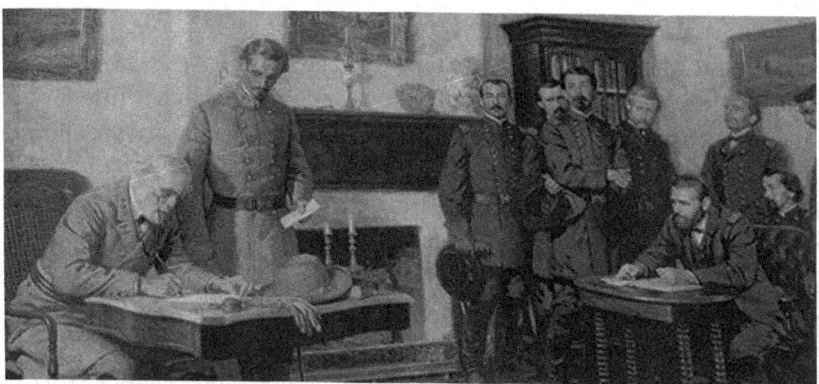

FIGURE 15.19 Vastly outnumbered by the Union army, the Confederate general Robert E. Lee (seated at the left) surrendered to Ulysses S. Grant at Appomattox Courthouse. (credit: "Alaskan Dude"/Wikimedia Commons)

Key Terms

Army of the Potomac   the Union fighting force operating outside Washington, DC
Army of the West   the Union fighting force operating in Kentucky, Tennessee, and the Mississippi River Valley
Confederacy   the new nation formed by the seceding southern states, also known as the Confederate States of America (CSA)
contrabands   enslaved people who escaped to the Union army's lines
Copperheads   Democrats who opposed Lincoln in the 1864 election
Crittenden Compromise   a compromise, suggested by Kentucky senator John Crittenden, that would restore the 36°30′ line from the Missouri Compromise and extend it to the Pacific Ocean, allowing slavery to expand into the southwestern territories
Emancipation Proclamation   signed on January 1, 1863, the document with which President Lincoln transformed the Civil War into a struggle to end slavery
Fort Sumter   a fort in the harbor of Charleston, South Carolina, where the Union garrison came under siege by Confederate forces in an attack on April 12, 1861, beginning the Civil War
general in chief   the commander of army land forces
Gettysburg Address   a speech by Abraham Lincoln dedicating the military cemetery at Gettysburg on November 19, 1863
greenbacks   paper money the United States began to issue during the Civil War
habeas corpus   the right of those arrested to be brought before a judge or court to determine whether there is cause to hold the prisoner
Sherman's March to the Sea   the scorched-earth campaign employed in Georgia by Union general William Tecumseh Sherman
total war   a state of war in which the government makes no distinction between military and civilian targets, and mobilizes all resources, extending its reach into all areas of citizens' lives

Summary

15.1 The Origins and Outbreak of the Civil War

The election of Abraham Lincoln to the presidency in 1860 proved to be a watershed event. While it did not cause the Civil War, it was the culmination of increasing tensions between the proslavery South and the antislavery North. Before Lincoln had even taken office, seven Deep South states had seceded from the Union to form the CSA, dedicated to maintaining racial slavery and White supremacy. Last-minute efforts to reach a compromise, such as the proposal by Senator Crittenden and the Corwin amendment, went nowhere. The time for compromise had come to an end. With the Confederate attack on Fort Sumter, the Civil War began.

15.2 Early Mobilization and War

Many in both the North and the South believed that a short, decisive confrontation in 1861 would settle the question of the Confederacy. These expectations did not match reality, however, and the war dragged on into a second year. Both sides mobilized, with advantages and disadvantages on each side that led to a rough equilibrium. The losses of battles at Manassas and Fredericksburg, Virginia, kept the North from achieving the speedy victory its generals had hoped for, but the Union did make gains and continued to press forward. While they could not capture the Southern capital of Richmond, they were victorious in the Battle of Shiloh and captured New Orleans and Memphis. Thus, the Confederates lost major ground on the western front.

15.3 1863: The Changing Nature of the War

The year 1863 proved decisive in the Civil War for two major reasons. First, the Union transformed the purpose of the struggle from restoring the Union to ending slavery. While Lincoln's Emancipation Proclamation actually succeeded in freeing few of the enslaved, it made freedom for African Americans a of the Union. Second, the tide increasingly turned against the Confederacy. The success of the Vicksburg Campaign had given the Union control of the Mississippi River, and Lee's defeat at Gettysburg had ended the attempted Confederate invasion of the North.

15.4 The Union Triumphant

Having failed to win the support it expected from either Great Britain or France, the Confederacy faced a long war with limited resources and no allies. Lincoln won reelection in 1864, and continued to pursue the Union campaign, not only in the east and west, but also with a drive into the South under the leadership of General Sherman, whose March to the Sea through Georgia destroyed everything in its path. Cut off and outnumbered, Confederate general Lee surrendered to Union general Grant on April 9 at Appomattox Court House in Virginia. Within days of Lee's surrender, Confederate troops had lay down their arms, and the devastating war came to a close.

Review Questions

1. Which of the following does *not* represent a goal of the Confederate States of America?
    A. to protect slavery from any effort to abolish it
    B. to protect the domestic slave trade
    C. to ensure that slavery would be allowed to spread into western territories
    D. to ensure that the international slave trade would be allowed to continue

2. Which was *not* a provision of the Crittenden Compromise?
    A. that the Five Civilized Tribes would be admitted into the Confederacy
    B. that the 36°30′ line from the Missouri Compromise would be restored and extended
    C. that Congress would be prohibited from abolishing slavery where it already existed
    D. that the interstate slave trade would be allowed to continue

3. Why did the states of the Deep South secede from the Union sooner than the states of the Upper South and the border states?

4. All the following were strengths of the Union *except* _____.
    A. a large population
    B. substantial industry
    C. an extensive railroad
    D. the ability to fight defensively, rather than offensively

5. All the following were strengths of the Confederacy *except* _____.
    A. the ability to wage a defensive war
    B. shorter supply lines
    C. the resources of the Upper South states
    D. a strong navy

6. What military successes and defeats did the Union experience in 1862?

7. Which of the following did the North *not* do to mobilize for war?
    A. institute a military draft
    B. form a military alliance with Great Britain
    C. print paper money
    D. pass the Homestead Act

8. Why is 1863 considered a turning point in the Civil War?

9. Which of the following is *not* a reason why many people opposed Lincoln's reelection in 1864?
   A. He appeared to have overstepped his authority by suspending the writ of habeas corpus.
   B. He issued the Emancipation Proclamation.
   C. He had replaced General George B. McClellan.
   D. He was seen as a power-hungry dictator.

10. What was General Sherman's objective on his March to the Sea?
    A. to destroy military and civilian resources wherever possible
    B. to free Black prisoners of war
    C. to join his army to that of General Grant
    D. to capture General Robert E. Lee

Critical Thinking Questions

11. Could the differences between the North and South have been worked out in late 1860 and 1861? Could war have been avoided? Provide evidence to support your answer.

12. Why did the North prevail in the Civil War? What might have turned the tide of the war *against* the North?

13. If you were in charge of the Confederate war effort, what strategy or strategies would you have pursued? Conversely, if you had to devise the Union strategy, what would you propose? How does your answer depend on your knowledge of how the war actually played out?

14. What do you believe to be the enduring qualities of the Gettysburg Address? Why has this two-minute speech so endured?

15. What role did women and African Americans play in the war?

The Era of Reconstruction, 1865–1877

FIGURE 16.1 In this political cartoon by Thomas Nast, which appeared in *Harper's Weekly* in October 1874, the "White League" shakes hands with the Ku Klux Klan over a shield that shows a couple weeping over a baby. In the background, a schoolhouse burns, and a lynched freedman is shown hanging from a tree. Above the shield, which is labeled "Worse than Slavery," the text reads, "The Union as It Was: This Is a White Man's Government."

CHAPTER OUTLINE

16.1 Restoring the Union
16.2 Congress and the Remaking of the South, 1865–1866
16.3 Radical Reconstruction, 1867–1872
16.4 The Collapse of Reconstruction

INTRODUCTION Few times in U.S. history have been as turbulent and transformative as the Civil War and the twelve years that followed. Between 1865 and 1877, one president was murdered and another impeached. The Constitution underwent major revision with the addition of three amendments. The effort to impose Union control and create equality in the defeated South ignited a fierce backlash as various terrorist and vigilante organizations, most notably the Ku Klux Klan, battled to maintain a pre–Civil War society in which White people held complete power. These groups unleashed a wave of violence, including lynching and arson, aimed at freed Black people and their White supporters. Historians refer to this era as Reconstruction, when an effort to remake the South faltered and ultimately failed.

The above political cartoon (Figure 16.1) expresses the anguish many Americans felt in the decade after the

Civil War. The South, which had experienced catastrophic losses during the conflict, was reduced to political dependence and economic destitution. This humiliating condition led many southern White people to vigorously contest Union efforts to transform the South's racial, economic, and social landscape. Supporters of equality grew increasingly dismayed at Reconstruction's failure to undo the old system, which further compounded the staggering regional and racial inequalities in the United States.

16.1 Restoring the Union

LEARNING OBJECTIVES

By the end of this section, you will be able to:
- Describe Lincoln's plan to restore the Union at the end of the Civil War
- Discuss the tenets of Radical Republicanism
- Analyze the success or failure of the Thirteenth Amendment

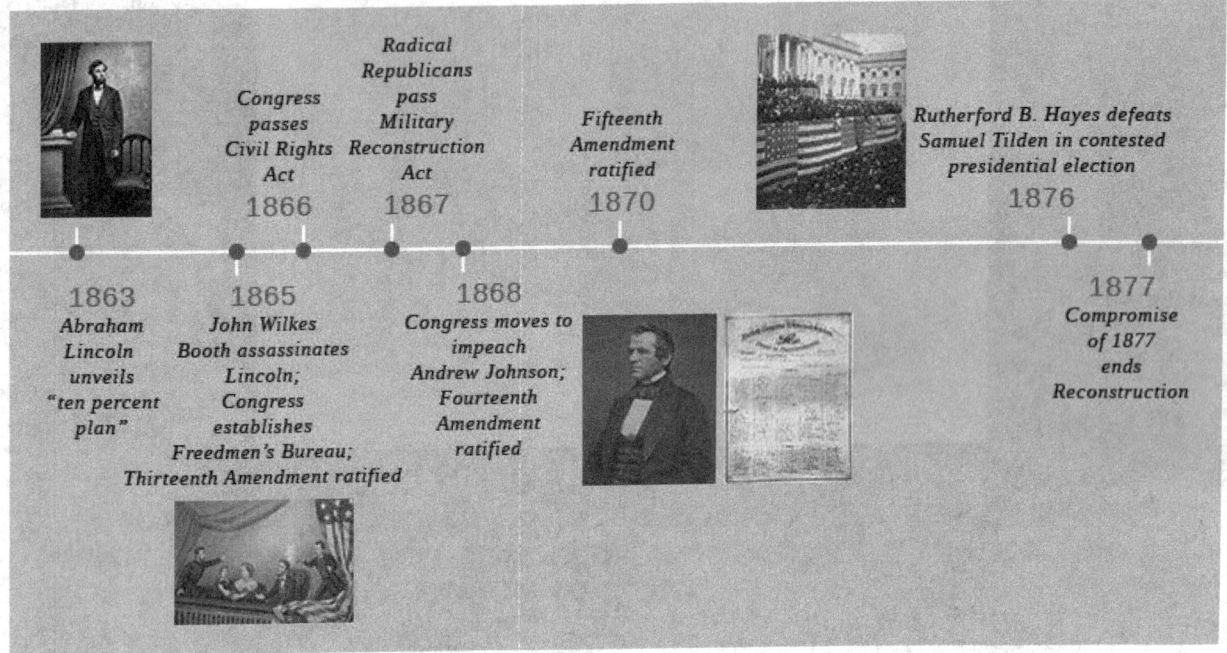

FIGURE 16.2

The end of the Civil War saw the beginning of the **Reconstruction** era, when former rebel Southern states were integrated back into the Union. President Lincoln moved quickly to achieve the war's ultimate goal: reunification of the country. He proposed a generous and non-punitive plan to return the former Confederate states speedily to the United States, but some Republicans in Congress protested, considering the president's plan too lenient to the rebel states that had torn the country apart. The greatest flaw of Lincoln's plan, according to this view, was that it appeared to forgive traitors instead of guaranteeing civil rights to formerly enslaved people. President Lincoln oversaw the passage of the Thirteenth Amendment abolishing slavery, but he did not live to see its ratification.

THE PRESIDENT'S PLAN

From the outset of the rebellion in 1861, Lincoln's overriding goal had been to bring the Southern states quickly back into the fold in order to restore the Union (Figure 16.3). In early December 1863, the president began the process of reunification by unveiling a three-part proposal known as the **ten percent plan** that outlined how the states would return. The ten percent plan gave a general pardon to all Southerners except high-ranking Confederate government and military leaders; required 10 percent of the 1860 voting population in the former rebel states to take a binding oath of future allegiance to the United States and the emancipation of the enslaved; and declared that once those voters took those oaths, the restored Confederate states would draft new state constitutions.

Access for free at openstax.org.

(a) (b)

FIGURE 16.3 Thomas Le Mere took this albumen silver print (a) of Abraham Lincoln in April 1863. Le Mere thought a standing pose of Lincoln would be popular. In this political cartoon from 1865 (b), Lincoln and his vice president, Andrew Johnson, endeavor to sew together the torn pieces of the Union.

Lincoln hoped that the leniency of the plan—90 percent of the 1860 voters did not have to swear allegiance to the Union or to emancipation—would bring about a quick and long-anticipated resolution and make emancipation more acceptable everywhere. This approach appealed to some in the moderate wing of the Republican Party, which wanted to put the nation on a speedy course toward reconciliation. However, the proposal instantly drew fire from a larger faction of Republicans in Congress who did not want to deal moderately with the South. These members of Congress, known as **Radical Republicans**, wanted to remake the South and punish the rebels. Radical Republicans insisted on harsh terms for the defeated Confederacy and protection for formerly enslaved people, going far beyond what the president proposed.

In February 1864, two of the Radical Republicans, Ohio senator Benjamin Wade and Maryland representative Henry Winter Davis, answered Lincoln with a proposal of their own. Among other stipulations, the Wade-Davis Bill called for a majority of voters and government officials in Confederate states to take an oath, called the **Ironclad Oath**, swearing that they had never supported the Confederacy or made war against the United States. Those who could not or would not take the oath would be unable to take part in the future political life of the South. Congress assented to the Wade-Davis Bill, and it went to Lincoln for his signature. The president refused to sign, using the pocket veto (that is, taking no action) to kill the bill. Lincoln understood that no Southern state would have met the criteria of the Wade-Davis Bill, and its passage would simply have delayed the reconstruction of the South.

THE THIRTEENTH AMENDMENT

Despite the 1863 Emancipation Proclamation, the legal status of enslaved people and the institution of slavery remained unresolved. The news of the Proclamation wouldn't even reach the entire country for another two and a half years. To deal with the remaining uncertainties, the Republican Party made the abolition of slavery a top priority by including the issue in its 1864 party platform. The platform read: "That as slavery was the cause, and now constitutes the strength of this Rebellion, and as it must be, always and everywhere, hostile to the principles of Republican Government, justice and the National safety demand its utter and complete extirpation from the soil of the Republic; and that, while we uphold and maintain the acts and proclamations by which the Government, in its own defense, has aimed a deathblow at this gigantic evil, we are in favor, furthermore, of such an amendment to the Constitution, to be made by the people in conformity with its provisions, as shall terminate and forever prohibit the existence of Slavery within the limits of the jurisdiction of the United States." The platform left no doubt about the intention to abolish slavery.

The president, along with the Radical Republicans, made good on this campaign promise in 1864 and 1865. A proposed constitutional amendment passed the Senate in April 1864, and the House of Representatives concurred in January 1865. The amendment then made its way to the states, where it swiftly gained the necessary support, including in the South. In December 1865, the Thirteenth Amendment was officially ratified and added to the Constitution. The first amendment added to the Constitution since 1804, it overturned a centuries-old practice by permanently abolishing slavery.

CLICK AND EXPLORE

Explore a comprehensive collection of documents, images, and ephemera related to Abraham Lincoln (http://openstax.org/l/15Lincoln) on the Library of Congress website.

President Lincoln never saw the final ratification of the Thirteenth Amendment. On April 14, 1865, the Confederate supporter and well-known actor John Wilkes Booth shot Lincoln while he was attending a play, *Our American Cousin*, at Ford's Theater in Washington. The president died the next day (Figure 16.4). Booth had steadfastly defended the Confederacy and White supremacy, and his act was part of a larger conspiracy to eliminate the heads of the Union government and keep the Confederate fight going. One of Booth's associates stabbed and wounded Secretary of State William Seward the night of the assassination. Another associate abandoned the planned assassination of Vice President Andrew Johnson at the last moment. Although Booth initially escaped capture, Union troops shot and killed him on April 26, 1865, in a Maryland barn. Eight other conspirators were convicted by a military tribunal for participating in the conspiracy, and four were hanged. Lincoln's death earned him immediate martyrdom, and hysteria spread throughout the North. To many Northerners, the assassination suggested an even greater conspiracy than what was revealed, masterminded by the unrepentant leaders of the defeated Confederacy. Militant Republicans would use and exploit this fear relentlessly in the ensuing months.

FIGURE 16.4 In *The Assassination of President Lincoln* (1865), by Currier and Ives, John Wilkes Booth shoots Lincoln in the back of the head as he sits in the theater box with his wife, Mary Todd Lincoln, and their guests, Major Henry R. Rathbone and Clara Harris.

Despite the Emancipation Proclamation and the ratification progress of the Thirteenth Amendment, slavery endured for some time. The news of the war's end and the freedom of the enslaved people traveled slowly, and in some cases was likely deliberately withheld. When Major General Gordan Granger arrived in Galveston, Texas to assert control, he brought with him a stunning announcement:

The people of Texas are informed that, in accordance with a proclamation from the Executive of the United States, all slaves are free. This involves an absolute equality of personal rights and rights of property between former masters and slaves, and the connection heretofore existing between them becomes that between employer and hired labor."

The date, June 19, 1865, would become the most popular annual celebration of the end of slavery, known as **Juneteenth**. The order was met with resistance and outright opposition. Some slaveholders chose to keep the news from enslaved people. And when people who learned about their emancipation decided to take advantage of their freedom, many were captured or killed. While the pathway to full freedom remained difficult, and discrimination and segregation would remain in place, newly freed Texans began organizing celebrations (also referred to as Jubilee Day and Emancipation Day) as early as 1866. Austin held its first Juneteenth celebration in 1867.

ANDREW JOHNSON AND THE BATTLE OVER RECONSTRUCTION

Lincoln's assassination elevated Vice President Andrew Johnson, a Democrat, to the presidency. Johnson had come from very humble origins. Born into extreme poverty in North Carolina and having never attended school, Johnson was the picture of a self-made man. His wife had taught him how to read and he had worked as a tailor, a trade he had been apprenticed to as a child. In Tennessee, where he had moved as a young man, he gradually rose up the political ladder, earning a reputation for being a skillful stump speaker and a staunch defender of poor southerners. He was elected to serve in the House of Representatives in the 1840s, became governor of Tennessee the following decade, and then was elected a U.S. senator just a few years before the country descended into war. When Tennessee seceded, Johnson remained loyal to the Union and stayed in the Senate. As Union troops marched on his home state of North Carolina, Lincoln appointed him governor of the then-occupied state of Tennessee, where he served until being nominated by the Republicans to run for vice president on a Lincoln ticket. The nomination of Johnson, a Democrat and a slaveholding southerner, was a pragmatic decision made by concerned Republicans. It was important for them to show that the party supported all loyal men, regardless of their origin or political persuasion. Johnson appeared an ideal choice, because his nomination would bring with it the support of both pro-Southern elements and the War Democrats who rejected the conciliatory stance of the Copperheads, the northern Democrats who opposed the Civil War.

Unexpectedly elevated to the presidency in 1865, this formerly impoverished tailor's apprentice and unwavering antagonist of the wealthy southern planter class now found himself tasked with administering the restoration of a destroyed South. Lincoln's position as president had been that the secession of the Southern states was never legal; that is, they had not succeeded in leaving the Union, therefore they still had certain rights to self-government as states. In keeping with Lincoln's plan, Johnson desired to quickly reincorporate the South back into the Union on lenient terms and heal the wounds of the nation. This position angered many in his own party. The northern Radical Republican plan for Reconstruction looked to overturn southern society and specifically aimed at ending the plantation system. President Johnson quickly disappointed Radical Republicans when he rejected their idea that the federal government could provide voting rights for formerly enslaved people. The initial disagreements between the president and the Radical Republicans over how best to deal with the defeated South set the stage for further conflict.

In fact, President Johnson's Proclamation of Amnesty and Reconstruction in May 1865 provided sweeping "amnesty and pardon" to rebellious Southerners. It returned to them their property, with the notable exception of the people they had enslaved, and it asked only that they affirm their support for the Constitution of the United States. Those Southerners exempted from this amnesty included the Confederate political leadership, high-ranking military officers, and persons with taxable property worth more than $20,000. The inclusion of this last category was specifically designed to make it clear to the southern planter class that they had a unique responsibility for the outbreak of hostilities. But it also satisfied Johnson's desire to exact vengeance on a class of people he had fought politically for much of his life. For this class of wealthy Southerners to regain their rights, they would have to swallow their pride and request a personal pardon from Johnson himself.

For the Southern states, the requirements for readmission to the Union were also fairly straightforward. States were required to hold individual state conventions where they would repeal the ordinances of secession and ratify the Thirteenth Amendment. By the end of 1865, a number of former Confederate leaders were in the Union capital looking to claim their seats in Congress. Among them was Alexander Stephens, the vice president of the Confederacy, who had spent several months in a Boston jail after the war. Despite the outcries of Republicans in Congress, by early 1866 Johnson announced that all former Confederate states had satisfied the necessary requirements. According to him, nothing more needed to be done; the Union had been restored.

Understandably, Radical Republicans in Congress did not agree with Johnson's position. They, and their northern constituents, greatly resented his lenient treatment of the former Confederate states, and especially the return of former Confederate leaders like Alexander Stephens to Congress. They refused to acknowledge the southern state governments he allowed. As a result, they would not permit senators and representatives from the former Confederate states to take their places in Congress.

Instead, the Radical Republicans created a joint committee of representatives and senators to oversee Reconstruction. In the 1866 congressional elections, they gained control of the House, and in the ensuing years they pushed for the dismantling of the old southern order and the complete reconstruction of the South. This effort put them squarely at odds with President Johnson, who remained unwilling to compromise with Congress, setting the stage for a series of clashes.

16.2 Congress and the Remaking of the South, 1865–1866

LEARNING OBJECTIVES
By the end of this section, you will be able to:
- Describe the efforts made by Congress in 1865 and 1866 to bring to life its vision of Reconstruction
- Explain how the Fourteenth Amendment transformed the Constitution

President Johnson and Congress's views on Reconstruction grew even further apart as Johnson's presidency progressed. Congress repeatedly pushed for greater rights for freed people and a far more thorough reconstruction of the South, while Johnson pushed for leniency and a swifter reintegration. President Johnson lacked Lincoln's political skills and instead exhibited a stubbornness and confrontational approach that aggravated an already difficult situation.

THE FREEDMEN'S BUREAU

Freed people everywhere celebrated the end of slavery and immediately began to take steps to improve their own condition by seeking what had long been denied to them: land, financial security, education, and the ability to participate in the political process. They wanted to be reunited with family members, grasp the opportunity to make their own independent living, and exercise their right to have a say in their own government.

However, they faced the wrath of defeated but un-reconciled southerners who were determined to keep Black people an impoverished and despised underclass. Recognizing the widespread devastation in the South and the dire situation of freed people, Congress created the Bureau of Refugees, Freedmen, and Abandoned Lands in March 1865, popularly known as the **Freedmen's Bureau**. Lincoln had approved of the bureau, giving it a charter for one year.

The Freedmen's Bureau engaged in many initiatives to ease the transition from slavery to freedom. It delivered food to Black people and White people alike in the South. It helped freed people gain labor contracts, a significant step in the creation of wage labor in place of slavery. It helped reunite families of freedmen, and it also devoted much energy to education, establishing scores of public schools where freed people and poor White people could receive both elementary and higher education. Respected institutions such as Fisk University, Hampton University, and Dillard University are part of the legacy of the Freedmen's Bureau.

In this endeavor, the Freedmen's Bureau received support from Christian organizations that had long advocated for abolition, such as the American Missionary Association (AMA). The AMA used the knowledge and skill it had acquired while working in missions in Africa and with Native American groups to establish and run schools for those freed from slavery in the postwar South. While men and women, White and Black, taught in these schools, the opportunity was crucially important for participating women (Figure 16.5). At the time, many opportunities, including admission to most institutes of higher learning, remained closed to women. Participating in these schools afforded these women the opportunities they otherwise may have been denied. Additionally, the fact they often risked life and limb to work in these schools in the South demonstrated to the nation that women could play a vital role in American civic life.

FIGURE 16.5 The Freedmen's Bureau, as shown in this 1866 illustration from *Frank Leslie's Illustrated Newspaper*, created many schools for Black elementary school students. Many of the teachers who provided instruction in these southern schools, though by no means all, came from northern states.

The schools that the Freedmen's Bureau and the AMA established inspired great dismay and resentment among the White populations in the South and were sometimes targets of violence. Indeed, the Freedmen's Bureau's programs and its very existence were sources of controversy. Racists and others who resisted this type of federal government activism denounced it as both a waste of federal money and a foolish effort that encouraged laziness among Black people. Congress renewed the bureau's charter in 1866, but President Johnson, who steadfastly believed that the work of restoring the Union had been completed, vetoed the re-chartering. Radical Republicans continued to support the bureau, igniting a contest between Congress and the president that intensified during the next several years. Part of this dispute involved conflicting visions of the proper role of the federal government. Radical Republicans believed in the constructive power of the federal government to ensure a better day for freed people. Others, including Johnson, denied that the government had any such role to play.

AMERICANA

The Freedmen's Bureau
The image below (Figure 16.6) shows a campaign poster for Hiester Clymer, who ran for governor of Pennsylvania in 1866 on a platform of White supremacy.

FIGURE 16.6 The caption of this image reads, "The Freedman's Bureau! An agency to keep the Negro in idleness at the expense of the White man. Twice vetoed by the President, and made a law by Congress. Support Congress & you support the Negro. Sustain the President & you protect the White man."

The image in the foreground shows an indolent Black man wondering, "Whar is de use for me to work as long as dey make dese appropriations." White men toil in the background, chopping wood and plowing a field. The text above them reads, "In the sweat of thy face shall thou eat bread. . . . The White man must work to keep his children and pay his taxes." In the middle background, the Freedmen's Bureau looks like the Capitol, and the pillars are inscribed with racist assumptions of things Black people value, like "rum," "idleness," and "White women." On the right are estimates of the costs of the Freedmen's Bureau and the bounties (fees for enlistment) given to both White and Black Union soldiers.

What does this poster indicate about the political climate of the Reconstruction era? How might different people have received this image?

BLACK CODES

In 1865 and 1866, as Johnson announced the end of Reconstruction, southern states began to pass a series of discriminatory state laws collectively known as **Black codes**. While the laws varied in both content and severity from state to state, the goal of the laws remained largely consistent. In effect, these codes were designed to maintain the social and economic structure of racial slavery in the absence of slavery itself. The laws codified White supremacy by restricting the civic participation of freed enslaved people—depriving them of the right to vote, the right to serve on juries, the right to own or carry weapons, and, in some cases, even the right to rent or lease land.

A chief component of the Black codes was designed to fulfill an important economic need in the postwar South. Slavery had been a pillar of economic stability in the region before the war. To maintain agricultural production, the South had relied on the enslaved to work the land. Now the region was faced with the daunting prospect of making the transition from a slave economy to one where labor was purchased on the open market. Not surprisingly, planters in the southern states were reluctant to make such a transition. Instead, they drafted Black laws that would re-create the antebellum economic structure with the façade of a free-labor system.

Black codes used a variety of tactics to tie formerly enslaved people to the land. To work, the formerly enslaved people were forced to sign contracts with their employer. These contracts prevented Black people from working for more than one employer. This meant that, unlike in a free labor market, Black people could not positively influence wages and conditions by choosing to work for the employer who gave them the best terms.

The predictable outcome was that formerly enslaved people were forced to work for very low wages. With such low wages, and no ability to supplement income with additional work, workers were reduced to relying on loans from their employers. The debt that these workers incurred ensured that they could never escape from their condition. Those formerly enslaved people who attempt to violate these contracts could be fined or beaten. Those who refused to sign contracts at all could be arrested for vagrancy and then made to work for no wages, essentially being reduced to the very definition of an enslaved person.

The Black codes left no doubt that the former breakaway Confederate states intended to maintain White supremacy at all costs. These draconian state laws helped spur the congressional Joint Committee on Reconstruction into action. Its members felt that ending slavery with the Thirteenth Amendment did not go far enough. Congress extended the life of the Freedmen's Bureau to combat the Black codes and in April 1866 passed the first Civil Rights Act, which established the citizenship of African Americans. This was a significant step that contradicted the Supreme Court's 1857 Dred Scott decision, which declared that Black people could never be citizens. The law also gave the federal government the right to intervene in state affairs to protect the rights of citizens, and thus, of African Americans. President Johnson, who continued to insist that restoration of the United States had already been accomplished, vetoed the 1866 Civil Rights Act. However, Congress mustered the necessary votes to override his veto. Despite the Civil Rights Act, the Black codes endured, forming the foundation of the racially discriminatory Jim Crow segregation policies that impoverished generations of African Americans.

THE FOURTEENTH AMENDMENT

Questions swirled about the constitutionality of the Civil Rights Act of 1866. The Supreme Court, in its 1857 decision forbidding Black citizenship, had interpreted the Constitution in a certain way; many argued that the 1866 statute, alone, could not alter that interpretation. Seeking to overcome all legal questions, Radical Republicans drafted another constitutional amendment with provisions that followed those of the 1866 Civil Rights Act. In July 1866, the Fourteenth Amendment went to state legislatures for ratification.

The Fourteenth Amendment stated, "All persons born or naturalized in the United States and subject to the jurisdiction thereof, are citizens of the United States and of the State wherein they reside." It gave citizens equal protection under both the state and federal law, overturning the Dred Scott decision. It eliminated the three-fifths compromise of the 1787 Constitution, whereby an enslaved person had been counted as three-fifths of a free White person, and it reduced the number of House representatives and Electoral College electors for any state that denied suffrage to any adult male inhabitant, Black or White. As Radical Republicans had proposed in the Wade-Davis bill, individuals who had "engaged in insurrection or rebellion [against] . . . or given aid or comfort to the enemies [of]" the United States were barred from holding political (state or federal) or military office unless pardoned by two-thirds of Congress.

The amendment also answered the question of debts arising from the Civil War by specifying that all debts incurred by fighting to defeat the Confederacy would be honored. Confederate debts, however, would not: "[N]either the United States nor any State shall assume or pay any debt or obligation incurred in aid of insurrection or rebellion against the United States, or any claim for the loss or emancipation of any slave; but all such debts, obligations and claims shall be held illegal and void." Thus, claims by former slaveholders requesting compensation for slave property had no standing. Any state that ratified the Fourteenth Amendment would automatically be readmitted. Most former Confederate states, except for Tennessee, refused to ratify the amendment in 1866.

President Johnson called openly for the rejection of the Fourteenth Amendment, a move that drove a further wedge between him and congressional Republicans. In late summer of 1866, he gave a series of speeches, known as the "swing around the circle," designed to gather support for his mild version of Reconstruction. Johnson felt that ending slavery went far enough; extending the rights and protections of citizenship to freed people, he believed, went much too far. He continued to believe that Black people were inferior to White people. The president's "swing around the circle" speeches to gain support for his program and derail the

Radical Republicans proved to be a disaster, as hecklers provoked Johnson to make damaging statements. Radical Republicans charged that Johnson had been drunk when he made his speeches. As a result, Johnson's reputation plummeted.

CLICK AND EXPLORE

Read the text of the Fourteenth Amendment (http://openstax.org/l/15Fourteena) and then view the original document (http://openstax.org/l/15Fourteenb) at Our Documents.

16.3 Radical Reconstruction, 1867–1872

LEARNING OBJECTIVES

By the end of this section, you will be able to:
- Explain the purpose of the second phase of Reconstruction and some of the key legislation put forward by Congress
- Describe the impeachment of President Johnson
- Discuss the benefits and drawbacks of the Fifteenth Amendment

During the Congressional election in the fall of 1866, Republicans gained even greater victories. This was due in large measure to the northern voter opposition that had developed toward President Johnson because of the inflexible and overbearing attitude he had exhibited in the White House, as well as his missteps during his 1866 speaking tour. Leading Radical Republicans in Congress included Massachusetts senator Charles Sumner (the same senator whom proslavery South Carolina representative Preston Brooks had thrashed with his cane in 1856 during the Bleeding Kansas crisis) and Pennsylvania representative Thaddeus Stevens. These men and their supporters envisioned a much more expansive change in the South. Sumner advocated integrating schools and giving Black men the right to vote while disenfranchising many southern voters. For his part, Stevens considered that the southern states had forfeited their rights as states when they seceded, and were no more than conquered territory that the federal government could organize as it wished. He envisioned the redistribution of plantation lands and U.S. military control over the former Confederacy.

Their goals included the transformation of the South from an area built on slave labor to a free-labor society. They also wanted to ensure that freed people were protected and given the opportunity for a better life. Violent race riots in Memphis, Tennessee, and New Orleans, Louisiana, in 1866 gave greater urgency to the second phase of Reconstruction, begun in 1867.

THE RECONSTRUCTION ACTS

The 1867 Military Reconstruction Act, which encompassed the vision of Radical Republicans, set a new direction for Reconstruction in the South. Republicans saw this law, and three supplementary laws passed by Congress that year, called the Reconstruction Acts, as a way to deal with the disorder in the South. The 1867 act divided the ten southern states that had yet to ratify the Fourteenth Amendment into five military districts (Tennessee had already been readmitted to the Union by this time and so was excluded from these acts). Martial law was imposed, and a Union general commanded each district. These generals and twenty thousand federal troops stationed in the districts were charged with protecting freed people. When a supplementary act extended the right to vote to all freed men of voting age (21 years old), the military in each district oversaw the elections and the registration of voters. Only after new state constitutions had been written and states had ratified the Fourteenth Amendment could these states rejoin the Union. Predictably, President Johnson vetoed the Reconstruction Acts, viewing them as both unnecessary and unconstitutional. Once again, Congress overrode Johnson's vetoes, and by the end of 1870, all the southern states under military rule had ratified the Fourteenth Amendment and been restored to the Union (Figure 16.7).

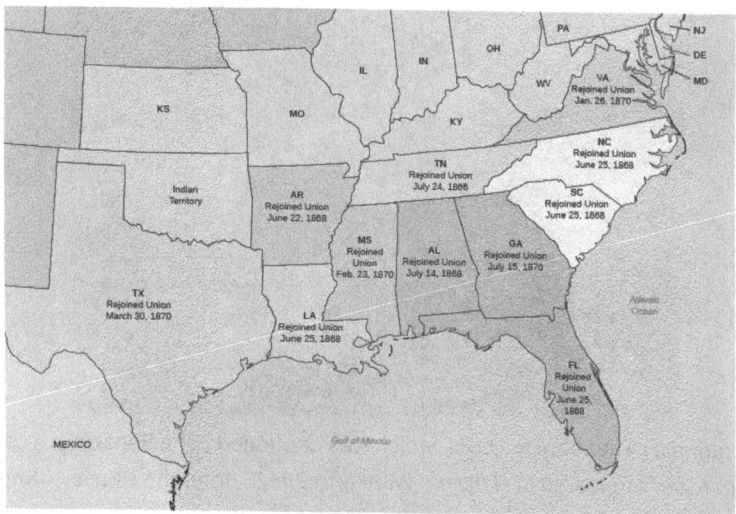

FIGURE 16.7 The map above shows the five military districts established by the 1867 Military Reconstruction Act and the date each state rejoined the Union. Tennessee was not included in the Reconstruction Acts as it had already been readmitted to the Union at the time of their passage.

THE IMPEACHMENT OF PRESIDENT JOHNSON

President Johnson's relentless vetoing of congressional measures created a deep rift in Washington, DC, and neither he nor Congress would back down. Johnson's prickly personality proved to be a liability, and many people found him grating. Moreover, he firmly believed in White supremacy, declaring in his 1868 State of the Union address, "The attempt to place the White population under the domination of persons of color in the South has impaired, if not destroyed, the kindly relations that had previously existed between them; and mutual distrust has engendered a feeling of animosity which leading in some instances to collision and bloodshed, has prevented that cooperation between the two races so essential to the success of industrial enterprise in the southern states." The president's racism put him even further at odds with those in Congress who wanted to create full equality between Black people and White people.

The Republican majority in Congress by now despised the president, and they wanted to prevent him from interfering in congressional Reconstruction. To that end, Radical Republicans passed two laws of dubious constitutionality. The Command of the Army Act prohibited the president from issuing military orders except through the commanding general of the army, who could not be relieved or reassigned without the consent of the Senate. The Tenure of Office Act, which Congress passed in 1867, required the president to gain the approval of the Senate whenever he appointed or removed officials. Congress had passed this act to ensure that Republicans who favored Radical Reconstruction would not be barred or stripped of their jobs. In August 1867, President Johnson removed Secretary of War Edwin M. Stanton, who had aligned himself with the Radical Republicans, without gaining Senate approval. He replaced Stanton with Ulysses S. Grant, but Grant resigned and sided with the Republicans against the president. Many Radical Republicans welcomed this blunder by the president as it allowed them to take action to remove Johnson from office, arguing that Johnson had openly violated the Tenure of Office Act. The House of Representatives quickly drafted a resolution to impeach him, a first in American history.

In impeachment proceedings, the House of Representatives serves as the prosecution and the Senate acts as judge, deciding whether the president should be removed from office (Figure 16.8). The House brought eleven counts against Johnson, all alleging his encroachment on the powers of Congress. In the Senate, Johnson barely survived. Seven Republicans joined the Democrats and independents to support acquittal; the final vote was 35 to 19, one vote short of the required two-thirds majority. The Radicals then dropped the impeachment effort, but the events had effectively silenced President Johnson, and Radical Republicans continued with their plan to reconstruct the South.

FIGURE 16.8 This illustration by Theodore R. Davis, which was captioned "The Senate as a court of impeachment for the trial of Andrew Johnson," appeared in *Harper's Weekly* in 1868. Here, the House of Representatives brings its grievances against Johnson to the Senate during impeachment hearings.

THE FIFTEENTH AMENDMENT

In November 1868, Ulysses S. Grant, the Union's war hero, easily won the presidency in a landslide victory. The Democratic nominee was Horatio Seymour, but the Democrats carried the stigma of disunion. The Republicans, in their campaign, blamed the devastating Civil War and the violence of its aftermath on the rival party, a strategy that southerners called "waving the bloody shirt."

Though Grant did not side with the Radical Republicans, his victory allowed the continuance of the Radical Reconstruction program. In the winter of 1869, Republicans introduced another constitutional amendment, the third of the Reconstruction era. When Republicans had passed the Fourteenth Amendment, which addressed citizenship rights and equal protections, they were unable to explicitly ban states from withholding the franchise based on race. With the Fifteenth Amendment, they sought to correct this major weakness by finally extending to Black men the right to vote. The amendment directed that "[t]he right of citizens of the United States to vote shall not be denied or abridged by the United States or by any State on account of race, color, or previous condition of servitude." Unfortunately, the new amendment had weaknesses of its own. As part of a compromise to ensure the passage of the amendment with the broadest possible support, drafters of the amendment specifically excluded language that addressed literacy tests and poll taxes, the most common ways Black people were traditionally disenfranchised in both the North and the South. Indeed, Radical Republican leader Charles Sumner of Massachusetts, himself an ardent supporter of legal equality without exception to race, refused to vote for the amendment precisely because it did not address these obvious loopholes.

Despite these weaknesses, the language of the amendment did provide for universal manhood suffrage—the right of all men to vote—and crucially identified Black men, including those who had been enslaved, as deserving the right to vote. This, the third and final of the Reconstruction amendments, was ratified in 1870 (Figure 16.9). With the ratification of the Fifteenth Amendment, many believed that the process of restoring the Union was safely coming to a close and that the rights of the formerly enslaved were finally secure. African American communities expressed great hope as they celebrated what they understood to be a national confirmation of their unqualified citizenship.

FIGURE 16.9 *The Fifteenth Amendment. Celebrated May 19th, 1870*, a commemorative print by Thomas Kelly, celebrates the passage of the Fifteenth Amendment with a series of vignettes highlighting Black rights and those who championed them. Portraits include Ulysses S. Grant, Abraham Lincoln, and John Brown, as well as Black leaders Martin Delany, Frederick Douglass, and Hiram Revels. Vignettes include the celebratory parade for the amendment's passage, "The Ballot Box is open to us," and "Our representative Sits in the National Legislature."

CLICK AND EXPLORE

Visit the Library of Congress (http://openstax.org/l/15Fifteen) to take a closer look at *The Fifteenth Amendment* by Thomas Kelly. Examine each individual vignette and the accompanying text. Why do you think Kelly chose these to highlight?

WOMEN'S SUFFRAGE

While the Fifteenth Amendment may have been greeted with applause in many corners, leading women's rights activists, who had been campaigning for decades for the right to vote, saw it as a major disappointment. More dispiriting still was the fact that many women's rights activists, such as Susan B. Anthony and Elizabeth Cady Stanton, had played a large part in the abolitionist movement leading up to the Civil War. Following the war, women and men, White and Black, formed the American Equal Rights Association (AERA) for the expressed purpose of securing "equal Rights to all American citizens, especially the right of suffrage, irrespective of race, color or sex." Two years later, with the adoption of the Fourteenth Amendment, section 2 of which specifically qualified the liberties it extended to "male citizens," it seemed as though the progress made in support of civil rights was not only passing women by but was purposely codifying their exclusion. As Congress debated the language of the Fifteenth Amendment, some held out hope that it would finally extend the franchise to women. Those hopes were dashed when Congress adopted the final language.

The consequence of these frustrated hopes was the effective split of a civil rights movement that had once been united in support of African Americans and women. Seeing this split occur, Frederick Douglass, a great admirer of Stanton, struggled to argue for a piecemeal approach that should prioritize the franchise for Black men if that was the only option. He insisted that his support for women's right to vote was sincere, but that getting Black men the right to vote was "of the most urgent necessity." "The government of this country loves women," he argued. "They are the sisters, mothers, wives and daughters of our rulers; but the negro is loathed. . . . The negro needs suffrage to protect his life and property, and to ensure him respect and education."

These appeals were largely accepted by women's rights leaders and AERA members like Lucy Stone and Henry Browne Blackwell, who believed that more time was needed to bring about female suffrage. Others demanded immediate action. Among those who pressed forward despite the setback were Stanton and Anthony. They felt greatly aggrieved at the fact that other abolitionists, with whom they had worked closely for years, did not demand that women be included in the language of the amendments. Stanton argued that the women's vote would be necessary to counter the influence of uneducated freedmen in the South and the waves of poor European immigrants arriving in the East.

In 1869, Stanton and Anthony helped organize the National Woman Suffrage Association (NWSA), an organization dedicated to ensuring that women gained the right to vote immediately, not at some future, undetermined date. Some women, including Virginia Minor, a member of the NWSA, took action by trying to register to vote; Minor attempted this in St. Louis, Missouri, in 1872. When election officials turned her away, Minor brought the issue to the Missouri state courts, arguing that the Fourteenth Amendment ensured that she was a citizen with the right to vote. This legal effort to bring about women's suffrage eventually made its way to the Supreme Court, which declared in 1874 that "the constitution of the United States does not confer the right of suffrage upon any one," effectively dismissing Minor's claim.

DEFINING AMERICAN

Constitution of the National Woman Suffrage Association

Despite the Fifteenth Amendment's failure to guarantee female suffrage, women did gain the right to vote in western territories, with the Wyoming Territory leading the way in 1869. One reason for this was a belief that giving women the right to vote would provide a moral compass to the otherwise lawless western frontier. Extending the right to vote in western territories also provided an incentive for White women to emigrate to the West, where they were scarce. However, Susan B. Anthony, Elizabeth Cady Stanton, and others believed that immediate action on the national front was required, leading to the organization of the NWSA and its resulting constitution. "ARTICLE 1.—This organization shall be called the National Woman Suffrage Association." "ARTICLE 2.—The object of this Association shall be to secure STATE and NATIONAL protection for women citizens in the exercise of their right to vote." "ARTICLE 3.—All citizens of the United States subscribing to this Constitution, and contributing not less than one dollar annually, shall be considered members of the Association, with the right to participate in its deliberations." "ARTICLE 4.—The officers of this Association shall be a President, Vice-Presidents from each of the States and Territories, Corresponding and Recording Secretaries, a Treasurer, an Executive Committee of not less than five, and an Advisory Committee consisting of one or more persons from each State and Territory." "ARTICLE 5.—All Woman Suffrage Societies throughout the country shall be welcomed as auxiliaries; and their accredited officers or duly appointed representatives shall be recognized as members of the National Association.
OFFICERS OF THE NATIONAL WOMAN SUFFRAGE ASSOCIATION." "PRESIDENT.
SUSAN B. ANTHONY, Rochester, N. Y."

How was the NWSA organized? How would the fact that it operated at the national level, rather than at the state or local level, help it to achieve its goals?

BLACK POLITICAL ACHIEVEMENTS

Black voter registration in the late 1860s and the ratification of the Fifteenth Amendment finally brought what Lincoln had characterized as "a new birth of freedom." **Union Leagues**, fraternal groups founded in the North that promoted loyalty to the Union and the Republican Party during the Civil War, expanded into the South after the war and were transformed into political clubs that served both political and civic functions. As centers of the Black communities in the South, the leagues became vehicles for the dissemination of information, acted as mediators between members of the Black community and the White establishment, and served other practical functions like helping to build schools and churches for the community they served. As extensions of the Republican Party, these leagues worked to enroll newly enfranchised Black voters, campaign for candidates, and generally help the party win elections (Figure 16.10).

FIGURE 16.10 *The First Vote*, by Alfred R. Waud, appeared in *Harper's Weekly* in 1867. The Fifteenth Amendment gave Black men the right to vote for the first time.

The political activities of the leagues launched a great many African Americans and formerly enslaved people into politics throughout the South. For the first time, Black people began to hold political office, and several were elected to the U.S. Congress. In the 1870s, fifteen members of the House of Representatives and two senators were Black. The two senators, Blanche K. Bruce and Hiram Revels, were both from Mississippi, the home state of former U.S. senator and later Confederate president Jefferson Davis. Hiram Revels (Figure 16.11), was a freeborn man from North Carolina who rose to prominence as a minister in the African Methodist Episcopal Church and then as a Mississippi state senator in 1869. The following year he was elected by the state legislature to fill one of Mississippi's two U.S. Senate seats, which had been vacant since the war. His arrival in Washington, DC, drew intense interest: as the *New York Times* noted, when "the colored Senator from Mississippi, was sworn in and admitted to his seat this afternoon . . . there was not an inch of standing or sitting room in the galleries, so densely were they packed. . . . When the Vice-President uttered the words, 'The Senator elect will now advance and take the oath,' a pin might have been heard drop."

FIGURE 16.11 Hiram Revels served as a preacher throughout the Midwest before settling in Mississippi in 1866. When he was elected by the Mississippi state legislature in 1870, he became the country's first African American senator.

DEFINING AMERICAN

Senator Revels on Segregated Schools in Washington, DC
Hiram R. Revels became the first African American to serve in the U.S. Senate in 1870. In 1871, he gave the following speech about Washington's segregated schools before Congress.

> Will establishing such [desegregated] schools as I am now advocating in this District harm our white friends? . . . By some it is contended that if we establish mixed schools here a great insult will be given to the white citizens, and that the white schools will be seriously damaged. . . . When I was on a lecturing tour in the state of Ohio . . . [o]ne of the leading gentlemen connected with the schools in that town came to see me. . . . He asked me, "Have you been to New England, where they have mixed schools?" I replied, "I have sir." "Well," said he, "please tell me this: does not social equality result from mixed schools?" "No, sir; very far from it," I responded. "Why," said he, "how can it be otherwise?" I replied, "I will tell you how it can be otherwise, and how it is otherwise. Go to the schools and you see there white children and colored children seated side by side, studying their lessons, standing side by side and reciting their lessons, and perhaps in walking to school they may walk together; but that is the last of it. The white children go to their homes; the colored children go to theirs; and on the Lord's day you will see those colored children in colored churches, and the white family, you will see the white children there, and the colored children at entertainments given by persons of their color." I aver, sir, that mixed schools are very far from bringing about social equality."

According to Senator Revels's speech, what is "social equality" and why is it important to the issue of desegregated schools? Does Revels favor social equality or social segregation? Did social equality exist in the United States in 1871?

Though the fact of their presence was dramatic and important, as the *New York Times* description above demonstrates, the few African American representatives and senators who served in Congress during Reconstruction represented only a tiny fraction of the many hundreds, possibly thousands, of Black people who served in a great number of capacities at the local and state levels. The South during the early 1870s brimmed with formerly enslaved and freeborn Black people serving as school board commissioners, county commissioners, clerks of court, board of education and city council members, justices of the peace, constables, coroners, magistrates, sheriffs, auditors, and registrars. This wave of local African American political activity contributed to and was accompanied by a new concern for the poor and disadvantaged in the South. The southern Republican leadership did away with the hated Black codes, undid the work of White supremacists, and worked to reduce obstacles confronting freed people.

Reconstruction governments invested in infrastructure, paying special attention to the rehabilitation of the southern railroads. They set up public education systems that enrolled both White and Black students. They established or increased funding for hospitals, orphanages, and asylums for the insane. In some states, the state and local governments provided the poor with basic necessities like firewood and even bread. And to pay for these new services and subsidies, the governments levied taxes on land and property, an action that struck at the heart of the foundation of southern economic inequality. Indeed, the land tax compounded the existing problems of White landowners, who were often cash-poor, and contributed to resentment of what southerners viewed as another northern attack on their way of life.

White southerners reacted with outrage at the changes imposed upon them. The sight of once-enslaved Black people serving in positions of authority as sheriffs, congressmen, and city council members stimulated great resentment at the process of Reconstruction and its undermining of the traditional social and economic foundations of the South. Indignant southerners referred to this period of reform as a time of "negro misrule." They complained of profligate corruption on the part of vengeful freed people and greedy northerners looking to fill their pockets with the South's riches. Unfortunately for the great many honest reformers, southerners did have a handful of real examples of corruption they could point to, such as legislators using state revenues to buy hams and perfumes or giving themselves inflated salaries. Such examples, however, were relatively few and largely comparable to nineteenth-century corruption across the country. Yet these powerful stories, combined with deep-seated racial animosity toward Black people in the South, led to Democratic campaigns to "redeem" state governments. Democrats across the South leveraged planters' economic power and wielded White vigilante violence to ultimately take back state political power from the Republicans. By the time President Grant's attentions were being directed away from the South and toward the Indian Wars in the West in 1876, power in the South had largely been returned to White people and Reconstruction was effectively abandoned. By the end of 1876, only South Carolina, Louisiana, and Florida still had Republican governments.

The sense that the South had been unfairly sacrificed to northern vice and Black vengeance, despite a wealth of evidence to the contrary, persisted for many decades. So powerful and pervasive was this narrative that by the time D. W. Griffith released his 1915 motion picture, *The Birth of a Nation*, White people around the country were primed to accept the fallacy that White southerners were the frequent victims of violence and violation at the hands of unrestrained Black people. The reality is that the opposite was true. White southerners orchestrated a sometimes violent and generally successful counterrevolution against Reconstruction policies in the South beginning in the 1860s. Those who worked to change and modernize the South typically did so under threats of violence. Black Republican officials in the South were frequently terrorized, assaulted, and even murdered with impunity by organizations like the Ku Klux Klan. When not ignoring the Fourteenth and Fifteenth Amendments altogether, White leaders often used trickery and fraud at the polls to get the results they wanted. As Reconstruction came to a close, these methods came to define southern life for African Americans for nearly a century afterward.

16.4 The Collapse of Reconstruction

LEARNING OBJECTIVES

By the end of this section, you will be able to:
- Explain the reasons for the collapse of Reconstruction
- Describe the efforts of White southern "redeemers" to roll back the gains of Reconstruction

The effort to remake the South generated a brutal reaction among southern White people, who were committed to keeping Black people in a subservient position. To prevent Black people from gaining economic ground and to maintain cheap labor for the agricultural economy, an exploitative system of sharecropping spread throughout the South. Domestic terror organizations, most notably the Ku Klux Klan, employed various methods (arson, whipping, murder) to keep freed people from voting and achieving political, social, or economic equality with their White neighbors.

BUILDING BLACK COMMUNITIES

The degraded status of Black men and women had placed them outside the limits of what antebellum southern White people considered appropriate gender roles and familial hierarchies. Slave marriages did not enjoy legal recognition. Enslaved men were humiliated and deprived of authority and of the ability to protect enslaved women, who were frequently exposed to the brutality and sexual domination of White enslavers and vigilantes alike. Enslaved parents could not protect their children, who could be bought, sold, put to work, brutally disciplined, and abused without their consent; parents, too, could be sold away from their children (Figure 16.12). Moreover, the division of labor idealized in White southern society, in which men worked the land and women performed the role of domestic caretaker, did not apply to the enslaved. Both enslaved men and women were made to perform hard labor in the fields.

FIGURE 16.12 After emancipation, many fathers who had been sold from their families as enslaved people—a circumstance illustrated in the engraving above, which shows an enslaved man forced to leave his wife and children—set out to find those lost families and rebuild their lives.

In the Reconstruction era, African Americans embraced the right to enjoy the family bonds and the expression of gender norms they had been systematically denied. Many thousands of freed Black men who had been separated from their families while enslaved took to the road to find their long-lost spouses and children and renew their bonds. In one instance, a journalist reported having interviewed a freed person who traveled over six hundred miles on foot in search of the family that was taken from him while in bondage. Couples that had been spared separation quickly set out to legalize their marriages, often by way of the Freedmen's Bureau, now that this option was available. Those who had no families would sometimes relocate to southern towns and cities, so as to be part of the larger Black community where churches and other mutual aid societies offered help and camaraderie.

SHARECROPPING

Most freed people stayed in the South on the lands where their families and loved ones had worked for generations while enslaved. They hungered to own and farm their own lands instead of the lands of White plantation owners. In one case, formerly enslaved people on the Sea Islands off the coast of South Carolina initially had hopes of owning the land they had worked for many decades after General Sherman directed that freed people be granted title to plots of forty acres.

The Freedmen's Bureau provided additional cause for such hopes by directing that leases and titles to lands in the South be made available to formerly enslaved people. However, these efforts ran afoul of President Johnson. In 1865, he ordered the return of land to White landowners, a setback for those freed people, such as those on the South Carolina Sea Islands, who had begun to cultivate the land as their own. Ultimately, there was no redistribution of land in the South.

The end of slavery meant the transition to wage labor. However, this conversion did not entail a new era of economic independence for formerly enslaved people. While they no longer faced relentless toil under the lash, freed people emerged from slavery without any money and needed farm implements, food, and other basic necessities to start their new lives. Under the **crop-lien system**, store owners extended credit to farmers under the agreement that the debtors would pay with a portion of their future harvest. However, the creditors charged high interest rates, making it even harder for freed people to gain economic independence.

Throughout the South, **sharecropping** took root, a crop-lien system that worked to the advantage of landowners. Under the system, freed people rented the land they worked, often on the same plantations where they had been enslaved. Some landless White citizens also became sharecroppers. Sharecroppers paid their landlords with the crops they grew, often as much as half their harvest. Sharecropping favored the landlords and ensured that freed people could not attain independent livelihoods. The year-to-year leases meant no incentive existed to substantially improve the land, and high interest payments siphoned additional money away from the farmers. Sharecroppers often became trapped in a never-ending cycle of debt, unable to buy their own land and unable to stop working for their creditor because of what they owed. The consequences of sharecropping affected the entire South for many generations, severely limiting economic development and ensuring that the South remained an agricultural backwater.

THE "INVISIBLE EMPIRE OF THE SOUTH"

Paramilitary White-supremacist terror organizations in the South helped bring about the collapse of Reconstruction, using violence as their primary weapon. The "Invisible Empire of the South," or **Ku Klux Klan**, stands as the most notorious. The Klan was founded in 1866 as an oath-bound fraternal order of Confederate veterans in Tennessee, with former Confederate General Nathan Bedford Forrest as its first leader. The organization—its name likely derived from *kuklos*, a Greek word meaning circle—devised elaborate rituals and grandiose names for its ranking members: Grand Wizard, Grand Dragon, Grand Titan, and Grand Cyclops. Soon, however, this fraternal organization evolved into a vigilante terrorist group that vented southern White people's collective frustration over the loss of the war and the course of Radical Reconstruction through acts of intimidation and violence.

The Klan terrorized newly freed Black people to deter them from exercising their citizenship rights and freedoms. Other anti-Black vigilante groups around the South began to adopt the Klan name and perpetrate acts of unspeakable violence against anyone they considered a tool of Reconstruction. Indeed, as historians have noted, Klan units around the South operated autonomously and with a variety of motives. Some may have sincerely believed they were righting wrongs, others merely satisfying their lurid desires for violence. Nor was the Klan the only racist vigilante organization. Other groups, like the Red Shirts from Mississippi and the Knights of the White Camelia and the White League, both from Louisiana, also sprang up at this time. The Klan and similar organizations also worked as an extension of the Democratic Party to win elections.

Despite the great variety in Klan membership, on the whole, the group tended to direct its attention toward persecuting freed people and people they considered **carpetbaggers**, a term of abuse applied to northerners accused of having come to the South to acquire wealth through political power at the expense of southerners. The colorful term captured the disdain of southerners for these people, reflecting the common assumption that these men, sensing great opportunity, packed up all their worldly possessions in carpetbags, a then-popular type of luggage, and made their way to the South. Implied in this definition is the notion that these men came from little and were thus shiftless wanderers motivated only by the desire for quick money. In reality, these northerners tended to be young, idealistic, often well-educated men who responded to northern campaigns urging them to lead the modernization of the South. But the image of them as swindlers taking advantage of the South at its time of need resonated with a White southern population aggrieved by loss and economic decline. Southern White people who supported Reconstruction, known as **scalawags**, also generated great hostility as traitors to the South. They, too, became targets of the Klan and similar groups.

The Klan seized on the pervasive but largely fictional narrative of the northern carpetbagger as a powerful tool for restoring White supremacy and overturning Republican state governments in the South (Figure 16.13). To preserve a White-dominated society, Klan members punished Black people for attempting to improve their station in life or acting "uppity." To prevent freed people from attaining an education, the Klan burned public schools. In an effort to stop Black citizens from voting, the Klan murdered, whipped, and otherwise intimidated freed people and their White supporters. It wasn't uncommon for Klan members to intimidate Union League members and Freedmen's Bureau workers. The Klan even perpetrated acts of political assassination, killing a sitting U.S. congressman from Arkansas and three state congressmen from South Carolina.

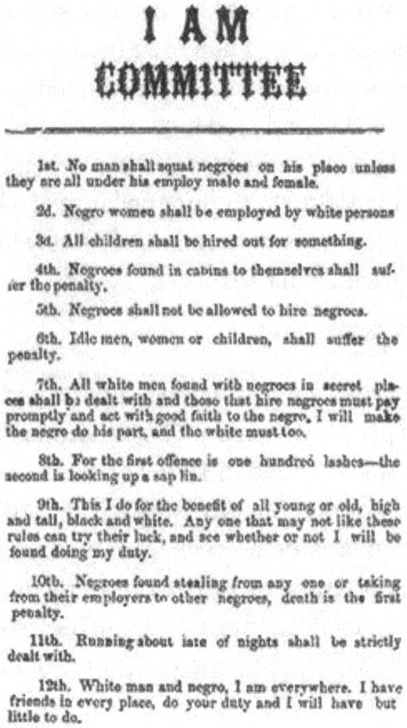

I AM COMMITTEE

1st. No man shall squat negroes on his place unless they are all under his employ male and female.

2d. Negro women shall be employed by white persons

3d. All children shall be hired out for something.

4th. Negroes found in cabins to themselves shall suffer the penalty.

5th. Negroes shall not be allowed to hire negroes.

6th. Idle men, women or children, shall suffer the penalty.

7th. All white men found with negroes in secret places shall be dealt with and those that hire negroes must pay promptly and act with good faith to the negro, I will make the negro do his part, and the white must too.

8th. For the first offence is one hundred lashes—the second is looking up a sap lin.

9th. This I do for the benefit of all young or old, high and tall, black and white. Any one that may not like these rules can try their luck, and see whether or not I will be found doing my duty.

10th. Negroes found stealing from any one or taking from their employers to other negroes, death is the first penalty.

11th. Running about late of nights shall be strictly dealt with.

12th. White man and negro, I am everywhere. I have friends in every place, do your duty and I will have but little to do.

FIGURE 16.13 The Ku Klux Klan posted circulars such as this 1867 West Virginia broadside to warn Black people and White sympathizers of the power and ubiquity of the Klan.

Klan tactics included riding out to victims' houses, masked and armed, and firing into the homes or burning them down (Figure 16.14). Other tactics relied more on the threat of violence, such as happened in Mississippi when fifty masked Klansmen rode out to a local schoolteacher's house to express their displeasure with the school tax and to suggest that she consider leaving. Still other tactics intimidated through imaginative trickery. One such method was to dress up as ghosts of slain Confederate soldiers and stage stunts designed to convince their victims of their supernatural abilities.

FIGURE 16.14 This illustration by Frank Bellew, captioned "Visit of the Ku-Klux," appeared in *Harper's Weekly* in 1872. A hooded Klansman surreptitiously points a rifle at an unaware Black family in their home.

Regardless of the method, the general goal of reinstating White supremacy as a foundational principle and returning the South to a situation that largely resembled antebellum conditions remained a constant. The Klan used its power to eliminate Black economic independence, decimate Black peoples' political rights, reclaim White dominance over Black women's bodies and Black men's masculinity, tear apart Black communities, and return Black people to earlier patterns of economic and political subservience and social deference. In this, they were largely successful.

CLICK AND EXPLORE

Visit [Freedmen's Bureau Online (http://openstax.org/l/15Freedmen)](http://openstax.org/l/15Freedmen) to view digitized records of attacks on freed people that were reported in Albany, Georgia, between January 1 and October 31, 1868.

The president and Congress, however, were not indifferent to the violence, and they worked to bring it to an end. In 1870, at the insistence of the governor of North Carolina, President Grant told Congress to investigate the Klan. In response, Congress in 1871 created the Joint Select Committee to Inquire into the Condition of Affairs in the Late Insurrectionary States. The committee took testimony from freed people in the South, and in 1872, it published a thirteen-volume report on the tactics the Klan used to derail democracy in the South through the use of violence.

MY STORY

Abram Colby on the Methods of the Ku Klux Klan

The following statements are from the October 27, 1871, testimony of fifty-two-year-old formerly enslaved Abram Colby, which the joint select committee investigating the Klan took in Atlanta, Georgia. Colby had been elected to the lower house of the Georgia State legislature in 1868. "On the 29th of October, they came to my house and broke my door open, took me out of my bed and took me to the woods and whipped me three hours or more and left me in the woods for dead. They said to me, "Do you think you will ever vote another damned Radical ticket?" I said, "I will not tell you a lie." They said, "No; don't tell a lie." . . . I said, "If there was an election to-morrow, I would vote the Radical ticket." They set in and whipped me a thousand licks more, I suppose. . . ." "They said I had influence with the negroes of other counties, and had carried the negroes against them. About two days before they whipped me they offered me $5,000 to turn and go with them, and said they would pay me $2,500 cash if I would turn and let another man go to the legislature in my place. . . ." "I would have come before the court here last week, but I knew it was no use for me to try to get Ku-Klux condemned by Ku-Klux, and I did not come. Mr. Saunders, a member of the grand jury here last week, is the father of one of the very men I knew whipped me. . . ." "They broke something inside of me, and the doctor has been attending to me for more than a year. Sometimes I cannot get up and down off my bed, and my left hand is not of much use to me.

—Abram Colby testimony, Joint Select Committee Report, 1872"

Why did the Klan target Colby? What methods did they use?

Congress also passed a series of three laws designed to stamp out the Klan. Passed in 1870 and 1871, the Enforcement Acts or "Force Acts" were designed to outlaw intimidation at the polls and to give the federal government the power to prosecute crimes against freed people in federal rather than state courts. Congress believed that this last step, a provision in the third Enforcement Act, also called the Ku Klux Klan Act, was necessary in order to ensure that trials would not be decided by White juries in southern states friendly to the Klan. The act also allowed the president to impose martial law in areas controlled by the Klan and gave President Grant the power to suspend the writ of habeas corpus, a continuation of the wartime power granted to President Lincoln. The suspension meant individuals suspected of engaging in Klan activity could be jailed indefinitely.

President Grant made frequent use of the powers granted to him by Congress, especially in South Carolina, where federal troops imposed martial law in nine counties in an effort to derail Klan activities. However, the federal government faced entrenched local organizations and a White population firmly opposed to Radical Reconstruction. Changes came slowly or not at all, and disillusionment set in. After 1872, federal government efforts to put down paramilitary terror in the South waned.

"REDEEMERS" AND THE END OF RECONSTRUCTION

While the president and Congress may have seen the Klan and other clandestine White supremacist, terrorist organizations as a threat to stability and progress in the South, many southern White people saw them as an instrument of order in a world turned upside down. Many White southerners felt humiliated by the process of Radical Reconstruction and the way Republicans had upended southern society, placing Black people in positions of authority while taxing large landowners to pay for the education of formerly enslaved people. Those committed to rolling back the tide of Radical Reconstruction in the South called themselves **redeemers**, a label that expressed their desire to redeem their states from northern control and to restore the antebellum social order whereby Black people were kept safely under the boot heel of White people. They represented the Democratic Party in the South and worked tirelessly to end what they saw as an era of "negro misrule." By 1877, they had succeeded in bringing about the "redemption" of the South, effectively destroying the dream of Radical Reconstruction.

Although Ulysses S. Grant won a second term in the presidential election of 1872, the Republican grip on national political power began to slip in the early 1870s. Three major events undermined Republican control. First, in 1873, the United States experienced the start of a long economic downturn, the result of economic instability in Europe that spread to the United States. In the fall of 1873, the bank of Jay Cooke & Company failed to meet its financial obligations and went bankrupt, setting off a panic in American financial markets. An economic depression ensued, which Democrats blamed on Republicans and which lasted much of the decade.

Second, the Republican Party experienced internal squabbles and divided into two factions. Some Republicans began to question the expansive role of the federal government, arguing for limiting the size and scope of federal initiatives. These advocates, known as Liberal Republicans because they followed classical liberalism in championing small government, formed their own breakaway party. Their ideas changed the nature of the debate over Reconstruction by challenging reliance on federal government help to bring about change in the South. Now some Republicans argued for downsizing Reconstruction efforts.

Third, the Grant administration became mired in scandals, further tarnishing the Republicans while giving Democrats the upper hand. One scandal arose over the siphoning off of money from excise taxes on whiskey. The "Whiskey Ring," as it was called, involved people at the highest levels of the Grant administration, including the president's personal secretary, Orville Babcock. Another scandal entangled Crédit Mobilier of America, a construction company and part of the important French Crédit Mobilier banking company. The Union Pacific Railroad company, created by the federal government during the Civil War to construct a transcontinental railroad, paid Crédit Mobilier to build the railroad. However, Crédit Mobilier used the funds it received to buy Union Pacific Railroad bonds and resell them at a huge profit. Some members of Congress, as well as Vice President Schuyler Colfax, had accepted funds from Crédit Mobilier in return for forestalling an inquiry. When the scam became known in 1872, Democratic opponents of Reconstruction pointed to Crédit Mobilier as an example of corruption in the Republican-dominated federal government and evidence that smaller government was better.

The Democratic Party in the South made significant advances in the 1870s in its efforts to wrest political control from the Republican-dominated state governments. The Ku Klux Klan, as well as other paramilitary groups in the South, often operated as military wings of the Democratic Party in former Confederate states. In one notorious episode following a contested 1872 gubernatorial election in Louisiana, as many as 150 freedmen loyal to the Republican Party were killed at the Colfax courthouse by armed members of the Democratic Party, even as many of them tried to surrender (Figure 16.15).

FIGURE 16.15 In this illustration by Charles Harvey Weigall, captioned "The Louisiana Murders—Gathering the Dead and Wounded" and published in *Harper's Weekly* in 1873, survivors of the Colfax Massacre tend to those involved in the conflict. The dead and wounded all appear to be Black, and two White men on horses watch over them. Another man stands with a gun pointed at the survivors.

In other areas of the South, the Democratic Party gained control over state politics. Texas came under Democratic control by 1873, and in the following year Alabama and Arkansas followed suit. In national politics, too, the Democrats gained ground—especially during the 1874 elections, when they recaptured control of the House of Representatives for the first time since before the Civil War. Every other southern state, with the exception of Florida, South Carolina, and Louisiana—the states where federal troops remained a force—also fell to the Democratic Party and the restoration of White supremacy. Southerners everywhere celebrated their "redemption" from Radical Republican rule.

THE CONTESTED ELECTION OF 1876

By the time of the 1876 presidential election, Reconstruction had come to an end in most southern states. In Congress, the political power of the Radical Republicans had waned, although some continued their efforts to realize the dream of equality between Black and White people. One of the last attempts to do so was the passage of the 1875 Civil Rights Act, which required equality in public places and on juries. This law was challenged in court, and in 1883 the Supreme Court ruled it unconstitutional, arguing that the Thirteenth and Fourteenth Amendments did not prohibit discrimination by private individuals. By the 1870s, the Supreme Court had also undercut the letter and the spirit of the Fourteenth Amendment by interpreting it as affording freed people only limited federal protection from the Klan and other terror groups.

The country remained bitterly divided, and this was reflected in the contested election of 1876. While Grant wanted to run for a third term, scandals and Democratic successes in the South dashed those hopes. Republicans instead selected Rutherford B. Hayes, the three-time governor of Ohio. Democrats nominated Samuel Tilden, the reform governor of New York, who was instrumental in ending the Tweed Ring and Tammany Hall corruption in New York City. The November election produced an apparent Democratic victory, as Tilden carried the South and large northern states with a 300,000-vote advantage in the popular vote. However, disputed returns from Louisiana, South Carolina, Florida, and Oregon, whose electoral votes totaled twenty, threw the election into doubt.

Hayes could still win if he gained those twenty electoral votes. As the Constitution did not provide a method to determine the validity of disputed votes, the decision fell to Congress, where Republicans controlled the Senate and Democrats controlled the House of Representatives. In late January 1877, Congress tried to break the deadlock by creating a special electoral commission composed of five senators, five representatives, and five justices of the Supreme Court. The congressional delegation represented both parties equally, with five Democrats and five Republicans. The court delegation had two Democrats, two Republicans, and one independent—David Davis, who resigned from the Supreme Court (and from the commission) when the Illinois legislature elected him to the Senate. After Davis's resignation, President Grant selected a Republican to take his place, tipping the scales in favor of Hayes. The commission then awarded the disputed electoral votes and the presidency to Hayes, voting on party lines, 8 to 7 (Figure 16.16). The Democrats called foul, threatening to hold up the commission's decision in the courts.

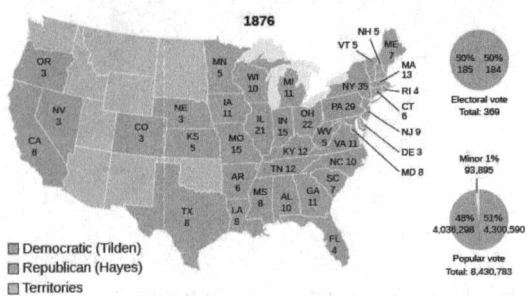

FIGURE 16.16 This map illustrates the results of the presidential election of 1876. Tilden, the Democratic candidate, swept the South, with the exception of the contested states of Florida, Louisiana, and South Carolina.

In what became known as the **Compromise of 1877**, Republican Senate leaders worked with the Democratic leadership so they would support Hayes and the commission's decision. The two sides agreed that one Southern Democrat would be appointed to Hayes's cabinet, Democrats would control federal patronage (the awarding of government jobs) in their areas in the South, and there would be a commitment to generous internal improvements, including federal aid for the Texas and Pacific Railway. Perhaps most important, all remaining federal troops would be withdrawn from the South, a move that effectively ended Reconstruction. Hayes believed that southern leaders would obey and enforce the Reconstruction-era constitutional amendments that protected the rights of freed people. His trust was soon proved to be misguided, much to his dismay, and he devoted a large part of his life to securing rights for freedmen. For their part, the Democrats took over the remaining southern states, creating what became known as the "Solid South"—a region that consistently voted in a bloc for the Democratic Party.

Key Terms

Black codes   laws some southern states designed to maintain White supremacy by keeping freed people impoverished and in debt

carpetbagger   a term used for northerners working in the South during Reconstruction; it implied that these were opportunists who came south for economic or political gain

Compromise of 1877   the agreement between Republicans and Democrats, after the contested election of 1876, in which Rutherford B. Hayes was awarded the presidency in exchange for withdrawing the last of the federal troops from the South

crop-lien system   a loan system in which store owners extended credit to farmers for the purchase of goods in exchange for a portion of their future crops

Freedmen's Bureau   the Bureau of Refugees, Freedmen, and Abandoned Lands, which was created in 1865 to ease Black peoples' transition from slavery to freedom

Ironclad Oath   an oath that the Wade-Davis Bill required a majority of voters and government officials in Confederate states to take; it involved swearing that they had never supported the Confederacy

Ku Klux Klan   a White vigilante organization that engaged in terroristic violence with the aim of stopping Reconstruction

Radical Republicans   northern Republicans who contested Lincoln's treatment of Confederate states and proposed harsher punishments

Reconstruction   the twelve-year period after the Civil War in which the rebel Southern states were integrated back into the Union

redeemers   a term used for southern White people committed to rolling back the gains of Reconstruction

scalawags   a pejorative term used for southern White people who supported Reconstruction

sharecropping   a crop-lien system in which people paid rent on land they farmed (but did not own) with the crops they grew

ten percent plan   Lincoln's Reconstruction plan, which required only 10 percent of the 1860 voters in Confederate states to take an oath of allegiance to the Union

Union Leagues   fraternal groups loyal to the Union and the Republican Party that became political and civic centers for Black people in former Confederate states

Summary

16.1 Restoring the Union

President Lincoln worked to reach his goal of reunifying the nation quickly and proposed a lenient plan to reintegrate the Confederate states. After his murder in 1865, Lincoln's vice president, Andrew Johnson, sought to reconstitute the Union quickly, pardoning Southerners en masse and providing Southern states with a clear path back to readmission. By 1866, Johnson announced the end of Reconstruction. Radical Republicans in Congress disagreed, however, and in the years ahead would put forth their own plan of Reconstruction.

16.2 Congress and the Remaking of the South, 1865–1866

The conflict between President Johnson and the Republican-controlled Congress over the proper steps to be taken with the defeated Confederacy grew in intensity in the years immediately following the Civil War. While the president concluded that all that needed to be done in the South had been done by early 1866, Congress forged ahead to stabilize the defeated Confederacy and extend to freed people citizenship and equality before the law. Congress prevailed over Johnson's vetoes as the friction between the president and the Republicans increased.

16.3 Radical Reconstruction, 1867–1872

Though President Johnson declared Reconstruction complete less than a year after the Confederate surrender, members of Congress disagreed. Republicans in Congress began to implement their own plan of bringing law and order to the South through the use of military force and martial law. Radical Republicans who advocated for a more equal society pushed their program forward as well, leading to the ratification of the Fifteenth Amendment, which finally gave Black men the right to vote. The new amendment empowered Black voters, who made good use of the vote to elect Black politicians. It disappointed female suffragists, however, who had labored for years to gain women's right to vote. By the end of 1870, all the southern states under Union military control had satisfied the requirements of Congress and been readmitted to the Union.

16.4 The Collapse of Reconstruction

The efforts launched by Radical Republicans in the late 1860s generated a massive backlash in the South in the 1870s as White people fought against what they considered "negro misrule." Paramilitary terrorist cells emerged, committing countless atrocities in their effort to "redeem" the South from Black Republican rule. In many cases, these organizations operated as an extension of the Democratic Party. Scandals hobbled the Republican Party, as did a severe economic depression. By 1875, Reconstruction had largely come to an end. The contested presidential election the following year, which was decided in favor of the Republican candidate, and the removal of federal troops from the South only confirmed the obvious: Reconstruction had failed to achieve its primary objective of creating an interracial democracy that provided equal rights to all citizens.

Review Questions

1. What was Lincoln's primary goal immediately following the Civil War?
   A. punishing the rebel states
   B. improving the lives of formerly enslaved people
   C. reunifying the country
   D. paying off the debts of the war

2. In 1864 and 1865, Radical Republicans were most concerned with _____.
   A. securing civil rights for formerly enslaved people
   B. barring ex-Confederates from political office
   C. seeking restitution from Confederate states
   D. preventing Andrew Johnson's ascent to the presidency

3. What was the purpose of the Thirteenth Amendment? How was it different from the Emancipation Proclamation?

4. Which of the following was *not* one of the functions of the Freedmen's Bureau?
   A. collecting taxes
   B. reuniting families
   C. establishing schools
   D. helping workers secure labor contracts

5. Which person or group was most responsible for the passage of the Fourteenth Amendment?
   A. President Johnson
   B. northern voters
   C. southern voters
   D. Radical Republicans in Congress

6. What was the goal of the Black codes?

7. Under Radical Reconstruction, which of the following did former Confederate states *not* need to do in order to rejoin the Union?
   A. pass the Fourteenth Amendment
   B. pass the Fifteenth Amendment
   C. revise their state constitution
   D. allow all freed men over the age of 21 to vote

8. The House of Representatives impeached Andrew Johnson over _____.
   A. the Civil Rights Act
   B. the Fourteenth Amendment
   C. the Military Reconstruction Act
   D. the Tenure of Office Act

9. What were the benefits and drawbacks of the Fifteenth Amendment?

10. Which of the following is *not* one of the methods the Ku Klux Klan and other terrorist groups used to intimidate Black people and White sympathizers?
    A. burning public schools
    B. petitioning Congress
    C. murdering freedmen who tried to vote
    D. threatening, beating, and killing those who disagreed with them

11. Which of the following was the term southerners used for a White southerner who tried to overturn the changes of Reconstruction?
    A. scalawag
    B. carpetbagger
    C. redeemer
    D. white knight

12. Why was it difficult for southern free Black people to gain economic independence after the Civil War?

Critical Thinking Questions

13. How do you think would history have been different if Lincoln had not been assassinated? How might his leadership after the war have differed from that of Andrew Johnson?

14. Was the Thirteenth Amendment a success or a failure? Discuss the reasons for your answer.

15. Consider the differences between the Thirteenth and Fourteenth Amendments. What does the Fourteenth Amendment do that the Thirteenth does not?

16. Consider social, political, and economic equality. In what ways did Radical Reconstruction address and secure these forms of equality? Where did it fall short?

17. Consider the problem of terrorism during Radical Reconstruction. If you had been an adviser to President Grant, how would you propose to deal with the problem?

Go West Young Man! Westward Expansion, 1840-1900

17

FIGURE 17.1 A widely held belief in the nineteenth century contended that Americans had a divine right and responsibility to settle the West with Protestant democratic values. Newspaper editor Horace Greely, who coined the phrase "Go west, young man," encouraged Americans to fulfill this dream. Artists of the day depicted this western expansion in idealized landscapes that bore little resemblance to the difficulties of life on the trail.

CHAPTER OUTLINE

17.1 The Westward Spirit
17.2 Homesteading: Dreams and Realities
17.3 Making a Living in Gold and Cattle
17.4 The Assault on American Indian Life and Culture
17.5 The Impact of Expansion on Chinese Immigrants and Hispanic Citizens

INTRODUCTION In the middle of the nineteenth century, farmers in the "Old West"—the land across the Allegheny Mountains in Pennsylvania—began to hear about the opportunities to be found in the "New West." They had long believed that the land west of the Mississippi was a great desert, unfit for human habitation. But now, the federal government was encouraging them to join the migratory stream westward to this unknown land. For a variety of reasons, Americans increasingly felt compelled to fulfill their "Manifest Destiny," a phrase that came to mean that they were expected to spread across the land given to them by God and, most importantly, spread predominantly American values to the frontier (Figure 17.1).

With great trepidation, hundreds, and then hundreds of thousands, of settlers packed their lives into wagons and set out, following the Oregon, California, and Santa Fe Trails, to seek a new life in the West. They imagined open lands, economic opportunity, and greater freedom to fulfill the democratic vision originally promoted by Thomas Jefferson despite Native American communities living in the region. Whatever their motivation, the great migration was underway. The American pioneer spirit was born.

17.1 The Westward Spirit

LEARNING OBJECTIVES

By the end of this section, you will be able to:
- Explain the evolution of American views about westward migration in the mid-nineteenth century
- Analyze the ways in which the federal government facilitated Americans' westward migration in the mid-nineteenth century

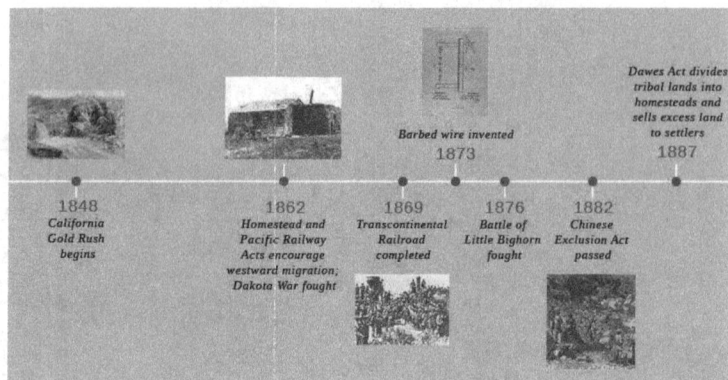

FIGURE 17.2 (credit "barbed wire": modification of work by the U.S. Department of Commerce)

While a small number of settlers had pushed westward before the mid-nineteenth century, the land west of the Mississippi was largely unexplored by the United States. Most Americans, if they thought of it at all, viewed this territory as an arid wasteland suitable only for American Indians. The reflections of early explorers who conducted scientific treks throughout the West tended to confirm this belief. Major Stephen Harriman Long, who commanded an expedition through Missouri and into the Yellowstone region in 1819–1820, frequently described the Great Plains as an arid and useless region, suitable as nothing more than a "great American desert." But, beginning in the 1840s, a combination of economic opportunity and ideological encouragement changed the way Americans thought of the West. The federal government offered a number of incentives, making it viable for Americans to take on the challenge of seizing these rough lands from their Native American and Hispanic owners. Still, most Americans who went west needed some financial security at the outset of their journey; even with government aid, the truly poor could not make the trip. The cost of moving an entire family westward, combined with the risks as well as the questionable chances of success, made the move prohibitive for most. While the economic Panic of 1837 led many to question the promise of urban America, and thus turn their focus to the promise of commercial farming in the West, the Panic also resulted in many lacking the financial resources to make such a commitment. For most, the dream to "Go west, young man" remained unfulfilled.

While much of the basis for westward expansion was economic, there was also a more philosophical reason, which was bound up in the American belief that the country—and the Indigenous peoples who populated it—were destined to come under the civilizing rule of Euro-American settlers and their superior technology, most notably railroads and the telegraph. While the extent to which that belief was a heartfelt motivation held by most Americans, or simply a rationalization of the conquests that followed, remains debatable, the clashes—both physical and cultural—that followed this western migration left scars on the country that are still felt today.

MANIFEST DESTINY

The concept of **Manifest Destiny** found its roots in the long-standing traditions of territorial expansion upon which the nation itself was founded. This phrase, which implies divine encouragement for territorial expansion, was coined by magazine editor John O'Sullivan in 1845, when he wrote in the *United States Magazine and Democratic Review* that "it was our manifest destiny to overspread the continent allotted by Providence for the free development of our multiplying millions." Although the context of O'Sullivan's original article was to encourage expansion into the newly acquired Texas territory, the spirit it invoked would subsequently be used to encourage westward settlement throughout the rest of the nineteenth century. Land developers, railroad magnates, and other investors capitalized on the notion to encourage westward settlement for their own financial benefit. Soon thereafter, the federal government encouraged this inclination as a means to further develop the West during the Civil War, especially at its outset, when concerns over the possible expansion of slavery deeper into western territories was a legitimate fear.

The idea was simple: Americans were destined—and indeed divinely ordained—to expand democratic institutions throughout the continent. As they spread their culture, thoughts, and customs, they would, in the process, expose the native inhabitants to Protestant institutions and, more importantly, new ways to develop the land. O'Sullivan may have coined the phrase, but the concept had preceded him: Throughout the 1800s, politicians and writers had stated the belief that the United States was destined to rule the continent. O'Sullivan's words, which resonated in the popular press, matched the economic and political goals of a federal government increasingly committed to expansion.

Manifest Destiny justified in Americans' minds their right and duty to govern any other groups they encountered during their expansion, as well as absolved them of any questionable tactics they employed in the process. While the commonly held view of the day was of a relatively empty frontier, waiting for the arrival of the settlers who could properly exploit the vast resources for economic gain, the reality was quite different. Hispanic communities in the Southwest, diverse tribes throughout the western states, as well as other settlers from Asia and Western Europe already lived in many parts of the country. American expansion would necessitate a far more complex and involved exchange than simply filling empty space.

Still, in part as a result of the spark lit by O'Sullivan and others, waves of Americans and recently arrived immigrants began to move west in wagon trains. They travelled along several identifiable trails: first the Oregon Trail, then later the Santa Fe and California Trails, among others. The Oregon Trail is the most famous of these western routes. Two thousand miles long and barely passable on foot in the early nineteenth century, by the 1840s, wagon trains were a common sight. Between 1845 and 1870, considered to be the height of migration along the trail, over 400,000 settlers followed this path west from Missouri (Figure 17.3). Despite emphasis on conflict with Native Americans in movies, tribe members often served as guides or traded with the emigrants.

FIGURE 17.3 Hundreds of thousands of people travelled west on the Oregon, California, and Santa Fe Trails, but their numbers did not ensure their safety. Illness, starvation, and other dangers—both real and imagined— made survival hard. But despite popular images of wagons circled to defend against Native American attacks, more Native people than emigrants died from the violence associated with the overland routes.(credit: U.S. National Archives and Records Administration)

DEFINING AMERICAN

Who Will Set Limits to Our Onward March?

"America is destined for better deeds. It is our unparalleled glory that we have no reminiscences of battle fields, but in defense [sic] of humanity, of the oppressed of all nations, of the rights of conscience, the rights of personal enfranchisement. Our annals describe no scenes of horrid carnage, where men were led on by hundreds of thousands to slay one another, dupes and victims to emperors, kings, nobles, demons in the human form called heroes. We have had patriots to defend our homes, our liberties, but no aspirants to crowns or thrones; nor have the American people ever suffered themselves to be led on by wicked ambition to depopulate the land, to spread desolation far and wide, that a human being might be placed on a seat of supremacy...."

"The expansive future is our arena, and for our history. We are entering on its untrodden space, with the truths of God in our minds, beneficent objects in our hearts, and with a clear conscience unsullied by the past. We are the nation of human progress, and who will, what can, set limits to our onward march? Providence is with us, and no earthly power can."

"—John O'Sullivan, 1839"

Think about how this quotation resonated with different groups of Americans at the time. When looked at through today's lens, the actions of the westward-moving settlers were fraught with brutality and racism. At the time, however, many settlers felt they were at the pinnacle of democracy, and that with no aristocracy or ancient history, America was a new world where anyone could succeed. Even then, consider how the phrase "anyone" was restricted by race, gender, and nationality. Also consider how the idea of "untrodden space" ignores specific groups of people.

CLICK AND EXPLORE

Visit Across the Plains in '64 (https://archive.org/details/acrossplainsin6400collrich) to follow one family making their way westward from Iowa to Oregon. Click on a few of the entries and see how the author describes their journey, from the expected to the surprising.

FEDERAL GOVERNMENT ASSISTANCE

To assist the settlers in their move westward and transform the migration from a trickle into a steady flow, Congress passed two significant pieces of legislation in 1862: the Homestead Act and the Pacific Railway Act. Born largely out of President Abraham Lincoln's growing concern that a potential Union defeat in the early stages of the Civil War might result in the expansion of slavery westward, Lincoln hoped that such laws would encourage the expansion of a "free soil" mentality across the West.

The Homestead Act allowed any head of household, or individual over the age of twenty-one—including unmarried women—to receive a parcel of 160 acres for only a nominal filing fee. All that recipients were required to do in exchange was to "improve the land" within a period of five years of taking possession. The standards for improvement were minimal: Owners could clear a few acres, build small houses or barns, or maintain livestock. Under this act, the government transferred over 270 million acres of public domain land to private citizens.

The Pacific Railway Act was pivotal in helping settlers move west more quickly, as well as move their farm products, and later cattle and mining deposits, back east. The first of many railway initiatives, this act commissioned the Union Pacific Railroad to build new track west from Omaha, Nebraska, while the Central Pacific Railroad moved east from Sacramento, California. The law provided each company with ownership of all public lands within two hundred feet on either side of the track laid, as well as additional land grants and payment through load bonds, prorated on the difficulty of the terrain it crossed. Because of these provisions, both companies made a significant profit, whether they were crossing hundreds of miles of open plains, or working their way through the Sierra Nevada Mountains of California. As a result, the nation's first transcontinental railroad was completed when the two companies connected their tracks at Promontory, Utah, in the spring of 1869. Other tracks, including lines radiating from this original one, subsequently created a network that linked all corners of the nation (Figure 17.4).

FIGURE 17.4 The "Golden Spike" connecting the country by rail was driven into the ground in Promontory, Utah, in 1869. The completion of the first transcontinental railroad dramatically changed the tenor of travel in the country, as people were able to complete in a week a route that had previously taken months.

In addition to legislation designed to facilitate western settlement, the U.S. government assumed an active role on the ground, building numerous forts throughout the West to aid settlers during their migration. Forts such as Fort Laramie in Wyoming (built in 1834) and Fort Apache in Arizona (1870) aimed to facilitate trade and limit conflict between migrants and local American Indian tribes. Others located throughout Colorado and Wyoming became important trading posts for miners and fur trappers. Those built in Kansas, Nebraska, and the Dakotas served primarily to provide relief for farmers during times of drought or related hardships. Forts constructed along the California coastline provided protection in the wake of the Mexican-American War as well as during the American Civil War. These locations subsequently serviced the U.S. Navy and provided important support for growing Pacific trade routes. Whether as army posts constructed to aid American migration, or as trading posts to further facilitate the development of the region, such forts proved to be vital contributions to westward migration.

WHO WERE THE SETTLERS?

In the nineteenth century, as today, it took money to relocate and start a new life. Due to the initial cost of relocation, land, and supplies, as well as months of preparing the soil, planting, and subsequent harvesting before any produce was ready for market, the original wave of western settlers along the Oregon Trail in the 1840s and 1850s consisted of moderately prosperous, White, native-born farming families of the East. But the passage of the Homestead Act and completion of the first transcontinental railroad meant that, by 1870, the possibility of western migration was opened to Americans of more modest means. What started as a trickle became a steady flow of migration that would last until the end of the century.

Nearly 400,000 settlers had made the trek westward by the height of the movement in 1870. The vast majority were men, although families also migrated, despite incredible hardships for women with young children. More recent immigrants also migrated west, with the largest numbers coming from Northern Europe and Canada. Germans, Scandinavians, and Irish were among the most common. These ethnic groups tended to settle close together, creating strong rural communities that mirrored the way of life they had left behind. According to U.S. Census Bureau records, the number of Scandinavians living in the United States during the second half of the nineteenth century exploded, from barely 18,000 in 1850 to over 1.1 million in 1900. During that same time period, the German-born population in the United States grew from 584,000 to nearly 2.7 million and the Irish-born population grew from 961,000 to 1.6 million. As they moved westward, several thousand immigrants established homesteads in the Midwest, primarily in Minnesota and Wisconsin, where, as of 1900, over one-third of the population was foreign-born, and in North Dakota, whose immigrant population stood at 45 percent at the turn of the century. Compared to European immigrants, those from China were much less numerous, but still significant. More than 200,000 Chinese arrived in California between 1876 and 1890, albeit for entirely different reasons related to the Gold Rush.

In addition to a significant European migration westward, several thousand African Americans migrated west following the Civil War, as much to escape the racism and violence of the Old South as to find new economic opportunities. They were known as **exodusters**, referencing the biblical flight from Egypt, because they fled the racism of the South, with most of them headed to Kansas from Kentucky, Tennessee, Louisiana, Mississippi, and Texas. Over twenty-five thousand exodusters arrived in Kansas in 1879–1880 alone. By 1890, over 500,000 Black people lived west of the Mississippi River. Although the majority of Black migrants became farmers, approximately twelve thousand worked as cowboys during the Texas cattle drives. Some also became "Buffalo Soldiers" in the wars against Native Americans. "Buffalo Soldiers" were African Americans allegedly so-named by various Native tribes who equated their black, curly hair with that of the buffalo. Many had served in the Union army in the Civil War and were now organized into six, all-Black cavalry and infantry units whose primary duties were to protect settlers during the westward migration and to assist in building the infrastructure required to support western settlement (Figure 17.5).

FIGURE 17.5 "Buffalo Soldiers," the first peacetime all-Black regiments in the U.S. Army, aided settlers, fought in the Indian Wars, and served as some of the country's first national park rangers.

CLICK AND EXPLORE

The Oxford African American Studies Center (http://openstax.org/l/homesteads) features photographs and stories about Black homesteaders. From exodusters to all-Black settlements, the essay describes the largely hidden role that African Americans played in western expansion.

While White easterners, immigrants, and African Americans were moving west, several hundred thousand Hispanics had already settled in the American Southwest prior to the U.S. government seizing the land during its war with Mexico (1846–1848). The Treaty of Guadalupe Hidalgo, which ended the war in 1848, granted American citizenship to those who chose to stay in the United States, as the land switched from Mexican to U.S. ownership. Under the conditions of the treaty, Mexicans retained the right to their language, religion, and culture, as well as the property they held. As for citizenship, they could choose one of three options: 1) declare their intent to live in the United States but retain Mexican citizenship; 2) become U.S. citizens with all rights under the constitution; or 3) leave for Mexico. Despite such guarantees, within one generation, these new Hispanic American citizens found their culture under attack, and legal protection of their property all but nonexistent.

17.2 Homesteading: Dreams and Realities

LEARNING OBJECTIVES

By the end of this section, you will be able to:
- Identify the challenges that farmers faced as they settled west of the Mississippi River
- Describe the unique experiences of women who participated in westward migration

As settlers and homesteaders moved westward to improve the land given to them through the Homestead Act, they faced a difficult and often insurmountable challenge. The land was difficult to farm, there were few building materials, and harsh weather, insects, and inexperience led to frequent setbacks. The prohibitive prices charged by the first railroad lines made it expensive to ship crops to market or have goods sent out. Although many farms failed, some survived and grew into large "bonanza" farms that hired additional labor and were able to benefit enough from economies of scale to grow profitable. Still, small family farms, and the settlers who worked them, were hard-pressed to do more than scrape out a living in an unforgiving environment that comprised arid land, violent weather shifts, and other challenges (Figure 17.6).

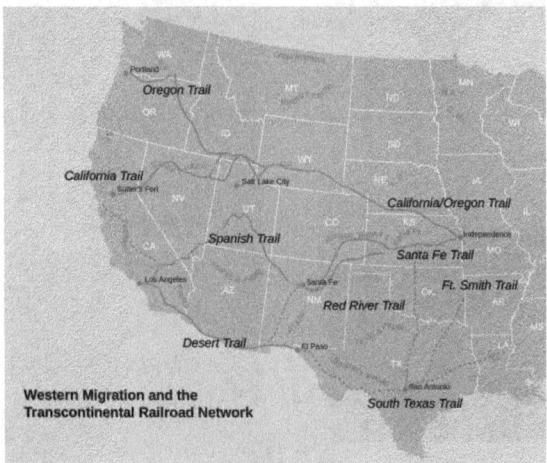

FIGURE 17.6 This map shows the trails (orange) used in westward migration and the development of railroad lines (blue) constructed after the completion of the first transcontinental railroad.

THE DIFFICULT LIFE OF THE PIONEER FARMER

Of the hundreds of thousands of settlers who moved west, the vast majority were homesteaders. These pioneers, like the Ingalls family of *Little House on the Prairie* book and television fame (see inset below), were seeking land and opportunity. Popularly known as "sodbusters," these men and women in the Midwest faced a difficult life on the frontier. They settled throughout the land that now makes up the Midwestern states of Wisconsin, Minnesota, Kansas, Nebraska, and the Dakotas. The weather and environment were bleak, and settlers struggled to eke out a living. A few unseasonably rainy years had led would-be settlers to believe that the "great desert" was no more, but the region's typically low rainfall and harsh temperatures made crop cultivation hard. Irrigation was a requirement, but finding water and building adequate systems proved too difficult and expensive for many farmers. It was not until 1902 and the passage of the Newlands Reclamation Act that a system finally existed to set aside funds from the sale of public lands to build dams for subsequent irrigation efforts. Prior to that, farmers across the Great Plains relied primarily on dry-farming techniques to grow corn, wheat, and sorghum, a practice that many continued in later years. A few also began to employ windmill technology to draw water, although both the drilling and construction of windmills became an added expense that few farmers could afford.

AMERICANA

The Enduring Appeal of *Little House on the Prairie*

The story of western migration and survival has remained a touchstone of American culture, even today. The television show *Frontier Life* on PBS is one example, as are countless other modern-day evocations of the settlers. Consider the enormous popularity of the *Little House* series. The books, originally published in the 1930s and 1940s, have been in print continuously. The television show, *Little House on the Prairie*, ran for over a decade and was hugely successful. Despite its popularity, *Little House on the Prairie* has created controversy more recently for its derogatory references to the Osage people. The books, although fictional, were based on Laura Ingalls Wilder's own childhood, as she travelled west with her family via covered wagon, stopping in Kansas, Wisconsin, South Dakota, and beyond (Figure 17.7).

(a)

(b)

FIGURE 17.7 Laura Ingalls Wilder (a) is the celebrated author of the *Little House* series, which began in 1932 with the publication of *Little House in the Big Woods*. The third, and best known, book in the series, *Little House on the Prairie* (b), was published just three years later.

Wilder wrote of her stories (http://openstax.org/l/ingallswilderbooks) , "As you read my stories of long ago I hope you will remember that the things that are truly worthwhile and that will give you happiness are the same now as they were then. Courage and kindness, loyalty, truth, and helpfulness are always the same and always needed." While Ingalls makes the point that her stories underscore traditional values that remain the same over time, this is not necessarily the only thing that made these books so popular. Perhaps part of their appeal is that they are adventure stories featuring encounters with severe weather, wild animals, and Native peoples. Does this explain their ongoing popularity? What other factors might make these stories appealing so long after they were originally written?

The first houses built by western settlers were typically made of mud and sod with thatch roofs, as there was little timber for building. Rain, when it arrived, presented constant problems for these **sod houses**, with mud falling into food, and vermin, most notably lice, scampering across bedding (Figure 17.8). Weather patterns not only left the fields dry, they also brought tornadoes, droughts, blizzards, and insect swarms. Tales of swarms of locusts were commonplace, and the crop-eating insects would at times cover the ground six to twelve inches deep. One frequently quoted Kansas newspaper reported a locust swarm in 1878 during which the insects devoured "everything green, stripping the foliage off the bark and from the tender twigs of the fruit trees, destroying every plant that is good for food or pleasant to the eye, that man has planted."

FIGURE 17.8 Sod houses were common in the Midwest as settlers moved west. There was no lumber to gather and no stones with which to build. These mud homes were vulnerable to weather and vermin, making life incredibly hard for the newly arrived homesteaders.

Farmers also faced the ever-present threat of debt and farm foreclosure by the banks. While land was essentially free under the Homestead Act, all other farm necessities cost money and were initially difficult to obtain in the newly settled parts of the country where market economies did not yet fully reach. Horses, livestock, wagons, wells, fencing, seed, and fertilizer were all critical to survival, but often hard to come by as the population initially remained sparsely settled across vast tracts of land. Railroads charged notoriously high rates for farm equipment and livestock, making it difficult to procure goods or make a profit on anything sent back east. Banks also charged high interest rates, and, in a cycle that replayed itself year after year, farmers would borrow from the bank with the intention of repaying their debt after the harvest. As the number of farmers moving westward increased, the market price of their produce steadily declined, even as the value of the actual land increased. Each year, hard-working farmers produced ever-larger crops, flooding the markets and subsequently driving prices down even further. Although some understood the economics of supply and demand, none could overtly control such forces.

Eventually, the arrival of a more extensive railroad network aided farmers, mostly by bringing much-needed supplies such as lumber for construction and new farm machinery. While John Deere sold a steel-faced plow as early as 1838, it was James Oliver's improvements to the device in the late 1860s that transformed life for homesteaders. His new, less expensive "chilled plow" was better equipped to cut through the shallow grass roots of the Midwestern terrain, as well as withstand damage from rocks just below the surface. Similar advancements in hay mowers, manure spreaders, and threshing machines greatly improved farm production for those who could afford them. Where capital expense became a significant factor, larger commercial farms—known as "**bonanza farms**"—began to develop. Farmers in Minnesota, North Dakota, and South Dakota hired migrant farmers to grow wheat on farms in excess of twenty thousand acres each. These large farms were succeeding by the end of the century, but small family farms continued to suffer. Although the land was nearly free, it cost close to $1000 for the necessary supplies to start up a farm, and many would-be landowners lured westward by the promise of cheap land became migrant farmers instead, working other peoples' land for a wage. The frustration of small farmers grew, ultimately leading to a revolt of sorts, discussed in a later chapter.

CLICK AND EXPLORE

Frontier House (http://openstax.org/l/homesteader) includes information on the logistics of moving across the country as a homesteader. Take a look at the list of supplies and gear. It is easy to understand why, even when the government gave the land away for free, it still took significant resources to make such a journey.

AN EVEN MORE CHALLENGING LIFE: A PIONEER WIFE

Although the West was numerically a male-dominated society, homesteading in particular encouraged the presence of women, families, and a domestic lifestyle, even if such a life was not an easy one. Women faced all the physical hardships that men encountered in terms of weather, illness, and danger, with the added complication of childbirth. Often, there was no doctor or midwife providing assistance, and many women died from treatable complications, as did their newborns. While some women could find employment in the newly settled towns as teachers, cooks, or seamstresses, they originally did not enjoy many rights. They could not sell property, sue for divorce, serve on juries, or vote. And for the vast majority of women, their work was not in towns for money, but on the farm. As late as 1900, a typical farm wife could expect to devote nine hours per day to chores such as cleaning, sewing, laundering, and preparing food. Two additional hours per day were spent cleaning the barn and chicken coop, milking the cows, caring for the chickens, and tending the family garden. One wife commented in 1879, "[We are] not much better than slaves. It is a weary, monotonous round of cooking and washing and mending and as a result the insane asylum is a third filled with wives of farmers."

Despite this grim image, the challenges of farm life eventually empowered women to break through some legal and social barriers. Many lived more equitably as partners with their husbands than did their eastern counterparts, helping each other through both hard times and good. If widowed, a wife typically took over responsibility for the farm, a level of management that was very rare back east, where the farm would fall to a son or other male relation. Pioneer women made important decisions and were considered by their husbands to be more equal partners in the success of the homestead, due to the necessity that all members had to work hard and contribute to the farming enterprise for it to succeed. Therefore, it is not surprising that the first states to grant women's rights, including the right to vote, were those in the Pacific Northwest and Upper Midwest, where women pioneers worked the land side by side with men. Some women seemed to be well suited to the challenges that frontier life presented them. Writing to her Aunt Martha from their homestead in Minnesota in 1873, Mary Carpenter refused to complain about the hardships of farm life: "I try to trust in God's promises, but we can't expect him to work miracles nowadays. Nevertheless, all that is expected of us is to do the best we can, and that we shall certainly endeavor to do. Even if we do freeze and starve in the way of duty, it will not be a dishonorable death."

17.3 Making a Living in Gold and Cattle

LEARNING OBJECTIVES

By the end of this section, you will be able to:
- Identify the major discoveries and developments in western gold, silver, and copper mining in the mid-nineteenth century
- Explain why the cattle industry was paramount to the development of the West and how it became the catalyst for violent range wars

Although homestead farming was the primary goal of most western settlers in the latter half of the nineteenth century, a small minority sought to make their fortunes quickly through other means. Specifically, gold (and, subsequently, silver and copper) prospecting attracted thousands of miners looking to "get rich quick" before returning east. In addition, ranchers capitalized on newly available railroad lines to move longhorn steers that populated southern and western Texas. This meat was highly sought after in eastern markets, and the demand created not only wealthy ranchers but an era of cowboys and cattle drives that in many ways defines how we think of the West today. Although neither miners nor ranchers intended to remain permanently in the West, many individuals from both groups ultimately stayed and settled there, sometimes due to the success of their gamble, and other times due to their abject failure.

THE CALIFORNIA GOLD RUSH AND BEYOND

The allure of gold has long sent people on wild chases; in the American West, the possibility of quick riches was no different. The search for gold represented an opportunity far different from the slow plod that homesteading farmers faced. The discovery of gold at Sutter's Mill in Coloma, California, set a pattern for such strikes that was repeated again and again for the next decade, in what collectively became known as the **California Gold Rush**. In what became typical, a sudden disorderly rush of prospectors descended upon a new discovery site, followed by the arrival of those who hoped to benefit from the strike by preying off the newly rich. This latter group of camp followers included saloonkeepers, prostitutes, store owners, and criminals, who all arrived in droves. If the strike was significant in size, a town of some magnitude might establish itself, and some semblance of law and order might replace the vigilante justice that typically grew in the small and short-lived mining outposts. This influx of settlers led to a massive loss of life for Native Americans in California that some scholars view as a genocide.

The original Forty-Niners were individual prospectors who sifted gold out of the dirt and gravel through "panning" or by diverting a stream through a sluice box (Figure 17.9). To varying degrees, the original California Gold Rush repeated itself throughout Colorado and Nevada for the next two decades. In 1859, Henry T. P. Comstock, a Canadian-born fur trapper, began gold mining in Nevada with other prospectors but then quickly found a blue-colored vein that proved to be the first significant silver discovery in the United States. Within twenty years, the **Comstock Lode**, as it was called, yielded more than $300 million in shafts that reached hundreds of feet into the mountain. Subsequent mining in Arizona and Montana yielded copper, and, while it lacked the glamour of gold, these deposits created huge wealth for those who exploited them, particularly with the advent of copper wiring for the delivery of electricity and telegraph communication.

(a)

(b)

FIGURE 17.9 The first gold prospectors in the 1850s and 1860s worked with easily portable tools that allowed anyone to follow their dream and strike it rich (a). It didn't take long for the most accessible minerals to be stripped, making way for large mining operations, including hydraulic mining, where high-pressure water jets removed sediment and rocks (b).

By the 1860s and 1870s, however, individual efforts to locate precious metals were less successful. The lowest-hanging fruit had been picked, and now it required investment capital and machinery to dig mine shafts that could reach remaining ore. With a much larger investment, miners needed a larger strike to be successful. This shift led to larger businesses underwriting mining operations, which eventually led to the development of greater urban stability and infrastructure. Denver, Colorado, was one of several cities that became permanent settlements, as businesses sought a stable environment to use as a base for their mining ventures.

For miners who had not yet struck it rich, this development was not a good one. They were now paid a daily or weekly wage to work underground in very dangerous conditions. They worked in shafts where the temperature could rise to above one hundred degrees Fahrenheit, and where poor ventilation might lead to long-term lung disease. They coped with shaft fires, dynamite explosions, and frequent cave-ins. By some historical accounts, close to eight thousand miners died on the frontier during this period, with over three times that number suffering crippling injuries. Some miners organized into unions and led strikes for better conditions, but these efforts were usually crushed by state militias.

Eventually, as the ore dried up, most mining towns turned into ghost towns. Even today, a visit through the American West shows old saloons and storefronts, abandoned as the residents moved on to their next shot at riches. The true lasting impact of the early mining efforts was the resulting desire of the U.S. government to bring law and order to the "Wild West" in order to more efficiently extract natural resources and encourage stable growth in the region. As more Americans moved to the region to seek permanent settlement, as opposed to brief speculative ventures, they also sought the safety and support that government order could bring. Nevada was admitted to the Union as a state in 1864, with Colorado following in 1876, then North Dakota, South Dakota, Montana, and Washington in 1889; and Idaho and Wyoming in 1890.

THE CATTLE KINGDOM

While the cattle industry lacked the romance of the Gold Rush, the role it played in western expansion should not be underestimated. For centuries, wild cattle roamed the Spanish borderlands. At the end of the Civil War, as many as five million longhorn steers could be found along the Texas frontier, yet few settlers had capitalized on the opportunity to claim them, due to the difficulty of transporting them to eastern markets. The completion of the first transcontinental railroad and subsequent railroad lines changed the game dramatically. Cattle ranchers and eastern businessmen realized that it was profitable to round up the wild steers and transport them by rail to be sold in the East for as much as thirty to fifty dollars per head. These ranchers and businessmen began the rampant speculation in the cattle industry that made, and lost, many fortunes.

So began the impressive cattle drives of the 1860s and 1870s. The famous Chisholm Trail provided a quick path from Texas to railroad terminals in Abilene, Wichita, and Dodge City, Kansas, where cowboys would receive their pay. These "cowtowns," as they became known, quickly grew to accommodate the needs of cowboys and the cattle industry. Cattlemen like Joseph G. McCoy, born in Illinois, quickly realized that the railroad offered a perfect way to get highly sought beef from Texas to the East. McCoy chose Abilene as a locale that would offer cowboys a convenient place to drive the cattle, and went about building stockyards, hotels, banks, and more to support the business. He promoted his services and encouraged cowboys to bring their cattle through Abilene for good money; soon, the city had grown into a bustling western city, complete with ways for the cowboys to spend their hard-earned pay (Figure 17.10).

FIGURE 17.10 Cattle drives were an integral part of western expansion. Cowboys worked long hours in the saddle, driving hardy longhorns to railroad towns that could ship the meat back east.

Between 1865 and 1885, as many as forty thousand cowboys roamed the Great Plains, hoping to work for local ranchers. They were all men, typically in their twenties, and close to one-third of them were Hispanic or African American. It is worth noting that the stereotype of the American cowboy—and indeed the cowboys themselves—borrowed much from the Mexicans who had long ago settled those lands. The saddles, lassos, chaps, and lariats that define cowboy culture all arose from the Mexican ranchers who had used them to great effect before the cowboys arrived.

Life as a cowboy was dirty and decidedly unglamorous. The terrain was difficult, but the longhorn cattle were hardy stock, and could survive and thrive while grazing along the long trail, so cowboys braved the trip for the promise of steady employment and satisfying wages. Eventually, however, the era of the free range ended. Ranchers developed the land, limiting grazing opportunities along the trail, and in 1873, the new technology of barbed wire allowed ranchers to fence off their lands and cattle claims. With the end of the free range, the cattle industry, like the mining industry before it, grew increasingly dominated by eastern businessmen. Capital investors from the East expanded rail lines and invested in ranches, ending the reign of the cattle drives.

AMERICANA

Barbed Wire and a Way of Life Gone

Called the "devil's rope" by Native Americans, barbed wire had a profound impact on the American West. Before its invention, settlers and ranchers alike were stymied by a lack of building materials to fence off land. Communal grazing and long cattle drives were the norm. But with the invention of barbed wire, large cattle ranchers and their investors were able to cheaply and easily parcel off the land they wanted—whether or not it was legally theirs to contain. As with many other inventions, several people "invented" barbed wire around the same time. In 1873, it was Joseph Glidden, however, who claimed the winning design and patented it. Not only did it spell the end of the free range for settlers and cowboys, it kept more land away from Native tribes(Figure 17.11).

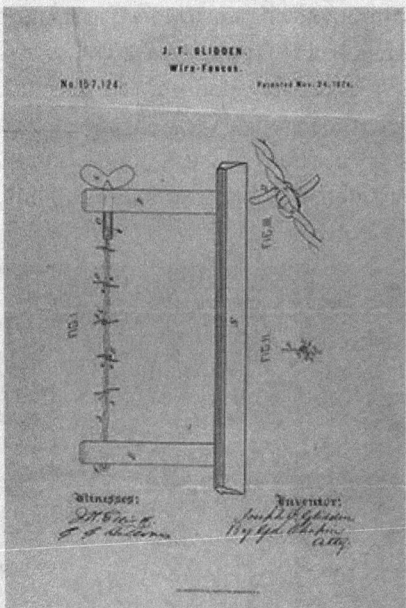

FIGURE 17.11 Joseph Glidden's invention of barbed wire in 1873 made him rich, changing the face of the American West forever. (credit: modification of work by the U.S. Department of Commerce)

In the early twentieth century, songwriter Cole Porter would take a poem by a Montana poet named Bob Fletcher and convert it into a cowboy song called, "Don't Fence Me In." As the lyrics below show, the song gave voice to the feeling that, as the fences multiplied, the ethos of the West was forever changed:

"Oh, give me land, lots of land, under starry skies above
Don't fence me in
Let me ride thru the wide-open country that I love
Don't fence me in . . .
Just turn me loose
Let me straddle my old saddle underneath the western skies
On my cayuse
Let me wander over yonder till I see the mountains rise

I want to ride to the ridge where the west commences
Gaze at the moon until I lose my senses
I can't look at hobbles and I can't stand fences
Don't fence me in.
"

VIOLENCE IN THE WILD WEST: MYTH AND REALITY

The popular image of the Wild West portrayed in books, television, and film has been one of violence and mayhem. The lure of quick riches through mining or driving cattle meant that much of the West did indeed consist of rough men living a rough life, although the violence was exaggerated and even glorified in the dime store novels of the day. The exploits of Wyatt Earp, Doc Holiday, and others made for good stories, but the reality was that western violence was more isolated than the stories might suggest. These clashes often occurred as people struggled for the scarce resources that could make or break their chance at riches, or as they dealt with the sudden wealth or poverty that prospecting provided.

Where sporadic violence did erupt, it was concentrated largely in mining towns or during range wars among large and small cattle ranchers. Some mining towns were indeed as rough as the popular stereotype. Men, money, liquor, and disappointment were a recipe for violence. Fights were frequent, deaths were commonplace, and frontier justice reigned. The notorious mining town of Bodie, California, had twenty-nine murders between 1877 and 1883, which translated to a murder rate higher than any other city at that time, and only one person was ever convicted of a crime. The most prolific gunman of the day was John Wesley Hardin, who allegedly killed over twenty men in Texas in various gunfights, including one victim he killed in a hotel for snoring too loudly (Figure 17.12).

FIGURE 17.12 The towns that sprouted up around gold strikes existed first and foremost as places for the men who struck it rich to spend their money. Stores, saloons, and brothels were among the first businesses to arrive. The combination of lawlessness, vice, and money often made for a dangerous mix.

Ranching brought with it its own dangers and violence. In the Texas cattle lands, owners of large ranches took advantage of their wealth and the new invention of barbed wire to claim the prime grazing lands and few significant watering holes for their herds. Those seeking only to move their few head of cattle to market grew increasingly frustrated at their inability to find even a blade of grass for their meager herds. Eventually, frustration turned to violence, as several ranchers resorted to vandalizing the barbed wire fences to gain access to grass and water for their steers. Such vandalism quickly led to cattle rustling, as these cowboys were not averse to leading a few of the rancher's steers into their own herds as they left.

One example of the violence that bubbled up was the infamous **Fence Cutting War** in Clay County, Texas

(1883–1884). There, cowboys began destroying fences that several ranchers erected along public lands: land they had no right to enclose. Confrontations between the cowboys and armed guards hired by the ranchers resulted in three deaths—hardly a "war," but enough of a problem to get the governor's attention. Eventually, a special session of the Texas legislature addressed the problem by passing laws to outlaw fence cutting, but also forced ranchers to remove fences illegally erected along public lands, as well as to place gates for passage where public areas adjoined private lands.

An even more violent confrontation occurred between large ranchers and small farmers in Johnson County, Wyoming, where cattle ranchers organized a "lynching bee" in 1891–1892 to make examples of cattle rustlers. Hiring twenty-two "invaders" from Texas to serve as hired guns, the ranch owners and their foremen hunted and subsequently killed the two rustlers best known for organizing the owners of the smaller Wyoming farms. Only the intervention of federal troops, who arrested and then later released the invaders, allowing them to return to Texas, prevented a greater massacre.

While there is much talk—both real and mythical—of the rough men who lived this life, relatively few women experienced it. While homesteaders were often families, gold speculators and cowboys tended to be single men in pursuit of fortune. The few women who went to these wild outposts were typically prostitutes, and even their numbers were limited. In 1860, in the Comstock Lode region of Nevada, for example, there were reportedly only thirty women total in a town of twenty-five hundred men. Some of the "painted ladies" who began as prostitutes eventually owned brothels and emerged as businesswomen in their own right; however, life for these young women remained a challenging one as western settlement progressed. A handful of women, numbering no more than six hundred, braved both the elements and male-dominated culture to become teachers in several of the more established cities in the West. Even fewer arrived to support husbands or operate stores in these mining towns.

As wealthy men brought their families west, the lawless landscape began to change slowly. Abilene, Kansas, is one example of a lawless town, replete with prostitutes, gambling, and other vices, transformed when middle-class women arrived in the 1880s with their cattle baron husbands. These women began to organize churches, school, civic clubs, and other community programs to promote family values. They fought to remove opportunities for prostitution and all the other vices that they felt threatened the values that they held dear. Protestant missionaries eventually joined the women in their efforts, and, while they were not widely successful, they did bring greater attention to the problems. As a response, the U.S. Congress passed both the Comstock Law (named after its chief proponent, anti-obscenity crusader Anthony Comstock) in 1873 to ban the spread of "lewd and lascivious literature" through the mail and the subsequent Page Act of 1875 to prohibit the transportation of women into the United States for employment as prostitutes. However, the "houses of ill repute" continued to operate and remained popular throughout the West despite the efforts of reformers.

CLICK AND EXPLORE

Take a look at the National Cowboy and Western Heritage Museum (http://openstax.org/l/natcowboy) to determine whether this site's portrayal of cowboy culture matches or contradicts the history shared in this chapter.

17.4 The Assault on American Indian Life and Culture

LEARNING OBJECTIVES

By the end of this section, you will be able to:
- Describe the methods that the U.S. government used to address the "Indian problem" during the settlement of the West
- Explain the United States policy of Americanization as it applied to Native peoples in the nineteenth century

As American settlers pushed westward, they inevitably came into conflict with Native tribes that had long been living on the land. Although the threat of attacks was quite slim and nowhere proportionate to the number of

U.S. Army actions directed against them, the occasional attack—often one of retaliation—was enough to fuel popular fear of Native peoples. The clashes, when they happened, were indeed brutal, although most of the brutality occurred at the hands of the settlers. Ultimately, the settlers, with the support of local militias and, later, with the federal government behind them, sought to eliminate the tribes from the lands they desired. This effort ultimately succeeded despite some Native military victories, and fundamentally changed the American Indian way of life.

CLAIMING LAND, RELOCATING LANDOWNERS

Back east, the popular vision of the West was of a vast and empty land. But of course this was an inaccurate depiction. On the eve of westward expansion, as many as 250,000 Native Americans, representing a variety of tribes, populated the Great Plains. Previous wars against tribes in the East in the early nineteenth century, as well as the failure of earlier treaties, led to a general policy of removal of these tribes west of the Mississippi. The Indian Removal Act of 1830 resulted in multiple forced removals, including the infamous "Trail of Tears," which saw nearly fifty thousand Cherokee, Seminole, Choctaw, Chickasaw, and Creek people relocated to what is now Oklahoma between 1831 and 1838. Building upon such a history, the U.S. government was prepared, during the era of western settlement, to deal with tribes that settlers viewed as obstacles to expansion.

As settlers sought more land for farming, mining, and cattle ranching, the first strategy employed to deal with the perceived "Indian problem" was to negotiate treaties to move tribes out of the path of White settlers. In 1851, the chiefs of most of the Great Plains tribes agreed to the First Treaty of Fort Laramie. This agreement established distinct tribal borders, essentially codifying the reservation system. In return for annual payments of $50,000 to the tribes (originally guaranteed for fifty years, but later revised to last for only ten) as well as the hollow promise of noninterference from westward settlers, the participating tribes agreed to stay clear of the path of settlement. Due to government corruption, many annuity payments never reached the tribes, and some reservations were left destitute and near starving. In addition, within a decade, as the pace and number of western settlers increased, even designated reservations became prime locations for farms and mining. Rather than waiting for new treaties, settlers—oftentimes backed by local or state militia units—simply attacked the tribes out of fear or to force them from the land. Some American Indians resisted, only to then face massacres.

In 1862, frustrated and angered by the lack of annuity payments, increasing hunger among their people, and the continuous encroachment on their reservation lands, Dakotas in Minnesota rebelled in what became known as the Dakota War or the War of 1862, killing the White settlers who moved onto their tribal lands. Over one thousand White settlers were captured or killed in the attack, before an armed militia regained control. Of the four hundred Sioux captured by U.S. troops, 303 were sentenced to death, but President Lincoln intervened, releasing all but thirty-eight of the men. Lincoln's government hanged the remaining thirty-eight Dakota men in the largest mass execution in the country's history. The government imprisoned other Dakota participants in the uprising, and banished their families from Minnesota. Settlers in other regions responded to news of this raid with fear and aggression. In Colorado, Arapahoe and Cheyenne tribes fought back against land encroachment; White militias then formed, decimating even some of the tribes that were willing to cooperate. One of the more vicious examples was near Sand Creek, Colorado, where Colonel John Chivington led a militia raid upon a camp in which the Cheyenne leader Black Kettle had already negotiated a peaceful settlement. The camp was flying both the American flag and the white flag of surrender when Chivington's troops murdered close to one hundred people, the majority of them women and children, and mutilated the bodies in what became known as the **Sand Creek Massacre**. For the rest of his life, Chivington would proudly display his collection of nearly one hundred Native American scalps from that day. Subsequent investigations by the U.S. Army condemned Chivington's tactics and their results; however, the raid served as a model for some settlers who sought any means by which to eradicate the perceived Indian threat. The incident highlighted growing disagreement between Americans in the eastern and western parts of the nation about how best to handle Indian affairs.

Hoping to forestall similar uprisings and all-out wars, the U.S. Congress commissioned a committee to investigate the causes of such incidents. The subsequent report of their findings led to the passage of two additional treaties: the Second Treaty of Fort Laramie and the Treaty of Medicine Lodge Creek, both designed to move the remaining tribes to even more remote reservations. The Second Treaty of Fort Laramie moved the remaining Lakota people to the Black Hills in the Dakota Territory and the Treaty of Medicine Lodge Creek moved the Cheyenne, Arapaho, Kiowa, and Comanche people to Indian Territory, later to become the State of Oklahoma.

The agreements were short-lived, however. With the subsequent discovery of gold in the Black Hills, settlers seeking their fortune began to move upon the newly granted Sioux lands with support from U.S. cavalry troops. By the middle of 1875, thousands of White prospectors were illegally digging and panning in the area. The Lakota people protested the invasion of their territory and the violation of sacred ground. The government offered to lease the Black Hills or to pay $6 million if the Indians were willing to sell the land. When the tribes refused, the government imposed what it considered a fair price for the land, ordered the Indians to move, and in the spring of 1876, made ready to force them onto the reservation.

In the Battle of Little Bighorn, perhaps the most famous battle of the American West, a Hunkpapa Lakota chief, Sitting Bull, urged Native Americans from all neighboring tribes to join his men in defense of their lands (Figure 17.13). At the Little Bighorn River, the U.S. Army's Seventh Cavalry, led by Colonel George Custer, sought a showdown. Driven by his own personal ambition, on June 25, 1876, Custer foolishly attacked what he thought was a minor encampment. Instead, it turned out to be a large group of Lakotas, Cheyennes, and Arapahos. The warriors—nearly three thousand in strength—surrounded and killed Custer and 262 of his men and support units, in the single greatest loss of U.S. troops to a Native American force in the era of westward expansion.

Look at these winter counts (http://openstax.org/l/wintercounts) by Lakota Chief American Horse at the National Museum of Natural History to explore a Lakota perspective on westward expansion.

FIGURE 17.13 The iconic Sitting Bull led Lakota, Cheyenne, and Arapaho warriors in what was the largest victory against American troops during Westward expansion. While the Battle of the Little Big Horn was a rout by the

Lakotas and their allies over Custer's troops, Native American resistance in the American West ultimately failed to halt American expansion.

AMERICAN INDIAN SUBMISSION

Despite their success at Little Bighorn, neither the Lakota people nor any other Plains tribes followed this battle with any other armed encounter. Rather, they either returned to tribal life or fled out of fear of remaining troops, until the U.S. Army arrived in greater numbers and began to exterminate Indian encampments and force others to accept payment for forcible removal from their lands. Sitting Bull himself fled to Canada, although he later returned in 1881 and subsequently worked in Buffalo Bill's Wild West show. In Montana, the Blackfoot and Crow were forced to leave their tribal lands. In Colorado, the Utes gave up their lands after a brief period of resistance. In Idaho, most of the Nez Perce gave up their lands peacefully, although in an incredible episode, a band of some eight hundred Indians sought to evade U.S. troops and escape into Canada.

> **MY STORY**
>
> ### I Will Fight No More: Chief Joseph's Capitulation
>
> Chief Joseph, known to his people as "Thunder Traveling to the Loftier Mountain Heights," was the chief of the Nez Perce tribe, and he had realized that they could not win against the White people. In order to avoid a war that would undoubtedly lead to the extermination of his people, he hoped to lead his tribe to Canada, where they could live freely. He led a full retreat of his people over fifteen hundred miles of mountains and harsh terrain, only to be caught within fifty miles of the Canadian border in late 1877. His speech has remained a poignant and vivid reminder of what the tribe had lost.
>
> "Tell General Howard I know his heart. What he told me before, I have it in my heart. I am tired of fighting. Our Chiefs are killed; Looking Glass is dead, Ta Hool Hool Shute is dead. The old men are all dead. It is the young men who say yes or no. He who led on the young men is dead. It is cold, and we have no blankets; the little children are freezing to death. My people, some of them, have run away to the hills, and have no blankets, no food. No one knows where they are—perhaps freezing to death. I want to have time to look for my children, and see how many of them I can find. Maybe I shall find them among the dead. Hear me, my Chiefs! I am tired; my heart is sick and sad. From where the sun now stands I will fight no more forever."
>
> "—Chief Joseph, 1877"

The final episode in the so-called Indian Wars occurred in 1890, at the **Wounded Knee Massacre** in South Dakota. On their reservation, the Lakota people had begun to perform the "Ghost Dance," which told of a Messiah who would deliver the tribe from its hardship, with such frequency that White settlers began to worry that another uprising would occur. The 7th Calvary prepared to round up the people performing the Ghost Dance. Frightened after the death of Sitting Bull at the hands of tribal police, a group of Lakota Ghost Dancers led by Bigfoot fled. When the 7th Cavalry caught up to them at Wounded Knee, South Dakota on December 29, 1890, the Lakotas prepared to surrender. Although the accounts are unclear, an apparent accidental rifle discharge by a young Lakota man preparing to lay down his weapon led the U.S. soldiers to begin firing indiscriminately upon the Native Americans. What little resistance the Lakotas mounted with a handful of concealed rifles at the outset of the fight diminished quickly, with the troops eventually massacring between 150 and 300 men, women, and children. The U.S. troops suffered twenty-five fatalities, some of which were the result of their own crossfire. Captain Edward Godfrey of the Seventh Cavalry later commented, "I know the men did not aim deliberately and they were greatly excited. I don't believe they saw their sights. They fired rapidly but it seemed to me only a few seconds till there was not a living thing before us; warriors, squaws, children, ponies, and dogs . . . went down before that unaimed fire." The United States awarded twenty of these soldiers the Congressional Medal of Honor, the nation's highest military honor. With this last show of brutality, the Indian Wars came to a close. U.S. government officials had already begun the process of seeking an alternative to the meaningless treaties and costly battles. A more effective means with which to address the public perception of the "Indian problem" was needed. **Americanization** provided the answer.

AMERICANIZATION

Through the years of the Indian Wars of the 1870s and early 1880s, opinion back east was mixed. There were many who felt, as General Philip Sheridan (appointed in 1867 to pacify the Plains Indians) allegedly said, that "the only good Indian was a dead Indian." But increasingly, several American reformers who would later form the backbone of the Progressive Era had begun to criticize the violence, arguing that the government should help the Native Americans through an Americanization policy aimed at assimilating them into American society. Individual land ownership, Christian worship, and education for children became the cornerstones of this new assault on Native life and culture.

Beginning in the 1880s, clergymen, government officials, and social workers all worked to assimilate Native peoples into American life. The government helped reformers remove Native American children from their homes and the cultural influence of their families and place them in boarding schools, such as the Carlisle Indian School, where they were forced to abandon their tribal traditions and embrace Euro-American social and cultural practices. Such schools acculturated Native American boys and girls and provided vocational training for males and domestic science classes for females. Boarding schools sought to convince Native children to abandon their language, clothing, and social customs for a more Euro-American lifestyle (Figure 17.14).

FIGURE 17.14 The federal government's policy towards Native Americans shifted in the late 1880s from the reservation system to assimilating them into the American ideal.

A vital part of the assimilation effort was land reform. During earlier negotiations, the government had recognized Native American communal ownership of land. Although many tribes recognized individual families' use rights to specific plots of land, the tribe owned the land. As a part of their plan to Americanize the tribes, reformers sought legislation to replace this concept with the popular Euro-American notion of real estate ownership and self-reliance. One such law was the Dawes Severalty Act of 1887, named after a reformer and senator from Massachusetts. In what was essentially a new version of the original Homestead Act, the Dawes Act permitted the federal government to divide the lands of any tribe and grant 160 acres of farmland or 320 acres of grazing land to each head of family, with lesser amounts to single persons and others. In a nod towards the paternal relationship with which White people viewed Native Americans—similar to the justification of the previous treatment of enslaved African Americans—the Dawes Act permitted the federal government to hold an individual Native American's newly acquired land in trust for twenty-five years. Only then would they obtain full title and be granted the citizenship rights that land ownership entailed. It would not be until 1924 that formal citizenship was granted to all Native Americans. Under the Dawes Act, Native Americans were assigned the most arid, useless land and "surplus" land went to White settlers. The government sold as much as eighty million acres of Native American land to White American settlers.

> **CLICK AND EXPLORE**
>
> Take a look at the Carlisle Industrial Indian School (http://openstax.org/l/carlisleschool), which attempted to assimilate Native American students from 1879 to 1918. Look through the photographs and records of the school to assess the school's impact on the student's cultural practices.

17.5 The Impact of Expansion on Chinese Immigrants and Hispanic Citizens

LEARNING OBJECTIVES

By the end of this section, you will be able to:

- Describe the treatment of Chinese immigrants and Hispanic citizens during the westward expansion of the nineteenth century

As White Americans pushed west, they not only collided with Native American tribes but also with Hispanic Americans and Chinese immigrants. Hispanics in the Southwest had the opportunity to become American citizens at the end of the Mexican-American war, but their status was markedly second-class. Chinese immigrants arrived en masse during the California Gold Rush and numbered in the hundreds of thousands by the late 1800s, with the majority living in California, working menial jobs. These distinct cultural and ethnic groups strove to maintain their rights and way of life in the face of persistent racism and entitlement. But the large number of White settlers and government-sanctioned land acquisitions left them at a profound disadvantage. Ultimately, both groups withdrew into homogenous communities in which their language and culture could survive.

CHINESE IMMIGRANTS IN THE AMERICAN WEST

The initial arrival of Chinese immigrants to the United States began as a slow trickle in the 1820s, with barely 650 living in the U.S. by the end of 1849. However, as gold rush fever swept the country, Chinese immigrants, too, were attracted to the notion of quick fortunes. By 1852, over 25,000 Chinese immigrants had arrived, and by 1880, over 300,000 Chinese lived in the United States, most in California. While they had dreams of finding gold, many instead found employment building the first transcontinental railroad (Figure 17.15). Some even traveled as far east as the former cotton plantations of the Old South, which they helped to farm after the Civil War. Several thousand of these immigrants booked their passage to the United States using a "credit-ticket," in which their passage was paid in advance by American businessmen to whom the immigrants were then indebted for a period of work. Most arrivals were men: Few wives or children ever traveled to the United States. As late as 1890, less than 5 percent of the Chinese population in the U.S. was female. Regardless of gender, few Chinese immigrants intended to stay permanently in the United States, although many were reluctantly forced to do so, as they lacked the financial resources to return home.

FIGURE 17.15 Building the railroads was dangerous and backbreaking work. On the western railroad line, Chinese migrants, along with other non-White workers, were often given the most difficult and dangerous jobs of all.

Prohibited by law since 1790 from obtaining U.S. citizenship through naturalization, Chinese immigrants faced harsh discrimination and violence from American settlers in the West. Despite hardships like the special tax that Chinese miners had to pay to take part in the Gold Rush, or their subsequent forced relocation into Chinese districts, these immigrants continued to arrive in the United States seeking a better life for the families they left behind. Only when the Chinese Exclusion Act of 1882 forbade further immigration from China for a ten-year period did the flow stop.

The Chinese community banded together in an effort to create social and cultural centers in cities such as San Francisco. In a haphazard fashion, they sought to provide services ranging from social aid to education, places of worship, health facilities, and more to their fellow Chinese immigrants. As Chinese workers began competing with White Americans for jobs in California cities, the latter began a system of built-in discrimination. In the 1870s, White Americans formed "anti-coolie clubs" ("coolie" being a racial slur directed towards people of any Asian descent), through which they organized boycotts of Chinese-produced products and lobbied for anti-Chinese laws. Some protests turned violent, as in 1885 in Rock Springs, Wyoming, where tensions between White and Chinese immigrant miners erupted in a riot, resulting in over two dozen Chinese immigrants being murdered and many more injured.

Slowly, racism and discrimination became law. The new California constitution of 1879 denied naturalized Chinese citizens the right to vote or hold state employment. Additionally, in 1882, the U.S. Congress passed the Chinese Exclusion Act, which forbade further Chinese immigration into the United States for ten years. The ban was later extended on multiple occasions until its repeal in 1943. Eventually, some Chinese immigrants returned to China. Those who remained were stuck in the lowest-paying, most menial jobs. Several found assistance through the creation of benevolent associations designed to both support Chinese communities and defend them against political and legal discrimination; however, the history of Chinese immigrants to the United States remained largely one of deprivation and hardship well into the twentieth century.

CLICK AND EXPLORE

The Central Pacific Railroad Photographic History Museum (http://openstax.org/l/railroadchina) provides a context for the role of the Chinese who helped build the railroads. What does the site celebrate, and what, if anything, does it condemn?

DEFINING AMERICAN

The Backs that Built the Railroad

Below is a description of the construction of the railroad in 1867. Note the way it describes the scene, the laborers, and the effort.

"The cars now (1867) run nearly to the summit of the Sierras. . . . four thousand laborers were at work—one-tenth Irish, the rest Chinese. They were a great army laying siege to Nature in her strongest citadel. The rugged mountains looked like stupendous ant-hills. They swarmed with Celestials, shoveling, wheeling, carting, drilling and blasting rocks and earth, while their dull, moony eyes stared out from under immense basket-hats, like umbrellas. At several dining camps we saw hundreds sitting on the ground, eating soft boiled rice with chopsticks as fast as terrestrials could with soup-ladles. Irish laborers received thirty dollars per month (gold) and board; Chinese, thirty-one dollars, boarding themselves. After a little experience the latter were quite as efficient and far less troublesome."

"—Albert D. Richardson, *Beyond the Mississippi*"

Several great American advancements of the nineteenth century were built with the hands of many other nations. It is interesting to ponder how much these immigrant communities felt they were building their own fortunes and futures, versus the fortunes of others. Is it likely that the Chinese laborers, many of whom died due to the harsh conditions, considered themselves part of "a great army"? Certainly, this account reveals the unwitting racism of the day, where workers were grouped together by their ethnicity, and each ethnic group was labeled monolithically as "good workers" or "troublesome," with no regard for individual differences among the hundreds of Chinese or Irish workers.

HISPANIC AMERICANS IN THE AMERICAN WEST

The Treaty of Guadalupe Hidalgo, which ended the Mexican-American War in 1848, promised U.S. citizenship to the nearly seventy-five thousand Hispanics now living in the American Southwest; approximately 90 percent accepted the offer and chose to stay in the United States despite their immediate relegation to second-class citizenship status. Relative to the rest of Mexico, these lands were sparsely populated and had been so ever since the country achieved its freedom from Spain in 1821. In fact, New Mexico—not Texas or California—was the center of settlement in the region in the years immediately preceding the war with the United States, containing nearly fifty thousand Mexicans. However, those who did settle the area were proud of their heritage and ability to develop *rancheros* of great size and success. Despite promises made in the treaty, these Californios—as they came to be known—quickly lost their land to White settlers who simply displaced the rightful landowners, by force if necessary. Repeated efforts at legal redress mostly fell upon deaf ears. In some instances, judges and lawyers would permit the legal cases to proceed through an expensive legal process only to the point where Hispanic landowners who insisted on holding their ground were rendered penniless for their efforts.

Much like Chinese immigrants, Hispanic citizens were relegated to the worst-paying jobs under the most terrible working conditions. They worked as *peóns* (manual laborers similar to enslaved people), *vaqueros* (cattle herders), and cartmen (transporting food and supplies) on the cattle ranches that White landowners possessed, or undertook the most hazardous mining tasks (Figure 17.16).

FIGURE 17.16 Mexican ranchers had worked the land in the American Southwest long before American "cowboys" arrived. In what ways might the Mexican *vaquero* pictured above have influenced the American cowboy?

In a few instances, frustrated Hispanic citizens fought back against the White settlers who dispossessed them of their belongings. In 1889–1890 in New Mexico, several hundred Mexican Americans formed **las Gorras Blancas** (the White Caps) to try and reclaim their land and intimidate White Americans, preventing further land seizures. White Caps conducted raids of White farms, burning homes, barns, and crops to express their growing anger and frustration. However, their actions never resulted in any fundamental changes. Several White Caps were captured, beaten, and imprisoned, whereas others eventually gave up, fearing harsh reprisals against their families. Some White Caps adopted a more political strategy, gaining election to local offices throughout New Mexico in the early 1890s, but growing concerns over the potential impact upon the territory's quest for statehood led several citizens to heighten their repression of the movement. Other laws passed in the United States intended to deprive Mexican Americans of their heritage as much as their lands. "Sunday Laws" prohibited "noisy amusements" such as bullfights, cockfights, and other cultural gatherings common to Hispanic communities at the time. "Greaser Laws" permitted the imprisonment of any unemployed Mexican American on charges of vagrancy. Although Hispanic Americans held tightly to their cultural heritage as their remaining form of self-identity, such laws did take a toll.

In California and throughout the Southwest, the massive influx of Anglo-American settlers simply overran the Hispanic populations that had been living and thriving there, sometimes for generations. Despite being U.S. citizens with full rights, Hispanics quickly found themselves outnumbered, outvoted, and, ultimately, outcast. Corrupt state and local governments favored White people in land disputes, and mining companies and cattle barons discriminated against them, as with the Chinese workers, in terms of pay and working conditions. In growing urban areas such as Los Angeles, *barrios*, or clusters of working-class homes, grew more isolated from the White American centers. Hispanic Americans, like the Native Americans and Chinese, suffered the fallout of the White settlers' relentless push west.

Key Terms

Americanization   the policy aimed at assimilating Native Americans into a middle class, Protestant version of the American way of life through boarding schools for Native American children and land allotment for Native American households

bonanza farms   large farms owned by speculators who hired laborers to work the land; these large farms allowed their owners to benefit from economies of scale and prosper, but they did nothing to help small family farms, which continued to struggle

California Gold Rush   the period between 1848 and 1849 when prospectors found large strikes of gold in California, leading others to rush in and follow suit; this period led to a cycle of boom and bust through the area, as gold was discovered, mined, and stripped

Comstock Lode   the first significant silver find in the country, discovered by Henry T. P. Comstock in 1859 in Nevada

exodusters   a term used to describe African Americans who moved to Kansas from the Old South to escape the racism there

Fence Cutting War   this armed conflict between cowboys moving cattle along the trail and ranchers who wished to keep the best grazing lands for themselves occurred in Clay County, Texas, between 1883 and 1884

las Gorras Blancas   the Spanish name for White Caps, the rebel group of Hispanic Americans who fought back against the appropriation of Hispanic land by White people; for a period in 1889–1890, they burned farms, homes, and crops to express their growing anger at the injustice of the situation

Manifest Destiny   the phrase, coined by journalist John O'Sullivan, which came to stand for the idea that White Americans had a calling and a duty to seize and settle the American West with Protestant democratic values

Sand Creek Massacre   a militia raid led by Colonel Chivington on a Cheyenne and Arapaho peoples camp in Colorado, flying both the American flag and the white flag of surrender; over one hundred men, women, and children were killed

sod house   a frontier home constructed of dirt held together by thick-rooted prairie grass that was prevalent in the Midwest; sod, cut into large rectangles, was stacked to make the walls of the structure, providing an inexpensive, yet damp, house for western settlers

Wounded Knee Massacre   an attempt to disarm a group of Lakota people near Wounded Knee, South Dakota, which resulted in members of the Seventh Cavalry of the U.S. Army opening fire and killing over 150 Lakota

Summary

17.1 The Westward Spirit

While a few bold settlers had moved westward before the middle of the nineteenth century, they were the exception, not the rule. The "great American desert," as it was called, was considered a vast and empty place, unfit for civilized people. In the 1840s, however, this idea started to change, as potential settlers began to learn more from promoters and land developers of the economic opportunities that awaited them in the West, and Americans extolled the belief that it was their Manifest Destiny—their divine right—to explore and settle the western territories in the name of the United States.

Most settlers in this first wave were White Americans of means. Whether they sought riches in gold, cattle, or farming, or believed it their duty to spread Protestant ideals to native inhabitants, they headed west in wagon trains along paths such as the Oregon Trail. European immigrants, particularly those from Northern Europe, also made the trip, settling in close-knit ethnic enclaves out of comfort, necessity, and familiarity. African Americans escaping the racism of the South also went west. In all, the newly settled areas were neither a fast track to riches nor a simple expansion into an empty land, but rather a clash of cultures, races, and traditions that defined the emerging new America.

17.2 Homesteading: Dreams and Realities

The concept of Manifest Destiny and the strong incentives to relocate sent hundreds of thousands of people west across the Mississippi. The rigors of this new way of life presented many challenges and difficulties to homesteaders. The land was dry and barren, and homesteaders lost crops to hail, droughts, insect swarms, and more. There were few materials with which to build, and early homes were made of mud, which did not stand up to the elements. Money was a constant concern, as the cost of railroad freight was exorbitant, and banks were unforgiving of bad harvests. For women, life was difficult in the extreme. Farm wives worked at least eleven hours per day on chores and had limited access to doctors or midwives. Still, they were more independent than their eastern counterparts and worked in partnership with their husbands.

As the railroad expanded and better farm equipment became available, by the 1870s, large farms began to succeed through economies of scale. Small farms still struggled to stay afloat, however, leading to a rising discontent among the farmers, who worked so hard for so little success.

17.3 Making a Living in Gold and Cattle

While homesteading was the backbone of western expansion, mining and cattle also played significant roles in shaping the West. Much rougher in character and riskier in outcomes than farming, these two opportunities brought forward a different breed of settler than the homesteaders. Many of the long-trail cattle riders were Mexican American or African American, and most of the men involved in both pursuits were individuals willing to risk what little they had in order to strike it rich.

In both the mining and cattle industries, however, individual opportunities slowly died out, as resources—both land for grazing and easily accessed precious metals—disappeared. In their place came big business, with the infrastructure and investments to make a profit. These businesses built up small towns into thriving cities, and the influx of middle-class families sought to drive out some of the violence and vice that characterized the western towns. Slowly but inexorably, the "American" way of life, as envisioned by the eastern establishment who initiated and promoted the concept of Manifest Destiny, was spreading west.

17.4 The Assault on American Indian Life and Culture

Settlers encroaching on Native American land created an "Indian problem" in the American West, which increasingly required government intervention. Violence between the United States and the Indian nations of the Plains marked westward expansion, and despite some Native victories, the Indian Wars ultimately transformed tribal cultures as the federal government forced tribes onto reservations. The violence of the Indian Wars also sparked debate about policy regarding Native Americans, and led to the rise of reformers in the East determined to solve the "Indian problem" peacefully.

Although the Americanization policy formulated by reformers ended the assault on American Indian life, it enhanced efforts to destroy Native cultures in an effort to assimilate Native peoples to an idealized Euro-American model. Although well-meaning people hoped to save Native Americans by preparing them for life in modern America, their boarding schools traumatized Native students, and their allotment policy impoverished Native peoples by selling surplus tribal lands to settlers.

17.5 The Impact of Expansion on Chinese Immigrants and Hispanic Citizens

In the nineteenth century, the Hispanic, Chinese, and White populations of the country collided. White people moved further west in search of land and riches, bolstered by government subsidies and an inherent and unshakable belief that the land and its benefits existed for their use. In some ways, it was a race to the prize: White Americans believed that they deserved the best lands and economic opportunities the country afforded, and did not consider prior claims to be valid.

Neither Chinese immigrants nor Hispanic Americans could withstand the assault on their rights by the tide of White settlers. Sheer numbers, matched with political backing, gave White people the power they needed to overcome any resistance. Ultimately, both ethnic groups retreated into urban enclaves, where their language and traditions could survive.

Review Questions

1. Which of the following does *not* represent a group that participated significantly in westward migration after 1870?
    A. African American "exodusters" escaping racism and seeking economic opportunities
    B. former Southern slaveholders seeking land and new financial opportunities
    C. recent immigrants from Northern Europe and Canada
    D. recent Chinese immigrants seeking gold in California

2. Which of the following represents an action that the U.S. government took to help Americans fulfill the goal of western expansion?
    A. the passage of the Homestead Act
    B. the official creation of the philosophy of Manifest Destiny
    C. the development of stricter immigration policies
    D. the introduction of new irrigation techniques

3. Why and how did the U.S. government promote western migration in the midst of fighting the Civil War?

4. What specific types of hardships did an average American farmer *not* face as he built his homestead in the Midwest?
    A. droughts
    B. insect swarms
    C. attacks from Native Americans
    D. limited building supplies

5. What accounts for the success of large, commercial "bonanza farms?" What benefits did they enjoy over their smaller family-run counterparts?

6. How did everyday life in the American West hasten equality for women who settled the land?

7. Which of the following groups was *not* impacted by the invention of barbed wire?
    A. ranchers
    B. cowboys
    C. farmers
    D. illegal prostitutes

8. The American cowboy owes much of its model to what other culture?
    A. Mexicans
    B. Native Americans
    C. Northern European immigrants
    D. Chinese immigrants

9. How did mining and cattle ranching transform individual "get rich quick" efforts into "big business" efforts when the nineteenth century came to a close?

10. Which of the following was *not* a primary method by which the American government dealt with American Indians during the period of western settlement?
    A. relocation
    B. appeasement
    C. extermination
    D. assimilation

11. What brought the majority of Chinese immigrants to the U.S.?
    A. gold
    B. work opportunities on the railroads
    C. the Homestead Act
    D. Chinese benevolent associations

12. How were Hispanic citizens deprived of their wealth and land in the course of western settlement?
    A. Native American raids
    B. land seizures
    C. prisoner of war status
    D. infighting

13. Compare and contrast the treatment of Chinese immigrants and Hispanic citizens to that of Native Americans during the period of western settlement.

Critical Thinking Questions

14. Describe the philosophy of Manifest Destiny. What effect did it have on Americans' westward migration? How might the different groups that migrated have sought to apply this philosophy to their individual circumstances?

15. Compare the myth of the "Wild West" with its reality. What elements of truth would these stories have contained, and what was fabricated or left out? What was life actually like for cowboys, ranchers, and the few women present in mining towns or along the cattle range?

16. What were the primary methods that the U.S. government, as well as individual reformers, used to deal with the perceived Indian threat to westward settlement? In what ways were these methods successful and unsuccessful? What were their short-term and long-term effects on Native Americans?

17. Describe the ways in which the U.S. government, local governments, and/or individuals attempted to interfere with the specific cultural traditions and customs of Native Americans, Hispanics, and Chinese immigrants. What did these efforts have in common? How did each group respond?

18. In what ways did westward expansion provide new opportunities for women and African Americans? In what ways did it limit these opportunities?

Industrialization and the Rise of Big Business, 1870-1900

18

FIGURE 18.1 The Electrical Building, constructed in 1892 for the World's Columbian Exposition, included displays from General Electric and Westinghouse, and introduced the American public to alternating current and neon lights. The Chicago World's Fair, as the universal exposition was more commonly known, featured architecture, inventions, and design, serving as both a showcase for and an influence on the country's optimism about the Industrial Age.

CHAPTER OUTLINE

18.1 Inventors of the Age
18.2 From Invention to Industrial Growth
18.3 Building Industrial America on the Backs of Labor
18.4 A New American Consumer Culture

INTRODUCTION "The electric age was ushered into being in this last decade of the nineteenth century today when President Cleveland, by pressing a button, started the mighty machinery, rushing waters and revolving wheels in the World's Columbian exhibition." With this announcement about the official start of the Chicago World's Fair in 1893 (Figure 18.1), the *Salt Lake City Herald* captured the excitement and optimism of the machine age. "In the previous expositions," the editorial continued, "the possibilities of electricity had been limited to the mere starting of the engines in the machinery hall, but in this it made thousands of servants do its bidding . . . the magic of electricity did the duty of the hour."

The fair, which commemorated the four hundredth anniversary of Columbus's journey to America, was a potent symbol of the myriad inventions that changed American life and contributed to the significant economic growth of the era, as well as the new wave of industrialization that swept the country. While businessmen capitalized upon such technological innovations, the new industrial working class faced enormous challenges. Ironically, as the World's Fair welcomed its first visitors, the nation was spiraling downward into the worst depression of the century. Subsequent frustrations among working-class Americans laid the groundwork for the country's first significant labor movement.

18.1 Inventors of the Age

LEARNING OBJECTIVES

By the end of this section, you will be able to:
- Explain how the ideas and products of late nineteenth-century inventors contributed to the rise of big business
- Explain how the inventions of the late nineteenth century changed everyday American life

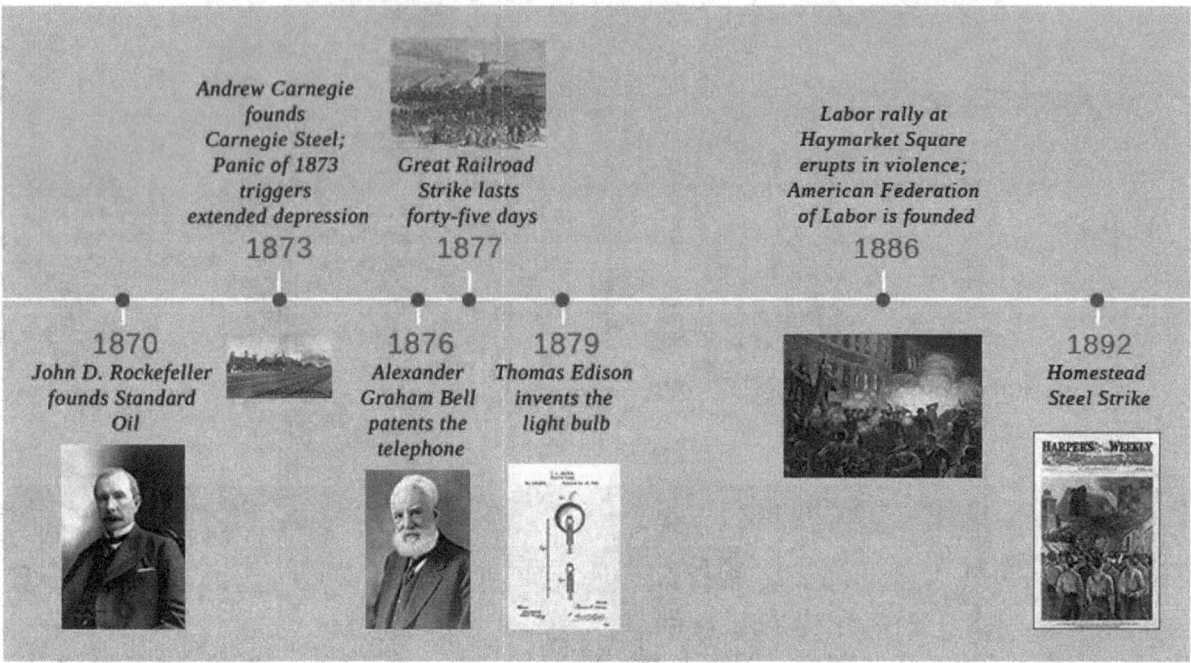

FIGURE 18.2

The late nineteenth century was an energetic era of inventions and entrepreneurial spirit. Building upon the mid-century Industrial Revolution in Great Britain, as well as answering the increasing call from Americans for efficiency and comfort, the country found itself in the grip of invention fever, with more people working on their big ideas than ever before. In retrospect, harnessing the power of steam and then electricity in the nineteenth century vastly increased the power of man and machine, thus making other advances possible as the century progressed.

Facing an increasingly complex everyday life, Americans sought the means by which to cope with it. Inventions often provided the answers, even as the inventors themselves remained largely unaware of the life-changing nature of their ideas. To understand the scope of this zeal for creation, consider the U.S. Patent Office, which, in 1790—its first decade of existence—recorded only 276 inventions. By 1860, the office had issued a total of 60,000 patents. But between 1860 and 1890, that number exploded to nearly 450,000, with another 235,000 in the last decade of the century. While many of these patents came to naught, some inventions became lynchpins in the rise of big business and the country's move towards an industrial-based economy, in which the desire for efficiency, comfort, and abundance could be more fully realized by most Americans.

AN EXPLOSION OF INVENTIVE ENERGY

From corrugated rollers that could crack hard, homestead-grown wheat into flour to refrigerated train cars and garment-sewing machines (Figure 18.3), new inventions fueled industrial growth around the country. As late as 1880, fully one-half of all Americans still lived and worked on farms, whereas fewer than one in seven—mostly men, except for long-established textile factories in which female employees tended to dominate—were employed in factories. However, the development of commercial electricity by the close of the century, to complement the steam engines that already existed in many larger factories, permitted more industries to concentrate in cities, away from the previously essential water power. In turn, newly arrived immigrants sought employment in new urban factories. Immigration, urbanization, and industrialization coincided to transform the face of American society from primarily rural to significantly urban. From 1880 to 1920, the number of industrial workers in the nation quadrupled from 2.5 million to over 10 million, while over the same period urban populations doubled, to reach one-half of the country's total population.

FIGURE 18.3 Advertisements of the late nineteenth century promoted the higher quality and lower prices that people could expect from new inventions. Here, a knitting factory promotes the fact that its machines make seamless hose, while still acknowledging the traditional role of women in the garment industry, from grandmothers who used to sew by hand to young women who now used machines.

In offices, worker productivity benefited from the typewriter, invented in 1867, the cash register, invented in 1879, and the adding machine, invented in 1885. These tools made it easier than ever to keep up with the rapid pace of business growth. Inventions also slowly transformed home life. The vacuum cleaner arrived during this era, as well as the flush toilet. These indoor "water closets" improved public health through the reduction in contamination associated with outhouses and their proximity to water supplies and homes. Tin cans and, later, Clarence Birdseye's experiments with frozen food, eventually changed how women shopped for, and prepared, food for their families, despite initial health concerns over preserved foods. With the advent of more easily prepared food, women gained valuable time in their daily schedules, a step that partially laid the groundwork for the modern women's movement. Women who had the means to purchase such items could use their time to seek other employment outside of the home, as well as broaden their knowledge through education and reading. Such a transformation did not occur overnight, as these inventions also increased expectations for women to remain tied to the home and their domestic chores; slowly, the culture of domesticity changed.

Perhaps the most important industrial advancement of the era came in the production of steel. Manufacturers and builders preferred steel to iron, due to its increased strength and durability. After the Civil War, two new processes allowed for the creation of furnaces large enough and hot enough to melt the wrought iron needed to produce large quantities of steel at increasingly cheaper prices. The Bessemer process, named for English inventor Henry Bessemer, and the open-hearth process, changed the way the United States produced steel and, in doing so, led the country into a new industrialized age. As the new material became more available, builders eagerly sought it out, a demand that steel mill owners were happy to supply.

In 1860, the country produced thirteen thousand tons of steel. By 1879, American furnaces were producing over one million tons per year; by 1900, this figure had risen to ten million. Just ten years later, the United States was the top steel producer in the world, at over twenty-four million tons annually. As production increased to match the overwhelming demand, the price of steel dropped by over 80 percent. When quality steel became cheaper and more readily available, other industries relied upon it more heavily as a key to their growth and development, including construction and, later, the automotive industry. As a result, the steel industry rapidly became the cornerstone of the American economy, remaining the primary indicator of industrial growth and stability through the end of World War II.

ALEXANDER GRAHAM BELL AND THE TELEPHONE

Advancements in communications matched the pace of growth seen in industry and home life. Communication technologies were changing quickly, and they brought with them new ways for information to travel. In 1858, British and American crews laid the first transatlantic cable lines, enabling messages to pass between the United States and Europe in a matter of hours, rather than waiting the few weeks it could take for a letter to arrive by steamship. Although these initial cables worked for barely a month, they generated great interest in developing a more efficient telecommunications industry. Within twenty years, over 100,000 miles of cable crisscrossed the ocean floors, connecting all the continents. Domestically, Western Union, which controlled 80 percent of the country's telegraph lines, operated nearly 200,000 miles of telegraph routes from coast to coast. In short, people were connected like never before, able to relay messages in minutes and hours rather than days and weeks.

One of the greatest advancements was the telephone, which Alexander Graham Bell patented in 1876 (Figure 18.4). While he was not the first to invent the concept, Bell was the first one to capitalize on it; after securing the patent, he worked with financiers and businessmen to create the National Bell Telephone Company. Western Union, which had originally turned down Bell's machine, went on to commission Thomas Edison to invent an improved version of the telephone. It is actually Edison's version that is most like the modern telephone used today. However, Western Union, fearing a costly legal battle they were likely to lose due to Bell's patent, ultimately sold Edison's idea to the Bell Company. With the communications industry now largely in their control, along with an agreement from the federal government to permit such control, the Bell Company was transformed into the American Telephone and Telegraph Company, which still exists today as AT&T. By 1880, fifty thousand telephones were in use in the United States, including one at the White House. By 1900, that number had increased to 1.35 million, and hundreds of American cities had obtained local service for their citizens. Quickly and inexorably, technology was bringing the country into closer contact, changing forever the rural isolation that had defined America since its beginnings.

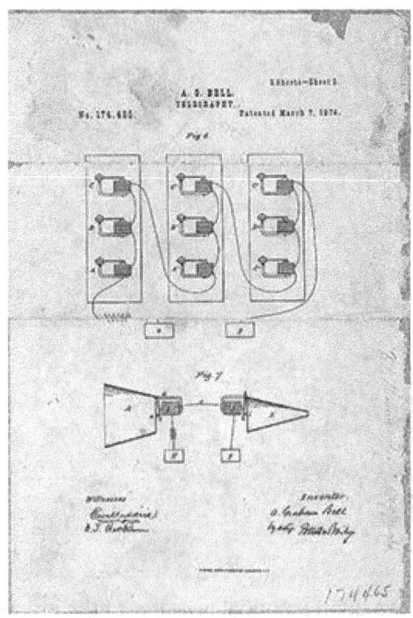

FIGURE 18.4 Alexander Graham Bell's patent of the telephone was one of almost 700,000 U.S. patents issued between 1850 and 1900. Although the patent itself was only six pages long, including two pages of illustrations, it proved to be one of the most contested and profitable of the nineteenth century. (credit: U.S. National Archives and Records Administration)

CLICK AND EXPLORE

Visit the Library of Congress (http://openstax.org/l/telephone) to examine the controversy over the invention of the telephone. While Alexander Graham Bell is credited with the invention, several other inventors played a role in its development; however, Bell was the first to patent the device.

THOMAS EDISON AND ELECTRIC LIGHTING

Although Thomas Alva Edison (Figure 18.5) is best known for his contributions to the electrical industry, his experimentation went far beyond the light bulb. Edison was quite possibly the greatest inventor of the turn of the century, saying famously that he "hoped to have a minor invention every ten days and a big thing every month or so." He registered 1,093 patents over his lifetime and ran a world-famous laboratory, Menlo Park, which housed a rotating group of up to twenty-five scientists from around the globe.

Edison became interested in the telegraph industry as a boy, when he worked aboard trains selling candy and newspapers. He soon began tinkering with telegraph technology and, by 1876, had devoted himself full time to lab work as an inventor. He then proceeded to invent a string of items that are still used today: the phonograph, the mimeograph machine, the motion picture projector, the dictaphone, and the storage battery, all using a factory-oriented assembly line process that made the rapid production of inventions possible.

FIGURE 18.5 Thomas Alva Edison was the quintessential inventor of the era, with a passion for new ideas and over one thousand patents to his name. Seen here with his incandescent light bulb, which he invented in 1879, Edison produced many inventions that subsequently transformed the country and the world.

In 1879, Edison invented the item that has led to his greatest fame: the practical incandescent light bulb. He allegedly explored over six thousand different materials for the filament, before stumbling upon carbonized cotton thread as the ideal substance. By 1882, with financial backing largely from financier J. P. Morgan, he had created the Edison Electric Illuminating Company, which began supplying electrical current to a small number of customers in New York City. Morgan guided subsequent mergers of Edison's other enterprises, including a machine works firm and a lamp company, resulting in the creation of the Edison General Electric Company in 1889.

The next stage of invention in electric power came about with the contribution of George Westinghouse. Westinghouse was responsible for making electric lighting possible on a national scale. While Edison used "direct current" or DC power, which could only extend two miles from the power source, in 1886, Westinghouse founded an electric company that promoted "alternating current" or AC power, which allowed for delivery over greater distances due to its wavelike patterns. The Westinghouse Electric Company delivered AC power, which meant that factories, homes, and farms—in short, anything that needed power—could be served, regardless of their proximity to the power source. A public relations battle ensued between the Westinghouse and Edison camps, coinciding with the invention of the electric chair as a form of prisoner execution. Edison publicly proclaimed AC power to be best adapted for use in the chair, in the hope that such a smear campaign would result in homeowners becoming reluctant to use AC power in their houses. Although Edison originally fought the use of AC power in other devices, he reluctantly adapted to it as its popularity increased.

CLICK AND EXPLORE

Not all of Edison's ventures were successful. Read about Edison's Folly (http://openstax.org/l/edisonfail) to learn the story behind his greatest failure. Was there some benefit to his efforts? Or was it wasted time and money?

18.2 From Invention to Industrial Growth

LEARNING OBJECTIVES

By the end of this section, you will be able to:
- Explain how the inventions of the late nineteenth century contributed directly to industrial growth in America
- Identify the contributions of Andrew Carnegie, John Rockefeller, and J. P. Morgan to the new industrial order emerging in the late nineteenth century
- Describe the visions, philosophies, and business methods of the leaders of the new industrial order

As discussed previously, new processes in steel refining, along with inventions in the fields of communications and electricity, transformed the business landscape of the nineteenth century. The exploitation of these new technologies provided opportunities for tremendous growth, and business entrepreneurs with financial backing and the right mix of business acumen and ambition could make their fortunes. Some of these new millionaires were known in their day as **robber barons**, a negative term that connoted the belief that they exploited workers and bent laws to succeed. Regardless of how they were perceived, these businessmen and the companies they created revolutionized American industry.

RAILROADS AND ROBBER BARONS

Earlier in the nineteenth century, the first transcontinental railroad and subsequent spur lines paved the way for rapid and explosive railway growth, as well as stimulated growth in the iron, wood, coal, and other related industries. The railroad industry quickly became the nation's first "big business." A powerful, inexpensive, and consistent form of transportation, railroads accelerated the development of virtually every other industry in the country. By 1890, railroad lines covered nearly every corner of the United States, bringing raw materials to industrial factories and finished goods to consumer markets. The amount of track grew from 35,000 miles at the end of the Civil War to over 200,000 miles by the close of the century. Inventions such as car couplers, air brakes, and Pullman passenger cars allowed the volume of both freight and people to increase steadily. From 1877 to 1890, both the amount of goods and the number of passengers traveling the rails tripled.

Financing for all of this growth came through a combination of private capital and government loans and grants. Federal and state loans of cash and land grants totaled $150 million and 185 million acres of public land, respectively. Railroads also listed their stocks and bonds on the New York Stock Exchange to attract investors from both within the United States and Europe. Individual investors consolidated their power as railroads merged and companies grew in size and power. These individuals became some of the wealthiest Americans the country had ever known. Midwest farmers, angry at large railroad owners for their exploitative business practices, came to refer to them as "robber barons," as their business dealings were frequently shady and exploitative. Among their highly questionable tactics was the practice of differential shipping rates, in which larger business enterprises received discounted rates to transport their goods, as opposed to local producers and farmers whose higher rates essentially subsidized the discounts.

Jay Gould was perhaps the first prominent railroad magnate to be tarred with the "robber baron" brush. He bought older, smaller, rundown railroads, offered minimal improvements, and then capitalized on factory owners' desires to ship their goods on this increasingly popular and more cost-efficient form of transportation. His work with the Erie Railroad was notorious among other investors, as he drove the company to near ruin in a failed attempt to attract foreign investors during a takeover attempt. His model worked better in the American West, where the railroads were still widely scattered across the country, forcing farmers and businesses to pay whatever prices Gould demanded in order to use his trains. In addition to owning the Union Pacific Railroad that helped to construct the original transcontinental railroad line, Gould came to control over ten thousand miles of track across the United States, accounting for 15 percent of all railroad transportation. When he died in 1892, Gould had a personal worth of over $100 million, although he was a deeply unpopular figure.

In contrast to Gould's exploitative business model, which focused on financial profit more than on tangible industrial contributions, Commodore Cornelius Vanderbilt was a "robber baron" who truly cared about the success of his railroad enterprise and its positive impact on the American economy. Vanderbilt consolidated several smaller railroad lines, called trunk lines, to create the powerful New York Central Railroad Company, one of the largest corporations in the United States at the time (Figure 18.6). He later purchased stock in the major rail lines that would connect his company to Chicago, thus expanding his reach and power while simultaneously creating a railroad network to connect Chicago to New York City. This consolidation provided more efficient connections from Midwestern suppliers to eastern markets. It was through such consolidation that, by 1900, seven major railroad tycoons controlled over 70 percent of all operating lines. Vanderbilt's personal wealth at his death (over $100 million in 1877), placed him among the top three wealthiest individuals in American history.

FIGURE 18.6 "The Great Race for the Western Stakes," a Currier & Ives lithograph from 1870, depicts one of Cornelius Vanderbilt's rare failed attempts at further consolidating his railroad empire, when he lost his 1866–1868 battle with James Fisk, Jay Gould, and Daniel Drew for control of the Erie Railway Company.

GIANTS OF WEALTH: CARNEGIE, ROCKEFELLER, AND MORGAN

The post-Civil War inventors generated ideas that transformed the economy, but they were not big businessmen. The evolution from technical innovation to massive industry took place at the hands of the entrepreneurs whose business gambles paid off, making them some of the richest Americans of their day. Steel magnate Andrew Carnegie, oil tycoon John D. Rockefeller, and business financier J. P. Morgan were all businessmen who grew their respective businesses to a scale and scope that were unprecedented. Their companies changed how Americans lived and worked, and they themselves greatly influenced the growth of the country.

Andrew Carnegie and *The Gospel of Wealth*

Andrew Carnegie, steel magnate, has the prototypical rags-to-riches story. Although such stories resembled more myth than reality, they served to encourage many Americans to seek similar paths to fame and fortune. In Carnegie, the story was one of few derived from fact. Born in Scotland, Carnegie immigrated with his family to Pennsylvania in 1848. Following a brief stint as a "bobbin boy," changing spools of thread at a Pittsburgh clothing manufacturer at age thirteen, he subsequently became a telegram messenger boy. As a messenger, he spent much of his time around the Pennsylvania Railroad office and developed parallel interests in railroads, bridge building, and, eventually, the steel industry.

Ingratiating himself to his supervisor and future president of the Pennsylvania Railroad, Tom Scott, Carnegie worked his way into a position of management for the company and subsequently began to invest some of his earnings, with Scott's guidance. One particular investment, in the booming oil fields of northwest Pennsylvania in 1864, resulted in Carnegie earning over $1 million in cash dividends, thus providing him with the capital necessary to pursue his ambition to modernize the iron and steel industries, transforming the United States in the process. Having seen firsthand during the Civil War, when he served as Superintendent of Military Railways and telegraph coordinator for the Union forces, the importance of industry, particularly steel, to the future growth of the country, Carnegie was convinced of his strategy. His first company was the J. Edgar Thompson Steel Works, and, a decade later, he bought out the newly built Homestead Steel Works from the Pittsburgh Bessemer Steel Company. By the end of the century, his enterprise was running an annual profit in excess of $40 million (Figure 18.7).

FIGURE 18.7 Andrew Carnegie made his fortune in steel at such factories as the Carnegie Steel Works located in Youngstown, Ohio, where new technologies allowed the strong metal to be used in far more applications than ever before. Carnegie's empire grew to include iron ore mines, furnaces, mills, and steel works companies.

Although not a scientific expert in steel, Carnegie was an excellent promoter and salesman, able to locate financial backing for his enterprise. He was also shrewd in his calculations on consolidation and expansion, and was able to capitalize on smart business decisions. Always thrifty with the profits he earned, a trait owed to his upbringing, Carnegie saved his profits during prosperous times and used them to buy out other steel companies at low prices during the economic recessions of the 1870s and 1890s. He insisted on up-to-date machinery and equipment, and urged the men who worked at and managed his steel mills to constantly think of innovative ways to increase production and reduce cost.

Carnegie, more than any other businessman of the era, championed the idea that America's leading tycoons owed a debt to society. He believed that, given the circumstances of their successes, they should serve as benefactors to the less fortunate public. For Carnegie, poverty was not an abstract concept, as his family had been a part of the struggling masses. He desired to set an example of philanthropy for all other prominent industrialists of the era to follow. Carnegie's famous essay, *The Gospel of Wealth*, featured below, expounded on his beliefs. In it, he borrowed from Herbert Spencer's theory of **social Darwinism**, which held that society developed much like plant or animal life through a process of evolution in which the most fit and capable enjoyed the greatest material and social success.

MY STORY

Andrew Carnegie on Wealth

Carnegie applauded American capitalism for creating a society where, through hard work, ingenuity, and a bit of luck, someone like himself could amass a fortune. In return for that opportunity, Carnegie wrote that the wealthy should find proper uses for their wealth by funding hospitals, libraries, colleges, the arts, and more. *The Gospel of Wealth* spelled out that responsibility.

"Poor and restricted are our opportunities in this life; narrow our horizon; our best work most imperfect; but rich men should be thankful for one inestimable boon. They have it in their power during their lives to busy themselves in organizing benefactions from which the masses of their fellows will derive lasting advantage, and thus dignify their own lives. . . ."

"This, then, is held to be the duty of the man of Wealth: First, to set an example of modest, unostentatious living, shunning display or extravagance; to provide moderately for the legitimate wants of those dependent upon him; and after doing so to consider all surplus revenues which come to him simply as trust funds, which he is called upon to administer, and strictly bound as a matter of duty to administer in the manner which, in his judgment, is best calculated to produce the most beneficial results for the community—the man of wealth thus becoming the mere agent and trustee for his poorer brethren, bringing to their service his superior wisdom, experience and ability to administer, doing for them better than they would or could do for themselves. . . ."

"In bestowing charity, the main consideration should be to help those who will help themselves; to provide part of the means by which those who desire to improve may do so; to give those who desire to use the aids by which they may rise; to assist, but rarely or never to do all. Neither the individual nor the race is improved by alms-giving. Those worthy of assistance, except in rare cases, seldom require assistance. The really valuable men of the race never do, except in cases of accident or sudden change. Every one has, of course, cases of individuals brought to his own knowledge where temporary assistance can do genuine good, and these he will not overlook. But the amount which can be wisely given by the individual for individuals is necessarily limited by his lack of knowledge of the circumstances connected with each. He is the only true reformer who is as careful and as anxious not to aid the unworthy as he is to aid the worthy, and, perhaps, even more so, for in alms-giving more injury is probably done by rewarding vice than by relieving virtue."

"—Andrew Carnegie, *The Gospel of Wealth*"

Social Darwinism added a layer of pseudoscience to the idea of the self-made man, a desirable thought for all who sought to follow Carnegie's example. The myth of the rags-to-riches businessman was a potent one. Author Horatio Alger made his own fortune writing stories about young enterprising boys who beat poverty and succeeded in business through a combination of "luck and pluck." His stories were immensely popular, even leading to a board game (Figure 18.8) where players could hope to win in the same way that his heroes did.

FIGURE 18.8 Based on a book by Horatio Alger, District Messenger Boy was a board game where players could

achieve the ultimate goal of material success. Alger wrote hundreds of books on a common theme: A poor but hardworking boy can get ahead and make his fortune through a combination of "luck and pluck."

John D. Rockefeller and Business Integration Models

Like Carnegie, John D. Rockefeller was born in 1839 of modest means, with a frequently absent traveling salesman of a father who sold medicinal elixirs and other wares. Young Rockefeller helped his mother with various chores and earned extra money for the family through the sale of family farm products. When the family moved to a suburb of Cleveland in 1853, he had an opportunity to take accounting and bookkeeping courses while in high school and developed a career interest in business. While living in Cleveland in 1859, he learned of Colonel Edwin Drake who had struck "black gold," or oil, near Titusville, Pennsylvania, setting off a boom even greater than the California Gold Rush of the previous decade. Many sought to find a fortune through risky and chaotic "wildcatting," or drilling exploratory oil wells, hoping to strike it rich. But Rockefeller chose a more certain investment: refining crude oil into kerosene, which could be used for both heating and lamps. As a more efficient source of energy, as well as less dangerous to produce, kerosene quickly replaced whale oil in many businesses and homes. Rockefeller worked initially with family and friends in the refining business located in the Cleveland area, but by 1870, Rockefeller ventured out on his own, consolidating his resources and creating the Standard Oil Company of Ohio, initially valued at $1 million.

Rockefeller was ruthless in his pursuit of total control of the oil refining business. As other entrepreneurs flooded the area seeking a quick fortune, Rockefeller developed a plan to crush his competitors and create a true **monopoly** in the refining industry. Beginning in 1872, he forged agreements with several large railroad companies to obtain discounted freight rates for shipping his product. He also used the railroad companies to gather information on his competitors. As he could now deliver his kerosene at lower prices, he drove his competition out of business, often offering to buy them out for pennies on the dollar. He hounded those who refused to sell out to him, until they were driven out of business. Through his method of growth via mergers and acquisitions of similar companies—known as **horizontal integration**—Standard Oil grew to include almost all refineries in the area. By 1879, the Standard Oil Company controlled nearly 95 percent of all oil refining businesses in the country, as well as 90 percent of all the refining businesses in the world. Editors of the *New York World* lamented of Standard Oil in 1880 that, "When the nineteenth century shall have passed into history, the impartial eyes of the reviewers will be amazed to find that the U.S. . . . tolerated the presence of the most gigantic, the most cruel, impudent, pitiless and grasping monopoly that ever fastened itself upon a country."

Seeking still more control, Rockefeller recognized the advantages of controlling the transportation of his product. He next began to grow his company through **vertical integration**, wherein a company handles all aspects of a product's lifecycle, from the creation of raw materials through the production process to the delivery of the final product. In Rockefeller's case, this model required investment and acquisition of companies involved in everything from barrel-making to pipelines, tanker cars to railroads. He came to own almost every type of business and used his vast power to drive competitors from the market through intense price wars. Although vilified by competitors who suffered from his takeovers and considered him to be no better than a robber baron, several observers lauded Rockefeller for his ingenuity in integrating the oil refining industry and, as a result, lowering kerosene prices by as much as 80 percent by the end of the century. Other industrialists quickly followed suit, including Gustavus Swift, who used vertical integration to dominate the U.S. meatpacking industry in the late nineteenth century.

In order to control the variety of interests he now maintained in industry, Rockefeller created a new legal entity, known as a **trust**. In this arrangement, a small group of trustees possess legal ownership of a business that they operate for the benefit of other investors. In 1882, all thirty-seven stockholders in the various Standard Oil enterprises gave their stock to nine trustees who were to control and direct all of the company's business ventures. State and federal challenges arose, due to the obvious appearance of a monopoly, which implied sole ownership of all enterprises composing an entire industry. When the Ohio Supreme Court ruled that the Standard Oil Company must dissolve, as its monopoly control over all refining operations in the U.S. was in violation of state and federal statutes, Rockefeller shifted to yet another legal entity, called a **holding company** model. The holding company model created a central corporate entity that controlled the operations of multiple companies by holding the majority of stock for each enterprise. While not technically a "trust" and therefore not vulnerable to anti-monopoly laws, this consolidation of power and wealth into one entity was on par with a monopoly; thus, progressive reformers of the late nineteenth century considered holding companies to epitomize the dangers inherent in capitalistic big business, as can be seen in the political cartoon below (Figure 18.9). Impervious to reformers' misgivings, other businessmen followed Rockefeller's example. By 1905, over three hundred business mergers had occurred in the United States, affecting more than 80 percent of all industries. By that time, despite passage of federal legislation such as the Sherman Anti-Trust Act in 1890, 1 percent of the country's businesses controlled over 40 percent of the nation's economy.

FIGURE 18.9 John D. Rockefeller, like Carnegie, grew from modest means to a vast fortune. Unlike Carnegie, however, his business practices were often predatory and aggressive. This cartoon from the era shows how his conglomerate, Standard Oil, was perceived by progressive reformers and other critics.

CLICK AND EXPLORE

The PBS video on Robber Barons or Industrial Giants (http://openstax.org/l/barons1) presents a lively discussion of whether the industrialists of the nineteenth century were really "robber barons" or if they were "industrial giants."

J. Pierpont Morgan

Unlike Carnegie and Rockefeller, J. P. Morgan was no rags-to-riches hero. He was born to wealth and became much wealthier as an investment banker, making wise financial decisions in support of the hard-working entrepreneurs building their fortunes. Morgan's father was a London banker, and Morgan the son moved to New York in 1857 to look after the family's business interests there. Once in America, he separated from the London bank and created the J. Pierpont Morgan and Company financial firm. The firm bought and sold stock in growing companies, investing the family's wealth in those that showed great promise, turning an enormous profit as a result. Investments from firms such as his were the key to the success stories of up-and-coming businessmen like Carnegie and Rockefeller. In return for his investment, Morgan and other investment bankers demanded seats on the companies' boards, which gave them even greater control over policies and decisions than just investment alone. There were many critics of Morgan and these other bankers, particularly among members of a U.S. congressional subcommittee who investigated the control that financiers maintained over key industries in the country. The subcommittee referred to Morgan's enterprise as a form of "money trust" that was even more powerful than the trusts operated by Rockefeller and others. Morgan argued that his firm, and others like it, brought stability and organization to a hypercompetitive capitalist economy, and likened his role to a kind of public service.

Ultimately, Morgan's most notable investment, and greatest consolidation, was in the steel industry, when he bought out Andrew Carnegie in 1901. Initially, Carnegie was reluctant to sell, but after repeated badgering by Morgan, Carnegie named his price: an outrageously inflated sum of $500 million. Morgan agreed without hesitation, and then consolidated Carnegie's holdings with several smaller steel firms to create the U.S. Steel Corporation. U.S. Steel was subsequently capitalized at $1.4 billion. It was the country's first billion-dollar firm. Lauded by admirers for the efficiency and modernization he brought to investment banking practices, as well as for his philanthropy and support of the arts, Morgan was also criticized by reformers who subsequently blamed his (and other bankers') efforts for contributing to the artificial bubble of prosperity that eventually burst in the Great Depression of the 1930s. What none could doubt was that Morgan's financial aptitude and savvy business dealings kept him in good stead. A subsequent U.S. congressional committee, in 1912, reported that his firm held 341 directorships in 112 corporations that controlled over $22 billion in assets. In comparison, that amount of wealth was greater than the assessed value of all the land in the United States west of the Mississippi River.

18.3 Building Industrial America on the Backs of Labor

LEARNING OBJECTIVES

By the end of this section, you will be able to:
- Explain the qualities of industrial working-class life in the late nineteenth century
- Analyze both workers' desire for labor unions and the reasons for unions' inability to achieve their goals

The growth of the American economy in the last half of the nineteenth century presented a paradox. The standard of living for many American workers increased. As Carnegie said in *The Gospel of Wealth*, "the poor enjoy what the rich could not before afford. What were the luxuries have become the necessaries of life. The laborer has now more comforts than the landlord had a few generations ago." In many ways, Carnegie was correct. The decline in prices and the cost of living meant that the industrial era offered many Americans relatively better lives in 1900 than they had only decades before. For some Americans, there were also increased opportunities for upward mobility. For the multitudes in the working class, however, conditions in the factories and at home remained deplorable. The difficulties they faced led many workers to question an industrial order in which a handful of wealthy Americans built their fortunes on the backs of workers.

WORKING-CLASS LIFE

Between the end of the Civil War and the turn of the century, the American workforce underwent a transformative shift. In 1865, nearly 60 percent of Americans still lived and worked on farms; by the early 1900s, that number had reversed itself, and only 40 percent still lived in rural areas, with the remainder living and working in urban and early suburban areas. A significant number of these urban and suburban dwellers earned their wages in factories. Advances in farm machinery allowed for greater production with less manual labor, thus leading many Americans to seek job opportunities in the burgeoning factories in the cities. Not surprisingly, there was a concurrent trend of a decrease in American workers being self-employed and an increase of those working for others and being dependent on a factory wage system for their living.

Yet factory wages were, for the most part, very low. In 1900, the average factory wage was approximately twenty cents per hour, for an annual salary of barely six hundred dollars. According to some historical estimates, that wage left approximately 20 percent of the population in industrialized cities at, or below, the poverty level. An average factory work week was sixty hours, ten hours per day, six days per week, although in steel mills, the workers put in twelve hours per day, seven days a week. Factory owners had little concern for workers' safety. According to one of the few available accurate measures, as late as 1913, nearly 25,000 Americans lost their lives on the job, while another 700,000 workers suffered from injuries that resulted in at least one missed month of work. Another element of hardship for workers was the increasingly dehumanizing nature of their work. Factory workers executed repetitive tasks throughout the long hours of their shifts, seldom interacting with coworkers or supervisors. This solitary and repetitive work style was a difficult adjustment for those used to more collaborative and skill-based work, whether on farms or in crafts shops. Managers embraced Fredrick Taylor's principles of **scientific management**, also called "stop-watch management," where he used stop-watch studies to divide manufacturing tasks into short, repetitive segments. A mechanical engineer by training, Taylor encouraged factory owners to seek efficiency and profitability over any benefits of personal interaction. Owners adopted this model, effectively making workers cogs in a well-oiled machine.

One result of the new breakdown of work processes was that factory owners were able to hire women and children to perform many of the tasks. From 1870 through 1900, the number of women working outside the home tripled. By the end of this period, five million American women were wage earners, with one-quarter of them working factory jobs. Most were young, under twenty-five, and either immigrants themselves or the daughters of immigrants. Their foray into the working world was not seen as a step towards empowerment or equality, but rather a hardship born of financial necessity. Women's factory work tended to be in clothing or textile factories, where their appearance was less offensive to men who felt that heavy industry was their purview. Other women in the workforce worked in clerical positions as bookkeepers and secretaries, and as salesclerks. Not surprisingly, women were paid less than men, under the pretense that they should be under the care of a man and did not require a living wage.

Factory owners used the same rationale for the exceedingly low wages they paid to children. Children were small enough to fit easily among the machines and could be hired for simple work for a fraction of an adult man's pay. The image below (Figure 18.10) shows children working the night shift in a glass factory. From 1870 through 1900, child labor in factories tripled. Growing concerns among progressive reformers over the safety of women and children in the workplace would eventually result in the development of political lobby groups. Several states passed legislative efforts to ensure a safe workplace, and the lobby groups pressured Congress to pass protective legislation. However, such legislation would not be forthcoming until well into the twentieth century. In the meantime, many working-class immigrants still desired the additional wages that child and women labor produced, regardless of the harsh working conditions.

FIGURE 18.10 A photographer took this image of children working in a New York glass factory at midnight. There, as in countless other factories around the country, children worked around the clock in difficult and dangerous conditions.

WORKER PROTESTS AND VIOLENCE

Workers were well aware of the vast discrepancy between their lives and the wealth of the factory owners. Lacking the assets and legal protection needed to organize, and deeply frustrated, some working communities erupted in spontaneous violence. The coal mines of eastern Pennsylvania and the railroad yards of western Pennsylvania, central to both respective industries and home to large, immigrant, working enclaves, saw the brunt of these outbursts. The combination of violence, along with several other factors, blunted any significant efforts to organize workers until well into the twentieth century.

Business owners viewed organization efforts with great mistrust, capitalizing upon widespread anti-union sentiment among the general public to crush unions through open shops, the use of strikebreakers, yellow-dog contracts (in which the employee agrees to not join a union as a pre-condition of employment), and other means. Workers also faced obstacles to organization associated with race and ethnicity, as questions arose on how to address the increasing number of low-paid African American workers, in addition to the language and cultural barriers introduced by the large wave of southeastern European immigration to the United States. But in large part, the greatest obstacle to effective unionization was the general public's continued belief in a strong work ethic and that an individual work ethic—not organizing into radical collectives—would reap its own rewards. As violence erupted, such events seemed only to confirm widespread popular sentiment that radical, un-American elements were behind all union efforts.

In the 1870s, Irish coal miners in eastern Pennsylvania formed a secret organization known as the **Molly Maguires**, named for the famous Irish patriot. Through a series of scare tactics that included kidnappings, beatings, and even murder, the Molly Maguires sought to bring attention to the miners' plight, as well as to cause enough damage and concern to the mine owners that the owners would pay attention to their concerns. Owners paid attention, but not in the way that the protesters had hoped. They hired detectives to pose as miners and mingle among the workers to obtain the names of the Molly Maguires. By 1875, they had acquired the names of twenty-four suspected Maguires, who were subsequently convicted of murder and violence against property. All were convicted and ten were hanged in 1876, at a public "Day of the Rope." This harsh reprisal quickly crushed the remaining Molly Maguires movement. The only substantial gain the workers had from this episode was the knowledge that, lacking labor organization, sporadic violent protest would be met by escalated violence.

Public opinion was not sympathetic towards labor's violent methods as displayed by the Molly Maguires. But the public was further shocked by some of the harsh practices employed by government agents to crush the labor movement, as seen the following year in the Great Railroad Strike of 1877. After incurring a significant pay cut earlier that year, railroad workers in West Virginia spontaneously went on strike and blocked the tracks (Figure 18.11). As word spread of the event, railroad workers across the country joined in sympathy, leaving their jobs and committing acts of vandalism to show their frustration with the ownership. Local citizens, who in many instances were relatives and friends, were largely sympathetic to the railroad workers' demands.

FIGURE 18.11 This engraving of the "Blockade of Engines at Martinsburg, West Virginia" appeared on the front cover of *Harper's Weekly* on August 11, 1877, while the Great Railroad Strike was still underway.

The most significant violent outbreak of the railroad strike occurred in Pittsburgh, beginning on July 19. The governor ordered militiamen from Philadelphia to the Pittsburgh roundhouse to protect railroad property. The militia opened fire to disperse the angry crowd and killed twenty individuals while wounding another twenty-nine. A riot erupted, resulting in twenty-four hours of looting, violence, fire, and mayhem, and did not die down until the rioters wore out in the hot summer weather. In a subsequent skirmish with strikers while trying to escape the roundhouse, militiamen killed another twenty individuals. Violence erupted in Maryland and Illinois as well, and President Hayes eventually sent federal troops into major cities to restore order. This move, along with the impending return of cooler weather that brought with it the need for food and fuel, resulted in striking workers nationwide returning to the railroad. The strike had lasted for forty-five days, and they had gained nothing but a reputation for violence and aggression that left the public less sympathetic than ever. Dissatisfied laborers began to realize that there would be no substantial improvement in their quality of life until they found a way to better organize themselves.

WORKER ORGANIZATION AND THE STRUGGLES OF UNIONS

Prior to the Civil War, there were limited efforts to create an organized labor movement on any large scale. With the majority of workers in the country working independently in rural settings, the idea of organized labor was not largely understood. But, as economic conditions changed, people became more aware of the inequities facing factory wage workers. By the early 1880s, even farmers began to fully recognize the strength of unity behind a common cause.

Models of Organizing: The Knights of Labor and American Federation of Labor

In 1866, seventy-seven delegates representing a variety of different occupations met in Baltimore to form the National Labor Union (NLU). The NLU had ambitious ideas about equal rights for African Americans and women, currency reform, and a legally mandated eight-hour workday. The organization was successful in convincing Congress to adopt the eight-hour workday for federal employees, but their reach did not progress much further. The Panic of 1873 and the economic recession that followed as a result of overspeculation on railroads and the subsequent closing of several banks—during which workers actively sought any employment regardless of the conditions or wages—as well as the death of the NLU's founder, led to a decline in their efforts.

A combination of factors contributed to the debilitating Panic of 1873, which triggered what the public referred to at the time as the "Great Depression" of the 1870s. Most notably, the railroad boom that had occurred from 1840 to 1870 was rapidly coming to a close. Overinvestment in the industry had extended many investors' capital resources in the form of railroad bonds. However, when several economic developments in Europe affected the value of silver in America, which in turn led to a de facto gold standard that shrunk the U.S. monetary supply, the amount of cash capital available for railroad investments rapidly declined. Several large business enterprises were left holding their wealth in all but worthless railroad bonds. When Jay Cooke &

Company, a leader in the American banking industry, declared bankruptcy on the eve of their plans to finance the construction of a new transcontinental railroad, the panic truly began. A chain reaction of bank failures culminated with the New York Stock Exchange suspending all trading for ten days at the end of September 1873. Within a year, over one hundred railroad enterprises had failed; within two years, nearly twenty thousand businesses had failed. The loss of jobs and wages sent workers throughout the United States seeking solutions and clamoring for scapegoats.

Although the NLU proved to be the wrong effort at the wrong time, in the wake of the Panic of 1873 and the subsequent frustration exhibited in the failed Molly Maguires uprising and the national railroad strike, another, more significant, labor organization emerged. The Knights of Labor (KOL) was more able to attract a sympathetic following than the Molly Maguires and others by widening its base and appealing to more members. Philadelphia tailor Uriah Stephens grew the KOL from a small presence during the Panic of 1873 to an organization of national importance by 1878. That was the year the KOL held their first general assembly, where they adopted a broad reform platform, including a renewed call for an eight-hour workday, equal pay regardless of gender, the elimination of convict labor, and the creation of greater cooperative enterprises with worker ownership of businesses. Much of the KOL's strength came from its concept of "One Big Union"—the idea that it welcomed all wage workers, regardless of occupation, with the exception of doctors, lawyers, and bankers. It welcomed women, African Americans, Native Americans, and immigrants, of all trades and skill levels. This was a notable break from the earlier tradition of craft unions, which were highly specialized and limited to a particular group. In 1879, a new leader, Terence V. Powderly, joined the organization, and he gained even more followers due to his marketing and promotional efforts. Although largely opposed to strikes as effective tactics, through their sheer size, the Knights claimed victories in several railroad strikes in 1884–1885, including one against notorious "robber baron" Jay Gould, and their popularity consequently rose among workers. By 1886, the KOL had a membership in excess of 700,000.

In one night, however, the KOL's popularity—and indeed the momentum of the labor movement as a whole—plummeted due to an event known as the **Haymarket affair**, which occurred on May 4, 1886, in Chicago's Haymarket Square (Figure 18.12). There, an anarchist group had gathered in response to a death at an earlier nationwide demonstration for the eight-hour workday. At the earlier demonstration, clashes between police and strikers at the International Harvester Company of Chicago led to the death of a striking worker. The anarchist group decided to hold a protest the following night in Haymarket Square, and, although the protest was quiet, the police arrived armed for conflict. Someone in the crowd threw a bomb at the police, killing one officer and injuring another. The seven anarchists speaking at the protest were arrested and charged with murder. They were sentenced to death, though two were later pardoned and one committed suicide in prison before his execution.

FIGURE 18.12 The Haymarket affair, as it was known, began as a rally for the eight-hour workday. But when police broke it up, someone threw a bomb into the crowd, causing mayhem. The organizers of the rally, although not responsible, were sentenced to death. The affair and subsequent hangings struck a harsh blow against organized

labor.

The press immediately blamed the KOL as well as Powderly for the Haymarket affair, despite the fact that neither the organization nor Powderly had anything to do with the demonstration. Combined with the American public's lukewarm reception to organized labor as a whole, the damage was done. The KOL saw its membership decline to barely 100,000 by the end of 1886. Nonetheless, during its brief success, the Knights illustrated the potential for success with their model of "industrial unionism," which welcomed workers from all trades.

AMERICANA

The Haymarket Rally

On May 1, 1886, recognized internationally as a day for labor celebration, labor organizations around the country engaged in a national rally for the eight-hour workday. While the number of striking workers varied around the country, estimates are that between 300,000 and 500,000 workers protested in New York, Detroit, Chicago, and beyond. In Chicago, clashes between police and protesters led the police to fire into the crowd, resulting in fatalities. Afterward, angry at the deaths of the striking workers, organizers quickly organized a "mass meeting," per the poster below (Figure 18.13).

FIGURE 18.13 This poster invited workers to a meeting denouncing the violence at the labor rally earlier in the week. Note that the invitation is written in both English and German, evidence of the large role that the immigrant population played in the labor movement.

While the meeting was intended to be peaceful, a large police presence made itself known, prompting one of the event organizers to state in his speech, "There seems to prevail the opinion in some quarters that this meeting has been called for the purpose of inaugurating a riot, hence these warlike preparations on the part of so-called 'law and order.' However, let me tell you at the beginning that this meeting has not been called for any such purpose. The object of this meeting is to explain the general situation of the eight-hour movement and to throw light upon various incidents in connection with it." The mayor of Chicago later corroborated accounts of the meeting, noted that it was a peaceful rally, but as it was winding down, the police marched into the crowd, demanding they disperse. Someone in the crowd threw a bomb, killing one policeman immediately and wounding many others, some of whom died later. Despite the aggressive actions of the police, public opinion was strongly against the striking laborers. The *New York Times*, after the events played out, reported on it with the headline

"Rioting and Bloodshed in the Streets of Chicago: Police Mowed Down with Dynamite." Other papers echoed the tone and often exaggerated the chaos, undermining organized labor's efforts and leading to the ultimate conviction and hanging of the rally organizers. Labor activists considered those hanged after the Haymarket affair to be martyrs for the cause and created an informal memorial at their gravesides in Park Forest, Illinois.

CLICK AND EXPLORE

This article about the "Rioting and Bloodshed in the Streets of Chicago" (http://openstax.org/l/haymarket) reveals how the *New York Times* reported on the Haymarket affair. Assess whether the article gives evidence of the information it lays out. Consider how it portrays the events, and how different, more sympathetic coverage might have changed the response of the general public towards immigrant workers and labor unions.

During the effort to establish industrial unionism in the form of the KOL, craft unions had continued to operate. In 1886, twenty different craft unions met to organize a national federation of autonomous craft unions. This group became the American Federation of Labor (AFL), led by Samuel Gompers from its inception until his death in 1924. More so than any of its predecessors, the AFL focused almost all of its efforts on economic gains for its members, seldom straying into political issues other than those that had a direct impact upon working conditions. The AFL also kept a strict policy of not interfering in each union's individual business. Rather, Gompers often settled disputes between unions, using the AFL to represent all unions of matters of federal legislation that could affect all workers, such as the eight-hour workday.

By 1900, the AFL had 500,000 members; by 1914, its numbers had risen to one million, and by 1920 they claimed four million working members. Still, as a federation of craft unions, it excluded many factory workers and thus, even at its height, represented only 15 percent of the nonfarm workers in the country. As a result, even as the country moved towards an increasingly industrial age, the majority of American workers still lacked support, protection from ownership, and access to upward mobility.

The Decline of Labor: The Homestead and Pullman Strikes

While workers struggled to find the right organizational structure to support a union movement in a society that was highly critical of such worker organization, there came two final violent events at the close of the nineteenth century. These events, the Homestead Steel Strike of 1892 and the Pullman Strike of 1894, all but crushed the labor movement for the next forty years, leaving public opinion of labor strikes lower than ever and workers unprotected.

At the Homestead factory of the Carnegie Steel Company, workers represented by the Amalgamated Association of Iron and Steel Workers enjoyed relatively good relations with management until Henry C. Frick became the factory manager in 1889. When the union contract was up for renewal in 1892, Carnegie—long a champion of living wages for his employees—had left for Scotland and trusted Frick—noted for his strong anti-union stance—to manage the negotiations. When no settlement was reached by June 29, Frick ordered a lockout of the workers and hired three hundred Pinkerton detectives to protect company property. On July 6, as the Pinkertons arrived on barges on the river, union workers along the shore engaged them in a gunfight that resulted in the deaths of three Pinkertons and six workers. One week later, the Pennsylvania militia arrived to escort strike-breakers into the factory to resume production. Although the lockout continued until November, it ended with the union defeated and individual workers asking for their jobs back. A subsequent failed assassination attempt by anarchist Alexander Berkman on Frick further strengthened public animosity towards the union.

Two years later, in 1894, the Pullman Strike was another disaster for unionized labor. The crisis began in the company town of Pullman, Illinois, where Pullman "sleeper" cars were manufactured for America's railroads. When the depression of 1893 unfolded in the wake of the failure of several northeastern railroad companies, mostly due to overconstruction and poor financing, company owner George Pullman fired three thousand of the factory's six thousand employees, cut the remaining workers' wages by an average of 25 percent, and then continued to charge the same high rents and prices in the company homes and store where workers were required to live and shop. Workers began the strike on May 11, when Eugene V. Debs, the president of the American Railway Union, ordered rail workers throughout the country to stop handling any trains that had Pullman cars on them. In practicality, almost all of the trains fell into this category, and, therefore, the strike created a nationwide train stoppage, right on the heels of the depression of 1893. Seeking justification for sending in federal troops, President Grover Cleveland turned to his attorney general, who came up with a solution: Attach a mail car to every train and then send in troops to ensure the delivery of the mail. The government also ordered the strike to end; when Debs refused, he was arrested and imprisoned for his interference with the delivery of U.S. mail. The image below (Figure 18.14) shows the standoff between federal troops and the workers. The troops protected the hiring of new workers, thus rendering the strike tactic largely ineffective. The strike ended abruptly on July 13, with no labor gains and much lost in the way of public opinion.

FIGURE 18.14 In this photo of the Pullman Strike of 1894, the Illinois National Guard and striking workers face off in front of a railroad building.

MY STORY

George Estes on the Order of Railroad Telegraphers

The following excerpt is a reflection from George Estes, an organizer and member of the Order of Railroad Telegraphers, a labor organization at the end of the nineteenth century. His perspective on the ways that labor and management related to each other illustrates the difficulties at the heart of their negotiations. He notes that, in this era, the two groups saw each other as enemies and that any gain by one was automatically a loss by the other.

"I have always noticed that things usually have to get pretty bad before they get any better. When inequities pile up so high that the burden is more than the underdog can bear, he gets his dander up and things begin to happen. It was that way with the telegraphers' problem. These exploited individuals were determined to get for themselves better working conditions—higher pay, shorter hours, less work which might not properly be classed as telegraphy, and the high and mighty Mr. Fillmore [railroad company president] was not going to stop them. It was a bitter fight. At the outset, Mr. Fillmore let it be known, by his actions and comments, that he held the telegraphers in the utmost contempt."

"With the papers crammed each day with news of labor strife—and with two great labor factions at each other's throats, I am reminded of a parallel in my own early and more active career. Shortly before the turn of the century, in 1898 and 1899 to be more specific, I occupied a position with regard to a certain class of skilled labor, comparable to that held by the Lewises and Greens of today. I refer, of course, to the telegraphers and station agents. These hard-working gentlemen—servants of the public—had no regular hours, performed a multiplicity of duties, and, considering the service they rendered, were sorely and inadequately paid. A telegrapher's day included a considerable number of chores that present-day telegraphers probably never did or will do in the course of a day's work. He used to clean and fill lanterns, block lights, etc. Used to do the janitor work around the small town depot, stoke the pot-bellied stove of the waiting-room, sweep the floors, picking up papers and waiting-room litter. . . ."

"Today, capital and labor seem to understand each other better than they did a generation or so ago. Capital is out to make money. So is labor—and each is willing to grant the other a certain amount of tolerant leeway, just so he doesn't go too far. In the old days there was a breach as wide as the Pacific separating capital and labor. It wasn't money altogether in those days, it was a matter of principle. Capital and labor couldn't see eye to eye on a single point. Every gain that either made was at the expense of the other, and was fought tooth and nail. No difference seemed ever possible of amicable settlement. Strikes were riots. Murder and mayhem was common. Railroad labor troubles were frequent. The railroads, in the nineties, were the country's largest employers. They were so big, so powerful, so perfectly organized themselves—I mean so in accord among themselves as to what treatment they felt like offering the man who worked for them—that it was extremely difficult for labor to gain a single advantage in the struggle for better conditions."

"—George Estes, interview with Andrew Sherbert, 1938"

18.4 A New American Consumer Culture

LEARNING OBJECTIVES

By the end of this section, you will be able to:
- Describe the characteristics of the new consumer culture that emerged at the end of the nineteenth century

Despite the challenges workers faced in their new roles as wage earners, the rise of industry in the United States allowed people to access and consume goods as never before. The rise of big business had turned America into a culture of consumers desperate for time-saving and leisure commodities, where people could expect to find everything they wanted in shops or by mail order. Gone were the days where the small general store was the only option for shoppers; at the end of the nineteenth century, people could take a train to the city and shop in large department stores like Macy's in New York, Gimbel's in Philadelphia, and Marshall Field's in Chicago. Chain stores, like A&P and Woolworth's, both of which opened in the 1870s, offered options to those who lived farther from major urban areas and clearly catered to classes other than the wealthy elite. Industrial advancements contributed to this proliferation, as new construction techniques permitted the building of stores with higher ceilings for larger displays, and the production of larger sheets of plate glass lent themselves to the development of larger store windows, glass countertops, and display cases where shoppers could observe a variety of goods at a glance. L. Frank Baum, of *Wizard of Oz* fame, later founded the National Association of Window Trimmers in 1898, and began publishing *The Store Window* journal to advise businesses on space usage and promotion.

Even families in rural America had new opportunities to purchase a greater variety of products than ever before, at ever decreasing prices. Those far from chain stores could benefit from the newly developed business of mail-order catalogs, placing orders by telephone. Aaron Montgomery Ward established the first significant mail-order business in 1872, with Sears, Roebuck & Company following in 1886. Sears distributed over 300,000 catalogs annually by 1897, and later broke the one million annual mark in 1907. Sears in particular understood that farmers and rural Americans sought alternatives to the higher prices and credit purchases they were forced to endure at small-town country stores. By clearly stating the prices in his catalog, Richard Sears steadily increased his company's image of their catalog serving as "the consumer's bible." In the process,

Sears, Roebuck & Company supplied much of America's hinterland with products ranging from farm supplies to bicycles, toilet paper to automobiles, as seen below in a page from the catalog (Figure 18.15).

FIGURE 18.15 This page from the Sears, Roebuck & Co. catalog illustrates how luxuries that would only belong to wealthy city dwellers were now available by mail order to those all around the country.

The tremendous variety of goods available for sale required businesses to compete for customers in ways they had never before imagined. Suddenly, instead of a single option for clothing or shoes, customers were faced with dozens, whether ordered by mail, found at the local chain store, or lined up in massive rows at department stores. This new level of competition made advertising a vital component of all businesses. By 1900, American businesses were spending almost $100 million annually on advertising. Competitors offered "new and improved" models as frequently as possible in order to generate interest. From toothpaste and mouthwash to books on entertaining guests, new goods were constantly offered. Newspapers accommodated the demand for advertising by shifting their production to include full-page advertisements, as opposed to the traditional column width, agate-type advertisements that dominated mid-nineteenth century newspapers (similar to classified advertisements in today's publications). Likewise, professional advertising agencies began to emerge in the 1880s, with experts in consumer demand bidding for accounts with major firms.

It may seem strange that, at a time when wages were so low, people began buying readily; however, the slow emergence of a middle class by the end of the century, combined with the growing practice of buying on credit, presented more opportunities to take part in the new consumer culture. Stores allowed people to open accounts and purchase on credit, thus securing business and allowing consumers to buy without ready cash. Then, as today, the risks of buying on credit led many into debt. As advertising expert Roland Marchand described in his *Parable on the Democracy of Goods*, in an era when access to products became more important than access to the means of production, Americans quickly accepted the notion that they could live a better lifestyle by purchasing the right clothes, the best hair cream, and the shiniest shoes, regardless of their class. For better or worse, American consumerism had begun.

AMERICANA

Advertising in the Industrial Age: Credit, Luxury, and the Advent of "New and Improved"

Before the industrial revolution, most household goods were either made at home or purchased locally, with limited choices. By the end of the nineteenth century, factors such as the population's move towards urban centers and the expansion of the railroad changed how Americans shopped for, and perceived, consumer goods. As mentioned above, advertising took off, as businesses competed for customers.

Many of the elements used widely in nineteenth-century advertisements are familiar. Companies sought to sell luxury, safety, and, as the ad for the typewriter below shows (Figure 18.16), the allure of the new-and-improved model. One advertising tactic that truly took off in this era was the option to purchase on credit. For the first time, mail order and mass production meant that the aspiring middle class could purchase items that could only be owned previously by the wealthy. While there was a societal stigma for buying everyday goods on credit, certain items, such as fine furniture or pianos, were considered an investment in the move toward entry into the middle class.

FIGURE 18.16 This typewriter advertisement, like others of the era, tried to lure customers by offering a new model.

Additionally, farmers and housewives purchased farm equipment and sewing machines on credit, considering these items investments rather than luxuries. For women, the purchase of a sewing machine meant that a shirt could be made in one hour, instead of fourteen. The Singer Sewing Machine Company was one of the most aggressive at pushing purchase on credit. They advertised widely, and their "Dollar Down, Dollar a Week" campaign made them one of the fastest-growing companies in the country.

For workers earning lower wages, these easy credit terms meant that the middle-class lifestyle was within their reach. Of course, it also meant they were in debt, and changes in wages, illness, or other unexpected expenses could wreak havoc on a household's tenuous finances. Still, the opportunity to own new and luxurious products was one that many Americans, aspiring to improve their place in society, could not resist.

Key Terms

Haymarket affair   the rally and subsequent riot in which several policemen were killed when a bomb was thrown at a peaceful workers rights rally in Chicago in 1886

holding company   a central corporate entity that controls the operations of multiple companies by holding the majority of stock for each enterprise

horizontal integration   method of growth wherein a company grows through mergers and acquisitions of similar companies

Molly Maguires   a secret organization made up of Pennsylvania coal miners, named for the famous Irish patriot, which worked through a series of scare tactics to bring the plight of the miners to public attention

monopoly   the ownership or control of all enterprises comprising an entire industry

robber baron   a negative term for the big businessmen who made their fortunes in the massive railroad boom of the late nineteenth century

scientific management   mechanical engineer Fredrick Taylor's management style, also called "stop-watch management," which divided manufacturing tasks into short, repetitive segments and encouraged factory owners to seek efficiency and profitability over any benefits of personal interaction

social Darwinism   Herbert Spencer's theory, based upon Charles Darwin's scientific theory, which held that society developed much like plant or animal life through a process of evolution in which the most fit and capable enjoyed the greatest material and social success

trust   a legal arrangement where a small group of trustees have legal ownership of a business that they operate for the benefit of other investors

vertical integration   a method of growth where a company acquires other companies that include all aspects of a product's lifecycle from the creation of the raw materials through the production process to the delivery of the final product

Summary

18.1 Inventors of the Age

Inventors in the late nineteenth century flooded the market with new technological advances. Encouraged by Great Britain's Industrial Revolution, and eager for economic development in the wake of the Civil War, business investors sought the latest ideas upon which they could capitalize, both to transform the nation as well as to make a personal profit. These inventions were a key piece of the massive shift towards industrialization that followed. For both families and businesses, these inventions eventually represented a fundamental change in their way of life. Although the technology spread slowly, it did spread across the country. Whether it was a company that could now produce ten times more products with new factories, or a household that could communicate with distant relations, the old way of doing things was disappearing.

Communication technologies, electric power production, and steel production were perhaps the three most significant developments of the time. While the first two affected both personal lives and business development, the latter influenced business growth first and foremost, as the ability to produce large steel elements efficiently and cost-effectively led to permanently changes in the direction of industrial growth.

18.2 From Invention to Industrial Growth

As the three tycoons profiled in this section illustrate, the end of the nineteenth century was a period in history that offered tremendous financial rewards to those who had the right combination of skill, ambition, and luck. Whether self-made millionaires like Carnegie or Rockefeller, or born to wealth like Morgan, these men were the lynchpins that turned inventors' ideas into industrial growth. Steel production, in particular, but also oil refining techniques and countless other inventions, changed how industries in the country could operate, allowing them to grow in scale and scope like never before.

It is also critical to note how these different men managed their businesses and ambition. Where Carnegie felt strongly that it was the job of the wealthy to give back in their lifetime to the greater community, his fellow tycoons did not necessarily agree. Although he contributed to many philanthropic efforts, Rockefeller's financial success was built on the backs of ruined and bankrupt companies, and he came to be condemned by progressive reformers who questioned the impact on the working class as well as the dangers of consolidating too much power and wealth into one individual's hands. Morgan sought wealth strictly through the investment in, and subsequent purchase of, others' hard work. Along the way, the models of management they adopted—horizontal and vertical integration, trusts, holding companies, and investment brokerages—became commonplace in American businesses. Very quickly, large business enterprises fell under the control of fewer and fewer individuals and trusts. In sum, their ruthlessness, their ambition, their generosity, and their management made up the workings of America's industrial age.

18.3 Building Industrial America on the Backs of Labor

After the Civil War, as more and more people crowded into urban areas and joined the ranks of wage earners, the landscape of American labor changed. For the first time, the majority of workers were employed by others in factories and offices in the cities. Factory workers, in particular, suffered from the inequity of their positions. Owners had no legal restrictions on exploiting employees with long hours in dehumanizing and poorly paid work. Women and children were hired for the lowest possible wages, but even men's wages were barely enough upon which to live.

Poor working conditions, combined with few substantial options for relief, led workers to frustration and sporadic acts of protest and violence, acts that rarely, if ever, gained them any lasting, positive effects. Workers realized that change would require organization, and thus began early labor unions that sought to win rights for all workers through political advocacy and owner engagement. Groups like the National Labor Union and Knights of Labor both opened their membership to any and all wage earners, male or female, Black or White, regardless of skill. Their approach was a departure from the craft unions of the very early nineteenth century, which were unique to their individual industries. While these organizations gained members for a time, they both ultimately failed when public reaction to violent labor strikes turned opinion against them. The American Federation of Labor, a loose affiliation of different unions, grew in the wake of these universal organizations, although negative publicity impeded their work as well. In all, the century ended with the vast majority of American laborers unrepresented by any collective or union, leaving them vulnerable to the power wielded by factory ownership.

18.4 A New American Consumer Culture

While tensions between owners and workers continued to grow, and wage earners struggled with the challenges of industrial work, the culture of American consumerism was changing. Greater choice, easier access, and improved goods at lower prices meant that even lower-income Americans, whether rural and shopping via mail order, or urban and shopping in large department stores, had more options. These increased options led to a rise in advertising, as businesses competed for customers. Furthermore, the opportunity to buy on credit meant that Americans could have their goods, even without ready cash. The result was a population that had a better standard of living than ever before, even as they went into debt or worked long factory hours to pay for it.

Review Questions

1. Which of these was *not* a successful invention of the era?
    A. high-powered sewing machines
    B. movies with sound
    C. frozen foods
    D. typewriters

2. What was the major advantage of Westinghouse's "alternating current" power invention?
   A. It was less prone to fire.
   B. It cost less to produce.
   C. It allowed machines to be farther from the power source.
   D. It was not under Edison's control.

3. How did the burst of new inventions during this era fuel the process of urbanization?

4. Which of the following "robber barons" was notable for the exploitative way he made his fortune in railroads?
   A. Jay Gould
   B. Cornelius Vanderbilt
   C. Andrew Carnegie
   D. J. Pierpont Morgan

5. Which of the following does *not* represent one of the management strategies that John D. Rockefeller used in building his empire?
   A. horizontal integration
   B. vertical integration
   C. social Darwinism
   D. the holding company model

6. Why was Rockefeller's use of horizontal integration such an effective business tool at this time? Were his choices legal? Why or why not?

7. What differentiated a "robber baron" from other "captains of industry" in late nineteenth-century America?

8. What was one of the key goals for which striking workers fought in the late nineteenth century?
   A. health insurance
   B. disability pay
   C. an eight-hour workday
   D. women's right to hold factory jobs

9. Which of the following was *not* a key goal of the Knights of Labor?
   A. an end to convict labor
   B. a graduated income tax on personal wealth
   C. equal pay regardless of gender
   D. the creation of cooperative business enterprises

10. What were the core differences in the methods and agendas of the Knights of Labor and the American Federation of Labor?

11. Which of the following did *not* contribute to the growth of a consumer culture in the United States at the close of the nineteenth century?
    A. personal credit
    B. advertising
    C. greater disposable income
    D. mail-order catalogs

12. Briefly explain Roland Marchand's argument in the *Parable of the Democracy of Goods*.

Critical Thinking Questions

13. Consider the fact that the light bulb and the telephone were invented only three years apart. Although it took many more years for such devices to find their way into common household use, they eventually wrought major changes in a relatively brief period of time. What effects did these inventions have on the lives of those who used them? Are there contemporary analogies in your lifetime of significant changes due to inventions or technological innovations?

14. Industrialization, immigration, and urbanization all took place on an unprecedented scale during this era. What were the relationships of these processes to one another? How did each process serve to catalyze and fuel the others?

15. Describe the various attempts at labor organization in this era, from the Molly Maguires to the Knights of Labor and American Federation of Labor. How were the goals, philosophies, and tactics of these groups similar and different? How did their agendas represent the concerns and grievances of their members and of workers more generally?

16. Describe the various violent clashes between labor and management that occurred during this era. What do these events reveal about how each group had come to view the other?

17. How did the new industrial order represent both new opportunities and new limitations for rural and working-class urban Americans?

18. How did the emergent consumer culture change what it meant to be "American" at the turn of the century?

ANSWER KEY for Chapters 1–18

Chapter 1

1. A 3. B 5. A 7. A 9. It was known that the Earth was round, so Columbus's plan seemed plausible. The distance he would need to travel was not known, however, and he greatly underestimated the Earth's circumference; therefore, he would have no way of recognizing when he had arrived at his destination. 11. D

Chapter 2

1. D 3. B 5. A 7. Luther was most concerned about indulgences, which allowed the wealthy to purchase their way to forgiveness, and protested the Church's taxation of ordinary Germans. Both wanted the liturgy to be given in churchgoers' own language, making scripture more accessible. 9. B 11. A 13. C

Chapter 3

1. C 3. As the Spanish tried to convert the Pueblo to Catholicism, the Native people tried to fold Christian traditions into their own practices. This was unacceptable to the Spanish, who insisted on complete conversion—especially of the young, whom they took away from their families and tribes. When adaptation failed, Native peoples attempted to maintain their autonomy through outright revolt, as with the Pueblo Revolt of 1680. This revolt was successful, and for almost twelve years the Pueblos' lives returned to normalcy. Their autonomy was short-lived, however, as the Spanish took advantage of continued attacks by the Pueblos' enemies to reestablish control of the region. 5. D 7. B 9. A 11. They encouraged colonization by offering headrights to anyone who could pay his own way to Virginia: fifty acres for each passage. They also used the system of indenture, in which people (usually men) who didn't have enough money to pay their own passage could work for a set number of years and then gain their own land. Increasingly, they also turned to enslaved Africans as a cheap labor source. 13. A 15. Native Americans didn't have any concept of owning personal property and believed that land should be held in common, for use by a group. They used land as they needed, often moving from area to area to follow food sources at different times of year. Europeans saw land as something individuals could own, and they used fences and other markers to define their property.

Chapter 4

1. C 3. Since the proprietors of the Carolina colonies were absent, English planters from Barbados moved in and gained political power, establishing slave labor as the predominant form of labor. In Pennsylvania, where prospective servants were offered a bounty of fifty acres of land for emigrating and finishing their term of labor, indentured servitude abounded. 5. B 7. B 9. B 11. The Freemasons were a fraternal society that originated in London coffeehouses in the early eighteenth century. They advocated Enlightenment principles of inquiry and tolerance. Masonic lodges soon spread throughout Europe and the British colonies, creating a shared experience on both sides of the Atlantic and spreading Enlightenment intellectual currents throughout the British Empire. Benjamin Franklin was a prominent Freemason. 13. D

Chapter 5

1. D 3. The Currency Act required colonists to pay British merchants in gold and silver instead of colonial paper money. With gold and silver in short supply, this put a strain on colonists' finances. The Sugar Act curtailed smuggling, angering merchants, and imposed stricter enforcement. Many colonists feared the loss of liberty with trials without juries as mandated by the Sugar Act. 5. B 7. D 9. A 11. The Committees of Correspondence provided a crucial means of communication among the colonies. They also set the foundation for a colonial government by breaking away from royal governmental structures. Finally, they promoted a

sense of colonial unity. **13**. A

Chapter 6

1. C   **3**. D   **5**. B   **7**. C   **9**. In the eighteenth century, militaries typically fought only in the summer months. On December 25 and 26, 1776, Washington triumphed over the Hessians encamped at Trenton by surprising them as they celebrated Christmas. Shortly thereafter, he used this same tactic to achieve victory at the Battle of Princeton.   **11**. The British southern strategy was to move the military theater to the southern colonies where there were more Loyalist colonists. Enslaved and Native American allies, the British hoped, would also swell their ranks. This strategy worked at first, allowing the British to take Charleston. However, British fortunes changed after Nathanael Greene took command of the southern Continental Army and scored decisive victories at the battles of Cowpens and Guilford. This set the stage for the final American victory at Yorktown, Virginia. The southern strategy had failed.   **13**. A

Chapter 7

1. A   **3**. Citizenship within a republic meant accepting certain rights and responsibilities as well as cultivating virtuous behavior. This philosophy was based on the notion that the success or failure of the republic depended upon the virtue or corruption of its citizens.   **5**. C   **7**. A   **9**. A group of farmers in western Massachusetts, including Daniel Shays, rebelled against the Massachusetts government, which they saw as unresponsive to their needs. Many were veterans of the Revolutionary War and faced tremendous debts and high taxes, which they couldn't pay with their worthless paper money. They felt that they didn't have a voice in the Massachusetts government, which seemed to cater to wealthy Boston merchants. They wanted their debts to be forgiven and the Massachusetts constitution to be rewritten to address their needs, and when these demands weren't met, they rebelled.   **11**. A

Chapter 8

1. B   **3**. Federalists believed in a strong federal republican government led by learned, public-spirited men of property. They believed that too much democracy would threaten the republic. The Democratic-Republicans, alternatively, feared too much federal government power and focused more on the rural areas of the country, which they thought were underrepresented and underserved. Democratic-Republicans felt that the spirit of true republicanism, which meant virtuous living for the common good, depended on farmers and agricultural areas.   **5**. D   **7**. D   **9**. A   **11**. The election was considered a revolution because, for the first time in American history, political power passed from one party to another. Jefferson's presidency was a departure from the Federalist administrations of Washington and Adams, who had favored the commercial class and urban centers of the country. The Democratic-Republican vision increased states' rights and limited the power of the federal government, lowering taxes and slashing the military, which Adams had built up.   **13**. B

Chapter 9

1. C   **3**. Industrialization made manufactured goods more abundant and more widely available. All but the poorest Americans were able to equip their homes with cookstoves, parlor stoves, upholstered furniture, and decorations such as wallpaper and window curtains. Even such formerly expensive goods as clocks were now affordable for most.   **5**. D   **7**. The federal government passed laws allowing people to sell back land they could not pay for and use the money to pay their debt. States made it more difficult to foreclose on mortgages and tried to make it easier for people to declare bankruptcy.   **9**. A   **11**. D   **13**. A successful northern manufacturer and inventor, Cooper valued hard work, thrift, and simplicity. He lived according to these values, choosing utilitarian, self-made furnishings rather than luxurious goods. Cooper's vision of hard work leading to respectability led him to found the Cooper Union for the Advancement of Science and Art; admission to this college, which was dedicated to the pursuit of technology, was based solely on merit.

Chapter 10

1. B **3.** A **5.** Northern manufacturers were expected to gain from the tariff because it made competing goods from abroad more expensive than those they made. Southern plantation owners expected the tariff would be costly for them, because it raised the price of goods they could only import. Southerners also feared the tariff represented an unwelcome expansion of federal power over the states. **7.** A **9.** The Petticoat affair divided those loyal to President Jackson from Washington, DC, insiders. When Washington socialite Peggy O'Neal's husband committed suicide and O'Neal then married John Eaton, a Tennessee senator with whom she was reportedly unfaithful to her husband, Jackson and those loyal to him defended Peggy Eaton against other Washington, DC, socialites and politicians. Martin Van Buren, in particular, supported the Eatons and became an important figure in Jackson's "Kitchen Cabinet" of select supporters and advisers. **11.** A **13.** Whigs opposed what they viewed as the tyrannical rule of Andrew Jackson. For this reason, they named themselves after the eighteenth-century British-American Whigs, who stood in opposition to King George. Whigs believed in an active federal government committed to internal improvements, including the establishment of a national bank. **15.** B **17.** D **19.** Tocqueville came to believe that democracy was an unstoppable force whose major benefit was equality before the law. However, he also described the tyranny of the majority, which overpowers the will of minorities and individuals.

Chapter 11

1. A **3.** Jefferson wanted Lewis and Clark to find an all-water route to the Pacific Ocean, strengthen U.S. claims to the Pacific Northwest by reaching it through an overland route, explore and map the territory, make note of its natural resources and wildlife, and make contact with Native American tribes with the intention of establishing trade with them. **5.** B **7.** C **9.** American slaveholders in Texas distrusted the Mexican government's reluctant tolerance of slavery and wanted Texas to be a new U.S. slave state. Most also disliked Mexicans' Roman Catholicism and regarded them as dishonest, ignorant, and backward. Belief in their own superiority inspired some Texans to try to undermine the power of the Mexican government. **11.** A **13.** The Chinese were seemingly more disciplined than the majority of the White miners, gaining a reputation for being extremely hard-working and frugal. White miners resented the mining successes that the Chinese earned. They believed the Chinese were unfairly depriving them of the means to earn a living. **15.** B

Chapter 12

1. A **3.** Some southerners believed that their region's monopoly over the lucrative cotton crop—on which both the larger American and Atlantic markets depended—and their possession of a slave labor force allowed the South to remain independent from the market revolution. However, the very cotton that provided the South with such economic potency also increased its reliance on the larger U.S. and world markets, which supplied—among other things—the food and clothes enslaved people needed, the furniture and other manufactured goods that defined the southern standard of comfortable living, and the banks from which southerners borrowed needed funds. **5.** Southern White people often used paternalism to justify the institution of slavery, arguing that enslaved people, like children, needed the care, feeding, discipline, and moral and religious education that they could provide. Enslaved people often used this misguided notion to their advantage: By feigning ignorance and playing into slaveholders' paternalistic perceptions of them, they found opportunities to resist their condition and gain a degree of freedom and autonomy. **7.** C **9.** B **11.** Many slaveholding expansionists believed that the events of the Haitian Revolution could repeat themselves in Cuba, leading to the overthrow of slavery on the island and the creation of an independent Black republic. Americans also feared that the British would seize Cuba—which, since Britain had outlawed slavery in its colonies in 1833, would result in all enslaved people on the island having free status.

Chapter 13

1. A **3.** They both emphasize the power of the individual over that of the majority. Evangelists of the Second

Great Awakening preached the power of personal spirituality, whereas transcendentalists were more concerned with the individual soul. **5.** C **7.** B **9.** At first, temperance reformers, who were predominantly led by Presbyterian ministers, targeted the middle and upper classes. When the movement veered toward teetotalism instead of temperance, the movement lost momentum. However, it was reborn with a focus on the working class in the 1840s. **11.** C **13.** C

Chapter 14

1. A **3.** This federal law appeared to northerners to be further proof of a "Slave Power" conspiracy and elite slaveholders' disproportionate influence over U.S. domestic policy. Northerners also resented being compelled to serve as de facto slave-catchers, as the law punished people not only for helping escaped enslaved people, but also for failing to aid in efforts to return them. Finally, the law rankled many northerners for the hypocrisy that it exposed, given southerners' arguments in favor of states' rights and against the federal government's meddling in their affairs. **5.** B **7.** C **9.** The Supreme Court decided that Dred Scott had not earned freedom by virtue of having lived in a free state; thus, Scott and his family would remain enslaved. More broadly, the Court ruled that Black people could never be citizens of the United States and that Congress had no authority to stop or limit the spread of slavery into American territories. **11.** B

Chapter 15

1. D **3.** Slavery was more deeply entrenched in the Deep South than it was in the Upper South or the border states. The Deep South was home to larger numbers of both slaveholders and enslaved people. Pro-Union sentiment remained strong in parts of the Upper South and border states, particularly those areas with smaller populations of slaveholders. **5.** D **7.** B **9.** C

Chapter 16

1. C **3.** The Thirteenth Amendment officially and permanently banned the institution of slavery in the United States. The Emancipation Proclamation had freed only those enslaved in rebellious states, leaving many enslaved people—most notably, those in the border states—in bondage; furthermore, it did not alter or prohibit the institution of slavery in general. **5.** D **7.** B **9.** The Fifteenth Amendment granted the vote to all Black men, giving formerly enslaved people and free Black people greater political power than they had ever had in the United States. Black people in former Confederate states elected a handful of Black U.S. congressmen and a great many Black local and state leaders who instituted ambitious reform and modernization projects in the South. However, the Fifteenth Amendment continued to exclude women from voting. Women continued to fight for suffrage through the NWSA and AWSA. **11.** C

Chapter 17

1. B **3.** During the first two years of the Civil War—when it appeared that the Confederacy was a formidable opponent—President Lincoln grew concerned that a Union defeat could result in the westward expansion of slavery. Thus, he hoped to facilitate the westward movement of White settlers who promoted the concept of free soil, which would populate the region with allies who opposed slavery. To encourage this process, Congress passed the Homestead Act and the Pacific Railway Act in 1862. The government also constructed and maintained forts that assisted in the process of westward expansion. **5.** Farmers who were able to invest a significant amount of capital in starting up large farms could acquire necessary supplies with ease. They also had access to new, technologically advanced farm machinery, which greatly improved efficiency and output. Such farmers hired migrant farmers to work their huge amounts of land. These "bonanza farms" were often quite successful, whereas family farms—unable to afford the supplies they needed for success, let alone take advantage of the technological innovations that would make their farms competitive—often failed. **7.** D **9.** In the cases of both mining and cattle ranching, diminishing resources played a key role. In mining, the first prospectors were able to pan for gold with crude and inexpensive materials, and therefore, almost anyone could head west and try his luck. Similarly, the quantity of cattle and the amount of grazing land meant that cowboys and would-be cattle barons had ample room to spread out. But as the easiest minerals were stripped away and large-scale ranchers purchased, developed, and fenced off grazing land, opportunities diminished. It took significantly more resources to tunnel down into a mine than it did to pan for gold; instead of individual prospectors, companies would assess a site's potential and then seek investment to hire workers and drill deep into the earth. Likewise, as the cattle trails were over-grazed, ranchers needed to purchase and privatize large swaths of land to prepare their cattle for market.   **11.** A   **13.** In all three cases, White settlers felt that they were superior to these ethnic groups and morally correct in their exploitation of the groups' land and labor. Whether mining sacred Sioux reservation lands for gold or forcing Chinese immigrants to pay a special fine to mine for gold, White settlers were confident that their goal of Manifest Destiny gave them the right to do as they wished. Hispanic Americans, unlike Chinese immigrants and Native Americans, were allowed citizenship rights, although racist laws and corrupt judges severely curtailed these rights. Chinese immigrants were ultimately denied entry to the United States through the Chinese Exclusion Act.

Chapter 18

1. B   **3.** New inventions fueled industrial growth, and the development of commercial electricity—along with the use of steam engines—allowed industries that had previously situated themselves close to sources of water power to shift away from those areas and move their production into cities. Immigrants sought employment in these urban factories and settled nearby, transforming the country's population from mostly rural to largely urban.   **5.** C   **7.** "Captains of industry" (such as Carnegie or Rockefeller) are noted for their new business models, entrepreneurial approaches, and, to varying degrees, philanthropic efforts, all of which transformed late nineteenth-century America. "Robber barons" (such as Gould) are noted for their self-centered drive for profit at the expense of workers and the general public, who seldom benefitted to any great degree. The terms, however, remain a gray area, as one could characterize the ruthless business practices of Rockefeller, or some of Carnegie's tactics with regard to workers' efforts to organize, as similar to the methods of robber barons. Nevertheless, "captains of industry" are noted for contributions that fundamentally changed and typically improved the nation, whereas "robber barons" can seldom point to such concrete contributions.   **9.** B   **11.** C

INDEX

A
abolitionist 342
Abu Ghraib 885
Afghan Northern Alliance 880
Age of Reason 103
agrarian society 19
al-Qaeda 878
alcalde 279
Alliance for Progress 786
American Equal Rights Association 419
American individualism 676
American Missionary Association 413
American Party 367
American River 286
American System 248
Americanization 453
antebellum 298
Anti-Federalists 185
Anti-Imperialist League 590
Antietam 388
appeasement 726
Army of the Potomac 388
Army of the West 389
Articles of Confederation 178
artisans 218
Atlanta Compromise 563

B
baby boom 770
bank runs 672
Banking Act of 1935 711
Barnburners 290
Battle of New Orleans 213
Bell 466
Beringia 8
bicameral 183
Big Three 741
Bill of Rights 193
Black Cabinet 715
Black codes 414
Black Death 18
Black Legend 49
Black Power 802

Black Pride 804
Black separatism 802
Black Tuesday 670
blacklist 762
Bleeding Kansas 366
bloody shirt campaign 526
bonanza farms 443
Bonus Army 679
boomerang generation 899
bootlegging 654
border ruffians 364
Boston Harbor 140
Boston Massacre 126
Boxer Rebellion 583
Brains Trust 697
Bucktails 246
Bull Run Creek 385
Bunker Hill 143
Bush Doctrine 879

C
California Gold Rush 445
Californios 284
Calvinism 40
carpetbaggers 425
Carter Doctrine 841
cash crop 298
charter schools 885
chasquis 13
chattel slavery 25
checks and balances 177
Chicano Movement 805
chinampas 12
circuit riders 327
Citizen Genêt affair 199
City Beautiful 510
civil service 525
civil unions 893
Civil Works Administration 702
Civilian Conservation Corps 702
Clark Memorandum 688
clear and present danger 617
code of deference 244
Coercive Acts 130

Cold War 758
collateralized debt obligations 889
colonization 340
Columbian Exchange 50
Comanche 278
Committee of Correspondence 129
Committee of Public Information 615
commodification 50
Compromise of 1850 292
Compromise of 1877 430
Comstock Lode 445
concurrent majority 317
Confederacy 382
confiscation acts 156
Connecticut Compromise 184
conscientious objectors 732
conservative Whigs 167
containment 758
Continental currency 159
contrabands 394
Contract with America 868
Contras 858
Copperheads 402, 411
Corps of Discovery 271
corrupt bargain 247
cotton boom 298
cotton gin 298
counterculture 816
counterinsurgency 787
coverture 169
Coxey's Army 540
credit default swaps 889
Crédit Mobilier of America scandal 525
Crittenden Compromise 381
crop-lien system 424
Crusades 20
Cumberland Road 232

D
D-day 743
Daughters of Liberty 119

Deep Throat 836
Defense of Marriage Act 900
deism 102
democracy 167
Democratic-Republicans 197
Depression of 1893 540
desegregation 776
deskilling 221
détente 829
direct primary 552
direct tax 116
Dixiecrats 824
dollar diplomacy 599
domestic slave trade 301
Dominion of New England 93
domino theory 758
Double V campaign 739
Dred Scott v. Sandford 368
Dunmore's Proclamation 144
Dust Bowl 683
Dutch West India Company 61

E

Edison 467
Electoral College 185
Emancipation Proclamation 395
Embargo Act of 1807 210
Emergency Banking Act 700
empresario 278
encomiendas 48
Enforcement Acts 427
English interregnum 87
Enlightenment 101
Enola Gay 747
Erie Canal 233
eugenicists 562
Executive Order 9066 740
executive privilege 836
exodusters 440
expatriate 655

F

Fair Deal 756
farm holidays 679
Farmerettes 619
Farmers' Alliance 537
federal minimum wage 756
Federalists 185
Fence Cutting War 448

feudal society 18
filibuster 275
Fire-Eaters 371
fireside chat 700
First Great Awakening 99
Five Civilized Tribes 258
flapper 650
flexible response 787
Florida land boom 668
Ford Hunger March 679
Fort Sumter 383
forty-niners 287
Fourteen Points 625
Franklin Delano Roosevelt 695
free moral agency 238
Free-Soil Party 290
Freedmen's Bureau 412
Freedom Riders 798
Freemasons 102
Freeport Doctrine 371
French and Indian War 105
Frontier Thesis 583

G

gender gap 869
general in chief 388
Gettysburg Address 397
GI Bill 755
Gilded Age 522
Giuseppe Zangara 698
Glass-Steagall Banking Act 702
globalization 32
Glorious Revolution 93
graft 505
Grange 536
Great Migration 500
Great Recession 890
Great Society 791
Greek civil war 759
Green Party 872
Greenback Party 537
greenbacks 392
greenhouse gases 894

H

habeas corpus 390
Half-Breeds 530
Harlem Hellfighters 619
Harlem Nine 777
Harpers Ferry 371

Haymarket affair 479
headright system 68
Heritage Foundation 852
Hessians 148
Higher Education Act 792
Hillarycare 867
Hippies 816
Hispaniola 34
HIV/AIDS 855
holding company 474
Hollywood 639
Homeland Security Act 882
Homestead Act 438
Hoover 666
Hoover Moratorium 688
horizontal integration 473
Huey "Kingfish" Long 711
hydroelectric power 707
hydropathy 339

I

identity politics 816
immediatism 343
impressment 200
Inca 50
indenture 67
Indian Removal Act 258
indirect tax 116
indulgences 39
initiative 552
Inquisition 21
instrumentalism 511
internment 740
interregnum 698
Intolerable Acts 131
Iron Curtain 758
Ironclad Oath 409
Irreconcilables 627

J

Jackie Robinson 774
Jesuits 63
Jim Crow 415
joint stock companies 44
José Martí 587
Juneteenth 411

K

Kamikaze 746
Kansas-Nebraska bill 363

Kellogg-Briand Pact 725
Kitchen Cabinet 252
Koran 20
Ku Klux Klan 425
Kyoto Protocol 894

L

labor theory of value 225
land fever 229
land offices 227
las Gorras Blancas 457
League of Nations 625
letters of marque 199
Levittown 768
liberty bonds 614
Liberty Party 290
Little Rock Nine 777
log cabin campaign 263
Long Telegram 758
Lost Generation 655
Louisiana Purchase 208
Loving v. Virginia 804
Loyalist 111

M

machine politics 504
machine tools 231
majority rule 167
malaria 595
Manhattan Project 747
Manifest Destiny 436
manumissions 174
Marbury v. Madison 208
maroon communities 77
Marshall Plan 759
Mary McLeod Bethune 715
mass incarceration 857
Massachusetts Circular 124
massive retaliation 765
materiel 728
Mayflower 45
McDonalds 768
Mecklenburg Resolves 144
mercantilism 50
Mexican Cession 286, 354
middle class 507
Middle Passage 77
military-industrial complex 765
millennialism 327
minutemen 142

miscegenation 370
missionaries 60
Missouri Compromise 276
mita 14
Model T 639
Mohawk and Hudson Railroad 234
Molly Maguires 477
Monarchy 166
monopoly 473
monster bank 254
Montesquieu 176
Montgomery Bus Boycott 778
Moral Majority 853
moral suasion 343
Mormons 334
Morrill Act 392
mourning wars 52
moving assembly line 640
muckrakers 550
Mugwumps 533
musket 78
Muslim 24
Mutually Assured Destruction 765

N

NAACP 564
national bank 196
National Labor Relations Board 712
National Organization for Women 822
National Recovery Administration 706
nativism 644
naturalism 512
naval quarantine 788
Navigation Acts 91
Negro nationalism 653
neutrality 609
New Deal 696
New Freedom 570
New Jersey Plan 184
new morality 650
New Nationalism 570
New Right 849
New York City Draft Riots 402
Niagara Movement 564
No Child Left Behind Act 884

no taxation without representation 119
non-importation movement 120
nonconformist 94
Northwest Passage 270
nullification 252

O

Obamacare 897
Okies 684
Open Door notes 592
Operation Desert Storm 862
Ostend Manifesto 319

P

Pancho Villa 608
Panic of 1819 278
Panic of 1873 531
Parents Music Resource Center 854
paternalism 303
patroonships 62
Peace Corps 786
Pentagon Papers 833
Petticoat affair 251
photojournalism 551
Phrenology 339
pietistic 332
Pilgrims 45
pink collar 674
plumbers 835
polygenism 318
polygyny 23
polytheistic 9
popular sovereignty 144
Populist Party 539
Port Huron Statement 806
pragmatism 511
privateers 43
probanza de mérito 35
Proclamation Line 114
Progressive Party 569
progressive tax 554
Progressivism 552
Prohibition 620
proportional representation 183
proprietary colonies 87
Protestant Reformation 39

Puritans 41
putting-out system 219

Q
Quartering Act 118
quipu 13

R
Radical Republicans 409
Radical Whigs 167
Rappites 332
Reaganomics 850
realism 511
recall 552
Reconquista 20
Reconstruction 408
Reconstruction Acts 416
Red Scare 630
Red Summer 629
redeemers 428
referendum 552
repartimiento 58
Report on Public Credit 194
Republic of Fredonia 279
Republic of Sonora 320
Republican Party 364
republicanism 144
Reservationists 627
Restoration colonies 87
return to normalcy 657
Revolution of 1800 206
Rhode Island system 220
Roanoke 43
robber barons 469
Rock and roll 770
Roosevelt Corollary 596
Rosie the Riveter 736
rotation in office 251
Rough Riders 588

S
sacraments 19
salutary neglect 92
Sand Creek Massacre 450
scalawags 425
scientific management 476
Scopes Monkey Trial 648
Scottsboro Boys 682
Second Great Awakening 326
Second Ku Klux Klan 646

second middle passage 308
second party system 263
Seneca Falls 346
Separatists 45
serfs 18
settlement house movement 498
Seward's Folly 581
Shakers 332
sharecropping 424
Sherman's March to the Sea 401
silent majority 823
Silent Sentinels 561
Slave Power 290, 358
Slavery 95
smallpox 52
Smoot-Hawley Tariff 688
social Darwinism 471, 511
social gospel 498
Social Register 507
Social Security 712
sod houses 442
Sons of Liberty 119
southern strategy 152, 823
Southern Tenant Farmers Union 705
Spanish-American War 568
specie 229
Speculation 668
sphere of influence 592
spoils system 246
Sputnik 766
Square Deal 567
stagflation 827
Stalwarts 530
Stamp Act 116
START 862
state-level reforms 552
states' rights 778
Stonewall Inn 820
Student Nonviolent Coordinating Committee (SNCC) 798
subprime mortgages 889
Suffolk Resolves 132
sugarcane 49
Supreme Court Packing Plan 713
Susquehannock 68

T
Taliban 879
Tallmadge Amendment 276
Tammany Hall 505
Tariff of Abominations 248
Taylorism 554
Tea Act of 1773 129
Tea Party 897
Teapot Dome scandal 658
teetotalism 338
Tejanos 278
temperance 337
ten percent plan 408
Tennessee Valley Authority 707
the Terror 198
thirteen colonies 144
three-fifths compromise 185
Timucua 59
Title VII 808
total war 390
Townshend 122
Trail of Tears 260
transcendentalism 328
Treaty of Paris 106
trust 473
Tulsa Massacre 629
Tuskegee Institute 731
tyranny of the majority 262

U
Underground Railroad 358
unicameral 177
Union Leagues 420
universal manhood suffrage 245
Urbanization 492

V
vertical integration 473
vice-admiralty courts 116
Victory Stamps 734
Vietnam Syndrome 857
Vietnamization 831
Virginia Plan 183

W
wampum 78
war on drugs 856
war on poverty 792
Washington Temperance

Society 338
Whigs 255
Wilmot Proviso 289
Wisconsin Idea 554
WMDs 880
Wobblies 559
Working Men's Party 225
Works Progress Administration 695, 711

Wounded Knee Massacre 452

X
XYZ affair 205

Y
yellow fever 595
yellow journalism 587
Yippies 825
Yom Kippur War 827
Yorktown 153
Yuppie 852

Z
Zimmermann telegram 611
zoot suits 739